Why
The King James
Version

A series of study notes, neither treatises nor essays, dealing with certain elementary problems and specific scriptural passages, involved in considering the preferential English translations of the Greek New Testament text, whether the King James Version (the Authorized Version), 1611—British; or the British Revised Version, 1880's; or the American Standard Version, 1900-1901; or the American Revised Standard Version, 1946-1952.

BY

J. REUBEN CLARK, JR.

CLASSICS IN MORMON LITERATURE

Deseret Book Company
Salt Lake City, Utah
1979

Library of Congress Cataloging in Publication Data

Clark, Joshua Reuben, 1871-1961.
    Why the King James version.

    (Classics in Mormon literature)
    Bibliography: p.
    Includes index.
    1.   Bible.   English—Versions—Authorized.   2.   Bible.
N.T.—Criticism, Textual.   I.   Title.   II.   Series.
[BS186.C57 1979]   220.5′2   79-15008
ISBN 0-87747-773-6

Other Volumes in the Classics
in Mormon Literature Series

An Approach to the Book of Mormon, by Hugh Nibley
The Gospel: God, Man, and Truth, by David H. Yarn, Jr.
Key to the Science of Theology and *A Voice of Warning,* by Parley P. Pratt
Outlines in Ecclesiastical History, by B. H. Roberts

PUBLISHER'S PREFACE TO "CLASSICS IN MORMON LITERATURE" EDITION

Since the first edition of *Why the King James Version* was published in 1956, numerous new translations and versions of the Bible have appeared. Each of these new works attempts, and with some reasonable success, to aid in understanding or clarifying the original meaning of the Bible text, or to manifest new fruits of scholastic endeavor. The entire spectrum of literary, textual, and theological questions relating to the Bible has been reexamined in recent years, but the net benefit is of only minor significance. The justifications presented for the multitude of new versions, however, remain primarily the same as those set forth more than two decades ago, when President J. Reuben Clark's work first appeared, and his examination and evaluation as presented in this volume remain acceptable and valid today.

Most of the issues are those of interpretation, although they may appear in a variety of forms. As Elder John A. Widtsoe once observed, "The translator at the best is only an interpreter of the text." (*Improvement Era,* March 1940, p. 161.) The message as reflected by translator-interpreters was President Clark's major concern, as he prepared his work. His preparations centered in the New Testament, for they constituted a part of his work that culminated in his classic volume *Our Lord of the Gospels.* Seeking to confirm his own spiritual perceptions about the message of the New Testament, he was reinforced in his feelings through his study of the King James Version.

iv

The question of the use and acceptance of the King James Version is further enhanced by the fact that it still remains the largest-selling version in the world today. And this in spite of the many different translations and versions that have received official recommendation or endorsement of many of the Christian churches.

One of the most important arguments used by President Clark for the use of the King James Version by the Latter-day Saints is that as it as "amended" in the Joseph Smith Translation, it is correct. He further demonstrates that the "essential verities" of Christ and his gospel are best preserved in the King James Version. The most common complaint against the King James Version, however, stems from its use of some archaic words and currently ungrammatical forms. President Clark wisely observed that "the chief reason the Bible King James Version is not understood is not because it is in archaic English, but because it is not read." Foremost of all the confirmatory material that makes up this volume, President Clark concludes with his personal witness of the Savior and his work. He has truly left us a scholarly and spiritual legacy: *Why the King James Version.*

PREFACE •

For this book I alone am responsible. It is not a Church publication. The work in its entirety is my own, save as specified in the *Acknowledgments*.

The book is not a treatise; it is not a series of essays. It is a collection of notes, somewhat classified, giving essential facts that the author wished to have available for himself, accompanied by his own reflections thereon as his work developed. The *Notes* are repetitious, rather highly so, both as to quotes and discussions. This is done both for the emphasis of particular matters, and also to have the quotes handily available where they seem pertinent.

He has, so far as possible, avoided paraphrasing, because he might distort the writers' meaning in his paraphrase. Effort has been made to follow quotes meticulously in punctuation, spelling, and of course in wording. Every pain has been taken in this regard.

The subject matter of the book is highly controversial. The *Notes* were prepared as personal background material in the author's preparation for the final text for his book, *Our Lord of The Gospels*. The *Notes* treat of matters concerning which he has always wished to have information, readily available.

It should be clearly in mind that *only the New Testament* is considered herein, save for a short discussion of the origin of writing and of modern criticism of the Old Testament.

As his study progressed, the author talked with some of his friends about the work he was doing, and they urged him so to prepare his studies that they might be printed. Yielding to these urgings, he redrafted the material he had already written and prepared the balance of his work in such form as to make it fairly readable if he should finally decide to print it. This arrangement required, to make it a little better understandable to readers, that there should be added in places the author's own views and comments on the facts and theories of his sources. This has caused the book to grow considerably in volume. However, he followed his plan of rearrangement of material till he finished what he set out to do. The book herein printed is the result.

Perhaps a beginning personal word will be pardoned.

All his life the author has rebelled against the effort of the "higher critics" to dilute and sometimes destroy the Word of God and, by some, to do away even with God himself and the Christ.

In his late teens or early twenties, the author met up with a book of scant scholarship, the character of which may be gathered from a few words from its concluding sentences. They read:

> ". . . the only men distinguished for their learning who now believe it [the Bible] to be the inspired word of God, are the men who are, either directly or indirectly, making their living out of it."

Scandalized by the book's treatment of the Holy Scriptures, the author was forced, in spiritual self-defense, to crystallize his early belief and to solidify his inborn faith in God and in his Son, Jesus the Christ.

He has been persuaded, by the reflections of maturing years, of the fundamental truths in Paul's statements to the Corinthians that "the foolishness of God is wiser than men" and "the wisdom of this world is foolishness with God." Finite man cannot rationalize the Infinite. The attempt to do so breeds mental chaos and great spiritual injury.

So believing, the author has, in his later years, done some reading in an effort to satisfy himself as to which of the generally used English translations of the New Testament, he might more fully rely upon (judged by his reading) as most accurately recording the words and an account of the works of our Lord and Master, barring the Inspired Version of Joseph Smith.

Believing that no one should inflict upon the public a serious book that does not serve a useful purpose, the author sends this book to the press somewhat harassed by the thought that it may not so serve. The subject matter covered herein is so great in its scope, and is of so difficult and intricate a character, involving so much scholarship that the author does not even measurably possess, that he has feared that what he says may be so inadequate as to waste the time of any one who might undertake to read it. Yet, its preparation has been of greatest value to him personally in helping to confirm and solidify his spiritual instincts regarding the New Testament record and message; and he has thought it might possibly serve a measurable purpose for some-one else.

The scholar who deals with the problems involved in the scientific study of the ancient manuscripts writ-ten in various ways and in various ancient languages, with their relative ages, origins, importance, and value, will hardly find the book of service.

The book is open to the criticism that its composi-tion is, on all technical questions, almost exclusively a matter of scissors and paste-pot. However, such is its avowed, deliberate character. Its value is probably directly proportionate to the quotations made from scholars who were fully qualified to speak.

The casual reader of light fiction will find the book insufferably dull. The general reader who is of a serious turn of mind, who has an interest in the Holy Scriptures, and who wishes to know something that is intelligible to him about the various translations of the Bible, may find herein something that will be interesting, possibly valuable.

The author, strictly a layman in such a labor, has found courage and a sustaining determination to go through with his undertaking from the words of a great scholar (Kenyon), who declares:

". . . any intelligent reader, without any knowledge of either Greek or Hebrew, can learn enough to understand the processes of criticism and the grounds on which the judgments of scholars must be based."

It is with this comfort and encouragement and in this spirit that this work has gone forward.

Still uncertain and undecided in his own mind, the author further imposed upon some of his friends by asking them to read the manuscript to see if they were still of the mind that it should be published as a book, and they, after so reading, have still encouraged him to have it printed.

The most this author may hope for is that his *Notes* will somehow provoke in some qualified scholars having a proper Gospel background, the desire and determination to go over the manuscripts and furnish us, under the influence and direction of the Holy Ghost, a translation of the New Testament that will give us an accurate translation that shall be pregnant with the great principles of the Restored Gospel. We shall then have a reliable record of the doings and sayings of our Lord and Master Jesus Christ.

So he commits the work to those who may be interested, hoping it may be of some use to them, as it has been to him, in stimulating and verifying instinctive spiritual convictions in the Holy Bible and its divine record, as it has come down to us over the centuries.

—J. R. C.

May 15, 1956.

ACKNOWLEDGMENTS ·

While I assume all and full responsibility for this book and for the views expressed herein, I must repeat my deep obligation, already expressed in the *Preface*, to my many friends, who, during the preparation of the book, have insistently encouraged me to go forward with it and then to print it. I forbear to mention them by name lest I might seem to involve them somehow in a responsibility for the book, its contents, and the views expressed in it, for which they may in no sense be properly charged.

But I may properly acknowledge the invaluable and unstinted help given me in connection with all technical matters having to do with the whole format of the book, — Elder Mark E. Petersen, — a wise and experienced printer; Elder Alva H. Parry, the experienced Manager of the Deseret Book Company, the publisher of the book; and Elder Thomas S. Monson, an experienced printer, Assistant Manager of the Deseret News Press, which printed the book. Their friendly, unstinted helpfulness has far exceeded their professional interest.

To my son, J. Reuben Clark III, I am indebted for the transliteration of the few Greek words I felt it was necessary that I should use; they are all in material I have quoted and are in the forms and the spelling given in the texts quoted.

I am quite unable to express the deep obligation I am under to Sister Rowena Miller, my secretary, who with a devotion and loyalty to her work, rarely equalled and never excelled, has prepared the copy for the press, including the making of the *Index*, has repeatedly checked all the quotations and citations, and has made herself so familiar with the subject matter of the book that she has given many valuable suggestions concerning it and its publication. She is entitled to full credit for "seeing it through the press."

OTHER ACKNOWLEDGMENTS •

I am deeply grateful—

To Professor Edward Robertson, the Librarian of The John Rylands Library, Manchester, for permission to print a reproduction of their Fragment of the Gospel of St. John;

To the University of Chicago Library for permission to print reproductions of pages of the Codex Sinaiticus, Codex Alexandrinus, Codex Vaticanus, Codex Ephraemi, and Erasmus New Testament Text.

To the Library of Congress, for the copy of Codex Bezae.

To Emery Walker (Ireland) Ltd., by Wilfred Merton, Director, in behalf of Sir Chester Beatty, for permission to print a reproduction of a page from the Chester Beatty Papyri.

I am also deeply grateful to the following copyright holders for permission to make the extensive quotes used in the *Notes*, credit to the individual authors being given in the book with each quotation:

G. Bell & Sons, Ltd., London,—Edward Miller, *A Guide to the Textual Criticism of the New Testament*, 1886; Frederick Henry Ambrose Scrivener, *A Plain Introduction to the Criticism of the New Testament For the Use of Biblical Students*, 4th ed. rev., Edward Miller, ed., 1894;

Deighton, Bell & Co., Ltd., Cambridge,—Frederick Henry Ambrose Scrivener, *A Plain Introduction to the Criticism of the New Testament For the Use of Biblical Students*, 2nd ed. rev., 1874; 3rd ed. rev., 1883;

Gerald Duckworth & Co. Ltd., London,—Frederic G. Kenyon, *The Text of the Greek Bible*, 1949;

E. P. Dutton & Co., Inc., New York,—Sir Frederic Kenyon, *The Story of the Bible*, 1949;

Eyre & Spottiswoode (Publishers) Ltd., London,— Sir Frederic Kenyon, *Our Bible and the Ancient Manuscripts*, 4th ed. rev., 1948; and "The Translators to the Reader," and other excerpts from the Variorum Bible (The Sunday School Centenary Bible, Authorized Version), 1880;

Funk & Wagnalls Company, New York,—*The New Schaff-Herzog Encyclopedia of Religious Knowledge*, 1908-1914;

Longmans, Green & Co., Inc., New York,—Alfred Edersheim, *The Life and Times of Jesus The Messiah*, 3rd ed., 1927;

John Murray, London,—John William Burgon, *The Revision Revised*, 1883; Sir Frederic Kenyon, *The Story of the Bible*, 1949;

The National Council of the Churches of Christ in the U.S.A., the Division of Christian Education of the National Council of the Churches of Christ in the U.S.A., and Thomas Nelson & Sons, New York,—*An Introduction to the Revised Standard Version of the New Testament*, 1946; American Standard Version, 1900-1901; and the Revised Standard Version, 1946-1952;

Pickering & Inglis, Ltd., Glasgow,— F. F. Bruce, *The Books and the Parchments*, 1950;

Charles Scribner's Sons, New York,—*Dictionary of the Bible*, One Volume Edition, edited by James Hastings; copyright 1909 by Charles Scribner's Sons, 1937 by A. W. Hastings, reprinted by permission of the publishers; and *Encyclopaedia of Religion and Ethics*, Volume IV, edited by James Hastings, 1928.

TABLE OF CONTENTS •

PREFACE v

ACKNOWLEDGMENTS xi

"THE TRANSLATORS TO THE READER" xxvii

THE PROBLEM. Why the King James Version 1

NOTE ONE. General Matters and Observations 8

Item 1. When Our New Testament Was Written 8
Kenyon's Views on Antiquity of Gospels, 9.

Item 2. Corruption of Early Scripture Manuscripts 12
Scrivener's Observations, 13; Editions of Scrivener's
Work, 14; Work of Burgon and Miller, 15.

Item 3. The Origin of Writing 16

Item 4. Search for Helpful Reference Books 19

Item 5. Quotation of Authorities 21

Item 6. The Scholars,—Scrivener, Burgon, Miller and
Kenyon, Who Are Mainly Quoted 23
Scrivener's Standing, 24; Work of Burgon, 25; Ken-
yon's Appraisal of Burgon, 25; Scrivener's Estimate of
Burgon, 27; Estimate of Kenyon, 28.

Item 7. The Making of the Revised Version, British
and American 29

Item 8. The Making of the Revised Standard Version,
American 31

Item 9. Some General Considerations 33

Item 10. Elements of Unfairness 35
The Title Pages, 38; Special Points in Title Pages, 41.

Item 11. The Revisers' Own Case 42

NOTE TWO. Elements of a Harmony and the Harmonies
Herein Relied Upon 44

Item 1. Chronological Harmony 44

Item 2. Idea of Harmony Is Old 44

Item 3. Harmonies Used 45

NOTE THREE. Christ's Ministry 48

    Item 1. Chronology of Christ's Ministry 48

    Item 2. Length of Ministry of Jesus 49
        The Problem Facing Jesus, 51.

    Item 3. Appraisal of Jesus 53
        Allen's Analysis, 55; Allen's Own Views, 57.

NOTE FOUR. The Authorized Version 60

NOTE FIVE. The Language of Jesus 62

NOTE SIX. The Language of the Earliest Recovered New
Testament Records 65

    Item 1. General Observations 65

    Item 2. The Syriac Versions 67

        Sub-item a. The Old Syriac 70

        Sub-item b. The Diatessaron by Tatian 73

        Sub-item c. The Peshitta (Also Called Peshito).... 75
        Miller's Comments, 76; Scrivener's Discussion—Anti-
        ochian Theory, 78; Other Syrian Texts, 80; Summary,
        81; Luke's Account, 82.

NOTE SEVEN. Number of Manuscripts of the New
Testament 84

NOTE EIGHT. Kinds and Groupings of Greek
Manuscripts 86

    Item 1. Classification of Manuscripts 86

    Item 2. Grouping of Manuscripts into Families, in
    1881 91

    Item 3. Re-grouping of Manuscripts into Families 92
        Kenyon's Grouping, 95; Byzantine, 95; Alexandrian,
        96; Caesarean, 96; Western, 97; Syriac, 97; Residual,
        98; Kenyon's Pre-Byzantine Authorities, 99.

NOTE NINE. Division of New Testament Into Paragraphs....101

NOTE TEN. Division of Chapters Into Verses 102

NOTE ELEVEN. Textual Criticism, Development of
Modern Criticism 103

    Item 1. Old Testament 103
        Early Critics, 104; Astruc, 104; Eichhorn, 104; Geddes,
        105; Ilgen, 105; de Wette, 105; Wellhausen, 106;
        Reuss-Graf, 106; Hupfeld, 106; Duhm, 107; Eerdmans,
        107.

    Item 2. New Testament 108
        Scrivener's Comment on Westcott-Hort System, 113.

NOTE TWELVE. Summary of Some Important Text Eliminations by the Extreme Textualists 119

NOTE THIRTEEN. The Antiquity Argument 122

Item 1. As of the Time of the Revised Version (British) 1880's, and of the American Standard Version (1900-1901) 122
Early Corruptions, 124; Necessity for More Information, 125.

Item 2. The Antiquity Argument as of the Present Date 126
Kenyon's Views, 126.

Item 3. Recognition that Later Manuscripts May Be Valuable 128

NOTE FOURTEEN. Manuscripts Underlying Our New Testament 130

Item 1. List of Some New Testament Greek Manuscripts that Critics Consider Important 130
Designations of Manuscripts, 132; Gregory's System, 133.

Item 2. The Papyri 134
Chester Beatty Manuscripts, 135.

Item 3. The Uncials 136
Codex Sinaiticus, 136; Codex Alexandrinus, 138; Codex Vaticanus, 139; Codex Ephraemi, 140; Codex Bezae, 141; Other Codices, 143.

Item 4. The Minuscules or Cursives 149

Item 5. The Lectionaries 151
Scrivener's Comments and Lists, 152.

NOTE FIFTEEN. Versions and Fathers 155
Versions, 156.

Item 1. Syriac Versions 156

Item 2. Armenian Versions 156

Item 3. Georgian Versions 157

Item 4. Coptic or Egyptian Versions...........................157
Sub-item a. Sahidic 158
Sub-item b. Bohairic 158
Sub-item c. Middle Egyptian 160

Item 5. Latin Versions 160
Sub-item a. The Old Latin 161
Sub-item b. The Vulgate 162

Item 6. Gothic Versions 164
    Scrivener's Discussion, 164.

Item 7. The Fathers 166

NOTE SIXTEEN. The Printed Bible 168

Item 1. The Gutenberg or Mazarin Bible, in Latin,
    1456 168

Item 2. The First Greek Bible, the Complutensian or
    Cardinal Ximenes Text, 1520 168

Item 3. The Erasmus Bible, in Greek, 1516 170

Item 4. The Editions of Robert Stephen, Theodore
    Beza, and the Elzevirs (Bonaventure and Abra-
    ham), 1546-1633 171
        Stephen (Stephanus) Bible, 171; Beza Bible, 171; El-
        zevir Bible, 172.

NOTE SEVENTEEN. English Versions 173

Item 1. English Manuscript Bibles 173

Item 2. The Printed Bible 175
Sub-item a. Tindale's Bible, the First English
    Bible Translated from Greek, 1526 175
Sub-item b. Coverdale's Bible, 1535 176
Sub-item c. Matthew's Bible, 1537 177
Sub-item d. Taverner's Bible, 1539 178
Sub-item e. The Great Bible, 1539-1541 178
Sub-item f. The Geneva Bible, 1557-1560 179
Sub-item g. The Bishops' Bible, 1568 180
Sub-item h. The Rheims or Douai Bible,
    1582-1609 181

**NOTE EIGHTEEN. The Authorized Version (A. V.) or
King James Version, 1611** 183

Item 1. The Preparation of the Text 183
        Division of Work, 184; Rules of Procedure, 184; Issues
        of Bible, 185.

Item 2. Source Materials of King James Version 185
Item 3. Modern Revisers' Justification 187
Item 4. Various Editions of the Authorized Version 188
Item 5. The Apocrypha 188
Item 6. Appraisal of Authorized Version 190
Item 7. Character of Greek Source Material for
Authorized Version 191

NOTE NINETEEN. The Byzantine Text 194

Resume of Printed Bible, 195; Manuscript Appraisal, 197; Scrivener's Comments, 197; Preparation of Manuscripts, 201; Imperfections in Sinaiticus Manuscript (א), 203; Imperfections of Vaticanus Manuscript (B), 206; Imperfections of the Two Manuscripts Compared, 207; Early Appearance of Various Types, 208; One Original Text Thesis, 209; Luke's Testimony, 211; "Welter" of Readings, 213; All Principal Types in Egypt, 213; Development of Texts, 214; Building Revised Standard Version Text, 216; Competitive Texts, 217; Egyptian Papyri, 217; The Uncial Texts in Greek, 219; The Syriac Versions, 222; Summary, 223.

NOTE TWENTY. The Inspired Version by the Prophet Joseph Smith 227

NOTE TWENTY-ONE. The Revised Versions, British and American 230

Item 1. General Observations 230
Item 2. Attitude and Possible Motives of Revisionists..233
Item 3. The Codex Sinaiticus (א) 235
Item 4. The Codex Vaticanus (B) 238

NOTE TWENTY-TWO. How Codices א and B (Sinaiticus and Vaticanus) Might Have Been Prepared 243

NOTE TWENTY-THREE. Reliability and Characteristics of Codices א and B (Sinaiticus and Vaticanus) 246

Item 1. Favorite Texts of Different Extreme Textualists 246
Item 2. Comparison of Texts א B A C D 246
Item 3. Special Comments on Texts א and B 248
Item 4. Arrangement of Columns in א and B 249

NOTE TWENTY-FOUR. Purity of the Text of the Codices א A B C D 252

Item 1. The Relative Corruption of These Texts 252
Item 2. Burgon's Collation of Luke 8:35-44 253
Item 3. Scrivener's Comments 255

NOTE TWENTY-FIVE. Tischendorf's Text— Sinaiticus (א) 258

Item 1. Scrivener's Comments 258
Item 2. Burgon's Comments 259

NOTE TWENTY-SIX. Westcott and Hort's New Greek Text 261

NOTE TWENTY-SEVEN. The Making of the Revised Versions, British and American 265

   Item 1. The Old Testament Text 265

   Item 2. The New Testament Text 265
      Resolutions for Guidance of Revisers, 266; Principles
      and Rules Governing Work of Revisers, 267; Time Con-
      sumed in Revision, 267; American-British Collabora-
      tion, 268.

   Item 3. Method of Work of Revisers 269

NOTE TWENTY-EIGHT. The Prefaces of the Revisions as Published by the Revisers 274

   Item 1. The Qualifications of the Revisers for Expressing Their Views, Revised Version 274

   Item 2. The Preface to the Old Testament, Revised
   Version 275

   Item 3. The Preface to the New Testament, Revised
   Version 276
      Summary Comments, 278.

   Item 4. The Preface to the Old Testament Revised
   Version 1900-1901 (American Standard Version)....282

   Item 5. The Preface to the New Testament Revised
   Version 1900-1901 (American Standard Version)....283

NOTE TWENTY-NINE. "Conjectural Emendation" in Determining the True Text 286

   Item 1. What is "Conjectural Emendation?" 286

   Item 2. Principle of "Conjectural Emendation" Not
   Generally Accepted 288

   Item 3. Problems and Dangers of "Conjectural
   Emendation" 291

   Item 4. Applicability of "Conjectural Emendation"
   to the Revised Version 292

   Item 5. Scrivener's Ultimate Views on "Conjectural
   Emendation" 296

   Item 6. Burgon's List of Textual Changes Made by
   Westcott and Hort on the Basis of "Conjectural
   Emendation" or "Ring of Genuineness" 297

NOTE THIRTY. The Use and Misuse of Marginal Notes........300

Item 1. Alterations Frequently Made Only in Marginal
Notes 300

Item 2. Luke 3:22, 10:41-42 Examined as to Different
Readings in the Manuscripts 302

Item 3. Treatment of Mark 6:11 303
Further on Marginal Notes, 304.

**NOTE THIRTY-ONE. New Renderings of Words; Matters
of Grammar** 306

Item 1. Some Miscellaneous Matters of Change 306

Item 2. Elimination of the Word "Charity" 308

Item 3. Elimination of Word "Miracles" 308

Item 4. Elimination and Changes of Other Important
Words 309

Item 5. Changing of "Lunatic" to "Epileptic". Effect on
Matt. 17:21 310

Item 6. Changes Made in Rom. 9:5, as Affecting
Christ's Godhood 312
Burgon Cites Authorities, 312.

Item 7. Changes in I Tim. 3:16 314

**NOTE THIRTY-TWO. Vital Omissions and Differences
Between Authorized and Revised Versions** 315

Item 1. Purpose of Note 315

Item 2. Vital Differences Between Authorized Version
and Revised Version 316

Sub-item a. Account of the Birth of Jesus,
Matt. 1:25 316

Sub-item b. Jesus, the Son of God, Mark 1:1 318

Sub-item c. Christ, the Creator, John 1:3-4 319

Sub-item d. The Son of Man, "in heaven,"
John 3:13 319

Sub-item e. The Lord's Prayer, Matt. 6:9-13,
Luke 11:2-4 321

Sub-item f. The Message of the Heavenly Host,
Luke 2:14 325
The Witness of Gospel Copies and Versions, 326; The
Testimony of the Fathers, 327; Other Illustrious Wit-
nesses, 328; Geographical Distribution of Witnesses,
329.

Sub-item g. The Institution of the Sacrament,
Luke 22:19-20 329

Sub-item h. The Agony in the Garden and the
Ministering Angel, Luke 22:43-44 331
Witnesses for the King James Text, 332; Burgon's
Comments on Revisers' Attitude, 333; Westcott-Hort's
Explanation of Omissions, 334.

Sub-item i. The Prayer on the Cross, Luke 23:24....334
Burgon's Discussion, 335; Witness of the Fathers, 336.

Sub-item j. Christ's Salutation to the Apostles in
the Upper Chamber, Luke 24:36 337

Sub-item k. Christ Displays His Hands and Feet,
Luke 24:40 337

Sub-item l. Casting Out Evil Spirits, Matt. 17:21....338

Sub-item m. "The Son of man is come to save,"
Matt. 18:11 340

Sub-item n. The Last Twelve Verses of the Gospel
of Mark, Mark 16:9-20 341
Burgon's Analysis of Designated Objections, 347.

NOTE THIRTY-THREE. Revised Standard Version
(American), Published February, 1946 351

Item 1. Character of the New Revised Standard
Version 351
The Revisers' "Introduction" Pamphlet, 352; The Language of the New Revision, 354.

Item 2. Organization for the Revised Standard
Version Project 356

Item 3. Reasons Assigned for Revision—Imperfections
of the Revised Version 358

Item 4. Source Materials Used for New Testament
Text Revision 361

Item 5. Canons of Criticism — Adoption of Westcott-
Hort's Greek Text 365

Item 6. New Source Material Available to Revised
Standard Version Translators 370

Item 7. Use of Source Materials 372

Item 8. Possible Aramaic Original Text 375

Item 9. The Seeming Real Reasons for the Revised
Standard Version 377

Item 10. Illustrative Text Changes 381

Item 11. Some Grammatical and Other Errors in the
Authorized Version 386

Item 12. Some General Impressions 391

NOTE THIRTY-FOUR. **Some Critical Omissions from and
Changes Made in the King James Version by the Earlier
Revisions and Retained and Added to by the Revised
Standard Version** 395

Item 1. "Conjectural Emendations" 395

Item 2. "Love" for "Charity" 398

Item 3. Elimination of "Miracles" from the New Text....398

Item 4. Casting Out of Evil Spirits, Matt. 17:14 ff. 399

Item 5. The Word "Inspiration," II Tim. 3:16 399

Item 6. The Godhood of Christ 400

Item 7. Special Vital Omissions 401

    Sub-item a. Account of the Birth of Jesus,
    Matt. 1:25 401

    Sub-item b. Jesus, the Son of God, Mark 1:1 402

    Sub-item c. Christ, the Creator, John 1:3-4 403

    Sub-item d. The Son of Man, "in heaven,"
    John 3:13 403

    Sub-item e. The Lord's Prayer, Matt. 6:9-13;
    Luke 11:2-4 404
    Luke's Account, 405.

    Sub-item f. The Message of the Heavenly Host,
    Luke 2:14 405

    Sub-item g. The Institution of the Sacrament,
    Luke 22:19-20 406
    Matthew's Account, 408; Mark's Account, 409.

    Sub-item h. The Agony in the Garden and the
    Ministering Angel, Luke 22:43-44 410

    Sub-item i. The Prayer on the Cross, Luke 23:34....411

    Sub-item j. Christ's Salutation to the Apostles
    in the Upper Chamber, Luke 24:36 412

    Sub-item k. Christ Displays His Hands and Feet,
    Luke 24:40 413

    Sub-item l. Casting Out Evil Spirits, Matt. 17:21....414
    Mark's Account, 414.

Sub-item m. The Son of Man is Come to Save,
   Matt. 18:11 415

Sub-item n. The Last Twelve Verses in Mark,
   Mark 16:9-20 416

SOME CLOSING OBSERVATIONS 418
   These Notes, 418; The Spirit of the Approach, 418; My
   Witness, 420.

APPENDIX A. Table of Chief Uncial Manuscripts 424

APPENDIX B. Table of Versions 426

APPENDIX C. Scrivener's List of Ecclesiastical Writers......427

BIBLIOGRAPHY 432

BIOGRAPHICAL NOTES 436

INDEX A. SUBJECTS 443

INDEX B. SCRIPTURAL REFERENCES 474

LIST OF ILLUSTRATIONS ·

King James (Authorized) Version, 1611...............*Frontispiece*

Chester Beatty Papyrus I ....*Facing Page* 8

Rylands Fragment of John 9

A—Codex Alexandrinus 136

C—Codex Ephraemi 137

Erasmus Bible 216

D—Codex Bezae 217

ℵ—Codex Sinaiticus 248

B—Codex Vaticanus 249

"THE TRANSLATORS TO THE READER"

Note: This document was issued in 1611 by the Translators of the Authorized Version, the King James Version. It is rarely printed but its witness of the scholarship of the translators (sometimes referred to in slighting terms) and of the reverential spirit in which they came to their translating tasks, made it seem desirable to print it as a part of this book, so making it more readily available. Those translators were neither unlearned nor devoid of reverence and amenability to the promptings of the Holy Spirit. They worked not only, but prayed also.

Zeal to promote the common good, whether it be by devising any thing ourselves, or revising that which hath been laboured by others, deserveth certainly much respect and esteem, but yet findeth but cold entertainment in the world. It is welcomed with suspicion instead of love, and with emulation instead of thanks: and if there be any hole left for cavil to enter, (and cavil, if it do not find an hole, will make one,) it is sure to be misconstrued, and in danger to be condemned. This will easily be granted by as many as know story, or have any experience. For was there ever any thing projected, that savoured any way of newness or renewing, but the same endured many a storm of gainsaying or opposition? A man would think that civility, wholesome laws, learning and eloquence, synods, and Churchmaintenance, (that we speak of no more things of this kind,) should be as safe as a sanctuary, and out of shot, as they say, that no man would lift up his heel, no, nor dog move his tongue against the motioners of them. For by the first we are distinguished from brute beasts led with sensuality: by the second we are bridled and restrained from outrageous behaviour, and from doing of injuries, whether by fraud or by violence: by the third we are enabled to inform and reform others by the light and feeling that we have attained

unto ourselves: briefly, by the fourth, being brought together
to a parley face to face, we sooner compose our differences,
than by writings, which are endless: and lastly, that the
Church be sufficiently provided for is so agreeable to good
reason and conscience, that those mothers are holden to be
less cruel, that kill their children as soon as they are born,
than those nursing fathers and mothers (wheresoever they be)
that withdraw from them who hang upon their breasts (and
upon whose breasts again themselves do hang to receive the
spiritual and sincere milk of the word) livelihood and support
fit for their estates. Thus it is apparent, that these things
which we speak of are of most necessary use, and therefore that
none, either without absurdity can speak against them, or without note of wickedness can spurn against them.

Yet for all that, the learned know, that certain worthy
men have been brought to untimely death for none other fault,
but for seeking to reduce their countrymen to good order and
discipline: And that in some Commonweals it was made a
capital crime, once to motion the making of a new law for the
abrogating of an old, though the same were most pernicious:
And that certain, which would be counted pillars of the State,
and patterns of virtue and prudence, could not be brought
for a long time to give way to good letters and refined speech;
but bare themselves as averse from them, as from rocks or
boxes of poison: And fourthly, that he was no babe, but a
great Clerk, that gave forth, (and in writing to remain to
posterity,) in passion peradventure, but yet he gave forth,
That he had not seen any profit to come by any synod or meeting of the Clergy, but rather the contrary: And lastly, against
Churchmaintenance and allowance, in such sort as the ambas-
sadors and messengers of the great King of kings should be
furnished, it is not unknown what a fiction or fable (so it is
esteemed, and for no better by the reporter himself, though
superstitious) was devised: namely, That at such time as the
professors and teachers of Christianity in the Church of Rome,
then a true Church, were liberally endowed, a voice forsooth
was heard from heaven, saying, Now is poison poured down

into the Church, &c. Thus not only as oft as we speak, as one
saith, but also as oft as we do any thing of note or consequence,
we subject ourselves to every one's censure, and happy is he
that is least tossed upon tongues; for utterly to escape the
snatch of them it is impossible. If any man conceit, that this
is the lot and portion of the meaner sort only, and that Princes
are privileged by their high estate, he is deceived. As *the
sword devoureth as well one as another,* as it is in *Samuel;*
nay, as the great commander charged his soldiers in a certain
battle to strike at no part of the enemy, but at the face; and
as the king of *Syria* commanded his chief captains *to fight
neither with small nor great, save only against the king of
Israel*: so it is too true, that envy striketh most spitefully
at the fairest, and the chiefest. *David* was a worthy prince,
and no man to be compared to him for his first deeds; and
yet for as worthy an act as ever he did, even for bringing
back the ark of God in solemnity, he was scorned and scoffed
at by his own wife. *Solomon* was greater than *David,* though
not in virtue, yet in power; and by his power and wisdom he
built a temple to the Lord, such an one as was the glory of
the land of Israel, and the wonder of the whole world. But
was that his magnificence liked of by all? We doubt of it.
Otherwise why do they lay it in his own son's dish, and call
unto him for easing of the burden? *Make,* say they, *the
grievous servitude of thy father, and his sore yoke, lighter.*
Belike he had charged them with some levies, and troubled
them with some carriages; hereupon they raise up a tragedy,
and wish in their heart the temple had never been built. So
hard a thing is it to please all, even when we please God best,
and do seek to approve ourselves to every one's conscience.

If we will descend to latter times, we shall find many the
like examples of such kind, or rather unkind, acceptance. The
first Roman Emperor did never do a more pleasing deed to
the learned, nor more profitable to posterity, for conserving
the record of times in true supputation, than when he corrected the Calendar, and ordered the year according to the
course of the sun: and yet this was imputed to him for nov-

elty, and arrogancy, and procured to him great obloquy. So
the first Christened Emperor (at the least wise, that openly
professed the faith himself, and allowed others to do the like,)
for strengthening the empire at his great charges, and pro-
viding for the Church, as he did, got for his labour the name
Pupillus, as who would say, a wasteful Prince, that had need
of a guardian or overseer. So the best Christened Emperor,
for the love that he bare unto peace, thereby to enrich both
himself and his subjects, and because he did not seek war, but
find it, was judged to be no man at arms, (though indeed he
excelled in feats of chivalry, and shewed so much when he
was provoked,) and condemned for giving himself to his ease,
and to his pleasure. To be short, the most learned Emperor
of former times, (at the least, the greatest politician,) what
thanks had he for cutting off the superfluities of the laws, and
digesting them into some order and method? This, that he
hath been blotted by some to be an Epitomist, that is, one that
extinguished worthy whole volumes, to bring his abridgments
into request. This is the measure that hath been rendered to
excellent Princes in former times, *cum bene facerent, male
audire,* for their good deeds to be evil spoken of. Neither is
there any likelihood that envy and malignity died and were
buried with the ancient. No, no, the reproof of *Moses* taketh
hold of most ages, *Ye are risen up in your fathers' stead, an
increase of sinful men. What is that that hath been done?
that which shall be done: and there is no new thing under
the sun,* saith the wise man. And St. *Stephen, As your fathers
did, so do ye.* This, and more to this purpose, his Majesty that
now reigneth (and long, and long, may he reign, and his offspring for ever, *Himself, and children, and children's children
always!*) knew full well, according to the singular wisdom
given unto him by God, and the rare learning and experience
that he hath attained unto; namely, That whosoever attempteth
any thing for the publick, (especially if it pertain to religion,
and to the opening and clearing of the word of God,) the same
setteth himself upon a stage to be glouted upon by every evil
eye; yea, he casteth himself headlong upon pikes, to be gored

by every sharp tongue. For he that meddleth with men's religion in any part meddleth with their custom, nay, with their freehold; and though they find no content in that which they have, yet they cannot abide to hear of altering. Notwithstanding his royal heart was not daunted or discouraged for this or that colour, but stood resolute, *as a statue immoveable, and an anvil not easy to be beaten into plates,* as one saith; he knew who had chosen him to be a soldier, or rather a captain; and being assured that the course which he intended made much for the glory of God, and the building up of his Church, he would not suffer it to be broken off for whatsoever speeches or practices. It doth certainly belong unto kings, yea, it doth specially belong unto them, to have care of religion, yea, to know it aright, yea, to profess it zealously, yea, to promote it to the uttermost of their power. This is their glory before all nations which mean well, and this will bring unto them a far more excellent weight of glory in the day of the Lord Jesus. For the Scripture saith not in vain, *Them that honour me I will honour*: neither was it a vain word that *Eusebius* delivered long ago, That piety toward God was the weapon, and the only weapon, that both preserved *Constantine's* person, and avenged him of his enemies.

But now what piety without truth? What truth, what saving truth, without the word of God? What word of God, whereof we may be sure, without the Scripture? The Scriptures we are commanded to search, *John* 5. 39; *Isai.* 8. 20. They are commended that searched and studied them, *Acts* 17. 11, and 8. 28, 29. They are reproved that were unskilful in them, or slow to believe them, *Matt.* 22. 29; *Luke* 24. 25. They can make us wise unto salvation, 2 *Tim.* 3. 15. If we be ignorant, they will instruct us; if out of the way, they will bring us home; if out of order, they will reform us; if in heaviness, comfort us; if dull, quicken us; if cold, inflame us. *Tolle, lege; tolle, lege;* Take up and read, take up and read the Scriptures, (for unto them was the direction,) it was said unto St. *Augustine* by a supernatural voice. *Whatsoever is in the Scriptures, believe me,* saith the same St. *Augustine, is high and divine;*

there is verily truth, and a doctrine most fit for the refreshing
and renewing of men's minds, and truly so tempered, that
every one may draw from thence that which is sufficient for
him, if he come to draw with a devout and pious mind, as true
religion requireth. Thus St. *Augustine.* And St. *Hierome, Ama*
Scripturas, et amabit te sapientia, &c. Love the Scriptures,
and wisdom will love thee. And St. *Cyrill* against *Julian, Even*
boys that are bred up in the Scriptures become most religious,
&c. But what mention we three or four uses of the Scripture,
whereas whatsoever is to be believed, or practised, or hoped
for, is contained in them? or three or four sentences of the
Fathers, since whosoever is worthy the name of a Father, from
Christ's time downward, hath likewise written not only of
the riches, but also of the perfection of the Scripture? *I adore*
the fulness of the Scripture, saith *Tertullian* against *Her-*
mogenes. And again, to *Apelles* an heretick of the like stamp
he saith, *I do not admit that which thou bringest in* (or con-
cludest) *of thine own* (head or store, *de tuo*) without Scripture.
So St. *Justin Martyr* before him; *We must know by all means*
(saith he) *that it is not lawful* (or possible) *to learn* (any
thing) *of God or of right piety, save only out of the Prophets,*
who teach us by divine inspiration. So St. *Basil* after *Ter-*
tullian, It is a manifest falling away from the faith, and a
fault of presumption, either to reject any of those things
that are written, or to bring in (upon the head of them,
ἐπεισαγεῖν) *any of those things that are not written.* We omit
to cite to the same effect St. *Cyrill* Bishop of *Jerusalem.* in his
4 *Catech.* St. *Hierome* against *Helvidius,* St. *Augustine* in his
third book against the letters of *Petilian,* and in very many
other places of his works. Also we forbear to descend to later
Fathers, because we will not weary the reader. The Scriptures then being acknowledged to be so full and so perfect,
how can we excuse ourselves of negligence, if we do not
study them? of curiosity, if we be not content with them?
Men talk much of εἰρεσιώνη, how many sweet and goodly things
it had hanging on it; of the Philosopher's stone, that it turn-
eth copper into gold; of *Cornucopia,* that it had all things

necessary for food in it; of *Panaces* the herb, that it was good for all diseases; of *Catholicon* the drug, that it is instead of all purges; of *Vulcan's* armour, that it was an armour of proof against all thrusts and all blows, &c. Well, that which they falsely or vainly attributed to these things for bodily good, we may justly and with full measure ascribe unto the Scripture for spiritual. It is not only an armour, but also a whole armoury of weapons, both offensive and defensive; whereby we may save ourselves, and put the enemy to flight. It is not an herb, but a tree, or rather a whole paradise of trees of life, which bring forth fruit every month, and the fruit thereof is for meat, and the leaves for medicine. It is not a pot of *Manna*, or a cruse of oil, which were for memory only, or for a meal's meat or two; but, as it were, a shower of heavenly bread sufficient for a whole host, be it never so great, and, as it were, a whole cellar full of oil vessels; whereby all our necessities may be provided for, and our debts discharged. In a word, it is a panary of wholesome food against fenowed traditions; a physician's shop (as St. *Basil* calls it) of preservatives against poisoned heresies; a pandect of profitable laws against rebellious spirits; a treasury of most costly jewels against beggarly rudiments; finally, a fountain of most pure water springing up unto everlasting life. And what marvel? the original thereof being from heaven, not from earth; the author being God, not man; the inditer, the Holy Spirit, not the wit of the Apostles or Prophets; the penmen, such as were sanctified from the womb, and endued with a principal portion of God's Spirit; the matter, verity, piety, purity, uprightness; the form, God's word, God's testimony, God's oracles, the word of truth, the word of salvation, &c.; the effects, light of understanding, stableness of persuasion, repentance from dead works, newness of life, holiness, peace, joy in the Holy Ghost; lastly, the end and reward of the study thereof, fellowship with the saints, participation of the heavenly nature, fruition of an inheritance immortal, undefiled, and that never shall fade away. Happy is the man that delighteth in the Scripture, and thrice happy that meditateth in it day and night.

But how shall men meditate in that which they cannot understand? How shall they understand that which is kept close in an unknown tongue? as it is written, *Except I know the power of the voice, I shall be to him that speaketh a barbarian, and he that speaketh shall be a barbarian to me.* The Apostle excepteth no tongue; not *Hebrew* the ancientest, not *Greek* the most copious, not *Latin* the finest. Nature taught a natural man to confess, that all of us in those tongues which we do not understand are plainly deaf; we may turn the deaf ear unto them. The *Scythian* counted the *Athenian,* whom he did not understand, barbarous: so the *Roman* did the *Syrian,* and the *Jew*: (even St. *Hierome* himself calleth the *Hebrew* tongue barbarous; belike, because it was strange to so many:) so the Emperor of *Constantinople* calleth the *Latin* tongue barbarous, though Pope *Nicolas* do storm at it: so the *Jews* long before *Christ* called all other nations *Lognasim,* which is little better than barbarous. Therefore as one complaineth that always in the Senate of *Rome* there was one or other that called for an interpreter; so lest the Church be driven to the like exigent, it is necessary to have translations in a readiness. Translation it is that openeth the window, to let in the light; that breaketh the shell, that we may eat the kernel; that putteth aside the curtain, that we may look into the most holy place; that removeth the cover of the well, that we may come by the water; even as *Jacob* rolled away the stone from the mouth of the well, by which means the flocks of *Laban* were watered. Indeed without translation into the vulgar tongue, the unlearned are but like children at *Jacob's* well (which was deep) without a bucket or something to draw with: or as that person mentioned by *Esay,* to whom when a sealed book was delivered with this motion, *Read this, I pray thee,* he was fain to make this answer, *I cannot, for it is sealed.*

While God would be known only in *Jacob,* and have his name great in *Israel,* and in none other place; while the dew lay on *Gideon's* fleece only, and all the earth besides was dry; then for one and the same people, which spake all of them the language of *Canaan,* that is, *Hebrew,* one and the same original in *Hebrew* was sufficient. But when the fulness of time drew near, that the Sun of righteousness, the Son of God, should come into the world, whom God ordained to be a reconciliation through faith in his blood, not of the *Jew* only, but also of the *Greek,* yea, of all them that were scattered abroad; then, lo, it pleased the Lord to stir up the spirit of a *Greek* prince, (*Greek* for descent and language,) even of *Ptolemy Philadelph* king of *Egypt,* to procure the translating of the book of God out of *Hebrew* into *Greek.* This is the translation of the *Seventy* interpreters, commonly so called, which prepared the way for our Saviour among the *Gentiles* by written preaching, as St. *John Baptist* did among the *Jews* by vocal. For the *Grecians,* being desirous of learning, were not wont to suffer books of worth to lie moulding in kings' libraries, but had many of their servants, ready scribes, to copy them out, and so they were dispersed and made common. Again the *Greek* tongue was well known and made familiar to most inhabitants in *Asia* by reason of the conquests that there the *Grecians* had made, as also by the colonies which thither they had sent. For the same causes also it was well understood in many places of *Europe,* yea, and of *Africk* too. Therefore the word of God, being set forth in *Greek,* becometh hereby like a candle set upon a candlestick, which giveth light to all that are in the house; or like a proclamation sounded forth in the marketplace, which most men presently take knowledge of; and therefore that language was fittest to contain the Scriptures, both for the first preachers of the Gospel to appeal unto for witness, and for the learners also of those times to make search and trial by. It is certain, that that translation was not so sound and so perfect, but that it needed in many places correction; and who had been so sufficient for this work as the Apostles or apostolick men? Yet it seemed good to the Holy Ghost and to them to take that which they found, (the same being for the greatest part true and sufficient,) rather than by making a new, in that new world and green age of the Church, to expose themselves to many exceptions and cavillations, as though they made a translation to serve their own turn; and therefore bearing witness to themselves, their witness not to be regarded. This may be supposed to be some cause, why the translation of the *Seventy* was allowed to pass for current. Notwithstanding, though it was commended generally, yet it did not fully content the learned, no not of the *Jews*. For not long after *Christ, Aquila* fell in hand with a new translation, and after him *Theodotion*, and after him *Symmachus*: yea, there was a fifth, and a sixth edition, the authors whereof were not known. These with the *Seventy* made up the *Hexapla*, and were worthily and to great purpose compiled together by *Origen*. Howbeit the edition of the *Seventy* went away with the credit, and therefore not only was placed in the midst by *Origen*, (for the worth and excellency thereof above the rest, as *Epiphanius* gathereth,) but also was used by the *Greek* Fathers for the ground and foundation of their commentaries. Yea, *Epiphanius* abovenamed doth attribute so much unto it, that he holdeth the authors thereof not only for interpreters, but also for prophets in some respect: and *Justinian* the Emperor, injoining the *Jews* his subjects to use especially the translation of the *Seventy*, rendereth this reason thereof, Because they were, as it were, enlightened with prophetical grace. Yet for all that, as the *Egyptians* are said of the Prophet to be men and not God, and their horses flesh and not spirit: so it is evident, (and St. *Hierome* affirmeth as much,) that the *Seventy* were interpreters, they were not prophets. They did many things well, as learned men; but yet as men they stumbled and fell, one while through oversight, another while through ignorance; yea, sometimes they may be noted to add to the original, and sometimes to take from it: which made the Apostles to leave them many times, when they left the *Hebrew*, and to deliver the sense thereof according to the truth of the word, as the Spirit gave them utterance. This may suffice touching the *Greek* translations of the Old Testament.

There were also within a few hundred years after *Christ* translations many into the *Latin* tongue: for this tongue also was very fit to convey the Law and the Gospel by, because in those times very many countries of the West, yea of the South, East, and North, spake or understood *Latin,* being made provinces to the *Romans.* But now the *Latin* translations were too many to be all good: for they were infinite; (*Latini interpretes nullo modo numerari possunt,* saith St. *Augustine.*) Again, they were not out of the *Hebrew* fountain, (we speak of the *Latin* translations of the Old Testament,) but out of the *Greek* stream; therefore the *Greek* being not altogether clear, the *Latin* derived from it must needs be muddy. This moved St. *Hierome,* a most learned Father, and the best linguist without controversy of his age, or of any other that went before him, to undertake the translating of the Old Testament out of the very fountains themselves; which he performed with that evidence of great learning, judgment, industry, and faithfulness, that he hath for ever bound the Church unto him in a debt of special remembrance and thankfulness.

Now though the Church were thus furnished with *Greek* and *Latin* translations, even before the faith of Christ was generally embraced in the Empire: (for the learned know, that even in St. *Hierome's* time the Consul of *Rome* and his wife were both Ethnicks, and about the same time the greatest part of the Senate also:) yet for all that the godly learned were not content to have the Scriptures in the language which themselves understood, *Greek* and *Latin,* (as the good lepers were not content to fare well themselves, but acquainted their neighbours with the store that God had sent, that they also might provide for themselves;) but also for the behoof and edifying of the unlearned, which hungered and thirsted after righteousness, and had souls to be saved as well as they, they provided translations into the vulgar for their countrymen, insomuch that most nations under heaven did shortly after their conversion hear *Christ* speaking unto them in their mother tongue, not by the voice of their minister only, but also by the written word translated. If any doubt hereof, he may be satisfied by examples enough, if enough will serve the turn. First, St. *Hierome* saith, *Multarum gentium linguis Scriptura ante translata docet falsa esse quæ addita sunt,* &c. That is, *The*

Scripture being translated before in the languages of many nations doth shew that those things that were added (by *Lucian* or *Hesychius*) *are false.* So St. *Hierome* in that place. The same *Hierome* elsewhere affirmeth that he, the time was, had set forth the translation of the *Seventy, suæ linguæ hominibus;* that is, for his countrymen of *Dalmatia.* Which words not only *Erasmus* doth understand to purport, that St. *Hierome* translated the Scripture into the *Dalmatian* tongue; but also *Sixtus Senesis,* and *Alphonsus a Castro,* (that we speak of no more,) men not to be excepted against by them of *Rome,* do ingenuously confess as much. So St. *Chrysostome,* that lived in St. *Hierome's* time, giveth evidence with him: *The doctrine of St. John* (saith he) *did not in such sort* (as the Philosophers' did) *vanish away: but the Syrians, Egyptians, Indians, Persians, Ethiopians, and infinite other nations, being barbarous people, translated it into their (mother) tongue, and have learned to be (true) Philosophers,* he meaneth Christians. To this may be added *Theodoret,* as next unto him both for antiquity, and for learning. His words be these, *Every country that is under the sun is full of these words,* (of the Apostles and Prophets;) *and the Hebrew tongue* (he meaneth the Scriptures in the *Hebrew* tongue) *is turned not only into the language of the Grecians, but also of the Romans, and Egyptians, and Persians, and Indians, and Armenians, and Scythians, and Sauromatians, and, briefly, into all the languages that any nation useth.* So he. In like manner *Ulpilas* is reported by *Paulus Diaconus* and *Isidore,* and before them by *Sozomen,* to have translated the Scriptures into the *Gothick* tongue: *John* Bishop of *Sevil* by *Vasseus,* to have turned them into *Arabick* about the Year of our Lord 717: *Beda* by *Cistertiensis,* to have turned a great part of them into *Saxon: Efnard* by *Trithemius,* to have abridged the French Psalter (as *Beda* had done the *Hebrew*) about the year 800: King *Alured* by the said *Cistertiensis,* to have turned the Psalter into *Saxon: Methodius* by *Aventinus* (printed at *Ingolstad*) to have turned the Scriptures into *Sclavonian: Valdo* Bishop of *Frising* by *Beatus Rhenanus,* to have caused about that time the Gospels to be translated into *Dutch* rhyme, yet extant in the library of *Corbinian*: *Valdus* by divers, to have turned them himself, or to have gotten them turned, into *French,* about the Year 1160: *Charles* the Fifth of that name, surnamed *The wise,* to have caused them to be turned into *French* about 200 years after *Valdus'* time; of which translation there be many copies yet extant, as witnesseth *Beroaldus.* Much about that time, even in our King *Richard* the Second's days, *John Trevisa* translated them into *English,* and many *English* Bibles in written hand are yet to be seen with divers; translated, as it is very probable, in that age. So the *Syrian* translation of the New Testament is in most learned men's libraries, of *Widminstadius'* setting forth; and the Psalter in *Arabick* is with many, of *Augustinus Nebiensis'* setting forth. So *Postel* affirmeth, that in his travel he saw the Gospels in the *Ethiopian* tongue: And *Ambrose Thesius* alledgeth the Psalter of the *Indians,* which he testifieth to have been set forth by *Potken* in *Syrian* characters. So that to have the Scriptures in the mother tongue is not a quaint conceit lately taken up, either by the Lord *Cromwell* in *England,* or by the Lord *Radevile* in *Polony,* or by the Lord *Ungnadius* in the Emperor's dominion, but hath been thought upon, and put in practice of old, even from the first times of the conversion of any nation; no doubt, because it was esteemed most profitable to cause faith to grow in men's hearts the sooner, and to make them to be able to say with the words of the Psalm, *As we have heard, so we have seen.*

Now the church of *Rome* would seem at the length to bear a motherly affection toward her children, and to allow them the Scriptures in the mother tongue: but indeed it is a gift, not deserving to be called a gift, an unprofitable gift: they must first get a licence in writing before they may use them; and to get that, they must approve themselves to their Confessor, that is, to be such as are, if not frozen in the dregs, yet soured with the leaven of their superstition. Howbeit it seemed too much to *Clement* the Eighth, that there should be any licence granted to have them in the vulgar tongue, and therefore he overruleth and frustrateth the grant of *Pius* the

Fourth. So much are they afraid of the light of the Scripture, (*Lucifugæ Scripturarum*, as *Tertullian* speaketh,) that they will not trust the people with it, no not as it is set forth by their own sworn men, no not with the licence of their own Bishops and Inquisitors. Yea, so unwilling they are to communicate the Scriptures to the people's understanding in any sort, that they are not ashamed to confess, that we forced them to translate it into *English* against their wills. This seemeth to argue a bad cause, or a bad conscience, or both. Sure we are, that it is not he that hath good gold, that is afraid to bring it to the touchstone, but he that hath the counterfeit; neither is it the true man that shunneth the light, but the malefactor, lest his deeds should be reproved; neither is it the plain-dealing merchant that is unwilling to have the weights, or the meteyard, brought in place, but he that useth deceit. But we will let them alone for this fault, and return to translation.

Many men's mouths have been opened a good while (and yet are not stopped) with speeches about the translation so long in hand, or rather perusals of translations made before: and ask what may be the reason, what the necessity, of the employment. Hath the Church been deceived, say they, all this while? Hath her sweet bread been mingled with leaven, her silver with dross, her wine with water, her milk with lime? (*lacte gypsum male miscetur*, saith St. *Irenee*.) We hoped that we had been in the right way, that we had had the Oracles of God delivered unto us, and that though all the world had cause to be offended, and to complain, yet that we had none. Hath the nurse holden out the breast, and nothing but wind in it? Hath the bread been delivered by the Fathers of the Church, and the same proved to be *lapidosus*, as *Seneca* speaketh? What is it to handle the word of God deceitfully, if this be not? Thus certain brethren. Also the adversaries of *Judah* and *Jerusalem*, like *Sanballat* in *Nehemiah*, mock, as we hear, both at the work and workmen, saying, *What do these weak Jews, &c.? will they make the stones whole again out of the heaps of dust which are burnt? although they build,*

yet if a fox go up, he shall even break down their stony wall.
Was their translation good before? Why do they now mend
it? Was it not good? Why then was it obtruded to the people?
Yea, why did the Catholicks (meaning Popish *Romanists*)
always go in jeopardy for refusing to go to hear it? Nay, if
it must be translated into *English,* Catholicks are fittest to
do it. They have learning, and they know when a thing is well,
they can *manum de tabula.* We will answer them both briefly:
and the former, being brethren, thus with St. *Hierome, Damna-
mus veteres? Minime, sed post priorum studia in domo Domini
quod possumus laboramus.* That is, *Do we condemn the ancient? In no case: but after the endeavours of them that were
before us, we take the best pains we can in the house of God.*
As if he said, Being provoked by the example of the learned
that lived before my time, I have thought it my duty to assay,
whether my talent in the knowledge of the tongues may be
profitable in any measure to God's Church, lest I should seem
to have laboured in them in vain, and lest I should be thought
to glory in men (although ancient) above that which was in
them. Thus St. *Hierome* may be thought to speak.

And to the same effect say we, that we are so far off from
condemning any of their labours that travelled before us in
this kind, either in this land, or beyond sea, either in King
Henry's time, or King *Edward's,* (if there were any translation, or correction of a translation, in his time,) or Queen
Elizabeth's of ever renowned memory, that we acknowledge
them to have been raised up of God for the building and furnishing of his Church, and that they deserve to be had of us
and of posterity in everlasting remembrance. The judgment
of *Aristotle* is worthy and well known: *If Timotheus had not
been, we had not had much sweet musick: But if Phrynis
(Timotheus'* master) *had not been, we had not had Timotheus.* Therefore blessed be they, and most honoured be their
name, that break the ice, and give the onset upon that which
helpeth forward to the saving of souls. Now what can be
more available thereto, than to deliver God's book unto God's
people in a tongue which they understand? Since of an hidden

treasure, and of a fountain that is sealed, there is no profit, as *Ptolemy Philadelph* wrote to the Rabbins or masters of the *Jews*, as witnesseth *Epiphanius*: and as St. *Augustine* saith, *A man had rather be with his dog than with a stranger* (whose tongue is strange unto him.) Yet for all that, as nothing is begun and perfected at the same time, and the latter thoughts are thought to be the wiser: so, if we building upon their foundation that went before us, and being holpen by their labours, do endeavour to make that better which they left so good; no man, we are sure, hath cause to mislike us; they, we persuade ourselves, if they were alive, would thank us. The vintage of *Abiezer*, that strake the stroke: yet the gleaning of grapes of *Ephraim* was not to be despised. See *Judges* 8. 2. *Joash* the king of *Israel* did not satisfy himself till he had smitten the ground three times; and yet he offended the Prophet for giving over then. *Aquila*, of whom we spake before, translated the Bible as carefully and as skilfully as he could; and yet he thought good to go over it again, and then it got the credit with the *Jews*, to be called κατ᾽ ἀκρίβειαν, that is, accurately done, as St. *Hierome* witnesseth. How many books of profane learning have been gone over again and again, by the same translators, by others? Of one and the same book of *Aristotle's* Ethicks there are extant not so few as six or seven several translations. Now if this cost may be bestowed upon the gourd, which affordeth us a little shade, and which to day flourisheth, but to morrow is cut down; what may we bestow, nay, what ought we not to bestow, upon the vine, the fruit whereof maketh glad the conscience of man, and the stem whereof abideth for ever? And this is the word of God, which we translate. *What is the chaff to the wheat? saith the Lord. Tanti vitreum, quanti verum margaritum!* (saith *Tertullian*.) If a toy of glass be of that reckoning with us, how ought we to value the true pearl! Therefore let no man's eye be evil, because his Majesty's is good; neither let any be grieved, that we have a Prince that seeketh the increase of the spiritual wealth of *Israel;* (let *Sanballats* and *Tobiahs* do so, which therefore do bear their just reproof;) but let us rather bless God from the ground of our heart for working this religious care in him to have the translations of the Bible maturely considered of and examined. For by this means it cometh to pass, that whatsoever is sound already, (and all is sound for substance in one or other of our editions, and the worst of ours far better than their authentick vulgar) the same will shine as gold more brightly, being rubbed and polished; also, if any thing be halting, or superfluous, or not so agreeable to the original, the same may be corrected, and the truth set in place. And what can the King command to be done, that will bring him more true honour than this? And wherein could they that have been set a work approve their duty to the King, yea, their obedience to God, and love to his Saints, more, than by yielding their service, and all that is within them, for the furnishing of the work? But besides all this, they were the principal motives of it, and therefore ought least to quarrel it. For the very historical truth is, that upon the importunate petitions of the Puritanes at his Majesty's coming to this crown, the conference at *Hampton-court* having been appointed for hearing their complaints, when by force of reason they were put from all other grounds, they had recourse at the last to this shift, that they could not with good conscience subscribe to the communion book, since it maintained the Bible as it was there translated, which was, as they said, a most corrupted translation. And although this was judged to be but a very poor and empty shift, yet even hereupon did his Majesty begin to bethink himself of the good that might ensue by a new translation, and presently after gave order for this translation which is now presented unto thee. Thus much to satisfy our scrupulous brethren.

Now to the latter we answer, That we do not deny, nay, we affirm and avow, that the very meanest translation of the Bible in *English,* set forth by men of our profession, (for we have seen none of their's of the whole Bible as yet) containeth the word of God, nay, is the word of God: As the King's speech which he uttered in Parliament, being translated into

French, Dutch, Italian, and *Latin,* is still the King's speech, though it be not interpreted by every translator with the like grace, nor peradventure so fitly for phrase, nor so expressly for sense, every where. For it is confessed, that things are to take their denomination of the greater part; and a natural man could say, *Verum ubi multa nitent in carmine, non ego paucis offendor maculis, &c.* A man may be counted a virtuous man, though he have made many slips in his life, (else there were none virtuous, for *in many things we offend all,*) also a comely man and lovely, though he have some warts upon his hand; yea, not only freckles upon his face, but also scars. No cause therefore why the word translated should be denied to be the word, or forbidden to be current, notwithstanding that some imperfections and blemishes may be noted in the setting forth of it. For what ever was perfect under the sun, where Apostles or apostolick men, that is, men endued with an extra-ordinary measure of God's Spirit, and privileged with the privilege of infallibility, had not their hand? The Romanists therefore in refusing to hear, and daring to burn the word translated, did no less than despite the Spirit of grace, from whom originally it proceeded, and whose sense and meaning, as well as man's weakness would enable, it did express. Judge by an example or two.

Plutarch writeth, that after that *Rome* had been burnt by the *Gauls,* they fell soon to build it again: but doing it in haste, they did not cast the streets, nor proportion the houses, in such comely fashion, as had been most sightly and con-venient. Was *Cataline* therefore an honest man, or a good patriot, that sought to bring it to a combustion? Or *Nero* a good Prince, that did indeed set it on fire? So by the story of *Ezra* and the prophecy of *Haggai* it may be gathered, that the temple built by *Zerubbabel* after the return from *Babylon* was by no means to be compared to the former built by *Solo-mon;* for they that remembered the former wept when they considered the latter. Notwithstanding might this latter either have been abhorred and forsaken by the *Jews,* or profaned by the *Greeks?* The like we are to think of translations. The translation of the *Seventy* dissenteth from the Original in many places, neither doth it come near it for perspicuity, gravity, majesty. Yet which of the Apostles did condemn it? Condemn it? Nay, they used it, (as it is apparent, and as St. *Hierome* and most learned men do confess;) which they would not have done, nor by their example of using of it so grace and commend it to the Church, if it had been unworthy the appellation and name of the word of God. And whereas they urge for their second defence to their vilifying and abusing of the *English* Bibles, or some pieces thereof, which they meet with, for that hereticks forsooth were the authors of the translations: (hereticks they call us by the same right that they call themselves catholicks, both being wrong:) we marvel what divinity taught them so. We are sure *Tertullian* was of another mind: *Ex personis probamus fidem, an ex fide personas?* Do we try men's faith by their persons? We should try their persons by their faith. Also St. *Augustine* was of another mind: for he, lighting upon certain rules made by *Tychonius* a *Donatist* for the better understanding of the word, was not ashamed to make use of them, yea, to insert them into his own book, with giving commendation to them so far forth as they were worthy to be commended, as is to be seen in St. *Augustine's* third book *De Doctr. Christ.* To be short, *Origen,* and the whole Church of God for certain hundred years, were of another mind: for they were so far from treading under foot (much more from burning) the translation of *Aquila* a proselyte, that is, one that had turned *Jew,* of *Symmachus,* and *Theodotion,* both *Ebionites,* that is, most vile hereticks, that they joined them together with the *Hebrew* original, and the translation of the *Seventy,* (as hath been before signified out of *Epiphanius,*) and set them forth openly to be considered of and perused by all. But we weary the unlearned, who need not know so much; and trouble the learned, who know it already.

Yet before we end, we must answer a third cavil and objection of their's against us, for altering and amending our translations so oft; wherein truly they deal hardly and strangely with us. For to whom ever was it imputed for a fault, (by such as were wise,) to go over that which he had done, and to amend it where he saw cause? St. *Augustine* was not afraid to exhort St. *Hierome* to a *Palinodia* or recantation. The same St. *Augustine* was not ashamed to retractate, we might say, revoke, many things that had passed him, and doth even glory that he seeth his infirmities. If we will be sons of the truth, we must consider what it speaketh, and trample upon our own credit, yea, and upon other men's too, if either be any way an hindrance to it. This to the cause. Then to the persons we say, that of all men they ought to be most silent in this case. For what varieties have they, and what alterations have they made, not only of their service books, portesses, and breviaries, but also of their *Latin* translation? The service book supposed to be made by St. *Ambrose,* (*Officium Ambrosianum,*) was a great while in special use and request: but Pope *Adrian,* calling a council with the aid of *Charles* the Emperor, abolished it, yea, burnt it, and commanded the service book of St. *Gregory* universally to be used. Well, *Officium Gregorianum* gets by this means to be in credit; but doth it continue without change or altering? No, the very *Roman* service was of two fashions; the new fashion, and the old, the one used in one Church, and the other in another; as is to be seen in *Pamelius* a Romanist, his preface before *Micrologus.* The same *Pamelius* reporteth out of *Radulphus de Rivo,* that about the year of our Lord 1277 Pope *Nicolas* the Third removed out of the churches of *Rome* the more ancient books (of service,) and brought into use the missals of the Friars Minorites, and commanded them to be observed there; insomuch that about an hundred years after, when the above named *Radulphus* happened to be at *Rome,* he found all the books to be new, of the new stamp. Neither was there this chopping and changing in the more ancient times only, but also of late. *Pius Quintus* himself confesseth, that every bishoprick almost had a peculiar kind of service, most unlike to that which others had; which moved him to abolish all other breviaries, though never so ancient, and privileged and pub-

lished by Bishops in their Dioceses, and to establish and ratify
that only which was of his own setting forth in the year 1568.
Now when the Father of their Church, who gladly would heal
the sore of the daughter of his people softly and slightly, and
make the best of it, findeth so great fault with them for their
odds and jarring; we hope the children have no great cause
to vaunt of their uniformity. But the difference that appear-
eth between our translations, and our often correcting of
them, is the thing that we are specially charged with; let us
see therefore whether they themselves be without fault this
way, (if it be to be counted a fault to correct,) and whether
they be fit men to throw stones at us: *O tandem major parcas
insane minori*: They that are less sound themselves ought not
to object infirmities to others. If we should tell them, that
Valla, Stapulensis, Erasmus, and *Vives,* found fault with their
vulgar translation, and consequently wished the same to be
mended, or a new one to be made; they would answer peradventure, that we produced their enemies for witnesses against
them; albeit they were in no other sort enemies, than as St.
Paul was to the *Galatians,* for telling them the truth: and
it were to be wished, that they had dared to tell it them
plainlier and oftener. But what will they say to this, That
Pope *Leo* the Tenth allowed *Erasmus'* translation of the New
Testament, so much different from the vulgar, by his apostolick letter and bull? That the same *Leo* exhorted *Pagnine* to
translate the whole Bible, and bare whatsoever charges was
necessary for the work? Surely, as the apostle reasoneth to
the *Hebrews,* that *if the former Law and Testament had been
sufficient, there had been no need of the latter*: so we may
say, that if the old vulgar had been at all points allowable, to
small purpose had labour and charges been undergone about
framing of a new. If they say, it was one Pope's private
opinion, and that he consulted only himself; then we are able
to go further with them, and to aver, that more of their chief
men of all sorts, even their own *Trent* champions, *Paiva* and
Vega, and their own inquisitor *Hieronymus ab Oleastro,* and
their own Bishop *Isidorus Clarius,* and their own Cardinal

Thomas a vio Cajetan, do either make new translations themselves, or follow new ones of other men's making, or note the
vulgar interpreter for halting, none of them fear to dissent
from him, nor yet to except against him. And call they this
an uniform tenor of text and judgment about the text, so
many of their worthies disclaiming the now received conceit?
Nay, we will yet come nearer the quick. Doth not their *Paris*
edition differ from the *Lovain,* and *Hentenius's* from them
both, and yet all of them allowed by authority? Nay, doth
not *Sixtus Quintus* confess, that certain Catholicks (he meaneth certain of his own side) were in such an humour of translating the Scriptures into *Latin,* that Satan taking occasion
by them, though they thought of no such matter, did strive
what he could, out of so uncertain and manifold a variety of
translations, so to mingle all things, that nothing might seem
to be left certain and firm in them, &c.? Nay further, did
not the same *Sixtus* ordain by an inviolable decree, and that
with the counsel and consent of his Cardinals, that the *Latin*
edition of the Old and New Testament, which the council of
Trent would have to be authentick, is the same without controversy which he then set forth, being diligently corrected
and printed in the printing-house of *Vatican?* Thus *Sixtus* in
his preface before his Bible. And yet *Clement* the Eighth, his
immediate successor to account of, publisheth another edition
of the Bible, containing in it infinite differences from that of
Sixtus, and many of them weighty and material; and yet this
must be authentick by all means. What is to have the faith
of our glorious Lord *Jesus Christ* with yea and nay, if this
be not? Again, what is sweet harmony and consent, if this
be? Therefore, as *Demaratus* of *Corinth* advised a great King,
before he talked of the dissensions among the *Grecians,* to
compose his domestick broils; (for at that time his queen and
his son and heir were at deadly feud with him) so all the
while that our adversaries do make so many and so various
editions themselves, and do jar so much about the worth and
authority of them, they can with no shew of equity challenge
us for changing and correcting.

But it is high time to leave them, and to shew in brief what we proposed to ourselves, and what course we held, in this our perusal and survey of the Bible. Truly, good Christian Reader, we never thought from the beginning that we should need to make a new translation, nor yet to make of a bad one a good one; (for then the imputation of *Sixtus* had been true in some sort, that our people had been fed with gall of dragons instead of wine, with wheal instead of milk;) but to make a good one better, or out of many good ones one principal good one, not justly to be excepted against; that hath been our endeavour, that our mark. To that purpose there were many chosen, that were greater in other men's eyes than in their own, and that sought the truth rather than their own praise. Again, they came, or were thought to come, to the work, not *exercendi causa,* (as one saith,) but *exercitati,* that is, learned, not to learn; for the chief overseer and ἐργοδιώκτης under his Majesty, to whom not only we, but also our whole Church was much bound, knew by his wisdom, which thing also *Nazianzen* taught so long ago, that it is a preposterous order to teach first, and to learn after; that τὸ ἐν πίθῳ κεραμίαν μανθάνειν, to learn and practise together, is neither commendable for the workman, nor safe for the work. Therefore such were thought upon, as could say modestly with St. *Hierome, Et Hebræum sermonem ex parte didicimus, et in Latino pene ab ipsis incunabulis, &c. detriti sumus; Both we have learned the Hebrew tongue in part, and in the Latin we have been exercised almost from our very cradle.* St. *Hierome* maketh no mention of the *Greek* tongue, wherein yet he did excel; because he translated not the Old Testament out of *Greek,* but out of *Hebrew.* And in what sort did these assemble? In the trust of their own knowledge, or of their sharpness of wit, or deepness of judgment, as it were in an arm of flesh? At no hand. They trusted in him that hath the key of *David,* opening, and no man shutting; they prayed to the Lord, the Father of our Lord, to the effect that St. *Augustine* did; *O let thy Scriptures be my pure delight; let me not be deceived in them, neither let me deceive by them.* In this confidence, and with this devotion, did they assemble together; not too many, lest one should trouble another; and yet many, lest many things haply might escape them. If you ask what they had before them; truly it was the *Hebrew* text of the Old Testament, the *Greek* of the New. These are the two golden pipes, or rather conduits, wherethrough the olive-branches empty themselves into the gold. St. *Augustine* calleth them precedent, or original, tongues; St. *Hierome*, fountains. The same St. *Hierome* affirmeth, and *Gratian* hath not spared to put it into his decree, That *as the credit of the old books* (he meaneth of the Old Testament) *is to be tried by the Hebrew volumes; so of the new by the Greek tongue,* he meaneth by the original *Greek.* If truth be to be tried by these tongues, then whence should a translation be made, but out of them? These tongues therefore (the Scriptures, we say, in those tongues) we set before us to translate, being the tongues wherein God was pleased to speak to his Church by his Prophets and Apostles. Neither did we run over the work with that posting haste that the *Septuagint* did, if that be true which is reported of them, that they finished it in seventy two days; neither were we barred or hindered from going over it again, having once done it, like St. *Hierome*, if that be true which himself reporteth, that he could no sooner write any thing, but presently it was caught from him, and published, and he could not have leave to mend it: neither, to be short, were we the first that fell in hand with translating the Scripture into *English,* and consequently destitute of former helps, as it is written of *Origen,* that he was the first in a manner, that put his hand to write commentaries upon the Scriptures, and therefore no marvel if he overshot himself many times. None of these things: The work hath not been huddled up in seventy two days, but hath cost the workmen, a slight as it seemeth, the pains of twice seven times seventy two days, and more. Matters of such weight and consequence are to be speeded with maturity: for in a business of moment a man feareth not the blame of convenient slackness. Neither did we think much to consult the translators or commentators,

Chaldee, Hebrew, Syrian, Greek, or *Latin;* no, nor the *Spanish, French, Italian,* or *Dutch;* neither did we disdain to revise that which we had done, and to bring back to the anvil that which we had hammered: but having and using as great helps as were needful, and fearing no reproach for slowness, nor coveting praise for expedition, we have at length, through the good hand of the Lord upon us, brought the work to that pass that you see.

Some peradventure would have no variety of senses to be set in the margin, lest the authority of the Scriptures for deciding of controversies by that shew of uncertainty should somewhat be shaken. But we hold their judgment not to be so sound in this point. For though *whatsoever things are necessary are manifest, as* St. *Chrysostome* saith; and, as St. *Augustine, in those things that are plainly set down in the Scriptures all such matters are found, that concern faith, hope, and charity*: Yet for all that it cannot be dissembled, that partly to exercise and whet our wits, partly to wean the curious from lothing of them for their every where plainness, partly also to stir up our devotion to crave the assistance of God's Spirit by prayer, and lastly, that we might be forward to seek aid of our brethren by conference, and never scorn those that be not in all respects so complete as they should be, being to seek in many things ourselves, it hath pleased God in his Divine Providence, here and there to scatter words and sentences of that difficulty and doubtfulness, not in doctrinal points that concern salvation, (for in such it hath been vouched that the Scriptures are plain,) but in matters of less moment, that fearfulness would better beseem us than confidence, and if we will resolve, to resolve upon modesty with St. *Augustine,* (though not in this same case altogether, yet upon the same ground,) *Melius est dubitare de occultis, quam litigare de incertis*: It is better to make doubt of those things which are secret, than to strive about those things that are uncertain. There be many words in the Scriptures, which be never found there but once, (having neither brother nor neighbour, as the *Hebrews* speak,) so that we cannot be holpen by

conference of places. Again, there be many rare names of
certain birds, beasts, and precious stones, &c., concerning
which the *Hebrews* themselves are so divided among themselves for judgment, that they may seem to have defined this
or that, rather because they would say something, than because they were sure of that which they said, as St. *Hierome*
somewhere saith of the *Septuagint*. Now in such a case doth
not a margin do well to admonish the Reader to seek further,
and not to conclude or dogmatize upon this or that peremptorily?
For as it is a fault of incredulity, to doubt of those things that
are evident; so to determine of such things as the Spirit of
God hath left (even in the judgment of the judicious) questionable, can be no less than presumption. Therefore as St. *Augustine* saith, that variety of translations is profitable for the finding out of the sense of the Scriptures: so diversity of
signification and sense in the margin, where the text is not so
clear, must needs do good; yea, is necessary, as we are persuaded. We know that *Sixtus Quintus* expressly forbiddeth that
any variety of readings of their vulgar edition should be put
in the margin; (which though it be not altogether the same
thing to that we have in hand, yet it looketh that way;) but we
think he hath not all of his own side his favourers for this
conceit. They that are wise had rather have their judgments
at liberty in differences of readings, than to be captivated to
one, when it may be the other. If they were sure that their
high priest had all laws shut up in his breast, as *Paul* the Second
bragged, and that he were as free from error by special privilege,
as the dictators of *Rome* were made by law inviolable, it were
another matter; then his word were an oracle, his opinion a
decision. But the eyes of the world are now open, God be
thanked, and have been a great while; they find that he is
subject to the same affections and infirmities that others be,
that his body is subject to wounds; and therefore so much as
he proveth, not as much as he claimeth, they grant and embrace.

Another thing we think good to admonish thee of, gentle
Reader, that we have not tied ourselves to an uniformity of
phrasing, or to an identity of words, as some peradventure

would wish that we had done, because they observe, that some learned men somewhere have been as exact as they could that way. Truly, that we might not vary from the sense of that which we had translated before, if the word signified the same thing in both places, (for there be some words that be not of the same sense every where,) we were especially careful, and made a conscience, according to our duty. But that we should express the same notion in the same particular word; as for example, if we translate the *Hebrew* or *Greek* word once by *purpose,* never to call it *intent;* if one where *journeying,* never *travelling;* if one where *think,* never *suppose;* if one where *pain,* never *ache;* if one where *joy,* never *gladness,* &c. thus to mince the matter, we thought to savour more of curiosity than wisdom, and that rather it would breed scorn in the atheist, than bring profit to the godly reader. For is the kingdom of God become words or syllables? Why should we be in bondage to them, if we may be free? use one precisely, when we may use another no less fit as commodiously? A godly Father in the primitive time shewed himself greatly moved, that one of newfangledness called κραββάτον, σκίμπους, though the difference be little or none; and another reporteth, that he was much abused for turning *cucurbita* (to which reading the people had been used) into *hedera*. Now if this happen in better times, and upon so small occasions, we might justly fear hard censure, if generally we should make verbal and unnecessary changings. We might also be charged (by scoffers) with some unequal dealing towards a great number of good *English* words. For as it is written of a certain great Philosopher, that he should say, that those logs were happy that were made images to be worshipped; for their fellows, as good as they, lay for blocks behind the fire: so if we should say, as it were, unto certain words, Stand up higher, have a place in the Bible always; and to others of like quality, Get you hence, be banished for ever; we might be taxed peradventure with St. *James's* words, namely, *To be partial in ourselves, and judges of evil thoughts*. Add hereunto, that niceness in words was always counted the next step to trifling; and so was to be curious about names too: also that we cannot follow a better pattern for elocution than God himself; therefore he using divers words in his holy writ, and indifferently for one thing in nature: we, if we will not be superstitious, may use the same liberty in our *English* versions out of *Hebrew* and *Greek*, for that copy or store that he hath given us. Lastly, we have on the one side avoided the scrupulosity of the Puritanes, who leave the old Ecclesiastical words, and betake them to other, as when they put *washing* for *baptism*, and *congregation* instead of *Church*: as also on the other side we have shunned the obscurity of the Papists, in their *azymes, tunike, rational, holocausts, prepuce, pasche,* and a number of such like, whereof their late translation is full, and that of purpose to darken the sense, that since they must needs translate the Bible, yet by the language thereof it may be kept from being understood. But we desire that the Scripture may speak like itself, as in the language of *Canaan*, that it may be understood even of the very vulgar.

Many other things we might give thee warning of, gentle Reader, if we had not exceeded the measure of a preface already. It remaineth that we commend thee to God, and to the Spirit of his grace, which is able to build further than we can ask or think. He removeth the scales from our eyes, the vail from our hearts, opening our wits that we may understand his word, enlarging our hearts, yea, correcting our affections, that we may love it above gold and silver, yea, that we may love it to the end. Ye are brought unto fountains of living water which ye digged not; do not cast earth into them, with the Philistines, neither prefer broken pits before them, with the wicked Jews. Others have laboured, and you may enter into their labours. O receive not so great things in vain: O despise not so great salvation. Be not like swine to tread under foot so precious things, neither yet like dogs to tear and abuse holy things. Say not to our Saviour with the *Gergesites*, Depart out of our coasts; neither yet with *Esau* sell your birthright for a mess of pottage. If light be come into the world, love not darkness more than light: if food, if clothing, be offered, go not naked, starve not yourselves. Remember the advice of *Nazianzene, It is a grievous thing* (or dangerous) *to neglect a great fair, and to seek to make markets afterwards*: also the encouragement of St. *Chrysostome, It is altogether impossible, that he that is sober* (and watchful) *should at any time be neglected*: lastly, the admonition and menacing of St. *Augustine, They that despise God's will inviting them shall feel God's will taking vengeance of them.* It is a fearful thing to fall into the hands of the living God; but a blessed thing it is, and will bring us to everlasting blessedness in the end, when God speaketh unto us, to hearken; when he setteth his word before us, to read it; when he stretcheth out his hand and calleth, to answer, Here am I, here we are to do thy will, O God. The Lord work a care and conscience in us to know him and serve him, that we may be acknowledged of him at the appearing of our Lord JESUS CHRIST, to whom with the Holy Ghost be all praise and thanksgiving.   Amen.

(*The Variorum Bible* (*The Sunday School Centenary Bible, Authorized Version*), Eyre and Spottiswoode, London, 1880.)

THE KING JAMES VERSION

Herein is a photostatic reproduction of two original leaves (four pages) of the black letter edition in Old English type of the King James Version of the Bible.

One leaf shows John 18:9-40 and 19:1-24; it is part of John's account of the trial and crucifixion of the Savior. The other leaf contains a portion of the Epistle of James, giving besides the royal law and the great sermon on faith and works, those famous passages which declare the motivating principle of the Last Dispensation, the Dispensation of the Fulness of Times:

"If any of you lack wisdom, let him ask of God, that giveth to all men liberally, and upbraideth not; and it shall be given him.

"But let him ask in faith, nothing wavering. For he that wavereth is like a wave of the sea driven with the wind and tossed.

"For let not that man think that he shall receive any thing of the Lord."

(From library of J. Reuben Clark, Jr.)

*Chap.17.
12.

9 That the ſaying might bee fulfilled which hee ſpake, * Of them which thou gaueſt me, haue I loſt none.

10 Then Simon Peter hauing a ſword, drew it, and ſmote the high Prieſts ſeruant, & cut off his right eare: The ſeruants name was Malchus.

11 Then ſaid Jeſus vnto Peter, Put vp thy ſword into the ſheath: the cup which my Father hath giuen me, ſhall I not drinke it?

12 Then the band and the captaine, and officers of the Jewes, tooke Jeſus, and bound him,

13 And led him away to Annas firſt, (for he was father in law to Caiaphas) which was the high Prieſt that ſame yeere. ||

|| And Annas ſent Chriſt bound vnto Caiaphas the high Prieſt, verſ. 24.
*Chap.11. 50.
* Mat.16. 48.

14 * Now Caiaphas was he which gaue counſell to the Jewes, that it was expedient that one man ſhould die for the people.

15 ¶ * And Simon Peter followed Jeſus, and ſo did another diſciple: that diſciple was knowen vnto the high Prieſt, and went in with Jeſus into the palace of the high Prieſt.

16 But Peter ſtood at the doore without. Then went out that other diſciple, which was knowen vnto the high Prieſt, and ſpake vnto her that kept the doore, and brought in Peter.

17 Then ſaith the damoſel that kept the doore vnto Peter, Art not thou alſo one of this mans diſciples? He ſayth, I am not.

18 And the ſeruants and officers ſtood there, who had made a fire of coales, (for it was colde) and they warmed themſelues: and Peter ſtood with them, and warmed himſelfe.

19 ¶ The high Prieſt then aſked Jeſus of his diſciples, and of his doctrine.

20 Jeſus anſwered him, I ſpake openly to the world, I euer taught in the Synagogue, and in the Temple, whither the Jewes alwayes reſort, and in ſecret haue I ſaid nothing.

21 Why aſkeſt thou me? Aſke them which heard me, what I haue ſaid vnto them: behold, they know what I ſaid.

|| Or, with a rod.

22 And when hee had thus ſpoken, one of the officers which ſtood by, ſtroke Jeſus || with the palme of his hand, ſaying, Anſwereſt thou the hie prieſt ſo?

23 Jeſus anſwered him, If I haue ſpoken euill, beare witneſſe of the euill: but if well, why ſmiteſt thou me?

* Mat.26. 57.

24 * Now Annas had ſent him bound vnto Caiaphas the high Prieſt.

25 And Simon Peter ſtood and warmed himſelfe: * They ſaid therefore vnto him, Art not thou alſo one of his diſciples? Hee denied it, and ſaid, I am not.

* Mat.26. 69.

26 One of the ſeruants of the high Prieſts (being his kinſman whoſe eare Peter cut off) ſaith, Did not I ſee thee in the garden with him?

27 Peter then denied againe, and immediatly the cocke crew.

28 ¶ * Then led they Jeſus from Caiaphas vnto || the hall of Judgement: And it was early, * and they themſelues went not into the Judgement hall, leſt they ſhould be defiled: but that they might eate the Paſſeouer.

* Mat.27. 2
|| Or, Pilates houſe.
* Acts 10. 28.

29 Pilate then went out vnto them, and ſaid, What accuſation bring you againſt this man?

30 They anſwered, & ſaid vnto him, If he were not a malefactor, we would not haue deliuered him vp vnto thee.

31 Then ſaid Pilate vnto them, Take ye him, and iudge him according to your law. The Jewes therefore ſaid vnto him, It is not lawfull for vs to put any man to death:

32 * That the ſaying of Jeſus might be fulfilled, which hee ſpake, ſignifying what death he ſhould die.

* Mat.10. 19.

33 * Then Pilate entred into the Judgement hall againe, and called Jeſus, and ſaid vnto him, Art thou the King of the Jewes?

* Matt.27. 11.

34 Jeſus anſwered him, Sayeſt thou this thing of thy ſelfe? or did others tell it thee of me?

35 Pilate anſwered, Am I a Jew? Thine owne nation, and the chiefe Prieſts haue deliuered thee vnto mee: what haſt thou done?

36 Jeſus anſwered, My kingdome is not of this world: if my kingdome were of this world, then would my ſeruants fight, that I ſhould not be deliuered to the Jewes: but now is my kingdome not from hence.

37 Pilate therefore ſaid vnto him, Art thou a King then? Jeſus anſwered, Thou ſaieſt that I am a King. To this ende was I borne, and for this cauſe came I into the world, that I ſhould beare witneſſe vnto the trueth: euery one that is of the trueth heareth my voyce.

38 Pilate ſaith vnto him, What is trueth? And when hee had ſaid this,

L 3　　　　　　　he

*Matth. 27. 15.

39 *But yee haue a custome that I should release vnto you one at the Passeouer: will ye therefore that I release vnto you the king of the Iewes?

*Act. 3. 14.

40 *Then cried they all againe, saying, Not this man, but Barabbas. Now Barabbas was a robber.

CHAP. XIX.

1 Christ is scourged, crowned with thornes, and beaten, 4 Pilate is desirous to release him, but being ouercome with the outrage of the Iewes, he deliuered him to bee crucified. 23 They cast lots for his garments. 26 He commendeth his mother to Iohn. 28 Hee dieth. 31 His side is pierced. 38 He is buried by Ioseph and Nicodemus.

*Matth. 27. 16.

THen *Pilate therfore tooke Iesus, and scourged him.

2 And the souldiers platted a crowne of thornes, and put it on his head, and they put on him a purple robe,

3 And said, haile king of the Iewes and they smote him with their hands.

4 Pilate therefore went foorth againe, and saith vnto them, Behold, I bring him foorth to you, that yee may know that I find no fault in him.

5 Then came Iesus foorth, wearing the crowne of thornes, and the purple robe: and Pilate saith vnto them, Behold the man.

6 When the chiefe Priests therefore and officers saw him, they cried out, saying, Crucifie him, crucifie him. Pilate saith vnto them, Take ye him, and crucifie him: for I find no fault in him.

7 The Iewes answered him, We haue a law, and by our law he ought to die, because hee made himselfe the Son of God.

8 When Pilate therefore heard that saying, he was the more afraid,

9 And went againe into the iudgement hall, & saith vnto Iesus, whence art thou? But Iesus gaue him no answere.

10 Then saith Pilate vnto him, Speakest thou not vnto me? knowest thou not, that I haue power to crucifie thee, and haue power to release thee?

11 Iesus answered, Thou couldest haue no power at all against me, except it were giuen thee from aboue: therfore

he that deliuered me vnto thee, hath the greater sinne.

12 And from thenceforth Pilate sought to release him: but the Iewes cried out, saying, If thou let this man goe, thou art not Cesars friend: whosoeuer maketh himselfe a king, speaketh against Cesar.

13 When Pilate therefore heard that saying, he brought Iesus foorth, and sate downe in the iudgement seate, in a place that is called the pauement, but in the Hebrew, Gabbatha.

14 And it was the preparation of the Passeouer, and about the sixt houre: and he saith vnto the Iewes, Beholde your King.

15 But they cried out, Away with him, away with him, crucifie him. Pilate saith vnto them, Shall I crucifie your King? The chiefe Priests answered, Wee haue no king but Cesar.

*Matth. 27. 31.

16 *Then deliuered he him therfore vnto them to bee crucified: and they tooke Iesus, and led him away.

17 And he bearing his crosse, went foorth into a place called the place of a skull, which is called in the Hebrewe, Golgotha:

18 Where they crucified him, and two other with him, on either side one, and Iesus in the middest.

19 And Pilate wrote a title, and put it on the crosse. And the writing was, IESVS OF NAZARETH, THE KING OF THE IEWES.

20 This title then read many of the Iewes: for the place where Iesus was crucified, was nigh to the citie, and it was written in Hebrewe, and Greeke, and Latine.

21 Then said the chiefe Priests of the Iewes to Pilate, Write not, The king of the Iewes: but that he said, I am King of the Iewes.

22 Pilate answered, What I haue written, I haue written.

*Matth. 27. 35.

23 *Then the souldiers, when they had crucified Iesus, tooke his garments, (and made foure parts, to euery souldier a part) and also his coat: Now the coat was without seame, || wouen from the top thorowout.

|| Or, wrought.

24 They said therefore among themselues, Let not vs rent it, but cast lots for it, whose it shall bee: * that the Scripture might bee fulfilled, which saith, They parted my raiment among them, and for my vesture they did cast lots

*Psal. 22. 18.

fer the word of exhortation, for I haue written a letter vnto you in few words.

23 Know yee, that our brother Timothie is set at libertie, with whom if he come shortly, I will see you.

24 Salute all them that haue the rule ouer you, and al the Saints. They of Italy salute you.

25 Grace be with you all. Amen.

¶ Written to the Hebrewes, from Italy, by Timothie.

¶ THE GENERALL
Epiſtle of Iames.

CHAP. I.

Wee are to reioyce vnder the Croſſe, 5 To aske patience of God, 13 And in our trials not to impute our weakeneſſe, or ſinnes vnto him, 19 but rather to hearken to the word, to meditate in it, and to doe thereafter. 26 Otherwiſe men may ſeeme, but neuer be truely religious.

Ames a seruant of God, and of the Lord Iesus Christ, to the twelue Tribes which are scattered abroad, greeting.

2 My brethren, count it all ioy when ye fall into diuers temptations.

3 Knowing this, that the trying of your faith worketh patience,

4 But let patience haue her perfect worke, that yee may be perfect, and entier, wanting nothing.

5 If any of you lacke wisedome, let him aske of God, that giueth to all men liberally, and vpbraydeth not : and it shalbe giuen him.

6 But let him aske in faith, nothing wauering : for he that wauereth is like a waue of the sea, driuen with the wind, and tossed

7 For let not that man thinke that he shall receiue any thing of the Lord.

8 A double minded man is vnstable in all his wayes.

9 Let the brother of low degree, ||reioyce in that he is exalted:

|| Or, glory.

10 But the rich, in that hee is made low : becauseas the floure of the grasse he shall passe away.

11 For the Sunne is no sooner risen with a burning heate, but it withereth the grasse ; and the flowre thereof falleth, and the grace of the fashion of it perisheth : so also shall the rich man fade away in his wayes.

12 Blessed is the man that endureth temptation : for when hee is tried, hee shall receiue the crowne of life, which the Lord hath promised to them that loue him.

13 Let no man say when he is tempted, I am tempted of God: for God cannot be tempted with ||euil, neither tempteth he any man.

|| Or, euils.

14 But euery man is tempted, when hee is drawen away of his owne lust, and entised.

15 Then when lust hath conceiued, it bringeth forth sinne : and sinne, when it is finished, bringeth foorth death.

16 Doe not erre, my beloued brethren.

17 Euery good gift, and euery perfect gift is from aboue, & commeth downe from the Father of lights, with whom is no variablenesse, neither shadow of turning.

18 Of his owne will begate hee vs, with the word of Trueth, that wee should bee a kinde of first fruits of his creatures.

19 Wherefore my beloued brethren, let euery man be swift to heare, slow to speake, slow to wrath.

20 For the wrath of man worketh not the righteousnesse of God.

21 Wherfore lay apart all filthinesse, and superfluitie of naughtinesse, and receiue with meekenesse the engrafted word, which is able to saue your soules.

22 But be ye doers of the word, and not

P

not hearers only, deceiuing your owne selues.

23 For if any be a hearer of the word and not a doer, he is like vnto a man beholding his naturall face in a glasse:

24 For he beholdeth himselfe, and goeth his way, and straightway forgetteth what maner of man he was.

25 But who so looketh into the perfect Law of libertie, and continueth therein, he being not a forgetfull hearer, but a doer of the worke, this man shall be blessed in his ||deed.

|| Or, doing.

26 If any man among you seeme to be religious, & bridleth not his tongue, but deceiueth his owne heart, this mans religion is vaine.

27 Pure religion and vndefiled before God and the Father, is this, to visit the fatherlesse and widowes in their affliction, and to keepe himselfe vnspotted from the world.

CHAP. II.

It is not agreeable to Christian profession to regard the rich, and to despise the poore brethren: 13 rather wee are to be louing, and mercifull: 14 And not to boast of faith where no deeds are, 17 which is but a dead faith, 19 the faith of deuils, 21 not of Abraham, 25 and Rahab.

My brethren, haue not the faith of our Lord Iesus Christ the Lord of glory, with respect of persons.

2 For if there come vnto your † assembly a man with a gold ring, in goodly apparell, and there come in also a poore man, in vile raiment:

† Gr, Synagogue.

3 And yee haue respect to him that weareth the gay clothing, and say vnto him Sit thou here ||in a good place: and say to the poore, Stand thou there, or sit here vnder my footstoole:

|| Or, well, or seemely.

4 Are yee not then partiall in your selues, and are become iudges of euill thoughts?

5 Hearken, my beloued brethren, Hath not God chosen the poore of this world, rich in faith, and heires of ||the kingdome, which hee hath promised to them that loue him?

|| Or, that.

6 But yee haue despised the poore. Doe not rich men oppresse you, and draw you before the Iudgement seats?

7 Do not they blaspheme that worthy Name, by the which ye are called?

8 If ye fulfil the royall Law, according to the Scripture, Thou shalt loue thy neighbour as thy selfe, ye doe well.

9 But if ye haue respect to persons, yee commit sinne, and are conuinced of the Law, as transgressours.

10 For whosoeuer shall keepe the whole Law, and yet offend in one point, he is guiltie of all.

11 For he ||that said, Doe not commit adulterie; said also, Doe not kill. Now if thou commit no adulterie, yet if thou kill, thou art become a transgressour of the Law.

|| Or, that Law which said.

12 So speake ye, & so do, as they that shalbe iudged by the Law of libertie.

13 For he shall haue iudgement without mercy, that hath shewed no mercy, & mercy || reioyceth against iudgement.

|| Or, glorieth.

14 What doeth it profit, my brethren, though a man say hee hath faith, and haue not workes? can faith saue him?

15 If a brother or sister be naked, and destitute of dayly food,

16 And one of you say vnto them, Depart in peace, bee you warmed and filled: notwithstanding yee giue them not those things which are needfull to the body: what doeth it profit?

17 Euen so faith, if it hath not works, is dead being † alone.

† Gr, by it selfe.

18 Yea, a man may say, Thou hast faith, and I haue workes: shew me thy faith ||without thy workes, and I will shew thee my faith by my workes.

|| Some copies reade, by thy works.

19 Thou beleeuest that there is one God, thou doest well: the deuils also beleeue, and tremble.

20 But wilt thou know, O vaine man, that faith without workes is dead?

21 Was not Abraham our father iustified by workes, when hee had offered Isaac his sonne vpon the Altar?

22 ||Seest thou how faith wrought with his workes, and by workes was faith made perfect?

|| Or, thou seest.

23 And the Scripture was fulfilled which saith, * Abraham beleeued God, and it was imputed vnto him for righteousnes: and he was called the friend of God.

*Gen. 15.6. rom. 4. 3. galat. 3. 6.

24 Ye see then, how that by workes a man is iustified, and not by faith onely.

25 Likewise also, was not Rahab the harlot iustified by workes, when she had receiued the messengers, and had sent them out another way?

26 For as the body without the ||spirit is

|| Or, breath

THE PROBLEM ·

Why the King James Version

Save for some few comments on the origin of writing and alphabets and on Old Testament criticism, these *Notes* relate exclusively to the New Testament which it is now proposed to name "The New Covenant."

The problem covered by these *Notes* is,—Shall the King James Version (also known as the Authorized Version) be abandoned and a Revised Version (one of the three of them, British and American) be adopted in its stead?

Both the King James Version and the Revised Versions are translations of Greek texts, recorded in handwritten manuscripts, either on papyrus (made from an Egyptian rush or reed) or on vellum (specially tanned skins of some animal).

The *King James Version* is a translation into English of a Greek text of the New Testament (also of the Old Testament) that had for some thousand or twelve hundred years come to be the accepted Greek text in the Greek-speaking and later the Protestant world.

The *Revised Versions* are translations into English of Greek texts of the New Testament that had virtually disappeared during this period of the thousand or twelve hundred years, but which came into prominence following critical agitation in the first half of the last century.

With the Reformation came popular demand for an English Bible. To that time Bibles were either Latin or Greek.

After several earlier English translations of this accepted Greek text,—Tindale's (1526), Coverdale's (1535), Matthew's (1537), Taverner's (1539), the Great Bible (1539-1541), the Geneva Bible (1557-1560), the Bishops' Bible (1568)—King James of England, that he might bring order and some kind of religious unity among his Protestant people, organized a committee to prepare an English version that might command the respect and support of the people. In 1611 this Committee submitted to King James an English translation of the generally accepted Greek text, the translation in no small part being based on some of the earlier English versions. This new translation met the general approval of the people and since that date has been known as the King James Version, or Authorized Version.

The Greek texts available to, and some at least used by the translators of the King James Version of 1611, were: that of Cardinal Ximenes — the Complutensian Polyglott (published in 1520) ; that of Erasmus (printed in 1516), begun after but published before the Complutensian; that of Robert Stephen (published in 1546 and 1549) ; and that of Beza (published in five editions, 1565 to 1598), which differed little from Stephen's. The Elzevirs — Bonaventure and Abraham — printers, brought out two editions, 1624 and 1633, made up of the texts of Stephen and Beza. All of these were Greek texts. The various English Bibles were based on one or more of these Greek texts, as they were available.

It seems now generally accepted that the translation of 1611 was based mainly on the Stephen text. The Elzevirs' 1633 edition spoke of their text as the *Received Text*, a designation that has come to be applied to the King James or Authorized Version of 1611.

However, for the balance of the seventeenth, the

eighteenth, and until the beginning of the nineteenth century, critical studies of the various available manuscripts were carried on, extensive collations of them were made,—the ground work had thus been laid for the vicious attack on the King James Version which began in the first half of the nineteenth century.

For over two hundred years the English Bible accepted and read was the King James Version.

The Inspired Version of the Prophet Joseph Smith fully supports, in all essential matters of the New Testament, the King James Version, which Version has thus been the accepted Bible text for the Church of Jesus Christ of Latter-day Saints from the Prophet's time on down, "as far as it is translated correctly," and the Prophet in his *Inspired Version* made relatively few changes in the New Testament.

The direct attack on the King James Version (after this two hundred years of supremacy) which finally led to the Revised Versions, began with Lachmann, a noted philologist and critic and a professor in Berlin, who proposed in a two-volume work (the first appearing in 1842 and the second in 1850) to discard the King James Version in favor of a new version to be founded on a supposedly lost fourth century Greek text but now discovered. His work is spoken of as "breaking the monopoly" of the King James Version. His claims were based (as the discussion finally developed) on two Greek manuscript texts now principally considered, the one now called the Alexandrinus (designated A) of the fifth century, and now in the British Museum; and the other the Vaticanus (designated B) of the late first half of the fourth century, i.e., by 350 A.D. This manuscript was then and is now in the Vatican at Rome. He had a few additional, but not important, other manuscripts.

Lachmann was followed by Samuel Prideaux Tregelles, who was brought up in the Society of Friends, but became later a lay member of the Church of England. He continued the attack on the King James Version and supported his contentions by reference to other early manuscripts that have, however, seemingly lost most of their importance in the later discussions on the matter. He is said to have "completely ignored" the King James Version.

The next and third important member of the attacking group that were making real war on the King James Version, was Tischendorf, who was a great scholar, though seemingly somewhat unstable in his views and conclusions. He discovered in a Mount Sinai monastery, St. Catherine, another early Greek manuscript dating back to about the time of Vaticanus, that is about 350 A.D. This manuscript has been called Sinaiticus (designated by א (*Aleph*), the first letter of the Hebrew alphabet). While following, in his earlier studies, the other critics in their war on the King James Version, it it said that toward the end of his life, he returned, in part at least, to the Received Text, the King James Version.

It appears that these three men, Lachmann, Tregelles, and Tischendorf, were scholars, not churchmen. Their approach was seemingly solely that of a scholar.

The final enemies of the King James Version, up to the beginning of the last quarter of the last century, were two professors of Cambridge (England), Brooke Foss Westcott, D.D. (Bishop of Durham; Regius Professor of Divinity, Cambridge), and Fenton John Anthony Hort, D.D. (Vicar of a parish near Cambridge; Hulsean Professor of Divinity, Cambridge). Relying principally on Sinaiticus (א) and Vaticanus (B) these two scholars fabricated a new Greek text, which became the basis of the Revised Versions,—the British of the 1880's, the American Standard Version of 1900-1901, and the Revised Standard Version of 1946-1952. One gets the impression that these Doctors were essentially scholars,— schoolmen — not churchmen.

The movement for a revised English Version took definite shape with the appointment of a Committee for that purpose in 1870 by the Convocation of the Province of Canterbury.

The Greek manuscripts principally used in making the Revisions (British and American) seem primarily to be the two already named, Vaticanus and Sinaiticus, and also Alexandrinus (already mentioned), though other early manuscripts, namely, Codex Ephraemi (designated C), fifth century, in Paris; Codex Bezae (designated D), fifth century, in Cambridge, England; and Codex Regius (designated L), eighth century, in Paris,—were also used in a confirmatory way. Codex Nitriensis (designated R), sixth century, in British Museum, and Codex Borgianus (designated T), fifth century, in Rome,—are also mentioned.

To these have been added, in the preparation of the Revised Standard Version, the rather recently discovered Egyptian papyri, the Chester Beatty manuscripts, which date from the early third (200 B.C.) to the fourth centuries,—the earliest considerable manuscripts thus far found. To what extent they were used is not definitely indicated.

With the appearance of the British Revision a vigorous storm of scholarly protest arose on the part of churchmen of the Church of England, as well as on the part of other scholars. Those supporting the new Revision became known as Extreme Textualists; those sup-

porting the King James Version, as Sound or High
Textualists. With the death of those supporting the
King James Version, the controversy died down. But
the people have clung to the King James Version, which
still remains their Bible. The conclusion finally reached
by a leading present-day scholar is declared to be that
the great King James Version, with its superlative
literary quality, will still be the Bible of the people; the
Revisions will be for the scholars.

In these *Notes*, the author will, on technical matters
(because he is not a linguist and for other reasons),
quote — sometimes very fully — the language of the
scholars themselves; let them tell their own story. He
will do as little summarizing and paraphrasing as he
can. Thus by design these *Notes* will be in no small part
a matter of "paste-pot and scissors." He will use
wherever possible the facts and admissions of the hostile
critics of the King James Version to establish its supremacy. He will aim to quote their own arguments on
the essentials of their case.

The effect of the position of the Extreme Textualists as set forth in their Revisions of the Bible, is to
weaken, if not destroy the Messiahship of Jesus. Incidents recorded in the King James Version have been
omitted from the Revised Version; substantial parts of
whole chapters—e.g., the last verses of Mark have been
omitted; doctrines and teachings have been changed;
doubts have been cast on fundamental expressions declaring the divinity and personality of Jesus the Christ;
faith-destroying questions have been raised by marginal
notes and by the text itself; the personality of Jesus in
its Christian concept has, in effect, been challenged.

That Jesus was the Christ, the Son of God; that he
made the atonement for the Fall of Adam; that he was

the First Fruits of the Resurrection and that his resurrection was a reality; that he was in fact the Savior of mankind, are all basic to the Restored Gospel. The Latter-day Saints cannot in any way sanction even the slightest derogation of these principles. The Prophet has put his stamp of approval upon all this as contained in the New Testament of the King James translation.

These *Notes* are designed to show that the King James Version is the best record to these ends that has yet been revealed through the Bible.

NOTE ONE ·

General Matters and Observations

Item 1. *When Our New Testament Was Written.*

Summary. This is a brief consideration of the historical criticism of the New Testament, dealing with when the New Testament Books were written. Contrary to the views held by historical critics of the school of Baur,— that the Gospels ("a tissue of falsifications," said they) were written in the second century, the more modern critics are falling back to the traditional dates which place the writings of the Gospels between the years 50 and 100 after Christ. The period of the explosion of the Baur doctrines has been spoken of as "an episode, during which science learnt much, and after which it must forget much." The date of the Synoptic Gospels (Matthew, Mark, and Luke) is placed at 65 to 75 A.D., and of the Gospel of John as late in the first century. (As to the language of the Sacred Autographs—the original records—see *Note Six* herein.) The language of the earliest records is a matter of controversy, but it is admitted that the Gospels appeared very early in Syriac, Greek, Latin, and Coptic (the language of the natives of Egypt).

Time and further reading have vindicated, for himself, the author's early spiritual instinct and have convinced him of the falsity and irreverence of the statements made by the writer quoted in the *Preface*.

Regarding the age of the Bible, Greek manuscripts of the New Testament (sometimes mere fragments) go back as far as the second century after Christ. In this connection it should be observed that modern discoveries have included a small papyrus fragment of John's Gospel (John 18:31-33, 37, 38) written in a hand (it is said) that can be confidently assigned to the first half of the second century (100-150 A.D.). This fragment

JOHN X, 31-XI, 10

CHESTER BEATTY PAPYRUS I

Fragment of Gospel of John. Early 3rd century. Part of 30 papyri leaves discovered (1931) "in Egypt (apparently in a cemetery or the ruins of a church in the neighborhood of Aphroditopolis)." "The earliest" of these papyri (parts of eleven codices) were "of the first half of the second century, the latest not later than the fourth." Said to be "most important Biblical discovery since that of the Codex Sinaiticus." Chester Beatty Library, Dublin, Ireland. See pp. 5 and 135, herein.

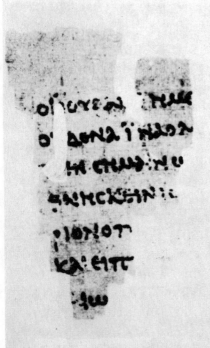 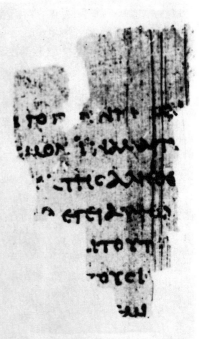

JOHN 18:31-33
(*recto*)

JOHN 18:37 and 38
(*verso*)

RYLANDS FRAGMENT OF JOHN

Greek papyrus. Found in Egypt. Written about 150 A.D., "when the ink of the original autograph can hardly have been dry." Earliest discovered manuscript. Proves "early circulation of the Fourth Gospel." Now in John Rylands Library, Manchester, England. See pp. 8 and 136, herein.

has a particular significance as showing that John's Gospel was written, and circulated as far as Egypt (where this fragment was found) before the end of the first half of the second century (before 150 A.D.), whereas certain critics have contended that John's Gospel was not written until towards the end of the second century. This discovery goes far towards confirming the traditional date of its composition,—the last years of the first century. (Sir Frederic Kenyon, *Our Bible and the Ancient Manuscripts*, 4th ed., rev. (London, Eyre & Spottiswoode, 1948), p. 128, cited hereinafter, *Our Bible;* Frederic G. Kenyon (Sir Frederic Kenyon), *The Text of the Greek Bible*, new ed. (London, Duckworth, 1949), pp. 75, 195, cited hereinafter as *The Text;* F. F. Bruce, *The Books and the Parchments* (London, Pickering & Inglis Ltd., 1950), p. 172, cited hereinafter as Bruce.)

Furthermore, scholars are now able confidently to affirm that: "The books of the New Testament were written between the years 50 and 100 after Christ." (Kenyon, *Our Bible*, p. 98.) This is another blow to the anti-Christian critics. Kenyon states:

"Since the publication of Harnack's *Chronologie der altchristlichen Litteratur* in 1897 it has been generally admitted that, with very few exceptions, the traditional dates of the New Testament books may be accepted as approximately correct. The doctrines of the school of Baur, which regarded the earliest Christian books as a tissue of falsifications of the second century, have been exploded. 'That time,' says Harnack, 'is over. It was an episode, during which science learnt much, and after which it must forget much.' Recent discoveries have only confirmed this conclusion." (*Our Bible*, p. 98, n. 1.)

Kenyon's Views on Antiquity of Gospels

Perhaps at this point two paragraphs might be added as indicating the latest (1949) views of some critics on the time when our New Testament texts were written. Kenyon says:

"As Christianity spread outwards from Palestine, through Syria, through Asia Minor, Italy, Roman Africa and Egypt, and converts were made not only among Greek-speaking Jews but among communities to whom Greek was less familiar, a demand grew up for the Scriptures in other languages. The three earliest, and therefore the most important for our purpose, were in the principal languages of the adjoining peoples—Syriac, Latin and Coptic (the language of the natives of Egypt). It is only lately that we have learnt much about the first versions in these tongues; for in each case the early version was eventually superseded by another, which became the accepted Bible of that people, and of the earlier translations relatively few manuscripts have survived, and most of these are only fragments. But it now seems certain that the books of the New Testament were translated into all these languages before the end of the third century, while the Syriac and Latin almost certainly go back to the second. The original translators must have used Greek manuscripts then existing; so that, so far as we can ascertain the original form of these various versions (itself not an easy task), we have the evidence of Greek manuscripts earlier than any which have come down to us. Further, these translations show us what kind of text was in use in the countries in which they were produced.

"If therefore we look back over the earliest generations of Christianity, from the time of our Lord to the date (somewhere about A.D. 325) when Christianity became the accepted religion of the Roman Empire, we see first of all a period of some forty years when the narrative of our Lord's life and teaching circulated orally, in the preaching of His disciples, or in written records which have not come down to us; and when St. Paul was writing his letters to various Christian churches which he and his companions had founded. Then, about the years 65 to 75, we have the composition of what are known as the three Synoptic Gospels, Mark, Luke and Matthew, Mark's being the earliest, and Matthew and Luke using him and also other narratives and collections of sayings. The Book of Acts belongs to the same period, being the second part of Luke's history. Revelation is now generally assigned to the time of the persecution of Domitian, about A.D. 95; and St. John's Gospel also must be late in the century. Then we have a period of rather over two

hundred years, when the various books circulated, either singly
in separate papyrus rolls or combined into small groups in papyrus codices, with no central control to ensure a uniform text,
but rather exposed to indefinite variation at the hands of local
scribes, and perhaps assuming a somewhat different character
in different parts of the world. During this period also translations were made into Syriac, Latin and Coptic. Meanwhile
Christianity was from time to time exposed to persecutions by
the Roman emperors and governors, when copies of the Scriptures were a special object of search and destruction, which increased the difficulty of securing an accurate transmission of
the text. Many churches must have been dependent on copies
locally made by inexperienced scribes; and though scholars or
bishops may from time to time have tried to secure and circulate
more correct copies, their efforts would probably have effect
only in their own neighbourhood. It is a period of confusion,
when people were thinking only of the substance of the Christian
teaching, and caring little for the verbal accuracy of the text;
and when there were no great libraries, as there were for pagan
literature, in which the books could be carefully copied and revised by skilled scholars. It is by realizing the conditions in
which Christians lived in these earliest centuries that we can
best understand the problems presented to us with regard to
the text of the Greek Bible." (Sir Frederic Kenyon, *The Story
of the Bible* (London, John Murray, 1949), pp. 34-37, cited hereafter as *The Story*.)

The foregoing statements, inferences, and implica-
tions in Kenyon's sentences,—that the original record
of Christ's teachings and works (the *Sacred Autographs*) were in Greek cannot be surely accepted. Other
authorities write equally persuasively to show that
the original records were in Aramaic, the language
of Jesus and the people among whom his ministry in
Palestine was performed. This whole matter is more
fully considered hereinafter. (See *Note Six*, herein.)

As Kenyon's discussions of matters concerning the
Bible text, particularly as affecting the Revised Version, will be so freely quoted in these *Notes*, perhaps
it would be well to observe that this course is followed

because, first, he is undoubtedly a scholar of great learning, ability, and distinction whose views demand consideration; but further and particularly because he seems to be so fully accepted by the modern revisionists, to be a sort of patron Saint to them, that his expressions, as against the position of the modern revisionists, become virtually "admissions against interest," as the lawyers say. His views are often so used in these *Notes.* (See *Note One, Item* 6, herein.)

Item 2.   Corruption of Early Scripture Manuscripts.

Summary. There was corruption of early manuscripts from various causes, some of which are listed. The Articles of Faith (the creed) of the Church of Jesus Christ of Latter-day Saints declares the Bible has been corrupted, and another statement of the Prophet Joseph Smith declares in general terms the source and causes of the corruptions. Scholars—Scrivener, Burgon, Miller—deal in considerable detail with the sources and causes that led to the corruptions indicated by the Prophet. Scrivener tells of the early tamperings with the Bible text, and also of the tampering with the writings of the early Fathers as they themselves complained, and names some of the early corrupting heretics,—Basilides, Valentinus, Marcion. He names Irenaeus as among those who contended against the heresies. Burgon and Miller devoted an entire work to a consideration of the corruptions of the Bible text.

The Eighth Article of Faith of the Church of Jesus Christ of Latter-day Saints declares: "We believe the Bible to be the word of God as far as it is translated correctly; we also believe the Book of Mormon to be the word of God." At another time, the Prophet Joseph Smith declared: "I believe the Bible as it read when it came from the pen of the original writers. Ignorant translators, careless transcribers, or designing and corrupt priests have committed many errors." (*Documentary History of the Church of Jesus Christ of Latter-*

day Saints, (Salt Lake City, Utah, Deseret News, 1912) Vol. VI, p. 57, cited hereinafter as *DHC*.)

SCRIVENER'S OBSERVATIONS

On the point of the early corruptions of the Scriptures by heretics, and others, and the effect thereof on early manuscripts as pure texts of the Scriptures, we may note the following brief observations by Dr. Scrivener:

"Besides the undesigned and, to a great extent, unavoidable differences subsisting between manuscripts of the New Testament within a century of its being written, the wilful corruptions introduced by heretics soon became a cause of loud complaint in the primitive ages of the Church. Dionysius, Bishop of Corinth, addressing the Church of Rome and Soter its Bishop (A.D. 168-176), complains that even his own letters had been tampered with. . . . Nor was the evil new in the age of Dionysius. Not to mention the Gnostics Basilides (A.D. 130?) and Valentinus (A.D. 150?) who published additions to the sacred text which were avowedly of their own composition, Marcion of Pontus, the arch-heretic of that period, coming to Rome on the death of its Bishop Hyginus (A.D. 142), brought with him that mutilated and falsified copy of the New Testament, against which the Fathers of the second century and later exerted all their powers, and whose general contents are known to us chiefly through the writings of Tertullian and subsequently of Epiphanius. It can hardly be said that Marcion deserves very particular mention in relating the history of the sacred text. Some of the variations from the common readings which his opponents detected were doubtless taken from manuscripts in circulation at the time, and, being adopted through no private preferences of his own, are justly available for critical purposes. . . . In similar instances the evidence of Marcion, as to matters of fact to which he could attach no kind of importance, is well worth recording: but where on the contrary the dogmas of his own miserable system are touched, or no codices or other witnesses countenance his changes (as is perpetually the case in his edition of S. Luke, the only Gospel—and that maimed or interpolated from the others—he seems to have acknowledged at all), his blasphemous extravagance may very well be forgotten. In such cases he does not so much as profess to follow anything more respectable than the capricious devices of his misguided fancy.

"Nothing throws so strong a light on the real state of the text in the latter half of the second century as the single notice of Irenæus (fl. 178) on Apoc. xiii. 18. This eminent person, the glory of the Western Church in his own age, whose five books against Heresies (though chiefly extant but in a bald old Latin version) are among the most precious reliques of Christian antiquity, had been privileged in his youth to enjoy the friendly intercourse of his master Polycarp, who himself had conversed familiarly with S. John and others that had seen the Lord (Euseb. *Eccl. Hist.* v. 20). Yet even Irenæus, though removed but by one stage from the very Apostles, possessed (if we except a bare tradition) no other means of settling discordant readings than are now open to ourselves; namely, to search out the best copies and exercise the judgment on their contents. His *locus classicus* must needs be cited in full, the Latin throughout, the Greek in such portions as survive." (Frederick Henry Ambrose Scrivener, *A Plain Introduction to the Criticism of the New Testament For the Use of Biblical Students,* 3rd ed. rev. (Cambridge, Deighton, Bell and Co., 1883), pp. 505-507, cited hereinafter as Scrivener; see also, *id.,* p. 511, for another statement by Dr. Scrivener.)

EDITIONS OF SCRIVENER'S WORK

Four editions of Dr. Scrivener's work have been issued: first edition, 1861; second edition, "thoroughly revised, enlarged, and brought down to the present date," Cambridge, Deighton, Bell and Co., 1874; third edition, "thoroughly revised, enlarged, and brought down to the present date," Cambridge, Deighton, Bell and Co., 1883; fourth edition, edited by Edward Miller, London, George Bell & Sons, 1894, in two volumes. The first three of these editions were, it appears, entirely the work of Dr. Scrivener, save for such incidental assistance as he might have called in. The fourth edition was only partly prepared at his death, but it was later finished by his life-long friend and full sympathizer, the Rev. Edward Miller, M.A. Rev. Miller indicates that because of the added discoveries which had been made it was necessary to rewrite some portions of Dr. Scrivener's third edition and he lists scholars whom he called to his assistance.

Since the third edition was the last edition which can be regarded as the work of Dr. Scrivener, and since the fourth edition contains material which he did not see, and upon which his great learning and judgment and wisdom were not bestowed (though apparently Rev. Miller is a very able scholar and called to his aid other scholars equally able), it has been decided to use in these *Notes* the text of the third edition, noting in appropriate places such changes as seem to be of any importance or significance as they appear in the fourth edition, cited hereinafter as Scrivener-Miller.

It might be added, though irrelevant to the foregoing, that some other reference books used in the preparation of these *Notes* are nearly half a century younger than the fourth edition of Scrivener, are written by those who hold opposite views from Dr. Scrivener in many respects, and are apparently among the latest words on textual criticism.

WORK OF BURGON AND MILLER

Messrs. Burgon and Miller have devoted an entire work (John William Burgon, *The Causes of the Corruption of the Traditional Text of the Holy Gospels*, Edward Miller, ed., London, George Bell and Sons, 1896) to a discussion of this subject of the corruption of scriptural texts. (See for summary of some causes, author's *On the Way to Immortality and Eternal Life* (Salt Lake City, Deseret Book Company, 1949), pp. 201 ff.)

Item 3.   The Origin of Writing.

Summary. The origin of writing as affecting the Five Books of Moses. While Old Testament writings are not directly concerned herein, yet the contention of "higher critics" that Moses could not have written the Pentateuch because writing was not known in Palestine at that time (1380 B.C.) so attacks the credibility of the whole Bible text that it ought to be noted that clay tablets discovered in Mesopotamia and Ur date back to 2100 B.C.; writings in Egypt date back as far as 3100 B.C.; Hittite and Crete writings dating in the second millennium B.C.; correspondence between the Egyptian Government and their Palestinian governors dating 1380 B.C. (about Joshua's time); inscriptions in the turquoise mines of Serabit (2200-2000 B.C.), written in an alphabet, the ancestor of the Hebrew, and derived from the Egyptian hieroglyphs, an alphabet thought also to be the ancestor of the Phoenician and therefore the Greek; inscriptions on tombs and pottery found at Byblos (on the Syrian coast) dating 1200-1000 B.C. Scholars affirm cumulative evidence sufficient to assure that writing not only in the Babylonian cuneiforms but in a script from which Hebrew eventually developed, existed at the time of the Exodus.

As bearing wholly upon the text of the Old Testament, particularly the Five Books of Moses, with which we are but indirectly concerned in these *Notes,*—a few words may be as well said here as elsewhere, regarding the contention of critics of the last quarter of the last century, that the Pentateuch of the Old Testament (the Five Books of Moses) could not have been written contemporaneously with the events recorded (much less by Moses), because writing was not at that time known in Palestine. (Kenyon, *Our Bible,* p. 4.)

This contention relates particularly to certain of the texts of the Old Testament. But because of the general tendency of the criticism to discredit the Bible as a whole, the following facts may be noted:

The view now generally accepted fixes the date of Joshua's conquest of Palestine at about 1380 B.C. Two views have been held as to the date of the Israelitish exodus: one somewhere between 1380 and 1362 B.C., the other between 1233 and 1223 B.C., but the general view is as stated. (Kenyon, *Our Bible*, p. 5; n. 2, p. 5.)

American scholars excavating in Mesopotamia (the valley of the Euphrates, lying north and east of Palestine) at Nippur, have uncovered thousands of clay tablets which can be dated about 2100 B.C. Sir Leonard Woolley discovered at Ur (the land of Abraham—Gen. 11:31), tablets of about the same date, while Langdon discovered at Kish, tablets that go back to "the middle of the fourth millennium or even earlier," B.C. (Kenyon, *Our Bible*, p. 4.)

From Egypt, from which the Israelites migrated, papyri manuscripts have been recovered that are datable about 2200-2000 B.C. These writings profess to quote teachings of one Kagemna on ethics and of Ptah-Hetep on gnomic philosophy (similar to Proverbs) and are datable about 3100 B.C. and 2880 B.C., respectively. The great Egyptian ritual work, the *Book of the Dead*, dates from 1580 to 1320 B.C.

Moses, trained in the royal courts, must have been familiar with Egyptian writing, and in all likelihood with Egyptian literature. He almost certainly could write; probably Aaron, too, and perhaps many others.

Writings of the Hittites and Cretes have been discovered in Asia Minor, in Northern Syria, and in Crete, that date back to the second millennium B.C.

At Tell el-Amarna (a city midway between Thebes and Memphis; ruled over about 1380 B.C. by Amenhotep IV, or Akhenaten, father-in-law of Tutankhamen), Egyptian papyri have been discovered containing correspondence between the king and the Egyptian governors of Palestine and Syria. This was "while the Hittites were conquering Damascus, and the Amorites were invading Phoenicia, Jerusalem, Lachish, Hazor, Megiddo, Gezer, are mentioned by name; and complaints are made of the assaults of the Habiru, who have been generally regarded as the Hebrews, though the identification is not accepted by all scholars." (Kenyon, *Our Bible*, pp. 5-6.) These were actual writings in Palestine of about Joshua's time. However, the language was Babylonian, not Hebrew.

Mention may be made of the Moabite Stone (which shows writing in Moab of about 890 B.C.), written in what is known as the Semitic alphabet, used in common by the Phoenicians, Aramaeans, and Hebrews; of the inscriptions (2200-2000 B.C.) in the turquoise mines in Serabit (located in the south end of the peninsula of Sinai), in an alphabet claimed to be the ancestor of the Hebrew alphabet and derived from the Egyptian hieroglyphs, thought also to be the ancestor of the Phoenician and therefore of the Greek. Kenyon also notes the inscriptions found on a royal sarcophagus at Byblos (1200-1000 B.C.) on the Syrian coast north of Beirut, and the inscriptions on pottery in Sinaitic-Hebrew script of about the thirteenth century B.C. at Tell Duweir (ancient Lachish), all still under discussion by specialists. Kenyon affirms that evidence is sufficient, in its cumulative effect, to assure that writing was known and commonly used in Palestine, not only in the Babylonian cuneiforms, but "in the script from which Hebrew eventually developed, from the time when the Hebrews entered Palestine after the Exodus." (*Our Bible*, p. 7.)

Kenyon closes his discussion of this whole question by noting the discovery at Ras-Shamra (a site not far from Alexandretta, on the north-west coast of Syria, the site identified as that of the ancient Phoenician city of Ugarit), of what seems to have been a library in which were found a quantity of clay tablets covered with cuneiform writing, not of the ordinary Babylonian type, but of a writing that was alphabetic in character, the language of which was an archaic form of Hebrew. The texts recorded on the tablets included some "literary and religious writings, among which occurred names familiar to us from the Old Testament." The city flourished about the beginning of the second millennium B.C. (*Our Bible*, pp. 7-9.)

Thus the rather elemental matter of criticism that the Hebrews had no knowledge of writing at the time when the first great books of the Old Testament were written is shown to be without foundation. (For article on "The Language of Homer's Heroes," (the Achaeans) by Jotham Johnson, see *Scientific American*, Vol. 190, No. 5 (May, 1954), pp. 70-74.)

Item 4. *Search for Helpful Reference Books.*

Summary. Efforts by author to get reference material, almost exclusively for the New Testament. The search for source books that could be successfully used by the author in his study of the matters considered has covered several years and has not been too fruitful, but enough books were finally secured to enable him to proceed as herein appearing.

It should be noted to begin with that hereafter these Notes deal almost exclusively with the New Testament. (But see *Note Eleven, Item 1,* for a short account of modern criticism of the Old Testament.)

As a matter of possible interest, it may be noted that several years ago, to aid him in his rebellion against this "higher criticism," the author began a search for reference works that would help him in his rebellion. He instituted searches for books—now out of print—in the great bookstores of New York and London. His success was scanty, but he did get some good books, and he used them to the maximum possible extent he could, but not being a linguist, his use of them has been greatly hampered. As is his custom, he began making notes of his reading. He talked about his plan with some of his friends. They encouraged him and suggested that he prepare something that might be published, they affirming they thought it would be helpful to others. In this view of possible publication, it occurred to him that his personal deficiencies might have this advantage: it has confined his use of available materials to such as he could himself understand reasonably well, which fact is something of a guarantee that the material presented will certainly come within the understanding of other ordinary laymen besides himself.

The author has been encouraged to go forward in his study, and enheartened (as already stated), by the words of a great scholar (Sir Frederic Kenyon, from whose writings he has already quoted and who will be used frequently hereinafter), who has said:

"... but any intelligent reader, without any knowledge of either Greek or Hebrew, can learn enough to understand the processes of criticism and the grounds on which the judgments of scholars must be based." (*Our Bible*, p. 18.)

The author might add that he began this study as something of a background to a chronological harmony of the Gospels that he began more than twenty-five years ago, when he taught a Sunday School class in the Twentieth Ward (Salt Lake City), but he laid it aside for ten years, then did a little more, then there was another period of cessation, and the last two or three years there has been more intensive work,—ninety percent of which has had to be done at night when the regular working days were over. He has tried to dig out and record a lot of things he, himself, has always wanted to know about the Bible. It may be these same things will be interesting to others.

It might be added that the work on these *Notes* was not seriously begun till 1949 and was substantially completed by October, 1953.

Item 5.   *Quotation of Authorities.*

Summary. Quotation from authorities,—*Extreme Textualists* and *High* or *Sound Textualists*,—the *Notes* are essentially and deliberately paste-pot and scissors production in all technical matters. The author's scholarship is wholly insufficient to enable him to handle the original sources even had they been available to him (as they were not). So he has had to rely upon the studies of recognized authorities in the field of Bible criticism. On technical matters, in order to be sure of his ground, he has quoted largely from these authorities.

Since the author's own scholarship is wholly insufficient to enable him to do any original research in this great field of human thought (which means the author has no standing in that field—and ought to have none), and since, as a matter of fact, original sources were not available to him even if he could have used them, he has quoted most extensively from writers who are learned and who have done the research necessary to give them a standing. He has quoted largely from the *High* or *Sound Textualists*, who compose the opposite school from the modernists, the "higher critics," who are called the *Extreme Textualists*. The High or Sound Textualists believe in Jesus as the Christ, in the full measure of his stature, as they understand it.

The author has tried, in these *Notes,* to be meticulously careful to make sure that all quotations are put within quotation marks, even parts of sentences running in the text. Through this means it will hardly be possible for the reader to fail to distinguish between the author's own comments and the observations of the scholars.

The quotations so used have mainly and directly to do with the Revised Version, printed in 1881 (New Testament) and 1885 (Old Testament) by the Oxford and Cambridge Universities (Oxford Press), the text being that arrived at by the Revisers working under the mandate of the Convocation of the Province of Canterbury of 1870.

However, the quotes and comments will be almost completely applicable to the American Standard Version, issued in 1901 (essentially, it was the same text as the Revised Version) when the agreement between the British and American scholars who collaborated in producing the Revised Version, permitted an American edition of the joint Version, — the American Standard Version.

Since, so far as noted, the recently issued Revised Standard Version (1946-1952) follows closely the two earlier Revisions—British and American—in certain essential changes made in the King James Version (the Authorized Version, sometimes spoken of as the *Textus Receptus*), a number of which will be specifically noted hereinafter, what is said regarding the British Revised Version will have a like application to this latest Revision.

As the author has said in the *Preface,* and in other places, these *Notes* cannot escape the charge that they are, in their technical discussions, almost exclusively a scissors and paste-pot production; the answer to this charge is: that is what they are intended to be, and they probably have value in the direct proportion that this is true.

Item 6.   The Scholars,—Scrivener, Burgon, Miller, and Kenyon, Who Are Mainly Quoted.

Summary.   The scholars most used and cited are Scrivener, Burgon, Miller, and Kenyon.   There is a general discussion of the use made of them, and of their relative values for these *Notes.*   The principal critical sources used in the *Notes* are named and a critical estimate of their attainments and reliability given, incorporating opinions of their opponents in scholastic theory and deductions.   As noted, those so named are Scrivener, Burgon, and Miller, who support the King James Version, and Kenyon, who supports the Revised Version, though in his more recent works he seems to be veering away somewhat from the allegiance he earlier gave to the Revised Version and to be returning to the King James Version for which he expresses the greatest admiration.

Since we shall quote from and cite so largely these men, it seems well to show at the beginning how they stood as among their antagonists and contemporaries,— that is, we shall qualify our witnesses — for the controversy was and is deep-rooted and it grew very bitter. As to two of these men (Scrivener and Burgon), we quote from Kenyon, who seems reasonably restrained in his general comments, though dogmatically certain when he has a point to support. Kenyon seems to line up with the Extreme Textualists. We have quoted very largely from him because he is a scholar recognized by the modern Extreme Textualists as not only of great ability, but as standing in a position of leadership amongst them, a sort of *exemplar.* His conclusions on critical matters seem generally accepted and his critical analysis of manuscripts adopted without serious question by the Extreme Textualist group.

Kenyon points out Scrivener's service in England along with Gregory's in Germany, in the work of listing the manuscripts of the New Testament which number increased enormously during the nineteenth century. (*The Text*, p. 67.) "For the full description of all MSS. reference must be made to the catalogues of Scrivener (*Plain Introduction to the Criticism of the New Testament*, 4th ed. by E. Miller, 1894, vol. I, pp. 90-376)." (*The Text*, p. 71.)

He lists Scrivener (along with Griesbach and Hort) as holding that as between Greek and Latin New Testament texts, "Greek is the main text, and that the Latin has been influenced by it," as against a number of other scholars holding the opposite view. (*The Text*, p. 94.)

He states Scrivener "elaborately studied" the Codex Bezae, and lists him as an authority in his "Bibliography" to his (Kenyon's) chapter, "The Manuscripts of the New Testament." (*The Text*, pp. 96, 110.) He speaks of Scrivener as one who "vehemently opposed" the theories of Westcott and Hort. (*Our Bible*, p. 114.)

Speaking of the work of Scrivener and Gregory in the cataloguing of manuscripts, he says:

"In England a similar service was rendered by F. H. A. Scrivener (1813-91), whose *Introduction to the Criticism of the New Testament*, first published in 1861 (fourth edition, 1894, by E. Miller, with chapters by other scholars) is still the fullest description, up to its date, of the textual materials for English readers." (*Our Bible*, p. 122.)

He also notes that in 1864, Scrivener issued "a new

edition, with full annotations" of the Codex Bezae. (*Our Bible*, p. 144.)

Finally, he speaks of the publication of the Revised Version (which was put through the press by Scrivener, though he had strongly opposed certain changes made in the Greek text by Hort), as follows:

"In Dr. Hort and Dr. Scrivener the New Testament Company possessed the two most learned textual critics then alive." (*Our Bible*, p. 238; see John William Burgon, *The Revision Revised* (London, John Murray, 1883), p. 231, cited hereafter as Burgon.)

The Revisionists of the 1880's used Dr. Scrivener and Dr. Hort to amass and present the evidence for and against all proposed changes in the Authorized Version. (*Note Twenty-seven*, p. 269; Burgon, p. 37.)

(See for an account of the various editions of Scrivener's great work, and of the text used herein, *A Plain Introduction to the Criticism of the New Testament for the Use of Biblical Students, Note One, Item 2, supra.*)

WORK OF BURGON

As to Burgon, Kenyon is less generous, for Burgon struck hard and made deep wounds. His philosophy was evidently that of the soldier: destroy your enemy!

KENYON'S APPRAISAL OF BURGON

Speaking of the battle between the proponents and opponents of the Received Text (our King James Version), Kenyon said:

"Dean J. W. Burgon, the protagonist of the former [the Received Text], was a doughty controversialist, and could deal a swashing blow with gusto. He had also behind him the sympathy of those who resented the changes in their beloved

Authorized Version and did not understand the reasons for them. Among scholars, however, he found little support, and though his disciple and assistant, E. W. Miller (who, besides directly controversial books, edited the fourth edition of Scrivener's useful *Introduction*), maintained the fight after his death, this conflict soon died down." (*The Text*, p. 170.)

He yields to Burgon the leadership of "a few scholars . . . who refused to abandon the 'received' text." (*The Story*, p. 87.) He lists Burgon along with Scrivener as one of those who "vehemently opposed" the theories of Westcott and Hort. (*Our Bible*, p. 114.) Again he says: "Other scholars who may be mentioned are J. W. Burgon, conspicuous for his vehement and even intemperate defence of the Received Text against the doctrines of Westcott and Hort." (*Our Bible*, p. 122.)

In another place, Kenyon says:

"Dean Burgon tilted desperately against the text of Westcott and Hort, and even went so far as to argue that these two documents [א and B] owed their preservation, not to the goodness of their text, but to its depravity, having been, so to speak, pilloried as examples of what a copy of the Scriptures ought not to be! In spite of the learning with which the Dean maintained his arguments, and of the support which equally eminent but more moderate scholars such as Dr. Scrivener gave to his conclusions, they have failed to hold their ground." (*Our Bible*, p. 140.)

Again he says:

"Dean Burgon of Chichester . . . assailed it [the Revised Version] vehemently in the *Quarterly Review* with a series of articles, the unquestionable learning of which was largely neutralised by the extravagance and intemperance of their tone. The Dean, however, was not alone in his dislike of the very numerous changes introduced by the Revisers into the familiar language of the English Bible, and there was a general unwillingness to adopt the new translation as a substitute for the Authorised Version in common use." (*Our Bible*, p. 242.)

The Dean is dead, but the people have largely vindicated his position. Their discernment was far greater than that of the Extreme Textualist scholars.

Further on, towards the end of his book, Kenyon, in summary says:

"More than fifty years have now passed since the publication of the Revised Version, and the dust of the original controversy has had time to die down. In less than that time the Authorised Version drove the Geneva Bible from the field; but there is no sign of a similar victory of the Revised over the Authorised....

"It is true that the Authorised Version has struck its roots too deeply into our language and literature, and is itself too great a monument of literary art, to be dispossessed without a preponderating balance of loss. We can no more do without the Authorised Version than we can do without Shakespeare and Bacon." (*Our Bible*, pp. 243-44.)

One uninfected with the spirit of Arianism, which still beclouds the minds and the spirit of the Extreme Textualists, would join in the concept put forth by Burgon and ignored by Kenyon, that God would not permit his Holy Words to be robbed of the great incidents and declarations that showed Jesus was the Christ. "The letter killeth, but the spirit giveth life." (II Cor. 3:6.)

SCRIVENER'S ESTIMATE OF BURGON

Having quoted so generously from Kenyon (who was of the opposite school from Burgon) regarding Burgon, and having quoted the commendatory observations which Kenyon makes seemingly reluctantly about Burgon, the appraisal of Burgon may appropriately be closed by quoting from Scrivener, the great scholar:

"Very many corrections have been made in the following Catalogue as well from investigations of my own as from information kindly furnished to me ... especially by Dean Burgon, to whom the present edition is more deeply indebted than it would be possible to acknowledge in detail. His series of Letters addressed to me in the *Guardian* newspaper (1873) contains but a part of the help he has afforded towards the preparation of this and the second edition. . . .

". . . Dean Burgon's brilliant monograph, 'The Last Twelve verses of the Gospel according to S. Mark vindicated against recent objectors and established' (Oxford and London, 1871), has thrown a stream of light upon the controversy, nor does the joyous tone of his book misbecome one who is conscious of having triumphantly maintained a cause which is very precious to him. We may fairly say that his conclusions have in no essential point been shaken by the elaborate and very able counter-plea of Dr. Hort." (Scrivener, pp. 178, 583.)

Because Dean Burgon wrote his attacks in a more or less popular style, and so measurably understandable to the layman, this author has quoted most generously from him in those parts of these *Notes* which deal with the Revised Versions as against the King James Version. His material is so well documented that it carries conviction on the points he discusses. In the quotations this author has tried to choose sections as relatively free from Greek terms as possible, to the detriment, at times, he is sure, of the fullest explanation. This resulted from the author's own ignorance of Greek and his belief that others who might read hereof would be perhaps also uninformed. This policy has necessitated a scantier use of Scrivener's work than he could have wished for.

ESTIMATE OF KENYON

As already stated, the author has made great use of Dr. Kenyon's studies, because he is recognized as a great scholar and seems to hold a position of leadership among the Extreme Textualists of today. His present conclusions and opinions have changed, it seems almost radically, from the conclusions and opinions of the Extreme Textualists of the last quarter of the last century. His extreme caution in urging his present views surely suggests a feeling on his part that further modifications must be made in the point of view of the early Extreme Textualists.

The Revisers of the latest American Version, the Revised Standard Version, pay to his views such great respect and follow him so closely in so many most important matters that he becomes their *exemplar*, almost of stature of a patron Saint.

Item 7. The Making of the Revised Version, British and American.

Summary. The making of the Revised Version, published in the early 1880's, and the American Standard Version of 1900-1901, is the product of Extreme Textualists' scholarship which seems largely to deny Jesus as the Christ. In 1870, the Convocation of the Province of Canterbury set up the machinery for a revision of the Authorized Version of the Bible (King James Version of 1611). The Extreme Textualists practically took over the work of this revision, which certainly tended to the destruction of Jesus as the Christ. While the initiation of the project was thus British, American scholars were invited to participate. These two groups of scholars differed in a number of matters, and it was agreed that no purely American edition should be issued for a specified period, which ended in 1900-1901. British edition—Revisers' dates—New Testament, November 11, 1880; Old Testament, July 10, 1884.

The Convocation of the Province of Canterbury (February, 1870) set up the machinery for a revision of the Authorized Version of the Bible, i.e., the King James translation of 1611. The "higher critics" (*Extreme Textualists*, as they have been named) seem to have been largely responsible for the impetus given to the movement at that time. These Extreme Textualists had been growing in strength since Jean Astruc (1684-1766) wrote about the Pentateuch, and Lachmann (1793-1851; his first book, 1831) attacked the New Testament. (Kenyon, *Our Bible*, p. 120.)

The Extreme Textualists and their collaborators took over the direction of the Revision for which the Convocation had planned. The Authorized Version (King James Version) was fatal to some of the beliefs, or disbeliefs, they seemed to foster.

A too largely sceptical Protestant clergy has followed along with the Extreme Textualists, in whose reasonings and conclusions they have, in good part, joined, until Jesus the Christ, the Messiah, the Atoning Sacrifice, the Redeemer of the World, the First Fruits of the Resurrection, the Son of God, has been pulled down toward the stature of Jesus of Nazareth, the man, a great and a good man, but all mortal. Faith in Christ largely lagging in them, a considerable part of the divines and scholars of the last four score years have written and spoken the arguments and doctrines of the Extreme Textualists until they are polluting with essentially anti-Christ and sometimes atheistic teachings, the very fountains of the true faith. Books and encyclopedic writings of the most noted divines and scholars may not now be surely relied upon for a fair presentation of the great spiritual problems (and there are problems, and they are great) and the solution of those same problems which now confront the Christian world.

These are the very scholars, along with other scholars who are not in the ministry, to whom Kenyon refers as dismissing serious consideration of Burgon and his associates.

The "Revisers' Preface" to the New Testament Revision bears date November 11, 1880; the Preface date of the Old Testament is July 10, 1884.

American scholars were invited to participate and did participate to some extent in the making of the Revised Version, made and published in Britain. At the time it was agreed among the two groups (British and American) that no purely American edition should be issued for a specified period. This period ended at the close of the century, and in 1900-1901 an American edition was issued. It was in substance the same as the Revised Version (British). The American edition was called the American Standard Version.

Item 8.   The Making of the Revised Standard Version, American.

Summary. The making of the Revised Standard Version (American), 1946-1952. This Version is in text, in great essentials, the same as the earlier British and American Versions. The National Council of the Churches of Christ in the U.S.A., having acquired control of the American Standard Version copyright, a committee was appointed to revise the American Standard Version if deemed necessary. The title page of this "New Covenant" bears date 1946.

Recently (1952-1953) wide propagandizing publicity has been given to a new translation of the Bible, known as the Revised Standard Version, in which have been retained vital changes which the Revised Version made in the King James Version. These changes consist in making omissions from and insertions into the text of the King James Version (the Authorized Version,—A.V., as it is frequently cited), particularly in the New Testament, with which alone we shall deal herein. The New Testament is now dubbed *The New Covenant*.

The title page of the whole Bible (Old and New Testaments) bears date 1952. The Preface is undated, but it states that its publication was authorized by "the National Council of the Churches of Christ in the U.S.A. in 1951." ("Preface," p. v.)

The title page to "The New Covenant / commonly called / The / New Testament / of our Lord and Savior / Jesus Christ / Revised Standard Version," bears date 1946.

It appears that in 1928, the copyright of the American Standard Version was acquired by the International Council of Religious Education, composed of "the educational boards of forty of the major Protestant denominations of the United States and Canada." This body appointed an "American Standard Bible Committee of scholars to have charge of the text, and authorized it to undertake further revision if deemed necessary." (*An Introduction to the Revised Standard Version of the New Testament*, by Members of the Revision Committee, Luther A. Weigle, Chairman (The International Council of Religious Education, 1946), p. 10, cited hereafter as *An Introduction.*)

The copyright of this revised text, dubbed "The New Covenant," was issued to the "Division of Christian Education of the National Council of the Churches of Christ in the United States of America."

This new translation (really a recension), like the Revised Version and the American Standard Version, is the product of the Extreme Textualists, and follows in essential matters the earlier translations (just named) made by other members of the same group in Britain (in the early 1880's) and in America (1900-1901). An outline of the steps leading to this new revision will be given later. (See *Note Thirty-three, infra.*)

Item 9. Some General Considerations.

> *Summary.* This *Item* contains: General observations on the effect of the extended use of the Revised Versions; the method of approach and what the Revisionists have actually done; domination of Westcott-Hort's work. The *Item* notes that the Revised Version is not really a revision of the King James Version, but is in fact a translation of a newly fabricated Greek text; that the Revised Standard Version is in fact a recension of the American Standard Version; that we stand in danger of a pollution of the sacred text of the Bible, by destroying the basic Christian concept that Jesus is the Christ. The author's study convinces him the King James Version is the best version of any yet produced, leaving out of account for the present, Joseph Smith's Inspired Version. The casual reader must be on guard not to be led astray by the fallacious reasonings of the Revisers. The revisions so far made are not really revisions of the King James Version, but a translation of a newly fabricated Greek text based on the great manuscripts,—Sinaiticus (ℵ) and Vaticanus (B). The new Revised Standard Version is really a revision (recension), not of the King James Version, but of the revisions of the 1880's in Britain and the American Standard Version, 1900-1901.

The problems which the use of this last text (the Revised Standard Version) would raise have led the author to believe that some observations about the history and text of the New Testament and about a few elementary matters involved in its translation into English, might be of some value to those who would find interest in the harmony of the Gospels, *Our Lord of The Gospels* (by the author and the preliminary print already issued),—a history of the life, mission, and teachings of our Lord and Savior, Jesus Christ, as recorded in the Gospels themselves and in the Book of Mormon.

A consideration of the doctrines of modern, so-called "higher criticism," fully persuades the author that we stand in danger of such a pollution of the sacred text by these Extreme Textualists as may weaken in the minds of many and destroy in the minds of some, the great fundamental fact that Jesus of Nazareth was indeed the Messiah, the Son of God, the Christ that was to come to earth to redeem men from the Fall and bring salvation and exaltation to the human family.

The author's own studies—superficial as they have had to be—have fortified his own convictions that the King James Version is the best version we have in English (not now considering the Prophet Joseph's Inspired Version). But the statements and arguments offered by the Extreme Textualists, to support their views and their new text, often appear so persuasive, particularly about matters that are inconsequential, that the author finds one must be on one's guard against the specious fallacies and errors which they put forth about matters of the essence,—fallacies and errors that scholars of the Sound or High Textualist group seem unreservedly to condemn and discard.

While the Revisers (British, early 1880's, and American, 1900-1901) began with a mandate to correct the errors and linguistic infelicities of the King James Version, they, in effect, adopted a new Greek text (largely based on Westcott and Hort's text), abandoning the Received Text (Textus Receptus) of which the King James Version (Authorized Version) was a translation. The Westcott-Hort Greek text was fabricated from an amalgamation of certain picked manuscripts, primarily B (Vaticanus) and ℵ (Sinaiticus), readings being added or invoked from now one, now another of other manuscripts that supported either or both of the two principal texts, or the conceptions of the fabricators. The new Greek text was based primarily upon this Greek text so prepared. A confidential copy of the Westcott and Hort Greek text was conveniently at hand when the British Revisers began their work and was made available to them. It seems clear that the Westcott-Hort text and its makers completely dominated the work of the Revisers. The Revision was essentially a translation of this new text.

In short, the Revised Version which the Revisers produced was, therefore, not a revised translation of the manuscripts of which the King James Version was a translation (the Textus Receptus), but a translation of a newly fabricated Greek text, and this new Greek text was in many vital matters different from the Textus Receptus.

The new version, the Revised Standard Version recently issued (1946-1952), is issued as a revision (perhaps better a *recension*) of the American Standard Version, which in effect is essentially a revision of the Revised Version of the early 1880's (British). The early Revisers used the Westcott and Hort text, with a very few other Greek texts, which were apparently of the same mold as Westcott and Hort's. All are texts largely acceptable to the Extreme Textualists.

Item 10.   *Elements of Unfairness.*

Summary. Elements of unfairness in work and propaganda of Revisers of the Revised Standard Version; they do not disclose the manuscripts they are using for their work; they emphasize unimportant changes and pass almost unnoticed the important ones; their essential motive could be to destroy Jesus as the Messiah; the title pages of the various Versions compared, with comments thereon. A revision of a translation of the Bible from

Greek into English is a fair enough undertaking if the reader may depend that such is the fact, but the Revised Standard Version while avowedly such a production (as the casual reader would understand) is not such in fact, but is a revision of an earlier revision that was based upon other Greek texts, indeed controlled by other Greek texts, than those from which came the King James Version. The Revisers go to great lengths in their propaganda, to build up the need for revision of the King James Version by playing up instances of bad grammar, archaic words (usually inconsequential), and like matters, but ignore great matters of substance, of omissions and insertions that vitally and negatively affect essential matters of Christian doctrine, such as that Jesus is the real Messiah "that was to come." A reading of the various title pages of the Revisions, and a rather casual analysis thereof show how the general reader might be misled as to the character of these revisions.

The making of a virtual recension of the text, not of the King James Version, but of the American Standard Version, is fair enough, if we are so informed, and the Extreme Textualist translators more or less frankly do affirm this was their course and purpose. But they talk all the way through their *Introduction* (see *Note Thirty-three*) in language that on its face could be interpreted as showing that what they were really doing was correcting the translation of the Greek manuscripts of which the King James Version is the translation—the Textus Receptus. But this they are not doing. No place has been noted where they name the manuscripts which they themselves are using, nor the text they are using, beyond saying they are revising the American Standard Version, though they do name and stress certain new manuscripts and papyri at their command which were not available to the earlier Revisers.

They go to great lengths to build up a case about the poor translation of the King James Version. They

say very little about the American Standard Version
or its need for revision; they mention it briefly and
call attention to a number of changes they have made;
but it gets little genuine criticism. On the other hand,
they belabor as much as they dare, the King James
Version, largely about matters that are more or less
inconsequential, matters of grammar, vocabulary, etc.
When it comes to vital matters of substance, they say
little or nothing about the changes that have been made
in the King James Version.

The general reader is likely to get the impression
that in their *Introduction* (a propaganda pamphlet)
the Revisers are telling about the important changes,
or at least informing us about the kind of essential
changes they are making in the King James Version.
But this is not the fact. Of course, this is not fair
on their part; it could be deception. One hesitates to
assign motives for actions, yet one may at least surmise.
The author's surmise is:

The fact of the situation is, as already pointed out
above, the Revisions of the last century have made no
essential headway with the great bulk of the people
who still cling to the King James Version. Kenyon has
freely admitted this fact. Therefore, they could scarcely hope to get anywhere with the general Bible-reading
public by a frank announcement that they were really
merely revising the earlier non-popular Revision. So
their propaganda is so worded as to give or leave the
impression that here was a revision of the King James
Version, which was to be more readable than the King
James Version. When the people read the Revision
carefully they will find that most, if not all of the great
errors of the earlier Revisions are retained which, in
many places, are calculated to destroy Jesus as the

Christ. This seems to be, or could be, their purpose. The whole problem could be as simple as that.

The Extreme Textualist is not, apparently cannot be, a true believer in Christ, a true Christian, in the sense in which true Christianity has been understood since Christ walked the earth. For the Extreme Textualist, Christ is gone; only a philosopher, a great teacher, a profound psychologist, a builder of an ethical code, remains—and sometimes some of them seem not too sure about his actual personality.

We have not had available any such criticism of the latest Extreme Textualist text—the Revised Standard Version of 1946-1952—as we had for the Revised Version (British), but since these new translators have perpetuated essential changes and omissions of the British Revision, the comments of the critics of the British (1880's) seem essentially, if not equally, applicable to the new text.

THE TITLE PAGES

We are not sure that some readers will understand the language of the title pages of the different versions.

The King James Version apparently had a title page, the essential parts of which, for our purposes, read as follows:

"The / Holy Bible / containing the / Old and New Testaments / translated out of the original tongues: and with / the former translations diligently compared / and revised, by His Majesty's special command / appointed to be read in Churches."

The title page of the New Testament part of the Bible of the King James Version reads as follows:

"The / New Testament / of / our Lord and Saviour Jesus Christ / translated out of the original Greek: and with / the former translations diligently compared / and revised, by his Majesty's special command / appointed to be read in Churches."

The title page of the American Standard Version reads:

"The / Holy Bible / containing the / Old and New Testaments / translated out of the original tongues / being the version set forth A. D. 1611 / compared with the most ancient authorities and revised / A. D. 1881-1885 / Newly Edited by the American Revision Committee / A. D. 1901 / Standard Edition."

The title page of the New Testament portion of the American Standard Version reads:

"The New Covenant / commonly called / The New Testament / of / our Lord and Saviour / Jesus Christ / translated out of the Greek / being the version set forth A. D. 1611 / compared with the most ancient authorities and revised / A. D. 1881 / Newly Edited by the New Testament Members of the / American Revision Committee / A. D. 1900 / Standard Edition."

The title page of the latest revision (recension), the Revised Standard Version, reads:

"The / Holy Bible / Revised Standard Version / containing the / Old and New Testaments / translated from the original tongues / being the version set forth A. D. 1611 / Revised A. D. 1881-1885 and A. D. 1901 / compared with the most ancient authorities / and revised A. D. 1952."

We quote again (see *Item 8*, p. 31, *supra*) from the title page of the Revised Standard Version of the New Testament:

"The New Covenant / commonly called / The / New Testament / of our Lord and Savior / Jesus Christ / Revised Standard Version / translated from the Greek / being the version set forth A. D. 1611 / revised A. D. 1881 and A. D. 1901 / compared with the most ancient authorities / and revised A. D. 1946."

It will be noted that the title pages of the whole

Bible and of the New Testament part of the *King James Version*, contain five elements:

1. Old Testament — translated from the original tongues.
   New Testament — translated from the original Greek.
2. Diligent comparison with other translations.
3. Revision.
4. His Majesty's special command.
5. Appointed to be read in Churches.

The American Standard Version has:

1. Old Testament — translation from the original tongues.
   New Testament — translation from the original Greek.
2. Reference to King James Version, A.D. 1611. Comparison with the most ancient authorities.
3. Revision—reference to English Revised Version.
4. Newly edited by American Revision Committee.
5. Absent.
6. The title given to the New Testament is changed to *The New Covenant, commonly called the New Testament.*

The Revised Standard Version has:

1. Old Testament—original tongues.
   New Testament—original Greek.
2. Reference to King James Version of 1611. Comparison with the most ancient authorities.
3. Revision—reference to Revision of 1881-1885 (British) and American Standard Version 1901.

4. No statement of the Revisers.
5. Absent.
6. The title given to the New Testament is *The New Covenant*.

SPECIAL POINTS IN TITLE PAGES

The casual reader might well infer from these title pages of these various Revisions that:

1. The King James Version—the Greek text thereof—was still the controlling text in these translations. This is not true. The Textus Receptus (the Greek text of the King James Version) has been as thoroughly discredited by the Revisers and as largely abandoned by them as expediency has permitted, and a new controlling Greek text (largely based on Westcott-Hort's) has been substituted. This most essential fact would not be suspected from the wording of the title pages. At best, these Revised title pages are not a full disclosure, and at worst they are a kind of deception; the people are not informed of the facts.

2. As a part of this situation, the reference to the "most ancient authorities," might be urged as putting the public on notice of what is carrying on, yet it gives no hint that the "most ancient authorities" used in the various Revisions have been substituted in this work of translation for the basic texts of the Authorized Version, the Textus Receptus.

3. The American Standard Version makes no reference on the title page to the Church or organization from which the Revisers get their authority. It is true that in the Preface to the New Testament the Revisers set out the organizations that are their sponsors, and in their *Introduction* to this Revision, the Revisers dis-

close names of those who did the actual work, but none of this information is on the title page (either as to individuals or as to an authorizing organization). The Bible-reading public is left in ignorance on these points.

4. The Revisers of both American Revisions (1901, 1946) are proposing to change the title of the New Testament to the New Covenant. No statement has been noted giving the reason for this change. The term *covenant* has a distinct religious flavor, connoting much: God's covenant with Abraham, God's covenant people, and so on. It is involved in the change from the Aaronic to the Melchizedek Priesthoods.

This whole procedure can hardly be characterized as frank dealing.

Item 11.   The Revisers' Own Case.

Summary. A pamphlet issued by makers of the Revised Standard Version sets out the Revisers' own case in behalf of their Revision. It does not carry conviction to some of us who read it. It fails to justify, satisfactorily, the great changes made in the King James Version text.

An Introduction to the Revised Standard Version of the New Testament, which these new translators have issued—a series of short, explanatory essays on various features of their work—contains nothing that disturbs the criticism of the Revised Version as hereinafter set out. As already pointed out, they call attention to new sources—manuscripts and papyri—at their disposal, but their essays make few specific references thereto.

It is the author's hope that his *Notes* (contained herein) will help our people who may read them to a renewed confidence in the King James Version, and so to a firmer testimony of the Messiahship of Jesus, by indicating to them that we may rely, as substantially declaring the Word of God, upon the great text of the King James Version, corrupted though it is from the original texts of the Sacred Autographs (which Autographs disappeared in the first two centuries of the Christian Era, — Kenyon, *The Text*, pp. 241-242; see also, pp. 65, 123, herein), especially where that Version is supported by the uncompleted Inspired Version of the Prophet Joseph Smith.

It is these considerations that have led the author to prepare these rather lengthy *Notes* in connection with the text of his harmony, *Our Lord of The Gospels*.

Here and there through the *Notes* the author has made observations on his own account, and set down some conclusions reached by himself. These will be the thoughts of a layman and will not interest the scholars, particularly the Extreme Textualists, but they may help some poor soul to keep the light of abiding faith shining for him through the clouds of doubt and unbelief that enshroud so much of the modern world,— a world that is weltering in apostasy from the true Christian faith and from the Christ who, as Peter declared nearly two thousand years ago, is the only "name under heaven given among men, whereby we must be saved." (Acts 4:12.)

NOTE TWO •
Elements of a Harmony and the Harmonies Herein Relied Upon

Item 1. *Chronological Harmony.*

The harmony developed and already printed (*Our Lord of The Gospels*) is a chronological harmony, that is, the incidents are arranged chronologically. In such harmonies the records of each incident in the Gospels are all brought together in one place, e.g., the records of the baptism of Jesus as found in Matthew, Mark, and Luke, are all collected in one place, and so of the other incidents of the Savior's life.

Item 2. *Idea of Harmony Is Old.*

The idea of a Gospel harmony is as old, certainly, as Tatian (150 or 160 A.D.), and his *Diatessaron*. (See for discussion of dates regarding Tatian, *Note Six, Item 2, Sub-item b, infra* p. 73.) We are not here concerned with the type of Tatian's harmony. John A. Broadus, in a list of the principal Gospel harmonies, names some 79 others, including: Eusebius (315 A.D.), Augustine (400 A.D.), Comestor (1180 A.D.), Perpinian (1330 A.D.), Gerson (1420 A.D.), then 8 others in the 1500's, 9 in the 1600's, 12 in the 1700's, and 45 in the 1800's. There have been a number of others in the 1900's as parts of student's and teacher's editions of the Bible. (John A. Broadus, *A Harmony of the Gospels in the Revised Version*, rev. ed., Archibald Thomas Robertson, ed. (New York, George H. Doran Company, 1920), pp. 279-280.)

Item 3.   Harmonies Used.

Summary. The principal harmonies used in the preparation of *Our Lord of The Gospels,* are the following:

ANDREWS (Samuel J.), *The Life of Our Lord Upon the Earth; Considered in its Historical, Chronological, and Geographical Relations.*

CLARK (George W.), *A New Harmony of the Four Gospels in English; According to the Common Version.*

ROBINSON (Edward), *A Harmony of the Four Gospels in English; According to the Common Version.*

STEVENS (William Arnold) and BURTON (Ernest DeWitt), *A Harmony of the Gospels for Historical Study.*

BROADUS (John A.), *A Harmony of the Gospels in the Revised Version, With New Helps for Historical Study,* ROBERTSON (Archibald Thomas) rev. ed.

ROBERTSON (Archibald T.), *A Harmony of the Gospels for Students of the Life of Christ.*

Because his scholarship would not take the author through original sources—indeed, as has been noted, original sources were not available to him, even though he could have used them, he has taken six harmonies and has arranged them, as nearly as might be, in parallel columns, and has then, with a few minor exceptions, arranged the one given in *Our Lord of The Gospels* in accordance with what seemed to be the views of the majority.

The harmonies so used are as follows:

(a) Samuel J. Andrews, *The Life of Our Lord Upon the Earth; Considered in its Historical, Chronological, and Geographical Relations,* rev. ed. (New York, Charles Scribner's Sons, 1891), first edition, 1862; member of Catholic Apostolic Church (*Irvingite*). (*The New Schaff-Herzog Encyclopedia of Religious Knowledge,* Samuel Macauley Jackson, ed. (New York and London, Funk and Wagnalls Company, 1908-1914), Vol. I, p. 174, hereafter cited as *Schaff-Herzog;* see *DHC,* Vol. IV, pp. 571-581.)

(b) George W. Clark, *A New Harmony of the Four Gospels in English; According to the Common Version*, rev. ed. (Philadelphia, American Baptist Publication Society, 1900), first edition, 1870; Baptist. (*Schaff-Herzog*, Vol. III, pp. 125-126.)

(c) Edward Robinson, *A Harmony of the Four Gospels in English; According to the Common Version*, M. B. Riddle, rev. ed. (Boston, New York, and Chicago, Houghton, Mifflin and Company, 1886); Dr. Robinson had first published a *Greek Harmony of the Gospels* (1845), before preparing his *English Harmony* (1846); Union Theological Seminary, New York; biblical scholar. The Schaffs say of him: "He is probably the most distinguished Biblical scholar whom America has produced, indeed, one of the most distinguished of the nineteenth century." (*Schaff-Herzog*, Vol. X, pp. 59-60.)

This *Harmony*, with "a Revision of the Arrangement," was used by the editors of the *Variorum Bible* (*The Sunday School Centenary Bible, Authorized Version*, London, Eyre and Spottiswoode, 1880); and was also used, it would seem, in subsequent editions of the *Variorum Teacher's Bible* (issued by the same printers) in 1893 and 1894 (*The E. & S. Teacher's Edition, The Holy Bible, Authorized Version*). It thus has the stamp of approval of very high authority.

(d) William Arnold Stevens and Ernest DeWitt Burton, *A Harmony of the Gospels for Historical Study*, 12th ed., rev. (New York, Chicago, Boston, Charles Scribner's Sons, 1904); first edition, 1894; Baptists. (*Schaff-Herzog*, Vol. XI, pp. 88-89; Vol. II, p. 316.)

(e) John A. Broadus, *A Harmony of the Gospels in the Revised Version, With New Helps for Historical Study*, Archibald Thomas Robertson, rev. ed. (New

York, George H. Doran Company, 1920); first edition, 1893; American Baptist. (*Schaff-Herzog*, Vol. II, p. 272.)

(f) Archibald T. Robertson, *A Harmony of the Gospels for Students of the Life of Christ (Based on the Broadus Harmony in the Revised Version)*, (New York, Richard R. Smith, Inc., 1930); first edition, 1922; Baptist. (*Schaff-Herzog*, Vol. X, p. 56.)

NOTE THREE ·

Christ's Ministry

Item 1. Chronology of Christ's Ministry.

Summary. The chronology of the harmony, *Our Lord of The Gospels,* is built on the theory that the event or sermon is of more importance than the order in which it occurred. All four Gospels are given equal importance as historical records.

It has been the author's thought that the exact order of events in the Savior's life is not of the last importance. Believing that the incidents attaching to his visit with the doctors at the Temple, when he was in Jerusalem attending the Passover at the age of twelve, show clearly that he was then fully conscious of his divine parenthood, the author has not been concerned with the consideration of those problems of the "higher critics" which relate to and deal with an alleged gradual growth in his mind (as they affirm) of the fact of his Messiahship. This elimination makes the task hereof much easier.

Moreover, the author has accepted the Gospel of John as containing accurate, historical data. (See *infra,* p. 59.) Apparently the harmonists used have given John the same standing. The contrary view discredits not only John, but also the synoptists Matthew, Mark, and Luke, for, obviously, the historical accuracy of John's record being cast in doubt, the way is opened for the development of that erroneous and Christianity-destroying contention that, after all, Christ did not in fact perform the miraculous acts the Gospels record, nor did he claim Messiahship for himself; that the miraculous events and the Messianic concept were but myths invented by the early Christian followers, perhaps by the Apostles themselves. If that view is accepted and then is run-through to its logical conclusion, it destroys Christ and the Christian faith. This erroneous concept of the Christ is in these *Notes* repudiated and discarded. (See *infra, Note Eleven.*)

Item 2.   Length of Ministry of Jesus.

Summary. These *Notes* adopt the traditional view that the ministry of Jesus occupied approximately three years, and discards the views of some higher critics that his mission lasted only one or two years. While his miles of travel could require much less time than three years, this was the smallest part of the problem, for he must convert the people that with his coming the old law was fulfilled, and that he brought a new covenant. How difficult this problem was is shown by the experiences and length of service it required to convert Peter. Furthermore, signs given and miracles performed by Jesus were not too effective in converting people, for many turned away from him when he failed to feed the great multitude following his feeding of the five thousand. It would seem from John's testimony that only a small part of the doings and sayings of Jesus were recorded and so come down to us.

Again, the author has followed the traditional view that the ministry of Jesus approximated three years, beginning when he was "about thirty years of age" (Luke 3:23), and finishing at or near the end of his thirty-third year (3 Nephi 8:2). The Book of Mormon record makes this fact clear. Scholars who would shorten the time to one, or between one and two years (e.g., Charles Augustus Briggs, *New Light on the Life of Jesus* (New York, Charles Scribner's Sons, 1909), p. 54), are not persuasive. They must rearrange, and in some places almost rewrite the Gospel records, and we

are much too far away from the time and the actual
words of the teachings of Christ, and from the semi-
current record of the incidents of his life, to make such
an effort either wise or fruitful in advancing the truths
of his life and message. The purpose of the effort to
shorten the time of his ministry seems to be to harmonize the Gospels with "higher criticism." But the
basis underlying the matters relied upon by the "higher
critics" is shifting so much, that, even if there is a
disposition to accept such an erroneous understanding,
it would be well to wait until we have the full argument
and facts before attempting so drastic an undertaking
as a virtual rewriting of the Gospels.

This shifting basis of the actual facts is shown, for
example, by the reported discovery, in the ruins of an
ancient building in Angora, of a column bearing an inscription that verifies Luke's account that, "there went
out a decree from Caesar Augustus, that all the world
should be taxed" (Luke 2:1), a passage the "higher
critics" have been wont to play upon as showing the
unreliability of the sacred New Testament record; and,
in the Old Testament field, by the more recent discovery (in a cave near the northern shore of the Dead
Sea) of manuscripts containing portions of Isaiah that
raise questions requiring a reappraisal of the conclusions heretofore reached by the "higher critics" on the
Isaiah texts. (William T. Ellis, "Roman Census That
Caused Famed Bethlehem Journey Proved by Ancient
Record," *The Washington Post*, December 19, 1926;
G. Ernest Wright, "A Phenomenal Discovery," *The
Biblical Archaeologist*, Vol. XI, No. 2 (May 1948), pp.
21-23; see also Edmund Wilson, "A Reporter at Large,
The Scrolls From the Dead Sea," *The New Yorker*, May
14, 1955.)

To those familiar with missionary work in the field, it is quite clear that even three years would be a short time for the carrying out of such a mission as the Gospels record. The travelling was rather extensive, even though within a small area. It could have been done in a shorter period than three years, but this is a smaller element of the problem. Jesus had the task of converting enough of those among whom he ministered, to form a nucleus for the work of the Apostles who were to carry on after his crucifixion and ascension. This task involved the overturning, the virtual outlawing, of the centuries-old Mosaic law of the Jews, and the substitution therefor of the Gospel of Christ.

THE PROBLEM FACING JESUS

It will be recalled that after the five thousand were fed, the multitude, following Jesus, came to Capernaum. There, accusing them of seeking him because he had fed them, Jesus preached to them the great sermon on the bread of life which he was to give. Then the record declares: "From that time many of his disciples went back, and walked no more with him." (John 6:66.) Miracles and signs held some for a time, but, as Jesus declared, 'it is a wicked and adulterous generation that asks for signs.' (Matt. 16:4.) A convert through miracles is likely to require continuing miracles to keep him converted.

So Jesus must root out from their minds the old covenant and convert them to the new.

As illustrating this point it would be well to have in mind how long it took Peter himself to be fully converted to the simple fact that the Gospel and its salvation were for all men. Peter had been with Jesus

(seemingly almost if not quite) constantly in his missionary work from its beginning; he had made at
Caesarea Philippi, the great declaration that Jesus was
the Christ (Matt. 16; Mark 8); he had seen the vision
of the beasts and creeping things of the earth let down
in a sheet, had been told to eat, had replied that he ate
not unclean things, and the voice of the Lord had come
to him, saying: "What God hath cleansed, that call not
thou common" (Acts 10); he had seen the conversion
and acceptance by Jesus, of the hated Samaritans, following his conversation with the Samaritan woman at
Jacob's well (John 4); he had witnessed the healing of
the daughter of the Syrophenician woman near Tyre
and Sidon (Matt. 15; Mark 7); he had seen Jesus
perform many, many other miracles, including the healing of his own mother-in-law, and afterwards all the
afflicted that were there present (Matt. 8; Mark 1;
Luke 4); he had himself healed the lame (Acts 3), and
one sick with the palsy for eight years (Acts 9), and
had even raised the dead (Acts 9), yet it was not until
this Peter was told of the vision of Cornelius and had
gone to him, that he was brought down to the humble
realization that the new Gospel was for all men. (Acts
10.)

This Gospel wiped away the Levitical rites and
ordinances as practiced among the Jews. Christ had
fulfilled the law. Jew and Gentile were equal under the
new covenant. So to Cornelius and his friends, "all here
present before God, to hear all things that are commanded thee of God," Peter, finally converted and understanding, "opened his mouth, and said, Of a truth
I perceive that God is no respecter of persons: But in
every nation he that feareth him, and worketh righteousness, is accepted with him." Peter then preached

Jesus the Christ and him crucified and resurrected. (Acts 10:33 ff.)

If it took all this to convert Peter, how great the task of bringing the people generally to a knowledge of the truth! Three years were short enough time for this great service, even by the Christ himself, for men's spirits must be led, they may not be coerced, even by Diety himself, as was shown when, in the Council of Heaven, one-third of the hosts rebelled, following Lucifer, the Son of the Morning. (D.C. 29:36.)

Moreover, on the question of the amount of missionary work that Jesus performed, we should have in mind the testimony that closes the Gospel of John: "And there are also many other things which Jesus did, the which, if they should be written every one, I suppose that even the world itself could not contain the books that should be written." (John 21:25.)

Finally, to the man of faith, there is the assurance that the records as originally written were of actual facts, for in the Upper Chamber on the night of the Last Supper, Jesus said to his Apostles: "But the Comforter, which is the Holy Ghost, whom the Father will send in my name, he shall teach you all things, and bring all things to your remembrance, whatsoever I have said unto you." (John 14:26.)

Item 3.   *Appraisal of Jesus.*

Summary. There are two schools of critics who deal with an appraisal of Jesus, differing as the approach to the problem differs. One discards all the miraculous elements of the Savior's life and experiences, their criticism going to explain away the miraculous elements; they affirm that Christ could not be both "the same unclouded thinker of the moral sayings and the apocalyptic fanatic of the eschatological passages," which, they affirm, were drawn from Jewish Apocalyptic writings. Says Allen, who is quoted: "The Gospels, as manipulated by the uncertain methods of this sort of criticism, seem capable of yielding a picture of any sort of Jesus that the critic desires." The other group of critics takes "a very much wider and more liberal historical background," accepting the miraculous elements of the life of Jesus (seemingly without too much enthusiasm). This group invokes the whole lessons and experiences of the Christian era to support their contentions. It is asserted that: "So long as NT critics start from different assumptions, and employ different methods, it is obvious that they will arrive at different conclusions." Great confusion results from these divergences. But even with these, everywhere is lacking the burning, living testimony, possessed by the Latter-day Saints, that Jesus is the Christ, the very Messiah for whom the Jewish prophets looked.

Perhaps something may be as well said here as elsewhere regarding the appraisal of Jesus, his personality, and his character, by certain critics. We shall note below certain phases of a discussion by Prof. Willoughby C. Allen, covering the general problem. He affirms that "surprisingly contradictory" results are reached in the historical field of the New Testament, resulting from the different approaches to the problems. He observes there are two classes of inquirers, broadly speaking. Because the Extreme Textualists seem to belong to the first class of inquirers and have permitted their theories to color their views about the New Testament texts, they seemingly supporting texts that will support their theories, we may profitably consider briefly these two critical approaches.

The one class affirms that Jesus was a man who developed as ordinary men develop, and that "the growth of His intellectual conceptions can be traced on psychological lines." These inquirers ask, first (Allen observes):

ALLEN'S ANALYSIS

"(a) Does a writer state as fact an event which lies outside the range of the known laws of Nature? Then, not only did the alleged event not happen, but some account must be given of the nature of the process which enabled the writer to state as fact what is incredible. Under this head the whole of the so-called miraculous element in the Gospels and Acts is removed from the sphere of history, and translated into the realm of myth, legend, popular exaggeration, symbolism, allegory, or transference of the miraculous from other departments of tradition into the life of Jesus. In the early days of criticism this generally led to the transference of the Gospels into the 2nd cent., in order to allow time for the growth of legend round the few traditional facts of the life of Jesus. More recently it has been argued that such growth may have been very rapid, and is consistent with a 1st cent. date for the Gospels. (b) The mental development of Jesus must be similar to our own, and it is not possible that He could have taught doctrines which appear to us to be logically inconsistent. This has been applied in particular, in recent times, to the problem of the eschatological teaching in the Gospels as compared with the moral teaching of Christ. Christ, it is argued, cannot have been both the same unclouded thinker of the moral sayings and the apocalyptic fanatic of the eschatological passages. We must, therefore, give up one of the two as historical, and the teaching generally chosen as most conveniently to be got rid of is the eschatological, which is then regarded as an intrusion into Christ's teaching of elements derived from Jewish Apocalyptic writings, remoulded in Christian circles. Of course, on lines like these the task of criticism is very largely one of explaining away the evidence which, at first sight, the Gospels set before us as to the facts of Christ's life.

"It would be impossible to give here an exhaustive list of all the ways in which criticism attempts to do this, but the following are some of them:—

"Adaptation of Christ's life to the narrative and prophecies of the OT. (This would account in part for the narrative of the Virginal conception, the stories of the Magi, and of the flight into Egypt, etc.) Adaptation to His life of heathen mythology (the Virgin birth). Adaptation to His life of the current Jewish doctrine of the Messiah. The attribution to Him of sayings prophetic of later events, *e.g.*, the manner of His death, or the fall of Jerusalem. The hardening into narratives of fact of words spoken by Him in allegory or metaphor." (Willoughby C. Allen, "Criticism (New Testament)," James Hastings, ed., *Encyclopaedia of Religion and Ethics* (New York, Charles Scribner's Sons, 1928), Vol. IV, pp. 319-320, cited hereafter as Hastings *Encyc.*)

All this destroys Jesus as the Christ.

After summarizing briefly the "difficulties which many will feel with criticism of this kind," Allen concludes:

"The Gospels, as manipulated by the uncertain methods of this sort of criticism, seem capable of yielding a picture of any sort of Jesus that the critic desires." (Allen, Hastings *Encyc.*, Vol. IV, p. 320a; italics ours.)

The foregoing concepts so described seem to be the concepts and attitudes of the Extreme Textualists.

Allen then discusses the investigators of the second class who take "a very much wider and more liberal historical background." Among the matters he points out, and which we may summarize, are,—that the Gospels give us a "picture of One whose personality, whilst truly human, yet transcends the limits of human personality as elsewhere known to us"; that the kind of evidence furnished by the Gospels is furnished in the history of the Christian Church; that these two sources furnish a continuously flowing "stream of evidence to a Person, dead yet living, human yet more than human"; that in view of the character of the subject matter of the enquiry, we cannot "apply to the Gospel evidence those rough and ready tests of the historical which critics of the first class are so eager to use"; while the critics of the first class say Christ did not perform miracles, therefore the account of them is very late, and is worthless as evidence, the critic of the second class asks why not a miracle (though the possible explanation they give is not much ahead of the position taken by the first class); that the critics of the first class find it impossible to accept that Christ taught the establishment of the Kingdom of God on earth to leaven human society and his second coming "on the clouds of heaven," these critics averring "Christ cannot have spoken these two divergent lines of teaching, we must choose between them," but, on the other hand, that the critics of the second class declare that these two classes of teaching "are ultimately harmonious."

This last conclusion we know to be sound under the principles of the Restored Gospel. Critics of this class seem to belong to the High or Sound Textualists.

Allen observes: "So long as NT critics start from different assumptions, and employ different methods, it is obvious that they will arrive at different conclusions."

ALLEN'S OWN VIEWS

Allen then puts forward, somewhat diffidently, considerations leading to the acceptance of the narratives of the Gospels as statements of historical facts, and suggests some such canons of criticism as these:

"(a) We are dealing with a record of One whose personality and force of character transcend, as is proved by the witness of history, all human knowledge. We cannot, therefore, rule out as evidence statements which ascribe to Him power and influence which are not found in normal experience of life. (b) There is, therefore, a general probability in favour of the credibility of the Gospel narratives. The area of uncertainty arises later in the attempt to reconstruct from them the original facts as they occurred." (Allen, Hastings *Encyc.*, Vol. IV, p. 320b.)

We who, in this, our day, have seen the miracles wrought by the administrations of the Priesthood, and have also heard the testimony of hosts of eyewitnesses to other miracles like those we have seen, have no difficulty with the Gospel narratives about miracles.

Allen instances as a case where the *actual* facts may be difficult to determine, the raising of Jairus' daughter, and the uncertainty as to what was the "death" or "life" involved in this occurrence.

He also discusses briefly the problem of the kind of approach to be used in a consideration of the Gospel narratives, — shall it be the attitude with which you approach normal ancient historical documents, or should there be a predisposition to accept them as accurate. In this connection he invokes the psychological fact of the influence of Christ's teachings upon mankind, and comments:

"If the Personality of Jesus acts upon consciousness through the whole period of history since His death in a way in which no other personality known to us has ever acted, then it will be clearly unscientific to apply to the record of His life the same axiomatic rules, as to what is or is not probable, that we are tempted to apply to the evidence as to the personality of ordinary individuals." (Allen, Hastings *Encyc.*, Vol. IV, p. 321a.)

Affirming that what has been said about the Gospels and their interpretation, applies to the Acts, Allen adds:

"Criticism of the Gospels and Acts which is based on quite unscientific presuppositions—that is the point—introduces hopeless confusion into NT criticism. It condemns offhand certain narratives as fictitious, and then invents the most improbable causes to account for their genesis and growth. This is not criticism based on principle, but arbitrary and captious rejection of evidence. We want, if possible, some sort of scientific method or principle, and this can be reached only by a preliminary investigation of all the facts. Christ as presented in the Gospels, Christ as experienced in history, Christ as experienced in modern life,—is this all of a piece, one long consecutive witness to a supernatural Christ? If so, whatever other method may be wrong, nothing can be more fundamentally unsound than the attempt to go to the Gospels and from the first to eliminate that element to which Gospels, history, modern consciousness, all alike bear testimony.

"The above considerations apply also to the Fourth Gospel." (Allen, Hastings *Encyc.,* Vol. IV, p. 321a.)

As one reads these summaries of the tenets of these different schools of criticism, one feels that the first school discussed by Allen is really anti-Christ and perhaps also atheistic. The second school is Christian, but its proponents seem almost wholly to lack what we of the Church call *testimony.* Members of this second school seem conscience-pricked into a weak defense of Jesus as the Christ, the Son of God, but they pitiably lack the living knowledge which permits men to say, "I know that Jesus is the Christ, the Son of the Living God." The Latter-day Saints are blessed with a living, burning testimony of the Messiahship of Jesus.

(See for a brief discussion of the "higher" or "historical" criticism which "seeks to answer a series of questions affecting the composition, editing, and collection of the Sacred Books" of the Old Testament, *infra, Note Eleven;* Strachan, Hastings *Encyc.,* Vol. IV, p. 314.)

NOTE FOUR ·
The Authorized Version

Summary. Reasons for using the Authorized Version.

A few preliminary words may be said here about the Authorized Version, or King James Version of the New Testament text; more will be said later. (See *Note Eighteen.*) This is the standard text used in these *Notes* in preference to the Revised Version, or the American Standard Version, or the Revised Standard Version, or any of the other more modern versions, because (1) the great bulk of our people know and use only the Authorized Version, and do not have access either to the Revised Versions (the accuracy of the text of which has been severely challenged by some critics, as hereinafter pointed out) or of the other versions; (2) references in our Standard Church Works and in our Church literature, are to the Authorized Version; (3) the Bible commentaries and Bible dictionaries are in good part keyed to the Authorized Version, though making use of the readings of other texts for critical purposes; (4) the Authorized Version stands as the greatest classic in English literature, and while containing some archaic words and presently ungrammatical forms, can yet be understood in all essential parts by the careful, thoughtful reader (the chief reason the Bible is not understood (as the Revisers complain) is not because it is in archaic English, but because it is not read); (5) the Authorized Version is to most of us *The Bible*, and we would feel we had been disloyal to the record of God's dealings with men if we were to use any other text (we love the Word of God as therein given); and (6) finally, for our Church membership, the Authorized Version is to be followed in preference to others because the Inspired Version by the Prophet Joseph Smith agrees with the Authorized Version in those essential particulars where other versions vary.

NOTE FIVE ·
The Language of Jesus

Summary. It seems almost unquestioned that Jesus spoke in Aramaic during his ministry in Palestine. It was the language of the people among whom he worked.

It should first be said that many scholars, possibly the most of them, treat the Greek texts as the original texts of the record of the ministry of Jesus. But this is not a universal concept.

In an article on "Language of Christ," Dr. G. H. Gwilliam, Rector of Remenham, Henley, makes these comments: After observing that "most scholars would admit that the vernacular of Palestine in the time of our Lord was Semitic, and not Greek," he notes that the practice of the scholars differs from their theory, "for in all kinds of theological writings, critical as well as devotional, the references to the text of the Gospels constantly assume that the Greek words are those actually uttered by our Lord. But if Greek was not commonly spoken in the Holy Land, it is improbable that He who ministered to the common people would have employed an uncommon tongue. It follows that the Greek words recorded by the Evangelists are not the actual words Christ spoke." Later in his discussion, Dr. Gwilliam says:

"However, the object of this article is not to deny that Christ knew, and sometimes spoke, Greek, but to reinforce the arguments by which we conclude that the vernacular of Palestine was Semitic, and that therefore Christ's teachings were, for the most part, delivered in a different tongue from that in which they have come to us in the Greek Gospels . . . . But all the evidence tends to the conviction that Christ habitually em-

THE LANGUAGE OF JESUS

ployed some form of the vernacular in his discourses, and not the alien language of Greece." (G. H. Gwilliam, "Language of Christ," James Hastings, ed., *Dictionary of the Bible, Complete in One Volume* (New York, Charles Scribner's Sons, 1920), pp. 530-531, cited hereafter as *HDB* (*Single Vol.*) ; see *An Introduction*, pp. 22 ff.)

Dr. James Hope Moulton, Greenwood Professor of Hellenistic Greek in the Victoria University of Manchester, writing on "Language of the NT," makes this statement:

"Jesus and the Apostles would use Aramaic among themselves, and in addressing the people in Judæa or Galilee, but Greek would often be needed in conversation with strangers. . . . Contributions of great value have recently been made to our knowledge of the Aramaic, in which nearly all the sayings of Christ must have been uttered, and in which Papias (as usually understood) shows they were first written down." (James Hope Moulton, "Language of the NT," *HDB* (*Single Vol.*), pp. 529b-530a.)

Edersheim says:

"If Greek was the language of the court and camp, and indeed must have been understood and spoken by most in the land, the language of the people, spoken also by Christ and His Apostles, was a dialect of the ancient Hebrew, the Western or Palestinian Aramaic. It seems strange, that this could ever have been doubted. A Jewish Messiah Who would urge His claim upon Israel in Greek, seems almost a contradiction in terms." (Alfred Edersheim, *The Life and Times of Jesus The Messiah*, 3rd ed., 28th imp. (New York, Longmans, Green and Co., 1927), Vol. I, pp. 129-30.)

Kenyon says:

"Aramaic was the language of the mass of the population of Mesopotamia, whence it spread, with dialectical varieties, over northern Syria and Palestine. . . . Palestinian Aramaic was no doubt the language habitually spoken by our Lord." (*The Text*, p. 112.)

Thus it is likely that we do not possess any saying,

and but few words (see *infra,* pp. 375 ff.) of the Savior in the language in which he spoke. The Greek so-called originals are in reality but translations of his words as spoken in Aramaic, in which language, if Papias (martyred 163 A.D.) is properly understood, they were also first written.

On this premise, the English text which we shall use —the Authorized Version—is but a translation of a translation of the original language in which Christ talked.

NOTE SIX •

The Language of the Earliest Recovered
New Testament Records

Item 1.   General Observations.

Summary. Bible critics (Protestant) generally affirm that the earliest records of Christ's ministry (the Sacred Autographs), which disappeared in the very early days of Christianity, were written in Greek, one critic assumes not far from 100 A.D. The greater part of their learned discussions on the New Testament would become inept and indeed largely fallacious if the earliest records were not in Greek. It seems clear that a Greek text (at least of John) was extant in the first half of the second century. The texts written in languages other than Greek are assumed to be translations of the Greek and are called *Versions.*

It must first be stated that the Extreme Textualists and indeed, it would appear, Bible critics generally, take the view that Greek is the language in which the Gospels were first recorded, so far as our present knowledge goes. The authorities seem to agree that the Sacred Autographs disappeared early in the days of the Apostolic Church, and that thus far no trace of them has been found.

Scrivener observes that the original autographs of the sacred writers "perished utterly in the very infancy of Christian history." (Scrivener, p. 2; and see *id.*, pp. 503, 503, n.i., 506, 515, 523, and 524; also pp. 43, 123, and 368, herein.)

The whole structure of modern criticism proceeds on the theory that the Greek is, for critical purposes, the original text.   Indeed, it would appear that if it should be found that the Greek text did not occupy this primal position, the whole superstructure of "higher criticism" would largely crumble to the ground.

Accordingly, as already stated, the "higher critics" cling, with greatest tenacity, to the premise that the Greek is the original text. This they assert and reassert with great vehemence and assurance.

From this premise it follows that all manuscripts in languages other than Greek are translations of the Greek. They are called *versions*, even though some of the *versions* may be found on manuscripts that are actually older than any Greek manuscript yet discovered.

However, one piece of evidence recently discovered shows a very early Greek text. In 1920, a papyri fragment 3½ by 2½ inches, was acquired by Dr. B. P. Grenfell for the John Rylands Library at Manchester. It contains parts of John 18:31-33, 37, 38, "in a hand which can be confidently assigned to the first half of the second century" (before 150 A.D.). (Kenyon, *The Text*, p. 195.) "Now we see that it was not only written, but had spread to a provincial town in Egypt, by the middle of the second century, which goes far towards confirming the traditional date of composition [Gospel of John], in the last years of the first century." (Kenyon, *Our Bible*, p. 128.) "It is the earliest extant fragment of the New Testament, and is a conclusive proof of the early date of the Fourth Gospel." (Kenyon, *The Story*, p. 126.)

(See for a plate showing both sides—*recto* and *verso* —of the fragment, Kenyon, *Our Bible*, p. 126; see for plate showing only the *recto*, Bruce, *The Books and the Parchments*, p. 172; see for brief notices and comments, Kenyon, *The Text*, pp. 75 and 195, where it is said (as already quoted) it is "in a hand which can be referred with some confidence to the first half of the second century.")

Thus it seems clear that a Greek text of the Gospels (at least of John) existed in the first half of the second century, that is, before A.D. 150. Kenyon postulates an original Greek text, "which cannot have been written very far from A.D. 100." (*Our Bible*, p. 155.)

We shall leave the question of the Greek text primacy stand there for the present, and turn to other texts.

We print herein (*Appendix B*), a table of *versions* published by Miller in 1886, which gives the "general dates" of the principal *versions* known then. As will be noted, these versions are classified as Syriac, Latin, Egyptian, and Single Versions. (Edward Miller, *A Guide to the Textual Criticism of the New Testament* (London, George Bell and Sons, 1886), p. 113, hereinafter cited as Miller.)

Item 2. The Syriac Versions.

Summary. It is seemingly possible that the Syriac versions were in the Aramaic which Jesus must have used and spoken, and that the original records of the works and teachings of Jesus were the basis of or actually were in the language of the Sacred Autographs. The "higher critics" argue for a Greek original record. Not all scholars are of this view; some seem to believe that the Aramaic was the language of the original records. The problems involved are briefly considered under three sub-headings noted hereinafter.

Since the Syriac *versions* are in Aramaic, the language in which Jesus and the Apostles spoke and taught, and since Syria is a near geographical neighbor of Palestine, we shall note some matters connected with Syriac *versions* that give to a layman grounds for the thought that perhaps these *versions* in their origin were not translations from the Greek, but original writings in Aramaic, though it may be that early Greek texts led to some changes in the early Aramaic texts.

It might be said here that the designation " 'Syriac' is the name generally given to Christian Aramaic. It is written in a distinctive variation of the Aramaic alphabet." (Bruce, p. 183.)

Stoutly maintaining that all Aramaic manuscripts are translations, Kenyon affirms: "There is, however, no *direct* connection between that original teaching [in Aramaic] and the Syriac Gospels . . . and there is no doubt that the Syrian Scriptures were translated from Greek. What is doubtful is the exact form in which they first circulated." (*The Text*, p. 112.) He also states that, "If we can ascertain with certainty what were the original words of the Syriac or Latin translations, we can generally know what was the Greek text which the translator had before him." (*Our Bible*, p. 155.)

The reasoning processes followed in this connection are the same found throughout the "higher criticism" field: reach your conclusion and then mass your evidence to prove it, sliding over or omitting the unfavorable evidences, and magnifying the favorable. To the layman the proper procedure would be to examine and classify the evidence and then reach a conclusion as to what the evidence shows. Necessarily, the handling of their evidence by these critics in the way stated, is not too persuasive.

Other scholars, however, are not so dogmatically sure that Kenyon's view is correct. Professor Millar Burrows (Yale University), in his chapter on "The Semitic Background of the New Testament," in the

Introduction to the Revised Standard Version, comments:

"Since the gospel was first proclaimed in Aramaic, it is not surprising that the recorded words of Jesus and the apostles retain even in translation much that is characteristic of the original Semitic sentence structure and idiom. Whether there was any direct translation of written Aramaic sources, in addition to the preservation of Semitic ways of speaking through tradition and oral translation, *is a question on which the members of our Committee do not agree,*" but they did not discuss the matter, because their responsibility "to translate the Greek text made such considerations irrelevant." (Millar Burrows, "The Semitic Background of the New Testament," *An Introduction,* pp. 27-28; italics ours.)

This same author had earlier observed in his chapter:

"The eternal gospel for all mankind had to be given in the first instance to a particular people in a particular land and at a particular time in history. That time was nearly two thousand years ago; that land was far-away Palestine; that people was the Jewish nation. The Aramaic language which they spoke and the Hebrew language in which their Scriptures were written both belonged to the family known as Semitic. Their whole cultural and spiritual heritage, for all the Persian and Greek elements it had assimilated, was basically Semitic. Both the form and the content of the New Testament can be understood only in the light of these facts." (Burrows, *An Introduction,* p. 22.)

Kenyon's handling of his evidence on this question is not always too persuasive to the layman.

The problems involved in the Syriac versions are complicated and difficult. For our purposes they will be grouped under three headings: The *Old Syriac,* the *Diatessaron,* and the *Peshitta,*—the groupings adopted by the modern Extreme Textualists, as represented by Kenyon.

Taking these in their order:

Sub-item a.   The Old Syriac.

Summary. The Old Syriac is witnessed by two texts,—
the Curetonian (designated *Cur.*) and the Sinaitic (designated *Sin.*). Scholars are not in agreement as to the
relationship or age of these two manuscripts, nor as to the
age of the affirmed original text of which these are the
record. The relationship of these and Tatian's Diatessaron
is a matter of speculative dispute. The *Cur.* and *Sin.*
manuscripts (as analyzed by scholars) seem to agree
rather with the Textus Receptus than with the uncials
Vaticanus and Sinaiticus.

The Old Syriac seems to be witnessed by two Syriac
texts,—the Curetonian (designated *Cur.*) and the Sinaitic (designated *Sin.*). The Curetonian is named for Dr.
Cureton who discovered it among a mass of Syriac
texts that were secured from the Nitrian Desert in
Egypt by the British Museum in 1842. Dr. Cureton
"contended that in this version we have the very words
of our Lord's discourses, in the identical language in
which they were originally spoken . . . that the original
of his version . . . must have been made earlier than the
original of the Peshitta, and that, in fact, the Peshitta
was a revision of the Old Syriac, just as the Vulgate
Latin was in part a revision of the Old Latin. . . . No
one now doubts that the Curetonian MS. represents a
version earlier than the Peshitta." (Kenyon, *Our Bible*,
pp. 161-62.)

It should be noted here that the Curetonian Manuscript contained part of the last twelve verses of Mark;
also the incident of the angel visiting and strengthening Jesus in Gethsemane and of the bloody sweat (Luke
22:43, 44) ; and also the words from the cross, "Father,
forgive them." (Luke 23:34.) The Curetonian also
has the doxology in the Lord's Prayer. (Matt. 6:13.)
(These matters will be discussed later.) (For a colla-

tion of *Cur.* and *Sin.* with other MSS.—‭א‬, B, A, D—
see Kenyon, *The Text*, pp. 118-121.)

The Gospels are called, "The Gospel of the Separated," from which Kenyon suggests the name was
given in contrast to Diatessaron, which "seems to show
that it is later than the Diatessaron." (*Our Bible*, p.
163.)

The Sinaitic Manuscript text was discovered (1892)
by two ladies (sisters), Mrs. Lewis and Mrs. Gibson, in
the same monastery on Mt. Sinai in which Tischendorf
had earlier discovered the great Codex Sinaiticus (‭א‬), of
which more will be said later. (Kenyon, *Our Bible*,
p. 161.)

Kenyon says "there is no doubt that the two MSS.
represent the same version, and that one of great
antiquity." He quotes Burkitt (whom he characterizes as "the best authority on the subject") as assign-
ing a date of 200 A.D. for these texts, which differ
one from the other to a considerable extent, *Sin.* being
classed as the older. *Sin.* is a palimpsest—that is, a
manuscript on which an erasure is made of the original
writing and another writing superimposed thereon. On
this manuscript the original were Gospel texts which
had been erased and a later text superimposed. (*Our
Bible*, pp. 161-163.)

Bruce observes: "The Lewis palimpsest [*Sin.*] has
traces of Palestinian dialect in its Syriac, which suggests that the translators of the Gospels into Syriac
were Palestinian Christians." (Bruce, p. 188.) Why
might it not be better to suggest that the erased text
was an original text in Syriac?

With reference to the date of the Syriac text (not
of the manuscripts), as just stated, Burkitt suggests
200 A.D. However, Bruce affirms, "The original Old

Syriac version of the Gospels was earlier than the introduction of Tatian's Diatessaron." (Bruce, p. 188; see
contra, Kenyon, above.) Treating the Old Syriac as a
translation, it is affirmed that the "translation must
have been made from Greek manuscripts in existence
in the second century, which thus carries us back to
a period long before our earliest Greek manuscripts."
(Kenyon, *The Story*, p. 91.)

However, as we shall shortly see, the Diatessaron is
placed in the 170's, perhaps early in that decade. This
is a century and a half earlier than the great uncials
Sinaiticus (‭א‬) and Vaticanus (B), both dated as early
in the 4th century, which along with Codex Alexandrinus (early 5th century) and a few other manuscripts of less importance, have been the basis for the
Extreme Textualists in their attack upon the Textus
Receptus (Authorized or King James Version). The
chief factor urged by the Extreme Textualists in favor
of these uncials was their age, it being assumed by the
critics that being the oldest they must be the best and
purest manuscripts. But these Syriac texts (which
agree rather with the Textus Receptus than the
uncials) and the recently discovered papyri (Chester
Beatty papyri and some others) of the early 3rd century, and some of the 4th, furnish earlier readings than
the uncials ‭א‬ and B and their associates, and these
earlier manuscripts challenge many conclusions reached
by the Extreme Textualists in favor of the uncials as
against the Textus Receptus or Byzantine text. (See
Kenyon, *The Story*, ch. X; see Scrivener, "The Curetonian Syriac," p. 319; the Sinaitic Syrian Manuscript
was not discovered until some 9 years after Scrivener's
third edition was issued—1883. In Scrivener's fourth
edition, edited by Miller, some doubt is cast upon the

antiquity of the Lewis manuscript as against the Peshitta, Scrivener-Miller, Vol. II, p. 37.)

Sub-item b.   The Diatessaron by Tatian.

Summary. There is a dispute as to the place where this harmony (for such it is) was written (Rome or Syria) and as to the time. There is also a dispute as to the possible textual influence which operated in the writing of the text, whether the so-called Western type or the Vaticanus-Sinaiticus type. One great scholar affirms that Tatian in his Diatessaron brings a "perplexing species of various readings" into his harmony.

One of the earliest Syriac texts is Tatian's *Diatessaron,*—a harmony of the Gospels. Tatian was born in the Euphrates valley, about 110 A.D. (Kenyon, *Our Bible,* p. 156); in another work, Kenyon gives his birth date as about 120 A.D. (*The Story,* p. 94.) He lived many years in Rome as a disciple of Justin Martyr, upon the martyrdom of whom (c. 165 A.D.) he returned from Rome to Syria (c. 172 A.D.). Tatian died about 180 A.D. By these dates, the *Diatessaron* was written during the 170's A.D.—if written in Syria. (Kenyon, *The Text,* pp. 112-113; see p. 44, herein.)

Dr. W. T. Davison places the date of writing c. 160 A.D., which would call for its writing in Rome. ("John, Gospel of," *HDB* (*Single Vol.*), p. 478b.)

Kenyon states:

"Whether he had prepared his Harmony of the Gospels before leaving Rome, or did so after his return to Syria, is unknown. In the former case it would no doubt have been made in Greek, in the latter probably in Syriac; and this is one of the questions in dispute among scholars." (*The Text,* p. 113.)

Curiously, a few pages farther on in his work, Kenyon positively affirms the harmony "was originally made in Rome from MSS. of the Western type." (*The Text,* p. 122, see *The Story,* pp. 93 ff.)

At still another place, Kenyon affirms: "Although Syriac is a dialect of Aramaic, akin to that in use in Palestine at the time of our Lord, the Gospels were not written in that language, and had therefore to be translated from the Greek for the benefit of the Christians of the Syriac Church." (*Our Bible*, p. 156.) Kenyon seems not meticulously careful about his dates.

Commenting on the writings of St. Ephraem of Syria—a writer of the fourth century—Kenyon says: "No responsible scholar could question the fact that the Diatessaron was actually a harmony of (or, more accurately, a narrative compiled from) the four canonical Gospels." (*Our Bible*, p. 158.)

If the Diatessaron was written in Syria, in Syriac, Kenyon's "reader" might wonder whether it might not have been based on Semitic texts existing in Syria at the time. Apparently there were such texts in existence and known now as Old Syriac, at the time the Diatessaron was written. (See *supra*.)

Scrivener does not give to the Diatessaron of Tatian the same importance given to it by the Extreme Textualists, who obviously regard it as in a more or less key position in the development of their theories about the Peshitta. In his "Preliminary Considerations" to his *Plain Introduction* Scrivener notes the work of Tatian as bringing a "perplexing species of various readings" in the harmony which he produced. (Scrivener, p. 12.)

Later in his Chapter II, "On the Greek Manuscripts of the New Testament," Scrivener speaks of Tatian's work in connection with the "division of the Gospels into larger chapters," and the giving of titles and placement of portions of the Gospel. But it has not been observed that Scrivener in any place gives to the Dia-

tessaron the serious consideration bestowed upon it by
Kenyon. (Scrivener, pp. 55-56.)

Sub-item c.   The Peshitta (Also Called Peshito).

> *Summary.* This version — variously dated and as-
> signed to different places of origin — is the subject of
> vigorous, even bitter controversy. The supporters of the
> primacy of the Vaticanus-Sinaiticus texts (primarily
> Drs. Westcott and Hort) have built a *myth* (so character-
> ized by scholars who are against the Authorized Version)
> that is founded on the character they give to the Peshitta.
> The whole matter is intricate and most difficult.

The two manuscripts, Curetonian and Sinaitic, are
classed as the *Old Syriac*, and the "higher critics"
affirm that the *Peshitta* is a revision of these texts,
perhaps with some such relationship between them and
the Peshitta as existed between the Old Latin and the
Vulgate. (Kenyon, *Our Bible*, p. 161; see Scrivener, pp.
311 ff., for his discussion of the *Peshito* (as he spells
it). Scrivener is not in accord with certain views of the
Extreme Textualists.)

The Extreme Textualists' present views of the
Peshitta are summarized thus by Kenyon:

> "Syria was a very definite province of the Christian Church,
> and might very naturally develop a local form of text; and so we
> find in the Old Syriac a text including many unquestionably early
> readings, some of which occur also in the Western group and
> others in the Neutral (or, as we prefer to call it, Alexandrian).
> It is a valuable witness, all the more because it incorporates
> elements of different types. Later, when Bishop Rabbula in
> the early fifth century undertook a revision of the texts then
> circulating in his diocese, he brought them more into con-
> formity with the Byzantine type, then acquiring dominance in
> the Church, and so produced the Peshitta, which became the
> generally 'received text' of Syrian Christianity." (*The Story*,
> p. 139.)

Kenyon characterizes Rabbula (Bishop of Edessa,

A.D. 411-435) as "the Jerome of the Syriac Church." However, it is affirmed that the "foundations" go back to a very early date, and that (which is significant), "on the whole it represents the Byzantine text in an early stage, but more ancient elements can sometimes be discerned in it." (*Our Bible*, pp. 163-164.)

It should always be in mind that *the Byzantine text is the Textus Receptus, that is, the text of which the Authorized (King James) Version is a translation; and is a text against which the Extreme Textualists are waging unrelenting war.* (Kenyon, *The Story*, p. 92.)

<h3 style="text-align:center">MILLER'S COMMENTS</h3>

Concerning this Extreme Textualist theory, set out above, Miller comments thus:

"We now come to the position resting upon the supposed posteriority of the so-called Syrian Text. Here again we are in the region of pure speculation unsustained by historical facts. Dr. Hort imagines first that there was a recension of the early Syrian Version, which this School maintains was represented by the Curetonian Version, somewhere between 250, A.D., and 350, at Edessa, or Nisibis, or Antioch. The result of this recension is said to have been the Peshito Version, which has hitherto been referred to the second century. We may remark, by the way, that the Peshito must be got rid of by Extreme Textualists, or it would witness inconveniently before the Fourth century to the 'Syrian' Text. Well indeed may Dr. Hort add 'even for conjecture the materials are scanty.' It would have been truer to the facts to have said, 'for such a conjecture there are no materials at all, and therefore it must be abandoned.'

"But Drs. Westcott and Hort also maintain that an authoritative recension of a much larger character was made after this at Antioch, and resulted in the formation of the 'Syrian' Text of the Gospels in Greek, which was formed upon the Vulgate, or common Syriac Version. What proof exists anywhere of such an important proceeding? A recension, be it observed, so thorough and so sweeping in its effects, that, according to the theory

under consideration, it must have placed the text it produced
in such a commanding situation that it has reigned for fifteen
centuries without a rival. How could this have occurred without an achievement so great and famous that the report of it
must have gone abroad? Surely this must have been another
Council of Nicæa, or at least a Council of Ariminum. Such results could not have issued from a mystery like that of the
viewless wind. Yet there is positively no record in the history—
not to speak of a Council of the Church—but of any single incident justifying the assumption that such an authoritative
revision ever took place. Never surely was there such an attempt before made to foist such pure fiction into history. But
besides that, the arguments for the formation of a new text in
the Fourth century thoroughly break down." (Miller, pp. 51-52.)

The validity of this criticism, voiced by Miller, has
been apparently accepted in its basic elements by the
Extreme Textualists, — at least by Kenyon, who deals
with it in this language:

"A greater difficulty (and it is a real one) in the theory is
that there is absolutely no historical confirmation of the Syrian
revision of the text, which is its corner-stone. It is rightly
urged that it is very strange to find no reference among the
Fathers to so important an event as an official revision of the
Bible text and its adoption as the standard text throughout the
Greek world. We know the names of the scholars who made
revisions of the Septuagint and of the Syriac version; but there
is no trace of those who carried out the far more important
work of fixing the shape of the Greek New Testament. Is not
the whole theory artificial and illusory, the vain imagining of
an ingenious mind, like so many of the products of modern
criticism, which spins endless webs out of its own interior, to
be swept away to-morrow by the ruthless broom of common
sense?

"Against this indictment may be placed the consideration
that even if we can find no historical reference to a revision,
yet the critical reasons which indicated the separation of the
Syrian text from the rest, and its inferiority in date, remain
untouched. . . . At the same time, it does seem possible that
the formal revision of the text at a set time in or about Antioch
may be a myth. . . . It seems possible that the Syrian text is
the result rather of a process continued over a considerable

period of time than of a set revision by constituted authorities.
. . . At a great centre of Christianity, such as Antioch, the
principle may have been established by general consent that the
best way to deal with divergences of readings was to combine
them, wherever possible, to smooth away difficulties and harshnesses, and to produce an even and harmonious text. . . . The
subsequent acceptance of the Antiochian or Syrian type as the
received text of the Greek New Testament must have been due
to the predominant influence of Constantinople. The Antiochian
revision aimed at producing a smooth, intelligible text, suitable
for popular use. Such a text, if once approved by metropolitan
churches so influential as Constantinople and Antioch, would
naturally become the received text of the whole Byzantine
Church." (*Our Bible*, pp. 115-16; see p. 355, herein.)

SCRIVENER'S DISCUSSION—ANTIOCHIAN THEORY

Scrivener has a considerable discussion of this whole
Antiochian theory, quoted *in extenso* hereinafter (*Note
Eleven, Item 2*, pp. 113 ff., herein). But a very pregnant
observation may be noted here. Speaking of the sur-
mised Antiochian revisions at the hands of the Syrian
bishops and Fathers of the Patriarchate of Antioch, who
(according to Hort) undertook an authoritative revision of the Greek text, which "was then taken as a
standard for a similar authoritative revision of the
Syriac text," which was later "subjected to a second
authoritative revision, carrying out more completely
the purposes of the first," Scrivener comments as
follows:

"Of this two-fold authoritative revision of the Greek text,
of this formal transmutation of the Curetonian Syriac into the
Peshito (for this is what Dr. Hort means, though his language
is a little obscure), although they must have been of necessity
public acts of great Churches in ages abounding in Councils
General or Provincial, not one trace remains in the history of
Christian antiquity; no one writer seems conscious that any
modification either of the Greek Scriptures or of the vernacular
translation was made in or before his times [*sic*]." (Scrivener,
p. 533.)

He had previously said of this system of Hort's: "We now come to the feature which distinguishes Dr. Hort's system from any hitherto propounded; by the acceptance or non-acceptance of which his whole edifice must stand or fall." (Scrivener, p. 533.) He adds a little later:

". . . regarding his speculative conjecture as undubitably true, Dr. Hort proceeds to name the text as it stood before his imaginary era of transfusion a *Pre-Syrian* text, and that into which it was changed, sometimes *Antiochian,* more often *Syrian*; while of the latter recension, though made deliberately, as our author believes, by the authoritative voice of the Eastern Church, he does not shrink from declaring that 'all distinctively Syrian readings must be at once rejected' (*ibid.* p. 119), thus making a clean sweep of all critical materials, Fathers, versions, manuscripts uncial or cursive, comprising about nineteen twentieths of the whole mass, which do not correspond with his preconceived opinion of what a correct text ought to be (*ibid.* p. 163)." (Scrivener, p. 534.)

Dr. Scrivener later speaks of this whole procedure as a "phantom scheme of Syrian revision." (Scrivener, p. 539.)

We might add here Scrivener's assertion that "Dr. Hort's system, therefore, is entirely destitute of historical foundation." (Scrivener, p. 537.)

Finally, we may again quote Scrivener on Hort's whole system:

"With all our reverence for his genius, and gratitude for much that we have learnt from him in the course of our studies, we are compelled to repeat as emphatically as ever our strong conviction that the hypothesis to whose proof he has devoted so many laborious years, is destitute not only of historical foundation, but of all probability resulting from the internal goodness of the text which its adoption would force upon us.

"This last assertion we will try to verify by subjoining a select number of those many passages in the N. T. wherein the two great codices ℵ and B, one or both of them, are witnesses for readings, nearly all of which, to the best of our judgment, are corruptions of the sacred originals." (Scrivener, pp. 542-543; see *Note Eleven, Item 2,* p. 117, herein.)

OTHER SYRIAN TEXTS

There are other Syrian texts which we may merely mention, because being late, they are of no real significance: the *Philoxenian* or *Harkleian Syriac,* and the *Palestinian Syriac.* (Kenyon, *The Text,* pp. 124-125; see Scrivener, pp. 325 ff., for his discussion of these texts, to which he adds a discussion of the Karkaphensian Syriac.)

We may close this brief summary of the Syriac scriptures with a quotation from Bruce, which presents in fervid, almost panicky language, the claim of the "higher critics" for an original Greek text. He says:

"Because the Syriac Bible is written in a variant dialect of the language that Jesus spoke, extreme views are sometimes expressed about the forms in which His sayings appear in the Syriac Gospels, as though His actual words in the language in which they were uttered might be found there. The ordinary reader, for example, may readily infer from the writings of Mr. George Lamsa that the Peshitta Gospels preserve the very words of our Lord better than the Greek Gospels do. This, of course, is quite wrong; the Peshitta New Testament is simply a translation of the Greek. Even the Old Syriac forms—Diatessaron and 'separate' Gospels alike—are translations of the Greek Gospels. The most we can say is that the Palestinian idioms in the Old Syriac Gospels may *possibly* go back to a living tradition of the original Gospel story and in particular of the words of Jesus. If the Syriac-speaking Churches were founded by Jewish Christians from Palestine, this is what we might expect." (Bruce, pp. 189-190.)

The concessions of the last two sentences will hardly make an effective cover-up if other discoveries of other Syriac manuscripts shall show that the Syriac texts were originals, not translations of Greek texts.

SUMMARY

Perhaps a layman may, without too much forward-ness, bring together in short summary, a few of the points noted above, in favor of an early, if not indeed an original Syriac text.

(a) Papias (martyred c. 163 A.D.) "as usually understood," shows that the words of Christ were first written down in Aramaic. (Moulton, *HDB* (*Single Vol.*), p. 530a.) The Syriac texts probably appeared early in the second century. (Miller, p. 98; Burgon, p. 9.)

(b) Hegesippus (flourished about the middle of the second century—wrote against Gnostics in 180 A.D.) quoted scripture from the Syriac, "and it was only in the last few years of Hegesippus's life that the Diatessaron appeared." (Bruce, p. 187.)

(c) There is evidence that the two Old Syriac texts, *Cur.* and *Sin.* do not represent all the Old Syriac Gospel Versions. (Bruce, p. 187.)

(d) John the Apostle may have used a Syrian text. (Miller, p. 75; Burgon, p. 9, who quotes Bp. Ellicott, writing in 1870, Bp. Ellicott later becoming a disciple of Westcott and Hort.) His Gospel was in Greek before 150 A.D. (See *supra, Note Six*, p. 66.)

(e) It is conceded that the Diatessaron if written in Syria, was probably in Syriac.

(f) There were Syriac texts in Syria prior to the writing of the Diatessaron.

(g) It is a fair inference that if written in Syria, Tatian would have used the Syrian texts available to him.

(h) Some "higher critics," while stoutly insisting that all Syriac texts are translations from a Greek original, yet reluctantly concede that "the Palestinian idioms in the Old Syriac Gospels may *possibly* go back to a living tradition of the original Gospel story and in particular of the words of Jesus," which, having in mind the migration of Palestinian Jews to Syria, "is what we might expect." (Bruce, pp. 189-190.)

The Syrians knew how to write and it is said they are meticulous scribes. It is inconceivable they would pass such precious truths down by *tradition* only instead of making a written record.

No positive evidence has been observed that the Syriac texts are translations, *versions*, of the Greek. All is inference only. To Kenyon's "reader," having in mind that Jesus and the Apostles spoke in Aramaic, that Syria, geographically, is near to Palestine, that the Syrians were meticulous in the preservation of their records, that the early Syriac texts are filled with Palestinian idioms, the inferences are all in favor of an original writing in Syriac. Such positive evidence as has been noted, supports the inference.

LUKE'S ACCOUNT

The possibility of this conclusion is certainly not lessened by the opening statements of Luke. He announced his reasons for his writings as follows:

"Forasmuch as many have taken in hand to set forth in order a declaration of those things which are most surely believed among us,

"Even as they delivered them unto us, which from the beginning were eyewitnesses, and ministers of the word;

"It seemed good to me also, having had perfect understanding of all things from the very first, to write unto thee in order, most excellent Theophilus,

"That thou mightest know the certainty of those things, wherein thou hast been instructed." (Luke 1:1-4.)

Again, to Kenyon's "reader" it is inconceivable that all of these accounts should have been written in Greek, as the theories of the Extreme Textualists—that all the original writings were in Greek—would require us to believe. True, Peter, Paul, and others were pushing out from Palestine and carrying the Gospel to Greek-speaking peoples. But they of these alien fields would not be undertaking "to set forth in order a declaration of those things which are most surely believed *among us, even as they delivered them unto us, which from the beginning were eyewitnesses,* and ministers of the word." Luke seems certainly to be speaking of the humble people among whom Christ moved and taught, people whose language was the Aramaic, to whom Jesus spoke (as seemingly all agree) in Aramaic, these people—eyewitnesses from the beginning—must have been the authors of these many accounts. Jesus worked among and taught the Jews—not the Greeks, nor a Greek-speaking world. The people who heard and followed and worshipped the Christ would have talked about him in their own language, they would have written one to another about him in their own tongue, they must use that tongue to tell others what he said to them in that tongue, to tell of the sacred spiritual intimacies they enjoyed with him, to tell of his healings, of his scorings of the priestly classes, the Scribes, the Pharisees, the Sadducees, and all the rest,—to say that they did all this in an alien tongue and not their own is, to Kenyon's "reader," to tax credulity to the breaking point and to exhaust the law of probabilities.

The first records of those who "from the beginning were eyewitnesses, and ministers of the word" surely must have been made in Aramaic in some form.

NOTE SEVEN ·

Number of Manuscripts of the New Testament

Summary. Most manuscripts are but fragments. The number is variously placed from a few thousand to as many as four thousand.

We might next note that Kenyon, writing on "Text of the New Testament," informs us, regarding the Greek manuscripts, that: "The last inventory of NT MSS (that of von Soden) contains 1716 copies of the Gospels, 531 of Acts, 628 of Pauline Epp., and 219 of Apoc." (F. G. Kenyon, "Text of the New Testament," *HDB* (*Single Vol.*) 1920, p. 918b.) If there are no duplications in the foregoing list, the total manuscripts would be 3094.

In 1883, Dean John William Burgon counted 2377; Dr. Frederick Henry Scrivener counted 2094 at about the same time. (Miller, p. 6.) In 1950, Bruce says: "The number of extant manuscripts of all or part of the New Testament writings runs to about 4000." (Bruce, p. 171.) Practically all manuscripts are fragmentary, that is, not complete. (See *infra*, p. 90, for an 1894 numbering, and p. 131, for another statement by Kenyon.)

It may be noted, and should be in mind that of the "Chief Uncial Manuscripts," only one (the Sinaiticus) is listed as containing the full New Testament text. (Miller, pp. 108-109.) All the others are deficient, lacking parts of the Gospels, or of Acts and the Catholic Epistles (the non-Pauline Epistles), or of the Pauline Epistles, or of the Apocalypse. The same is generally true among the cursive manuscripts, though a small minority contain the complete New Testament. (*The Text*, p. 104.) Sometimes two or three pages make up the total manuscript; sometimes even fragments of a page, or pages, make up a listed manuscript. (See *infra*, Appendix A.)

Scrivener, speaking of the matter of identity in wording of these various texts, says:

"The more numerous and venerable the documents within our reach, the more extensive is the view we obtain of the variations (or VARIOUS READINGS as they are called) that prevail in manuscripts. If the number of these variations was rightly computed at thirty thousand in Mill's time, a century and a half ago, they must at present [1883] amount to at least fourfold that quantity." (Scrivener, p. 3.)

NOTE EIGHT ·
Kinds and Groupings of Greek Manuscripts

Item 1. *Classification of Manuscripts.*

Summary. Greek manuscripts are classified first as to the style of writing as either uncials (capital letters of large size, each letter formed separately) or as minuscules (small letters written with a running hand), commonly called cursives. Such manuscripts are also classified as to the materials upon which the writing is placed,—that is, papyrus (a material made from the pith of the papyrus plant) or vellum (made from the skin of calves, sheep, and other animals). Papyrus was generally used until about the third century after Christ, when vellum came into use. The vellums were small sheets bound together like a book and were called codices (singular, codex). The papyrus was prepared and preserved as rolls until about the third century after Christ, when this material also was bound as sheets in a book and called codices also. One such papyrus codex dates back to the end of the second century after Christ. The early Christian Church seems to have used codices of papyrus. A summary tabulation is given of the more important Greek manuscripts, and the language of versions is noted.

It may be noted here that the Greek manuscripts of the New Testament are classified according to their styles of writing, and are of two kinds: (1) those written in *uncials*, i.e., in capital letters of large size, there being no separation of words and no punctuation, each letter being formed separately; and (2) those written (beginning about the 9th century) in a running hand called *minuscule*, commonly called *cursives*. (Kenyon, *HDB* (*Single Vol.*), p. 917b; Miller, p. 105.)

Manuscripts are also classified according to the materials of which they were made. These materials were either papyrus or vellum.

In the ancient world—Graeco-Roman, Palestinian, and Syrian—books were written on papyrus, which was made from the pith of the papyrus plant. The pith was cut into thin slips which were joined together by glue, water, and pressure into thin sheets, which sheets in turn were joined together in long rolls on which the writing was inscribed in columns. The papyrus grew plentifully in the Nile. Dampness destroys the papyrus and dryness tends to make it brittle. Apparently for these reasons, papyri are found only in Egypt and in some parts of Palestine, where the climatic conditions have been favorable over the centuries. In Egypt papyrus rolls have been found (written in Egyptian hieroglyphics or some like form of writing) that date back 2000 years B.C. "It is from the graves and ruins and rubbish-heaps of Egypt that writings on papyrus have been restored to us in great numbers." (Kenyon, *The Story*, p. 21.) Seemingly, the period of greatest productivity of surviving Egyptian papyrus rolls is from 300 B.C. to 640 A.D. In dimension the papyrus roll varied in length up to 30 to 35 feet, in height from 5 inches for a pocket volume, up to 15 inches, but normally about 10 inches. Papyrus was also fabricated into sheets of varying dimensions that were bound together book-like as codices. (Kenyon, *The Story*, pp. 22-23; *Our Bible*, p. 13.)

Beginning about the second century B.C., vellum began to be used for making books. This is prepared from the skin of calves, sheep, and other animals. Seemingly it was first used by King Eumenes of Pergamum (from which we get our word *parchment*), who wished to establish a library. His rival, Ptolemy of Egypt, refused to let him have the necessary papyrus, whereupon he invented vellum. However, papyrus continued to be the predominant writing material until about the third century after Christ, when vellum, because it was more durable, came into general use. The vellum or parchment was arranged in sheets and quires and bound together much the same as modern books. These books are called *codices*.

They were frequently quite bulky. The Codex Sinaiticus (see *infra*), when complete probably had 720 leaves, or 1440 pages, measuring 15 by 13½ inches; the Vaticanus (see *infra*), about 820 leaves, 1640 pages, 10½ by 10 inches; the Alexandrinus, about 820 leaves, 1640 pages, 12½ by 10½ inches. (Kenyon, *The Story*, p. 27.)

By the third century, Christians particularly, had come to making codices (as bound books) out of papyrus. We have one papyrus codex that seems to go back to the end of the second century. One of these codices ran to as many as 118 leaves, formed of 59 sheets of papyrus laid one upon another and folded in the middle. But smaller quires were the rule, from 8 to 12 leaves. The early Church seems principally to have employed papyrus codices for their use. (See for a brief but clear and excellent discussion of this subject, Kenyon, *The Story*, ch. III.)

Dr. Scrivener, in his masterful work, *A Plain Introduction to the Criticism of the New Testament*, Third Edition, Revised (Cambridge, Deighton, Bell and Co., 1883), devoted Chapter II of his book to a discussion, "On the Greek Manuscripts of the New Testament." (See *infra*, Note Fourteen, p. 152.)

Section I of this chapter treats: "On the general character of Manuscripts of the Greek Testament."

Section II gives a "Description of the Uncial Manuscripts of the Greek Testament," and lists and describes the various manuscripts, classifying them as follows:

"Manuscripts of the Gospels,"
"Manuscripts of the Acts and Catholic Epistles" (Epistles of James, Peter, John, and Jude),
"Manuscripts of the Pauline Epistles," and
"Manuscripts of the Apocalypse."

Section III treats: "On the Cursive Manuscripts of the Greek Testament":

"Manuscripts of the Gospels,"
"Manuscripts of the Acts and Catholic Epistles,"
"Manuscripts of St. Paul's Epistles," and
"Manuscripts of the Apocalypse."

Section IV is written "On the Lectionaries, or Manuscript Service-books of the Greek Church":

"Evangelistaria or Evangeliaria, containing Lessons from the Gospels," and
"Lectionaries containing the Apostolos or Praxapostolos."

Dr. Scrivener concludes his listings and description thus:

"The total number of manuscripts we have recorded in the preceding catalogues are 61 uncial and 642 cursive of the Gospels; 14 uncial and 252 cursive of the Acts and Catholic Epistles; 22 uncial and 295 cursive of S. Paul; 5 uncial and 111 cursive of the Apocalypse; 339 Evangelistaria; and 82 Lectionaries of the Praxapostolos. In calculating this total of 1817 manuscripts we have deducted 78 duplicates, and must bear in mind that a few of the codices, whose present locality is unknown, may have reappeared under other heads." (Scrivener, p. 307; see p. 153, herein.)

In his "Index I," Scrivener gives the following:

*"Index of about 1429 separate Greek Manuscripts of the New
Testament described in Chapter II, Sections II, III, IV, arranged
according to the countries wherein they are now deposited.*

"Denmark 3 MSS.; England 373; France 238; Germany 96;
Greece 1+; Holland 6; Ireland 3; Italy 417; Russia 79; Scot-
land 8; Spain 23; Sweden 7; Switzerland 15; Turkey 120; United
States 3; Unknown 37." (Scrivener, p. 661.)

The fourth edition (Scrivener-Miller, Vol. I, pp.
377, 410) gives the following tabulations:

UNCIALS:—

Evangelia	71
Acts and Catholic Epistles	19
St. Paul's Epistles	27
Apocalypse	7
Total	124

CURSIVES:—

Evangelia	1321
Acts and Catholic Epistles	420
St. Paul's Epistles	491
Apocalypse	184
Evangelistaria	963
Apostolos	288
Total	3667
Grand Total	3791

TOTAL NUMBER OF GREEK MSS., ARRANGED ACCORDING TO COUNTRIES

British Empire	438	Brought forward	1788
Belgium (2), Denmark (3), Holland (7), Sweden (7)	19	Palestine	260
		Russia	104
		Spain	34
Egypt	26	Switzerland	15
France	324	Turkey (Oriental Monasteries)	724
Germany	140	United States	17
Greece	197	Places unknown	30
Italy	644		
Carried forward	1788	Total	2972

As already stated, translations of these Greek manuscripts are known as *versions;* a revised text or edition of a version, is known as a *recension.* There are very many versions, — the English Bible (the Authorized Version) being one of them, and the English translation of the Latin version, the Vulgate (the Douay Version), used by the Catholic Church, is another. There are also Syriac, Georgian, Ethiopic, Arabic, Persian, and Gothic versions. (Kenyon, *HDB* (*Single Vol.*), pp. 919b-923b; *Our Bible*, pp. 169-170.)

Item 2. Grouping of Manuscripts into Families, in 1881.

Summary. The grouping of manuscripts by Westcott and Hort was as follows: The Syrian family, the Neutral family, the Alexandrian family, and the Western family.

Dr. Kenyon tells us that Westcott and Hort have grouped these manuscripts and versions as follows:

"(α) The *Syrian* family, often headed in the Gospels by the manuscripts A and C, but more fully and characteristically represented by the later uncials, such as EFKMS, etc., and by the great mass of the minuscules [cursives], by the Peshitta version, and by most of the Fathers from Chrysostom downwards; from this family, in its fully developed form, is descended the TR [*i.e.,* the *Textus Receptus* or Received Text, described below, of which the Authorized Version is an English translation]. (β) The *Neutral* family, of which the main representative is B [the Vatican Manuscript], often supported by א [the Sinaitic text discovered by Tischendorf], by LRTZ, by the minuscule Evan. 33, and some other minuscules in a lesser degree, by Boh. and sometimes Sah. and frequently by the quotations of Origen; in Acts, Epp., and Apoc., A and C generally join this group. (γ) The *Alexandrian* family, a sort of subspecies of β [the group preceding], not continuously found in any one MS, but represented by the readings of some MSS of the β group when they differ among themselves, and especially when they differ from B; LT, and AC when they are not Syrian, may be taken as the leading members of the family. (δ) The

Western family, headed by D among the uncials (with E² in Acts and D₂ in Paul.) and Evan. 473 among a small group of minuscules, but most authentically represented by the Old Latin and Old Syriac versions, and especially by *k* and Syr.-Sin.; it also largely colours Sah., and is found in almost all the early Fathers, notably Justin, Irenæus, Cyprian, and Clement." (Kenyon, *HDB* (*Single Vol.*), pp. 925b-926a; for a discussion, somewhat skeptical in character, of the value and accuracy of detailed family manuscript classifications, see Scrivener, pp. 553 ff., and Burgon, *note*, p. 95.)

As is more or less obvious, the letters and abbreviations used in the foregoing quotation are used to designate different Greek manuscripts and versions. The uncials "are indicated by the capital letters, first of the Latin alphabet, then of the Greek, and finally of the Hebrew, for which it is now proposed to substitute numerals preceded by 0. . . . The minuscule MSS are usually indicated by Arabic numerals, separate series being formed for the four divisions of the NT." H. von Soden has proposed a new system, but it is said to be more cumbersome than the previous system. Another system which "has received the adhesion of most NT scholars," has been issued by Gregory. (Kenyon, *HDB* (*Single Vol.*), pp. 917b, 918b.)

Item 3. Re-grouping of Manuscripts into Families.

Summary. The primacy, given by Westcott and Hort to Vaticanus (B), followed and supported by Sinaiticus (‭א‬), then by Alexandrinus (A), with a very few others attached, controlled the work of these scholars. These were grouped as the Neutral text. Further study and discovery has destroyed this primacy of ‭א‬ and B by "showing that it was at any rate of restricted circulation, and that it had rivals of at least equal age." The character of Vaticanus and Sinaiticus "is better to be explained as the result of skilled editing of well-selected authorities on a definite principle." Westcott and Hort's groupings have been broken down. Kenyon sets out the re-grouping which further study "appears" to justify as follows: the Byzantine known as the "received text"; the Alexandrian, substantially identical with Westcott and Hort's "Neutral"; the Caesarean, which in character, lies between the Alexandrian and the Western; the Western, which modern criticism criticizes; and the Syriac. All these classifications are admittedly faulty and seemingly must be regarded as tentative. Kenyon finally proposes, — the Vaticanus-Sinaiticus group; the Western group; the Syriac group; the Caesarean group; and a "Residual group."

The foregoing grouping of Westcott and Hort was made as of the 1880's. It was built around what they called the *Neutral* text, and that text in turn was built around, first the Codex Vaticanus (B), which they seem to have regarded and treated as the purest text discovered. As a second source in purity (as estimated by them), they used Codex Sinaiticus (א), but B seems generally, if not always, to have been the controlling text. Codex Alexandrinus (A) apparently came along third, but seemingly without any decisive influence in cases of difference. Then trailed along a few other manuscripts, used and approved when convenient, and disapproved and seemingly sometimes condemned, at least in parts, when their testimony went in the wrong direction, to which extent they were considered as depraved texts.

As hereinafter stated (*Note Eleven*), the great war (begun by Lachmann) was against the Textus Receptus, — the Authorized or King James Version, which was belittled, sometimes, a layman would think, maligned. (Miller, p. 38; Kenyon, *Our Bible*, p. 120.)

But further study and added discoveries of additional manuscript material has brought about a regrouping of the manuscripts. The *Neutral* text of Westcott and Hort has not only lost its position of primacy, but has been virtually abandoned. Kenyon says:

"If the present state of opinion with regard to the several textual groups be compared with that formulated by Westcott and Hort half a century ago, it will be seen that there have been several modifications. It does not now seem probable that the β text (Hort's Neutral) can be regarded as having descended without editorial intervention and substantially unaltered from the original, but rather that it owes its present form to competent editorial treatment in accordance with the principles of trained textual scholarship." (*The Text*, pp. 242-43.)

In another place, Kenyon comments:

"In short, the general tendency was to weaken the position of exclusive superiority claimed by Westcott and Hort for the Neutral text, by showing that it was at any rate of restricted circulation, and that it had rivals of at least equal age." (*The Story*, p. 129.)

Again:

"The course both of discoveries and of critical study has made it increasingly difficult to believe that the Vaticanus and its allies represent a stream of tradition that has come down practically uncontaminated from the original sources. . . . The uniformity of character which on the whole marks the Vaticanus and Sinaiticus is better to be explained as the result of skilled editing of well-selected authorities on a definite principle. Therefore, while respecting the authority due to the age and character of this recension, we shall be disposed to give more consideration than Westcott and Hort did to other early readings which found a home in the Western, Syriac, or Cæsarean texts." (*The Story*, p. 143; see p. 127, herein.)

Once more:

"Thus while the discoveries of the last fifty years have shaken the exclusive predominance which Westcott and Hort assigned to the Vaticanus-Sinaiticus text, they have shattered to pieces the unity of the so-called Western text." (*The Story*, p. 131.)

Kenyon uses many expressions throughout his work indicating that the Neutral Family text (really the foundation of the Revised Versions) must be abandoned as defined and valued by Westcott and Hort, that it

breaks up into other families, and that the B and ℵ
texts are not uncontaminated records but are the result
of revisions and combinations of other texts.

We quoted above (*Note Eight, Item 2*, p. 91) Kenyon's statement as to the family groupings worked out
by Westcott and Hort. These groupings have been
broken down in part and rearranged by Kenyon. We
shall quote *in extenso* his summary dealing with this
subject, because it is one of the latest, if not the latest,
grouping by any modern scholar (*Our Bible*, 1948
reprint) :

KENYON'S GROUPING

"It will have been seen that the picture presented by Westcott and Hort in 1881, though in the main holding its ground,
has undergone certain modifications as the result of the discoveries of the last fifty years. It would be rash to claim that
finality has yet been reached; but at each stage of the journey
it is useful to sum up the results which *appear* to have been
reached, if only to serve as a basis for further examination, or
as an hypothesis by which future discoveries may be tested.

"The classification now suggested is as follows:

BYZANTINE

"(a) *Byzantine,* a title which seems preferable to Hort's
'Syrian,' as avoiding confusion with 'Syriac' and as more de-
scriptive of the text which came to be generally adopted in
the Byzantine Church. This is the text found in the vast majority of later MSS., which from them passed into the earliest
printed texts, and which was the universally 'received text,'
until it was challenged by modern scholarship and by the results of modern discoveries. Its characteristic features are
verbal revision in the direction of smoothness, intelligibility,
ease of comprehension, concordance between different narratives of the same event. It seems to be the result of a long-
continued process of minor revision in the interests of the
ordinary reader. The earliest traces of it appear in the quotations of Chrysostom, who worked at Antioch until 398 and

then at Constantinople until 407, and it seems to have established itself in the Metropolitan Church in the course of the next centuries, until by the eighth it is found in practically complete possession of the Greek world. The oldest and most important MSS. which show readings of this type are A and C in the Gospels, W except in Mark, and the purple MSS. N, O, Σ, Φ; after these follow the great mass of later uncials and minuscules. It can now, however, generally be discarded when it comes into competition with the earlier families.

ALEXANDRIAN

"(β) *Alexandrian*, substantially identical with Hort's 'Neutral.' The latter title is better avoided, since it now appears that this type of text cannot claim an uncontaminated descent from the originals, but is rather the result of skilled editorial handling of good materials; also that it is not a text universally current in Egypt (though that is its main home), but is rather the product of a well-equipped scriptorium in a particular place, which can hardly be other than Alexandria. To this family belong in the first line the great uncials B and ℵ, often supported by L R T Z, also by A and C except in the Gospels, by the minuscules 33, 81 and 157, and the Coptic versions, both Sahidic and Bohairic. Of the Fathers, Origen is the one who most often has readings of this type.

CAESAREAN

"(γ) *Cæsarean*.—The discovery of this family of text has been described above (p. 117). So far, its character has only been established in Mark, the Gospel which (being the shortest and containing the least of our Lord's teaching) appears to have had the least circulation in the early Church, and so escaped revision and corruption. Here it is found in the Codex Koridethianus (Θ), the groups of minuscules known as Family 1 and Family 13, the Chester Beatty papyrus P^{45}, the Armenian and Georgian versions, and the quotations in the later works of Origen and in Eusebius. It clearly established itself in the library at Cæsarea, where Origen and Eusebius worked, but there is evidence, especially in P^{45}, of its circulation in Egypt, and that may well be its original home. In character it lies between the Alexandrian and Western.

WESTERN

"(δ) *Western*. As stated above, it was formerly the custom to label as 'Western' any reading which was earlier than 'Syrian,' but was not found in the 'Neutral' authorities. In this way it was argued that the Western text was in early times prevalent, not only in the West, but also in Syria and even in Egypt; that it was in fact the original form of text, from which the 'Neutral' was derived by drastic editorial revision. But the growth of evidence and investigation has shown that in this sense no such thing as a Western text exists at all. The Syriac and Egyptian variants from the 'Neutral' or Alexandrian text do not by any means always or generally coincide with those of the Latin authorities; and it is not possible to trace them to a common source, or reconstruct a Western text on these lines at all. On the other hand, if it is once recognised that it is not necessary to group in a single family all readings with early attestation which do not belong to the Alexandrian family, it is easy to segregate one group of these which have a common character, and whose attestation is definitely Western. This is the type of text found in Codex Bezæ and the other Græco-Latin uncials D_2 E_3 F_2 G_3, the African form of the Old Latin version, especially in the MSS. *k* and *e*, and the quotations in Cyprian, Priscillian, Tyconius and Primasius. It is a type marked by striking variations from all other groups, especially in the Gospels and Acts. In the Acts especially it abounds with variants which some have thought superior to the Alexandrian and Byzantine texts, and which, if not original, must be due to deliberate alterations by someone who regarded himself as having authoritative information. Specimens of these variants will be found in Appendix I.

SYRIAC

"(ε) *Syriac*.—It seems necessary to separate the Old Syriac version from the Western family with which it was formerly associated. It is in fact nearer akin to the Alexandrian type, though independent of it; and such infusion of Western readings as it has may well be attributed to the influence of Tatian's Diatessaron. It may therefore be regarded rather as the local text of the Church of Edessa, influenced at first by the Western text imported by Tatian from Rome, and eventually revised under Byzantine influences by Rabbula into the form of the

Peshitta, which became the authorised Bible of the Syrian Church.

"When, however, all these families have been marked off and labelled, it must be recognised that they have not exhausted the early history of the New Testament text. No one of these families can be taken as containing the whole authentic truth; all reach back to a period of uncertainty out of which they gradually emerged; and they do not all between them cover the whole of the material. In addition to the readings which can be attributed with some certainty to one or the other family, there is a residue of unassigned readings, relics of a time when there was much variation among the texts of the sacred books (especially the Gospels) circulating among the widely scattered Christian communities, out of which the families or types which we have now learned to discern were gradually formed. If this be so, we must recognise that absolute certainty in details is unattainable; that even if the Alexandrian type (or the Western or Cæsarean, if anyone prefers it) is generally superior, it cannot always be right, and we must be prepared to consider alternative readings on their merits. We must be content to know that the general authenticity of the New Testament text has been remarkably supported by the modern discoveries which have so greatly reduced the interval between the original autographs and our earliest extant manuscripts, and that the differences of reading, interesting as they are, do not affect the fundamental doctrines of the Christian faith." (Kenyon, *Our Bible*, (1948 reprint) pp. 177-79; see *Note Nineteen*, pp. 194 ff.)

Thus it does seem to Kenyon's "reader" that pretty much the whole edifice built by Westcott and Hort and their fellow Extreme Textualists with such intricate care and ingenious supposition, with so much "conjectural emendation," with so much general conjecture, and super-abundance of "ifs," has fallen, or is falling, like a house of cards, without noise and with little dust, and that "higher criticism" is off to a new start that does not begin (as we shall read later) with a besmirching of the great Authorized Version. We are now to let the great unlearned public continue to be edified and built up spiritually by the King James Version, while scholars enjoy the various Revisions.

KENYON'S PRE-BYZANTINE AUTHORITIES

Kenyon has this further classification of what he terms pre-Byzantine authorities (it must be remembered that he is giving essentially the views of the Extreme Textualists who would bury the Byzantine text, but which, like Banquo's ghost, will not down):

"Thus while the discoveries of the last fifty years have shaken the exclusive predominance which Westcott and Hort assigned to the Vaticanus-Sinaiticus text, they have shattered to pieces the unity of the so-called Western text. [See p. 94, herein.] In place of these two families, with the somewhat shadowy 'Alexandrian' text, as envisaged by the two Cambridge scholars, we now seem to find our pre-Byzantine authorities falling into at least five categories; (1) the Vaticanus-Sinaiticus group, with its home in Egypt, and almost certainly in Alexandria, since it is difficult to imagine such splendid manuscripts being produced except in a great capital; it is a group obviously of great importance, being headed by these two outstanding manuscripts, supported by a number of early though fragmentary uncials and a few minuscules, and by the Bohairic and generally the Sahidic version, and to it the name *Alexandrian* may more appropriately, and with less appearance of begging the question, be applied than that of Neutral; (2) the true *Western* group, headed by the Codex Bezæ, the other Græco-Latin uncials, and the Old Latin version, especially in that earliest form of it which appears to be associated with Africa and to have been used by Cyprian; (3) the *Syriac* group, represented mainly by the Old Syriac version and the other versions (Georgian, Armenian) which appear to have been derived from it; (4) the *Cæsarean* group, as yet not fully worked out, but which may in part be extracted, as described above, from the Chester Beatty papyrus, the Washington and Koridethi codices, and Families 1 and 13, with the quotations in some of the works of Origen and Eusebius; and (5) a residue of unassorted readings, found in early authorities, but which it is quite inadmissible to claim as 'Western' now that we realize that not everything that is not Neutral is Western." (*The Story*, pp. 131-132.)

Having in mind the all-out espousal of the Westcott-Hort thesis by the Extreme Textualists, it is not difficult to understand how they still cling with a slipping hold to א and B as the "outstanding manuscripts." (*The Story*, p. 131.) It is hard to admit one has made an egregious mistake. But their own concessions, grudgingly made, suggest they must come to it.

NOTE NINE ·

Division of New Testament Into Paragraphs

It might be noted in passing, that Bengel (1734) "introduced the division of the New Testament into paragraphs, with which we have become familiar," and that Wetstein was "the first to cite the Manuscripts under their present designation, quoting from A to O of the Uncials in the Gospels, and 1-112 of the Cursives." (Miller, pp. 15-16.)

NOTE TEN •

Division of Chapters Into Verses

In Stephen's fourth edition of his text (published in 1551), the chapters into which Cardinal Hugo, of Santo Caro, had divided the books of the Bible, were now subdivided into verses. Dr. Gregory is quoted as declaring "that Stephen Langton was the author of the present division into Chapters," though there was some sort of division into chapters from the first. (Miller, pp. 10-11.)

NOTE ELEVEN •
Textual Criticism, Development of Modern Criticism

Miller, writing of the situation in the 1880's affirmed there were two chief schools of textual criticism — *The School of Extreme Textualism* (*Extreme Textualists*) and *The Rival School of Sound or High Textualism*. (Miller, pp. 38 ff.; see *supra Note Three*.)

These two schools had for years waged a fierce controversy over the text of the New Testament, — the *Extreme Textualists* trying to discredit and break down the Authorized Version (King James Version), and the *Rival School of Sound or High Textualism* seeking to sustain it. (Miller, pp. 60 ff.; Burgon, pp. 96-97.)

Item 1. Old Testament.

Summary. Modern criticism began about the middle of the 18th century. Earlier critics lived in the eleventh century, but their work seems rather desultory. The French scientist and court physician, Jean Astruc (1684-1766), wrote about 1753. Others are named as following Astruc: Eichhorn, Alexander Geddes, Ilgen, de Wette, Wellhausen, Eduard Reuss, Vatke, Graf, Hupfeld, Duhm. These critics have advanced theories then abandoned them, then they have re-theorized and re-abandoned; it appears that not yet has any discussion of the books of the Old Testament found general acceptance.

While in these *Notes* we are concerned primarily with the New Testament, yet it would seem wise to make some observations regarding the Old Testament.

Dr. James Strachan (Professor of Hebrew and Biblical Criticism, Magee College, Londonderry), writing in Hastings' *Encyclopaedia of Religion and Ethics, sub voce* "Criticism (Old Testament)," has briefly traced the history of modern criticism which began about the middle of the 18th century. The following is a precis of his discussion:

EARLY CRITICS

He first notes some earlier critics, such as Theodore of Mopsuestia, who did some work on the Psalms; Ibn Ezra, a scholarly Jew (1070-1138), who notes some anachronisms in the Pentateuch; Luther, who was fearless in his expressions concerning certain books of the Canon, and who was not disturbed by the suggestion that Moses may not have written the Pentateuch; Spinoza, who "anticipated not a few of the modern critical results"; and Richard Simon, who also worked on the Pentateuch.

ASTRUC

Dr. Strachan names the French scientist and court physician, Jean Astruc, a Catholic, as the discoverer of "the critical secret," and the creator of the "*novum organum* which was 'to destroy and to overthrow, to build and to plant.' " Astruc studied the Pentateuch and carried his work through all of Genesis and a part of Exodus, "as far as the point where the distinction of Divine names appears to cease (Ex 6)," the two Divine names used being Elohim and Jehovah. The conclusion was suggested from this study that Genesis was composed of two or three memoirs. (His book was printed after some hesitancy, in 1753.)

EICHHORN

Eichhorn is named next by Dr. Strachan. He followed along the general lines of Astruc, and expressed the belief ("long since antiquated") that the last four books of the Pentateuch "were compiled from separate writings of Moses and some of his contemporaries."

GEDDES

Alexander Geddes is named next. He repudiated the findings of Astruc and Eichhorn that there were two fundamental documents in Genesis, and affirmed that the book was made up of a "collection of loose scraps, of various age and worth, probably compiled in the time of Solomon." He applied the same theory to other books of the Old Testament. His conclusions acquired the name of the "Fragment Hypothesis," which met its "death-blow at the hands of the greatest OT scholar of last century, Heinrich Ewald of Gottingen," *in a work written when he was nineteen years old.*

ILGEN

Ilgen, "Eichhorn's successor at Jena," announced there were two writers in Genesis who used the word *Elohim.* Hupfeld independently reached the same conclusion some fifty years later. The "higher critics" appear now to accept this conclusion, "as one of the assured results of criticism."

DE WETTE

In 1805, de Wette argued that Deuteronomy was distinct in origin and purpose from the rest of the Pentateuch, fixing its origin in the time of Josiah (621 B.C.), and of the reformation of that time. This is said by Dr. Strachan, to be "universally regarded as the key to the interpretation of the spiritual evolution of Israel."

The critics next affiliated the Book of Joshua with the Pentateuch.

Wellhausen

Wellhausen followed and, neglecting Ilgen's work, proposed one undivided Elohist document which he named the "Book of Origins," as the "groundwork" of the Hexateuch. He contended that the so-called Jahwist sections were additions to the Elohist as supplements. This was called the "Supplement Hypothesis," and had the support of some scholars, but "it has now no more than a historical interest."

Reuss-Graf

In 1834, Eduard Reuss, acting on the premise that a nation would not begin its history with a whole system of law which prophets following would ignore (this concept seems to eliminate all divine intervention in the giving of the law), propounded the hypothesis that "in the true historical sequence the Prophets are earlier than the Law, and the Psalms later than both." A year later Vatke propounded practically the same theory. This theory was published by K. H. Graf, a pupil of Reuss, and became known as the "Grafian Hypothesis."

Hupfeld

Hupfeld, having cast aside the "Supplement Hypothesis" of Ewald, revived the almost forgotten theory of Ilgen,—that there were two distinct Elohist writers in the Pentateuch. His theory was that "the productions of three originally independent writers (now known as J, E, and P) were at length combined by an editor, who —fortunately for us—left his sources much as he found them, being content to establish a merely superficial unity. . . . The inference was inevitable that these three strata of legislation belong to three widely separated ages."

Graf's suggestion that the Priestly Code was partly historical and partly legal and that the first was pre-exilic and the second post-exilic, has not been accepted. The critics were for some time divided as to whether the whole of Deuteronomy was pre-exilic or post-exilic, but now are in practically unanimous agreement that it is post-exilic. (Babylonish captivity,—from about 600 B.C. to 536 B.C.)

DUHM

Duhm attacked the concept of the traditional succession of Mosaism, Prophecy, Judaism, and affirmed that the great prophets "are not the children of the Law, but the inspired creators of the religion of Israel. Prophecy is the supreme initial fact which transcends explanation." The results of Duhm's work are affirmed to support the Grafian hypothesis.

Wellhausen's book of 1878, in behalf of the new hypothesis, "removed OT criticism from the rank of a subordinate question to the centre of theological discussion."

EERDMANS

Prof. B. D. Eerdmans (writing 1908-10) has abandoned the Graf-Wellhausen-Kuenen hypothesis and declared his intention of reexamining the fundamentals of the theories of that school. (James Strachan, "Criticism (Old Testament)," Hastings *Encyc.*, Vol. IV, pp. 314-319.)

So the critics theorize and abandon, re-theorize and re-abandon. The essential matter would seem to be not who wrote or when they were written, but do they contain the Word of God and a record of his dealings with his children.

Item 2.   New Testament.

Summary. Criticism is classified as "literary" and "historical." Scholars regard the criticism in the historical field as "surprisingly contradictory," though in the "literary" field agreement is largely reached; but the whole field is "strangely bewildering." Sources of Gospel accounts are not likely to be successfully determined. The Extreme Textualists in their order are Lachmann, Tregelles, Tischendorf, Westcott and Hort. The more modern Kenyon apparently is trying to steer a middle course between the two schools. The Extreme Textualists claimed a primacy for the manuscripts Vaticanus (B) and Sinaiticus (ℵ). Among the opposing school, the Sound or High Textualists, may be mentioned Burgon, Miller, and in a less pronounced way, the great scholar Scrivener. Comments are given upon the two schools and some of their adherents. Scrivener's dissertation (extracts from) on Westcott and Hort's work and thesis.

Turning now to the New Testament:

Here, also, the criticism is classified as both "literary" and "historical." Professor Willoughby C. Allen (Rector of Saham Toney, Norfolk, formerly Lecturer in Theology and in Hebrew at Exeter College, Oxford), writing in Hastings' *Encyclopaedia, sub voce* "Criticism (New Testament)," comments, regarding criticism of the Gospels and Acts: "To the dispassionate inquirer the present state of this department of investigation must be strangely bewildering," not in the field of "literary" criticism, where agreement has been largely reached, but in the field of "historical" criticism, where "results are surprisingly contradictory." The following comments are a precis of Prof. Allen's discussion:

As to the Synoptic Gospels (Matthew, Mark, and

Luke), the critics generally agree that Mark was used
by Matthew and Luke; that the last two had available
a collection of the Savior's sayings (undiscovered as
yet) designated as Q; that a third written source was
used by Luke; and that some effort is made to show
that Mark was made up of two documents.

As to John, some scholars (Allen names Wellhausen
and Spitta) try to find traces of composite scholarship,
"but it may be questioned whether the unity of the book
is not too apparent to be lightly shaken."

Attempts to dissect Acts into sections coming from
different sources, seem not to have been too successful,
except perhaps as to the "We" sections.

Allen observes:

"The use of Mark in Matthew and Luke has been rather
observed than discovered; and, if Mark did not exist, literary
analysis certainly could not reconstruct it out of the later Gospels. For that very reason, attempts to reconstruct Q can be
at the best but tentative. The attempted analysis of these books
into sources which are not now extant is a matter of great
difficulty, arising from the fact that the writers have so re-cast
any sources which they may have used that reconstruction of
them is now almost impossible. It is for that reason that attempts on purely literary grounds to re-discover sources used
in the Acts are little likely to succeed." (Allen, Hastings
Encyc., Vol. IV, p. 319b.)

It seems that the first considerable person who
might be called an *Extreme Textualist*, was K. Lachmann (first book, 1831); he was followed by Samuel
Prideaux Tregelles (d. 1875); next came Constantine
Tischendorf, the discoverer of the Codex Sinaiticus (‫א‬)
at the Monastery of St. Catherine, on Mount Sinai, in
1859. (See *infra*, *Note Twenty-five*, *Item 1*, p. 258.)
The seemingly two most effective members of this
school thereafter were Bishop B. F. Westcott and Dr.

F. J. A. Hort (Cambridge), who elaborated and published (Hort writing and Westcott collaborating) a Greek text of the New Testament in 1881 (May 12th). (Miller, pp. 20-30; Kenyon, *HDB* (*Single Vol.*), p. 925.)

This school (the Extreme Textualists) claimed a primacy for the B manuscript (in the Vatican at Rome) and for the Sinaitic manuscript (ℵ), which was discovered by Tischendorf. (See *infra*, *Note Thirteen*, pp. 122 ff.) This Sinaitic manuscript was given by the Convent to Alexander II., Emperor of Russia, and was lodged in St. Petersburg (Petrograd). (Miller, p. 24; Kenyon, *HDB* (*Single Vol.*), p. 925.) It has since been purchased by the British Government and British interests and is now in the British Museum in London. (Kenyon, *Our Bible*, pp. 130-131.)

As already stated, this school (Extreme Textualist) has made constant war, without quarter, against the Authorized Version, the King James translation. Kenyon speaks of the work of Lachmann as doing a "very great service in breaking the monopoly of the TR" (*Textus Receptus*, the basis of the Authorized Version); of the work of Tregelles as "completely ignoring the TR"; and of the work of Westcott and Hort against the proponents of the Textus Receptus, as "in the opinion of nearly all students of the subject," a decisive triumph. (Kenyon, *HDB* (*Single Vol.*), pp. 925, 926b; but see Burgon, pp. 242-43, 253; and for observations on German influence in modern criticism, Extreme Textualists, see Burgon, pp. 21, n. 2, 236, and 517; and his observations to the point that the Authorized Version (Textus Receptus) must somehow be gotten rid of if the Revised Version is to stand, Burgon, pp. 296-97.)

It may not be going too far afield for a layman to

say (it is believed to be within the facts) that the recognition of this 'decisive triumph' is in no small part the result of the loss by a considerable part of the Christian clergy, of faith in the divinity of Jesus the Christ.

As Caesar said, "Men willingly believe that which they wish [to believe]." ("*Libenter homines id quod volunt credunt.*" *De Bello Gallico*, Bk. iii, sec. 18.)

In contemplating the spiritual ruin that must follow the abandonment of the Christ Jesus, some scriptures come to mind: Peter, bearing witness of Jesus the Christ to the Sanhedrin: "Neither is there salvation in any other: for there is none other name under heaven given among men, whereby we must be saved." (Acts 4:12.) Paul declared to the Corinthians: "For the preaching of the cross is to them that perish foolishness; but unto us which are saved it is the power of God." (I. Cor. 1:18.) Ezekiel voiced a great principle that has application to the tragic falling away from Jesus that now flows over Christendom: "Mischief shall come upon mischief, and rumour shall be upon rumour; then shall they seek a vision of the prophet; but the law shall perish from the priest, and counsel from the ancients." (Ezek. 7:26.) But we have the great hope voiced by Isaiah and fulfilled in the opening of the Last Dispensation: "Therefore, behold, I will proceed to do a marvellous work among this people, even a marvellous work and a wonder: for the wisdom of their wise men shall perish, and the understanding of their prudent men shall be hid." (Isa. 29:14; see *Note Eight, supra,* for the present state of criticism affecting the text of the Authorized Version.)

As has been repeatedly indicated in all the preceding pages, the various Revised Versions (British, 1880's, American, 1901 and 1946) are essentially a translation of a Greek text fabricated by Westcott and Hort and founded primarily on Codices B and א, with incorporations from a few other codices that supported the readings of these two, but especially founded on Codex B.

It will be recalled that as between the Textus Receptus (King James Version) and the Revised Versions, Kenyon declared, "in the opinion of nearly all students of the subject," the Revisers scored a decisive triumph. (Kenyon, *HDB* (*Single Vol.*), p. 926b.)

It will also be remembered from the preceding pages, that the severest critic against the original Revised Version (British, 1881) was Dean Burgon who is characterized by Kenyon as "a doughty controversialist," who could "deal a swashing blow with gusto," but who 'found little support among scholars,' and who assailed vehemently the Revised Version with "unquestionable learning" which was "largely neutralised by the extravagance and intemperance of their tone." (*Note One*, pp. 25-26.) That he assailed the new Version with vehemence is abundantly proved by his writings, as has already appeared and will appear later.

But the conclusions he reached on the fundamental weakness of Westcott and Hort's theories and procedures in building their text have been seemingly fully concurred in by Dr. Scrivener, whom Kenyon characterized, along with Hort, as "the two most learned textual critics then alive" (as of the date of the Revision). (*Note One*, p. 25.) Of Scrivener's work — *Introduction to the Criticism of the New Testament* (fourth edition, 1894)—Kenyon declares it "is still [1948] the fullest description, up to its date, of the textual materials for English readers." (*Note One*, p. 24.)

Scrivener's judicial and dispassionate criticism of Westcott and Hort's system, its difficulties, its dilemmas, the peculiar characteristics of their reasonings and the virtual repudiation of their final conclusions as illogical, unsound, and unsupported, while of some length, is worth quoting here in essential part.

SCRIVENER'S COMMENT ON WESTCOTT-HORT SYSTEM

After discussing the bringing together of the various books which now make up the Bible and the time at which there came to be a single volume, Scrivener observes, as to the great texts ℵ and B on which Westcott and Hort place such reliance as having a more or less undisturbed descent from the Sacred Autographs:

"Hence it is not unreasonable to suspect that our great codices (ℵABC), which originally contained the whole N.T., may have been transcribed in their several parts from copies differing from each other in genius and in date. With such a possibility before us we ought not to be perplexed if the character of the text whether of Cod. A or of Cod. B differs in the Gospels from that which it bears in the Acts and the Epistles." (Scrivener, p. 532.)

After a brief similar comment upon differences with other texts, Scrivener continues:

"At this remote period, during the first half of the second century, must have originated the wide variations from the prevailing text on the part of our primary authorities, both manuscripts and versions, which survive in Cod. Bezæ of the Greek, and in the Old Latin codices or at least in some of them." (Scrivener, p. 532.)

After discussing the "Western" text, its early readings, its characteristics, its 'enrichment' by variations (quoting Hort), and interpolations, Scrivener leads to Hort's proposed Antiochian text prepared (according to Hort) by the "Syrian bishops and Fathers of the Patriarchate of Antioch," by asserting:

"We now come to the feature which distinguishes Dr. Hort's system from any hitherto propounded; by the acceptance or non-acceptance of which his whole edifice must stand or fall." (Scrivener, p. 533; see p. 79, herein.)

After numbering and briefly noting the various steps incident to the development of this Antiochian text, Scrivener says:

". . . although they [the essential revisions in the Syrian text which Dr. Hort assumes must have taken place in the framing of the final text] must have been of necessity public acts of great Churches in ages abounding in Councils General or Provincial, not one trace remains in the history of Christian antiquity; no one writer seems conscious that any modification either of the Greek Scriptures or of the vernacular translation was made in or before his times [*sic*]. . . . Yet regarding his speculative conjecture as undubitably true, Dr. Hort proceeds to name the text as it stood before his imaginary era of transfusion a *Pre-Syrian* text, and that into which it was changed, sometimes *Antiochian,* more often *Syrian;* while of the latter recension, though made deliberately, as our author believes, by the authoritative voice of the Eastern Church, he does not shrink from declaring that 'all distinctively Syrian readings must be at once rejected' (*ibid.* p. 119), thus making a clean sweep of all critical materials, Fathers, versions, manuscripts uncial or cursive, comprising about nineteen twentieths of the whole mass, which do not correspond with his preconceived opinion of what a correct text ought to be (*ibid.* p. 163)." (Scrivener, pp. 533-534; see pp. 78-79, herein.)

Stating that "but one or two steps yet remain in this thorough elimination of useless elements," Scrivener notes "a few authorities still survive which are honoured as *Pre-Syrian,* and continued unaffected by the phantom revisions, which, for critical purposes, have reduced their colleagues to ignominious silence."

Scrivener then notes that Hort has reserved the

Western, Alexandrian, and Neutral groups as being "tolerably void of corruption as regards the substance." He then discusses in some summary critical detail, these three types (Western, Neutral, Alexandrian); notes the preferential position Hort gives to the Neutral א B and comments thereon and upon the writers thereof. He says Hort is "very glad when he can to find friends for his favourite," and does not disparage inferior manuscripts if they support his favorites, but if "the worst comes to the worst" and his favorite B stands without support, it still must be accepted, especially in the Gospels.

Scrivener then compares the theories of Hort and Griesbach, and the critical relationship between them and the handicap under which Griesbach labored in advancing his theories because he did not have all the manuscripts available to Hort, but notes the difficulties in which Hort found himself. He notes, commenting upon Hort's scheme, that "nothing less than the exigency of his case could have driven our author [Hort] to encumber himself with a scheme fraught with difficulties too great even for his skill to overcome. Dr. Hort's system, therefore, is entirely destitute of historical foundation. He does not so much as make a show of pretending to it." (Scrivener, pp. 534-537.)

Scrivener continues with a discussion of the arguments of some two other Revisers regarding the Syrian texts and their comparative ages.

Commenting upon the "double edge" of Hort's conflation (fusing together) of two texts (Luke 24:53), Scrivener says that other conflations he refers to "prove nothing to any one who has not made up his mind beforehand as to what the reading ought to be," and notes certain tendencies of copyists. (Scrivener, p. 539.)

Further commenting upon the supporting arguments of the two other Revisers (referred to above) touching their assertion that there is no historical trace of any distinctively Syrian reading prior to "the middle of the third century," Scrivener notes that this "is the earliest period assigned by Dr. Hort for the inception of his phantom scheme of Syrian revision," the Antiochian text. (Scrivener, p. 539; see p. 79, herein.)

Scrivener follows this with comments on the inadequate study made of the writings of Irenaeus, Hippolytus, Clement, Origen, and states that such study as had been made "would suffice to prove that their evidence is by no means exclusively favourable to Dr. Hort's opinions, a fact for which we will allege but one instance out of many, the support given to the Received text by Hippolytus in that grand passage, John iii. 13." (Scrivener, p. 540.)

Scrivener then notes the necessity for a study by "scholars yet young," of the cursive manuscripts, the Thebaic New Testament, and the Memphitic (Bohairic) also. He follows this with some discussion of the internal evidence characterized (as he quotes) "a very delicate and difficult domain of textual criticism, and can only draw our conclusions with the utmost circumspection and reserve." (Scrivener, pp. 540-541.)

In further comment upon the use of internal evidence, Scrivener says:

"It is sometimes said that all reasoning is analytical, not synthetical; the reducing a foregone conclusion to the first principles on which it rests, rather than the building upon those first principles the materials wherewith to construct the conclusion." (Scrivener, p. 541.)

He then affirms that in Dr. Hort's work, regarding Cod. B, "those lines of thought are closely followed which most readily lead up to the theory of that manuscript's practical impeccability." He also notes that where because of the "precariousness of Intrinsic [sic] evidence" a decision must be made upon a diversity of judgment, "in such cases the ultimate decision must rest with the individual critic: 'in almost all texts variations occur where personal judgment inevitably takes a large part in the final decision. . . . Different minds will be impressed by different parts of the evidence as clearer than the rest, and so virtually ruling the rest: here therefore personal discernment would seem the surest ground for confidence' (*ibid.* p. 65). For the critic's confidence perhaps, not for that of his reader." (Scrivener, pp. 541-542.)

After paying tribute to Dr. Hort's fullness of learning, patience of research, keenness of intellectual power, "and especially for a certain marvellous readiness in accounting after some fashion for every new phenomenon which occurs, however apparently adverse to the acceptance of his own theory," Scrivener closes this general discussion with the following comments:

"With all our reverence for his genius, and gratitude for much that we have learnt from him in the course of our studies, we are compelled to repeat as emphatically as ever our strong conviction that the hypothesis to whose proof he has devoted so many laborious years, is destitute not only of historical foundation, but of all probability resulting from the internal goodness of the text which its adoption would force upon us.

"This last assertion we will try to verify by subjoining a select number of those many passages in the N.T. wherein the two great codices ℵ and B, one or both of them, are witnesses for readings, nearly all of which, to the best of our judgment, are corruptions of the sacred originals." (Scrivener, pp. 542-543; see p. 79, herein.)

In coming to the end of this summary discussion by Scrivener of certain phases of the work of Westcott and

Hort, one comes necessarily—when Scrivener quotes Hort's conclusion regarding the place and function of the individual critic—to the criticism of Burgon regarding the "individual mind" and "conjectural emendation." For a true exercise of such functions by a translator, he must have inspiration and revelation, and where doctrinal matters are involved the translator must know the true doctrine. (See *Note Twenty-nine.*)

NOTE TWELVE ·

Summary of Some Important Text Eliminations by the Extreme Textualists

Summary. Summary by Miller of some vital Biblical passages that have been tampered with by Westcott and Hort, as the text appears in the Authorized Version (King James Version, the Textus Receptus).

The school of the Extreme Textualists would seemingly eliminate from the Bible the following (among many others) vital passages, as summarized by Miller. They are merely noted here, that at this point some idea may be gathered as to the injuries the Extreme Textualists have inflicted upon the people. Some of the more important of these passages will be treated more fully later.

"(a) The Last Twelve Verses of the Gospel according to St. Mark must be cast aside, and an abrupt close made after the words, 'for they were afraid.'

"(b) In the Lord's Prayer as given by St. Luke (xi. 2-4), the following clauses must be excised:—'Our . . . . which art in Heaven'; 'Thy will be done, as in Heaven, so on earth';— 'but deliver us from evil.'

"(c) The Doxology must be omitted from the Lord's Prayer in St. Matthew (vi. 13), and so all record of it lost in the Gospels.

"(d) Vv. 43, 44 must no longer be reckoned in the 22nd chapter of St. Luke, and thereby the account must disappear of the strengthening Angel and the 'Bloody Sweat,' as well as the evangelical record of 'the Agony in the Garden.'

"(e) The first of our Lord's seven Sayings from the Cross (St. Luke xxiii. 34) must be regarded as unauthentic, 'Father, forgive them, for they know not what they do.'

"(f) Also St. Luke's assertion of the Ascent into Heaven (xxiv. 51),—an omission of the more importance, because St. Mark's account of the same event, which included also the session at the Right Hand of GOD, is supposed under these principles to have vanished with the last twelve verses of his Gospel.

"(g) St. Luke's recital of the Institution of the Holy Sacrament (xxii. 19, 20) must be lost, except as far as 'This is My Body.'

"These seven instances, which might be multiplied extensively by the addition of other omissions,—such as of the descending angel and the cure wrought in the pool of Bethesda, of the last cry in St. Mark's description of the centurion's faith, of the greater part of St. Luke's account of the Inscription on the Cross, of St. Peter's visit to the Sepulchre in the same Gospel, of the salutation, 'Peace be unto you,' of the Lord shewing His Hands and His Feet, of the word 'broken,' whereby a gash is made and a blank space left in St. Paul's grand version of the Institution of the Holy Sacrament, and others too numerous to recount here—not to do more than allude to startling statements, such as that our Lord's Side may have been pierced before death, and that the sun was eclipsed at the full,—may teach all who revere and love the Word of God what precious points are at stake. If the changes advocated by the modern school leave enough behind in Holy Writ to support without doubt the essentials of the Faith of Christendom, yet they are so momentous in themselves as to produce a painful wrench in earnest affections which have attached themselves to words familiar and deeply loved from childhood, and to prove that, at least to first appearance, general and special attention should be directed to what may really be a corruption of the Holy Scriptures. Besides this, the number of alterations, amounting in the most moderate of the new recensions to 5,337, reveals the formidable nature of the operations that are threatened. If the majority of these alterations are small, it must be remembered that the instance taken is one which presents much less change than other editions of the New Testament. Enough is shown to establish beyond doubt that it is the duty of all Christians, who take an intelligent interest in the controversies of their day, not to sit still when such concerns are in jeopardy." (Miller, pp. 1-4.)

As stated above, certain of these matters will

receive more extensive treatment, hereinafter. (*Infra,* pp. 315, ff.)

The school of the Extreme Textualists, with their destructive, as well as constructive principles, naturally led to the creation of a group who, while they are not unwilling to adopt changes in the Received Text (Textus Receptus) which a consideration of all the evidence justifies or requires, yet they are unwilling to cast away the Received Text as being (to all intents and purposes) unreliable, indeed, almost spurious, as in effect contended by the Extreme Textualists. This second group, as already stated, is designated as the Rival School of Sound or High Textualists. (Miller, pp. 60 ff.) This school numbered among its members such distinguished scholars as Dr. F. H. A. Scrivener, Dean Burgon (Dean of Chichester), Canon Cook, Bishops Christopher and Charles Wordsworth, Dr. J. G. Reiche, and many others. (Miller, pp. 30-35.) These men have all passed on, and apparently none of their stature have yet taken their places, though it is to be noted that a scanty and desultory criticism of the Revised Standard Version has been made. It is to be hoped that a group of scholars will appear who can handle adequately this latest assault on the citadel of Christianity.

NOTE THIRTEEN •

The Antiquity Argument

Item 1. *As of the Time of the Revised Version (British) 1880's, and of the American Standard Version (1900-1901).*

Summary. The Extreme Textualists declared for the primacy of the Manuscripts Vaticanus (B) and Sinaiticus (ℵ), seemingly on the ground that these were the oldest known Greek manuscripts. The discovery of the Chester Beatty Manuscripts and others (also in Greek) and ante-dating these two, has materially weakened this position. The antiquity argument is discussed in the light of the conditions existing in the early Christian Church, including the early corruption of the scriptures, often by heretics, sometimes by churchmen, innocently or ignorantly, sometimes by design by those who were not classed as heretics. Comments on the effect and possible design upon Christian faith of the Westcott-Hort contentions regarding the Vaticanus and Sinaiticus manuscripts. The Prophet Joseph's estimate of Biblical corruptions.

To the author, a layman of scanty scholastic equipment and no facilities, to Kenyon's "reader," the basic difference between the two schools — the Extreme Textualists and the Rival School of Sound or High Textualists—seems to come to this:

The Extreme Textualists declared that the then oldest *discovered* Greek manuscript B, the Vatican manuscript, and its companion ℵ, the Sinaitic manuscript (discovered by Tischendorf), should be regarded as the controlling texts, and seemingly that the New Testament should be essentially a translation of these manuscripts. The ostensible reason given for this contention seems to have been the antiquity of the texts. The

Sound or High Textualists contended for the primacy of the Received Text, or Traditional Text, which Miller describes as follows:

"The Received Text of the sixteenth and seventeenth centuries represented with general, but far from invariable accuracy, the Traditional Text of the previous ages of the Church." (Miller, pp. 12-13.)

Perhaps a few words of a general character from a layman on this matter of antiquity, the age of manuscripts, may be said here. (See *infra*, pp. 249, 255.)

Under all the circumstances attaching to the recording of the sayings and events of the Savior's earthly mission and the preservation of that record, the mere age of a manuscript by itself can hardly be advanced as an evidence of record truthfulness when that age is two and a half centuries after Christ lived and moved in mortality.

As already pointed out (*supra*, p. 65) Dr. Scrivener affirms that the original autographs of the sacred writers, in whatever language written, "perished utterly in the very infancy of Christian history." (Scrivener, p. 2.) This fact seems now to be recognized by the critics generally. So all we have, at the very best, are copies or versions of these autographs.

The two manuscripts to be considered later (Sinaiticus and Vaticanus) seem generally admitted to be the oldest Greek vellum manuscripts so far known. They are believed to have been written about the middle of the fourth century. The earlier papyrus manuscripts —Chester Beatty Manuscripts—were not known in 1880, but their existence completely destroys the argument of mere date, for "the earliest [of these] is of the first half of the second century, the latest not later than the fourth: most are of the third." (See *Note*

Fourteen, p. 131, herein.) On this ground of antiquity, two scholars, particularly — Westcott and Hort — declared that אֹ and B should be the controlling texts, merely (it seems, in the last analysis) because in age they were the oldest manuscripts discovered. To rid themselves of the embarrassment of the early and older Aramaic text (Old Syriac, the Diatessaron, and the Peshito, *supra, Note Six*) these two scholars developed theories (*supra,* pp. 91 ff.), which are characterized by hostile critics as unsupported, fantastic suppositions. "They assume everything. They prove nothing." (Burgon, p. 264, and see pp. 114 ff.)

EARLY CORRUPTIONS

However, from almost the earliest times the Scriptures were corrupted. (See *infra,* p. 256.) The changing of sacred writings had very early become so common that Dionysius, bishop of Corinth, writing to the bishop of Rome (Soter) in the second century, complained that his own letters had been tampered with (168-176 A.D.). Heretics produced their own corrupted texts. Irenaeus (fl. 178 A.D.), "the glory of the Western Church in his own age," who "had been privileged in his youth to enjoy the friendly intercourse of his master Polycarp, who himself had conversed familiarly with S. John and others that had seen the Lord," had no text to which he could refer as authentic, and was forced to settle discordant readings, as scholars today settle them, that is, "to search out the best copies and exercise the judgment on their contents." (Scrivener, pp. 505-507; see *supra,* pp. 12 ff., for fuller discussion and citation.)

As to the two texts (אֹ and B) that were so strongly urged by their proponents as controlling texts on account of their age, it should be observed that their proponents affirm as to B (Vaticanus), that it is controlling because, as they theorized it out, B was the pre-Peshito text of which the Peshito text was a translation. The High or Sound Textualists scoffed at this claim, which they said utterly lacks all proof and rests only upon *ifs* and deductions. Prebendary Scrivener has this to say regarding the work of Westcott and Hort:

". . . barely the smallest vestige of historical evidence has ever been alleged in support of the views of these accomplished editors, their teaching must either be received as intuitively true, or *dismissed from our consideration as precarious, and even visionary.*" (Scrivener, p. 531; italics supplied by Burgon, p. iv; see also, Burgon, p. 264; and for the "fable of 'the *Syrian* text'", Burgon, p. 343; also pp. 296, 316, and 350, herein.)

NECESSITY FOR MORE INFORMATION

Having in mind the utter disappearance of the Sacred Autographs, the corruptions that crept into the surviving copies by the insertions and omissions made by heretics, by churchmen seeking to advance their own doctrines and interpretations, by copyists, etc., all of which sources of corruption were in full bloom for possibly two and a half centuries before א and B were written, then surely it requires more than *ifs* and *conjectures* (*infra, Note Twenty-nine*, p. 286) to justify the conclusion that these two texts (which are at best only copies of other texts) are copies of the true texts, out of the multitude of texts then in existence, most of them and probably all of them more or less corrupted, all just because they are the oldest vellum copies of other early texts yet undiscovered. The law of probability makes sport of such a conclusion. Surely there must be some proof, not merely somebody's guess or opinion that א or B or both, are descended (and the only ones descended) from the purest of the numerous earlier texts that existed in the fourth century. As one notes the character of the havoc which those two texts work upon vital portions of the Scriptures as contained in the Authorized Version (*infra, Note Twelve* and *Note Thirty-two*), portions that are basic to the Christian faith of the whole Christian Era, one can but wonder if there be not behind this movement of the Extreme Textualists a deliberate purpose and intent to destroy the Christian faith, as it has existed over the centuries. Their whole attitude towards Christian Scriptures is not without a strong color favoring such a suggestion. In view of all this uncertainty and doubt about the sacred text of the Bible and the accuracy thereof as we have it, we can see clearly the inspired wisdom of the Prophet Joseph when he said, "I believe the Bible as it read when it came from the pen of the original writers. Ignorant translators, careless transcribers, or designing and corrupt priests have committed many errors." (*DHC*, Vol. VI, p. 57.)

Item 2.   The Antiquity Argument as of the Present Date.

Summary. Kenyon discounts the authority given by Westcott and Hort to the manuscripts Vaticanus and Sinaiticus. The Prophet Joseph in his Inspired Version follows essentially in all vital matters the King James Version as against the Revised Versions (Westcott and Hort's text, essentially).

Since the foregoing was written, we have found confirmation of our views in the following statement of Kenyon, already partly quoted above:

KENYON'S VIEWS

"The general conclusion to which we seem to be led is that there is no royal road to the recovery of the original text of the New Testament. Fifty years ago it seemed as if Westcott and Hort had found such a road, and that we should depart from the Codex Vaticanus (except in the case of obvious scribal blunders) at our peril. The course both of discoveries and of critical study has made it increasingly difficult to believe that the Vaticanus and its allies represent a stream of tradition that has come down practically uncontaminated from the original sources. Based as they must have been on a multitude of different rolls, it would have been a singularly happy accident if all had been of the same character, and all deriving without contamination from the originals. The uniformity of character which on the whole marks the Vaticanus and Sinaiticus is better to be explained as the result of skilled editing of well-selected authorities on a definite principle. Therefore, while respecting the authority due to the age and character of this recension, we shall be disposed to give more consideration than Westcott and Hort did to other early readings which found a home in the Western, Syriac, or Cæsarean texts." (Kenyon, *The Story*, p. 143; see p. 94, herein.)

For our part, we feel assured that the Lord would not have permitted his children to go forward for seventeen or eighteen centuries and then have established his Church in the Last Dispensation upon a text (the Authorized Version) containing such vitally erroneous doctrines as the Extreme Textualists would now try to make us believe the Authorized Version contains. This conclusion becomes for us a demonstration when we consider that the Inspired Version, in all great essential differences between the Authorized and Revised Versions, follows the Authorized Version, not the Revised Version. Of course, if there is no such personage as our Lord and Savior, Jesus Christ, the Messiah that atoned for the sins of the world (as the Extreme Textualists seem to contemplate) but only a Jesus of Nazareth, a very wise man of exceptional psychic powers, then this argument has no value, and we have lost the Christian faith of nearly two millenniums. (For a development of this idea, see *supra*, pp. 53 ff.)

The Extreme Textualists of the Westcott-Hort era gave little if any value to any manuscript that had not a considerable antiquity, unless it supported their favorite text. As indicated above, their chief weapon against the Textus Receptus was that it was based on late manuscripts.

Item 3. Recognition that Later Manuscripts May Be Valuable.

Summary. In the controversies of the 1880's, the later manuscripts were generally discredited or ignored. The more modern critics give greater weight to them, even the Extreme Textualists adopting them when it suits their purpose. The dating of these later manuscripts is so uncertain as to make them largely valueless for critical purposes. The standing of Vaticanus (B) and Sinaiticus (א) is breaking down.

There has been a little yielding on this point of antiquity by the Extreme Textualists of this generation. For example, Kenyon, speaking of the *Bodleian Genesis* (tenth century), affirms: "In spite of its late date, its text is valuable." Again: "The dating of Greek minuscules is very dubious, and those who know most are apt to be the least confident about it; and when it is known, it is of little value for textual purposes." The *Codex Marchalianus* (sixth century) "is therefore a principal authority for the text of the Hexapla [Origen's polyglot] in the Prophets." In another place he says: "As a rule, the older the manuscript the greater the chances of its being correct, though this is a rule to which there are many exceptions." (Kenyon, *The Text*, pp. 51, 69, 53; *The Story*, p. 7.)

Thus the antiquity argument in favor of א B has lost much of its potency.

However, it is interesting to note with what tenacity the Extreme Textualists cling to their love for א B, and for still other manuscripts; and later manuscripts, seem still to be given a standing by them for critical purposes in proportion as they agree or disagree with these two manuscripts. But this reverence seems to be breaking down.

NOTE FOURTEEN ·
Manuscripts Underlying Our New Testament

Item 1. List of Some New Testament Greek Manuscripts that Critics Consider Important.

Summary. A list of the New Testament manuscripts that critics consider important, include those given in the text classified as indicated. They are (as already pointed out) papyri (written on papyrus) ; uncials (written on vellum) ; minuscules or cursives (written on vellum) ; and uncial and cursive penmanship. The periods when these various types of manuscripts were principally used are noted. The manner in which manuscripts are listed, and the different systems that have been used in such listing are given. The system of Gregory now generally in use is noted, and the way in which manuscripts are designated under this system. The Greek manuscripts of the New Testament are classified under three main heads: papyri, uncials, minuscules (cursives).

It is useful to have in mind some of the New Testament Greek manuscripts which seem to be considered by the critics as being most important.

They will be listed under the classifications which the critics apparently use: *Papyri* (written on papyrus) ; *Uncials* (written on vellum) ; and *Minuscules* or *Cursives* (also written on vellum). (See *supra, Note Eight*, pp. 86 ff., for a brief explanation of these record materials.)

A word may be added regarding uncials and minuscules or cursives. *Uncial* manuscripts are written all in large capitals, quite distinct, mostly separately formed, occasionally links between them, no punctuation nor sentence beginning or ending. The New Testament Greek manuscripts were written in uncials until the ninth century.

Uncial writing was then replaced by the *minuscule* or *cursive* style of writing, which shortly replaced the uncial style. It was a running script, said to be derived from a style of writing in use for non-literary purposes. This style continued until the invention of printing. The great mass of New Testament manuscripts which we now have, are written in this script. There are said to be about 212 *uncial* manuscripts of the New Testament now known, of which only some 60 are more than mere fragments; the *minuscules* number some 4,000. (Kenyon, *The Text*, pp. 36-38; *The Story*, pp. 26-27; *Our Bible*, pp. 14-15, 128.)

No attempt will be made to discuss these manuscripts. The study of them is the whole business of the critics. The problems involved are many and most difficult. The study of these problems requires a knowledge of the ancient dead languages which few only possess. We are not of the few.

The purpose of listing them is to enable a reader who comes to them in his reading to have at least a general idea of what his author is talking about.

As already noted (*Note Eight*), papyrus manuscripts are both on rolls and in codices. They cover the period prior to the introduction of the use of vellum. It is only during the last quarter of a century that the most important papyri have been discovered; these are codices. The most numerous are the Chester Beatty papyri. These were discovered (1931) "in Egypt (apparently in a cemetery or the ruins of a church in the neighbourhood of Aphroditopolis)." The papyri recovered are a part of eleven codices, "the earliest is of the first half of the second century, the latest not later than the fourth: most are of the third." This is said to be "the most important Biblical discovery since that of the Codex Sinaiticus, and has given us our earliest evidence of the text of the N.T." (Kenyon, *The Text*, pp. 39, 73; see also *id.* p. 193; see pp. 134-135, herein.)

Three other codices (vellum) are listed by Extreme Textualists as of the last importance: *Codex Sinaiticus* (discovered by Tischendorf, of early fourth century, now in Britain), *Codex Vaticanus* (in the Vatican Library, of early fourth century), and *Codex Alexandrinus* (in the British Museum, of the early fifth century).

Designations of Manuscripts

Before beginning our short listing of manuscripts, it will be useful very briefly to refer to the way in which manuscripts are designated for convenient reference.

Apparently our present cataloguing system goes back to J. J. Wetstein (a disciple of Bentley) in 1751-52. His system indicated the uncials by capital letters, and the minuscules by Arabic numerals. New Testament papyri were not then known. There were some refinements in his system unnecessary to note here.

About a century later, J. M. A. Scholz undertook an extension of the list, which had grown considerably. The Latin capitals had all been used, then the Greek capitals were added, and subsequently the Hebrew were used in a few cases.

Large additions were made to these lists in the nineteenth century. These were separately numbered by Scrivener in England and Gregory in Germany. It was finally agreed that Gregory should make and keep the official list. However, the manuscripts became so numerous that the system began to break down. The same symbol was used to designate different manuscripts, and the same manuscript was designated by different symbols.

The result was that H. von Soden in his critical edition of the New Testament (1902-13) introduced a new method of enumeration, said to be ingenious but "intolerably complicated." It undertook by enumerating symbols to indicate the date of each manuscript, by a very elaborate, complicated arrangement of the letters and numbers given to a manuscript; the manuscripts were divided into categories, and then the categories were divided; manuscripts with commentaries attached had a different numbering; and there were other cataloguing refinements.

GREGORY'S SYSTEM

To avoid the introduction of this new impractical system, Gregory consulted the principal students of textual criticism in Europe and America, and produced an amended form with the fewest possible changes, which followed the accepted form.

"The principles on which his list is formed are as follows: (1) Papyri are denoted by a P (preferably of 'antique' form, *P*) followed by a number; (2) Uncials are denoted by numbers in thick ('clarendon') type preceded by 0; but for the first forty-five of them their old designations by Latin or Greek capital letters are retained (Hebrew in the case of א only); this involves double designations in the case of eight letters only, D, E, F, G, H, K, L, P, the duplicates being distinguished as D_2 or D^{paul}, etc.; the long series of fragments previously grouped under the letters, O, T, W and Θ are abolished, thus setting free those letters for substantial MSS. recently discovered; (3) minuscule MSS. are indicated by Arabic numerals, as before, but in a continuous numeration, so that the designations of Gospel MSS. are unchanged, while those of the other groups follow on or fill accidental gaps. This system, which is easily intelligible and involves the minimum of change in familiar

symbols, has been generally accepted, and is used in the following list, the numbers of von Soden being added for the benefit
of those who wish to refer to his edition. Gregory's list was
continued after his death by von Dobschutz, and the addition
of newly discovered MSS. is now in the hands of Dr. H.
Lietzmann." (Kenyon, *The Text,* ed. 1936, pp. 70-71.)

The Greek manuscripts (New Testament) are classified under three main heads, *Papyri, Uncials,* and *Minuscules.* A fourth class may be added, the *Lectionaries,*
"manuscripts (generally of late date) in which the Bible
text is arranged for ritual use in the service of the
Church." (*The Text,* p. 66.)

We may list the following manuscripts:

Item 2.   The Papyri.

Summary. Contains a list of important papyri manuscripts (9 manuscripts).

P^5. (Sod. ε 02). *British Museum Pap. 782.* 3rd century. First discovered example of "single-quire form of
papyrus codex .... Its text agrees generally with that of
א." Fragment of the Gospel of John. (Kenyon, *The
Text,* p. 71.)

P^{13}. (Sod. α 1034). *British Museum Pap. 1532.* Late
3rd or 4th century. Fragment of Hebrews. Contains
parts lacking in B. (*The Text,* pp. 71-72.)

P^{15-30}. Papyri fragments from Oxyrhynchus; unimportant. (*The Text,* p. 72.)

P^{38}. *Michigan Pap. 1571.* Contains Acts with mutilations. Probably 4th century. "(Sanders dates it early
3rd, Hunt and Schubart early 4th, Wilcken 4th or 5th).
The text is substantially that of Codex Bezae (D)." The
text shows wide divergence from א B type and from type
eventually appearing in the Received Text,—Authorized

Version. Shows such a text was in existence in Egypt at the early date of early 3rd to 4th or 5th centuries. (*The Text*, pp. 72, 90.)

CHESTER BEATTY MANUSCRIPTS

P[45]. *Chester Beatty Pap. I.* Portions of 30 leaves of a codex originally containing all four Gospels and Acts. Early 3rd century. As already stated, Kenyon, who edited the Chester Beatty Papyri, considers these papyri, with **P**[46] and **P**[47], "the most important Biblical discovery since that of the Codex Sinaiticus, and has given us our earliest evidence of the text of the N.T." (*The Text*, pp. 72-73; see pp. 131-132, herein.)

P[46]. *Chester Beatty Pap. II.* Eighty-six leaves, slightly mutilated. Thirty of the leaves in the University of Michigan. Early 3rd century. Contains all general Epistles of Paul; the Pastoral Epistles were apparently never included. There were ten leaves in the original acquisition by Beatty; the University of Michigan subsequently obtained 30 more leaves. Kenyon edited them all. "In general, the readings of the papyrus agree more with the Alexandrian group represented by ℵ A B than with the Western group represented by D F G, though (especially in Romans) there are a noticeable number of agreements with the latter." (*The Text*, pp. 73-74.)

P[47]. *Chester Beatty Pap. III.* Ten leaves of codex of Revelation. 3rd century. Text agrees more with four earliest manuscripts (ℵ A C P) than with group headed by 046 or than with mass of later manuscripts. (*The Text*, p. 74.)

P[48]. *Papyrus 1165* of the Societa Italiana, Florence. 3rd century. Fragment containing parts of Acts. Text definitely of Codex Bezae type. Valuable because D is deficient in this part of Acts. Another early witness for Bezae. (*The Text*, pp. 74-75.)

P[52]. *Papyrus Ryl. Gk. 457.* John Rylands Library at Manchester. Early 2nd century. Small fragment ($3\frac{1}{2}$ by $2\frac{1}{2}$ inches), containing John 18:31-33, 37-38, written on both sides of the sheet, *recto* and *verso*. The oldest of all the manuscripts so far discovered, "by at least fifty years." Bruce quotes Dr. H. Guppy (Rylands Librarian) as saying it was "written 'when the ink of the original autograph can hardly have been dry.'" Kenyon notes its importance as "proof of the early circulation of the Fourth Gospel." Found in Egypt. (Kenyon, *The Text*, p. 75; *Our Bible*, pp. 126, 128; Bruce, p. 172.)

Item 3. The Uncials.

Summary. Contains a list of important uncial manuscripts (29 manuscripts).

CODEX SINAITICUS

א. *Codex Sinaiticus.* (Sod. δ 2). Vellum. Now in British Museum. Early 4th century. Could not have been earlier than the second quarter of the 4th century, "hardly be much earlier than A.D. 340." (Kenyon, *The Text*, pp. 75-82; *Our Bible*, p. 131.) One of the two oldest known vellum manuscripts. Discovered by Tischendorf in a monastery (St. Catherine) at the foot of Mt. Sinai. (For account of its discovery, see *infra Note Twenty-one, Item 3*; pp. 235 ff.; for account of its acquisition by British Museum, see Kenyon, *Our Bible*, pp. 130-31, quoted *infra* p. 237.) According to Tischendorf (the discoverer) and Lake (who edited it), four scribes were employed in the preparation of the codex.

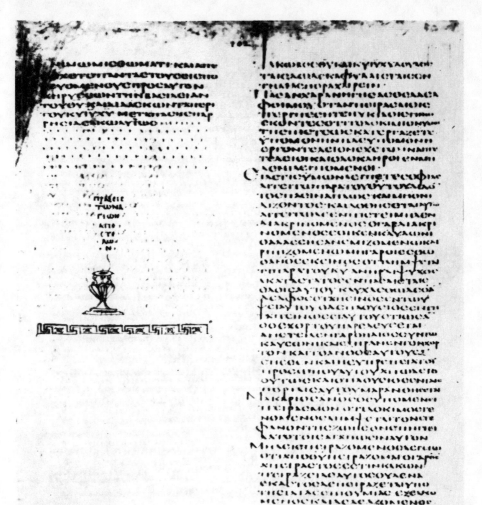

Courtesy, University of Chicago Library

James 1:1-15

A—CODEX ALEXANDRINUS

Greek vellum. Uncial. Early 5th century. Presented to James I of England by Patriarch of Alexandria through British Ambassador to Constantinople. Origin unknown, but "everything points to Egypt." Tradition says written by a noble lady of Egypt named Thecla. "Beyond all doubt, disfigured by the fewest blemishes of any" of ancient manuscripts. In British Museum. See p. 138, herein.

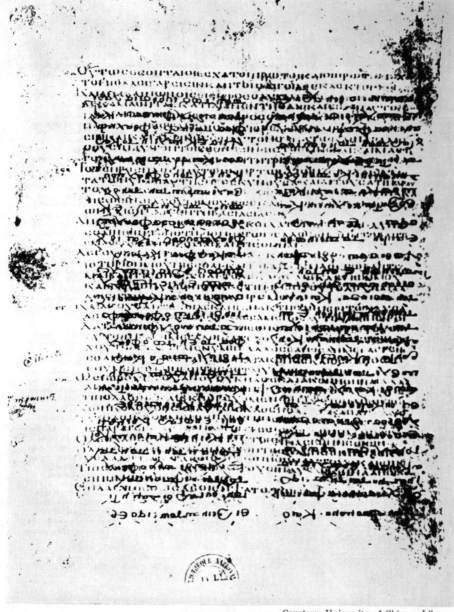

Matt. 20:16-34

C—CODEX EPHRAEMI

Greek vellum. Uncial. 5th century. Palimpsest (original writing washed off and then written over with another text); so made in 12th century. Originally one column containing both Testaments; rewritten in two columns containing works of Ephraim Syrus. Origin unknown. In 16th century belonged to Medici family; brought to France by Catherine de Medici. In Bibliotheque Nationale, Paris. See p. 140, herein.

"Several correctors have also been at work on it, some contemporary (or identical) with the original scribes, and others
later. By far the most important of the corrections are those
made by a group of scholars (denoted by the symbol $\aleph^{ca}$ or
$\aleph^{cb}$), one of whom wrote notes at the end of Esdras and
Esther, stating that the MS. was collated with an exceedingly
early copy corrected by the hand of the martyr Pamphilus, with
an autograph note by him saying that he corrected it in prison
from Origen's own copy of the Hexapla. This note is probably
of the sixth or early seventh century, and makes it extremely
probable that the MS. was then at Cæsarea, where the library
of Pamphilus was, and also that the corrections in these hands
were taken from a very early MS. which itself was only by one
step removed from Origen. This gives exceptional value to this
group of corrections. In general $\aleph$ has the same type of text
as B, but according to Ropes it is superior in the Prophets and
in Chronicles and 2 Esdras. In Tobit it has a different recension." (Kenyon, *The Text*, pp. 47-48; see *id.*, 80-81.)

"Preponderance of opinion" favors Egypt as place
of origin, and if Egypt, then in Alexandria. Sinaiticus
has "kinship" in text with Vaticanus, the two "form the
head and main substance of a group which in the opinion
of many presents the most authentic text of the N.T.
Substantially it is the text represented in our Revised
Version." (*The Text*, p. 81; see p. 217, *infra.*)

Scrivener's appraisal of the text is not so favorable.
He says:

"With regard to the deeply interesting question as to the
critical character of Cod. $\aleph$, although it strongly supports the
Codex Vaticanus in many characteristic readings, yet it cannot
be said to give its exclusive adherence to any of the witnesses
hitherto examined. It so lends its grave authority, now to one
and now to another, as to convince us more than ever of the
futility of seeking to derive the genuine text of the New Testament from any one copy, however ancient and, on the whole,
trustworthy." (Scrivener, p. 93; the 4th ed. adds the following
clause: ". . . when evidence of a wide and varied character is at
hand" (Scrivener-Miller, Vol. I, p. 97); and see p. 220, *infra.*)

CODEX ALEXANDRINUS

A. *Codex Alexandrinus*. (Sod. δ 4). Vellum. British Museum (Royal MS. D.v-viii). Early 5th century. Contains both Testaments "nearly complete"; some lost by mutilation. Five scribes were employed; three took part in New Testament; a fourth the Old Testament. Several correctors have been over the manuscripts,—the original scribes (A¹), and also Aᵃ, "who is nearly contemporary with the MS." Origin—"everything points to Egypt." Tradition says written by Thecla, a noble lady of Egypt, about A.D. 325, but date is too early. (Kenyon, *The Text*, pp. 82-84.)

"In the N.T. it is Alexandrian (*i.e.*, akin to א B) except in the Gospels, where it shows signs of the Antiochian revision which eventually produced the received ecclesiastical text [Textus Receptus]." (*The Text*, p. 84.)

Scrivener says:

"The Codex Alexandrinus has been judged to be carelessly written; many errors of transcription no doubt exist, but not more than in other copies of the highest value (e.g. Cod. א, and possibly even Cod. B)." (Scrivener, p. 100; in the 4th ed., the last clause reads: "many errors of transcription no doubt exist, but not so many as in some copies (e.g. Cod. א), nor more than in others (as Cod. B)." Scrivener-Miller, Vol. I, p. 104.)

Burgon says, comparing Codices א and B and C, "our own A being, beyond all doubt, disfigured by the fewest blemishes of any." (Burgon, p. 14.)

Kenyon continues:

"Its modern history begins with Cyril Lucar, who was Patriarch of Alexandria before being translated to Constantinople in 1621. He offered it to the British Ambassador, Sir Thomas Roe, as a gift to James I; but by the time it reached England in 1627 Charles I was on the throne, and the binding which it then received bears the initials C. R. In 1757 it passed with the rest of the Royal Library to the newly founded British Museum." (Kenyon, *The Text*, p. 84.)

CODEX VATICANUS

B. *Codex Vaticanus*. (Sod. δ 1). Vatican Library, Rome (Vat. gr. 1209). Vellum. Early 4th century (first half). Contains both Testaments, but in the New Testament nothing remains after Hebrews 9:14. A later scribe has gone over the manuscript, spoiling appearance. Seemingly two scribes for Old Testament, one for New Testament, and two correctors, "one (B^2) about contemporary." Place of origin, Hort thought Rome, others southern Italy or Caesarea, but Kenyon thinks Egypt and Alexandria. Said to have been first of great uncials to reach Europe, but "last to become fully known." Apparently manuscript was in the Vatican, possibly 1475 A.D., certainly in 1481 A.D. Collations were made in 1669, 1720, and 1780, but not published. Napoleon took it to Paris, but it was returned to Italy. Access to it was denied to foreign scholars. Tischendorf gained access to it in 1866, published an edition in 1867. The New Testament was finally published 1868. (Kenyon, *The Text*, pp. 85-87.)

This manuscript was the foundation of Westcott and Hort's text, which was the basis, along with ℵ, of the Revised Version (British 1880's, American 1900-1901) of which the Revised Standard Version of 1946 (American) is merely a recension.

This text (B) will be of the principal matters hereinafter considered in these *Notes*.

Scrivener has considerable to say about this text, both on its own account and in comparison with ℵ. (See Scrivener, pp. 101 ff., 527 ff.) One comment is worth repeating here (though quoted later):

"One marked feature, characteristic of this copy, is the great number of its omissions, which has induced Dr. Dobbin to speak of it as presenting 'an abbreviated text of the New Testament:' and certainly the facts he states on this point are startling enough. He calculates that Codex B leaves out words or whole clauses no less than 330 times in Matthew, 365 in Mark, 439 in Luke, 357 in John, 384 in the Acts, 681 in the surviving Epistles; or 2556 times in all." (Scrivener, p. 116.)

Dr. Hort belittles the significance of these omissions which he affirms are found in other good documents. (Scrivener, p. 116, n. 1.)

B$_2$. *Codex Vaticanus 2066.* "The great Codex Vaticanus being deficient in the Apocalypse, the letter B was formerly assigned in that book to another Vatican MS. Since, however, this MS. is of quite different date and character, it is better to avoid confusion. It is described below as 046." Vellum. (Kenyon, *The Text*, p. 88.)

CODEX EPHRAEMI

C. *Codex Ephraemi.* (Sod. δ 3). Vellum. Bibliotheque Nationale, Paris. 5th century. Converted into a palimpsest in twelfth century, the original Testaments (both) being washed off and some works of Ephraim Syrus written over it. Many leaves thrown away; the remaining portions very incomplete. Text of mixed character, "is therefore a witness to the variety of texts which were in circulation in the early centuries." Belonged in the sixteenth century to the Medici family; was brought to France by Catherine de Medici. "Every book of the New Testament is represented except 2 Thess. and 2 John, but none is perfect." (*The Text*, pp. 88-89.)

Saying this Codex is of "first-rate importance," Scrivener gives a full list of the passages it contains, "that it may not be cited *e silentio* for what it does not exhibit." (Scrivener, p. 117, n. 2.)

Codex Bezae

D. *Codex Bezae.* (Sod. δ 5). Vellum. University Library at Cambridge (England). Contains Gospels, Acts, with small fragments of Catholic Epistles (James, Peter, John) in Greek and Latin. Probably 5th century, but difficult to date. Presented to University by great Reformation scholar, Theodore Beza, in 1581. Some passages in Matthew, John, Acts, lost by mutilation. Catholic Epistles all lost but the Latin text of 3 John 11-15. Place of origin doubtful; one critic (Clark) urged Egypt, but Kenyon doubts this, but says Northern Africa is possible. Sicily is advocated by some; Sardinia also mentioned. But evidence insufficient to decide question. The text has wide divergences, both from the Alexandrian type headed by א B and from the Textus Receptus. (*The Text*, pp. 89-90.)

Scrivener considers it has a "Western origin." (For a description of the codex, see Scrivener, pp. 120 ff., 123.)

Kenyon says:

"In Acts the variations are so numerous that it is necessary to recognize drastic editorial action, either by the editor of the D-text in additions and variations, as generally held, or by the editor of the א B-text in excisions, as maintained by Prof. A. C. Clark in his recent edition of the book." (*The Text*, p. 92.)

Examples of such editorial action are then given. (*The Text*, pp. 92-94.)

The manuscript has been corrected by many hands; Scrivener said nine (Scrivener, p. 125), but his descriptions and datings are said to be "untrustworthy." The "most active" is D^g, held to be contemporary with the manuscript. (*The Text*, p. 94.)

It is disputed whether the Greek of D is a recension of the Greek Gospel and Acts, "or is the result of retro-

active influences from versions in other tongues." Some
critics say the Greek is the main text, and that the Latin
has been influenced by it; other critics take the opposite
view. The latest editor (Prof. Clark) considers the Latin is a "servile translation" of the Greek and of little
value. (*The Text*, pp. 94-95; Scrivener, p. 126.)

Some have held the text is descended "from a bilingual Graeco-Syriac MS., probably produced at Antioch."
(*The Text*, p. 95.)

". . . It is of course possible that the D text, in the course
of its ancestry, has been subject to influences of all these various
kinds, Greek, Latin and Syriac; and this possibility, while it
hardly affects the problem of the larger variants, throws some
doubt on the value of the MS. in respect of verbal variations."
(*The Text*, p. 95.)

Scrivener quotes approvingly Davidson's comment:

"Its singularly corrupt text, in connexion with its great
antiquity, is a curious problem, which cannot easily be solved."
(Scrivener, p. 126; for further comments on this point, see
Scrivener-Miller, Vol. I, p. 130.)

It is unnecessary to trace its history more than to say
that Beza is said to have discovered it in the monastery
of St. Irenaeus in 1562. It had been previously collated
by someone for Robert Stephanus, who used it in his 1550
edition.

"It has been elaborately studied by Scrivener, Rendel Harris,
Chase, Weiss, Ropes and Clark, and has held a foremost place
in textual discussion since the time of Westcott and Hort."
(*The Text*, p. 96; see Scrivener, pp. 120 ff.)

It is suggested that the Codex D was taken to the
Council of Trent in 1546 "to confirm the Latin reading in
John xxi. 22, 'sic eum volo,' which D alone may seem to
do." (Scrivener, p. 122, n. 2.)

This manuscript will frequently be noted hereinafter.

(See for its use in making the Received Text, Kenyon, *The Story*, p. 46.)

D$_2$. *Codex Claromontanus.* (Sod. α 1026). Vellum. Bibliotheque Nationale in Paris. 6th century. Pauline Epistles in Greek and Latin, Greek on left-hand pages. Written probably in Italy; possibly in Sardinia. The Latin, which is independent of the Greek text, "is generally a good example of the Old Latin version." (*The Text*, pp. 96-97; Scrivener, p. 163.)

OTHER CODICES

E. *Codex Basiliensis.* (Sod. ε 55). Vellum. In library of University of Basle. 8th century. "Of no great value." (*The Text*, p. 97.)

However, Scrivener's estimate is different. He says: "This copy is one of the most notable of the second-rate uncials." (Scrivener, p. 127; the 4th ed. substitutes *later* for *second-rate*, Scrivener-Miller, Vol. I, p. 131.)

He closes his discussion:

"The value of this codex, as supplying materials for criticism, is considerable. It approaches more nearly than some others of its date to the text now commonly received, and is an excellent witness for it." (Scrivener, pp. 127-128.)

Perhaps this is the reason for Kenyon's slighting remark.

E$_2$. *Codex Laudianus.* (Sod. α 1001). Vellum. In the Bodleian Library (University of Oxford). Probably 7th century. In Latin and Greek, the latter akin to D. Is "earliest MS. that contains the eunuch's confession of faith." (Acts 8:37.) Possibly written in Sardinia. Used by Bede. (*The Text*, pp. 97-98; Scrivener, p. 159.)

E$_3$. *Codex Sangermanensis.* (Sod. α 1027). Vellum. In Leningrad. 9th or 10th century. Copy of D$_2$ "made later than the fifth corrector of that MS." (*The Text*, p. 98; Scrivener, p. 166, "Greek-Latin Manuscript.")

F_2. *Codex Augiensis.* (Sod. α 1029). Vellum. 9th century. In Trinity College, Cambridge. Came from abbey of Reichenau; possibly written there. Contains Pauline Epistles, lacking part of Romans. Belongs to same group as D_2. (*The Text*, p. 98; Scrivener, p. 167, "Greek-Latin Manuscript.")

G_3. *Codex Boernerianus.* (Sod. α 1028). Vellum. In National Library at Dresden. 9th century. Contains Pauline Epistles, with Latin interlinear text. Closely akin to F_2. Both may be copies of same original. Originally part of same manuscript as Δ (Codex Sangallensis) of the Gospels; possibly written at St. Gall where Codex Sangallensis now is. (*The Text*, p. 98; Scrivener, p. 169.)

H_3. *Codex Coislinianus 202.* (Sod. α 1022). Vellum. 6th century. 41 leaves of Pauline Epistles; 8 in monastery of the Laura on Mt. Athos (whole manuscript once there), 22 in Paris, 3 in Leningrad, 3 at Moscow, 3 at Kieff, and 2 at Turin. Contains scattered portions of Epistles, ending with Titus, where a note is appended saying:

". . . that it was corrected from the copy in the library of Cæsarea, written by the holy Pamphilus. It contains the colometrical edition of the Epistles prepared in the 4th century by Euthalius of Sulca, who was also the author of a division of the Acts and Catholic Epistles into sections, which is probably the basis of the later section-numeration found in B. The text is therefore of some importance." (*The Text*, pp. 98-99; Scrivener, p. 172.)

I. *Codex Washingtonianus II.* (Sod. α 1041). Vellum. In Freer Museum at Washington. Probably 7th century. Manuscript much mutilated, with fragments of all Pauline Epistles except Romans. "The text is strongly Alexandrian in character, and agrees with א and A more than with B." (*The Text*, p. 99.)

K. *Codex Cyprius*. (Sod. ε 71). Vellum. In Bibliotheque Nationale, Paris. 9th century. "A complete copy of the Gospels, and a typical representative of the normal ecclesiastical or Byzantine text." (*The Text*, p. 99; Scrivener, p. 132.)

L. *Codex Regius*. (Sod. ε 56). Vellum. In Bibliotheque Nationale, Paris. 8th century. Contains Gospels, in text "which has largely escaped the Byzantine revision." Often agrees with B. Forms part of Alexandrian group.

"It is remarkable as containing both the shorter ending of Mk. referred to in the margin of the R.V. and then the ordinary last twelve verses, with a note prefixed to each saying that it is found in some copies." (*The Text*, pp. 99-100.)

Scrivener says:

"It is but carelessly written, and abounds with errors of the ignorant scribe, who was more probably an Egyptian than a native Greek." (Scrivener, p. 133.)

N. *Codex Purpureus Petropolitanus*. (Sod. ε 19). Written in silver on purple vellum. 182 leaves at Leningrad, 33 leaves at Patmos, 6 in the Vatican, 4 in the British Museum, 2 in Vienna, and 1 in Genoa, in all 228 leaves out of a probable 462. 6th century. Contains portions of all four Gospels. Probably from Constantinople. Probably divided up by Crusaders. Most of surviving portions acquired by Russian Government in 1896 from Sarumsahly (Caesarea in Cappadocia). Text of Byzantine type "in a rather early stage of its evolution." (*The Text*, p. 100.)

Scrivener says: "It exhibits strong Alexandrian forms." (Scrivener, p. 136.)

O. *Codex Sinopensis*. (Sod. ε 21). In Bibliotheque Nationale, Paris. 6th century. 43 leaves of St. Matthew (mainly 13-24). Written in letters of gold on purple vellum. Close akin to N and Σ (Codex Rossanensis). (*The Text*, p. 100.)

Under "O", Scrivener lists several small fragments. (Scrivener, p. 137.)

P₂. *Codex Porphyrianus*. (Sod. α 3). Vellum. Leningrad. 9th century. Palimpsest. Contains Acts, Epistles, and Apocalypse. "Valuable as one of the few uncial MSS. of the latter book." Text grouped with earlier uncials א A C. (*The Text*, p. 100.)

R. *Codex Nitriensis*. (Sod. ε 22). Vellum. In British Museum. 6th century. Palimpsest of Luke. Imperfect, about half preserved. Is aligned with א B family. (*The Text*, pp. 100-01; Scrivener, p. 139.)

T. *Codex Borgianus*. (Sod. ε 5). Vellum. In library of the Propaganda at Rome. 5th century. 17 leaves from John and Luke, Greek and Sahidic on opposite pages. Text closely associated with א B. (*The Text*, p. 101; Scrivener, pp. 141 ff., where several other manuscripts bearing a T, sub-numbered, are discussed.)

W. *Codex Washingtonianus I*. (Sod. ε 014). Vellum. In Freer Museum at Washington. Late 4th or 5th century. Gospels in Western order (Matthew, John, Luke, Mark). Text of varied character, part Byzantine, part Alexandrian, part akin to Old Latin version, part Caesarean. "Remarkable" addition to end of Mark (see *The Text*, p. 101, for Greek text thereof). With Old Testament manuscripts, acquired by Mr. Freer in Egypt in 1906. (*The Text*, pp. 101-102; see also *id*. pp. 54-55.)

Z. *Codex Dublinensis*. (Sod. ε 26). Vellum. Trinity College, Dublin. 6th century. Palimpsest. Contains 295 verses of Matthew. Large uncials of Egyptian type, and Egyptian text. Many agreements with ℵ. (*The Text*, p. 102.)

Scrivener says:

"In regard to the text, it agrees much with Codd. ℵBD: with Cod. A it has only 23 verses in common: yet in them A and Z vary 14 times. Mr. Abbott adds that while ℵBZ stand together 10 times against other uncials, BZ are never alone, but ℵZ against B often. It is freer than either of them from transcriptural errors. Codd. ℵBCZ combine less often than ℵBDZ. On examining Cod. Z throughout 26 pages, he finds it alone 13 times, differing from ℵ 30 times, from B 44 times, from Stephen's text 95 times. Thus it approaches nearer to ℵ than to B." (Scrivener, p. 149.)

Δ. *Codex Sangallensis*. (Sod. ε 76). Vellum. At St. Gall. Probably 9th century. Graeco-Latin copy of Gospels. Latin interlined with Greek. Matthew, Luke, John text "is ordinary," Mark is Alexandrian type. Little value. (*The Text*, p. 102; Scrivener, p. 150.)

Θ. *Codex Koridethianus*. (Sod. ε 050). Vellum. At Tiflis. 9th century. Contains Gospels. Scribe poorly acquainted with Greek. Interesting text. Belongs to Caesarean family. Other than Mark, text is in close conformity with the Received Text. (*The Text*, pp. 102-03.)

Λ. *Codex Tischendorfianus III*. (Sod. ε 77). Vellum. In the Bodleian. 9th century. Contains Luke and John. Along with 12 minuscules, it has a subscription affirming its text was derived "from the ancient copies at Jerusalem." (*The Text*, p. 103; Scrivener, p. 154.)

Ξ. *Codex Zacynthius*. (Sod. A¹). Vellum. In library of the British and Foreign Bible Society. 8th century. Palimpsest. Contains most of Luke, with marginal commentary. Text related to B. Same section division as B and text akin. (*The Text*, p. 103.)

As to the relation between Ξ and the Received Text, Scrivener says:

"The character of the variations of Cod. Ξ from the Received text may be judged of by the estimate made by some scholar, that 47 of them are transpositions in the order of the words, 201 are substitutions of one word for another, 118 are omissions, while the additions do not exceed 24 (Christian Remembrancer, Jan. 1862)." (Scrivener, pp. 156-157.)

Σ. *Codex Rossanensis.* (Sod. ε 18). Silver letters on purple vellum. At Rossano in Calabria. 6th century. Contains Matthew and Mark. Sister manuscript of N (*supra*). (*The Text*, p. 103.)

Φ. *Codex Beratinus.* (Sod. ε 17). Silver letters on purple vellum. At Berat, Albania. 6th century. Forms part of group of N, O, and Σ. Byzantine text in early stage. "Remarkable" for long insertion in Matthew 20:28, also found in D. (*The Text*, p. 103.)

Ψ. *Codex Laurensis.* (Sod. δ 6). Vellum. In monastery of the Laura on Mount Athos. 8th or 9th century. Contains Gospels from Mark 9 onwards, Acts, and Epistles. Agrees with L in inserting short ending before long one in Mark, which has a non-Byzantine character, but with readings characteristic of ℵ B and D type. (*The Text*, pp. 103-04.)

046. *Codex Vaticanus 2066.* (Sod. α 1070). In Vatican Library. 8th century. Contains Apocalypse, which heads group of about 40 minuscules, with a recension of text different from early uncials and later ecclesiastical text. (*The Text*, p. 104.)

Item 4.   The Minuscules or Cursives.

Summary. Contains a list of important minuscule (cursive) manuscripts—very few (12) are noted.

Kenyon introduces his listing of the minuscules with this paragraph:

"The latest catalogue of minuscule manuscripts reaches a total of 2,401. Only a small minority of these contain the complete New Testament. Manuscripts of the four Gospels are by far the most numerous; others contain either the Acts and Catholic Epistles, or the Pauline Epistles, or the Apocalypse, or some combination of these. . . . An overwhelming majority contain the common ecclesiastical text, which, originating in a revision which seems to have begun in Syria at the end of the fourth century, was generally adopted throughout the Church, and is known as the Byzantine or Received Text. The object of textual criticism is to get behind this revision, and to ascertain the text of the earliest centuries. It is therefore interested mainly in those MSS. which, of whatever date, appear to have in some degree escaped this revision and to preserve some evidences of earlier texts. It is with these, or with some of these, that the following brief list is concerned." (*The Text*, pp. 104-05.)

The last two sentences of the above give the key to the whole Extreme Textualist theory and treatment of the manuscripts of the New Testament: rule out or discredit all manuscripts that do not support their theory and note and magnify all those that do. This is not the technique of the true scientist, and "higher criticism" seems to aspire to that status.

Of the considerable number of *minuscules* mentioned by Kenyon, we shall note a very few.

1. (Sod. δ 254). At Basle. 12th century. Erasmus used this with others in preparing the first printed Greek Testament. Kenyon says, "If he had made it his chief authority for the Gospels, the text of our ordinary Bibles would have been very different from what it is; but in

fact he followed mainly another Basle MS., 2, which contains the ordinary Byzantine text." This manuscript is said to belong to the Caesarean text. Is part of Family 1. (*The Text*, p. 105.)

2. (Sod. ε 1214). At Basle. 15th century. "Only notable as having been Erasmus' principal authority in the Gospels." (*The Text*, p. 105.)

13. (Sod. ε 368). At Paris. 12th century. Belongs to Ferrar group or Family 13, and is considered as forming part of the Caesarean group. (*The Text*, pp. 105-06.)

33. (Sod. δ 48). At Paris. 9th century. "Considered by Eichhorn and Hort to be the best of all the minuscules of the Gospels, its text being of the same type as that of B." (*The Text*, p. 106.)

[It is interesting to note, first, that in the 9th century, the B text was thus in some circulation, so was not unknown. This means, apparently, that the Church— East and West—could have a choice of the text it wished and thought best, B or Byzantine, and with this choice available, the Church took the Byzantine. See below, manuscript 157.]

61. (Sod. ε 603). At Dublin. 15th or 16th century. Of importance historically because containing I John 5:7-8 (the Three Heavenly Witnesses) which Erasmus omitted in his first New Testament, but promised to insert if a Greek text was produced that contained it. This manuscript being produced, he inserted the passages in his third edition. Manuscript 629 also has the passage. (*The Text*, p. 106.)

81. (Sod. α 162). At British Museum. Contains best text of Acts of all minuscules, ranking with leading uncials. (*The Text*, p. 106.)

157. (Sod. ε 207). "Specially mentioned by Hort, as in the same class as 33." (*The Text*, p. 107; and see *supra* 33 and comment.)

346. (Sod. ε 226). At Milan. 12th century. Family 13. Only Greek manuscript which in Matt. 1:16 has the same reading as the Curetonian Manuscript of the Old Syriac (see *supra*). (*The Text*, p. 107.)

383. (Sod. α 353). At Oxford. 13th century. Contains many readings of Codex Bezae (see *supra*) in Acts 13-22. (*The Text*, p. 107.)

565. (Sod. ε 93). Leningrad. 9th-10th century. Has gold letters on purple vellum with colophon (inscription at end of book) stating it was copied and corrected from manuscripts from Jerusalem. "Good text with ancient readings, and in Mark is akin to the Caesarean type." (*The Text*, p. 107.)

579. (Sod. ε 376). At Paris. 13th century. Double ending to Mark as in L (*supra*). (*The Text*, p. 107.)

614. (Sod. α 364). At Milan. 11th century. Manuscript of Acts and Paul of Codex Bezae type, "and useful for the end of Acts, where D is deficient." (*The Text*, p. 107.)

Item 5. The Lectionaries.

Summary. Contains some important Lectionaries (a book or table of lessons used in a church service, of which there are some 1609 manuscripts). Scrivener has discussed these and classified them in considerable detail.

Lectionaries (a book or table of lessons used in a church service). Concerning these Kenyon makes the following observations:

"There remain only the Lectionaries, of which the latest catalogue enumerates 1609. These have an importance of their

own in connection with liturgical history and also with the history
of the text during the Middle Ages. In general, they give only
the ordinary ecclesiastical type of text, but a recent study by
E. C. Colwell and D. W. Riddle has shown that the lections
from Mark include a high proportion of readings of the ℵ B,
and not a few of the Codex Bezae type. . . . It seems clear that
there was a definite lectionary text, since a comparison of lectionaries shows a high level of uniformity; but it is also clear
that different parts of it were compiled at different times or
from different sources. Thus the lections from Mark for Satur-
day and Sunday do not show anything like the same high proportion of ℵ B readings as the lections for the other days of
the week; and the lections from the other Gospels are generally
of the Received Text type. This is in accordance with a phenomenon observed elsewhere, and to which reference will be
made again, that the text of Mark has much more often escaped
the Byzantine revision than that of the other Gospels, which
were more popular and in more general use." (*The Text*, pp.
108-09.)

SCRIVENER'S COMMENTS AND LISTS

As we have already quoted (see pp. 88-89, herein),
Scrivener, in Chapter II of his *Plain Introduction*,
devotes Section II thereof to a "Description of the Uncial
Manuscripts of the Greek Testament," Section III, "On
the Cursive Manuscripts of the Greek Testament," Section IV, "On the Lectionaries, or Manuscript Service-
books of the Greek Church." These three Sections cover
some 220 pages, most of it in 10-point print.

Section II is divided into:

"Manuscripts of the Gospels," (pp. 87-159),
"Manuscripts of the Acts and Catholic Epistles," (pp.
159-162),
"Manuscripts of the Pauline Epistles," (pp. 162-175),
"Manuscripts of the Apocalypse," (pp. 175-177).

Section III is divided into:

"Manuscripts of the Gospels," (pp. 179-246),

"Manuscripts of the Acts and Catholic Epistles," (pp. 246-264),
"Manuscripts of St. Paul's Epistles," (pp. 264-273),
"Manuscripts of the Apocalypse," (pp. 273-278).

Section IV is divided into:

"Evangelistaria or Evangeliaria, containing Lessons from the Gospels," (pp. 280-301),
"Lectionaries containing the Apostolos or Praxapostolos," (pp. 301-307).

Dr. Scrivener begins his Section III (*Cursive Manuscripts*) by noting that they were written from the tenth down to the fifteenth century, that they are too numerous to be "minutely described" in a work such as he is writing, and that he will describe the few he mentions "with all possible brevity, dwelling only on a few which present points of especial interest." He notes the importance of the lectionaries of the Greek Church and comments upon the way in which they may be of service. (Scrivener, pp. 178, 279.)

He closes his listings and discussions of this voluminous material with this paragraph, which gives an idea of the immensity of this field of investigation:

"The total number of manuscripts we have recorded in the preceding catalogues are 61 uncial and 642 cursive of the Gospels; 14 uncial and 252 cursive of the Acts and Catholic Epistles; 22 uncial and 295 cursive of S. Paul; 5 uncial and 111 cursive of the Apocalypse; 339 Evangelistaria; and 82 Lectionaries of the Praxapostolos. In calculating this total of 1817 manuscripts we have deducted 78 duplicates, and must bear in mind that a few of the codices, whose present locality is unknown, may have reappeared under other heads." (Scrivener, p. 307; see p. 89, herein.)

The fourth edition (Scrivener-Miller, Vol. I, p. 377), gives the following tabulation:

UNCIALS:—

Evangelia 71
Acts and Catholic Epistles 19
St. Paul's Epistles 27
Apocalypse 7

    Total 124

CURSIVES:—

Evangelia 1321
Acts and Catholic Epistles 420
St. Paul's Epistles 491
Apocalypse 184
Evangelistaria 963
Apostolos 288

    Total 3667

    Grand Total 3791

Some of the manuscripts of various sorts listed by Kenyon have been discovered since Scrivener wrote his book

NOTE FIFTEEN •
Versions and Fathers

Summary. Herein discussed are the various versions and writings of the Fathers. It should be in mind always that Protestant scholars seem generally to consider that the original records, the Sacred Autographs, were written in Greek. A version is a translation of the Greek text into some other language. The early spread of the teachings of Jesus is noted. Kenyon's views given as to needs for earliest versions.

It must be remembered that all the authorities herein cited and used proceed on the theory that the New Testament was originally written in Greek, and that every text in any other language is mediately or immediately a translation of the Greek text, that is, a *version*. (See *Note Six* above for suggestions that the original Sacred Autographs—that is, the original records of the Savior's mission and teachings, could have been in some form of Aramaic.)

It is pointed out by the scholars that the Gospel message was carried outward fanlike from Palestine, being first preached in the East, "in the languages of those countries which lay nearest to Judaea." But almost at the same time, it spread to other regions. It is said the New Testament was translated into Syriac and Latin by about 150 A.D., and into Egyptian somewhere near 200 A.D. (Kenyon, *Our Bible*, pp. 155-156.) The disciples and those who succeeded them, took literally the Lord's command: "Go ye into all the world, and preach the gospel to every creature. He that believeth and is baptized shall be saved; but he that believeth not shall be damned." (Mark 16:15-16.)

Because, say the scholars, to the westward of Palestine, Greek was understood by the people generally (under their theory that the original script was Greek and so readable by all) the earliest need for translations was in other directions:

". . . three were earliest in urgency and of chief importance: Syriac, for the countries spreading from Antioch to the Euphrates valley; Coptic, for Egypt, which bordered Palestine on the south-west, and where a strong Hellenistic colony was surrounded by a native Egyptian population; and Latin, not only or even primarily for Italy, where much of the population spoke Greek, but certainly for the flourishing provinces of Roman Africa and Roman Gaul." (*The Text,* pp. 111-112.)

Versions

We shall name the important *versions* usually listed:

Item 1. Syriac.

Already sufficiently noted and discussed. (See *Note Six, Item 2,* pp. 67 ff., above; see also Scrivener's comments, pp. 164 ff., herein.)

Item 2. Armenian.

This is said to have been written about 400 A.D., apparently in a corrupted form which was revised on receiving a 'corrected' text from Constantinople. Original version probably made from Syriac. "The revision after 431 would probably have been from MSS. of the Byzantine type, and this seems to be confirmed by the existing MSS." (*The Text,* p. 126.)

This is an interesting statement since it indicates that the discredited (by the Extreme Textualists) Byzantine type was in circulation less than a century after their favorite ℵ and B texts were prepared. The two types of texts seem to have been before the Church from almost the beginning of textual variations.

One Armenian text (989) has an interesting addition to the *pericope adulterae* (John 7:53-8:1-11) as usually recorded. This text says that what the Lord wrote on the ground was the sins of the woman's accusers. (*The Text*, p. 127.)

Other characteristics of the Armenian text need not be mentioned. (See Scrivener, p. 407; but see Scrivener's comment, pp. 165 ff., *infra*.)

Item 3.   Georgian.

But recently come under study by the scholars, it is said that the Gospels and Pauline Epistles were always in separate manuscripts. The earliest and best manuscript of the Gospels is the Adysh Manuscript, written about 897 A. D. The second group is headed by the Opiza Manuscript (913) and the Tbet' Manuscript (995). All other manuscripts represent 11th century revisions from Greek manuscripts of the Byzantine type, which became the accepted text of the Georgian Church. One scholar's (Blake) conclusion is that the old Georgian version "was one of the best witnesses to the Caesarean text." It has been "corrected" by Byzantine copies of the Adysh. This text came from an Armenian text "greatly revised in the MSS." (Kenyon, *The Text*, pp. 127-129; see Scrivener, p. 411; and see Scrivener's comments, pp. 165 ff., herein.)

Item 4.   Coptic or Egyptian Versions.

Coptic is the ancient language of Egypt, "formerly written in hieroglyphic, hieratic, or demotic, but here written in Greek characters, with the addition of six letters to represent sounds not used in Greek. In this form it was the language and the script of the native Christian Church in Egypt." It began to be used in the latter part of the second century. In a primitive form it is found on a papyrus in the British Museum, written on the back of a horoscope, date of which is either 95 or 155, probably the first.

There are two main Egyptian dialects: *Sahidic*, used in Southern or Upper Egypt, and *Bohairic*, used in Lower or Northern Egypt. Other less important dialects were spoken in the area between these two, known as *Akhmimic* and *Fayyumic*. The Bohairic became the one commonly used, but the Sahidic is the older.

The translation into the Egyptian vernacular probably was not later than the first quarter of the third century. (Kenyon, *The Text*, p. 129; see for a general discussion of these versions, Scrivener, pp. 365 ff., where he gives an account of Egyptian writing and changes and development therein.)

Sub-item a.   Sahidic.

The text is said to be predominantly associated with the ℵ B or Alexandrian type. It is denied that the text forms a part of one group with D and the Old Latin. (See for discussion of particular readings, Kenyon, *The Text*, pp. 131-33.)

Scrivener calls this, in the alternative, the *Thebaic Version*. He gives a short account of the exploitation of the text by various scholars, with an appraisal of the value of each, notes the different arrangement of the Gospels, and gives a comparative text of Acts 17:12-16 in the two languages, Memphitic and Thebaic. (Scrivener, pp. 392 ff.)

Sub-item b.   Bohairic.

There are a considerable number of manuscripts. In the Horner edition (1898-1905), 46 manuscripts were used for the Gospels, and 34 for the other books. The best manuscripts are dated from 1174 to 1320, though one manuscript seems to go back to 889. The text is to be associated with ℵ B family. " . . . both forms of the Coptic Gospels are to be reckoned as equally in the main supporters of the Alexandrian type, with a similar proportion of minor non-Alexandrian variants." Hoskier assigns the date of the Bohairic Version to about 200-250, "and argues that it had a considerable influence on the text of ℵ." (Kenyon, *The Text*, pp. 133-34.)

Scrivener speaks of this version as the *Memphitic Version*, in an alternative with Bahiric (spelled with an *a* instead of an *o* as by Kenyon). (In the fourth edition, the designation *Memphitic* is dropped, and *Bohairic* used, with a foot-note reading: "Memphitic (Lightfoot), Coptic (Tischendorf and others)." Scrivener-Miller, Vol. II, p. 106.)

Scrivener gives a considerable account of this version and the various publications of the text. He seems to entertain a rather high regard for the version. He gives a list of the Memphitic manuscripts to be found in European libraries, stating that though probably very imperfect, they will yet be found much fuller than any which has heretofore been given. He lists his manuscripts under: A. *The Gospels;* B. *The Pauline Epistles, Catholic Epistles and Acts;* C. *The Apocalypse.* He gives the location of the manuscripts he lists. (Scrivener, pp. 373 ff.) He notes:

"From this account of the MSS it appears that, with the single exception of the Apocalypse, the Memphitic New Testament, as far back as we can trace its history, contained all the books of our present Canon." (Scrivener, p. 389.)

Sub-item c.   Middle Egyptian.

So little is known of these dialects as to make it unprofitable to discuss them, says Kenyon, who adds that the underlying text is substantially the same as the Sahidic.   (*The Text*, pp. 134-135.)

Scrivener discusses other Coptic versions under the heading, "The Bashmuric or Elearchian Version," concerning which there appears to have been in Scrivener's time, considerable controversy.   In the fourth edition, this is discussed under the headings: "The Fayoum Version," and "The Middle Egyptian or Lower Sahidic Version." (Scrivener, pp. 401 ff.; Scrivener-Miller, Vol. II, pp. 140 ff.)

The other Eastern versions listed as Ethiopic, Arabic, and Persian, are said to have no textual importance. (Kenyon, *The Text*, pp. 134 ff.; Scrivener, pp. 409 ff., 414 ff., 413.)

The Ethiopic preserved the Book of Enoch, which was supposed to be wholly lost until in 1773 a traveller named James Bruce brought a manuscript from Abyssinia. In 1886 a small vellum book containing the opening 32 chapters was discovered; it probably is of the 6th century. The Chester Beatty manuscripts contain several leaves of a codex of the book,—date 4th or 5th century. (Kenyon, *The Text*, pp. 134-35.)

Item 5.   Latin.

Since the English Bible of today is a translation of a Greek text, though the Latin text is said to have played a part in the Authorized Version translation (Miller, p. 12), it is not necessary here to consider the Latin manuscripts, a translation of which is the English Bible used by the Roman Church. However, a short paragraph from Kenyon will indicate the place and importance of the

Latin text in the history of Christian civilization in Western Europe. Kenyon says:

"The Latin versions have a double importance and a special interest. In their earlier forms they throw valuable (though somewhat puzzling) light on the original text of the New Testament and its fortunes in the early centuries. In its later form, the Vulgate of St. Jerome, it became the accepted Bible of the Western world for over a thousand years, and is the Bible of the Church of Rome to-day. It was also the text from which all translations of the Scriptures into English were made before the sixteenth century. As an element in the history of religion and of civilization, it is of unique importance." (Kenyon, *The Text,* pp. 135-36.)

The sources of the modern Latin Bible are given thus:

Sub-item a.   The Old Latin.

Place of writing (the Extreme Textualists would say place of translation from the Greek) is unknown. Rome is doubted. Africa or Gaul are suggested. Some Latin text of the Pauline Epistles seems to have been in Carthage at the time of the Scillitan martyrs as early as 180 (see for account of martyrdom, *Schaff-Herzog,* Vol. X, *sub voce* "Scilli, Martyrs of"), and (seemingly) in Lyons and Vienne in 177; Tertullian was using a Latin text (c. 150-220), as also Cyprian, bishop of Carthage (c. 200-258). It seems clear that a good part of the New Testament circulated in Africa in the first half of the 3rd century. On the evidence he adduces, Kenyon says: "It is to Africa that we must assign the beginnings of the Latin Bible as we know it, though it is possible that a version was simultaneously in existence in southern Gaul." (*The Text,* p. 137.) This "African form" of the Old Latin is closely related to Codex Bezae, and supports D in many places.

There are several pre-Vulgate texts which are not African. Scholars differ as to whether they are a revision of the African text or an independent version. They are of a different type of text from those found in Egypt, "of which the foremost representatives are ℵ B." (Kenyon, *The Text*, pp. 137-138.)

Kenyon lists some of the Latin manuscripts dating from the fourth century on. He states that the majority of these have mixed texts. (*The Text*, pp. 138-141.)

Scrivener discusses this Old Latin Version and notes the confusion that existed in the Latin text prior to Jerome's work, begun about 382 A.D., under the direction of the Bishop of Rome, Damasus. Scrivener adds a list of the Old Latin manuscripts of the Gospels, some 38, which "compared with what extracts we obtain from the Latin Fathers, comprise all we know of the version before Jerome." (Scrivener, pp. 338 ff., 347, 348.)

In the fourth edition (Scrivener-Miller, Vol. II, p. 54) a paragraph has been added to the third edition which begins as follows: "To these thirty-eight codices must be added extracts from the Latin Fathers, of which the Latin interpreter of Irenaeus, Tertullian, Cyprian, Augustine, Priscillian, and Primasius are the most important for the history of the version." The remainder of the paragraph gives some detail regarding the additional codices to which reference is made in this new paragraph of this fourth edition.

Sub-item b.   The Vulgate.

In 382 A.D., Pope Damasus invited Jerome, the leading Biblical scholar of his day, to make a revision of the Latin Bible with a view to putting an end to the confusion resulting from the great variety of conflicting texts. Jerome seems to have revised the Latin text through reference and use of Greek texts, making as few changes as possible in the familiar text.

In 384 Jerome submitted a revision of the Gospels and in 391 the remaining books. Jerome's revision contained much of the Old Latin, with the addition of new material from Greek manuscripts, which in some cases were different from any manuscripts we know. It is affirmed that the manuscripts he used were of the ℵ B L class.

The whole Bible (including the Old Testament) was completed about 404.

The new revision made its way slowly. It is said to have "suffered much contamination" from the Old Latin, which in outlying areas continued to be used in the 12th and 13th centuries. Thus "in a much corrupted form," the Vulgate became the Bible of the Middle Ages in the Western World. (Kenyon, *The Text*, pp. 143-44.)

Unsuccessful attempts were made to revise it in the 9th and 13th centuries.

This Vulgate was "the first book produced by the printing-press, the famous Gutenberg or Mazarin Bible of 1456." The first authorized edition was published in 1590 by Pope Sixtus V. But his successor, Clement VIII, caused a new edition to be published and this "became (and remains) the official Bible of the Church of Rome." (*The Text*, p. 144; see for a discussion of the Vulgate in the Middle Ages, Kenyon, *Our Bible*, pp. 180 ff.)

However, in the Old Testament, Jerome made "a very slight revision of the Old Latin Psalter, with reference only to the LXX; this version is still in use at St. Peter's, and is known as the *Roman* Psalter." (Kenyon, *The Text*, pp. 58-59.)

The best Vulgate manuscript is said to be Codex

Amiatinus (A), in the Laurentian Library at Florence. (*The Text*, p. 145.)

(For a study on the Latin texts, see Scrivener, beginning on p. 338; for a discussion of Jerome's work and the Vulgate which came from it, see Scrivener, pp. 348 ff. This chapter was revised in the fourth edition, "but incorporating, where possible, Dr. Scrivener's language," by Rev. H. J. White, under the direction of the Right Rev. John Wordsworth, D.D., Bishop of Salisbury, who, "since the publication of the third edition of this book," had done "exhaustive work on the Old Latin Versions and the Vulgate, commenced before for the University of Oxford." Scrivener-Miller, Vol. II, p. 41.)

Item 6. *Gothic.*

In the 4th century, Bishop Ulfilas made a translation for the Goths in Moesia. Only fragments exist.

"It was made from the Greek in both Testaments; in the Old Testament from a Lucianic text of the LXX, and in the New Testament from a text predominantly of the Byzantine type, with a sprinkling of earlier readings." (Kenyon, *The Text*, p. 149.)

(See Scrivener, pp. 138 ff., for a description of *Codex Guelpherbytanus* A (P) and *Codex Guelpherbytanus* B (Q); P is assigned to the sixth, and Q to the fifth century; and pp. 405 ff., for a scholarly discussion of the Gothic Version, noting some manuscripts (which Scrivener says must be called fragments) which "approach nearer to the received text, in respect of their readings, than the Egyptian or one or two other versions of about the same age,"—5th and 6th centuries.)

SCRIVENER'S DISCUSSION

This discussion of *versions* can be appropriately closed with Scrivener's comment about them:

"(1). It may be found as difficult to arrive at the primitive text of a version, as of the Greek original itself; the variations in its different copies are often quite as considerable, and suspicious of subsequent correction, whether from the Greek or from some other version, are as plausible to raise and as hard to refute. This is preeminently the case in regard to the Latin version, especially in its older form; but the Peshito Syriac, the Armenian, the Georgian and almost every other have been brought into discredit, on grounds more or less reasonable, by those whose purpose it has served to disparage their importance.

"(2). Although several of the ancient versions, and particularly the Latin, are rendered more closely to the original than would be thought necessary or indeed tolerable in modern times, yet it is often by no means easy to ascertain the precise Greek words which the translator had in his copy. While versions are always of weight in determining the authenticity of sentences or clauses inserted or omitted by Greek manuscripts, and in most instances may be employed even for arranging the order of words, yet every language differs so widely in spirit from every other, and the genius of one version is so much at variance with that of others, that too great caution cannot be used in applying this kind of testimony to the criticism of the Greek. The Aramæan idiom, for example, delights in a graceful redundancy of pronouns, which sometimes affects the style of the Greek Testament itself (e.g. Matth. viii. 1; 5): so that the Syriac ought to have no influence in deciding a point of this kind, inasmuch as the translator would naturally follow the usage of his own language, rather than regard the precise wording of his original.

"(3). Hence it follows that no one can form a trustworthy judgment respecting the evidence afforded by any version, who is not master of the language in which it was written. In a past generation, critics contented themselves with using Latin versions of the Egyptian, Æthiopic, &c., to their own and their readers' cost. The insertion or absence of whole clauses, indeed, are patent facts which cannot be mistaken, but beyond such matters the unskilled enquirer ought not to venture. The immediate result of this restriction may be to confine the student to the full use of the Syriac and Latin versions; a few Biblical scholars, as Bishop Lightfoot and especially the Rev. S. C. Malan, have made good progress in the ancient Egyptian; the rest of us must remain satisfied with a confession of ignorance, or apply our best diligence to remedy it." (Scrivener, pp. 310-311; the foregoing discussion is revised in the fourth edition. Scrivener-Miller, Vol. II, pp. 1-5.)

Item 7. The Fathers.

Summary. The Fathers who are invoked to learn and verify early texts.

In addition to the foregoing sources for reaching the primal text of the New Testament, we have the testimony of early Christian writers,—the Fathers. This patristic evidence is not seemingly wholly trustworthy as to its exactness. The Fathers evidently quoted often from a memory that was not always conspicious for its accuracy. Then copyists of the patristic writings were not always either skilled or too careful, so they altered the writings as originally penned by the Fathers. So the first problem to meet in the use of these sources is to establish the original text of the Fathers.

The earlier Fathers used texts that considerably antedate any manuscript that we now possess. In the sub-Apostolic age, quotations from the scriptures are rare, and their value is more to establish the existence of New Testament books than to establish the exactness of the text quoted.

These patristic writings are of the "greatest value in determining the time and place at which the principal types of text came into existence or were current." (Kenyon, *The Text*, p. 150.)

Kenyon makes use of the writings of the Fathers to assist in substantiating his theories of the various families into which he divides the Greek manuscripts. (*The Text*, pp. 150 ff.; see pp. 151-152 for brief biography of Origen, "the greatest scholar among the early Greek Fathers.")

Kenyon concludes his short discussion of the patristic writings with this paragraph:

"After the first quarter of the fifth century the Fathers lose much of their value for our present purpose. The Byzantine revision was establishing itself in the East, and the Vulgate in the West, and the writings of the Fathers throw less and less light on the subject with which we are concerned, *the recovery of the earliest form of the Greek Scriptures*." (*The Text*, p. 153; italics ours.)

In this last clause you have the whole aim of modern criticism. (See for a confirmatory statement touching the Revised Standard Version, *An Introduction*, pp. 27-28, quoted later.)

Scrivener treats the value of patristic evidence in much the same vein. He gives a list of some one hundred eighty odd of the more important Fathers, Greek and Latin, printed as Appendix C. (Scrivener-Miller, Vol. II, pp. 172-174; and see Scrivener, 3rd ed., pp. 416 ff.)

NOTE SIXTEEN •
The Printed Bible

The following printed Bibles are noted:

Item 1.   The Gutenberg or Mazarin Bible, in Latin, 1456.

> *Summary.* Issued early in 1456. A print of the Vulgate in folio.

Until the fifteenth century, the Bible books circulated solely in manuscripts.   Those noted above are a few regarded as most important out of thousands that had been made, most of them that are now existent being only fragments, some of them scraps of parts of a page, as for example the oldest fragment yet discovered, the Rylands Fragment. (*Note Fourteen*, p. 134.)

The earliest printed Bible (issued early in 1456) was a print of the Vulgate, in folio, large type, known as the Gutenberg (from the supposed name of the printer) or Mazarin Bible (from the name of the owner of the copy which first drew attention in later times).   Present scholarship believes the book was printed by Fust and Schoeffer in Mainz.   (Kenyon, *The Text*, p. 154.)

Item 2.   The First Greek Bible, the Complutensian or Cardinal Ximenes Text, 1520.

> *Summary.* Finished in 1514, published in 1520. Seemingly it is a print of the generally accepted text, which is the basis of the Authorized or King James Version (Textus Receptus). Matter briefly discussed as to source texts.

The first Greek text was not printed till over fifty years after the first Latin Bible,—the Gutenberg Bible.

The texts with which we are most concerned, because they were the Greek texts of which the Authorized or King James Version is a translation, are described as follows:

The Cardinal Ximenes Text, which was based upon a number of earlier manuscripts (all Ximenes could find), was finished in 1514 and published in 1520. This Greek text is known as the Complutensian Polyglott. It was built "from selected Manuscripts of great age and accuracy, supplied by Pope Leo X., who was the patron of the undertaking. Attempts have been made without success to ascertain what these Manuscripts were." This "is admitted to be a fair but not by any means a faultless edition of the text that had already been in vogue, as is universally admitted, for upwards of a thousand years." (Miller, pp. 7-8.)

However, the Revisers of the Revised Version speak slightingly of this text (with the texts of Stephanus and of Beza) affirming that it was "founded for the most part on manuscripts of late date, few in number, and used with little critical skill. But in those days it could hardly have been otherwise." ("Revisers' Preface" (to the New Testament), Revised Version, *The Parallel Bible* (London, Henry Frowde and C. J. Clay and Son, 1885), p. v.)

Assuming the editors of the Polyglott were wrong and that the Revisers were right as to the age of the manuscripts used to build the Polyglott, this fact should be noted: it is certainly not impossible that the manuscripts used by Ximenes to build his text were in themselves as ancient or possibly more ancient than any now extant, specifically than א and B to be noted later (and see *supra*, *Note Fourteen*, pp. 136 ff.); or in the alternative, that they were copies (as ℵ and B are copies) of other manuscripts which were older than the ℵ and B copies.

As showing the multiplicity of copies anciently, it is interesting to note that according to Burgon, ". . . we are unacquainted with *one single instance* of a known MS. copied from another known MS." (Burgon, p. 256; but see *supra*, p. 143, Codex E₃.)

Item 3.   The Erasmus Bible, in Greek, 1516.

Summary. Erasmus Greek Bible printed in Germany before the end of February, 1516. There was a rivalry between this Bible and the Complutensian as to which should be published first. The matter of source texts is briefly discussed. Editions of this work were published in 1516, 1522, and 1535.

The Erasmus edition was printed in Germany before the end of February, 1516. It anticipated the printing of the Complutensian edition, which was waiting for the approval of the Pope. Erasmus "seems to have used what copies he could procure, but in a few cases where he either found or supposed his Greek authorities to be deficient, he translated from the Vulgate into Greek." It appears that in a controversy between Erasmus and some of his critics as to the text, Erasmus invoked "the celebrated Vatican Codex (B)" which "was on this occasion for the first time appealed to on a point of textual criticism." Editions of the Erasmus text were published, the first, February, 1516, the third in 1522, then a fourth, and the last, in 1535. (Miller, pp. 8-9.) The statement made in the "Revisers' Preface" to the Revised Version text is misleading as to the use of early manuscripts. (See Revised Version (1881), "Revisers' Preface" (to the N.T.), I, 1.)

Item 4.   The Editions of Robert Stephen, Theodore Beza, and the Elzevirs (Bonaventure and Abraham), 1546-1633.

   Summary.   See Miller's discussion of these various editions.

Miller's comments on these various texts are as follows:

STEPHEN (STEPHANUS) BIBLE

"The two first of Stephen, published at Paris respectively in 1546 and 1549, were most elegantly printed with type cast at the expense of Francis I., and are known to connoisseurs by the title 'O mirificam' from the opening words expressing an encomium upon that king's liberality. The third, in folio, came out in 1550, and for the first time in the history of editions of the Greek Testament contained various readings. Reference was made to sixteen authorities, viz., the Complutensian Polyglott and fifteen manuscripts, amongst which the Codex Bezæ (D), now at Cambridge, is thought to have been numbered. Erasmus is not mentioned, although Stephen's two earliest editions were mainly grounded upon Erasmus' readings; and his third, according to Dr. Scrivener's computation, differs from them conjointly in only 361 places. Robert Stephen did not collate his authorities himself, but employed the services of his son Henry.

"His record of readings in the margin of his folio caused great offence to the doctors of the Sorbonne, and Stephen withdrew to Geneva to escape their enmity. Here he published in 1551 his fourth edition, almost unchanged in the Greek text from the previous one, but with one remarkable alteration. The chapters, into which Cardinal Hugo, of Santo Caro, had divided the books of the Bible in the thirteenth century, were in this edition first subdivided into verses. His son Henry said that his father made the subdivision 'whilst riding' from Paris to Lyons, probably during the intervals of his exercise. His object was to facilitate reference in a Concordance which he had in prospect.

BEZA BIBLE

"Beza's text did not differ much from Stephen's. He published five editions, slightly varying upon one another, and rang-

ing from 1565 to 1598. Of these the fourth, published in 1589,
has the highest reputation, the fifth having been produced in
'extreme old age.' Besides the advantage of Stephen's collections, Beza was the possessor of two very important MSS., the
one already mentioned (D of the Gospels and Acts), which was
presented by him to the University of Cambridge, and the Codex
Claromontanus (D of St. Paul's Epistles) at Paris, both of which
contained Greek and Latin texts, being therefore 'bilingual'
manuscripts.

ELZEVIR BIBLE

"The Elzevirs—Bonaventure and Abraham—brought out two
editions at their celebrated press, one in 1624, and the other in
1633. Their text was made up from those of Stephen and Beza.
The latter edition was remarkable from the expression 'Received
Text' occurring for the first time. Addressing the reader they
said, 'So you have now a text universally received, in which we
give no alteration or corruption.'

"The text of Stephen, which was afterwards carefully repro-
duced by Mill, has been generally taken in England as the standard or 'Received' text, and that of the Elzevirs has been thus
regarded on the continent. The translators, however, of our
Authorized Version did not adhere exclusively to any one of the
chief editions. When their authorities were at variance, they
sometimes in their interpretation of the 'Received Text' followed
Beza, sometimes Stephen, sometimes the Complutensians, Erasmus, or the Latin Vulgate." (Miller, pp. 10-12.)

As already quoted (*supra*, p. 123), "the Received
Text of the sixteenth and seventeenth centuries repre-
sented with general, but far from invariable accuracy,
the Traditional Text of the previous ages of the Church."
(Miller, pp. 12-13; for a scholarly summary of these early
editions of the Greek New Testament, see Scrivener, ch.
V, p. 422; see also, Kenyon, *The Text*, pp. 154 ff., *Our
Bible*, pp. 74 ff., 102 ff.)

NOTE SEVENTEEN •

English Versions

English Versions of the Bible may be divided into two classes: Manuscript Bibles and Printed Bibles.

Dr. Kenyon (of the Department of Manuscripts in the British Museum) has traced the English translations as set out below. (F. G. Kenyon, "English Versions," *HDB* (*Single Vol.*), pp. 219-230.)

Item 1. English Manuscript Bibles.

Summary. Of the earliest English manuscript Bibles there may be named, each more or less fragmentary and partial translations, Caedmon, Bede, Alfred the Great, with his English translations of the Decalogue, the summary of the Mosaic law, and the letter of the Council of Jerusalem, which he prefixed to his own code of laws; the Lindisfarne Gospels, Ælfric's translation of the Heptateuch, with epitomes of the Book of Kings and brief versions of Esther, Judith, and Maccabees. During the period of the Conquest, a French version of the Apocalypse was translated into English. Later English versions of the Psalter appeared, the most noteworthy being by Richard Rolle, translated from the Latin (14th century) about which time also appeared a narrative of the Life of Christ made by a rearrangement of the Gospels. Finally the Wyclif Bible appeared (about 1380), an English translation of the Latin Vulgate—the first complete translation of the Old and New Testaments.

We may pass with mere mention the early more or less fragmentary and partial translations of parts of the Bible by Caedmon (7th century), a manuscript; Bede (d. 735), a manuscript; Alfred the Great (849-901), who, to his code of laws, prefixed English translations of the Decalogue, a summary of the Mosaic law, and the letter of the Council of Jerusalem (Acts 15:23-29).

Then came the Lindisfarne Gospels (in Northumbrian and Mercian dialects),—"the earliest extant translation of the Gospels into English," which were followed in the tenth century by a translation by Ælfric (about 990) of the Heptateuch, and "homilies containing epitomes of the Books of Kings and Job, and brief versions of Esther, Judith, and Maccabees," which are the "earliest extant English version of the narrative books of the OT." During the period of the Norman Conquest, the biblical literature was mainly in French. A French version of the Apocalypse was translated into English, one version of which appeared later in the Wyclif Bible. (Kenyon, *HDB* (*Single Vol.*), p. 220b.)

The French versions largely disappeared in England in the 14th century, during which period two English versions of the Psalter appeared, the more noteworthy being by Richard Rolle (d. 1349), hermit of Hampole, in Yorkshire, translated from the Latin, the English following the Latin verse by verse. During this same century, an English narrative of the Life of Christ appeared, made up of a rearrangement of the Gospels. Another incomplete translation appeared about the same time. (Kenyon, *HDB* (*Single Vol.*), pp. 220b, 221a.)

This, in summary, brings us to the Wyclif Bible, the first English translation of the complete Old Testament and New Testament,—the New Testament was translated first (about 1380), presumably by Wyclif himself, the Old Testament between 1382 and 1384, supposedly by Nicholas Hereford. It appeared in various editions so as to appeal to all classes of people. A second version of Wyclif's Bible was published after his death, in which the English text (clearly based on the first Wyclif version), was revised and cured of many defects. Its authorship

is unknown, though some have ascribed it to John Purvey. This version had a wide circulation among the high
and the low. "Copies are still in existence which formerly had for owners Henry VI., Henry VII., Edward VI.,
and Elizabeth." (A Catholic writer has sought to disprove that Wyclif translated a version of the Bible, but
Dr. Kenyon seems effectively to dispose of that writer's
claim.) Wyclif's translation was of the Latin Vulgate;
he does not seem to have had either Hebrew or Greek
texts. Wyclif's Bible was the last English Manuscript
Bible. All the foregoing translations were made from
the Latin Vulgate, and seemingly all were manuscripts.
(Kenyon, *HDB* (*Single Vol.*), pp. 219-223b; see also,
Kenyon, *Our Bible*, pp. 194-209; *The Story*, pp. 47 ff.)

Item 2.   The Printed Bible.

Sub-item a.   Tindale's Bible, the First English Bible Translated from Greek, 1526.

Summary. Tindale's Bible, the first English Bible
translated from Greek; first English Bible printed (1526).
He also translated the Pentateuch from the Hebrew. Tindale was finally seized, brought to trial, condemned, strangled, and burnt at the stake.

In 1526 the first regular English version of the Bible
was printed. This marked the beginning of a new era
of English versions. This was Tindale's translation. The
first printed edition appeared in 1526. With the vicissi-
tudes, hardships, and persecutions that were attendant
upon Tindale and his translations and printing labors, inflicted by those opposing the Reformation, we are not
here concerned. He was finally seized, brought to trial,
condemned, strangled, and burnt at the stake, October
6, 1536. (See John Fox, *Book of Martyrs*, Charles A.
Goodrich, ed. (Edwin Hunt, Middletown, 1833), pp.
258 ff.)

Several editions of his Bible were printed, the finally completed work, in 1535. The translation seems to have been a good one as shown by the considerable use made of it in the Authorized Version (A.V.). It is said that Tindale's Bible . . .

"... was the first English printed NT; it laid the foundations, and much more than the foundations, of the AV of 1611; it set on foot the movement which went forward without a break until it culminated in the production of that AV; and it was the first English Bible that was translated directly from the original language. All the English manuscript Bibles were translations from the Vulgate; but Tindale's NT was taken from the Greek, which he knew from the editions by Erasmus, published in 1516, 1519, and 1522. As subsidiary aids he employed the Latin version attached by Erasmus to his Greek text, Luther's German translation of 1522, and the Vulgate; but it has been made abundantly clear that he exercised independent judgment in his use of these materials, and was by no means a slavish copier of Luther." (Kenyon, *HDB* (*Single Vol.*), p. 223b.)

Tindale also printed in 1530, an English translation of the Pentateuch from the Hebrew. In 1531 he printed an English translation of the Book of Jonah.

Sub-item b. *Coverdale's Bible, 1535.*

Summary. Printed 1535. Dedicated to Henry VIII. Rearranged books of the Bible.

Coverdale's Bible was printed in 1535. It was the first complete English Bible produced, Tindale's Bible being composed of the New Testament and some portions of the Old Testament as noted above. Coverdale and Tindale are supposed to have been associated in Tindale's translation of the Pentateuch. Coverdale worked under the patronage of Cromwell. The Bible was dedicated to Henry VIII, who had condemned Tindale's Bible. In his version of Tindale's work, Coverdale used the Zurich German Bible of Zwingli, a Latin version of Pagninus, the Vulgate, and Luther's translation. He seems to have made little use of Greek or Hebrew texts.

Coverdale's Bible is said to be "epoch-making" because of his rearranging of the Books of the Bible. In the Vulgate, circulating in the West, and (contrary to the opinion of Jerome, its translator), the books of the Apocrypha were interspersed among the other books of the Old Testament. This was true also of the LXX (Septuagint). Wyclif's Bible (a translation of the Vulgate) followed the same arrangement. Luther placed the Apocrypha apart in his translation and likewise separated Hebrews, James, Jude and the Apocalypse in the New Testament. In his table of contents, Tindale followed Luther's arrangement. Coverdale arranged his Old Testament books into five parts, and added the New Testament. "So far as concerns the English Bible, Coverdale's example was decisive," in relation to the matter of framing the canon. (Kenyon, *HDB* (*Single Vol.*), pp. 224-225a.)

Sub-item c.   Matthew's Bible, 1537.

Summary. Matthew's Bible appeared in 1537. Largely made up of portions of Tindale's and Coverdale's Bibles, except that the historical books were new translations, translator unknown. No such person known as Thomas Matthew, the supposed translator; translation accredited by tradition to John Rogers.

Matthew's Bible appeared in 1537, the year of Coverdale's second edition. Like Coverdale's translation, the title page recited that it was printed with the King's "lycence." It was largely made of portions of Tindale's translation and of Coverdale's, though the historical books were in great part a new translation, the origin thereof being unknown. While the title page says the translation was by one Thomas Matthew, yet no such person is known and the work is accredited, by tradition, to John Rogers. (Kenyon, *HDB* (*Single Vol.*), p. 225.)

Sub-item d.   Taverner's Bible, 1539.

Summary.   Taverner's Bible, based on Matthew's Bible.

Taverner's Bible (1539) was based upon Matthew's Bible. Some verbal corrections, to make better English, were made in the Old Testament, and Taverner, being a good Greek scholar, revised some of the New Testament text in accordance with the reading of the Greek text. This Bible is said to have had "no influence" on the development of an acceptable English Bible. (Kenyon, *HDB* (*Single Vol.*) p. 225.)

Sub-item e.   The Great Bible, 1539-1541.

Summary.   A complete revision of Matthew's Bible by Coverdale (1539-1541). Thomas Cromwell (Earl of Essex) declared that a copy should be set up in every parish church; it thus became "the first (and only) English Bible formally authorized for public use."

At the invitation of Thomas Cromwell (Earl of Essex) and Thomas Cranmer (Archbishop of Canterbury), Coverdale undertook a complete revision of Matthew's Bible that, apparently, had not been so successful as they wished. This revision was ready in 1538, printed in 1539. Cromwell issued "an injunction" that a copy should be set up in every parish church. It thus became "the first (and only) English Bible formally authorized for public use." The translation is said to have had considerable merit. Coverdale, while not equal to Tindale in scholarship, still had scholarship enough "to choose and follow the best authorities." Taking Tindale's translation and his own previous version, he revised these texts with reference to the Hebrew, Greek, and Latin, with special assistance in the Old Testament from the superior Latin translation by Sebastian Munster. In the New Testament he used Erasmus. He retained familiar Latin phrases, and introduced a considerable number of words and sentences from the Vulgate, not found in the Hebrew or Greek.

The first edition being rapidly exhausted, a second edition was issued which is sometimes known as Cranmer's Bible, because he wrote the prologue appearing therein.

Henry VIII in his later years reacted against Protestantism. In 1543 a proclamation was issued against Tindale's and in 1546 against Coverdale's Bible. And some were destroyed. At Henry's death (1547) new editions were issued of Tindale's, Coverdale's, Matthew's, and the Great Bible. Following Mary's accession to the throne (1553), all circulation of English translations was stopped. (Kenyon, *HDB* (*Single Vol.*), pp. 225-226a.)

Sub-item f. The Geneva Bible, 1557-1560.

Summary. The Geneva Bible by W. Whittingham (1557). First version printed in Roman type and in which the text was divided into verses. Besides Whittingham, Thomas Sampson and A. Gilby participated in the work. It became the Bible of the Puritans.

Geneva had become the "rallying place of the more advanced members of the Protestant party in exile." They fell under the strong rule of Calvin. There his relative, W. Whittingham, "a Fellow of All Soul's College, Oxford, and subsequently dean of Durham," published in 1557 a small octavo volume of the New Testament. It was the first version printed in Roman type and in which the text was divided into verses (following R. Stephanus in his Graeco-Latin text).

The translator stated he had used in his work the "original Greek" and translations into other tongues. Calvin wrote a preface.

It was at once made the basis of a revised version of both Testaments by a group of Puritan scholars. The details of the work are not recorded. Among those participating besides Whittingham, were Thomas Sampson (at one time dean of Chichester, later dean of Christ Church), and A. Gilby (of Christ's College). The complete Bible was put upon the market in 1560. The New Testament had been considerably revised. The Psalter was added in 1559. The type and verse-division followed Whittingham's 1557 version.

The revisers of Whittingham's text made the Great Bible their basis for the Old Testament and Matthew's Bible for the New Testament. They also used the Latin Bible of Leo Juda (1544) and Pagninus (1527). They also consulted the scholars, including Calvin and Beza, the latter's "reputation stood highest among all the Biblical scholars of the age." There were copious marginal notes.

This version was very popular and was, for a century, the Bible of the people. During the Civil War in Britain this was the Bible of the Puritans. It is said over 160 editions were issued. Laurence Tomson made a revision of the New Testament in 1576, which became popular and was sometimes bound in with the Genevan Old Testament. (Kenyon, *HDB* (*Single Vol.*), pp. 226b-227a.)

Sub-item g. The Bishops' Bible, 1568.

Summary. The Geneva Bible being a Puritan Bible, the Church of England prelates desired their own Bible. This was made by the Episcopal Bishops under the leadership of the Archbishop of Canterbury. The Great Bible was to be taken as a basis. It supplanted the Great Bible as the official version, and was so used till the King James Version.

The Geneva Bible, as indicated, was essentially a Puritan Bible. It naturally was not much favored by the clergy of the Church of England. Accordingly, the idea of a Bible translated by the Bishops of the Church was revived. Under the leadership of the Archbishop of Canterbury, a new translation of the Bible was undertaken. The Great Bible (1539-1541) was to be taken as the basis for the new version. The Old Testament was indifferently done; the New Testament was much better. The Geneva Bible and other versions were used in the work of translating. It contained notes. The Bishops' Bible supplanted the Great Bible as the official version. Alterations were made in a second edition printed in 1569. A third edition was printed in 1572. This version was used as the official text till the version of 1611 (King James), "of which it formed the immediate basis." (Kenyon, *HDB* (*Single Vol.*), p. 227a.)

Sub-item h.   The Rheims or Douai Bible, 1582-1609.

Summary. A Catholic version of the Bible in English issued by English Catholic refugees on the continent. It takes its name from the place of translation and issuance.

This was a Catholic version of the Bible in English, issued by English Catholic refugees on the continent who established an English College at Douai. The version was prepared in Douai though the first edition of the New Testament was issued in 1582 from Rheims, a temporary home of the College. It was the work of Gregory Martin, formerly a Fellow of St. John's College, Oxford. The Old Testament text was published in 1609. The Latin Vulgate was the basis of this version, little attention being given either to the Hebrew or Greek originals. The style was largely influenced by the Latin. It was used by the Authorized Version translators who took from it many of the Latin words they used. (Kenyon, *HDB* (*Single Vol.*), p. 227.)

NOTE EIGHTEEN •

The Authorized Version (A.V.) or
King James Version, 1611

Item 1.   The Preparation of the Text.

Summary. King James, following failure of the
Hampton Court Conference, took an active part in moving
forward on the suggestion made at the Conference that a
translation of the Bible be prepared calculated to heal
differences between Anglican and Puritan elements of
the Church. Noted are the personnel and organization
of the translation groups, which were to be made up of
scholars from the two universities. The translators, beginning their labors near the end of 1607, finished in about
two years. The text was revised by a group working about
nine months; final revision was by a small group; it was
printed and issued in 1611. It was printed in black letter
type, in the largest folio volume of all the series of English
Bibles.

In 1604, James I held the Hampton Court Conference,
called to settle differences between the Puritan and Anglican elements of the Church. In the course of the
Conference, the President of the Corpus Christi College,
Oxford (Dr. Reynolds), the leader of the moderate Puritan party, referred to the imperfections and disagree-
ments of the existing English versions of the Bible, and
suggested a new version to be prepared by the best scholars of the country. The Conference was a failure and
did nothing about the suggestion of Dr. Reynolds. But
King James moved forward.

Dr. Kenyon has given the essential facts of the preparation of the version as follows:

"He [the King] took an active part in the preparation of instructions for the work, and to him appears to be due the credit of two features which went far to secure its success. He suggested that the translation should be committed in the first instance to the universities (subject to subsequent review by the bishops and the Privy Council, which practically came to nothing), and thereby secured the services of the best scholars in the country, working in co-operation; and (on the suggestion of the bishop of London) he laid down that no marginal notes should be added, which preserved the new version from being the organ of any one party in the Church.

DIVISION OF WORK

"Ultimately it was arranged that six companies of translators should be formed, two at Westminster, two at Oxford, and two at Cambridge. The companies varied in strength from 7 to 10 members, the total (though there is some little doubt with regard to a few names) being 47. The Westminster companies undertook Gn.-2 Kings and the Epistles, the Oxford companies the Prophets and the Gospels, Ac., and Apoc., and the Cambridge companies 1 Chron.-Eccles. and the Apocrypha.

RULES OF PROCEDURE

"A series of rules was drawn up for their guidance. The Bishops' Bible was to be taken as the basis. The old ecclesiastical terms were to be kept. No marginal notes were to be affixed, except for the explanation of Hebrew or Greek words. Marginal references, on the contrary, were to be supplied. As each company finished a book, it was to send it to the other companies for their consideration. Suggestions were to be invited from the clergy generally, and opinions requested on passages of special difficulty from any learned man in the land. 'These translations to be used when they agree better with the text than the Bishops' Bible, namely, Tindale's, Matthew's, Coverdale's, Whitchurch's [i. e., the Great Bible], Geneva.' The translators claim further to have consulted all the available versions and commentaries in other languages, and to have repeatedly revised their own work, without grudging the time which it required. The time occupied by the whole work is stated by themselves as two years and three-quarters. The several companies appear to have begun their labours about the end of 1607, and to have taken two years in completing their several shares. A final revision, occupying nine months, was then made by a smaller body, consisting of two representatives from each company, after which it was seen through the press by Dr. Miles Smith and Bishop Bilson; and in 1611 the new version, printed by R. Barker, the king's printer, was given to the world in a large folio volume (the largest of all the series of English Bibles) of black letter type.

ISSUES OF BIBLE

"The details of its issue are obscure. There were at least two issues in 1611, set up independently, known respectively as the 'He' and 'She' Bibles, from their divergence in the translation of the last words of Ruth 3:15; and bibliographers have differed as to their priority, though the general opinion is in favour of the former. Some copies have a wood-block, others an engraved title-page, with different designs. The title-page was followed by the dedication to King James, which still stands in our ordinary copies of the AV, and this by the translators' preface (believed to have been written by Dr. Miles Smith), which is habitually omitted. (It is printed in the present King's Printers' Variorum Bible, and is interesting and valuable both as an example of the learning of the age and for its description of the translators' labours.) For the rest, the contents and arrangement of the AV are too well known to every reader to need description." (Kenyon, *HDB* (*Single Vol.*), p. 227.)

Item 2.   Source Materials of King James Version.

Summary. It differed in method of preparation from the Tindale, Coverdale, and Matthew Bibles (each the work of a single scholar) ; from the Geneva and Douai Bibles (each the work of a small group) ; from the Bishops' Bible (the work of a larger group, working without adequate supervision). It was the work of a carefully selected group of scholars. The text owed much to its predecessors. The merits of earlier translations are noted; it observes the sense of "solemnity" of the 1611 translators. In a literary way it "was the noblest literary achievement of the age in which they lived. . . . (it) is the finest example of Jacobean prose, and has influenced incalculably the whole subsequent course of English literature."

Kenyon continues his discussion (*HDB* (*Single Vol.*), p. 227):

"Nor is it necessary to dwell at length on the characteristics of the translation. Not only was it superior to all its predecessors, but its excellence was so marked that no further revision was attempted for over 250 years. Its success must be attributed to the fact which differentiated it from its predecessors, namely, that it was not the work of a single scholar (like Tindale's, Coverdale's, and Matthew's Bibles), or of a small group (like the Geneva and Douai Bibles), or of a larger number of men working independently with little supervision (like the Bishops' Bible), but was produced by the collaboration of a carefully selected band of scholars, working with ample time and with full and repeated revision. Nevertheless, it was not a new translation. It owed much to its predecessors. The translators themselves say, in their preface: 'We never thought from the beginning that we should need to make a new translation, nor yet to make of a bad one a good one, . . . but to make a good one better, or out of many good ones one principal good one, not justly to be excepted against; that hath been our endeavour, that our mark.' The description is very just. The foundations of the AV were laid by Tindale, and a great part of his work continued through every revision. Each succeeding version added something to the original stock, Coverdale (in his own and the Great Bible) and the Genevan scholars contributing the largest share; and the crown was set upon the whole by the skilled labour of the Jacobean divines, making free use of the materials accumulated by others, and happily inspired by the gift of style which was the noblest literary achievement of the age in which they lived. A sense of the solemnity of their subject saved them from the extravagances and conceits which sometimes mar that style; and, as a result, they produced a work which, from the merely literary point of view, is the finest example of Jacobean prose, and has influenced incalculably the whole subsequent course of English literature. On the character and spiritual history of the nation it has left an even deeper mark, to which many writers have borne eloquent testimony; and if England has been, and is, a Bible-reading and Bible-loving country, it is in no small measure due to her possession of a version so nobly executed as the AV.

" . . . The Bishops' Bible, hitherto the official version, ceased to be reprinted, and the AV no doubt gradually replaced it in churches as occasion arose. In domestic use its fortunes were for a time more doubtful, and for two generations it existed concurrently with the Geneva Bible; but before the century was out its predominance was assured." (Kenyon, *HDB (Single Vol.)*, pp. 227b-228b.)

Item 3.   Modern Revisers' Justification.

Summary. The Extreme Textualists have made unrelenting war on the Authorized or King James Version. Their own explanation in their Preface to the Revised Version is given.

As appears elsewhere herein (*Note Twelve*), the Extreme Textualists have made unrelenting war on the Authorized Version. Having this in mind the following paragraph from the Revised Version staff (given in their "Revisers' Preface" to the N.T.) is of interest:

"That Translation was the work of many hands and of several generations. The foundation was laid by William Tyndale. His translation of the New Testament was the true primary Version. The Versions that followed were either substantially reproductions of Tyndale's translation in its final shape, or revisions of Versions that had been themselves almost entirely based on it. Three successive stages may be recognised in this continuous work of authoritative revision: first, the publication of the Great Bible of 1539-41 in the reign of Henry VIII; next, the publication of the Bishops' Bible of 1568 and 1572 in the reign of Elizabeth; and lastly, the publication of the King's Bible of 1611 in the reign of James I. Besides these, the Genevan Version of 1560, itself founded on Tyndale's translation, must here be named; which, though not put forth by authority, was widely circulated in this country, and largely used by King James' Translators. Thus the form in which the English New Testament has now been read for 270 years was the result of various revisions made between 1525 and 1611; and the present Revision is an attempt, after a long interval, to follow the example set by a succession of honoured predecessors." ("Revisers' Preface" (to the N.T.), p. v. For the need of a new revision, Church sponsored, see Burgon, p. 126.)

Item 4.   Various Editions of the Authorized Version.

> *Summary.* First printed in 1611; there was an Oxford edition in 1701, in which Archbishop Ussher's dates of Bible chronology appeared. There were other Cambridge and Oxford editions.

Quarto and octavo editions of the Authorized Version were published in 1612, after which numerous editions were issued, into which many printing inaccuracies crept. In 1701 an Oxford edition was issued "in which Archbishop Ussher's dates for Scripture chronology were printed in the margin, where they thenceforth remained." Two editions, Cambridge in 1762 and Oxford in 1769, carefully revised the text, modernized the spelling, corrected the punctuation, and considerably altered the marginal notes. These editions "formed the standard for subsequent reprints of the AV, which differ in a number of details, small in importance but fairly numerous in the aggregate, from the original text of 1611." (Kenyon, *HDB* (*Single Vol.*), p. 228b.)

Item 5.   The Apocrypha.

> *Summary.* In 1666 the Apocrypha was omitted, though previously omitted from some editions of other Bibles. The Nonconformists made objections to the Apocrypha. It was omitted from a 1782 edition in America. Note the attitude of the British and Foreign Bible Society. The books of the Apocrypha are named. The declaration of the Council of Trent thereon is given. The Prophet Joseph Smith's revelation and opinion on the Apocrypha are considered.

Kenyon comments here:

"In 1666 appeared the first edition of the AV from which the Apocrypha was omitted. It had previously been omitted from some editions of the Geneva Bible, from 1599 onwards. The Nonconformists took much objection to it, and in 1664 the Long Parliament forbade the reading of lessons from it in public; but the lectionary of the English Church always included lessons from it. The example of omission was followed in many editions subsequently. The first edition printed in America (apart from a surreptitious edition of 1752), in 1782, is without it. In 1826 the British and Foreign Bible Society, which has been one of the principal agents in the circulation of the Scriptures throughout the world, decided never in future to print or circulate copies containing the Apocrypha; and this decision has been carried into effect ever since." (Kenyon, *HDB* (*Single Vol.*), pp. 228b-229a.)

The Apocrypha here mentioned included: First and Second Esdras, Tobit, Judith, the rest of the chapters of the Book of Esther (following Chapter 10:3 of the Authorized Version), Wisdom of Solomon, the Wisdom of Jesus the Son of Sirach or Ecclesiasticus, Baruch, the Song of the Three Holy Children (which was inserted between verses 23 and 24, Chapter 3 of Daniel), the History of Susanna, the Story of Bel and the Dragon (cut off from the end of Daniel), Prayer of Manasses, king of Judah (when he was held captive in Babylon), the First and Second Maccabees. All of the foregoing except the Prayer of Manasses and the First and Second Esdras, were declared canonical by the Council of Trent, April 15, 1546, and are found in the Catholic Bible. (Ira Maurice Price, "Apocrypha," *HDB* (*Single Vol.*), pp. 42-43.)

On March 9, 1833, the Prophet Joseph received the following revelation while he was engaged in studying the Apocrypha:

"Verily, thus saith the Lord unto you concerning the Apocrypha—There are many things contained therein that are true, and it is mostly translated correctly;

"There are many things contained therein that are not true, which are interpolations by the hands of men.

"Verily, I say unto you, that it is not needful that the Apocrypha should be translated.

"Therefore, whoso readeth it, let him understand, for the Spirit manifesteth truth;

"And whoso is enlightened by the Spirit shall obtain benefit therefrom;

"And whoso receiveth not by the Spirit, cannot be benefited. Therefore it is not needful that it should be translated. Amen." (D. C., Sec. 91.)

Concerning the Apocrypha, the Prophet Joseph, Sidney Rigdon, and F. G. Williams wrote to W. W. Phelps, and others in Zion (Missouri), June 25, 1833:

"We have not found the Book of Jasher, nor any other of the lost books mentioned in the Bible as yet; nor will we obtain them at present. Respecting the Apocrypha, the Lord said to us that there were many things in it which were true, and there were many things in it which were not true, and to those who desire it, should be given by the Spirit to know the true from the false." (*DHC*, Vol. I, p. 363.)

Item 6. Appraisal of Authorized Version.

> *Summary.* The Extreme Textualist views and views of the Sound or High Textualists.

Kenyon's concluding paragraph on the King James Version may well be quoted here:

"So far as concerned the translation of the Hebrew and Greek texts which lay before them, the work of the authors of the AV, as has been shown above, was done not merely well but excellently. There were, no doubt, occasional errors of interpretation; and in regard to the OT in particular the Hebrew scholarship of the age was not always equal to the demands made upon it. But such errors as were made were not of such magnitude or quantity as to have made any extensive revision necessary or desirable even now, after a lapse of nearly three hundred years. There was, however, another defect, less important (and indeed necessarily invisible at the time), which the lapse of years ultimately forced into prominence, namely, in the text (and especially the Greek text) which they translated. As has been shown elsewhere (Text of the NT), criticism of the Greek text of the

NT had not yet begun. Scholars were content to take the text as it first came to hand, from the late MSS which were most readily accessible to them. The NT of Erasmus, which first made the Greek text generally available in Western Europe, was based upon a small group of relatively late MSS, which happened to be within his reach at Basle. The edition of Stephanus in 1550, which practically established the 'Received Text' which has held the field till our own day, rested upon a somewhat superficial examination of 15 MSS, mostly at Paris, of which only two were uncials, and these were but slightly used. None of the great MSS which now stand at the head of our list of authorities was known to the scholars of 1611. None of the ancient versions had been critically edited; and so far as King James' translators made use of them (as we know they did), it was as aids to interpretation, and not as evidence for the text, that they employed them. In saying this there is no imputation of blame. The materials for a critical study and restoration of the text were not then extant; and men were concerned only to translate the text which lay before them in the current Hebrew, Greek, and Latin Bibles. Nevertheless it was in this inevitable defectiveness of text that the weakness lay which ultimately undermined the authority of the AV." (Kenyon, *HDB* (*Single Vol.*), p. 229a.)

These observations set out the views and conclusions of the Extreme Textualists. The Rival School of Sound or High Textualists would not accept these views and conclusions without serious curtailment as to facts and conclusions. These matters will receive some consideration later.

Item 7.   *Character of Greek Source Material for Authorized Version.*

Summary. Opinions of Kenyon and Burgon.

Regarding Kenyon's statement that none of the great texts now heading the list of manuscripts (he doubtless had in mind ℵ and B) were "known to the scholars of 1611," it should be remembered that Erasmus knew of the Vaticanus manuscript. (Scrivener, p. 105.)

Other scholars do not share Dr. Kenyon's almost flippant discrediting of the manuscripts behind the Authorized Version. John William Burgon (Dean of Chichester), of whom we have already read, quotes Dr. Hort (one of the two men primarily responsible for the new Greek text which forms the basis for the Revised Version) as follows: "The fundamental Text of *late extant Greek MSS.* generally is *beyond all question identical* with the dominant Antiochian or Græco-Syrian Text of the *second half of the fourth century.*" (Burgon, p. 257; see p. 211, herein.) This is the text of the Authorized Version.

Burgon himself comments upon this same point as follows:

"The one great Fact, which especially troubles him [Dr. Hort] and his joint Editor [Dr. Westcott],—(as well it may)—is *The Traditional Greek Text* of the New Testament Scriptures. Call this Text Erasmian or Complutensian,—the Text of Stephens, or of Beza, or of the Elzevirs,—call it the 'Received,' or the *Traditional Greek Text,* or whatever other name you please; —the fact remains, that a Text *has* come down to us which is attested by a general consensus of ancient Copies, ancient Fathers, ancient Versions. This, at all events, is a point on which, (happily,) there exists entire conformity of opinion between Dr. Hort and ourselves. Our Readers cannot have yet forgotten his virtual admission that,—*Beyond all question* the *Textus Receptus* is *the dominant Græco-Syrian Text of* A.D. 350 *to* A.D. 400.

"Obtained from a variety of sources, this Text proves to be essentially *the same* in all. That it requires Revision in respect of many of its lesser details, is undeniable: but it is at least as certain that it is an excellent Text as it stands, and that the use of it will never lead critical students of Scripture seriously astray,—which is what no one will venture to predicate concerning any single Critical Edition of the N.T. which has been published since the days of Griesbach, by the disciples of Griesbach's school." (Burgon, p. 269.)

Mr. Burgon follows these observations with a searching and destructive criticism of the bases upon which the new Greek text (the basis of the Revised Version) is built.

On the question of the Greek text which was the basis of the Authorized Version, the following note by Burgon is of interest:

"It were unhandsome, however, to take leave of the learned labours of Prebendary Scrivener and Archdeacon Palmer, without a few words of sympathy and admiration. Their volumes (mentioned at the beginning of the present Article) are all that was to have been expected from the exquisite scholarship of their respective editors, and will be of abiding interest and value. *Both* volumes should be in the hands of every scholar, for neither of them supersedes the other. Dr. Scrivener has (with rare ability and immense labour) set before the Church, *for the first time, the Greek Text which was followed by the Revisers of* 1611, viz. Beza's N. T. of 1598, supplemented in above 190 places from other sources; every one of which the editor traces out in his *Appendix,* pp. 648-56. At the foot of each page, he shows what changes have been introduced into the Text by the Revisers of 1881.—Dr. Palmer, taking *the Text of Stephens* (1550) as his basis, presents us with the Readings adopted by the Revisers of the 'Authorized Version,' and relegates the displaced Readings (of 1611) to the foot of each page.—We cordially congratulate them both, and thank them for the good service they have rendered." (Burgon, pp. 49-50, n. 2; see "Revisers' Preface" (to the N.T.), sec.'s I and II.)

NOTE NINETEEN •
The Byzantine Text

Summary. Considered in this *Note* are:—Definition of *Byzantine* and *Textus Receptus*. Early editions of the printed Bible,—Mazarin or Gutenberg Bible, the Complutensian Polyglott, the Erasmus Bible, the Robert Estienne or Stephanus Bible; the seemingly new attitude of the Extreme Textualists, with their new classification of manuscripts; Scrivener's comments thereon and on the adoption or rejection of manuscripts on the basis of agreement or non-agreement of a proposed thesis; the characterization of manuscripts by the Extreme Textualists; early existence of the Byzantine text, and the variations made in seemingly all texts; the present writer's position; representation of various "family" readings from the earliest manuscripts on down for centuries, sometimes competing in the same manuscript, and the readings of one type text seem as ancient as others, particularly as to the ℵ and B; position of Kenyon, who is largely quoted among the Extreme Textualists, on the ℵ B group; establishment of original Greek text; the first texts; Luke's declaration about texts; possibility of all texts descending from one text; early multiplicity of texts, and the use thereof by early writers as shown by Beatty texts; methods by which variant texts might have been developed; modern Revisers use same methods for building their Revised Version, that they condemn as methods improperly used by earlier scholars. Some comparison of statements about competitive texts,—the early papyri, the uncials, the Westcott-Hort Antiochian myth, the Syriac versions, the Armenian version, the Coptic or Egyptian versions. A summary of results following consideration of statements about competition among texts.

Byzantine is the name (derived from the ancient name of Constantinople) by which the standard ecclesiastical text is generally known, by the Extreme Textualists at any rate. Other critics speak of the final text as the *Textus Receptus* (Received Text). These two names

—Byzantine and Textus Receptus—refer to the same text. (Kenyon, *The Story*, pp. 39-40, 92; *The Text*, p. 203.) It seems desirable to give a brief summary of the history of this Textus Receptus, as it was finally translated into the King James Version, the Authorized Version.

To begin with, it may be again said (in resume) that the first complete printed book after the invention of printing, was the Latin Vulgate. (See *Note Sixteen*; *The Text*, p. 154.) The book is known as the Mazarin Bible (frequently referred to as the Gutenberg Bible, named from the printers). The book in Latin was in circulation by August, 1456. Of the forty copies known, the United States purchased one for the Library of Congress at a cost of some $300,000.00. (Kenyon, *The Story*, pp. 42-43.)

In 1502, Cardinal Ximenes, Archbishop of Toledo, began to prepare an edition of a Greek Bible, accompanied by a Hebrew text of the Old Testament, and a Latin text of the whole Bible. The printing of the New Testament was finished earliest, in 1514, but publication was delayed until the Old Testament was completed in the middle of 1517. The book was given to the public in 1522. This is known as the *Complutensian Polyglott*, so named from the Latin name for Alcala, where the preparation of the text was carried on. (*The Text*, p. 155.)

However, a printer in Basle, Froben by name, had heard of the Cardinal's project, and arranged with Erasmus ("the foremost scholar of the Reformation") to prepare an edition of the Greek New Testament. Erasmus began his work in 1515, September; it was finished and published in March, 1516. Erasmus is said to have had for his work only "a handful of manuscripts, mostly of quite late date"; for the Gospels he is said to have had only one manuscript of the 15th century; his manuscript of Revelation was said to be deficient, and that he supplied the deficiency by a translation of his own from a Latin text. "Nevertheless his edition became the basis of the Greek text in universal use down to our own day." Erasmus produced five more editions; in the one of 1527, he consulted the Complutensian. Continental printers used the Erasmus text. (Kenyon, *The Story*, pp. 43-45; *The Text*, pp. 155 ff.)

It seems clear that in the course of his work, Erasmus had placed before him for consideration, a considerable number (365, it is stated) of readings from B (Vaticanus), of which number apparently some were used. (Scrivener, p. 105.)

In 1550, the French printer, Robert Estienne, or Stephanus, issued an edition of the Greek Testaments. His chief source was the Erasmus edition, though he used also the Complutensian, and fifteen manuscripts which he had from Paris, among which was the Codex Bezae ("of this little use was made"), the rest being late manuscripts. (Kenyon, *The Text*, p. 156.)

It appears to Kenyon's "reader" that the Extreme Textualists, having been driven, from their supposedly highly fortified position behind the א B codices, out into the open text field again, are now building up a new attack against the Textus Receptus by treating that text as if originating in the Erasmus text and so ignoring all the antecedents of the pre-Erasmus text. Yet at the same time, these critics claim all the manuscripts, early and late, they can for א B texts, not only noting but emphasizing them, if they favor א B, and then re-classify those they cannot claim into other groups, mentioning with scant notice all of the early texts favoring the Byzantine text, as if of no consequence.

SCRIVENER'S COMMENTS

We may well quote here some observations of Scrivener (acknowledged as one of the greatest scholars of his time) on this general subject of appraising manuscripts:

"The point on which we insist is briefly this:—that the evidence of ancient authorities is anything but unanimous; that they are perpetually at variance with each other, even if we limit the term ancient within the narrowest bounds. Shall it include, among the manuscripts of the Gospels, none but the five oldest copies Codd. ℵ A B C D? The reader has but to open the first recent critical work he shall meet with, to see them scarcely ever in unison; perpetually divided two against three, or perhaps four against one. All the readings these venerable monuments contain must of course be *ancient,* or they would not be found where they are; but they cannot all be true. So again, if our search be extended to the versions and primitive Fathers, the same phenomenon unfolds itself, to our grievous perplexity and disappointment. . . . It is not at all our design to seek our readings from the later uncials, supported as they usually are by the mass of cursive manuscripts; but to employ their confessedly secondary evidence in those numberless instances wherein their elder brethren are hopelessly at variance. We do not claim for the recent documents the high consideration and deference fitly reserved for a few of the oldest; just as little do we think it right to pass them by in silence, and allow to them no more weight or importance than if they had never been written. 'There are passages,' to employ the words of a very competent judge, 'where the evidence of the better cursives may be of substantial use in confirming a good reading, or in deciding us between two of nearly equal merit to place one in the text and assign the other to the margin.'" (Scrivener, pp. 522-524.)

In his note to the foregoing observations, Scrivener adds:

"I suppose too that Mr. Hammond means much the same thing when he says 'It seems almost superfluous to affirm that *every element of evidence must be allowed its full weight;* but it is a principle that must not be forgotten' (*Outlines of Textual Criticism,* p. 93, 2nd edition). Truly it is not superfluous to insist on this principle when we so perpetually find the study of the cursive manuscripts disparaged by the use of what we

may venture to call the Caliph Omar's argument, that if they
agree with the older authorities their evidence is superfluous, if
they contradict them, it is necessarily false." (Scrivener, n. 1,
p. 524.)

A little later in his discussion, Scrivener says:

"Hence it follows that in judging of the character of a various
reading proposed for our acceptance, we must carefully mark
whether it comes to us from many directions or from one. . . .

"It is strange, but not more strange than needful, that we are
compelled in the cause of truth to make one stipulation more:
namely, that this rule be henceforth applied impartially in all
cases, as well when it will tell in favour of the Received text, as
when it shall help to set it aside. To assign a high value to cursive
manuscripts of the best description (such as 1. 33. 69. 157. Evst.
259, or 61 of the Acts), and to such uncials as L R Δ, or even as ℵ
or C, whensoever they happen to agree with Cod. B, and to treat
their refined silver as though it had been suddenly transmuted
into dross when they come to contradict it, is a practice too
plainly unreasonable to admit of serious defence, and can only
lead to results which those who uphold it would be the first
to deplore." (Scrivener, pp. 555-556.)

In the seeming majority of cases, the measuring rod
applied by the Extreme Textualists to the value of a
manuscript, is its *agreement* with the favorite texts ℵ B;
agreements with other texts get scant notice. The expressions used covering this agreement are: "agrees
generally," "agrees more," the text "is akin to," "is
substantially," "largely escaped," "rather early stage of
its evolution," "close akin," "closely associated," "close
conformity," etc., etc., frequently with no statement as
to the character of the remainder of the text. What is
the character of the remainder of the text? Surely the
manuscript would be as good a witness for the other text
as for the ℵ B text. One can but wonder. In at least
one case (E, Codex Basiliensis), Kenyon characterizes
the text, in a two-line description of it, as "of no great

value," (*The Text*, p. 97) while Scrivener affirms it has "considerable" value and is an "excellent witness" for the "commonly received" text, that is, the Byzantine or Textus Receptus. (Scrivener, p. 128.)

This seems an almost perfect example of the way Extreme Textualists use and dispose of manuscripts that do not support their favorite texts.

This shuffling of evidence and values is a delusive procedure, not justified on the record; it misleads the public. (See *supra*, *Note Eight*; Kenyon, *The Story*, p. 131.)

As to the early existence of the Byzantine text, Burgon quotes Dr. Hort as saying: "The fundamental Text of *late extant Greek MSS.* generally is *beyond all question identical* with the dominant Antiochian or Græco-Syrian Text of the *second half of the fourth century*." (See *The New Testament in the Original Greek*, rev. by Brooke Foss Westcott and Fenton John Anthony Hort (Cambridge and London, Macmillan and Co., 1881), Vol. II, Introduction, Appendix, p. 92; see also p. 192, herein.)

Burgon interprets this as Dr. Hort's admission that the "Traditional Greek Text of the New Testament,—the TEXTUS RECEPTUS, in short,—is, according to Dr. Hort, 'BEYOND ALL QUESTION' the 'TEXT OF THE SECOND HALF OF THE FOURTH CENTURY.'" (Burgon, pp. 257-258.)

Yet along with this procedure, the Extreme Textualists speak of the residue after their reclassification, thusly:

"It is, I think, just this unassorted residue that gives us the clue to the early history of the text of the New Testament. . . . Scholars need to apply the increased knowledge which we now possess of this period to the problems of the New Testament text, and to use both imagination and common sense in interpreting them. . . .

"The four Gospels were composed in different times and places over perhaps a third of a century, and for a time circulated separately among a number of other narratives of our Lord's life (of which the newly discovered fragment of an unknown Gospel may have been one). . . . The apostles were scattered, and even the leaders of the Church in Jerusalem had neither the power nor the means to impose uniformity. . . .

"In these circumstances, is it surprising if in the first two centuries a large number of minor variations, and some of greater magnitude, found their way into the copies of the Scripture which circulated in the towns and villages of Palestine, Syria, Egypt, Asia Minor, Italy, Africa, and even farther afield? Rather we have to be thankful that greater and more serious corruption did not creep in." (Kenyon, *The Story*, pp. 132-136; see *Note Eight*, p. 99.)

As will be seen from *Note Eight*, the Extreme Textualists have reshuffled the manuscripts into proposed new families, but they still belittle the text and its foundation manuscripts of which the Authorized Version is a translation.

Obviously a critical examination of this problem is not within the purpose of this work, nor is it within our abilities or resources. But Kenyon's "any intelligent reader" (we hope to qualify under this specification) "without any knowledge of either Greek or Hebrew, can learn enough to understand the processes of criticism and the grounds on which the judgments of scholars must be based." (Kenyon, *Our Bible*, p. 18; see p. 20, herein.)

This is our justification for the audacious effrontery which characterizes what follows, as well as a very large part of the contents of all these *Notes*.

But having ventured so far in this *Note* and in the others, we may venture still farther, into almost forbidden areas. We might begin with Bruce's affirmation firmly fixed in our minds, to show how thin and uncertain is the footing on which we walk: "But, so far as the present writer knows, there is no living scholar who holds the antiquity of the Byzantine text." (Bruce, p. 178.)

A few words more, before beginning our adventure, about matters primarily affecting the character and standing of the great manuscripts ℵ (Sinaiticus) and B (Vaticanus). They are two of five that have a privileged place in certain textual criticism. The five are ℵ, B, A, C, and D. The materials given in the next few pages will suggest several matters that bear upon the credibility that ℵ B are entitled to receive as manuscripts that should control the New Testament English text.

PREPARATION OF MANUSCRIPTS

So far as has been observed, there is, certainly as to these great manuscripts, no word or even suggestion touching the point of who actually directed the preparation of any of them; or of who chose the manuscript or manuscripts which should be used in making the new manuscript, save perhaps of the Septuagint and the Peshitta text (Kenyon, *The Text*, p. 24; *The Story*, p. 139; *Our Bible*, p. 115); or of who checked the manuscript as written to see if it followed copy — and concededly we have no manuscript which is not a copy of some other manuscript or manuscripts which have not yet been discovered (but see *The Text*, p. 98, Codex E_3, p. 143, herein; and see as to certain cursives, Burgon, p. 80, and p. 332, herein); or of who passed upon the alterations or omissions that the scribe made from the manuscript or manuscripts from which he was copying to make his own manuscript, and obviously this is a most important element; or what was the condition as to legibility of the manuscript or manuscripts used as copy (apparently the great bulk of existing manuscripts are

mere fragments) and we have today no copy that is not
(to a greater or less extent) defaced and mutilated,
from which some portions have not been destroyed or
lost,— and so of many, many other matters that would
be involved in the making of a manuscript.

Furthermore, with one exception as to the great
uncials (or indeed as to any other manuscript) there
has been observed but one in which the scribe who
actually wrote the manuscript may possibly be identified.
This is the Codex Alexandrinus (A). As to this there is
a "tradition" that this was written by "Thecla [the
martyr], a noble lady of Egypt" who gave it to the
"patriarchal cell of Alexandria." (*The Text*, p. 84.)

Nothing is known of the training and capabilities of
any of the scribes who copied or prepared the manuscripts. The manuscripts almost universally testify to
carelessness in copying,—all kinds of errors, omissions,
duplications, additions, appear to be the rule, not the
exception. It seems clear that frequently more than one
scribe was used in writing a manuscript. The manuscripts have been gone over, sometimes repeatedly, by
different scribes, and changes made by subsequent and
also unknown scribes, sometimes centuries after the
original writing.

The thousands of existing manuscripts (from a fraction of a page to a practically full text,—see *Note Seven*
for number of manuscripts) have been found in all sorts
of places, the last great manuscripts discovered of the
New Testament (the Chester Beatty papyri) seem to
have come from an old rubbish heap, possibly of a church,
in Egypt. The place of the writing of these manuscripts,
the purpose thereof, who wished to have the manuscripts
prepared, the circumstances attending upon the writing,
whether for profit or from a pious motive, the period of

the writing, the time consumed in their preparation,—these and scores of other details are wholly unknown. Aside from a few characterized as great, the manuscripts are but scraps of papyri or vellum, sometimes containing a few pages, more or less casually discovered, for the most part, in out of the way, obscure places, where they have lain over the centuries, unknown, forgotten.

Under these circumstances, this "reader" finds it impossible to be too reliant as touching the differences or even the agreements of the various texts.

Of the five manuscripts just noted, א, B, A, C, D, there are, as already stated, two of prime importance in connection with Extreme Textual criticism. Kenyon (who might be designated the *exemplar* of the modern Revisers) says:

"Here it will be sufficient to state that it [א] is closely allied to the Vaticanus, and that these two fourth-century MSS. form the head and main substance of a group which in the opinion of many presents the most authentic text of the N.T. Substantially it is the text represented in our Revised Version." (*The Text*, p. 81; see pp. 137, 217, 219 ff., herein.)

IMPERFECTIONS IN SINAITICUS MANUSCRIPT (א)

Touching the Codex Sinaiticus (א): this was discovered (1844) by Tischendorf in a monastery on Mount Sinai, in an incident filled both with romance and near tragedy. This story has been recounted heretofore (*Note Fourteen*) and hereafter (*Notes Twenty-one to Twenty-four*). Nothing is known concerning this manuscript prior to its discovery by Tischendorf in the monastery. Our knowledge of it is deficient as to all the matters concerning its preparation that have been noted above.

Regarding the manuscript Vaticanus (B), nothing is known of its history prior to its deposit in the Vatican

Library about 1448. Its history since that time is sufficiently set forth heretofore (*Note Fourteen*) and hereafter (*Notes Twenty-one to Twenty-four*). Like the
Codex Sinaiticus, there is complete ignorance as to all
the matters touching its preparation which have been
noted above.

However, a speculation by the scholar Edward Miller
is of interest. Calling attention to the destruction of the
Holy Scriptures incident to the persecutions under Diocletian and Galerius and to the command of Constantine
issued to Eusebius that he prepare for the Emperor and
send to him fifty copies of the Holy Scriptures, Miller
suggests that these two manuscripts—Sinaiticus and
Vaticanus—were two of the fifty copies so prepared and
sent, and therefore these two manuscripts are in fact but
one, so far as origin is concerned, and so are but one witness to the text they carry, and not two. (Miller, p. 81;
see *Notes Twenty-two and Twenty-three, Item 3.*)

However, the study of the manuscripts themselves by
the scholars, seems to disclose certain facts that are of
great interest, as relating to their reliability. Regarding
Sinaiticus, Scrivener says:

"The whole manuscript is disfigured by corrections, a few
by the original scribe, or by the usual *comparer* (*see* p. 53) ;
very many by an ancient and elegant hand of the sixth century
(אᵃ), whose emendations are of great importance; some again
by a hand but little later (אᵇ) ; far the greatest number by a
scholar of the seventh century (אᶜ), who often cancels the
changes introduced by אᵃ; others by as many as eight several
later writers." (Scrivener, p. 90.)

The function of the comparer (so titled by Scrivener)
—he was a skillful person appointed for the task, "was
to amend manifest errors, sometimes also to insert orna-
mented capitals in places which had been reserved for

them; in later times (and as some believe at a very early period) to set in stops, breathings and accents; in copies destined for ecclesiastical use to arrange the musical notes that were to guide the intonation of the reader." (Scrivener, p. 53.)

In this manuscript (Sinaiticus) there are no breathings and accents, except in portions of Tobit (Old Testament); "the apostrophus and the single point for punctuation are entirely absent for pages together," but "thickly studded" in places where "a later hand has been unusually busy"; there are no capitals, though initial letters have been specially treated, the manuscript contains Ammonian sections and Eusebian canons, though Tischendorf "is positive" that these and certain notes are not "by the original scribe." (Scrivener-Miller, Vol. I, pp. 92-93.)

(Ammonius of Alexandria, 3rd century, possibly a younger contemporary of Origen, made an attempt, said to be one of the earliest, to make a harmony of the Gospels, in which "he put beside the text of the Gospel of Matthew the parallel passages from the three other Gospels." These groupings were known as *Ammonian sections.* Eusebius, "availing himself of the work of Ammonius, divided the text of each Gospel into sections," which varied greatly in length. These are called *Eusebian canons.* The system seems to have been complicated. *Schaff-Herzog,* "Ammonius of Alexandria," Vol. I, p. 156; "Bible Text," Vol. II, p. 101; "Eusebius of Cæsarea," Vol. IV, p. 209.)

Tischendorf 'persuaded himself' that "four several scribes had been engaged upon" the manuscript. While other scholars were not able to follow Tischendorf in this conclusion, yet they have agreed seemingly "that at least two, and probably more, persons have been employed on the several parts of the volume." (Scrivener-Miller, Vol. I, p. 96.)

Scrivener's summary comment on this codex reads as follows:

"With regard to the deeply interesting question as to the critical character of Cod. ℵ, although it strongly supports the Codex Vaticanus in many characteristic readings, yet it cannot be said to give its exclusive adherence to any of the witnesses hitherto examined. It so lends its grave authority, now to one and now to another, as to convince us more than ever of the futility of seeking to derive the genuine text of the New Testament from any one copy, however ancient and, on the whole, trustworthy." (Scrivener, p. 93; see pp. 137, 220, 237, herein; the fourth edition adds the following clause: "when evidence of a wide and varied character is at hand." Scrivener-Miller, Vol. I, p. 97.)

IMPERFECTIONS OF VATICANUS MANUSCRIPT (B)

Concerning the Codex Vaticanus (B), the following details may be noted: From the original B manuscript of the New Testament there were missing the latter part of the Epistle to the Hebrews and the Apocalypse (the Catholic Epistles had followed the Acts). (Scrivener, p. 102.) These missing parts are believed to have been added in the fifteenth century from "a manuscript belonging to Cardinal Bessarion." Scrivener conjectures that the Cardinal brought B with him into the west of Europe. (Scrivener, p. 101.) Capital letters were "totally wanting . . . for some centuries," though the ones later added were probably inserted by the corrector. (Scrivener, pp. 102, 104.) Stops were inserted by a later hand; "breathings and accents are now universally allowed to have been added by a later hand" than the original penman, either in the eighth or tenth or eleventh century, the same hand having also retraced the text, who may also have attempted a critical revision (Scrivener, p. 103); except ℵ it is the only manuscript omitting the last twelve verses of Mark—the writer left a blank column (Scrivener, p. 104) ; it has been called "an abbreviated text of the New Testament"; words or whole clauses are omitted, "330 times in Matthew, 365 in Mark, 439 in Luke, 357 in John, 384 in the Acts, 681 in the surviving Epistles; and 2556 times in all." (Scrivener, p. 116.) Apparently there were four writers involved in the completed text of B as we now have it; the original writer, his contemporary reviser ("both of whom supplied words or letters here and there in the margin or between the lines") ; a third scribe made corrections, and finally the correction of the scribe who retraced. (Scrivener, p. 112.) Tischendorf has "a decided opinion," that the scribe who made B is one of the four who wrote ‭א‬. (Scrivener, p. 113.) Later editors have placed "on the page with the rest of their text readings which are known or credibly stated to be of decidedly later date." (Scrivener, p. 114.) The differences between ‭א‬ and B in many characteristics and singular readings are "more patent and perplexing than ever." (Scrivener, p. 515.)

Imperfections of the Two Manuscripts Compared

As already stated, all of the matters, listed above regarding the place of the origin and preparation of the B manuscript, are wholly wanting. (For a more complete discussion of this manuscript see *Notes Twenty-one, Twenty-two, Twenty-three, and Twenty-four, infra.*)

This much it has been deemed desirable to say here about these two manuscripts because these are the prime reliance of all modern Revisers. The reader will be interested in the *Notes* hereof just referred to.

Before leaving this particular consideration, the reader will also be interested in the following comments

upon these manuscripts, which the Revisers primarily
depend upon.

One critic (Burgon) says:

*"It is easier to find two consecutive verses in which the two
MSS. [א B] differ, the one from the other, than two consecutive
verses in which they entirely agree."* (Scrivener, p. 515, n. 1.)

Regarding Codex B, Scrivener says:

"One marked feature, characteristic of this copy, is the
great number of its omissions, which has induced Dr. Dobbin to
speak of it as presenting 'an abbreviated text of the New Testament:' and certainly the facts he states on this point are
startling enough. He calculates that Codex B leaves out words
or whole clauses no less than 330 times in Matthew, 365 in
Mark, 439 in Luke, 357 in John, 384 in the Acts, 681 in the
surviving Epistles; or 2556 times in all." (Scrivener, p. 116.)

The same scribe also repeatedly re-wrote words and
clauses. (Scrivener, p. 116.)

Another quotation from Burgon, vigorously phrased,
but clearly stating his own views:

"We venture to assure him [Bp. Ellicott], without a particle
of hesitation, that א B D are *three of the most scandalously
corrupt copies extant:*—exhibit *the most shamefully mutilated*
texts which are anywhere to be met with:—have become, by
whatever process (for their history is wholly unknown), the
depositories of the largest amount of *fabricated readings,* ancient *blunders,* and *intentional perversions of Truth,*—which
are discoverable in any known copies of the Word of GOD."
(Burgon, p. 16; see his "Preface," pp. x-xi; for sources of corruption, *id.*, pp. 334-36.)

EARLY APPEARANCE OF VARIOUS TYPES

Kenyon's "reader" will be impressed, on the strength
of the description of the various manuscripts as heretofore listed (see *Notes Fourteen and Fifteen*), with the
fact, as it seems to this "reader," that each family of
manuscripts now listed had some representation in one

or more manuscripts practically from the earliest times; that from early times, these variant texts came into competition one with another and often in the same areas and frequently in the same manuscript; that, specifically, while under this competition, the ℵ B type fell into the rear (as to popular favor at any rate), yet that the Byzantine type gained constantly and finally virtually crowded out for centuries the other type. On the surface at any rate, one could find at least a semblance of justification for Burgon's sarcastic appraisal that "these two Manuscripts are indebted for their preservation, *solely to their ascertained evil character,*" or as stated in his "Table of Contents": "their very preservation being probably attributable solely to the patent foulness of the Text they exhibit" (Burgon, pp. xxxvii, 319; see Kenyon, *Our Bible,* p. 140), for ℵ was holed-up in a monastery at Mt. Sinai, say from 350 A.D. to 1844 A.D., apparently unknown to scholars and unesteemed by its owners and custodians, while B slumbered in the Vatican Library from 1448 (nothing is known of its history before that date, from the probable time of its writing, say 350 A.D. till 1448) till say 1866 (Tischendorf's inspection) save for a slight use by Erasmus in 1535. (Scrivener, pp. 87, 101, 105; Kenyon, *The Text,* pp. 86-87.)

That there was some competition among various texts seems admitted by some critics at least, as will appear a little later.

ONE ORIGINAL TEXT THESIS

There are a few points we might briefly consider in a preliminary way; some of them have already been touched upon. We shall quote freely from Kenyon's works, because (as already stated) modern critics following Extreme Textualist views seem to consider him as

their authority. Regarding this diversity of texts, he lays
down this basic premise:

"At the first each book had its single original text, which
it is now the object of criticism to recover; but in the first two
centuries this original text disappeared under a mass of variants, created by errors, by conscious alterations, and by
attempts to remedy the uncertainties thus created." (*The Text*,
pp. 241-42.)

The same general purpose of establishing the original Greek text was affirmed by the Revisers who produced the Revised Standard Version. (*An Introduction*,
p. 28.) Kenyon elaborates this idea in his discussion of
the "families" into which the manuscripts may be
grouped. (*The Text*, pp. 11 ff.)

This thesis assumes, apparently, that all existing
manuscripts of any one book were copies of, or perhaps
descended from, the first original manuscript which from
a variety of causes became corrupted—*depraved* is the
word they use—as time went on, and finally disappeared,
as Kenyon says, and seemingly the critics agree, "in the
first two centuries."

It might be well to repeat here the comments of
Kenyon already made on this question of continuous line
of descent from the original manuscripts, the Sacred
Autographs. His comments follow:

"The general conclusion to which we seem to be led is that
there is no royal road to the recovery of the original text of
the New Testament. Fifty years ago it seemed as if Westcott
and Hort had found such a road, and that we should depart
from the Codex Vaticanus (except in the case of obvious scribal
blunders) at our peril. The course both of discoveries and of
critical study has made it increasingly difficult to believe that the
Vaticanus and its allies represent a stream of tradition that has
come down practically uncontaminated from the original sources.
Based as they must have been on a multitude of different rolls,

it would have been a singularly happy accident if all had been
of the same character, and all deriving without contamination
from the originals. The uniformity of character which on the
whole marks the Vaticanus and Sinaiticus is better to be explained as the result of skilled editing of well-selected authorities on a definite principle. Therefore, while respecting the
authority due to the age and character of this recension, we
shall be disposed to give more consideration than Westcott and
Hort did to other early readings which found a home in the
Western, Syriac, or Cæsarean texts." (Kenyon, *The Story*, p.
143; see pp. 94, 127, herein.)

This seems to put an end to the loudly-proclaimed
primacy and legitimacy of the Sinaiticus and Vaticanus
texts.

LUKE'S TESTIMONY

But, Kenyon's "reader" asks, might there not have
been more than one person, indeed might there not have
been several persons (does not Luke so state) writing
an original account of Christ's labors and teachings, or
of some part or incident or incidents thereof? We now
appeal to four—Matthew, Mark, Luke, and John, to
which may be added Acts. There must have been others
(some postulate a Q text as the basis for some of the
Gospels). (Allen, Hastings *Encyc.*, Vol. IV, p. 319b.)

Luke expressly says there were many:

"Forasmuch as many have taken in hand to set forth in
order a declaration of those things which are most surely believed among us,

"Even as they delivered them unto us, which from the
beginning were eyewitnesses, and ministers of the word;

"It seemed good to me also, having had perfect understanding of all things from the very first, to write unto thee in order,
most excellent Theophilus,

"That thou mightest know the certainty of those things,
wherein thou hast been instructed." (Luke 1:1-4.)

In this connection it is worth while to recall Paul's words to Timothy:

"The cloke that I left at Troas with Carpus, when thou comest, bring with thee, and the books, but especially the parchments." (II Tim. 4:13.)

It may well be that the "parchments" were scriptures, Gospel records. Luke's testimony is as set out above. So he decides to add his own account to the "many" already existing. There is nothing in Luke's statement that would suggest that he was speaking of copies of a single original. Luke says, "as many have taken in hand to set forth in order a declaration of those things which are most surely believed among us." These "declarations" must surely have been individual originals, not copies of one original. We certainly might assume that Luke himself made use of these various earlier accounts, which, as to Luke, would be originals.

A Kenyon "reader" might certainly question whether all the variant readings of the thousands of New Testament manuscripts now known (fragmentary as the bulk of them are) must necessarily be considered as having descended from a "single original text" of each book, or whether some other "original text," not a copy of the "single original text," might not have been resorted to for a reading different from that coming down from the "single original text" or from any other "original" source; and the "reader" asks, can it be definitely said in fact that the other records could not have been more accurate than the postulated "single original text" of the critics? On the facts, it would seem to the "reader" that the chance of other "original texts" is far more probable than the chance that all variant readings come from corruptions of a "single original text." (For a discussion of sources of Gospel texts, see *A Dictionary of Christ and the Gospels*, James Hastings, ed. (New York, Charles Scribner's Sons, 1908), for the following discussions: Willoughby C. Allen, "Matthew, Gospel According to," Vol. II; Arthur J. MacLean, "Mark, Gospel According to," Vol. II; Arthur Wright, "Luke, Gospel According to," Vol. II; R. H. Strachan, "John, Gospel of (I.: Critical article)," Vol. I; William Ralph Inge, "John, Gospel of (II.: Contents)," Vol. I.)

"WELTER" OF READINGS

All the authorities agree that soon after the Apostles disappeared there rapidly developed a multiplicity of texts. By the fourth century, says Kenyon, "they had to deal with a great welter of various readings and of mixed texts." (*The Text*, p. 248.)

The makers of manuscripts began to draw from the various texts before them in making their own, the critics affirm.

"Such interchange of influence has indeed to be recognized as a constant factor in textual history. Hardly any manuscript is free from influences from authorities of a different complexion from itself. The readings characteristic of each family have for the most part to be extracted from manuscripts which in the main have been revised into conformity with the prevalent text,—generally and increasingly the Received Text, which ultimately submerged all others, leaving only here and there a few relics, like the wandering blocks of geology, of a more primeval form." (*The Text*, pp. 249-250. It is hoped Kenyon's textual criticism is better than his geology seems to be.)

ALL PRINCIPAL TYPES IN EGYPT

Referring to the popular critical theory held in the last quarter of the last century by the Extreme Textualists,—that in Egypt there was preserved a text that came down largely in an uncorrupted state until it found record in the Vaticanus (B) Manuscript,—Kenyon adds, after calling attention to the Chester Beatty papyri and affirming that whether these papyri were "regarded as good or bad . . . ." yet—

"What is significant is that they prove that in Egypt in the early part of the third century readings were in circulation which were derived from, or which eventually became attached to, all the principal families, together with a not inconsiderable number of which no other witness has survived. In the Gospels the Chester Beatty papyrus has readings which we associate with the β, γ, and δ texts, in varying proportions in the different books." (*The Text,* pp. 250-251.)

Kenyon is here referring to his proposed classification of texts. The δ group includes the Codex Bezae which became one of the sources (apparently a minor source) of the Byzantine text as finally developed. (*The Text,* pp. 213, ff.)

As to Codex Bezae, Kenyon observes, speaking of the manuscripts available to Stephanus, "One of these was really old, that which is now known as the Codex Bezae, but for reasons which will appear later little use was made of it." (*The Story,* p. 46.)

Kenyon had previously observed:

"But to whichever family a critic may give his general preference, it by no means follows that he should regard it as always right. . . . He had to make a number of choices where the balance of probability was quite undetermined, and, being human, he cannot always have chosen right. Therefore a modern editor must be free to consider readings with an open mind, whether he finds them in a manuscript predominantly of β or γ or δ character." (*The Text,* p. 250.)

DEVELOPMENT OF TEXTS

Kenyon's views as to the way in which his α and β and δ texts were developed are stated thus:

"When an editor set himself to deal with the varied material that he found before him, he could approach his task in several different ways. To some (and this was the commonest type) the governing idea was to make the text plain and easy. To this end the order of words was altered, names and pronouns were introduced, normal phrases were substituted for less usual ones, words which might be misunderstood or misinterpreted in an unorthodox manner were omitted or changed, narratives in one Gospel were assimilated to those in another, inexact quotations from the Old Testament were made exact, alternative readings in different manuscripts were combined, and so on. The result was an easy, intelligible text, at some sacrifice of character, and ultimately differing considerably in detail, though not in essential teaching, from the original. In this way such a text as the α text was produced.

"Another editor, of more independent frame of mind, might treat the text more freely, varying phrases to suit his own taste, importing short passages from other sources, amplifying the narrative for the sake of effect, including rather than omitting, and attaching little importance to accuracy of transmission, though with no doctrinal motives. This would be the genesis of the δ text. At the opposite extreme to him would be the trained scholar, whose guiding principle would be accuracy, not edification, who would be thinking of the author rather than of the reader. He would be careful to consult the oldest manuscripts accessible to him, and would compare their variant readings in the light of critical science, considering which was most likely to give the author's original words. He would tend to omit superfluities or insufficiently attested words or passages, and to prefer the more difficult reading to the easier, as more likely to have been altered. These are the lines on which the closest approximation to the original would be arrived at. They are the established principles of textual science, which are applied to the editing of classical texts; and it is because the β text [essentially the Revised Version] appears to have been formed on these lines that most modern scholars, even if they are not satisfied that it has preserved the authentic original substantially in uncontaminated integrity, nevertheless hold that on the whole it offers us the purest text." (*The Text,* pp. 248-249.)

For other expressions by Kenyon upon the value of the Sinaiticus and Vaticanus texts, we refer to *Note Eight,* p. 94, and *Note Thirteen,* p. 127.

With reference to the Byzantine text, or as Kenyon classifies it, the α text, he says:

"This is the text found in the great majority of manuscripts, entrenched in print by Erasmus and Stephanus, and known as the Textus Receptus or Received Text, as opposed to the critical editions of modern times. It is Bengel's 'Asiatic,' Semler's 'Oriental,' Griesbach's 'Constantinopolitan,' Hort's 'Syrian,' von Soden's 'K,' and it is the text translated in our Authorized Version." (*The Text,* pp. 197-198.)

Kenyon's "reader" is not too much impressed with this purely speculative (as it seems) account of how the Textus Receptus (α text) was developed. The description seems to be another effort to discredit that text, because it does not support the critics' favorite.

BUILDING REVISED STANDARD VERSION TEXT

In passing it may be briefly said that the foregoing account regarding the production of Kenyon's family α (Textus Receptus) almost perfectly describes the processes used by the latest modern Revisers of that text,— particularly (by admission) the Revisers who produced the Revised Standard Version of 1946. More will be said of this matter later (*Note Thirty-three*), but it might be said now that the recent Revisers admittedly and boastfully make changes to make the text more readable, i.e., to make the text plain and "easy to read"; the language of the King James is too "elegant" for the New Testament; they have made changes of so-called "mistranslations," which have altered, doctrinally, the Authorized Version text; they have corrected the "mistakes in English grammar" of the King James translation; they have made changes where the Authorized Version "gives an inaccurate picture of the underlying Greek text," (which, of course, the Revisers do not have); they have elimi-

ΕΠΙΣΤΟΛΗ ΤΟΥ ΑΓΙΟΥ
ΑΠΟΣΤΟΛΟΥ ΙΑΚΩΒΟΥ

EPISTOLA BEATI APO
STOLI IACOBI

Iacobus dei ac domini Iesu Christi seru⁹, duodecim tribubus, q̃ sunt i dispersióe, salutē. Pro summo gaudio ducite fratres mei, quoties in tētationes incideritis uarias. illud scientes, q d'explo ratio fidei uestræ, parit patiétiā. cætex̃ pa tiétia opus p̃fectũ habeat, ut sitis p̃fecti, & integri. & nulla in parte diminuti. Q d' si cui uestrū deest sapientia, postulet ab eo q dat, nēpe deo, q dat incq̃ oibus sim/ pliciter, & nõ improperat. ac dabit ci, sed postulet fide, nihil hæsitans. Nā qui hæsi tat, is similis est fluctui maris, qui uentis agit & impetu rapit. Ne uero existimet homo ille, se qcq̃ accepturũ a dño. Vir animo duplici, incõstás est in oibus uijs suis. Glorietur autē frater qui est humi/ lis in sublimitate sua. Contra qui diues est, in humiliatióe sui, quoniā ueluti flos herbæ p̃teribit. Exortus est enim sol cũ æstu & exaruit herba, & flos illi⁹ decidit, & decor aspectus illius perijt. Sic & diues in abūdantia sua marcescet. Beatus uir q suffert tentationem, quoniā cũ ,pbatus erit, accipiet coronã uitæ quam promisit dñs ijs a quibus fuerit dilectus. Ne quis cũ tentatur dicat se a deo tentari. Nā de us ut a malis tentari non potest, ita nec ipse quēcq̃ tentat, Imo unusquisq̃ tenta
o tur, dum

James 1:1-13

ERASMUS BIBLE IN GREEK AND LATIN

1516 (February). First Greek Bible actually published; printed in Germany. Greek Complutensian Bible prepared by 1514, but not actually published till 1520. Both Complutensian and Erasmus texts were essentially Byzantine. Erasmus Bible was foundation of Textus Receptus, in translation the Authorized or King James Version. See pp. 216 and 170, herein.

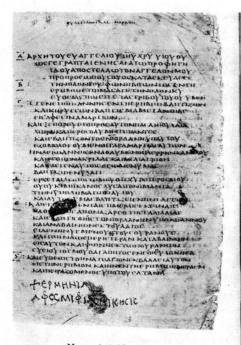
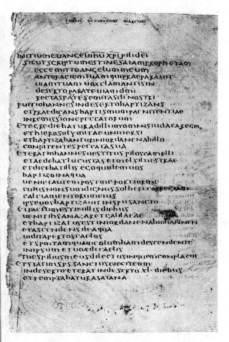

MARC 1:1-13

MARC 1:1-13

Mark 1:1-13

D—CODEX BEZAE

Greek and Latin vellum. Uncial. Probably 5th century. Greek on left page, Latin on right. Origin doubtful,—Egypt, northern Africa, possibly Sicily, Sardinia, Antioch. Dispute as to which text the prime one, the other being the translation thereof. Beza said to have discovered it in Monastery of St. Irenaeus in 1562. University Library at Cambridge, England. See pp. 218 and 141, herein.

nated anachronisms; they have revised and edited the proper names in the Authorized Version, particularly when the Aramaic is involved; they have altered pronouns, tenses of verbs, etc., etc. But more to the point, they, too, have made changes so that the text expresses their own theological ideas. If a text can be depraved by such means, this new translation gives us an extremely depraved text as against one that has been accepted for centuries. One modern writer says that the modern Revisers have made 30,000 changes in the New Testament of the Authorized Version, the King James text. (Dwight MacDonald, quoting Allen Wikgren, "The Bible in Modern Undress," *The New Yorker*, November 14, 1953.)

COMPETITIVE TEXTS

But we return to the matter of competitive texts for a few observations:

It should be recalled that as to the ℵ and B texts (upon the antiquity of which so much weight has been given to the point that, more or less, principally more, they control in the attempted reconstruction of the theoretical original Greek text), the best guess as to their age is that they were written during the second quarter of the fourth century, say prior to 350 A.D. (But see *The Text*, p. 81.) Of them, Kenyon says: "These two fourth-century MSS. form the head and main substance of a group which in the opinion of many presents the most authentic text of the N.T. Substantially it is the text represented in our Revised Version [British]." (*The Text*, p. 81; see p. 137, herein.)

EGYPTIAN PAPYRI

As we have already seen, the Michigan papyrus (dated variously from early 3rd to 4th or 5th centuries) has a text substantially that of Codex Bezae. We repeat, this Codex Bezae is one of those from which Textus Receptus was constructed, though scantily used. It could be of the century before א or B or contemporary with them, or a little later. It is a corrupt text, a mixture, but so is א. (See *supra, Note Fourteen,* p. 134, and *supra, Note Nineteen,* p. 203.)

Another papyrus (**P**⁴⁶ Chester Beatty Pap. II) dated early 3rd century, one hundred years before Sinaiticus, is said to agree more with the Alexandrian group than with the Western, which latter includes D—the Codex Bezae—but in Romans, there are "a noticeable number of agreements with the latter," that is, the group that includes D. Thus in the 3rd century (200 A.D., plus) a part at least of the Codex Bezae—one of the sources of the Byzantine text—was in circulation in Egypt. (*The Text,* pp. 73-74; see p. 135, herein.)

Still another papyrus (**P**⁴⁷ Chester Beatty Pap. III) 3rd century, throws into competition in its text, the texts of the favorite א A C P manuscripts, and the Byzantine ("the mass of later MSS.") text, which are both in the same manuscript. (See Kenyon, *Our Bible,* p. 177.) Finally, **P**⁴⁸, 3rd century, is "a text definitely of the Codex Bezae type." (*The Text,* p. 74.)

Thus of these early papyri, 3rd century, the majority mentioned contain seemingly Byzantine readings (Codex Bezae type, though it must not be forgotten that Codex Bezae also contained readings of the B type), as in **P**⁴⁸, some such readings in preponderance, others to a substantial degree, and all, it seems, in competition in the text itself with the א B type. *All these are of the century before א B were written.*

Kenyon's "reader" must be permitted to observe that

on this evidence the *antiquity* of one type is at least as
great as that of the others, and that, at this time, the ℵ B
type was in a position to gain prestige as much as the
Byzantine. The "reader" is not unmindful that according to the critics the Byzantine type shows a development
of text in certain particulars which the ℵ B type lacks.
It would seem this might conceivably bring the result
(which the critics apparently contend for) that the ℵ B
type text is nearer its earlier forms than is the Byzantine
to its antecedents. But why not apply this conclusion to
the Byzantine text? One seems as good a guess as the
other. One still has in the early papyri the two types
running side by side, with apparently nothing to indicate
the one was a better text than the other, though the subsequent history of the two types shows that the Church
preferred the Byzantine as the better. No discussion has
been noted that would really show that the changes made
by the editors (of the Byzantine text) who worked with
this "welter" of manuscripts, were surely the result of
caprice or literary or theological considerations, rather
than that they were founded on some earlier text not now
known. The explanation offered by the Extreme Textualists on this point seems a bit too easy and convenient, to ignore too many other possibilities, in order
to be really persuasive.

THE UNCIAL TEXTS IN GREEK

We will now note some of the uncials.

First, as to the Sinaiticus, we have seen no statement
directly touching the presence of Byzantine passages in
this text, but Kenyon says, "it is closely allied to the Vaticanus ... In Acts and Epistles it is habitually to be found
in the same group with A and B, though not without some
variations." (*The Text*, pp. 81-82.)

While Scrivener says:

"It so lends its grave authority, now to one and now to another, as to convince us more than ever of the futility of seeking to derive the genuine text of the New Testament from any one copy, however ancient and, on the whole, trustworthy." (Scrivener, p. 93; see p. 137, herein.) The fourth edition adds the following clause: "when evidence of a wide and varied character is at hand." (Scrivener-Miller, Vol. I, p. 97.)

A straight-forward statement as to the presence or absence in ℵ of Byzantine readings, and of the extent thereof, would be interesting. All discussions noted leave this question open.

Next, as to Codex Alexandrinus, A, dated early 5th century, a little over half a century later than ℵ or B, this Codex is said to be "Alexandrian (i.e., akin to ℵ B) except in the Gospels, where it shows signs of the Antiochian revision which eventually produced the received ecclesiastical text." (*The Text*, p. 84.) This is certainly evidence for the Byzantine text, and that too in the Gospels. Kenyon says that the Alexandrinus (early 5th century) and Codex C (Codex Ephraemi, 5th century) "contain a considerable number of readings" of the Byzantine type α. Why should this evidence be submerged or cast aside, and the ℵ B emphasized? (*The Text*, p. 201; see p. 138, herein.) Here again are the two types side-by-side, so to speak, of which the one type—the ℵ B —did not prosper in popular use and the Byzantine did, to the development of the Textus Receptus. (*The Text*, pp. 82 ff.) Kenyon's reference to "the Antiochian revision" as if to an historic fact, is curious, because in his book, *Our Bible,* he declares, regarding an "Antiochian revision," "there is absolutely no historical confirmation of the Syrian revision of the text . . . . it does seem possible that the formal revision of the text at a set time in or about Antioch may be a myth." (*Our Bible*, p. 115; see p. 77, herein; Dr. Kenyon does not seem always to remember at one time what he has written at another time.)

The Codex Bezae (dated 5th century) has a difficult, confusing text in both Greek and Latin. Here also are the two types, in the same text, "showing the widest divergences both from the Alexandrian type headed by ℵ B and from the type which eventually prevailed in the Greek Church and which appears in our Received Text and Authorized Version." (*The Text*, p. 90.) It is difficult to understand this "divergence" except on the premise that both texts were in the manuscript.

It may be again noted that the Codex Bezae was one of the codices upon which the Textus Receptus was built, though it was scantily used. (*Note Sixteen*, p. 171.)

The Codex Purpureus Petropolitanus of the 6th century has a text which "is of Byzantine type, in a rather early stage of its evolution"; and see along with this codex, the Codex Sinopensis (6th century), Codex Rossanensis (6th century), Codex Beratinus (6th century), while the Codex Washingtonianus I, late 4th or 5th century, had a text partly Byzantine, partly Alexandrian, partly Caesarean, and the Codex Dublinensis, 6th century, had a text "with many agreements with ℵ." (*The Text*, p. 102; see pp. 145-148, herein.)

Of Codex Basiliensis (8th century), while Kenyon says of it: "Of no great value," (*The Text*, p. 97; see p. 198 herein) Scrivener (as already noted) says its value "is considerable" and "approaches more nearly than some others of its date to the text now commonly received, and is an excellent witness for it." (Scrivener, p. 128.)

To these might be added the Codex Zacynthius (8th

century), which Kenyon says was related to B. Scrivener points out it has relatively few changes from the Byzantine text.

Thus by the end of the 8th century we have a manuscript that is virtually the Textus Receptus, the Authorized Version. By this time, it would seem, the Byzantine text had more or less attained its development. The ℵ B texts, while existing, were seemingly not in general use.

In the next century (9th) the Codex Cyprius gave "a complete copy of the Gospels, and a typical representative of the normal ecclesiastical or Byzantine text" (*The Text*, p. 99; see p. 145, herein), and see also the Codex Koridethianus (9th century), where "in the Gospels other than Mark its text has been revised into closer conformity with the Received Text." (*The Text*, pp. 102-103.)

This is a very interesting comment,—a text has been "revised" to conform to the Received Text. The author wonders whether it would be possible to consider that a full Received Text has been changed so as to incorporate some ℵ B readings. The "reader" can only wonder as to this and many other kindred comments,—whether the form of the statement of fact is not consciously framed to carry a definite impression which the actual facts do not justify.

The Syriac Versions

The foregoing relates to the uncials written in Greek, but we must not overlook the Versions,—particularly the Syriac. Whatever may have been the type of text of the Old Syriac, it is interesting to note that, "in general . . . while the version cannot be reckoned wholly with either the ℵ B group or the D group, it shows a preponderance of agreement with the latter," that is, the Byzantine-

Codex Bezae type of text. Seemingly, this (the Old Syriac) dates "from the last quarter of the second century." (*The Text*, pp. 117, 121.) Thus both types, on this assumption, were extant in versions as early as A.D. 175.

The Diatessaron of Tatian is placed about 160 A.D. to 170 A.D. If, as some assume, this harmony was based on the Old Syriac Version, then that Version was written at least as early as the beginning of the third quarter of the second century, say about 150 A.D. to 175 A.D. But Kenyon says it "was not made from OS." (*The Text*, p. 121.)

The Peshitta was apparently used by Chrysostom, "who was born and worked at Antioch until 398." So this text, which was essentially Byzantine, was in use in Syria, becoming the "official Bible of the Syriac Church." This would be within half a century of the ℵ B manuscripts. Kenyon, in commenting about this situation, which seems exceedingly involved and uncertain as he presents it, still clings to the Antiochian revision. Miller's comment must be well based: "The Peshito must be got rid of by Extreme Textualists, or it would witness inconveniently before the Fourth century to the 'Syrian' Text. Well indeed may Dr. Hort add 'even for conjecture the materials are scanty.' " Nor may we forget that Kenyon says, "there is absolutely no historical confirmation of the Syrian revision of the text," and that a "formal revision of the text at a set time in or about Antioch may be a myth." (*The Text*, pp. 122-123, 152; Miller, p. 51; *Our Bible*, p. 115; and see *Note Six*, and pp. 76-79, 220-221, herein.)

SUMMARY

The Armenian version is dated about 400 A.D., and apparently witnesses the Byzantine type. The early

Coptic or Egyptian versions (dated, in the earliest forms, in the latter part of the second century (100-200 A.D.) seem to have been a mixture of ℵ B D (Bezae) and Old Latin. Thus at this early date the types are intermingled, though Kenyon asserts the text is preponderantly ℵ B. (*The Text*, pp. 125-129, 131-132.) But what were the unpreponderant texts? We might be told; it would be interesting. (And note the comment at the end of the comment on the uncials, p. 222, *supra.*)

Thus the Codex Bezae type text (it seems likely of the Byzantine type; if it were otherwise, we should probably have been told) in some of its portions appeared in the Egyptian papyri along with the rival B type text in the latter part of the 2nd century (that is, the late 100's-plus A.D.). It is not clear from the discussions noted that ℵ may not have had some Byzantine readings (350 A.D.). One is inclined to think if Byzantine texts were wholly absent we would have been told. The Codex A did have "ancestral readings" (5th century) of the Byzantine type, particularly in the Gospels. The Codex Bezae of the 5th century was one of the codices out of which the Textus Receptus was built, though scantily used. In the Codex Basiliensis of the 8th century we are approaching the final form of the Byzantine text. And in the 9th century we have the Codex Cyprius—"*a typical representative of the normal ecclesiastical or Byzantine text.*" (Kenyon, *The Text*, p. 99; italics ours.)

As the years grew, the Church seems largely to have repudiated or rejected the B type text, though, all along the way, texts occasionally appeared akin to the ℵ and B type: Codex Borgianus (5th century), Codex Nitriensis (6th century), Codex Dublinensis (6th century), Codex Zacynthius (8th century), and Codex Laurensis (8th or 9th century).

Apparently by the 9th century—up to which time the texts of the two types, Byzantine and B type, had frequently existed side by side, though apparently the ℵ B type was not generally known in any such form as B had crystallized it in the 4th century—the Church was casting off the ℵ B readings, and adopting the Byzantine. Thus in a competition of centuries, when they were centuries nearer the Sacred Autographs than we are now, and when both texts were known and available, the Church finally fixed upon the Byzantine text.

Speaking of the α text (the name he has assigned to the Byzantine type), Kenyon says:

"As has already been said, the α text is found in by far the greater number of our extant authorities, but some of the earlier ones show it less fully developed. Thus A and C in the Gospels contain a considerable number of readings of this type. So does W, except in Mk. So do the purple MSS. N O Σ Φ. It is fully established in the later uncials E, F, G, H, K, M, S, U, V, Y, Ω, which Legg classes together as representing this type of text. Of the minuscules all may be assumed to have this text until the contrary has been demonstrated; the most important of the exceptional minuscules will be specified later as belonging to other groups; and even these have not wholly escaped its influence. The only attempt to classify this great mass of materials is that made by von Soden, which has been described above; it will be remembered that his main divisions are K^1, of which the earliest representative (Ω) is of the eighth century; K^x, which was dominant from the tenth to the twelfth century; and K^r, which prevailed from the thirteenth century onwards; each of these having many subdivisions.

"The relatively late date and secondary character of the α text must now be taken as established." (*The Text,* pp. 201-202.)

But on the evidence Kenyon submits, it is a little difficult for his "reader" to justify the conclusion about the late date of the Byzantine text or of its "secondary character," since Byztantine readings seem as early as any others and are with the others in the same manuscripts, sometimes seem to be called to witness the presence of the ℵ B text. It does seem clear to Kenyon's "reader" that such readings are *secondary* chiefly because the Extreme Textualists have found it convenient, perhaps necessary, so to designate them in order to support their favorites, the ℵ and B texts.

The writer should and does apologize for expressing so definitely his own views on this highly difficult, specialized, controversial field, in and about which the most learned and profound scholars differ so widely. But this "reader," after examining and considering as carefully as he might, the arguments and conclusions reached by the various scholars felt that some other "reader" might be interested in the views of this "reader" writer. He feels clearly that the evidence given, and the agreements based thereon by the Extreme Textualists do not sustain the conclusions reached by them. We do not yet have the final word on this controversy.

NOTE TWENTY •
The Inspired Version by the Prophet Joseph Smith

Summary. The Prophet Joseph Smith began, but, it seems, never completed an Inspired Version of the Bible. It perhaps might be appropriately termed a recension. It followed the King James Version in most matters, though containing an entirely new version of the opening chapters of Genesis. There was also considerable change in the twenty-fourth chapter of Matthew.

Following the versions in a chronological order, another version should be mentioned here,—the Inspired Version by the Prophet Joseph Smith. This is not a translation in the usual sense (so far as our records show) although what purports to be a printing of the version is so titled. In fact, this version, if it had been a translation from Greek or other manuscripts, would have been rather a recension than a version, because it is founded upon, indeed is an amended Authorized Version. Except in the opening chapters of Genesis, it follows closely the Authorized Version text, the alterations made here and there in the Authorized Version text being seemingly for purposes of clarification, largely of doctrinal problems, or of additions to the same purpose.

Perhaps the most extensive change made in any other one place than in Genesis, occurs in the twenty-fourth chapter of Matthew, where the subject matter has been so rearranged as more clearly to distinguish the two main themes of the discourse, the one, the signs preceding and the destruction of Jerusalem, and the other, the signs of the Second Coming.

The Genesis portion is designated (in the Pearl of Great Price) as the Book of Moses and covers the ground covered by and includes chapters 1 to 5 of Genesis and down through chapter 6, verse 13.

This Book of Moses, together with the Book of Abraham (a translation by the Prophet, of a papyrus), the revision of the twenty-fourth chapter of Matthew, and some other documents ("Extracts from the History of Joseph Smith, the Prophet"—now also printed separately under the title, *Joseph Smith Tells His Own Story*—and the Articles of Faith) are published (first edition, 1851) as The Pearl of Great Price.

The Church of Jesus Christ of Latter-day Saints has never issued the Inspired Version of the whole Bible, since apparently the Prophet Joseph never finally finished his revision. (See *DHC*, Vol. I, pp. 215, 324.) However, the Reorganized Church has printed an edition of the Bible with a title page which recites: "The /Holy Scriptures/ Translated and Corrected/ by the/ Spirit of Revelation/ by/ Joseph Smith, Jr./ The Seer."

So much of the revision as is covered by the Book of Moses and by the twenty-fourth chapter of Matthew (as these are printed in the Pearl of Great Price) is accepted by the Latter-day Saints.

The Authorized Version so amended, the Pearl of Great Price (just described), the Book of Mormon, and the Doctrine and Covenants, constitute the accepted Scriptures of the Church. To these Scriptures are added from time to time other revelations and inspired writings or utterances of the presiding authority of the Church.

The first recorded revelation received by the Prophet Joseph Smith in connection with this revision came sometime in 1830. The Prophet records preparing to "recommence" work on this revision ("translation" as he termed it) on September 12, 1831. (*DHC*, Vol. I, pp. 98, 215.)

An entry in his journal under date of February 2, 1833, affirms:

"I completed the translation and review of the New Testament, on the 2nd of February, 1833, and sealed it up, no more to be opened till it arrived in Zion." (*DHC*, Vol. I, p. 324.)

It was the Prophet's intention to publish together the New Testament text and the Book of Mormon, apparently in Zion, but the persecutions of the Saints in Missouri and their drivings did not permit the accomplishment of this purpose. (*DHC*, Vol. I, p. 341. See for discussion and facts, *DHC*, Vol. I, pp. 132, 211, 215; B. H. Roberts, *A Comprehensive History of The Church of Jesus Christ of Latter-day Saints*, Century I (Salt Lake City, Deseret News Press, 1930), Vol. I, pp. 238 ff., 247, 271; Joseph Fielding Smith, *Essentials in Church History*, 5th ed. (Salt Lake City, Deseret News Press, 1935), p. 138.)

NOTE TWENTY-ONE ·
The Revised Versions, British and American

Item 1. General Observations.

Summary. It would have been rather a recension than a revision, if instructions had been strictly followed. The work is essentially the offspring of the modern "lower" textual criticism, dealing with texts. Independent study and investigation being impossible, the criticism of the Revised Version will primarily consist in quoting the criticism of acknowledged scholars. The general plan of treatment herein is given.

The British New Testament Preface date is November 11, 1880, Oxford Press, 1881. The Old Testament Preface date is July 10, 1884, Oxford Press, 1885. The equivalent American New Testament Revision has no Preface date, but the title page gives 1881, "Newly Edited by the New Testament Members of the American Revision Committee, A.D. 1900, Standard Edition," Thomas Nelson & Sons, press. The American Old Testament Revision also has no Preface date, but the title page gives 1881-1885, "Newly Edited by the American Revision Committee, A.D. 1901, Standard Edition," Thomas Nelson & Sons, press.

If instructions issued to the Revisers for this first revision had been strictly followed, it would appear this work should have been called a *recension,* not a *version.*

Quite clearly, it seems to the layman, the Revised Version is the offspring of modern criticism.

In strict parlance the "lower" or textual criticism deals with the language, form, and wording of the texts themselves; the "higher" or historical criticism, deals with the authorship of the sacred books, etc. Popularly the term "higher criticism" covers both sorts, and is so used in these *Notes*, though usually when so used herein, reference is generally to criticism of the texts, though both kinds may be covered.

The author should at this point repeat, and repeat again, that his scholarship does not qualify him to examine the original manuscripts, and to analyze and to comment thereon. Moreover, the manuscripts are not available to him, even if he were able to use them. So the pages that follow (as already pointed out) will be made up, in the far larger part (as have many that have preceded in these *Notes*), of quotations from recognized scholars who have treated the subjects that will be discussed herein. The author is emboldened to proceed by Kenyon's comment (already repeatedly quoted) as to what an "intelligent reader" might do, hoping the author may qualify under that description.

The author has already, in a quotation from Miller (*supra, Note Twelve*) listed some seven most important scriptural texts, which, in the Revised Version, have either been omitted, or seriously questioned as to their genuineness, or changed by the Extreme Textualists, usually referred to herein as the "higher critics," though in the classification of literary and historical criticism as the "lower" critics. The scholars point out many places, other than those mentioned herein, where, by omissions or doubt-raising marginal notes (frequently misleading, as the critics allege), the accuracy of the Authorized Version is brought into question.

These alterations and doubt-casting marginal notes are so important that it seems well to give the criticisms of the Sound or High Textualists (the opposite of the

Extreme Textualists) upon a number of the more vital of them. To avoid all misconception, it seems wise again insistently to point out that the manuscripts upon which an independent judgment might be formed are not available to the author, and that if they had been at his command, his scholarship is so scant he could not have used them. These two facts are stressed and should not be forgotten.

Nevertheless, because the scriptures affected are so vital, it seems wisdom, since we cannot make our own independent analysis of the various manuscripts, to quote generously from the views of the Sound Textualists, that we may have some idea of the damage which the Extreme Textualists are inflicting upon some of the fundamental beliefs of the Christian world. The views of the Extreme Textualists are calculated largely if not completely to destroy Christ and the Christianity of two thousand years of building. This must not be.

This will result (as already repeatedly pointed out) in a largely paste-pot-and-scissors operation herein, but it will be accurate.

As bearing upon this whole general matter, it might be noted that the Sound Textualists (Burgon, pp. 1, 2, 6) insistently urge that the Revisers departed from their instructions to revise the Authorized Version, and, violative of their instructions, devoted themselves primarily to the building of a new Greek text, and then translating it.

As a groundwork for the discussion of a few of the attacks of the Extreme Textualists on the Authorized Version, we refer to *Note Eleven* for an account of the development of modern criticism—what it seeks to do. The author will in addition, also give some consideration to observations already made touching on the history and character of the two Greek texts ℵ and B; as well as call attention to some of the principles applied by the compilers of the new Greek text in their work of compilation. The author will then note what scholars have to say about some changes made (additions or omissions) by the Revisers in their production of the Revised Version.

Item 2.   Attitude and Possible Motives of Revisionists.

Summary. Revision was under the influence and to a great extent the direction of Extreme Textualists, the earliest of whom were avowedly seeking to destroy the position among Christians held by the Authorized Version. Westcott and Hort's new Greek text, fabricated by them, based primarily on ℵ and B seemed to control the new Revision, though since then these manuscripts have lost some of their former importance, even among Extreme Textualists.

We return to the text of the Revised Version which was prepared and issued, certainly under the influence, if not under the positive guidance and direction of the Extreme Textualists (the critics of the first class described by Allen, *Note Eleven*), and who entertained concepts just indicated as belonging to that class. Under such conditions we must not be surprised if the new Version shall eliminate or cast doubt upon passages and expressions that over the centuries have become hallowed.

As already pointed out, open war was declared on the Authorized Version (Textus Receptus, King James Version) more than one hundred years ago. (*Supra, Note Eleven.*)   As noted there, it has been said that Lachmann (1793-1851) 'broke the monopoly of the TR' (Lachmann's text, 1831); Tregelles (1813-1875) 'completely ignored the TR' (1857-1872); and Westcott and

Hort are credited with having 'scored a decisive triumph' against the defenders of the Authorized Version. As already suggested, we shall see that it was the new Greek text (fabricated by Westcott and Hort) that was to control the work of the Revisers, and we shall quote at some length the opinion of some scholars upon the character of this new Greek text and the manuscripts upon which it rests. Tischendorf (1815-1874) was "the most conspicuous figure in this school." (Miller, p. 23; see *supra*, see for estimate of Tischendorf, *infra*, pp. 258 ff.)

When in 1870 (February 10), the Convocation of the Southern Province (Burgon, p. 2)—The Convocation of the Province of Canterbury ("Revisers' Preface" (to the N.T.), vi-b; see *infra*, pp. 265 ff.) set up the machinery for a revision of the King James translation of the Bible (hereinafter considered), the onslaught of the Extreme Textualists had grown and crystallized into what has been characterized (as to codices א and B, Sinaiticus and Vaticanus) as 'worship' on the part of Tregelles (Burgon, p. 333) and "superstitious reverence" on the part of Westcott and Hort. (Burgon, p. 95.) This new Greek text, fabricated by Drs. Westcott and Hort, would appear to be based primarily on Vaticanus.

This new Greek text (Westcott and Hort) becomes important to us, as indeed do the codices just named, primarily because of the effect they are exercising upon the English versions of the Holy Bible, an influence which it may perhaps be happily said, seems to be on the wane.

While many of the extravagant claims made by the Extreme Textualists for the Codices א B have been largely abandoned by at least some of the present members of that group, yet these codices are still given a primacy position in arguments by their proponents that the Sound Textualists will not concede. Recent discoveries have

driven back the Extreme Textualists from their most advanced position as to the value of these codices, but they
still give them a preferential position, and still use them
more or less as standards for comparison and evaluation.
It seems useful, therefore, to give in some considerable
detail the arguments and considerations which may be
made against these codices on the merits.

Kenyon claims that the "relative lateness" of the Byzantine or Received Text has been regarded by almost all
scholars as proved, but that this does not dispose of the
contentions as to the relative value of texts which "still
remains the outstanding issue in the criticism of the New
Testament." (Kenyon, *The Text*, pp. 170-171.) We venture to refer to *Note Nineteen* where the author has
brought together some facts that are not consistent with
the alleged lateness of the Byzantine text.

We shall therefore quote extensively from the arguments of the Sound Textualists against the positions
claimed by the Extreme Textualists for their favorite
אַ B texts.

It is worth while here to devote a little space to the
history of these two codices upon which so much reliance
is placed by the Extreme Textualists, even though rather
extensive reviews of and comments on these two codices
(אַ B) have been hereinbefore made.

Item 3.   The Codex Sinaiticus (אַ).

Summary. Brief history of Codex. It is now in the
hands of the British Government.

The following is a brief description by Scrivener of
this codex and its discovery, which has in it something
of the romantic. It is a dramatic story.

"אַ (*Aleph*). CODEX SINAITICUS, now at St. Petersburg, the
justly celebrated copy which has for the last quarter of a cen-

tury attracted such general attention in the learned world. From
Tischendorf's Notitia Ed. Cod. Sinaitici (pp. 5, 6) we gained in
1860 some insight into the history of its discovery. When travelling in 1844 under the patronage of his own sovereign, King
Frederick Augustus of Saxony, he picked out of a basket full
of papers destined to light the oven of the Convent of St. Cathar-
ine on Mount Sinai, the 43 leaves of the Septuagint which he
published in 1846 as the Codex Friderico-Augustanus (*see* p.
30). These, of course, he easily got for the asking, but finding
that further portions of the same codex (e.g. the whole of
Isaiah and 1, 4 Maccabees) were extant, he rescued them from
their probable fate, by enlightening the brotherhood as to their
value. He was permitted to copy one page of what yet remained,
containing the end of Isaiah and the beginning of Jeremiah,
which he afterwards published in the first volume of his Monumenta Sacra Inedita (1855), pp. xxxx. and 213-16; and he
departed in the full hope that he should be allowed to purchase
the whole: but he had taught the monks a sharp lesson, and
neither then, nor on his subsequent visit in 1853, could he gain
any tidings of the leaves he had left behind; he even seems to
have concluded that they had been carried into Europe by some
richer or more fortunate collector. At the beginning of 1859,
after the care of the seventh edition of his N.T. was happily
over, he went for a third time into the East, under the well-
deserved patronage of the Emperor of Russia, the great pro-
tector of the Oriental Church; and the treasure which had been
twice withdrawn from him as a private traveller, was now, on
the occasion of some chance conversation, spontaneously put into
the hands of one sent from the champion and benefactor of the
oppressed Church. Tischendorf touchingly describes his sur-
prise, his joy, his midnight studies over the priceless volume
(*'quippe dormire nefas videbatur'*) on that memorable 4th of
February, 1859. The rest was easy; he was allowed to copy
his prize at Cairo, and ultimately to bring it to Europe, as a
tribute of duty and gratitude to the Emperor Alexander II. To
that monarch's wise munificence both the larger edition (1862),
and the smaller of the New Testament only (1863), are mainly
due.

"The Codex Sinaiticus is $13\frac{1}{2}$ inches in length by $14\frac{7}{8}$ inches
high, and consists of $345\frac{1}{2}$ leaves of the same beautiful vellum
as the Cod. Friderico-Augustanus which is really a part of it
(*see* p. 30), whereof 199 contain portions of the Septuagint
version, $147\frac{1}{2}$ the whole New Testament, Barnabas' Epistle,

and a considerable fragment of Hermas' Shepherd. It has subsequently appeared that the Russian Archimandrite (now Bishop) Porphyry had brought with him from Sinai in 1845 some pieces of Genesis xxiii. 19—xxiv. 19, 25-36 and of Numbers v. 26—vi. 17; 22—vii. 12, which had been applied long before to the binding of other books. Each page comprises four columns (*see* p. 27), with 48 lines in each column, of those continuous, noble, simple uncials (*compare* Plate IV. 11 a *with* 11 b) which we have described so minutely in the preceding section pp. 32—9). The poetical books of the Old Testament, however, being written in *stichoi*, admit of only two columns on a page (*above*, p. 51). The order of the sacred books is remarkable, though not unprecedented (p. 70). St. Paul's Epistles precede the Acts, and, amongst them, that to the Hebrews follows 2 Thess., standing on the same page with it (p. 71). Although this manuscript has hitherto been inspected by few Englishmen (Tregelles, however, and Dean Stanley were among the number), yet its general aspect has grown familiar to us by the means of photographs of its most important pages taken for the use of private scholars, as well as from the *facsimiles* contained in Tischendorf's several editions. . . .

"With regard to the deeply interesting question as to the critical character of Cod. ℵ, although it strongly supports the Codex Vaticanus in many characteristic readings, yet it cannot be said to give its exclusive adherence to any of the witnesses hitherto examined. It so lends its grave authority, now to one and now to another, as to convince us more than ever of the futility of seeking to derive the genuine text of the New Testament from any one copy, however ancient and, on the whole, trustworthy." (Scrivener, pp. 87-89, 93; see p. 137, herein; the fourth edition adds the following clause: "when evidence of a wide and varied character is at hand." Scrivener-Miller, Vol. I, p. 97.)

This codex is now in the hands of the British Government. Its acquisition is narrated by Kenyon as follows:

"In 1933 it became known that the Soviet Government was not unwilling to sell it, having little use for Bibles and much for money. Indeed, negotiations had previously been opened with an American syndicate; but the financial crisis supervened, and America's difficulty gave England an unhoped-for opportunity. After prolonged negotiations a bargain was concluded by which it passed into the possession of the Trustees of the British

Museum for the sum of £100,000 (much less than the sum contemplated in the American negotiations), of which half was
guaranteed by the British Government. Accordingly, just before Christmas, 1933, the great Bible entered the British Museum, amid scenes of much popular excitement." (Kenyon, *Our
Bible,* pp. 130-31.)

Kenyon has his joke about us and our purchase of a
copy of the Mazarin (Gutenberg) Bible. He says, noting
that we paid about $300,000 for our one copy of the
Gutenberg Bible, there being some 39 other copies:

"If that [$300,000] was a fair market price for a printed
Bible, of which many other copies existed, and of no textual
importance, the £100,000 [about $500,000] paid for the unique
Codex Sinaiticus, more than 1,100 years older and one of the most
valuable witnesses to the text of the Bible, seems a very good
bargain." (*The Story,* p. 43.)

Comments upon this codex will be quoted later. (See
infra, p. 243.) Some of the characteristics and imperfections of this codex have been already given in *Note
Nineteen.*

Item 4. The Codex Vaticanus (B).

Summary. Brief history of Codex. In the Vatican at
Rome.

The following account of Codex Vaticanus is given
by Scrivener. There is less romance than is incident to
Codex Sinaiticus, but there is equal interest.

"B. CODEX VATICANUS 1209 is perhaps the oldest [the
fourth edition adds "large"] vellum manuscript in existence,
and is the glory of the great Vatican Library at Rome. To this
legitimate source of deep interest must be added the almost romantic curiosity which has been excited by the jealous watchful-
ness of its official guardians. . . . This book seems to have been
brought into the Vatican Library shortly after its establishment
by Pope Nicolas V. in 1448, but nothing is known of its previous history. It is entered in the earliest Catalogue of that

Library, made in 1475. Since the missing portions at the end
of the New Testament are believed to have been supplied in
the fifteenth century from a manuscript belonging to Cardinal
Bessarion, we may be allowed to conjecture, if we please, that
this learned Greek brought the Codex into the west of Europe.
Although this book has not even yet been as thoroughly collated,
or rendered as available as it might be to the critical student,
its general character and appearance are sufficiently well known.
It is a quarto volume, arranged in quires of five sheets or ten
leaves each, like Codex Marchalianus of the Prophets written
in the sixth or seventh century and Cod. Rossanensis of the
Gospels to be described hereafter (p. 157), not of four or three
sheets as Cod. ℵ (p. 93), the ancient, perhaps the original, numbering of the quires being often found in the margin. The New
Testament fills 142 out of its 759 thin and delicate vellum leaves,
said to be made of the skins of antelopes: it is bound in red
morocco, being ten and a half inches high, ten broad, four and
a half thick. It once contained the whole Bible in Greek, the
Old Testament of the Septuagint version (a tolerably fair representation of which was exhibited in the Roman edition as early
as 1587), except the books of the Maccabees and the Prayer of
Manasses. The first forty-six chapters of Genesis (the manuscript begins at *polin*, Gen. xlvi. 48) and Psalms cv.—cxxxvii.
[the fourth edition adds: "also the books of the Maccabees"]
are wanting. The New Testament is complete down to Hebr. ix.
14 *katha*: the rest of the Epistle to the Hebrews (the Catholic
Epistles had followed the Acts, *see* p. 71), and the Apocalypse,
being written in the later hand alluded to above. The peculiar
arrangement of three columns on a page, or six on the opened
leaf of the volume, is described by eye-witnesses as very striking
(*see above*, p. 27) : in the poetical books of the Old Testament
(since they are written *sticheros*) only two columns fill a page.
The *facsimile* copper-plate in Mai's larger edition of the Codex
Vaticanus, and the uncouth tracing by Zacagni in 1704, repeated
both by Horne and Tregelles, have been strongly censured by
recent observers. . . . All who have inspected the Codex are
loud in their praises of the fine thin vellum, the clear and elegant
hand of the first penman, the simplicity of the whole style of
the work: capital letters, so frequent in the Codex Alexandrinus,
were totally wanting in this document for some centuries. In
several of these particulars our manuscript resembles the Herculanean rolls, and thus asserts a just claim to high antiquity,
which the absence of the divisions into *kephalia*, of the sections

and canons, and the substitution in their room of another scheme of chapters of its own (described above, p. 54), beyond question tend very powerfully to confirm. Each column contains forty-two [the fourth edition adds, "ordinarily"] lines, each line from sixteen to eighteen letters, of a size somewhat less than in Cod. A, much less than in Cod. ℵ (though they all vary a little in this respect),with no intervals between the words, a space of the breadth of half a letter being left at the end of a sentence, and a little more at the conclusion of a paragraph; the first letter of the new sentence occasionally standing a little out of the line (*see* pp. 49, 90). It has been doubted whether any of the stops are *primâ manu,* and (contrary to the judgment of Birch and others) the breathings and accents are now universally allowed to have been added by a later hand. This hand, referred by some to the eighth century (although Tischendorf, with Dr. Hort's approval, assigns it to the tenth or eleventh), retraced, with as much care as such an operation would permit, the faint lines of the original writing (the ink whereof was perhaps never quite black), the remains of which can even now be seen by a keen-sighted reader by the side of the thicker and more modern strokes; and, anxious at the same time to represent a critical revision of the text, the writer left untouched such words or letters as he wished to reject. In these last places, *where no breathings or accents and scarcely any stops have ever been detected,* we have an opportunity of seeing the manuscript in its primitive condition, before it had been tampered with by the later scribe. . . .

"Tischendorf says truly enough that something like a history might be written of the futile attempts to collate Cod. B, and a very unprofitable history it would be. The manuscript is first distinctly heard of (for it does not appear to have been used for the Complutensian Polyglott) through Sepulveda, to whose correspondence with Erasmus attention has been seasonably recalled by Tregelles. . . .

"Those who agree the most unreservedly respecting the age of the Codex Vaticanus, vary widely in their estimate of its critical value. By some it has been held in such undue esteem that its readings, if probable in themselves, and supported (or even though not supported) by two or three other copies and versions, have been accepted in preference to the united testimony of all authorities besides: while others have spoken of its text as one of the most vicious extant. Without anticipating what must be discussed hereafter (Chap. VII.) we may say at once, that neither of these views can commend itself to impartial judges: that, while we accord to Cod. B at least as much weight as to any single document in existence, we ought never to forget that it is but one out of many, several of them being nearly (and one quite) as old, and in other respects hardly less worthy of confidence than itself. One marked feature, characteristic of this copy, is the great number of its omissions, which has induced Dr. Dobbin to speak of it as presenting 'an abbreviated text of the New Testament:' and certainly the facts he states on this point are startling enough. . . . " (Scrivener, pp. 101-116.)

To this sentence, Dr. Scrivener adds the following note:

"Even Bp. Lightfoot, a strong and consistent admirer of the manuscript, speaks of its 'impatience of apparently superfluous words' (Epistle to the Colossians, p. 316). Dr. Hort (Introduction, p. 235) pleads that such facts 'have no bearing on either the merits or the demerits of the scribe of B, except as regards the absolutely singular readings of B,' whereas multitudes of these omissions are found in other good documents." (Scrivener, p. 116, n. 1.)

This "reader" can but ask,—How much weight or cogency must we give an argument justifying or excusing deficiencies or imperfections in one codex, which is based upon the ground that equivalent deficiencies or imperfections exist in other codices? It is old wisdom that "two wrongs do not make a right."

Dr. Scrivener continues:

". . . He [Dr. Dobbin] calculates that Codex B leaves out words or whole clauses no less than 330 times in Matthew, 365 in Mark, 439 in Luke, 357 in John, 384 in the Acts, 681 in the surviving Epistles; or 2556 times in all. That no small proportion of these are mere oversights of the scribe seems evident from a circumstance that has only come to light of late years, namely, that this same scribe has repeatedly written words and clauses *twice over*, a class of mistakes which Mai and the collators have seldom thought fit to notice, inasmuch as the false addition has not been retraced by the second hand, but which

by no means enhances our estimate of the care employed in
copying this venerable record of primitive Christianity. Hug
and others have referred the origin of Codex B to Egypt, but
(unlike in this respect to Codex A) its history does not confirm
their conjecture, and the argument derived from orthography
or grammatical forms, is now well understood to be but slight
and ambiguous. Dr. Hort, on no very substantial grounds, is
'inclined to surmise that B and ℵ were both written in the West,
probably at Rome' (Introduction, pp. 265-7)." (Scrivener, pp.
116-117; Scrivener-Miller, Vol. I, pp. 105-109, 119-121; see
infra, pp. 243 ff.; *supra, Note Fourteen*, p. 138.)

NOTE TWENTY-TWO •

How Codices ℵ and B (Sinaiticus and Vaticanus) Might Have Been Prepared

Summary. It is suggested by Miller that the two Codices ℵ (Sinaiticus) and B (Vaticanus) might have been prepared at the same time responsive to an order from the Emperor Constantine to send him "fifty magnificent copies of the Holy Scriptures." It is contended these two codices are not to be regarded as two witnesses but one to the text they reproduce.

Concerning the possible origin of the two codices, Codex Vaticanus and Codex Sinaiticus, the comments of Edward Miller, M.A., (a scholar of learning and distinction) are of great interest:

"So we are brought from Origen to Eusebius. And indeed, the veneration and affection entertained by the latter for the great teacher has been expressed by him frequently in his history. Cæsarea was the adopted home of the latter days of Origen. He must have spent most of his last twenty years in that city. It was his refuge after troubles in Alexandria: there he was at length ordained. His spirit must have lived on amongst his admirers: and in Eusebius of Cæsarea we see a virtual successor to his main opinions and tenets.

"But during the lifetime of these men a catastrophe occurred which must have affected very greatly the transmission of the Holy Scriptures. The persecution of Diocletian and Galerius, notwithstanding the care taken and the firmness shewn even unto death, must have caused the destruction of a large number of manuscripts. Hesychius, Lucian, and Pamphilus suffered martyrdom. And after the storm passed over, there must have been a serious lack of copies of the Holy Scriptures for use in the Church, especially where the large increase of converts added to the number of congregations, and caused the building of fresh churches.

"Towards the end of this long period of history, and whilst Constantine was in the midst of his Semiarian stage, he gave the celebrated order to Eusebius, probably between A.D. 330 and 340, to send him fifty magnificent copies of the Holy Scriptures. They were to be written on the best vellum by skilful and accomplished penmen, and in a form well fitted for use. Orders were at the same time issued to the Governor of the province to supply the materials for the work, which was to be accomplished with all possible speed. Two carriages were placed at the disposal of Eusebius for conveying the copies to Constantinople, and he sent them off soon under the charge of a deacon.

"Now there are various reasons for supposing that B and א were amongst these fifty manuscripts. They are referred by the best judges to about the period of Constantine's letter, to speak generally. In Tischendorf's opinion, which is confirmed by Dr. Scrivener, the scribe of B wrote six 'conjugate leaves' of א. These manuscripts are unrivalled for the beauty of their vellum and for their other grandeur, and are just what we should expect to find amongst such as would be supplied in obedience to an imperial command, and executed with the aid of imperial resources. They are also, as has been already stated, sister manuscripts, as may be inferred from their general resemblance in readings. They abound in omissions, and show marks of such carelessness as would attend an order carried out with more than ordinary expedition. And even the corrector, who always followed the copyist, did his work with similar carelessness to the scribe whom he was following. Besides which, it is expressly stated in א that it was collated with a very old manuscript corrected by Pamphilus after the Hexapla of Origen. And Cæsarea was the place where manuscripts of Pamphilus and Origen would be found.

"There is therefore very considerable foundation for the opinion entertained by many that these two celebrated manuscripts owe their execution to the order of Constantine, and show throughout the effects of the care of Eusebius, and the influence of Origen, whose works formed the staple of the Library of Pamphilus, in the city where they were most likely written.

"Such was probably the parentage, and such the production of these two celebrated manuscripts, which are the main exponents of a form of Text differing from that which has come down to us from the Era of Chrysostom, and has since that time till very recent years been recognized as mainly supreme in the Church. And the question arises, which of the two was the generally accredited Text in the period which has just passed under review." (Miller, pp. 80-83.)

In a footnote to the end of the third full paragraph of the foregoing quotation, the author says:

"Eusebius sent them, *trissa kai tetrassa.* 'Vit. Const.,' iv. 37. There are three interpretations of these words: (1) 'in triple or quadruple sheets,' in that case it would have been probably *triploa kai tetraploa*: (2) 'written in three or four vertical columns respectively' (Canon Cook), which would exactly describe ℵ and B, only a preposition would be wanted to turn the adjectival into an adverbial expression: (3) combined with *pentekonta somatia en diphtherais egkataskeyois* (c. 36), 'we sent abroad the collections [of writings] in richly adorned cases, three or four in a case' (Archdeacon Palmer, quoted by Dr. Scrivener). After examining the letters, I am convinced that my friend Archdeacon Palmer is right." (Miller, p. 82; see also, Burgon, p. 26, n.; and Scrivener, p. 113.)

Mr. Burgon observes regarding these two codices:

"These two famous manuscripts, because they are disfigured exclusively by the self-same mistakes, are convicted of being descended (and not very remotely) from the self-same very corrupt original. . . . Codd. B and ℵ, as already hinted, are not to be reckoned as two witnesses." (Burgon, p. 257; see also *id.*, pp. 318, 339.)

No direct comment by the Extreme Textualists upon these speculations has been observed. Whether they have not considered them of sufficient importance to call for notice, or whether the suggestions have a possible merit that is so difficult to disprove, as to make adverse comment unwise, we have no means of knowing.

NOTE TWENTY-THREE ·

Reliability and Characteristics of Codices ℵ and B (Sinaiticus and Vaticanus)

Item 1.   Favorite Texts of Different Extreme Textualists.

Summary. Tregelles, Tischendorf, Westcott and Hort, and now seemingly Kenyon each had or has a special text or texts to which each gave first choice or support.

Of the more noteworthy Extreme Textualists of the last century, each of them, beginning with Tregelles, seems to have had a favorite text, based on the principle of "antiquity." "Tregelles worshipped 'codex B,'" supposedly of the fourth century; Tischendorf entertained a like feeling for Sinaiticus of the same period; while Westcott and Hort rendered like homage to Vaticanus (B). (Burgon, pp. 333, 95; and see *id.*, pp. 300, 343.)

Today, Kenyon is giving great prominence to recently discovered Egyptian papyri, particularly the Chester Beatty papyri. Each of these scholars has had his favorite text.

Item 2.   Comparison of Texts ℵ B A C D.

Summary. Burgon asserts that ℵ B C D, especially ℵ B, have established a "tyrannical ascendency . . . ." which can only be fitly spoken of as a blind superstition." Observations by Tischendorf, Burgon, and Scrivener on these manuscripts are given.

Westcott and Hort produced a Greek text of their own (founded on B), which has come under severe scholarly criticism. To these two, ℵ and B, should be added the Alexandrian Codex (A), the "rescript codex" (C), both supposedly of the fifth century, and one codex, Bezae (D), probably of the sixth century. (See *Note Nineteen, supra.*)

Concerning these five codices, Burgon (1883) says:

"Singular to relate, the first, second, fourth, and fifth of these codices (B ℵ C D), but especially B and ℵ, have within the last twenty years established a tyrannical ascendency over the imagination of the Critics, which can only be fitly spoken of as a blind superstition." (Burgon, p. 11.)

If Miller's conjecture regarding the common origin of ℵ B is correct, then they should not be regarded as two distinct codices, but as two copies of an earlier codex which was not faithfully copied either by the scribe or scribes copying ℵ or by the copyist or copyists of B, or else each was corrupt in accordance with the manuscripts from which they were copied.

Tischendorf is quoted as saying the two codices (ℵ and B) were partly written by the same scribe. (Burgon, p. 12.)

To the foregoing comment on these codices (ℵ and B), may be added the following comments by Dr. Scrivener on their origin, preparation, and relationship to other codices:

"We are thus warranted, as well from direct evidence as from the analogy of the Old Testament, to believe that Eusebius mainly resorted for his Constantinopolitan Church-books to the codices of Pamphilus, which might once have belonged to Origen. What critical corrections (if any) he ventured to make in the text on his own judgment is not so clear. Not that there is the least cause to believe, with Dr. Nolan (*Inquiry into the Integrity of the Greek Vulgate*, p. 27), that Eusebius had either the power or the will to suppress or tamper with the great doctrinal texts 1 John v. 7, 8; 1 Tim. iii. 16; Acts xx. 28; yet we cannot deny that his prepossessions may have tempted him to arbitrary alterations in other passages, which had no direct bearing on the controversies of his age. Codd. ℵ B are quite old enough to have been copied under his inspection, and it is certainly very remarkable that these two early manuscripts omit one whole paragraph (Mark xvi. 9-16) with his sanction, if not after his example. . . . The relation in which Cod. ℵ stands to the other four chief manuscripts of the Gospels, may be roughly estimated from analysing the transcript of four pages first published by Tischendorf, as well as in any other way. Of the 312 variations from the common text therein noted, ℵ stands alone in 45, in 8 agrees with ABCD united (much of C, however, is lost in these passages), with ABC together 31 times, with ABD 14, with AB 13, with D alone 10, with B alone but once (Mark i. 27), with C alone once: with several authorities against AB 39 times, with A against B 52, with B against A 98. Hence, while the discovery of this precious document has unquestionably done much to uphold Cod. B (which is the more correctly written, and doubtless the more valuable of the two) in many of its more characteristic and singular readings, it has made the mutual divergencies of the very oldest critical authorities more patent and perplexing than ever." (Scrivener, pp. 513-515.)

Item 3.   Special Comments on Texts ℵ and B.

> *Summary.* Character and inter-relationships of these two texts.

Dr. Scrivener adds to this, in a footnote, the following from Mr. Burgon in further adverse appraisal of ℵ B:

"And that too hardly to the credit of either of them. 'Ought it not,' asks Dean Burgon, 'sensibly to detract from our opinion of the value of their evidence to discover that *it is easier to find two consecutive verses in which the two MSS. differ, the one from the other, than two consecutive verses in which they entirely agree?* . . . On every such occasion only one of them can possibly be speaking the truth. Shall I be thought unreasonable if I confess that these perpetual inconsistencies between Codd. B and A—grave inconsistencies, and occasionally even gross ones,—altogether destroy my confidence in either?' (*Last Twelve Verses of S. Mark*, pp. 77-8)." (Scrivener, p. 515, n. 1.)

On this question of the origin and relationship to the

James 2:6—3:13

ℵ — Codex Sinaiticus

Greek vellum. Uncial. Discovered by Tischendorf in Monastery of St. Catherine, Mt. Sinai. Can "hardly be much earlier than A.D. 340." Has rare arrangement of four columns to page. One of two codices (other Vaticanus) made basis of Revised Version texts. In British Museum. Origin uncertain; some believe Egypt. See pp. 249 and 136, herein.

Iac. 1, 1-11   1, 11-19   1, 19-27

James 1:1-27

B—CODEX VATICANUS

Greek vellum. Uncial. Early 4th century, first half. Origin unknown; Hort thought Rome, others southern Italy or Caesarea, others Egypt and Alexandria. Possibly in Vatican in 1475 A.D. Foundation (along with Sinaiticus) of Westcott-Hort's text, on which Revised Versions are based. In Vatican, Rome. One of few manuscripts written in three columns. See pp. 249 and 139, herein.

Sacred Autographs of ℵ B, Burgon makes these statements:

"For we decline to admit that the texts exhibited by B ℵ can have 'diverged from a point near the sacred autographs, and never come into contact subsequently.' We are able to show, on the contrary, that the readings they jointly embody afford the strongest presumption that the MSS. which contain them are nothing else but specimens of those 'corrected,' i.e. *corrupted* copies, which are known to have abounded in the earliest ages of the Church. From the prevalence of identical depravations in either, we infer that they are, on the contrary, derived from the same not very remote depraved original: and therefore, that their coincidence, when they differ from all (or nearly all) other MSS., so far from marking 'two primitive and entirely separate lines of transmission' of the inspired autographs, does but mark what was derived from the same corrupt common ancestor; whereby the supposed two independent witnesses to the Evangelic verity become resolved into *a single witness to a fabricated text of the IIIrd century.*" (Burgon, pp. 27-28, n.)

As several times pointed out above, the Extreme Textualists today seem now to have abandoned this direct descent idea, though still holding for the superiority of ℵ B. The concept seems now to be that these two texts are the product of considerable editing of the same sort as that which resulted in the Westcott-Hort text. (*Note Twenty-four, Item 1*, p. 252.)

Item 4. *Arrangement of Columns in ℵ and B.*

Summary. Arrangement of columns in ℵ and B, and the significance thereof as indicating their separate origins, which is a critical point with the Extreme Textualists.

Some point has been made as to the arrangement of the columns in the two codices ℵ and B, as showing their separate origins, which is, of course, a critical point with the Extreme Textualists. Concerning this, Dr. Scrivener says, minimizing the importance of the columnar arrangement as a determining factor as to separate origins, and discussing the form and age of codices generally:

"Little needs be said respecting the *form* of manuscripts, which in this particular much resemble printed books. A few are in large folio; the greater part in small folio or quarto, the prevailing shape being a quarto whose height but little exceeds its breadth; some are in octavo, a not inconsiderable number smaller still. In some copies the sheets have marks in the lower margin of their first or last pages, like the *signatures* of a modern volume, the folio at intervals of four, the quarto at intervals of eight leaves, as in the Codex Bezae of the Gospels and Acts (D), and the Codex Augiensis of St. Paul's Epistles (F). Not to speak at present of those manuscripts which have a Latin translation in a column parallel to the Greek, as the Codex Bezae, the Codex Laudianus of the Acts, and the Codices Claromontanus and Augiensis of St. Paul, many copies of every age have two Greek columns on each page; of these the Codex Alexandrinus is the oldest: the Codex Vaticanus has three columns on a page, the Codex Sinaiticus four. The unique arrangement of these last two has been urged as an argument for their higher antiquity, as if they were designed to imitate *rolled* books, whose several skins or leaves were fastened together lengthwise, so that their contents always appeared in parallel columns; they were kept in scrolls which were unrolled at one end for reading, and when read rolled up at the other. This fashion prevails in the papyrus fragments yet remaining, and in the most venerated copies of the Old Testament preserved in Jewish synagogues." (Scrivener, pp. 27-28.)

Dr. Scrivener adds in a note:

"The manuscript in four columns is quite unique, but, besides the Cod. Vaticanus, the Vatican Dio Cassius, the Milan fragment of Genesis, and two copies of the Samaritan Pentateuch at Nablous described by Tischendorf (Cod. Frid.-Aug. Proleg. § 11) are arranged in *three* columns. Tischendorf has more recently discovered a similar arrangement in two palimpsest leaves of Wisdom and Ecclesiasticus from which he gives extracts (Not. Cod. Sinait. p. 49); in a Latin fragment of the Pentateuch, seen by him at Lyons in 1843; in a Greek Evangelistarium of the eighth century, and a Patristic manuscript at Patmos of the ninth (*ibid.* p. 10); so that the argument drawn from the *triple* columns must not be pressed too far. He adds also a Turin copy of the Minor Prophets in Greek (Pasinus, *Catalogue,* 1749), and a Nitrian Syriac codex in the British Museum 'quem circa finem quarti saeculi scriptum esse subscriptio testatur' (Monum. sacra inedita, Vol. I. Proleg. p. xxxxi). To this not slender list Mr. E. Maude Thompson enables us to annex B. M. Addit. 24142, a Flemish Latin Bible of the eleventh century. The late Lord Ashburnham in 1868 printed his Old Latin fragments of Leviticus and Numbers, also in three columns, with a *facsimile* page; and the famous Utrecht Psalter, assigned by some to the sixth century, by others to the ninth or tenth, is written with three columns on a page, although it bears marks of having been transcribed from an archetype which contained only two." (Scrivener, pp. 27-28, n. 2; the fourth edition is amplified by Miller with added corroborative data. Scrivener-Miller, Vol. I, p. 28, n. 2; see also *id.*, p. 513, n. 2.)

The foregoing analyses seem to discredit the force of any argument for the separate origin of ℵ and B based upon the columnar arrangement of the texts.

Speaking generally as to the antiquity of the ℵ B texts, and having in mind the "welter" of early manuscripts and their disappearance, what sound, reasonable basis is there for assuming that, since these two manuscripts have survived out of all the manuscripts representing other texts (for example the early Syrian texts) these two must of necessity represent the oldest and most authentic texts of the Sacred Autographs? To state the deduction is to discard it.

NOTE TWENTY-FOUR •

Purity of the Text of the Codices ℵ A B C D

Item 1. The Relative Corruption of These Texts.

Summary. The relative corruption of texts ℵ A B C D, as viewed by scholars noting wide variations among them.

Of the four codices (ℵ B C D), drawn under discussion by Dr. Scrivener, D is declared by Burgon to be the most depraved (Burgon, p. 12), and Scrivener is quoted as saying regarding the same manuscript:

"We find ourselves confronted with a text, the like to which we have no experience of elsewhere .... so wide are the variations in the diction, so constant and inveterate the practice of expounding the narrative by means of interpolations which seldom recommend themselves as genuine by even a semblance of internal probability." (Burgon, p. 13.)

Regarding Codex ℵ and the other three mentioned, Burgon says:

"Next to D, the most untrustworthy codex is ℵ, which bears on its front a memorable note of the evil repute under which it has always laboured: viz. it is found that at least *ten* revisers between the IVth and the XIIth centuries busied themselves with the task of correcting its many and extraordinary perversions of the truth of Scripture.—Next in impurity comes B:—then, the fragmentary codex C: our own A being, beyond all doubt, disfigured by the fewest blemishes of any." (Burgon, pp. 13-14; see p. 138, herein.)

Later, Burgon makes this comment regarding the four codices named above, plus A (Alexandrinus):

"Let no one suppose that we deny their extraordinary

value,—their unrivalled critical interest,—nay, their actual *use* in helping to settle the truth of Scripture. What we are just now insisting upon is only the *depraved text* of codices ℵ A B C D,—especially of ℵ B D. And because this is a matter which lies at the root of the whole controversy, and because we cannot afford that there shall exist in our reader's mind the slightest doubt on *this* part of the subject, we shall be constrained once and again to trouble him with detailed specimens of the contents of ℵ B, &c., in proof of the justice of what we have been alleging. We venture to assure him, without a particle of hesitation, that ℵ B D are *three of the most scandalously corrupt copies extant*:—exhibit *the most shamefully mutilated* texts which are anywhere to be met with:—have become, by whatever process (for their history is wholly unknown), the depositories of the largest amount of *fabricated readings,* ancient *blunders,* and *intentional perversions of Truth,*—which are discoverable in any known copies of the Word of God." (Burgon, pp. 15-16; see his "Preface," pp. x-xi; and for sources of corruption, *id.,* pp. 334-336.)

Item 2.   Burgon's Collation of Luke 8:35-44.

Summary. This is an example of the care of Burgon's investigations and of his scholarship. Scrivener comments on some other passages also given as examples of Dr. Hort's methods, saying: "Even if the reader has not gone with me in every case, more than enough has been alleged to prove to demonstration that the true and pure text of the sacred writers is not to be looked for in ℵ or B, in ℵ B, or B D, or B L, or any like combination of a select few authorities, but demands, in every fresh case as it arises, the free and impartial use of every available source of information."

To show the kind of careful investigation and scrutiny of texts which lie behind Burgon's conclusions, we may note the following collation made by him:

"But in fact take a single page of any ordinary copy of the Greek Testament,—Bp. Lloyd's edition, suppose. Turn to page 184. It contains ten verses of S. Luke's Gospel, ch. viii. 35 to 44. Now, proceed to collate those ten verses. You will make the notable discovery that, within those narrow limits, by codex D alone the text has been depraved 53 times, resulting in no less than 103 corrupt readings, 93 *of which are found only in* D. The words omitted by D are 40: the words added are 4. Twenty-five words have been substituted for others, and 14 transposed. Variations of case, tense, &c., amount to 16; and the phrase of the Evangelist has been departed from 11 times. Happily, the other four 'old uncials' are here available. And it is found that (within the same limits, and referred to the same test,) A exhibits 3 omissions, 2 of which are *peculiar to* A.—B omits 12 words, 6 of which are *peculiar to* B: substitutes 3 words: transposes 4: and exhibits 6 lesser changes—2 of them being its own peculiar property.—ℵ has 5 readings (affecting 8 words) *peculiar to itself*. Its omissions are 7: its additions, 2: its substitutions, 4: 2 words are transposed; and it exhibits 4 lesser discrepancies.—C has 7 readings (affecting 15 words) *peculiar to itself*. Its omissions are 4: its additions, 7: its substitutions, 7: its words transposed, 7. It has 2 lesser discrepancies, and it alters the Evangelist's phrase 4 times.

"But (we shall be asked) what amount of *agreement*, in respect of 'Various Readings,' is discovered to subsist between these 5 codices? for *that*, after all, is the practical question. We answer,—A has been already shown to stand alone twice: B, 6 times: ℵ, 8 times: C, 15 times; D, 93 times.—We have further to state that A B stand together by themselves once: B ℵ, 4 times: B C, 1: B D, 1: ℵ C, 1: C D, 1.—A ℵ C conspire 1: B ℵ C, 1: B ℵ D, 1: A B ℵ C, *once* (viz. in reading *erotesen*, which Tischendorf admits to be a corrupt reading): B ℵ C D, also *once*.—The 5 'old uncials' therefore (A B ℵ C D) combine, and again stand apart, with singular impartiality.—Lastly, they are *never once* found to be in accord in respect of *any single* '*various Reading*.'—Will any one, after a candid survey of the premises, deem us unreasonable, if we avow that such a specimen of the *concordia discors* which everywhere prevails between the oldest uncials, but which especially characterizes ℵ B D, indisposes us greatly to suffer their unsupported authority to determine for us the Text of Scripture?" (Burgon, pp. 16-17.)

This careful examination and analysis compels Kenyon's "reader" to ponder carefully before accepting any conclusion of the Extreme Textualists that runs contrary to conclusions of such scholarly study.

Item 3.   Scrivener's Comments.

Dr. Scrivener makes these comments upon the same general question:

"The point on which we insist is briefly this:—that the evidence of ancient authorities is anything but unanimous; that they are perpetually at variance with each other, even if we limit the term ancient within the narrowest bounds. Shall it include, among the manuscripts of the Gospels, none but the five oldest copies Codd. אABCD? The reader has but to open the first recent critical work he shall meet with, to see them scarcely ever in unison; perpetually divided two against three, or perhaps four against one. All the readings these venerable monuments contain must of course be *ancient*, or they would not be found where they are; but they cannot all be true. So again, if our search be extended to the versions and primitive Fathers, the same phenomenon unfolds itself, to our grievous perplexity and disappointment." (Scrivener, pp. 522-23; see p. 197, herein.)

To this may be added Dr. Scrivener's observations, made a little later on in his book:

"The student may try the same experiments on two other passages often urged in this debate, Matth. v. 22, for which he will find the materials above, p. 501, and Matth. xix. 17, which will be discussed in Chap. IX. We freely admit that these are but a few out of many cases where the statements of ancient writers about whose date there can be no question are borne out by the readings of the more ancient codices, especially of א or B, or of the two united. Undoubtedly this circumstance lends a weight and authority to these manuscripts, and to the few which side with them, which their mere age would not procure for them: it does not entitle them to be regarded as virtually the only documents worthy of being consulted in the recension of the sacred text; as qualifying to be sole arbiters in critical questions relating to the New Testament, against whose decision there can be no appeal. Yet nothing less than this is claimed in behalf of one or two of them by their devoted admirers." (Scrivener, p. 527.)

Still later, he says:

"With all our reverence for his [Dr. Hort's] genius, and gratitude for much that we have learnt from him in the course of our studies, we are compelled to repeat as emphatically as ever our strong conviction that the hypothesis to whose proof he has devoted so many laborious years, is destitute not only of historical foundation, but of all probability resulting from the internal goodness of the text which its adoption would force upon us." (Scrivener, p. 542.)

To this last, Scrivener, adds the following note:

"For reasons which will be readily understood, we have quoted sparingly from the trenchant article in the *Quarterly Review*, April 1882 [Burgon], but the following summary of the consequences of a too exclusive devotion to Codd. ℵ B seems no unfit comment on the facts of the case: 'Thus it would appear that the Truth of Scripture has run a very narrow risk of being lost for ever to mankind. Dr. Hort contends that it more than half lay *perdu* on a forgotten shelf in the Vatican Library; —Dr. Tischendorf that it had found its way into a waste-paper basket in the convent of S. Catherine at the foot of Mount Sinai,—from which he rescued it on the 4th February 1859:— neither, we venture to think, a very likely supposition. We incline to believe that the Author of Scripture hath not by any means shown Himself so unmindful of the safety of the Deposit as these learned persons imagine' (p. 365)." (Scrivener, p. 542, n. 1.)

Dr. Scrivener continues:

"This last assertion we will try to verify by subjoining a select number of those many passages in the N.T. wherein the two great codices ℵ and B, one or both of them, are witnesses for readings, nearly all of which, to the best of our judgment, are corruptions of the sacred originals." (Scrivener, pp. 542-43.)

After several pages of collations to prove his affirmations, Dr. Scrivener comments further:

"Enough of the weary and ungracious task of finding fault. The foregoing list of errors patent in the most ancient codices might be largely increased: two or three more will occur incidentally in Chapter IX. (1 Cor. xiii. 3; Phil. ii. 1; 1 Pet. i. 23; *see* also pp. 500, 565). Even if the reader has not gone with me in every case, more than enough has been alleged to prove to demonstration that the true and pure text of the sacred writers is not to be looked for in א or B, in אB, or BD, or BL, or any like combination of a select few authorities, but demands, in every fresh case as it arises, the free and impartial use of every available source of information. Yet after all, Cod. B is a document of such value, that it grows by experience even upon those who may have been a little prejudiced against it by reason of the excessive claims of its too zealous friends." (Scrivener, p. 552.)

These careful, judicious comments relieve us of the necessity of regarding the estimates of these two texts (א B) by the Extreme Textualists, as necessarily controlling the wording of the Sacred Text. This is particularly true for Latter-day Saints, who can call to their assistance the text of the Inspired Version.

NOTE TWENTY-FIVE •

Tischendorf's Text—Sinaiticus ℵ

Item 1.   Scrivener's Comments.

Summary. Scrivener's comments which discredit Tischendorf's predilection for the ℵ text.

Dr. Scrivener comments upon Tischendorf's use and estimate of Sinaiticus as follows:

"The results of this excessive and irrational deference to one of our chief codices, that which he was so fortunate as to bring to the light twenty-five years ago, appears plainly in Tischendorf's eighth edition of the New Testament. That great critic had never been conspicuous for stability of judgment. His third edition was constructed almost without any reference to the cursive manuscripts, which, unless they be, what no one asserts or imagines, merely corrupt copies, or copies of copies, of existing uncials, must needs be the representatives of yet older codices which have long since perished: 'respectable ancestors' (as one has quaintly put the matter) 'who live only in their descendants' (Long, *Ciceronis Verrin. Orat.*, Præf. p. vi.). In Tischendorf's seventh edition, completed in 1859, that error was rectified, and the sum of textual variations between the third and seventh edition in consequence amounted to 1296, in no less than 595 of which (430 of the remainder being mere matters of spelling) he returned to the readings of the Received text, which he had before deserted, but to which fresh materials and larger experience had brought him back. In the eighth edition another disturbing element is introduced, and that edition differs from his seventh in as many as 3369 places, to the scandal of the science of Comparative Criticism, as well as to his own grave discredit for discernment and consistency. The evidence of Cod. ℵ, supported or even unsupported by one or two authorities of any description, proved with him sufficient to outweigh all other witnesses, whether manuscripts, versions, or ecclesiastical writers." (Scrivener, pp. 528-529.)

Item 2. Burgon's Comments.

Summary. Burgon comments more vigorously upon Tischendorf's attitude towards אּ, and makes special reference to individual passages showing the unsound and unreasonableness of Tischendorf's conclusions on the אּ text.

Mr. Burgon has this to say about Tischendorf and his last edition of the New Testament, first quoting Bp. Ellicott:

" 'The case of Dr. Tischendorf' (proceeds Bp. Ellicott) 'is still more easily disposed of. *Which* of this most inconstant Critic's texts are we to select? Surely not the last, in which an exaggerated preference for a single Manuscript which he has had the good fortune to discover, has betrayed him into an almost child-like infirmity of critical judgment. Surely also not his seventh edition, which . . . exhibits all the instability which a comparatively recent recognition of the authority of cursive manuscripts might be supposed likely to introduce.' With Dr. Tischendorf,— (whom one vastly his superior in learning, accuracy, and judgment, has generously styled 'the first Biblical Critic in Europe') —'*the evidence of codex* אּ, supported or even unsupported by one or two other authorities of any description, is sufficient to outweigh any other witnesses,— whether Manuscripts, Versions, or ecclesiastical Writers.' " (Burgon, pp. 22-23.)

Upon these criticisms, Mr. Burgon comments with a citation of authorities:

"We need say no more. Until the foregoing charge has been disproved, Dr. Tischendorf's last edition of the N.T., however precious as a vast storehouse of materials for criticism,—however admirable as a specimen of unwearied labour, critical learning, and first-rate ability,—must be admitted to be an utterly unsatisfactory exhibition of the inspired Text. It has been ascertained that his discovery of codex אּ caused his 8th edition (1865-72) to differ from his 7th in no less than 3505 places,— 'to the scandal of the science of Comparative Criticism, as well as to his own grave discredit for discernment and consistency.' But, in fact, what is to be thought of a Critic who,—because the last verse of S. John's Gospel, in אּ, seemed to himself to be *written with a different pen* from the rest,—has actually *omitted that verse* (xxi. 25) *entirely,* in defiance of *every known Copy, every known Version,* and the explicit testimony of *a host of Fathers?* Such are Origen (in 11 places),—Eusebius (in 3),— Gregory Nyss. (in 2),—Gregory Nazian.,—ps.-Dionys. Alex.,— Nonnus,—Chrysostom (in 6 places),—Theodorus Mops. (in 2), —Isidorus,—Cyril Alex. (in 2),—Victor Ant.,—Ammonius,— Severus,—Maximus,—Andreas Cretensis,—Ambrose,—Gaudentius, — Philastrius, — Sedulius, — Jerome, — Augustine (in 6 places). [Burgon's specific cited references are omitted.] That Tischendorf was a critic of amazing research, singular shrewdness, indefatigable industry; and that he enjoyed an unrivalled familiarity with ancient documents; no fair person will deny. But (in the words of Bishop Ellicott, whom we quote so perseveringly for a reason not hard to divine,) his 'great inconstancy,'—his 'natural want of sobriety of critical judgment,'— and his 'unreasonable deference to the readings found in his own codex Sinaiticus;'—to which should be added *'the utter absence in him of any intelligible fixed critical principles;'*— all this makes Tischendorf one of the worst of guides to the true Text of Scripture." (Burgon, pp. 23-24.)

The citation of Bp. Ellicott by Burgon, arises from the fact that Bp. Ellicott, at some time after he wrote as quoted, became one of the chief protagonists for the Revised Version of the 1880's (British), which (as has been repeatedly noted) relied to a great extent for the primacy for which the Revisers contended, upon this very text (אּ) for the importance of which Bp. Ellicott was forced to contend in supporting the Revised Version. Bp. Ellicott was Chairman of the revising body. (*Note Twenty-seven,* p. 269.)

We should note that Scrivener points out that in Tischendorf's seventh edition of his text, he returned to the Received Text, in "no less than 595" cases. (Scrivener, p. 529.)

NOTE TWENTY-SIX •
Westcott and Hort's New Greek Text

Summary. In this *Note* is set out the influence of Westcott and Hort's new Greek text, and something about its fabrication. Hort's text is based mainly upon B. An advance copy of this text was supplied to the British Revisers of the Bible in the 1880's. Dr. Scrivener's comments are given on the preparation of the Westcott-Hort text, the preparation occupying 25 years, and its distribution before and at the time of the Revision, to which are added Burgon's comments thereon.

Because it appears to have exercised such a great influence in the preparation of the text of the Revised Version, there may be especially noted here the new Greek text fabricated by Westcott and Hort, to which reference has heretofore been repeatedly made, with considerable comment. The title page of this text reads:

"The New Testament / in the Original Greek / the text revised by / Brooke Foss Westcott D.D. / and / Fenton John Anthony Hort D.D. / Text / Cambridge and London / Macmillan and Co. / 1881 / All rights reserved."

This text is described by Scrivener as follows:

" *The New Testament in the original Greek. The text revised by Brooke Foss Westcott, D.D.* [Regius Professor of Divinity in the University of Cambridge], *and Fenton John Anthony Hort, D.D.* [Hulsean Professor of Divinity there], Vol. I, Cambridge and London, 1881'. *Introduction and Appendix,* in a separate volume, by Dr. Hort only, 1881." (Scrivener, p. 488.)

The manuscript mostly relied upon, and indeed controlling, in the fabrication of this new Greek text, was B, as already repeatedly noted. (See pp. 238 ff., *supra.*)

Concerning an advance copy of this text (which was placed at the disposal of the Revisers), Dr. Scrivener (one of the Revisers) writes as follows:

"The simple manual text of the Greek New Testament, of which the above comprises an instalment, has been in preparation for twenty years. It is yet unpublished [1874], but has been placed in the hands of a few scholars, especially of the editors' colleagues in the work of revising the Authorised version of the English Bible, in a limited and private issue, with such brief remarks prefixed as may suffice to explain its nature and distinctive purpose. Although the book is marked 'Confidential,' the writer of these pages has been permitted to state the textual readings which it exhibits in such passages as may be discussed throughout the remaining chapters of the present volume. That he has not felt at liberty to quote from the Prefatory matter has occasionally been as unjust to its joint-authors as inconvenient to himself.

"So far as appears from their Preface, the editors have not made any great additions of their own to the mass of collated materials for the revision of the sacred text. Those which exist ready at hand have been verified as far as possible, and the whole mass of evidence, both documentary and internal, has been thoroughly and deliberately weighed by them, separately and in conference, with an amount of care and diligence that have been hitherto unexampled. Hence it follows that even when full Prolegomena shall have been provided, and the Appendix of select various readings and discussions upon them added, the work will still convey to an uninitiated reader but a feeble notion of the time and thought which have been freely bestowed upon it, and that too by men who are in every way fit for the task they have undertaken. Whether we are or are not prepared to assent to their conclusions in each separate case, must largely depend on the judgment we may have formed as to the general principles on which they act. Summary and dogmatical rejection of their verdict upon any considerable point would be as unjust to the eminent persons who have anxiously arrived at it, as it would be a decisive proof of incompetency or of invincible prejudice on the part of those who should venture to set it aside." (Scrivener, 2nd ed., pp. 431-432.)

In his third edition, Scrivener expresses his appraisal of the work of Doctors Westcott and Hort as follows:

"This important and comprehensive work, the joint labour of two of our best living scholars toiling, now separately, now in counsel, for five and twenty years, was published, the text a few days earlier than the Revised English Version (May 17, 1881), the Introduction about four months later. The text, or one almost identical with it, had been submitted to the Revisers of the N.T., and to a few other Biblical students, several years before, so that the general tenor and spirit of our authors' judgment was known to many: the second edition of my present work was enriched by the free permission granted by them to announce their conclusions regarding passages which come up for discussion in Chapter IX. and elsewhere. Drs. Westcott and Hort depart more widely from the *textus receptus* than any previous editor had thought necessary; nor can they be blamed for carrying out their deliberate convictions, if the reasons they allege shall prove sufficient to justify them. Those reasons are given at length by Dr. Hort in his 'Introduction,' a treatise whose merits may be frankly acknowledged by persons the least disposed to accept his arguments: never was a cause, good or bad in itself, set off with higher ability and persuasive power. On the validity of his theory we shall have much to say in Chapters VII. and IX., to which we here refer once for all. The elegant volume which exhibits the Greek text contains in its margin many alternative readings, chiefly recorded in passages wherein a difference of opinion existed between the two illustrious editors. Words or passages supposed to be of doubtful authority are included in brackets ([ ]), those judged to be probably or certainly spurious—and their number is ominously large—in double brackets ([ ]). Mark xvi. 9-20; John vii. 53-viii. 11 are banished to the end of their respective Gospels, as if they did not belong to them. Finally, quotations from and even slight allusions to the Old Testament, in great but judicious plenty, are printed in a kind of uncial letter, to the great benefit of the student." (Scrivener, pp. 488-489.)

Copies of this Westcott-Hort text were communicated to each of the members of the Committee (not alone to Dr. Scrivener), "under pledge that they should neither show nor communicate its contents to any one else." (Burgon, p. 24.)

One brief comment (Kenyon would perhaps call it

"vehement and intemperate") by Burgon may be noted here on this new Greek text. He says:

"I pointed out that 'the New Greek Text,'—which, in defiance of their instructions, the Revisionists of 'the Authorized English Version' had been so ill-advised as to spend ten years in elaborating,—was a wholly untrustworthy performance: was full of the gravest errors from beginning to end: had been constructed throughout on an entirely mistaken Theory. Availing myself of the published confession of one of the Revisionists, I explained the nature of the calamity which had befallen the Revision. I traced the mischief home to its true authors,— Drs. Westcott and Hort; a copy of whose unpublished Text of the N.T. (the most vicious in existence) had been confidentially, and under pledges of the strictest secrecy, placed in the hands of every member of the revising Body. I called attention to the fact that, unacquainted with the difficult and delicate science of Textual Criticism, the Revisionists had, in an evil hour, surrendered themselves to Dr. Hort's guidance: had preferred his counsels to those of Prebendary Scrivener, (an infinitely more trustworthy guide) : and that the work before the public was the piteous—but *inevitable*—result. All this I explained in the October number of the 'Quarterly Review' for 1881." (Burgon, "Preface," pp. xi-xii.)

NOTE TWENTY-SEVEN •

The Making of the Revised Versions, British and American

Perhaps at this point it would be well to note some of the essential facts involved in the actual work of the Revisers (British Revision). We shall be concerned primarily with the work of revising the New Testament, since these *Notes* have to do only with the Four Gospels.

Item 1.   The Old Testament Text.

Summary. While not immediately and only remotely involved in these *Notes*, yet the statements made in the Preface to the Old Testament text may be noted.

But in passing it may be observed that in their Preface to the Old Testament, the Revisers observe:

"The Received, or, as it is commonly called, the Massoretic Text of the Old Testament Scriptures has come down to us in manuscripts which are of no very great antiquity, and which all belong to the same family or recension. . . . But as the state of knowledge on the subject is not at present such as to justify any attempt at an entire reconstruction of the text on the authority of the Versions, the Revisers have thought it most prudent to adopt the Massoretic Text as the basis of their work, and to depart from it, as the Authorised Translators had done, only in exceptional cases." ("Revisers' Preface" (to the O.T.), p. vii.)

Item 2.   The New Testament Text.

Summary. The Preface (quoted in part) to the New Testament text of the Revision gives the origin of the Revision movement, its avowed purpose, and the *modus operandi* of the work of the Committee. Texts used by the American collaborating Revisers are not given.

With the New Testament text a far different system

was followed. In their Preface to the New Testament, the Revisers give in some detail the origin of the revision movement, its announced purpose, and the *modus operandi* of the Revisers' work. A few passages will be quoted bearing upon this. The Revisers record:

"The present Revision had its origin in action taken by the Convocation of the Province of Canterbury in February 1870, and it has been conducted throughout on the plan laid down in Resolutions of both Houses of the Province, and, more particularly, in accordance with Principles and Rules drawn up by a special Committee of Convocation in the following May. Two Companies, the one for the revision of the Authorised Version of the Old Testament, and the other for the revision of the same Version of the New Testament, were formed in the manner specified in the Resolutions, and the work was commenced on the twenty-second day of June 1870. Shortly afterwards, steps were taken, under a resolution passed by both Houses of Convocation, for inviting the co-operation of American scholars; and eventually two Committees were formed in America, for the purpose of acting with the two English Companies, on the basis of the Principles and Rules drawn up by the Committee of Convocation.

RESOLUTIONS FOR GUIDANCE OF REVISERS

"The fundamental Resolutions adopted by the Convocation of Canterbury on the third and fifth days of May 1870 were as follows:—

" '1. That it is desirable that a revision of the Authorised Version of the Holy Scriptures be undertaken.

" '2. That the revision be so conducted as to comprise both marginal renderings and such emendations as it may be found necessary to insert in the text of the Authorised Version.

" '3. That in the above resolutions we do not contemplate any new translation of the Bible, or any alteration of the language, except where in the judgement of the most competent scholars such change is necessary.

" '4. That in such necessary changes, the style of the language employed in the existing Version be closely followed.

" '5. That it is desirable that Convocation should nominate a body of its own members to undertake the work of revision, who shall be at liberty to invite the co-operation of any eminent for scholarship, to whatever nation or religious body they may belong.'

PRINCIPLES AND RULES GOVERNING WORK OF REVISERS

"The Principles and Rules agreed to by the Committee of Convocation on the twenty-fifth day of May 1870 were as follows:—

" '1.	To introduce as few alterations as possible into the Text of the Authorised Version consistently with faithfulness.

" '2.	To limit, as far as possible, the expression of such alterations to the language of the Authorised and earlier English Versions.

" '3.	Each Company to go twice over the portion to be revised, once provisionally, the second time finally, and on principles of voting as hereinafter is provided.

" '4.	That the Text to be adopted be that for which the evidence is decidedly preponderating; and that when the Text so adopted differs from that from which the Authorised Version was made, the alteration be indicated in the margin.

" '5.	To make or retain no change in the Text on the second final revision by each Company, except *two thirds* of those present approve of the same, but on the first revision to decide by simple majorities.

" '6.	In every case of proposed alteration that may have given rise to discussion, to defer the voting thereupon till the next Meeting, whensoever the same shall be required by one third of those present at the Meeting, such intended vote to be announced in the notice for the next Meeting.

" '7.	To revise the headings of chapters and pages, paragraphs, italics, and punctuation.

" '8.	To refer, on the part of each Company, when considered desirable, to Divines, Scholars, and Literary Men, whether at home or abroad, for their opinions.' . . .

TIME CONSUMED IN REVISION

"The whole time devoted to the work has been ten years and a half. The First Revision occupied about six years; the Second, about two years and a half. The remaining time has been spent in the consideration of the suggestions from America on the Second Revision, and of many details and reserved questions arising out of our own labours. As a rule, a session of four days has been held every month (with the exception of August and September) in each year from the commencement of the work in June 1870. The average attendance for the whole time has been sixteen each day; the whole Company consisting at first of twenty-seven, but for the greater part of the time of twenty-four members, many of them residing at great distances from London. Of the original number four have been removed from us by death.

"At an early stage in our labours, we entered into an agreement with the Universities of Oxford and Cambridge for the conveyance to them of our copyright in the work. This arrangement provided for the necessary expenses of the undertaking; and procured for the Revised Version the advantage of being published by Bodies long connected with the publication of the Authorised Version." ("Revisers' Preface" (to the N.T.), pp. vi-vii; cf. *Note Thirty-three*, pp. 352 ff.)

AMERICAN-BRITISH COLLABORATION

The Preface contains the following statement as to the way in which the American and British Committees collaborated:

"Our communications with the American Committee have been of the following nature. We transmitted to them from time to time each several portion of our First Revision, and received from them in return their criticisms and suggestions. These we considered with much care and attention during the time we were engaged on our Second Revision. We then sent over to them the various portions of the Second Revision as they were completed, and received further suggestions, which, like the former, were closely and carefully considered. Last of all, we forwarded to them the Revised Version in its final form; and a list of those passages in which they desire to place on record their preference of other readings and renderings will be found at the end of the volume. We gratefully acknowledge their care, vigilance, and accuracy; and we humbly pray that their labours and our own, thus happily united, may be permitted to bear a blessing to both countries, and to all English-speaking people throughout the world." ("Revisers' Preface" (to the N.T.), p. vii.)

No statement has been noted as to the Greek texts used by the American Revisers in their work beyond the notice on the title page: "Translated Out of the

Greek Being the Version Set Forth A.D. 1611 Compared
With the Most Ancient Authorities and Revised A.D.
1881." (American Standard Version of the New Testament, 1900.)

From this it would appear that probably they had
access to B ℵ D C A, but whether to Westcott and Hort's
revised Greek text does not appear, from the Revised
Version text or from explanations. However, as already
pointed out, this latter text (Westcott and Hort) was
placed at the disposal of the English Revisers, and seemingly exercised a great influence upon them. (*Supra,
Note Twenty-six.*)

Item 3.   Method of Work of Revisers.

Summary. Statements by Bp. Ellicott, Chairman of
the Revising body are quoted, likewise Dr. Newth's statement on the attendance at meetings of members of the
Revising body. Burgon's explanation and comments,
quoting various members of the Committee are given, in
which he relieves Scrivener from any responsibility for
the final form of the Revised Version as to its "spurious
'Readings.'" Burgon asserts that the traditional text has
been departed from nearly 6000 times, "almost invariably
for the worse."

Some further details accessible to us, of the method
of work of the Revisers, have been recorded. The Bishop
of Gloucester and Bristol (the Right Rev. Charles John
Ellicott, D.D.) is quoted as saying (Bishop Ellicott was
Chairman of the Revising Body):

"Whether any *Textual* Changes are proposed? The evidence
for and against is briefly stated, and the proposal considered. The
duty of stating this evidence is by tacit consent devolved upon
(*sic*) two members of the Company, who from their previous
studies are specially entitled to speak with authority upon such
questions,—Dr. Scrivener and *Dr. Hort,*—and who come prepared to enumerate particularly the authorities on either side.
Dr. Scrivener opens up the matter by stating the facts of the

case, and by giving his judgment on the bearings of the evidence. Dr. Hort follows, and mentions any additional matters that may call for notice; and, if differing from Dr. Scrivener's estimate of the weight of the evidence, gives his reasons and states his own view. After discussion, the vote of the Company is taken, and the proposed Reading accepted or rejected. *The Text being thus settled*, the Chairman asks for proposals on the Rendering." (Burgon, pp. 37-38; see also *id.*, pp. 38-39.)

Dr. Newth is cited for the statement that of the twenty-eight members of the Commission (Synod), the "average attendance *was not so many as sixteen, —* concerning whom, moreover, the fact has transpired that some of the most judicious of their number often *declined to give any vote at all.*" (Burgon, p. 109.) "Dr. Hort is calculated to have *talked for three years* out of the ten." (Burgon, p. 365.)

Dean Burgon quotes from Dr. Newth's *Lectures on Bible Revision,* as follows:

"As the general Rules under which the Revision was to be carried out had been carefully prepared, no need existed for any lengthened discussion of preliminary arrangements, and the Company upon its first meeting was able to enter at once upon its work. . . . The portion prescribed for the first session was Matt. i. to iv. . . . The question of the spelling of proper names . . . being settled, the Company proceeded to the actual details of the Revision, and in a surprisingly short time settled down to an established method of procedure. . . . . All proposals made at the first Revision were decided by simple majorities. . . . *The questions which concerned the Greek Text were decided for the most part at the First Revision.*" (Burgon, p. 369, n. 1.)

As to the attitude of the various Revisers on the acceptability of their work, Dean Burgon comments as follows:

"On a review of all that has happened, from first to last, we can but feel greatly concerned: greatly surprised: most of all, disappointed. We had expected a vastly different result. It is partly (not quite) accounted for, by the rare attendance in the Jerusalem Chamber [place of meeting] of some of the names on which we had chiefly relied. Bishop Moberly (of Salisbury) was present on only 121 occasions: Bishop Wordsworth (of S. Andrews) on only 109: Archbishop Trench (of Dublin) on only 63: Bishop Wilberforce on only *one*. The Archbishop, in his Charge, adverts to 'the not unfrequent sacrifice of grace and ease to the rigorous requirements of a literal accuracy;' and regards them 'as pushed to a faulty excess.' Eleven years before the scheme for the present 'Revision' had been matured, the same distinguished and judicious Prelate, (then Dean of Westminster,) persuaded as he was that a Revision *ought* to come, and convinced that in time it *would* come, deprecated its being attempted *yet*. His words were,—'Not however, I would trust, as yet: for we are not as yet *in any respect prepared for it. The Greek, and the English* which should enable us to bring this to a successful end might, it is to be feared, be wanting alike.' Archbishop Trench, with wise after-thought, in a second edition, explained himself to mean *'that special Hellenistic Greek, here required.'*

"The Bp. of S. Andrews has long since, in the fullest manner, cleared himself from the suspicion of complicity in the errors of the work before us,—as well in respect of the 'New Greek Text' as of the 'New English Version.' In the Charge which he delivered at his Diocesan Synod, (22nd Sept. 1880,) he openly stated that two years before the work was finally completed, he had felt obliged to address a printed circular to each member of the Company, in which he strongly remonstrated against the excess to which changes had been carried; and that the remonstrance had been, for the most part, unheeded. Had this been otherwise, there is good reason to believe that the reception which the Revision has met with would have been far less unfavourable, and that many a controversy which it has stirred up, would have been avoided. We have been assured that the Bp. of S. Andrews would have actually resigned his place in the Company at that time, if he had not been led to expect that some opportunity would have been taken by the Minority, when the work was finished, to express their formal dissent from the course which had been followed, and many of the conclusions which had been adopted.

"Were certain other excellent personages, (Scholars and Divines of the best type) who were often present, disposed at this late hour to come forward, they too would doubtless tell

us that they heartily regretted what was done, but were powerless to prevent it. It is no secret that Dr. Lee,—the learned
Archdeacon of Dublin,—(one of the few really competent members of the Revising body,)—found himself perpetually in the
minority.

"The same is to be recorded concerning Dr. Roberts, whose
work on the Gospels (published in 1864) shows that he is not
by any means so entirely a novice in the mysteries of Textual
Criticism as certain of his colleagues.—One famous Scholar
and excellent Divine,—a Dean whom we forbear to name,—
with the modesty of real learning, often withheld what (had
he given it) would have been an adverse vote.—Another learned
and accomplished Dean (Dr. Merivale), after attending 19
meetings of the Revising body, withdrew in disgust from them
entirely. He disapproved *the method* of his colleagues, and was
determined to incur no share of responsibility for the probable
result of their deliberations.—By the way,—What about a certain solemn Protest, by means of which the Minority had resolved *liberare animas suas* concerning the open disregard shown
by the Majority for the conditions under which they had been
entrusted with the work of Revision, but which was withheld
at the last moment? Inasmuch as their reasons for the course
they eventually adopted seemed sufficient to those high-minded
and honourable men, we forbear to challenge it. Nothing however shall deter us from plainly avowing our own opinion that
human regards scarcely deserve a hearing when GOD's Truth
is imperilled. And that the Truth of GOD's Word in countless
instances *has been* ignorantly sacrificed by a majority of the
Revisionists—(out of deference to a worthless Theory, newly
invented and passionately advocated by two of their body),—
has been already demonstrated; as far, that is, as demonstration is *possible* in this subject matter.

"As for Prebendary Scrivener,—*the only really competent
Textual Critic of the whole party*,—it is well known that he
found himself perpetually outvoted by two-thirds of those present. We look forward to the forthcoming new edition of his
Plain Introduction, in the confident belief that he will there
make it abundantly plain that he is in no degree responsible
for the monstrous Text which it became his painful duty to
conduct through the Press on behalf of the entire body, of
which he continued to the last to be a member. It is no secret
that, throughout, Dr. Scrivener pleaded in vain for the general

view we have ourselves advocated in this and the preceding Article." (Burgon, pp. 228-231.)

Regarding Dr. Scrivener, Dean Burgon makes the following further comments:

"It cannot be too plainly or too often stated that learned Prebendary Scrivener is *wholly guiltless* of the many spurious 'Readings' with which a majority of his co-Revisionists have corrupted the Word of GOD. He pleaded faithfully,—but he pleaded in vain.—It is right also to state that the scholarlike Bp. of S. Andrews (Dr. Charles Wordsworth) has fully purged himself of the suspicion of complicity, by his printed (not published) remonstrances with his colleagues.—The excellent Bp. of Salisbury (Dr. Moberly) attended only 121 of their 407 meetings; and that judicious scholar, the Abp. of Dublin (Dr. Trench) only 63." (Burgon, p. 106, n. 1; see also further comments *id.*, pp. 2 and 246, n. 1.)

Dean Burgon affirms, "The traditional Text has been departed from by them nearly 6000 times, — almost invariably *for the worse.*" (Burgon, p. 107.)

Regarding these changes Dr. Wordsworth is quoted as saying:

"We meet in every page with small changes which are vexatious, teasing, and irritating; even the more so because they are small (as small insects sting most sharply), *which seem almost to be made merely for the sake of change.*" (Burgon, p. 226, n. 1; and see *id.*, pp. 223 ff.)

NOTE TWENTY-EIGHT •

The Prefaces of the Revisions As Published by the Revisers

It would be useful to look at the methods and procedure of the British Revisers as set out in the Prefaces to their work. These Prefaces are very revealing.

Item 1.   The Qualifications of the Revisers for Expressing Their Views, Revised Version.

> *Summary.* They were by training and scholarship supposedly fitted to express their views in good clear English, and as Churchmen they should have been in a most humble, reverential attitude.

In this relation, we should have in mind the following situation. We refer again to the discussion heretofore given (*Notes Three and Eleven*) on Textual Criticism for the attitude of the Extreme Textualists upon Christ and his work. The writers of these Prefaces were scholars of great repute and many of them learned divines of high place in the Church of England. (*Note Twenty-seven.*) By training and by profession they were masters of languages, ancient and modern. They must be presumed to know the meaning of words. The use of words had been their business over the long and exacting hours they record as spending at their work. They must have written their Prefaces with the intent that their words would express their real intent and their full feeling.

Item 2.   The Preface to the Old Testament, Revised Version.

Summary. The Preface is noteworthy for what it does not say. Some deficiencies in expression and attitude noted since the text must stand as the promulgation of the Word of God.

We may so proceed to their Prefaces. The closing words of the "Revisers' Preface" to their work of revision of the Old Testament are not without interest.

After first briefly recording changes in the personnel of the revising committee and noting the time spent upon their work, the concluding paragraph of the Preface reads thusly:

"The labour therefore has been great, but it has been given ungrudgingly; and now with a feeling of deep thankfulness to Almighty God, and the earnest hope that their endeavours may with His blessing tend to a clearer knowledge of the Old Testament Scriptures, the Revisers bring their long task to a close. Jerusalem Chamber, Westminster Abbey, 10 July, 1884." ("Revisers' Preface" (to the O.T.), p. x.)

It may be noted as to this paragraph of the Preface to the Old Testament in the Revised Version, that no hope is expressed therein that a truer record of the words of the Almighty has been made, or a hope that a more accurate account of the happenings recorded in the Old Testament has been worked out, or that the Revisionists asked for the guidance of the Holy Spirit in their arduous and important work, or that they considered they had such aid, or that their "deep thankfulness to Almighty God" was for his aid in making a correct translation, but rather thankfulness that their work was done. They have an "earnest hope," not a prayer, that their Revision will bring a clear knowledge of the Scriptures, not a burning testimony of the truth thereof.

We note these deficiencies.

So much for the Preface to the Old Testament.

Item 3. The Preface to the New Testament, Revised Version.

Summary. The bulk of the Preface is devoted to matters of scholarship, as might have prefaced the translation of a classic work of history or literature. The spiritual elements of the work are reserved for the last three paragraphs. Each paragraph is analyzed and appraised in turn. The first two of these last three paragraphs contain no mention or direct reference to Christ. The third paragraph contains the only mention of Christ in the entire Preface, and is found in a prayer "to Almighty God, that the Gospel of our Lord and Saviour Jesus Christ may be more clearly and more freshly shewn forth to all who shall be readers of this Book." A summary of the deficiencies of the Preface as to Jesus the Christ, his personality, mission, resurrection, atonement, is given.

Now we turn to the Preface to the New Testament.

The New Testament British Revision had been finished a little over three and a half years earlier than the Old Testament Revision. (The New Testament Preface is dated "Jerusalem Chamber, Westminster Abbey, 11th November 1880"; the Old Testament Preface, as just stated, bears date July 10, 1884.)

The bulk of both British Prefaces is devoted to problems of scholarship. These problems are treated and discussed as they might be in a translation of a classic work of literature or history, though there is in the discussion an undercurrent of responsibility and restraint that attests a realization by the Revisers that, at least from the viewpoint of the Bible reader, they were dealing with a work that was something more than just literature: they so testify. Nevertheless, the dominant factor of the whole work (as disclosed in the Prefaces of the British Revisers) was scholarship, not spirituality.

The spiritual element of the British Revisers was reserved, even for mere mention, to the three paragraphs that closed their Preface. These read:

"We now conclude, humbly commending our labours to Almighty God, and praying that his favour and blessing may be vouchsafed to that which has been done in his name. We recognised from the first the responsibility of the undertaking; and through our manifold experience of its abounding difficulties we have felt more and more, as we went onward, that such a work can never be accomplished by organised efforts of scholarship and criticism, unless assisted by Divine help.

"We know full well that defects must have their place in a work so long and so arduous as this which has now come to an end. Blemishes and imperfections there are in the noble Translation which we have been called upon to revise; blemishes and imperfections will assuredly be found in our own Revision. All endeavours to translate the Holy Scriptures into another tongue must fall short of their aim, when the obligation is imposed of producing a Version that shall be alike literal and idiomatic, faithful to each thought of the original, and yet, in the expression of it, harmonious and free. While we dare to hope that in places not a few of the New Testament the introduction of slight changes has cast a new light upon much that was difficult and obscure, we cannot forget how often we have failed in expressing some finer shade of meaning which we recognised in the original, how often idiom has stood in the way of a perfect rendering, and how often the attempt to preserve a familiar form of words, or even a familiar cadence, has only added another perplexity to those which already beset us.

"Thus, in the review of the work which we have been permitted to complete, our closing words must be words of mingled thanksgiving, humility, and prayer. Of thanksgiving, for the many blessings vouchsafed to us throughout the unbroken progress of our corporate labours; of humility, for our failings and imperfections in the fulfilment of our task; and of prayer to Almighty God, that the Gospel of our Lord and Saviour Jesus Christ may be more clearly and more freshly shewn forth to all who shall be readers of this Book." ("Revisers' Preface" (to the N.T.), pp. xi-xii.)

Those three paragraphs are more significant for what they do not say than for what they say.

The first paragraph commends their labors to Almighty God and prays and asks his blessings upon what has been done in his name. It also declares recognition of their responsibility and that their work could not be done "by organised efforts of scholarship and criticism, unless assisted by Divine help." There is no mention of nor direct reference to Christ, whose life, mission, and teachings the New Testament records.

The second paragraph affirms that a work "so long and so arduous" as this, must have "defects" and "blemishes," and notes the character of some of them; expresses the hope that "the introduction of slight changes has cast a new light upon much that was difficult and obscure"; but states these changes have sometimes added new "perplexities." Still no mention of or reference to the Christ.

The third paragraph speaks of thanksgiving for the many blessings vouchsafed to the Revisers "throughout the unbroken progress of our corporate labours" (the source of the blessings is not indicated); "humility, for our failings and imperfections in the fulfilment of our task" (this is a phrase of somewhat cloudy meaning); and a prayer "to Almighty God, that the Gospel of our Lord and Saviour Jesus Christ may be more clearly and more freshly shewn forth to all who shall be readers of this Book."

SUMMARY COMMENTS

At last in the entire New Testament Preface comes a mention of the Christ, but only in the naming of his Gospel.

Surely this is a remarkable document to introduce a Version of the New Testament, the inspired account of the life, mission, works, and teachings of the Christ,—the only adequate source of such an account that exists, covering Palestine.

Recalling what we have already set out about the scholarship and literary attainments of the Revisers, we may note, in addition to what we have already said, the following matters. We do not wish to be either trivial or captious.

1. There is no statement in the Prefaces and no necessary implication that the Revisers invoked at any time in their long labors or relied upon the Holy Spirit to guide them in their work. They may have earnestly prayed to the Lord at the beginning of each session for the presence and help of the Holy Ghost, but their Prefaces do not so state,—the Holy Ghost which Jesus told the Apostles 'would teach them all things, and bring all things to their remembrance, whatsoever he had said unto them.' (John 14:26.) The Holy Ghost was worth remembering and soliciting. There is no statement or comment indicating that the Revisers took advantage of the repeated promises of Jesus to his Apostles: "And whatsoever ye shall ask in my name, that will I do, that the Father may be glorified in the Son" (John 14:13). And again (later in the same evening, in the Upper Chamber), there is nothing to show that they remembered the words of the Christ, "Whatsoever ye shall ask the Father in my name, he will give it you." (John 16:23.) Their full record of proceedings may show all this was done (unfortunately their full record is not available to us to verify, or otherwise, our supposition), but their Preface does not show it, nor is it either intimated or indicated.

But such an invocation for Divine help to do work of such transcendent importance as the Revisers were essaying to accomplish, would have been the natural and inevitable approach of men of normal faith. It should be noted that while the Preface contains the statement: "Different schools of criticism have been represented among us, and have together contributed to the final result," ("Revisers' Preface" (to the N.T.), p. viii) nevertheless the majority of the Revisers were seemingly Extreme Textualists (as will hereinafter appear), and apparently were not willing to accept the Jesus of the New Testament accounts as given in the Authorized Version, as these accounts have been accepted and interpreted over the centuries (see *supra*, p. 53 ff.), and one of the members of the revising group (unnamed) is spoken of as "one who openly denies the eternal Godhead of our LORD JESUS CHRIST." (Burgon, p. 344; see *infra*, p. 287.)

So it seems likely that the Revisers overlooked the appeal to the Father through the Son. Once again, they seemed not to remember the words spoken by the Christ to his disciples during the last night before the Crucifixion, first in the Upper Chamber (John 14:13), then on the way to the Garden (John 15:16), and later as they lingered in the Garden: "Verily, verily, I say unto you, Whatsoever ye shall ask the Father in my name, he will give it you." (John 16:23.)

Naturally none would so appeal who did not believe in the divinity of the Son.

Burgon, commenting on this matter of prayer and referring to the presence of a Unitarian among the Revisers says:

"But even if this Unitarian had been an eminent Scholar, my objection would remain in full force; for I hold, (and surely so do you!), that the right Interpretation of GOD'S Word may not be attained without the guidance of the HOLY SPIRIT, whose aid must first be invoked by faithful prayer." (Burgon, p. 507, and see Burgon's note, beginning p. 504, for comments by Bp. Wilberforce in his work, *Chronicle of Convocation* (Feb. 1871), and by Bp. Wordsworth in his *Address on the Revised Version*, 1881.)

2. As to the *thankfulness* expressed,—it is not specifically addressed to or towards anyone, either the Father, or the Son, or the Holy Ghost. Seemingly it is just a general impulse of gratitude, not directed even to Divine influence. The natural thing, for men of normal faith, would have been to address the Father through his Son, thanking him for his help which it would have been the natural thing for devout men to seek in such a work. Of course, as honest men, they would not claim they had been blessed with Divine inspiration, if they did not ask for it, and if they did not believe they had received it.

3. As already stated, the description of their humility is a bit cloudy and uncertain. Apparently their "failings and imperfections" made them humble, whether scholastically or spiritually, they do not tell us.

4. Finally, they do pray to Almighty God, but not through the Son, that the Gospel of our Lord Jesus Christ (this identifies the Gospel intended) "may be more clearly and more freshly shewn forth" to men. The word *freshly* is a little difficult to grasp, unless it means a *fresh*, that is *new*, Gospel or Gospel principle. It seems from what they did, that this is probably what they meant, for we shall see they did thrust in some *fresh* ideas that are calculated to destroy the Christian faith of centuries. (See *infra*, pp. 300 ff.)

On this question of *freshness*, the observations of Burgon on the changes they made and wished to make are worth quoting:

"The correction of known Textual errors of course we eagerly expected: and on every occasion when the Traditional Text was altered, we as confidently depended on finding a record of the circumstance inserted with religious fidelity into the margin,—as agreed upon by the Revisionists at the outset. In both of these expectations however we found ourselves sadly disappointed. The Revisionists have *not* corrected the 'known Textual errors.' On the other hand, besides silently adopting most of those wretched fabrications which are just now in favour with the German school, they have encumbered their margin with those other Readings which, after due examination, *they had themselves deliberately rejected.* For why? Because, in their collective judgment, 'for the present, it would not be safe to accept one Reading to the absolute exclusion of others.' A fatal admission truly! What are found in the margin are therefore *'alternative Readings,'*—in the opinion of these self-constituted representatives of the Church and of the Sects." (Burgon, p. 236.)

Item 4. The Preface to the Old Testament Revised Version 1900-1901 (American Standard Version).

Summary. It is even less spiritual than the British edition. It could have been written by a pagan or an atheist.

But the American Revisers seem even more remotely removed from any apparent awareness that Divine inspiration might have been implored to assist them in their work of revision. The Preface to their edition of the Revised Version of the Old Testament deals wholly with their differences with the English Revisers, some of the differences appearing to us laymen to be captious, technical, and trivial. The concluding paragraph of this Preface is interesting and revealing as to the mental and spiritual attitude of the Revisers. It reads:

"Earnestly hoping that our work may contribute to the better understanding of the Old Testament, we commend it to the considerate judgment of all students of the Sacred Scriptures." ("Preface" (to the O. T.), A.S.V., p. vii.)

This conclusion might have been written by an atheist or a pagan. Was it? It is weak beyond measure to have been the words of men of God. It is wholly devoid of expressed faith or reverence.

Item 5. The Preface to the New Testament Revised Version 1900-1901 (American Standard Version).

Summary. Comments are made on the publication procedures of the Revised Version in Britain and America. There is the same absence of spirituality as in the British Preface. The absence of the words *Jesus* or *Christ* in Preface is noted; the "words of Christ" are mentioned in the one phrase. There is no mention of God except in the concluding paragraph. There is no evidence of a feeling of necessity to invoke Divine guidance in their work to obtain true meaning. Concluding comments.

The American Revisers' Preface to the New Testament text is largely devoted to an explanation and attempted justification (which may be good) for the changes they have made in the original Revised Version issued in England. This original print of the British Version was, it will be recalled, the joint work of English and American scholars. Changes in the Authorized Version text which were suggested by the American scholars and which were unacceptable to the British scholars, were printed in the original British Press' edition, as Appendices. In this American Version, the Appendix disappears and its material is seemingly incorporated in the text as changes in the text or as footnotes.

It should be recalled that as part of the arrangement between the American and British scholars covering the preparation of the original Revised Version text printed in England (1881 and 1885) it was stipulated that no American edition should be issued for fourteen years. This arrangement was observed by the American Committee.

The work of the American scholars in the preparation of the American edition of the Revised Version, was seemingly largely, as already stated, the inclusion either in the text or as notes, of the American preferences. There is little in the Preface to lead one to believe that the Revisers had any concern other than either improving the English of the Authorized Version (according to their ideas—some of them apparently good—of improvement) or improving the mechanics of the printer in the printers' page,—titles and headings, arrangement of footnotes, spelling, and like matters. There is in the Preface evidence that they appreciated that they were dealing "with a venerable monument of English usage, and have been careful not to obliterate the traces of its historic origin and descent" (this last clause is muddy as to its meaning), that is, it appears they thoroughly understood they were dealing with a piece of great literature, but there is no suggestion that they were concerned over the fact (which apparently they did not appreciate) that they were dealing with the Word of God. Neither the words *Jesus* or *Christ* appear once in the Preface, except in the phrase " 'words' of Christ," and these occur in a reference to a 'grouping of references topically.' No mention is made of God, except in the concluding paragraph, to be quoted hereinafter. There is no indication that where the Revisers had different views about the text, they ever felt it necessary to invoke Divine help to obtain the true meaning. The best that can be said is that they appreciated they were engaged in an absorbing intellectual exercise. ("Preface" (to the N.T.), A.S.V., p. iv.)

The concluding paragraph of the American Preface is written in the spirit of their work. It reads:

"The present volume, it is believed, will on the one hand bring a plain reader more closely into contact with the exact thought of the sacred writers than any version now current in Christendom, and on the other hand prove itself especially serviceable to students of the Word. In this belief the editors bid it anew God-speed, and in the realization of this desired result they will find their all-sufficient reward." ("Preface" (to the N.T.), A.S.V., p. v.)

One expression of the Preface,—"the exact *thought* of the sacred writers" (italics ours) : Were the words of the Lord in the Good Book, his commandments, were the burning invectives against the Pharisees, and the sacred record of the Lord's mighty miracles, and the eternal principles of the Lord's Gospel,—were all these but the *thought* of the writers, or were the sacred words of the Testament the recording of facts and eternal truths? The Latter-day Saint knows that the Testament is a sacred record of facts, incidents, and eternal truths.

Scholastically, these Revisers may have been all that could be desired (some critics think otherwise,—Burgon, p. 124), but they have given us no real evidence that spiritually they had the faith or the conviction that the true Christian should and does possess.

NOTE TWENTY-NINE •

"Conjectural Emendation" in Determining the True Text

Item 1. What is "Conjectural Emendation?"

> *Summary.* Shortly put: "Conjectural emendations" are changes in the text either by omissions, additions, or alterations for which there is no authority in any of the known manuscripts. Renewed reference is made to the influences dominating the making of the Revised Version. The responsibility of the Church of England for the Revision. Changes by "divination." The "individual mind" element.

In the fabrication of their new Greek text, Westcott and Hort made certain changes in their new text as against the language of the older texts by what they termed "conjectural emendations."

Shortly and generally put, "conjectural emendations" are apparently changes in the text either by omissions, additions, or alterations, for which there is no authority in the known manuscripts. It should be foremost in mind in what is said in the following pages under this heading, that, as already pointed out, the new Greek text (the Westcott and Hort Greek text) appears to be the basic and controlling text of the Revised Version, and that the Westcott and Hort text is in turn primarily based on the Codex Vaticanus (B). The influence of Dr. Hort upon the revision of the Authorized Version text, as set out above, lends strong color to the charge that he it was who dominated the whole Revision. The comments made by Scrivener and by Burgon, and by others quoted by them, are aimed at the unreliability of this new Greek text

(Westcott and Hort) for a final determination, and this in turn means the unreliability therefor of the Revised Version based thereon.

First, the character of the omissions and questionable texts of the Revised Version give a semblance of justification at least for the observations of Burgon on the attitude of Westcott and Hort on the essential point of Christ's divinity.

Burgon vigorously, almost viciously, points out that the Church of England has become a party to this sacrilegious procedure, through its Bishops and Doctors who "have not scrupled to enter into an irregular alliance with Sectarians,—yes, have even taken into partnership with themselves one who openly denies the eternal Godhead of our LORD JESUS CHRIST." (Burgon, p. 344; and see *id.*, p. 353.)

The phrase "conjectural emendation" appears to describe a procedure by which the framers of the text—in our discussion here, the Westcott and Hort new Greek text—arrive at their decisions as to the true text by a sort of divination. They may use this divination to reach a decision as between two or more texts, or to arrive at a text that is different from all other known texts. In the last analysis the decision seems to rest upon the "individual mind" of the translator, assuming he is an acceptable translator.

In the pages that follow, the critics of this new text give reasons for their objection to this system, and illustrate their objections. The nubbin of the criticism is given by Burgon in these words:

"If these distinguished Professors have enjoyed a Revelation as to what the Evangelists actually wrote, they would do well to acquaint the world with the fact at the earliest possible moment. If, on the contrary, they are merely relying on their own inner consciousness for the power of divining the truth of Scripture at a glance,—they must be prepared to find their decrees treated with the contumely which is due to imposture, of whatever kind." (Burgon, p. 95, n. 1; see *id.*, pp. 289, 290.)

Item 2. Principle of "Conjectural Emendation" Not Generally Accepted.

> *Summary.* Considered: recognition of textual errors in all extant documents. Changes by this method run counter to the witness of the Fathers. Scrivener's observations on the general principle.

As just stated, the new Greek text (Westcott and Hort), upon which the Revised Version is mainly based (Burgon, pp. 294 and 320) was, according to its critics, built by its framers on theories and principles which have not been generally used or accepted by textual critics. It is a little difficult, from materials available to the author, accurately to define or understand the matters and problems involved, but the system seems to be based upon the fixing at times of the true text by "conjectural emendation," which it seems may go as far as to recognize "places in which we are *constrained by overwhelming evidence* to recognize the existence of Textual error in *all* extant documents" (Burgon, p. 355, quoting Drs. Hort and Westcott), or as Drs. Westcott and Hort are quoted as saying, "the prevalent assumption, that throughout the N.T. the true text is to be found *somewhere* among recorded readings, *does not stand the test of experience.*" (Burgon, pp. 28, n., 294, 320, 355, quoting Drs. Hort and Westcott.)

Dean Burgon states that one of those *places* is found (according to Drs. Westcott and Hort) in II Peter 3:10, which reads: "But the day of the Lord will come as a thief in the night; in the which the heavens shall pass away with a great noise, and the elements shall melt with fervent heat, the earth also and the works that are therein shall be burned up."

After noting some possible explanation for certain variant readings of this text in the manuscripts, Burgon comments:

"But what is there in all this to make one distrust the Traditional reading?—supported as it is by the whole mass of Copies: by the Latin,—the Coptic,—the Harkleian,—and the Æthiopic Versions:—besides the only Fathers who quote the place; viz. Cyril seven times, and John Damascene once? . . . As for pretending, at the end of the foregoing enquiry, that 'we are *constrained by overwhelming evidence* to recognize the existence of textual error *in all extant documents*,'—it is evidently a mistake. Nothing else is it but a misstatement of facts." (Burgon, pp. 355-356.)

It might be here noted that Dean Burgon affirms Dr. Hort is all but wholly deficient in producing evidence for his conclusions regarding textual readings he adopts. (Burgon, p. 305.)

Regarding the determination of text by "conjecture," we quote below Prebendary Scrivener,—as already observed, he is an outstanding scholar of strictest integrity as shown by the fact that he was chosen to carry through the press the new Greek text of the Revised Version, with many readings of which he did not agree (Burgon, p. 231; and see *id.*, xii; p. 10, n. 1; p. 13, n. 1; p. 49, n. 2; p. 106, n. 1; p. 108; p. 237, n. 3; and pp. 246-247). Because the comments are so searchingly made, yet with a scholarly restraint that is strongly persuasive of their soundness, we have made somewhat extensive extracts. Scrivener says:

"It is now agreed among competent judges that *Conjectural Emendation* must never be resorted to, even in passages of acknowledged difficulty; the absence of proof that a reading proposed to be substituted for the common one is actually supported by some trustworthy document being of itself a fatal objection to our receiving it. Those that have been hazarded aforetime by celebrated scholars, when but few codices were known or actually collated, have seldom, very seldom, been confirmed by subsequent researches: and the time has now fully come when, in the possession of abundant stores of variations collected from memorials of almost every age and country, we are fully authorised in believing that the reading which no manuscript, or old version, or primitive Father has borne witness to, however plausible and (for some purposes) convenient, cannot safely be accepted as genuine or even as probable; even though there may still remain a few passages respecting which we cannot help framing a shrewd suspicion that the original reading differed from any form in which they are now presented to us.

"In no wise less dangerous than bare conjecture destitute of external evidence, is the device of Lachmann (*see* p. 480) for unsettling by means of emendation (*emendando*), without reference to the balance of conflicting testimony, the very text he had previously fixed by revision (*recensendo*) through the means of critical authorities: in fact the earlier process is but so much trouble misemployed, if its results are liable to be put aside by abstract judgment or individual prejudices. Not that the most sober and cautious critic would disparage the fair use of internal evidence, or withhold their proper influence from those reasonable considerations which in practice cannot, and in speculation should not, be shut out from every subject on which the mind seeks to form an intelligent opinion. Whether we will or not, we unconsciously and almost instinctively adopt that one of two opposite statements, *in themselves pretty equally attested to,* which we judge the better suited to recognised phenomena, and to the common course of things. I know of no person who has affected to construct a text of the N.T. on diplomatic grounds exclusively, without paying some regard to the character of the sense produced; nor, were the experiment tried, would any one find it easy to dispense with discretion and the dictates of good sense: nature would prove too strong for the dogmas of a wayward theory. 'It is difficult not to indulge in *subjectiveness,* at least in some measure,' writes Dr. Tregelles (*Account of Printed Text,* p. 109): and, thus qualified, we may add that it is one of those difficulties a sane man would not wish to overcome." (Scrivener, pp. 490-492.)

Item 3.   Problems and Dangers of "Conjectural Emendation."

Summary. Scrivener's comments thereon, including the non-appealing character of such emendations, (which he characterizes as "guess work") to scholars generally.

On the problems and dangers involved in "conjectural emendation," Scrivener continues:

"The foregoing remarks may tend to explain the broad distinction between mere conjectural emendation, which must be utterly discarded, and that just use of internal testimony which he is the best critic who most judiciously employs. They so far resemble each other, as they are both products of the reasoning faculty exercising itself on the sacred words of Scripture: they differ in this essential feature, that the one proceeds in ignorance or disregard of evidence from without, while the office of the other has no place unless where external evidence is evenly, or at any rate not very unevenly, balanced. What degree of preponderance in favour of one out of several readings, all of them affording some tolerable sense, shall entitle it to reception as a matter of right; to what extent canons of subjective criticism may be allowed to eke out the scantiness of documentary authority; are points that cannot well be defined with strict accuracy. Men's decisions respecting them will always vary according to their temperament and intellectual habits; the judgment of the same person (the rather if he be by constitution a little unstable) will fluctuate from time to time as to the same evidence brought to bear on the self-same passage. Though the *canons* or rules of internal testimony be themselves grounded either on principles of common sense, or on certain peculiarities which all may mark in the documents from which our direct proofs are derived (*see below*, p. 499); yet has it been found by experience (what indeed we might have looked for beforehand), that in spite, perhaps in consequence, of their extreme simplicity, the application of these canons has proved a searching test of the tact, the sagacity, and the judicial acumen of all that handle them. For the other functions of an editor accuracy and learning, diligence and zeal are sufficient: but the delicate adjustment of conflicting probabilities calls for no mean exercise of a critical genius. This innate faculty we lack in Wetstein, and notably in Scholz; it was highly developed in

Mill and Bengel, and still more in Griesbach. His well-known power in this respect is the main cause of our deep regret for the failure of Bentley's projected work, with all its faults whether of plan or execution." (Scrivener, pp. 492-493.)

Dr. Scrivener follows these comments by laying down seven rules governing internal evidence which, as he affirms:

". . . being founded in the nature of things, are alike applicable to all subjects of literary investigation, though their general principles may need some modification in the particular instance of the Greek Testament." (Scrivener, p. 493.)

Our purpose here does not require that we should list these rules. But he makes these general comments:

"There are texts, no doubt, some of those for example which Dr. Westcott and Dr. Hort have branded with a marginal † in their edition; e.g. Acts vii. 46; xiii. 32; xix. 40; xxvi. 28; Rom. viii. 2; 1 Cor. xii. 2 (where Eph. ii. 11 might suggest *hoti pote*) ; 1 Tim. vi. 7, and especially in the kindred Epistles, 2 Pet. iii. 10; 12; Jude 5; 22, 23, wherein, whether from internal difficulties or from the actual state of the external evidence, we should be very glad of more light than our existing authorities will lend us. *What I most urge is the plain fact, that the conjectures, even of able and accomplished men, have never been such as to approve themselves to any but their authors, much less to commend themselves to the judgment of scholars as intuitively true.*" (Scrivener, p. 490, n. 2; italics ours.)

The second edition contains the following sentence:

"A conspicuous instance of the vast difference between amending by guess-work and amending by means of fresh manuscript readings will appear in the case of Mark vi. 20, examined below in Chap. IX." (Scrivener, 2nd ed., p. 433, n. 1; and see pp. 581 ff. (3rd ed.) for a discussion of Mark 6:20.)

Item 4. Applicability of "Conjectural Emendation" to the Revised Version.

Summary. This *Item* notes: Hort's seeming estimate of such emendations, the place of the "individual mind";

his collaboration with others in these "emendations,"—analogous to revelation. Burgon's analysis is given of Hort's description of the processes incident to such "emendations," with particular reference to a few chosen scripture passages. Necessity of proof for "emendations."

As to the applicability of this "conjectural emendation," this "guess-work," to the new Greek text of Westcott and Hort, and therefore to the Revised Version which is based upon that text, the following statements by Hort (quoted by Burgon) containing his own, at least implied, estimates of his (Hort's) work, are of interest. These statements involve comments upon the *conjectural* theory itself, and upon the *individual mind* which uses the theory. Hort says (as quoted) in what, under the circumstances, may well be regarded as an appraisement of his own capabilities:

"The *Art of Conjectural Emendation* depends for its success so much on personal endowments, fertility of resource in the first instance, and even more an appreciation of language too delicate to acquiesce in merely plausible corrections, that it is easy to forget its true character as a critical operation founded on knowledge and method." (Burgon, p. 351.)

Again:

"But *we are obliged to come to the individual mind* at last; and canons of Criticism are useful only as warnings against *natural illusions*, and aids to circumspect consideration, not as absolute rules to prescribe the final decision. It is true that no *individual mind* can ever work with perfect uniformity, or free itself completely from *its own idiosyncrasies*. Yet a clear sense of the danger of *unconscious caprice* may do much towards excluding it. We trust also that the present Text has escaped some risks of this kind by being the joint production of two Editors of different habits of mind." (Burgon, p. 25, see *id.*, p. 253.)

Dr. Hort refers here to the collaboration of himself and Dr. Westcott in the preparation of their new Greek text.

Dean Burgon seems aptly to have challenged that this kind of complex raises the question of whether one so commenting claims revelation as his guide. (*Supra*, p. 287.)

On another occasion, Dr. Hort (as quoted) said:

"Every binary group (of MSS.) *containing* B is found to offer a large proportion of Readings, which, on the closest scrutiny, have THE RING OF GENUINENESS: while it is difficult to find any Readings so attested which LOOK SUSPICIOUS after full consideration," as to which judgment, it appears, Dr. Hort affirms: "We are obliged to *come to the individual mind at last.*" (Burgon, p. 307.)

First, on this matter of the "ring of genuineness," Dean Burgon says:

"The man who finds '*no marks of either Critical or Spiritual insight*' in the only Greek Text which was known to scholars till A.D. 1831,—(although he confesses that 'the text of Chrysostom and other Syrian Fathers of the IVth century is substantially identical with it'); and vaunts in preference '*the bold vigour*' and '*refined scholarship*' which is exclusively met with in certain depraved uncials of the same or later date:—the man who thinks it not unlikely that the incident of the piercing of our SAVIOUR'S side (*allos de labon logchen k.t.l.*) was actually found in the genuine Text of S. Matt. xxvii. 49, *as well as* in S. John xix. 34: —the man who is of opinion that the incident of the Woman taken in Adultery (filling 12 verses), 'presents serious differences from the diction of S. John's Gospel,'—treats it as 'an insertion in a comparatively late Western text' and declines to retain it even within brackets, on the ground that it 'would fatally interrupt' the course of the narrative if suffered to stand:—the man who can deliberately separate off from the end of S. Mark's Gospel, and print separately, S. Mark's last 12 verses, (on the plea that they 'manifestly cannot claim any apostolic authority; but are doubtless founded on some tradition of the Apostolic age;')—yet who straightway proceeds to annex, *as an alternative Conclusion* (*allos*), 'the wretched supplement derived from codex L:'—the man (lastly) who, in defiance of 'solid reason and pure taste,' finds music in the 'utterly marred' 'rhythmical arrangement' of the Angels' Hymn on the night of the Nativity:—such an one is not entitled to a hearing when he talks about *'the ring of genuineness.'* He has already effectually put himself out of Court. He has convicted himself of a natural infirmity of judgment,—has given proof that he labours under a peculiar Critical inaptitude for this department of enquiry,—which renders his decrees nugatory, and his opinions worthless." (Burgon, pp. 309-310; for additional examples of the same sort, see citations to Burgon's text itself in his note, p. 315.)

Next, to Dr. Hort's observation that we "come to the individual mind at last," Dean Burgon makes this following answering comment:

"A somewhat insecure safeguard surely! May we be permitted without offence to point out that the 'idiosyncrasies' of an 'individual mind' (to which we learn with astonishment 'we are obliged to come at last') are probably the very worst foundation possible on which to build the recension of an inspired writing? With regret we record our conviction, that these accomplished scholars have succeeded in producing a Text vastly more remote from the inspired autographs of the Evangelists than any which has appeared since the invention of printing. When full Prolegomena have been furnished we shall know more about the matter; but to judge from the Remarks which the learned Editors (Revisionists themselves) have subjoined to their elegantly-printed volume, it is to be feared that the fabric will be found to rest too exclusively on vague assumption and unproved hypothesis. In other words, a painful apprehension is created that their edition of 'The New Testament in the original Greek' will be found to partake inconveniently of the nature of a work of the Imagination. As codex ℵ proved fatal to Dr. Tischendorf, so is codex B evidently the rock on which Drs. Westcott and Hort have split. Did it ever occur to those learned men to enquire how the Septuagint Version of the *Old* Testament has fared at the hands of codex B? They are respectfully invited to address themselves to this very damaging enquiry." (Burgon, pp. 25-29.)

Later, Dr. Burgon adds this comment, following a partial repetition of the comments of Dr. Hort upon the "individual mind," and having in mind Dr. Westcott's collaboration in the preparation of the new Greek text and Dr. Hort's contention about the safeguard this afforded (*supra*):

". . . we can but avow our conviction that the safeguard is altogether inadequate. When two men, devoted to the same pursuit, are in daily confidential intercourse on such a subject, the *'natural illusions'* of either have a marvellous tendency to communicate themselves. Their Reader's only protection is rigidly to *insist* on the production of *Proof* for everything which these authors say." (Burgon, p. 251.)

Item 5.   Scrivener's Ultimate Views on "Conjectural Emendation."

On the general subject of "conjectural emendation," and particularly as it applies to the new Greek text of Westcott and Hort, Burgon quotes from Scrivener the passages set out below, after making the following introductory statement:

"*The following is* PREBENDARY SCRIVENER'S *recently published estimate of the System on which* DRS. WESTCOTT AND HORT *have constructed their* 'Revised Greek Text of the New Testament' (1881).—*That System, the Chairman of the Revising Body* (BISHOP ELLICOTT) *has entirely adopted (see below, pp. 391 to 397), and made the basis of his Defence of* THE REVISERS *and their* 'New Greek Text.'" (Burgon, p. iv.)

"But there is little hope for the stability of their imposing structure, if its foundations have been laid on the sandy ground of ingenious conjecture: and since barely the smallest vestige of historical evidence has ever been alleged in support of the views of these accomplished editors, their teaching must either be received as intuitively true, or dismissed from our consideration as precarious, and even visionary. . . .

"Dr. Hort's system, therefore, is entirely destitute of historical foundation. . . .

". . . we are compelled to repeat as emphatically as ever our strong conviction that the hypothesis to whose proof he has devoted so many laborious years, is destitute not only of historical foundation, but of all probability resulting from the internal goodness of the text which its adoption would force upon us. . . .

" 'We cannot doubt that it [Luke 23:34] comes from an extraneous source' (Hort, *Notes,* p. 68). Nor can we on our part doubt that the system which entails such consequences is hopelessly self-condemned." (Scrivener, pp. 531, 537, 542, 604; see herein, pp. 79, 117, 125, 255, 316, 350.)

Item 6.   Burgon's List of Textual Changes Made by West-cott and Hort on the Basis of "Conjectural Emenda-tion" or "Ring of Genuineness."

Summary. The writer's concluding observations.

The *conjectural* theory, as applied by the editors of the new Greek text, calls for omissions as well as emendations. Here again Dr. Burgon comments in a most thoroughgoing and succinct way that gives a general view of the whole matter. He introduces a footnote on the subject with these words:

"It is notorious that, on the contrary, Dr. Hort is frequently constrained to admit that *the omitted words* actually *have* 'the ring of genuineness.' The words which he insists on thrusting out of the Text are often conspicuous *for the very quality* which (by the hypothesis) was the warrant for their exclusion. Of this, the Reader may convince himself by referring to the note at foot of the present page." (Burgon, pp. 310-311.)

His note reads:

"In S. Matth. i. 25,—the omission of *'her first-born:'*—in vi. 13, the omission of the *Doxology*:—in xii. 47, the omission of *the whole verse*:—in xvi. 2, 3, the omission of our Lord's memorable words concerning the *signs of the weather*:—in xvii. 21, the omission of the mysterious statement, *'But this kind goeth not out save by prayer and fasting:'*— in xviii. 11, the omission of the precious words *'For the Son of man came to save that which was lost.'*

"In S. Mark xvi. 9-20, the omission of the *'last Twelve Verses,'*—('the contents of which are *not such as could have been invented* by any scribe or editor of the Gospel,'—W. and H. p. 57). All admit that *ephoboynto gar* is an impossible ending.

"In S. Luke vi. 1, the suppression of the unique *deyteroproto;* ('the very obscurity of the expression attesting strongly to its genuineness,'—Scrivener, p. 516, and so W. and H. p. 58) :— ix. 54-56, the omitted *rebuke to the 'disciples James and John:'* —in x. 41, 42, the omitted *words concerning Martha and Mary*: —in xxii. 43, 44, the omission of the *Agony in the Garden,—* (which nevertheless, *'it would be impossible to regard* as a product of the inventiveness of scribes,'—W. and H. p. 67) :— in xxiii. 17, a memorable clause omitted:—in xxiii. 34, the omission of our Lord's *prayer for His murderers,—*(concerning which Westcott and Hort remark that *'few verses of the Gospels bear in themselves a surer witness to the truth of what they record than this'*—p. 68) :—in xxiii. 38, the statement that the Inscription on the Cross was *'in letters of Greek, and Latin, and Hebrew'*:—in xxiv. 12, *the visit of Peter to the Sepulchre.* Bishop Lightfoot remarks concerning S. Luke ix. 56: xxii. 43, 44: and xxiii. 34,—*'It seems impossible to believe that these incidents are other than authentic.'*—(p. 28.)

"In S. John iii. 13, the solemn clause *'which is in heaven:'*— in v. 3, 4, the omitted incident of *the troubling of the pool:*— in vii. 53 to viii. 11, *the narrative concerning the woman taken in adultery* omitted,—concerning which Drs. W. and H. remark that *'the argument which has always told most in its favour in modern times is its own internal character.* The story itself has justly seemed *to vouch for its own substantial truth,* and the words in which it is clothed to harmonize with those of other Gospel narratives'—(p. 87). Bishop Lightfoot remarks that *'the narrative bears on its face the highest credentials of authentic history,'* — (p. 28)." (Burgon, n. 1, pp. 311-312; see also *id.,* n. 1, p. 315, n. 1, p. 317.)

It is interesting to note that the Revisers who produced the late Revised Standard Version seem to make a point of the fact (as stated by Frederick C. Grant— one of the Revisers) that:

"I find that we have adopted only one conjectural emendation (in Jude 5, 'he who . . .'), and this is one that Hort discussed in his notes, and favored." (Frederick C. Grant, "The Greek Text of the New Testament," *An Introduction,* p. 41.)

If this statement is accurate (we have not attempted to check it, but we are not persuaded of its accuracy), then the Extreme Textualists seem to have abandoned the depraving principle of "conjectural emendation," and its partner the "ring of genuineness." (See *Note Thirty-four, Item 1,* for a discussion of the "conjectural emendation" of Jude.)

Perhaps this concluding observation is not out of place: of all the causes and sources alleged by the critics as depraving the manuscripts of the New Testament (Westcott and Hort) no one of them could be more evident, if indeed so evident, as this principle of "conjectural emendation." Indeed not a few of the practices described as depraving the sacred texts generally might, perhaps appropriately, be brought together under this designation.

NOTE THIRTY •
The Use and Misuse of Marginal Notes

We may now note some of the results on the Authorized Version text which followed the revision thereof by the use (as a guide) of the Westcott and Hort new Greek text.

Item 1.   *Alterations Frequently Made Only in Marginal Notes.*

> *Summary.* Alterations are frequently made only through the use of marginal notes. Some changes in the Authorized Version, sometimes appear in marginal notes only. Effect of marginal notes upon the uninformed reader is stated. In the Revised Version, the inclusion in a marginal note of omitted portions of the text seems normally to indicate rejection of the words so included, concerning which practice reference is made to the instructions given to the Revisers to control their work. Real effect of marginal notes.

It may be said, in the first place, that apparently the Revisers did not usually adopt in the Revised Version text itself, the readings of the new Greek text. These new Greek text readings were in many instances indicated in the margins of the Revised Version text, frequently, perhaps usually, preceded by the words, "some ancient authorities," say so-and-so, though often such "ancient authorities" include only one or both of the codices ℵ and B.

Upon this problem of marginal notes and readings and the effect which they may have upon the unschooled reader, as also upon the character of the notes and their integrity, the author will quote several passages from

Dean Burgon, who has examined the matter with care. The author does this because it will give the reader in the minimum space a view of the shocking array of suggested omissions and changes found in the Revised Version.

Dr. Scrivener's comment on marginal notes is brief but it clearly states his well considered opinion:

". . . the various readings recorded in the margin are nothing better than *rejected* readings, deliberately refused a place in the text, and set in the margin, if sometimes too lightly, yet always in a spirit of fairness to the unlearned reader of Holy Scripture." (Scrivener, "Preface," p. ix.)

On these marginal notes in the Revised Version, Dean Burgon expresses serious exception, because he affirms they mislead the uninformed reader and raise in him unnecessary and unjustified doubts. Invoking the mandate given to the Revisers touching their handling of the Authorized Version text (see *Note Twenty-seven*), he says:

"Above all,—*Who* was to foresee that instead of removing *'plain* and *clear errors'* from our Version [as their mandate directed], the Revisionists,—(besides systematically removing out of sight so many of the genuine utterances of the SPIRIT,)— would themselves introduce a countless number of blemishes, unknown to it before? Lastly, how was it to have been believed that the Revisionists would show themselves industrious in sowing broadcast over four continents doubts as to the Truth of Scripture, which it will never be in their power either to remove or to recal [sic]? *Nescit vox missa reverti.*

"For, the ill-advised practice of recording, in the margin of an English Bible, certain of the blunders—(such things cannot by any stretch of courtesy be styled 'Various Readings')— which disfigure 'some' or 'many' 'ancient authorities,' can only result in hopelessly unsettling the faith of millions. It cannot be defended on the plea of candour,—the candour which is determined that men shall 'know the worst.' *'The worst'* has NOT *been told*: and it were dishonesty to insinuate that *it has*. If all the cases were faithfully exhibited where 'a few,' 'some,' or 'many ancient authorities' read differently from what is exhibited in the actual Text, not only would the margin prove insufficient to contain the record, but *the very page itself* would not nearly suffice. Take a single instance (the first which comes to mind), of the thing referred to. Such illustrations might be multiplied to any extent." (Burgon, pp. 114-115.)

Item 2.   Luke 3:22, 10:41-42 Examined as to Different Readings in the Manuscripts.

Summary. Authorities cited and discussed by Burgon.

Burgon continues:

"In S. Luke iii. 22, (in place of 'Thou art my beloved Son; *in Thee I am well pleased,*') the following authorities of the IInd, IIIrd and IVth centuries, read,—*'this day have I begotten Thee:'* viz.—codex D and the most ancient copies of the old Latin (a, b, c, ff², l),—Justin Martyr in three places (A.D. 140),—Clemens Alex. (A.D. 190),—and Methodius (A.D. 290) among the Greeks. Lactantius (A.D. 300),—Hilary (A.D. 350),—Juvencus (A.D. 330),—Faustus (A.D. 400), and—Augustine amongst the Latins. The reading in question was doubtless derived from the *Ebionite Gospel* (IInd cent.). Now, we desire to have it explained to us *why* an exhibition of the Text supported by such an amount of first-rate primitive testimony as the preceding, obtains *no notice whatever* in our Revisionists' margin,—if indeed it was the object of their perpetually recurring marginal annotations, to put the unlearned reader on a level with the critical Scholar; to keep nothing back from him; and so forth? . . . It is the gross one-sidedness, the patent *unfairness,* in a critical point of view, of this work, (which professes to be nothing else but *a Revision of the English Version of* 1611,)— which chiefly shocks and offends us.

"For, on the other hand, of what possible use can it be to encumber the margin of S. Luke x. 41, 42 (for example), with the announcement that 'A few ancient authorities read *Martha, Martha, thou art troubled: Mary hath chosen &c.*' (the fact being, that D *alone* of MSS. omits *'careful and'* . . . *'about many things. But one thing is needful, and'* . . .)? With the record of this circumstance, is it reasonable (we ask) to choke up our English margin,—to create perplexity and to insinuate doubt? The author of the foregoing marginal Annotation was of course aware that the same 'singular codex' (as Bp. Ellicott styles cod. D) omits, in S. Luke's Gospel alone, no less than

1552 words: and he will of course have ascertained (by counting) that the words in S. Luke's Gospel amount to 19,941. Why then did he not tell *the whole* truth; and instead of '&c.,' proceed as follows? — 'But inasmuch as cod. D is so scandalously corrupt that about *one word in thirteen* is missing throughout, the absence of nine words in this place is of no manner of importance or significancy. The precious saying omitted is above suspicion, and the first half of the present Annotation might have been spared.' . . . We submit that a Note like that, although rather 'singular' in style, really *would* have been to some extent helpful,—if not to the learned, at least to the unlearned reader. . . .

"We shall of course be indignantly called upon to explain what we mean by so injurious—so damning—an imputation? For all reply, we are content to refer to the sample of our meaning which will be found below, in pp. 137-8. The exposure of what has there been shown to be the method of the Revisionists in respect of S. Mark vi. 11, might be repeated hundreds of times. It would in fact *fill a volume.* We shall therefore pass on, when we have asked the Revisionists in turn—*How they have dared* so effectually to blot out those many precious words from the Book of Life, that no mere English reader, depending on the Revised Version for his knowledge of the Gospels, can by possibility [*sic*] suspect their existence? . . . Supposing even that it *was* the calamitous result of their mistaken principles that they found themselves constrained on countless occasions, to omit from their Text precious sayings of our LORD and His Apostles,—what possible excuse will they offer for not having preserved a record of words so amply attested, *at least in their margin?*" (Burgon, pp. 115-118.)

Item 3.   Treatment of Mark 6:11.

Summary. Analyzed and discussed by Burgon with citation of authorities.

It might be well to show here what happened to Mark 6:11, in the Revised Version:

"But serious as this is, *more* serious (if possible) is the unfair *Suppression systematically practised* throughout the work before us. 'We have given alternative Readings in the margin,' —(says Bishop Ellicott on behalf of his brother-Revisionists,)— '*wherever they seem to be of sufficient importance or interest*

to deserve notice.' (iii. 1.) From which statement, readers have
a right to infer that whenever 'alternative Readings' are *not*
'given in the margin,' it is because such Readings do *not* 'seem
to be of *sufficient importance or interest to deserve notice.'* Will
the Revisionists venture to tell us that,—(to take the first instance of unfair Suppression which presents itself,)—our LORD'S
saying in S. Mark vi. 11 is not 'of sufficient importance or interest to deserve notice'? We allude to the famous words,—
'Verily I say unto you, It shall be more tolerable for Sodom and
Gomorrah in the day of judgment, than for that city:'—words
which are not only omitted from the 'New English Version,' but
*are not suffered to leave so much as a trace of themselves in
the margin.* And yet, the saying in question is attested by the
Peschito and the Philoxenian Syriac Versions: by the Old Latin:
by the Coptic, Æthiopic and Gothic Versions:—by 11 uncials
and by the whole bulk of the cursives:—by Irenæus and by
Victor of Antioch. So that whether Antiquity, or Variety of
Attestation is considered,—whether we look for Numbers or
for Respectability,—the genuineness of the passage may be regarded as *certain.* Our complaint however is *not* that the
Revisionists entertain a different opinion on this head from ourselves: but that they give the reader to understand that the
state of the Evidence is such, that it is quite 'safe to accept'
the shorter reading,—'to the *absolute exclusion* of the other.'
—So vast is the field before us, that this single specimen of what
we venture to call 'unfair Suppression,' must suffice. (Some will
not hesitate to bestow upon it a harsher epithet.) It is in truth
by far the most damaging feature of the work before us, that
its Authors should have so largely and so seriously *falsified the
Deposit;* and yet, (in clear violation of the IVth Principle or
Rule laid down for their guidance at the outset,) have suffered
no trace to survive in the margin of the deadly mischief which
they have effected." (Burgon, pp. 137-138.)

FURTHER ON MARGINAL NOTES

On the question of marginal notes, the Dean comments
still further:

"The marginal readings, which our Revisers have been so ill-
advised as to put prominently forward, and to introduce to the
Reader's notice with the vague statement that they are sanctioned
by 'Some' (or by 'Many') 'ancient authorities,'—are specimens
arbitrarily selected out of an immense mass; are magisterially

recommended to public attention and favour; *seem* to be invested with the sanction and authority of Convocation itself. And this becomes a very serious matter indeed. No hint is given *which be* the 'ancient Authorities' so referred to:—nor what proportion they bear to the 'ancient Authorities' producible on the opposite side:—nor whether they are the *most* 'ancient Authorities' obtainable:—nor what amount of attention their testimony may reasonably claim. But in the meantime a fatal assertion is hazarded in the Preface (iii. 1.), to the effect that *in cases where 'it would not be safe to accept one Reading to the absolute exclusion of others,' 'alternative Readings'* have been given 'in the margin.' So that the 'Agony and bloody sweat' of the World's REDEEMER (Lu. xxii. 43, 44),— and His Prayer for His murderers (xxiii. 34),—and much beside of transcendent importance and inestimable value, may, *according to our Revisionists,* prove to rest upon no foundation whatever. At all events, *'it would not be safe,'* (i.e. *it is not safe*) to place absolute reliance on them. Alas, how many a deadly blow at Revealed Truth hath been in this way aimed with fatal adroitness, which no amount of orthodox learning will ever be able hereafter to heal, much less to undo!" (Burgon, pp. 131-132; and see *id.,* p. 175.)

NOTE THIRTY-ONE •

New Renderings of Words; Matters of Grammar

Summary. Critics of the Revisers' changes in the Authorized Version stress the relative unimportance of errors in Greek grammar, Greek tenses, articles, pronouns, particles, prepositions, etc., etc., as urged by the Revisers; they complain against the use of a multiplicity of unimportant and often misleading and unnecessarily doubt-inspiring marginal notes and glosses and charge the Revisers with ignorance of Hellenistic Greek; they complain against the translation of the same Greek word with the same English word, ignoring the context. Burgon, in his criticisms, uses the following matters and passages, among others: Mark 1:18 (*left* for *forsook*). He also comments on *tomb* for *sepulchre*, the elimination of the word *charity*, the substitution of *sign* for *miracle*. He notes the treatment of the words *grace, disciple, Paradise, Baptist, Bishop, Gospel, Church, hypocrite, Scripture, Angel*. He points out that the words *lunatic* and *epileptic* have been tampered with; he discusses Matt. 17:21, citing authorities, notes virtual elimination of the word *everlasting*, discusses the change in II Tim. 3:16, in connection with the word *inspiration*, and notes the changing of *doctrine* to *teaching*, discusses the marginal note on Romans 9:5, with elaborate citation of authorities, and again reviews his controversy with Bp. Ellicott over the translation of I Tim. 3:16.

Item 1. *Some Miscellaneous Matters of Change.*

There are several general matters to which the critics of the Revised Version refer, with complaint. Some of them relate to the technical matters of Greek grammar— e.g., the Greek tenses, articles, pronouns, particles, prepositions, etc. A strenuous criticism is voiced against the multiplicity of unimportant and often misleading and unnecessarily doubt-inspiring marginal notes and glosses, as already noted. The translators are charged with want of "familiarity with Hellenistic Greek," and a comparison is drawn between the translators of 1611 (the Authorized Version translators) and the Revised Version translators, and the practice of the latter always to translate the same Greek word with the same English word, irrespective of the requirements of the context. (Burgon, pp. 153 ff., 183 ff., 187 ff.)

As illustrative of this criticism, the following may be noted:

"But take a more interesting example. In S. Mark i. 18, the A.V. has, 'and straightway they *forsook*' (which the Revisionists alter into *'left'*) 'their nets.' Why? Because in verse 20, the same word *aphentes* will recur; and because the Revisionists propose to let the statement ('they *left* their father Zebedee') stand. They 'level up' accordingly; and plume themselves on their consistency." (Burgon, p. 193.)

(It seems to the author that no one with any feeling for the English language would undertake to say that "they left their nets" is equivalent to "they forsook their nets.")

"We venture to point out, however, that the verb *aphienai* is one of a large family of verbs which,—always retaining their own essential signification,—yet depend for their English rendering entirely on the context in which they occur." (Burgon, p. 193.)

Special note is taken of the substitution of *tomb* for *sepulchre*, when speaking of the burial place of the Savior (*id.* pp. 197-198); of the use of *teaching* for *doctrine*, so that "the Revisers have well-nigh extirpated 'DOCTRINE' from the N. T." They instance (*inter alia*) in this connection, the substitution of *teaching* for *doctrine* in Paul's expression, "the *doctrine* of baptisms." (Heb. 6:2; Burgon, p. 199.) (We may observe that English-wise there is certainly a fundamental difference between *teaching* and *doctrine*.)

Item 2.   Elimination of the Word Charity.

Burgon's comments on the elimination of the words *charity* and *miracles* from the *Revised Version* are worth quoting in full:

"Having said so much about the proposed rendering of such unpromising vocables as *mnemeion—didache—phiale,* it is time to invite the Reader's attention to the calamitous fate which has befallen certain other words of infinitely greater importance.

"And first for *Agape*—a substantive noun unknown to the heathen, even as the sentiment which the word expresses proves to be a grace of purely Christian growth. What else but a real calamity would be the sentence of perpetual banishment passed by our Revisionists on 'that most excellent gift, the gift of *Charity*,' and the general substitution of 'Love' in its place? Do not these learned men perceive that 'Love' is not an equivalent term? Can they require to be told that, because of S. Paul's exquisite and life-like portrait of 'CHARITY,' and the use which has been made of the word in sacred literature in consequence, it has come to pass that the word *'Charity'* connotes many ideas to which the word 'Love' is an entire stranger? that 'Love,' on the contrary, has come to connote many unworthy notions which in *'Charity'* find no place at all? And if this be so, how can our Revisionists expect that we shall endure the loss of the name of the very choicest of the Christian graces,—and which, if it is nowhere to be found in Scripture, will presently come to be only traditionally known among mankind, and will in the end cease to be a term clearly understood? Have the Revisionists of 1881 considered how firmly this word *'Charity'* has established itself in the phraseology of the Church,—ancient, mediæval, modern,—as well as in our Book of Common Prayer? how thoroughly it has vindicated for itself the right of citizenship in the English language? how it has entered into our common vocabulary, and become one of the best understood of 'household words'? Of what can they have been thinking when they deliberately obliterated from the thirteenth chapter of S. Paul's 1st Epistle to the Corinthians the ninefold recurrence of the name of 'that most excellent gift, the gift of CHARITY'?" (Burgon, pp. 201-202.)

Item 3.   Elimination of Word Miracles.

Burgon's comments here are as follows:

"With equal displeasure, but with even sadder feelings, we recognize in the present Revision a resolute elimination of 'MIR-ACLES' from the N.T.—Not so, (we shall be eagerly reminded,) but only of their *Name*. True, but the two perforce go together, as every thoughtful man knows. At all events, the getting rid of *the Name*,—(except in the few instances which are enumer-ated below,)—will in the account of millions be regarded as the getting rid of *the thing*. And in the esteem of all, learned and unlearned alike, the systematic obliteration of the signifying word from the pages of that Book to which we refer exclusively for our knowledge of the remarkable thing signified, — can-not but be looked upon as a memorable and momentous circum-stance. Some, it may be, will be chiefly struck by the foolishness of the proceeding: for at the end of centuries of familiarity with such a word, we are no longer *able* to part company with it, even if we were inclined. The term has struck root firmly in our Literature: has established itself in the terminol-ogy of Divines: has grown into our common speech. But further, even were it possible to get rid of the words 'Miracle' and 'Miraculous,' what else but abiding inconvenience would be the result? for we must still desire to speak about *the things;* and it is a truism to remark that there are no other words in the language which connote the same ideas. What therefore has been gained by substituting *'sign'* for *'miracle'* on some 19 or 20 occasions—('this beginning of *his signs* did JESUS,'—'this is again the *second sign* that JESUS did')—we really fail to see." (Burgon, pp. 202-203.)

There is of course an obvious difference in meaning in English between the word *sign* and the word *miracle* which no one can overlook. The *signs* of the coming of our Lord are wars, etc., etc., but these are not *miracles*.

Item 4. Elimination and Changes of Other Important Words.

Dean Burgon continues:

"That the word in the original is *semeion,* and that *semeion* means 'a sign,' we are aware. But what then? Because (*h*)*agge-los*, in strictness, means 'a messenger,' — *graphe*, 'a writing,' — (*h*)*ypokrites*, 'an actor,'—*ekklesia*, 'an assembly,'—*eyaggelion*, 'good tidings,'—*episkopos*, 'an overseer,'—*baptistes*, 'one that

dips,'—*paradeisos,* 'a garden,'—*mathetes,* 'a learner,'—*charis,*
'favour:'—are we to forego the established English equivalents
for these words, and never more to hear of 'grace,' 'disciple,'
'Paradise,' 'Baptist,' 'Bishop,' 'Gospel,' 'Church,' 'hypocrite,'
'Scripture,' 'Angel'? Is it then desired to revolutionize our sacred terminology? or at all events to sever with the Past, and
to translate the Scriptures into English on etymological principles? We are amazed that the first proposal to resort to such
a preposterous method was not instantly scouted by a large majority of those who frequented the Jerusalem Chamber.

"The words under consideration are not only not equivalent,
but they are quite dissimilar. All *'signs'* are not *'Miracles,'*
though all *'Miracles'* are undeniably *'signs.'* Would not a marginal annotation concerning the original word, as at S. Luke
xxiii. 8, have sufficed? And *why* was the term *'Miracle'* as the
rendering of *semeion* spared only on *that* occasion in the Gospels; and *only* in connection with S. Peter's miracle of healing
the impotent man, in the Acts? We ask the question not caring
for an answer. We are merely bent on submitting to our Readers,
whether,—especially in an age like the present of widespread
unbelief in the Miraculous,—it was a judicious proceeding in
our Revisionists almost everywhere to substitute 'Sign' for
'Miracle' as the rendering of *semeion.*" (Burgon, pp. 203-204.)

Glosses seem to have raised questions about the Holy
Ghost, to the point of casting question on the composition
of the Trinity by making Holy Ghost and Holy Spirit
equivalent. (Burgon, pp. 204-205.)

*Item 5. Changing of Lunatic to Epileptic. Effect on
Matt. 17:21.*

Again, in reciting the instance of the lunatic brought
to the Savior after the Apostles had failed to heal him,
the Revisers have changed *lunatic* to *epileptic,* thus seeking (it would appear) to destroy the idea of demoniacal
possession. And to support this view, the Revisers have
entirely omitted Matt. 17:21, where the Savior (answering the enquiry as to why they could not cure the sick
man) declared: "Howbeit this kind goeth not out but

by prayer and fasting." Upon this latter passage
Burgon comments:

"Consider our LORD'S solemn words in Mtt. xvii. 21,—'*But
this kind goeth not out save by prayer and fasting,*'—12 words
left out by the R.V., though witnessed to by *all the Copies but
3*: by the Latin, Syriac, Coptic, and Armenian Versions: and
by the following Fathers:—(1) Origen, (2) Tertullian, (3) the
Syriac Clement, (4) the Syriac *Canons of Eusebius,* (5) Athanasius, (6) Basil, (7) Ambrose, (8) Juvencus, (9) Chrysostom,
(10) *Opus imp.,* (11) Hilary, (12) Augustine, (13) J. Damascene, and others. Then (it will be asked), why have the Revisionists left them out? Because (we answer) they have been
misled by B and ℵ, Cureton's Syriac and the Sahidic, — as
untrustworthy a quaternion of witnesses to the text of Scripture as could be named." (Burgon, p. 206, n. 1, see *Note
Thirty-two, Item 2,* pp. 338-339.)

Still another: Obedient to or in consonance with the
"modern Thought," the Revisers, on "a supposed distinction between the import of the epithets 'ETERNAL' and
'EVERLASTING,'" have eliminated, in large part, the term
everlasting from the Scriptures as a translation of
aionios. (Burgon, p. 207.)

The word *inspiration* has been tampered with in the
statement of Paul:

"All scripture is given by inspiration of God, and is profitable for doctrine. . . ." (II Tim. 3:16.)

The Revisers have rendered it:

"Every scripture inspired of God *is also profitable* for
teaching," &c., which, it is pointed out, might "imply that
a distinction is drawn by the Apostle himself between inspired and uninspired Scripture." This change is
seriously questioned by Bishop Middleton on grammatical
grounds. (Burgon, pp. 208-209.)

Note also the effect here of substituting *teaching* for
doctrine.

Item 6.   Changes Made in Rom. 9:5, as Affecting Christ's Godhood.

Finally, for our purposes, we quote the following as showing in what manner the Revisers stand, in at least one instance; other instances have been all but equally demolished:

"A MARGINAL ANNOTATION set over against Romans ix. 5 is the last thing of this kind to which we shall invite attention. S. Paul declares it to be Israel's highest boast and glory that of them, 'as concerning the flesh [came] CHRIST, *who is over all* [things], *God blessed for ever!* Amen.' A grander or more unequivocal testimony to our LORD'S eternal GODhead is nowhere to be found in Scripture. Accordingly, these words have been as confidently appealed to by faithful Doctors of the Church in every age, as they have been unsparingly assailed by unbelievers. The dishonest shifts by which the latter seek to evacuate the record which they are powerless to refute or deny, are paraded by our ill-starred Revisionists in the following terms:—

" 'Some modern Interpreters place a full stop after *flesh,* and translate, *He who is God over all be (is) blessed for ever*: or, *He who is over all is God, blessed for ever.* Others punctuate, *flesh, who is over all. God be (is) blessed for ever.'*

"Now this is a matter,—let it be clearly observed,—which, (as Dr. Hort is aware,) 'belongs to *Interpretation,*—and *not to Textual Criticism.*' What business then has it in these pages at all? Is it then the function of Divines appointed *to revise the Authorized Version,* to give information to the 90 millions of English-speaking Christians scattered throughout the world as to the unfaithfulness of *'some modern Interpreters'*? We have hitherto supposed that it was *'Ancient* authorities' exclusively,— (whether 'a few,' or 'some,' or 'many,')—to which we are invited to submit our judgment. How does it come to pass that *the Socinian gloss* on this grand text (Rom. ix. 5) has been brought into such extraordinary prominence? Did our Revisionists consider that their marginal note would travel to earth's remotest verge,—give universal currency to the view of 'some modern Interpreters,'—and in the end 'tell it out among the heathen' also?

BURGON CITES AUTHORITIES

"We refer to Manuscripts,—Versions,—Fathers: and what

do we find? (1) It is demonstrable that *the oldest Codices, besides the whole body of the cursives*, know nothing about the method of 'some modern Interpreters.' — (2) 'There is absolutely not a shadow, *not a tittle of evidence, in any of the ancient Versions*, to warrant what they do.'—(3) How then, about the old Fathers? for the sentiments of our best modern Divines, as Pearson and Bull, we know by heart. We find that the expression *'who is over all* [things], *God blessed for ever*, is expressly acknowledged to refer to our SAVIOUR by the following 60 illustrious names:—

"Irenæus,—Hippolytus in 3 places,—Origen,—Malchion, in the name of six of the Bishops at the Council at Antioch, A.D. 269,—ps.-Dionysius Alex., twice,—the *Constt. App.*,—Athanasius in 6 places,—Basil in 2 places,—Didymus in 5 places,—Greg. Nyssen. in 5 places,—Epiphanius in 5 places,—Theodorus Mops.,—Methodius,—Eustathius,—Eulogius, twice,—Caesarius, 3 times,—Theophilus Alex., twice,—Nestorius,—Theodotus of Ancyra,—Proclus, twice,—Severianus Bp. of Gabala,—Chrysostom, 8 times,—Cyril Alex., 15 times,—Paulus Bp. of Emesa,—Theodoret, 12 times,—Gennadius, Abp. of C.P.,—Severus, Abp. of Antioch,—Amphilochius,—Gelasius Cyz.,—Anastasius Ant., —Leontius Byz., 3 times,—Maximus,—J. Damascene, 3 times. Besides of the Latins, Tertullian, twice,—Cyprian,—Novatian, twice,—Ambrose, 5 times,—Palladius the Arian at the Council of Aquileia,—Hilary, 7 times,—Jerome, twice,—Augustine, about 30 times,—Victorinus,—the *Breviarium*, twice,—Marius Mercator,—Cassian, twice,—Alcimus Avit.,—Fulgentius, twice,—Leo, Bp. of Rome, twice,—Ferrandus, twice,—Facundus:—to whom must be added 6 ancient writers, of whom 3 have been mistaken for Athanasius,—and 3 for Chrysostom. All these see in Rom. ix. 5, a glorious assertion of the eternal GODhead of CHRIST. [Burgon's specific citations omitted.]

"Against such an overwhelming torrent of Patristic testimony,—for we have enumerated *upwards of sixty* ancient Fathers—it will not surely be pretended that the Socinian interpretation, to which our Revisionists give such prominence, can stand. But why has it been introduced *at all?* We shall have every Christian reader with us in our contention, that such perverse imaginations of 'modern Interpreters' are not entitled to a place in the margin of the N.T. For our Revisionists to have even given them currency, and thereby a species of sanction, constitutes in our view a very grave offence. A public retractation and a very humble Apology we claim at their hands. Indifferent Scholarship, and mistaken views of Textual Criti-

cism, are at least venial matters. But *a Socinian gloss gratui-
tously thrust into the margin of every Englishman's N.T.* admits
of no excuse—is not to be tolerated on *any* terms. It would by
itself, in our account, have been sufficient to determine the fate
of the present Revision." (Burgon, pp. 210-214; see *Note Thirty-
four, Item 6.*)

Item 7.   Changes in I Tim. 3:16.

As a final word, reference may be made to Dean Burgon's reply to Bp. Ellicott, covering some 76 pages, on
the text of I Tim. 3:16, which, in the *Authorized Version* reads:

". . . great is the mystery of godliness: God was manifest
in the flesh, justified in the Spirit, seen of angels, preached unto
the Gentiles, believed on in the world, received up into glory."

In the *Revised Version* it reads:

". . . great is the mystery of godliness; He who was manifested in the flesh, justified in the spirit, seen of angels, preached
among the nations, believed on in the world, received up in
glory." (Burgon, pp. 425 ff.)

The *Inspired Version* of the Prophet Joseph follows
the Authorized Version.

To the layman, Dean Burgon seems adequately to
establish his points which our Inspired Version supports.

It might be noted here that the *Revised Standard
Version* still further perverts the meaning of this declaration of Paul's. The text now appears:

"Great indeed, we confess, is the mystery of our religion:
He was manifested in the flesh,
vindicated in the Spirit,
seen by angels,
preached among the nations,
believed on in the world,
taken up in glory."

This seems successfully to eliminate all reference to
the Godhood of Christ.

NOTE THIRTY-TWO ·

Vital Omissions and Differences Between Authorized and Revised Versions

Item 1. Purpose of Note.

> *Summary.* To show by a few of the many, the kind
> of changes which the Revisers have made in our Bible.
> Dr. Scrivener's comments are given on the whole of Dr.
> Hort's system which is basic to the Revised Version.

It seems desirable to note a few, out of the multitude, of the instances where the Revisers have omitted or changed vital parts of the New Testament record. Many, not mentioned here, have been hereinbefore pointed out and discussed.

It will be in mind that in this *Note*, we deal only with the British Revision of the 1880's, and the American Revision of 1900-1901.

It is sufficient now to request attention to the kind of incidents mentioned and to note how well these omissions would feed doubts as to the Messiahship of Jesus. The analysis of the status of the authorities on the scriptural passages involved, gives color to the suggestion that the Revisers were not filled with that knowledge that Jesus was the Christ that brought so many of the early Christians to a martyr death.

The instances referred to follow, but before beginning their consideration, we may well repeat here Prebendary Scrivener's comments (already quoted) on the lack of evidence to support conclusions reached by the Revisers, as embodied in the text and marginal notes of the Revised Version (British). Scrivener says:

"But there is little hope for the stability of their imposing structure, if its foundations have been laid on the sandy ground of ingenious conjecture: and since barely the smallest vestige of historical evidence has ever been alleged in support of the views of these accomplished editors, their teaching must either be received as intuitively true, or dismissed from our consideration as precarious, and even visionary. . . .

"Dr. Hort's system, therefore, is entirely destitute of historical foundation. . . .

". . . we are compelled to repeat as emphatically as ever our strong conviction that the hypothesis to whose proof he has devoted so many laborious years, is destitute not only of historical foundation, but of all probability resulting from the internal goodness of the text which its adoption would force upon us. . . .

" 'We cannot doubt that it [Luke 23:34] comes from an extraneous source' (Hort, *Notes*, p. 68). Nor can we on our part doubt that the system which entails such consequences is hopelessly self-condemned." (Scrivener, pp. 531, 537, 542, 604; see herein, pp. 79, 117, 125, 255, 296, 350.)

Item 2. Vital Differences Between Authorized Version and Revised Version.

Summary. Some special instances, from among many, noted by critics of vital differences between the Authorized Version and the Revised Version. As to each incident listed, Burgon has analyzed the text, noted and discussed the differences, and in almost every case exhaustively cited authorities in favor of the reading of the Authorized Version.

We shall now call a special attention to a few out of the many instances, noted by critics, of vital differences between the Authorized Version and the Revised Version.

Sub-item a. Account of the Birth of Jesus, Matt. 1:25.

The King James (Authorized) Version reads:

"And knew her not till she had brought forth her firstborn son: and he called his name Jesus."

The Inspired Version of the Prophet Joseph reads:

"And knew her not until she had brought forth her first-born son; and they called his name Jesus." (Matt. 2:8.)

The Revised Version reads:

". . . and knew her not till she had brought forth a son: and he called his name Jesus."

The American Standard Version follows the Revised Version.

The change could have a considerable bearing on the dogma of the perpetual virginity of Mary.

Concerning this change made by the Revisers, Dean Burgon comments:

"And so much for the first, second, and third Critical annotations, with which the margin of the revised N.T. is disfigured. Hoping that the worst is now over, we read on till we reach ver. 25, where we encounter a statement which fairly trips us up: viz.,—'And knew her not *till she had brought forth a son.*' No intimation is afforded of what has been here effected; but in the meantime every one's memory supplies the epithet ('her first-born') which has been ejected. Whether something very like indignation is not excited by the discovery that these important words have been surreptitiously withdrawn from their place, let others say. For ourselves, when we find that only א B Z and two cursive copies can be produced for the omission, we are at a loss to understand of what the Revisionists can have been dreaming. Did they know that,—besides the Vulgate, the Peschito and Philoxenian Syriac, the Æthiopic, Armenian, Georgian, and Slavonian Versions,—a whole torrent of Fathers are at hand to vouch for the genuineness of the epithet they were so unceremoniously excising? They are invited to refer to ps.-Tatian,—to Athanasius,—to Didymus,—to Cyril of Jer.,—to Basil,—to Greg. Nyss.,—to Ephraem Syr.,—to Epiphanius,—to Chrysostom,—to Proclus,—to Isidorus Pelus.,—to John Damasc.,—to Photius,—to Nicetas:—besides, of the Latins, Ambrose,—the *Opus imp.*,—Augustine,—and not least to Jerome—eighteen Fathers in all. And how is it possible, (we ask,) that two copies of the IVth century (B א) and one of the VIth (Z)—all three without a character—backed by a few copies of the old Latin, should be supposed to be any counterpoise at all for such an array of first-rate contemporary evidence as the foregoing?" (Burgon, pp. 122-124.)

To the foregoing, Burgon adds a quote from Bp. Ellicott, Chairman of the Revisers' Committee, indicating the Bishop's estimate of British scholarship. The Bishop is quoted as saying:

"For any authoritative Revision, we are not yet mature: either in Biblical learning or Hellenistic scholarship." (Burgon, p. 124.)

Sub-item b.   Jesus, the Son of God, Mark 1:1.

The King James (Authorized) Version reads:

"The beginning of the gospel of Jesus Christ, the Son of God."

The Inspired Version follows the Authorized Version.

The Revised Version has the same reading, but a marginal note says:

"Some ancient authorities omit *the Son of God.*"

The American Standard Version follows the Revised Version.

Dean Burgon comments:

"From the first verse of S. Mark's Gospel we are informed that 'Some ancient authorities omit *the Son of God.*' Why are we *not* informed that every known uncial Copy *except one of bad character,* — every cursive *but two,* — *every Version,* — and the following Fathers, — all *contain* the precious clause: viz. Irenæus, — Porphyry, — Severianus of Gabala, — Cyril Alex., — Victor Ant., — and others, — besides Ambrose and Augustine among the Latins : — while the supposed adverse testimony of Serapion and Titus, Basil and Victorinus, Cyril of Jer. and Epiphanius, proves to be all a mistake? To speak plainly, since the clause is above suspicion, *Why are we not rather told so?*" (Burgon, p. 132.)

Sub-item c.   Christ, the Creator, John 1:3-4.

The King James (Authorized) Version reads:

"All things were made by him; and without him was not any thing made that was made. In him was life. . . . "

The Inspired Version of the Prophet Joseph reads:

"All things were made by him; and without him was not anything made which was made."

The Revised Version reads:

"All things were made by him; and without him was not anything made that hath been made. In him was life . . ." The marginal note in the Revised Version reads as to "by him": "Or, *through*" him; and as a note to "was not anything made," the Revised Version states, "Or, *was not anything made. That which hath been made was life in him; and the life &c.*"

The American Standard Version reads:

"All things were made through him; and without him was not anything made that hath been made. In him was life. . . ." The marginal note as to "was not anything made," agrees with the Revised Version.

Dean Burgon comments:

"In the 3rd verse of the first chapter of S. John's Gospel, we are left to take our choice between,—'without Him was not anything made that hath been made. In him was life; and the life,' &c., — and the following absurd alternative, — 'Without him was not anything made. *That which hath been made was life in him;* and the life,' &c. But we are *not* informed that this latter monstrous figment is known to have been the importation of the Gnostic heretics in the IInd century, and to be as destitute of authority as it is of sense. *Why is prominence given only to the lie?*" (Burgon, p. 132.)

Sub-item d.   The Son of Man, "in heaven," John 3:13.

The King James (Authorized) Version reads:

"And no man hath ascended up to heaven, but he that came down from heaven, even the Son of man which is in heaven."

The Inspired Version reads:

"I tell you, No man hath ascended up to heaven, but he who came down from heaven, even the Son of Man who is in heaven."

The Revised Version reads:

"And no man hath ascended into heaven, but he that descended out of heaven, even the Son of man, which is in heaven." The marginal note reads: "Many ancient authorities omit *which is in heaven.*"

The American Standard Version reads:

"And no one hath ascended into heaven, but he that descended out of heaven, even the Son of man, who is in heaven." The marginal note reads: "Many ancient authorities omit *who is in heaven.*"

Dean Burgon discusses this change as follows (his specific references are omitted):

"At S. John iii. 13, we are informed that the last clause of that famous verse ('No man hath ascended up to heaven, but He that came down from heaven, even the Son of Man—*which is in heaven*'), is not found in 'many ancient authorities.' But why, in the name of common fairness, are we not *also* reminded that this, (as will be found more fully explained in the note overleaf,) is *a circumstance of no Textual significancy whatever?*

"Why, above all, are we not assured that the precious clause in question (*o on en to oyrano*) *is* found in every MS. in the world, except five of bad character? — is recognized by *all* the Latin and *all* the Syriac versions; as well as by the Coptic,—Æthiopic,—Georgian,—and Armenian?—is either quoted or insisted upon by Origen, —Hippolytus, —Athanasius, —Didymus, — Aphraates the Persian, — Basil the Great, — Epiphanius, — Nonnus,— ps.-Dionysius Alex.,— Eustathius;— by Chrysostom, — Theodoret, — and Cyril, each 4 times; by Paulus, Bishop of Emesa (in a sermon on Christmas Day, A.D. 431) ; — by Theodorus Mops., — Amphilochius, — Severus, — Theodorus Heracl.,—Basilius Cil.,—Cosmas,—John Damascene, in 3 places, —and 4 other ancient Greek writers;—besides Ambrose,—Novatian, — Hilary, — Lucifer, — Victorinus, —Jerome, — Cassian, —

Vigilius,— Zeno,— Marius,— Maximus Taur.,— Capreolus,—Augustine, &c.:—is acknowledged by Lachmann, Tregelles, Tischendorf: in short, is *quite above suspicion*: why are we not told *that?* Those 10 Versions, those 38 Fathers, that host of Copies in the proportion of 995 to 5,—*why*, concerning all these is there not so much as a hint let fall that such a mass of counter-evidence exists? . . . Shame,—yes, *shame* on the learning which comes abroad only to perplex the weak, and to unsettle the doubting, and to mislead the blind! Shame,—yes, *shame* on that two-thirds majority of well-intentioned but most incompetent men, who, — finding themselves (in an evil hour) appointed to correct *'plain and clear errors'* in the *English* 'Authorized Version,'—occupied themselves instead with *falsifying the inspired Greek Text* in countless places, and branding with suspicion some of the most precious utterances of the SPIRIT! Shame,—yes, *shame* upon them!

"Why then, (it will of course be asked,) is the margin — (a) of S. Mark i.1 and—(b) of S. John i.3, and—(c) of S. John iii. 13, encumbered after this discreditable fashion? It is (we answer) only because *the Text of Drs. Westcott and Hort* is thus depraved in all three places. Those Scholars enjoy the unenviable distinction of having dared to expel from S. John iii. 13 the words *o on en to oyrano*, which Lachmann, Tregelles and Tischendorf were afraid to touch. Well may Dean Stanley have bestowed upon Dr. Hort the epithet of *'fearless'!* . . . If report speaks truly, it is by the merest accident that the clause in question still retains its place in *the Revised Text.*" (Burgon, pp. 132-135.)

Sub-item e. The Lord's Prayer, Matt. 6:9-13, Luke 11:2-4.

The King James (*Authorized*) Version of Matt. 6:9-13 reads:

"Our Father which art in heaven, Hallowed be thy name. Thy kingdom come. Thy will be done in earth, as it is in heaven. Give us this day our daily bread. And forgive us our debts, as we forgive our debtors. And lead us not into temptation, but deliver us from evil: For thine is the kingdom, and the power, and the glory, for ever. Amen."

In the *Inspired Version*, Matt. 6:10-15 is given thus:

"Our Father who art in heaven, Hallowed be thy name.

322 NOTE 32. VITAL CHANGES IN REVISED VERSIONS

Thy kingdom come. Thy will be done on earth, as it is done in heaven. Give us this day, our daily bread. And forgive us our trespasses, as we forgive those who trespass against us. And suffer us not to be led into temptation, but deliver us from evil. For thine is the kingdom, and the power, and the glory, forever and ever, Amen."

The Revised Version of Matt. 6:9-13 reads:

"Our Father which art in heaven, Hallowed be thy name. Thy kingdom come. Thy will be done, as in heaven, so on earth. Give us this day our daily bread. And forgive us our debts, as we also have forgiven our debtors. And bring us not into temptation, but deliver us from the evil one." The marginal notes to this in the Revised Version read as follows: "our daily bread,"—"Gr. *our bread for the coming day*"; "the evil one,"—"Or, *evil*"; and "Many authorities, some ancient, but with variations, add *For thine is the kingdom, and the power, and the glory, for ever. Amen.*"

The American Standard Version of Matt. 6:9-13 follows the Revised Version, except as noted below:

"Which" is changed to "who" in "Our Father who art in heaven . . .", and adds the following marginal note: "Or, *our needful bread.*"

The King James (Authorized) Version of Luke 11:2-4 reads:

"Our Father which art in heaven, Hallowed be thy name. Thy kingdom come. Thy will be done, as in heaven, so in earth. Give us day by day our daily bread. And forgive us our sins; for we also forgive every one that is indebted to us. And lead us not into temptation; but deliver us from evil."

The Inspired Version of Luke 11:2-4 reads:

"Our Father who art in heaven, hallowed be thy name. Thy kingdom come. Thy will be done as in heaven, so in earth. Give us day by day our daily bread. And forgive us our sins; for we also forgive every one who is indebted to us. And let us not be led into temptation; but deliver us from evil; for thine is the kingdom and power. Amen."

It will be noted the Prophet Joseph retained: "who (which) art in heaven"; changed "lead us not into temptation," to "suffer (let) us not be led into temptation," and retained the full "Doxology" in Matthew and inserted a part into Luke.

As to Luke 11:2-4 the *Revised Version* reads:

"Father, Hallowed be thy name. Thy kingdom come. Give us day by day our daily bread. And forgive us our sins; for we ourselves also forgive every one that is indebted to us. And bring us not into temptation." Marginal notes in the Revised Version, to this text, read as follows: To "Father," — "Many ancient authorities read *Our Father, which art in heaven.* See Matt. vi. 9"; to "Thy kingdom come,"—"Many ancient authorities add *Thy will be done, as in heaven, so on earth.* See Matt. vi. 10"; to "Our daily bread,"—"Gr. *our bread for the coming day";* to "into temptation,"—"Many ancient authorities add *but deliver us from the evil* one (or *from evil*). See Matt. vi. 13."

The American Standard Version follows the Revised Version except as noted below:

"Which" is changed to "who" in "Our Father, *who* art in heaven . . ." and adds to the marginal notes: "Or, *Our needful bread,* as in Mt. 6:11."

On these changes, Dean Burgon comments:

"An instructive specimen of depravation follows, which can be traced to Marcion's mutilated recension of S. Luke's Gospel. We venture to entreat the favour of the reader's sustained attention to the license with which the LORD'S Prayer as given in S. Luke's Gospel (xi. 2-4), is exhibited by codices ℵ A B C D. For every reason one would have expected that so precious a formula would have been found enshrined in the 'old uncials' in peculiar safety; handled by copyists of the IVth, Vth, and VIth centuries with peculiar reverence." (Burgon, p. 34.)

After a summary critical examination of the Greek texts of the five texts named, Dean Burgon continues:

"So then, these five 'first-class authorities' are found to throw themselves into *six different combinations* in their de-

partures from S. Luke's way of exhibiting the Lord's Prayer,—
which, among them, they contrive to falsify in respect of no
less than 45 words; and yet *they are never able to agree among
themselves as to any single various reading*: while *only once*
are more than two of them observed to stand together,—viz.
in the unauthorized omission of the article. In respect of 32
(out of the 45) words, *they bear in turn solitary evidence.* What
need to declare that it is *certainly false* in every instance?
Such however is the infatuation of the Critics, that the vagaries
of B are all taken for gospel. Besides omitting the 11 words
which B omits jointly with א, Drs. Westcott and Hort erase
from the Book of Life those other 11 precious words which
are omitted by B only. And in this way it comes to pass that
the mutilated condition to which the scalpel of Marcion the
heretic reduced the Lord's Prayer some 1730 years ago, (for
the mischief can all be traced back to *him!*), is palmed off on
the Church of England by the Revisionists as the work of the
Holy Ghost!" (Burgon, pp. 35-36.)

Later in his book, Dean Burgon returns to this subject, with particular reference to the closing words of
the Lord's prayer:

"Are we to regard it as a kind of *set-off* against all that goes
before, that in an age when the personality of Satan is freely
called in question, 'THE EVIL ONE' has been actually *thrust into
the Lord's Prayer?* A more injudicious and unwarrantable in-
novation it would be impossible to indicate in any part of the
present unhappy volume. The case has been argued out with
much learning and ability by two eminent Divines, Bp. Lightfoot and Canon Cook. The Canon remains master of the field.
That *the change ought never to have been made* is demonstrable.
The grounds of this assertion are soon stated. To begin, (1) It
is admitted on all hands that it must for ever remain a matter
of opinion only whether in the expression *apo toy poneroy*, the
nominative case is *to poneron* (as in S. Matth. v. 37, 39: Rom.
xii. 9), or *o poneros* (as in S. Matth. xiii. 19, 38: Eph. vi. 16),
—either of which yields a good sense." (Burgon, pp. 214-215.)

After pointing to the effect of the proposed change
upon the Church of England formularies and its effect
upon what he calls the Christian baptism ceremony, Burgon continues:

"Then further—(6), What more unlikely than that our Lord would end with giving such prominence to that rebel Angel whom by dying He is declared to have 'destroyed'? (Heb. ii. 14: 1 John iii. 8.) For, take away the Doxology (as our Revisionists propose), and we shall begin the Lord's Prayer with 'Our Father,' and literally end it with—*the Devil!*—But above all, — (7) Let it never be forgotten that this is *the pattern Prayer,* a portion of every Christian child's daily utterance,— the most sacred of all our formularies, and by far the most often repeated,—into which it is attempted in this way to introduce a startling novelty. Lastly—(8), When it is called to mind that nothing short of *necessity* has warranted the Revisionists in introducing a single change into the A.V.,—'*clear and plain errors*'—and that no such plea can be feigned on the present occasion, the liberty which they have taken in this place must be admitted to be absolutely without excuse. . . . Such at least are the grounds on which, for our own part, we refuse to entertain the proposed introduction of the Devil into the Lord's Prayer. From the position we have taken up, it will be found utterly impossible to dislodge us." (Burgon, p. 216.)

Sub-item f.   The Message of the Heavenly Host, Luke 2:14.

The King James (*Authorized*) *Version* reads:

"Glory to God in the highest, and on earth peace, good will toward men."

The Inspired Version is practically the King James (Authorized) Version, reading:

"Glory to God in the highest; and on earth, peace; good will to men."

The Revised Version text is as follows:

"Glory to God in the highest, And on earth peace among men in whom he is well pleased." The marginal notes in the Revised Version comment: to "peace,"—"Many ancient authorities read *peace, good pleasure among men*"; to "men,"— "Gr. *men of good pleasure.*"

The American Standard Version follows the Revised Version.

Dean Burgon makes another exhaustive analysis of this proposed Revised Version change. Because the analysis shows the tremendous amount of work that has gone into the Dean's criticism of the Revised Version text, it is quoted here in full. The analysis reads (his specific references are omitted):

"A more grievous perversion of the truth of Scripture is scarcely to be found than occurs in the proposed revised exhibition of S. Luke ii. 14, in the Greek and English alike; for indeed not only is the proposed Greek text (*en anthropois eydokias*) impossible, but the English of the Revisionists ('*peace among men in whom he is well pleased*') 'can be arrived at' (as one of themselves has justly remarked) 'only through some process which would make any phrase bear almost any meaning the translator might like to put upon it.' More than that: the harmony of the exquisite three-part hymn, which the Angels sang on the night of the Nativity, becomes hopelessly marred, and its structural symmetry destroyed, by the welding of the second and third members of the sentence into one. Singular to relate, the addition of *a single final letter (s)* has done all this mischief. Quite as singular is it that we should be able at the end of upwards of 1700 years to discover what occasioned its calamitous insertion. From the archetypal copy, by the aid of which the old Latin translation was made, (for the Latin copies *all* read '*pax hominibus bonæ voluntatis,*') the preposition *en* was evidently away,—absorbed apparently by the *an* which immediately follows. In order therefore to make a sentence of some sort out of words which, without *en*, are simply unintelligible, *eydokia* was turned into *eydokias*. It is accordingly a significant circumstance that, whereas there exists *no* Greek copy of the Gospels which *omits* the *en*, there is scarcely a Latin exhibition of the place to be found which contains it. To return however to the genuine clause,—'Good-will towards men' (*en anthropois eydokia*).

THE WITNESS OF GOSPEL COPIES AND VERSIONS

"Absolutely decisive of the true reading of the passage —irrespectively of internal considerations—ought to be the consideration that it is vouched for *by every known copy* of the Gospels of whatever sort, excepting only ℵ A B D: the first and third of which, however, were anciently corrected and brought into conformity with the Received Text; while the second (A) is observed to be so inconstant in its testimony, that in the primitive 'Morning-hymn' (given in another page of the same codex, and containing a quotation of S. Luke ii. 14), the correct reading of the place is found. D's complicity in error is the less important, because of the ascertained sympathy between that codex and the Latin. In the meantime the two Syriac Versions are a full set-off against the Latin copies; while the hostile evidence of the Gothic (which this time sides with the Latin) is more than neutralized by the unexpected desertion of the Coptic version from the opposite camp. The Armenian, Georgian, Æthiopic, Slavonic and Arabian versions, are besides all with the Received Text. It therefore comes to this: — We are invited to make our election between every other copy of the Gospels,— every known Lectionary,—and (not least of all) the ascertained ecclesiastical usage of the Eastern Church from the beginning, —on the one hand: and the testimony of four Codices without a history or a character, which concur in upholding a patent mistake, on the other. Will any one hesitate as to which of these two parties has the stronger claim on his allegiance?

THE TESTIMONY OF THE FATHERS

"Could doubt be supposed to be entertained in any quarter, it must at all events be borne away by the torrent of Patristic authority which is available on the present occasion:—

"In the IInd century, — we have the testimony of (1) Irenæus.

"In the IIIrd, — that of (2) Origen in 3 places, — and of (3) the *Apostolical Constitutions* in 2.

"In the IVth,—(4) Eusebius,—(5) Aphraates the Persian, —(6) Titus of Bostra, each twice;—(7) Didymus in 3 places; —(8) Gregory of Nazianzus,—(9) Cyril of Jerusalem,—(10) Epiphanius twice; — (11) Gregory of Nyssa 4 times, — (12) Ephraem Syrus,—(13) Philo bishop of Carpasus,—(14) Chrysostom, in 9 places,—and (15) a nameless preacher at Antioch, —all these, *contemporaries* (*be it remembered*) of B *and* ℵ, are found to bear concurrent testimony in favour of the commonly received text.

"In the Vth century,—(16) Cyril of Alexandria, on no less than 14 occasions, vouches for it also;—(17) Theodoret on 4; —(18) Theodotus of Ancyra on 5 (once in a homily preached

before the Council of Ephesus on Christmas-day, A.D. 431) ;—
(19) Proclus archbishop of Constantinople;— (20) Paulus
bishop of Emesa (in a sermon preached before Cyril of Alexandria on Christmas-day, A.D. 431) ;—(21) the Eastern bishops
at Ephesus collectively, A.D. 431 (an unusually weighty piece
of evidence) ;—and lastly, (22) Basil of Seleucia. Now, let it
be remarked that *these were contemporaries of codex* A.

"In the VIth century, — the Patristic witnesses are (23)
Cosmas, the voyager, 5 times,—(24) Anastasius Sinaita,—(25)
Eulogius archbishop of Alexandria: *contemporaries, be it re-
membered, of codex* D.

"In the VIIth,—(26) Andreas of Crete twice.

"And in the VIIIth,—(27) Cosmas bishop of Maiuma near
Gaza, — and his pupil (28) John Damascene, — and (29) Germanus archbishop of Constantinople.

OTHER ILLUSTRIOUS WITNESSES

"To these 29 illustrious names are to be added unknown
writers of uncertain date, but *all* of considerable antiquity; and
some are proved by internal evidence to belong to the IVth or
Vth century,— in short, to be of the date of the Fathers whose
names 16 of them severally bear, but among whose genuine
works their productions are probably *not* to be reckoned. One
of these was anciently mistaken for (30) Gregory Thaumaturgus: a second, for (31) Methodius: a third, for (32) Basil.
Three others, with different degrees of reasonableness, have
been supposed to be (33, 34, 35) Athanasius. One has passed
for (36) Gregory of Nyssa; another for (37) Epiphanius;
while no less than eight (38 to 45) have been mistaken for
Chrysostom, some of them being certainly his contemporaries.
Add (46) one anonymous Father, and (47) the author of the
apocryphal *Acta Pilati*,—and it will be perceived that 18 ancient authorities have been added to the list, every whit as
competent to witness what was the text of S. Luke ii. 14 at the
time when A B ℵ D were written, as Basil or Athanasius, Epiphanius or Chrysostom themselves. *For our present purpose*
they are *Codices* of the IVth, Vth, and VIth centuries. In this
way then, far more than *forty-seven* ancient witnesses have come
back to testify to the men of this generation that the commonly
received reading of S. Luke ii. 14 is *the true reading*, and that
the text which the Revisionists are seeking to palm off upon
us is *a fabrication and a blunder*. Will any one be found to
maintain that the authority of B and ℵ is appreciable, when

confronted by the first 15 *contemporary Ecclesiastical Writers* above enumerated? or that A can stand against the 7 which follow?

GEOGRAPHICAL DISTRIBUTION OF WITNESSES

"This is not all however. Survey the preceding enumeration geographically, and note that, besides 1 name from Gaul, —at least 2 stand for Constantinople,— while 5 are dotted over Asia Minor: — 10 at least represent Antioch; and — 6, other parts of Syria:—3 stand for Palestine, and 12 for other Churches of the East:—at least 5 are Alexandrian,—2 are men of Cyprus, and—1 is from Crete. If the articulate voices of so many illustrious Bishops, coming back to us in this way from every part of ancient Christendom and all delivering the same unfaltering message,—if *this* be not allowed to be decisive on a point of the kind just now before us, then pray let us have it explained to us,—What amount of evidence *will* men accept as final? It is high time that this were known. . . . The plain truth is, that a case has been established against א A B D and the Latin version, which amounts to *proof* that those documents, even when they conspire to yield the self-same evidence, are not to be depended on as witnesses to the text of Scripture. The history of the reading advocated by the Revisionists is briefly this:—*It emerges into notice in the IInd century; and in the Vth, disappears from sight entirely.*" (Burgon, pp. 41-46.)

So much for the Revised Version's attempted corruption of the message of the heavenly hosts. If anything of this sort can be proved beyond reasonable question it would seem this has been so proved. One cannot consider the meticulous care that attaches to Burgon's work without being profoundly impressed with its reliability.

Sub-item g.   The Institution of the Sacrament, Luke 22:19-20.

The King James (Authorized) Version text reads:

"And he took bread, and gave thanks, and brake it, and gave unto them, saying, This is my body which is given for you: this do in remembrance of me. Likewise also the cup after supper, saying, This cup is the new testament in my blood, which is shed for you."

The Inspired Version (disregarding punctuation changes) reads as the Authorized Version text except that "*it*" is omitted after "brake."

The Revised Version reads:

"And he took bread, and when he had given thanks, he brake it, and gave to them, saying, This is my body which is given for you: this do in remembrance of me. And the cup in like manner after supper, saying, This cup is the new covenant in my blood, even that which is poured out for you." The marginal notes to the Revised Version are: to "bread,"—"Or, *a loaf*"; to "which,"—"Some ancient authorities omit *which is given for you . . . which is poured out for you*"; to "covenant," —"Or, *testament*."

The American Standard Version follows the Revised Version, except that the marginal note to "covenant," is omitted.

That is, under these proposed changes, the whole sacrament under the Revised Versions would consist of: "And he took bread, and when he had given thanks, he brake it, and gave to them, saying, This is my body." The element of blood would be lost.

After listing a total of 16 omissions, beginning with the one noted above, Dean Burgon comments:

"On an attentive survey of the foregoing sixteen instances of unauthorized Omission, it will be perceived that the 1st passage (S. Luke xxii. 19, 20) must have been eliminated from the Text because the mention of *two* Cups seemed to create a difficulty. . . . In the meantime, so far are Drs. Westcott and Hort from accepting the foregoing account of the matter, that they even style the 1st 'a *perverse interpolation:*' in which view of the subject, however, they enjoy the distinction of standing entirely alone. . . .

"The *sole* authority for just half of the places above enumerated is *a single Greek codex*,—and that, the most depraved of all,—viz. Beza's D. It should further be stated that the only allies discoverable for D are a few copies of the old Latin. What we are saying will seem scarcely credible: but it is a plain fact, of which any one may convince himself who will be at the pains to inspect the critical apparatus at the foot of the pages of Tischendorf's last (8th) edition. Our Revisionists' notion, therefore, of what constitutes 'weighty evidence' is now before the Reader. If, in *his* judgment, the testimony of *one single manuscript,* (and *that* manuscript the Codex Bezæ (D),) —does really invalidate that of *all other Manuscripts and all other Versions* in the world,—then of course, the Greek Text of the Revisionists will in his judgment be a thing to be rejoiced over. But what if he should be of opinion that such testimony, in and by itself, is simply worthless? We shrewdly suspect that the Revisionists' view of what constitutes 'weighty Evidence' will be found to end where it began, viz. in the Jerusalem Chamber. . . .

"Now, that ecclesiastical usage and the parallel places would seriously affect such precious words as are found in S. Luke xxii. 19, 20,—was to have been expected. Yet has the type been preserved all along, from the beginning, with singular exactness; except in one little handful of singularly licentious documents, viz. in D a ff² i l, which *leave all out*;—in b e, which substitute verses 17 and 18;—and in 'the singular and sometimes rather wild Curetonian Syriac Version,' which, retaining the 10 words of ver. 19, substitutes verses 17, 18 for ver. 20. Enough for the condemnation of D survives in Justin,—Basil, —Epiphanius,— Theodoret,— Cyril,— Maximus,— Jerome. But why delay ourselves concerning a place vouched for *by every known copy of the Gospels except* D? Drs. Westcott and Hort entertain *'no moral doubt* that the [32] words [given at foot] were absent from the original text of S. Luke'; in which opinion, happily, *they stand alone.* But why did our Revisionists suffer themselves to be led astray by such blind guidance?" (Burgon, pp. 76-79.)

Sub-item h.   *The Agony in the Garden and the Ministering Angel, Luke 22:43-44.*

The King James (Authorized) Version reads:

"And there appeared an angel unto him from heaven, strengthening him. And being in an agony he prayed more earnestly: and his sweat was as it were great drops of blood falling down to the ground."

The Inspired Version of the Prophet follows the Au-

thorized Version text, with the slight change of "his sweat was as it were" to "he sweat as it were."

The Revised Version reads:

"And there appeared unto him an angel from heaven, strengthening him. And being in an agony he prayed more earnestly: and his sweat became as it were great drops of blood falling down upon the ground." The marginal note in the Revised Version reads: "Many ancient authorities omit ver. 43, 44."

The American Standard Version follows the Revised Version.

Dean Burgon's comment on this proposed omission is thus:

"The 2nd has been suppressed because the incident was deemed derogatory to the majesty of GOD Incarnate. . . .

"The next place is entitled to far graver attention, and may on no account be lightly dismissed, seeing that these two verses contain the sole record of that 'Agony in the Garden' which the universal Church has almost erected into an article of the Faith.

"That the incident of the ministering Angel, the Agony and bloody sweat of the world's Redeemer (S. Luke xxii. 43, 44), was anciently absent from certain copies of the Gospels, is expressly recorded by Hilary, by Jerome, and others. Only necessary is it to read the apologetic remarks which Ambrose introduces when he reaches S. Luke xxii. 43, to understand what has evidently led to this serious mutilation of Scripture, —traces of which survive at this day exclusively in *four* codices, viz. A B R T. Singular to relate, in the Gospel which was read on Maundy-Thursday these two verses of S. Luke's Gospel are thrust in between the 39th and the 40th verses of S. Matthew xxvi. Hence, 4 cursive copies, viz. 13-69-124-346—(confessedly derived from a common ancient archetype, and therefore not four witnesses but only one),—actually exhibit these two Verses in that place.

WITNESSES FOR THE KING JAMES TEXT

"But will any unprejudiced person of sound mind entertain a doubt concerning the genuineness of these two verses, witnessed to as they are by *the whole body of the Manuscripts,* uncial as well as cursive, and *by every ancient Version? . . .* If such a thing were possible, it is hoped that the following enumeration of ancient Fathers, who distinctly recognize the place under discussion, must at least be held to be decisive: —viz.

"Justin M.,—Irenæus in the IInd century:—

"Hippolytus,—Dionysius Alex.,—ps. Tatian, in the IIIrd:—

"Arius, — Eusebius, — Athanasius, — Ephraem Syr., — Didymus, — Gregory Naz., — Epiphanius, — Chrysostom, — ps.-Dionysius Areop., in the IVth:—

"Julian the heretic,— Theodorus Mops.,— Nestorius,— Cyril Alex.,— Paulus, bishop of Emesa,— Gennadius,— Theodoret,— and several Oriental Bishops (A.D. 431), in the Vth:—besides

"Ps.-Cæsarius, — Theodosius Alex., — John Damascene, — Maximus,—Theodorus hæret.,—Leontius Byz.,—Anastasius Sin., —Photius: and of the Latins, Hilary,—Jerome,—Augustine,— Cassian,—Paulinus,—Facundus.

BURGON'S COMMENTS ON REVISERS' ATTITUDE

"It will be seen that we have been enumerating *upwards of forty famous personages from every part of ancient Christendom,* who recognize these verses as genuine; fourteen of them being as old,—some of them, a great deal older,—than our oldest MSS.—*Why* therefore Drs. Westcott and Hort should insist on shutting up these 26 precious words—this article of the Faith—in double brackets, in token that it is 'morally certain' that verses 43 and 44 are of spurious origin, we are at a loss to divine. We can but ejaculate (in the very words they proceed to disallow),—'FATHER, forgive them; for they know not what they do.' But our especial concern is with *our Revisionists;* and we do not exceed our province when we come forward to reproach them sternly for having succumbed to such evil counsels, and deliberately branded these Verses with their own corporate expression of doubt. For unless *that* be the purpose of the marginal Note which they have set against these verses, we fail to understand the Revisers' language and are wholly at a loss to divine what purpose that note of theirs can be meant to serve. It is prefaced by a formula which, (as we learn from their own Preface,) offers to the reader the 'alternative, of *omitting* the Verses in question: implies that '*it would not be safe*' any longer to accept them,—as the Church has hitherto done,—with undoubting confidence. In a word,—*it brands them with suspicion. . . .* We have been so full on this subject, —(not half of our references were known to Tischendorf,)— because of the unspeakable preciousness of the record; and because we desire to see an end at last to expressions of doubt and uncertainty on points which really afford not a shadow of pretence for either. These two Verses were excised through mistaken piety by certain of the orthodox, — jealous for the honour of their LORD, and alarmed by the use which the impugners of His GODhead freely made of them. Hence Ephraem (*Carmina Nisibena,* p. 145) puts the following words into the mouth of Satan, addressing the host of Hell: — 'One thing I witnessed in Him which especially comforts me. I saw Him praying; and I rejoiced, for His countenance changed and He was afraid. *His sweat was drops of blood,* for He had a presentiment that His day had come. This was the fairest sight of all,—unless, to be sure, He was practising deception on me. For verily if He hath deceived me, then it is all over,—both with me, and with you, my servants!'" (Burgon, pp. 76, 79-82.)

WESTCOTT-HORT'S EXPLANATION OF OMISSIONS

The justification for the proposed omission of these verses, is thus (as quoted) given by Drs. Westcott and Hort:

" 'The documentary evidence clearly designates [these verses] as *an early Western interpolation,* adopted in eclectic texts.'—'They can only be *a fragment from the Traditions,* written or oral, which were for a while at least *locally current:'*—an 'evangelic Tradition,' therefore, *'rescued from oblivion by the Scribes of the second century.'* " (Burgon, p. 81, n. 15.)

Sub-item i. The Prayer on the Cross, Luke 23:34.

The King James (Authorized) Version reads:

"Then said Jesus, Father, forgive them; for they know not what they do."

The Prophet Joseph in his *Inspired Version,* gives the Authorized Version reading, but inserts in brackets following "they know not what they do," the following explanation: "Meaning the soldiers who crucified him."

The Revised Version reads:

"And Jesus said, Father, forgive them; for they know not what they do." The marginal note reads: "Some ancient authorities omit *And Jesus said, Father, forgive them; for they know not what they do.*"

The American Standard Version follows the Revised Version.

BURGON'S DISCUSSION

Discussing this doubt thus cast upon this scripture, Dean Burgon says:

"Next in importance after the preceding, comes the Prayer which the SAVIOUR of the World breathed from the Cross on behalf of His murderers (S. Luke xxiii. 34). These twelve precious words, — ('Then said JESUS, FATHER, forgive them; for they know not what they do,')—like those twenty-six words in S. Luke xxii. 43, 44 which we have been considering already, Drs. Westcott and Hort enclose within double brackets in token of the 'moral certainty' they entertain that the words are spurious. And yet these words are found in *every known uncial* and in *every known cursive Copy,* except four; besides being found *in every ancient Version.* And *what,*— (we ask the question with sincere simplicity,) — *what* amount of evidence is calculated to inspire undoubting confidence in any existing Reading, if not such a concurrence of Authorities as this? . . . We forbear to insist upon the probabilities of the case. The Divine power and sweetness of the incident shall not be enlarged upon. We introduce no considerations resulting from Internal Evidence. True, that 'few verses of the Gospels bear in themselves a surer witness to the Truth of what they record, than this.' (It is the admission of the very man who has nevertheless dared to brand it with suspicion.) But we reject his loathsome patronage with indignation. 'Internal Evidence,' — 'Transcriptional Probability,'—and all such 'chaff and draff,' with which he fills his pages *ad nauseam,* and mystifies nobody but himself,—shall be allowed no place in the present discussion. Let this verse of Scripture stand or fall as it meets with sufficient external testimony, or is forsaken thereby. How then about the *Patristic* evidence,—for this is all that remains unexplored?

WITNESS OF THE FATHERS

"Only a fraction of it was known to Tischendorf. We find our SAVIOUR'S Prayer attested,—

"In the IInd century by Hegesippus,— and by Irenæus:—

"In the IIIrd, by Hippolytus,—by Origen,—by the *Apostolic Constitutions*,—by the *Clementine Homilies*,—by ps.-Tatian,— and by the disputation of Archelaus with Manes:—

"In the IVth, by Eusebius, — by Athanasius, — by Gregory Nyss.,—by Theodorus Herac.,—by Basil,—by Chrysostom,—by Ephraem Syr.,— by ps.-Ephraim,— by ps.-Dionysius Areop.,— by the Apocryphal *Acta Pilati*,—by the *Acta Philippi*,—and by the Syriac *Acts of the App.*, — by ps.-Ignatius, — and ps.-Justin:—

"In the Vth, by Theodoret,—by Cyril,—by Eutherius:—

"In the VIth, by Anastasius Sin.,—by Hesychius:—

"In the VIIth, by Antiochus mon.,—by Maximus,—by Andreas Cret.:—

"In the VIIIth, by John Damascene, — besides ps.-Chrysostom,—ps.-Amphilochius,—and the *Opus imperf.*

"Add to this, (since Latin authorities have been brought to the front), — Ambrose, — Hilary, — Jerome, — Augustine, — and other earlier writers.

"We have thus again enumerated *upwards of forty* ancient Fathers. And again we ask, With what show of reason is the brand set upon these 12 words? Gravely to cite, as if there were anything in it, such counter-evidence as the following, to the foregoing torrent of Testimony from every part of ancient Christendom: — viz: 'B D, 38, 435, a b d and one Egyptian version'—might really have been mistaken for a *mauvaise plaisanterie*, were it not that the gravity of the occasion effectually precludes the supposition. How could our Revisionists *dare* to insinuate doubts into wavering hearts and unlearned heads, where (as here) they were *bound* to know, there exists *no manner of doubt at all?*" (Burgon, pp. 82-85; Burgon's specific citations omitted.)

The Dean then discusses with equal cogency the suggested omission of the Inscription on the cross, and the visit of Peter to the sepulchre. (Burgon, pp. 85-90, listing his authorities.)

Sub-item j.   Christ's Salutation to the Apostles in the Upper Chamber, Luke 24:36.

The King James (Authorized) Version reads:

"And as they thus spake, Jesus himself stood in the midst of them, and saith unto them, Peace be unto you."

The Inspired Version reads:

"And as they thus spake, Jesus himself stood in the midst of them, and said unto them, Peace be unto you."

The Revised Version reads:

"And as they spake these things, he himself stood in the midst of them, and saith unto them, Peace be unto you." The marginal note reads: "Some ancient authorities omit *and saith unto them, Peace be unto you."*

The American Standard Version follows the Revised Version.

Regarding this note which would omit this greeting, Burgon says:

". . . And yet the precious words . . . (Lu. xxiv. 36) are vouched for by 18 uncials (with ℵ A B at their head), and *every known cursive copy* of the Gospels: by all the Versions: and (as before) by Eusebius,—and Ambrose,—by Chrysostom, —and Cyril,—and Augustine." (Burgon, p. 90.)

Sub-item k.   Christ Displays His Hands and Feet, Luke 24:40.

The King James (Authorized) Version reads:

"And when he had thus spoken, he shewed them his hands and his feet."

The Inspired Version follows the Authorized Version text.

The Revised Version reads:

"And when he had said this, he shewed them his hands and his feet." The marginal note reads: "Some ancient authorities omit ver. 40."

The American Standard Version reads:

"And when he had said this, he showed them his hands and his feet." The marginal note follows the Revised Version.

Touching this record of the display by the resurrected Christ of his hands and feet, and the proposed deletion thereof by the Revisionists, Burgon says:

"The words are found in 18 uncials (beginning with א A B), and in every known cursive: in the Latin,—the Syriac, —the Egyptian,—in short, *in all the ancient Versions.* Besides these, ps.-Justin, — Eusebius, — Athanasius, — Ambrose (in Greek),— Epiphanius,—Chrysostom,— Cyril,—Theodoret,—Ammonius, — and John Damascene — quote them. What but the veriest trifling is it, in the face of such a body of evidence, to bring forward the fact that D and 5 copies of the old Latin, with Cureton's Syriac (of which we have had the character already), *omit* the words in question?" (Burgon, pp. 90-91.)

Sub-item l. Casting Out Evil Spirits, Matt. 17:21.

The King James (Authorized) Version text reads:

"Howbeit this kind goeth not out but by prayer and fasting."

The Inspired Version of the Prophet Joseph Smith gives the text of the Authorized Version.

The Revised Version text omits this verse entirely, with a marginal note:

"Many authorities, some ancient, insert ver. 21 *But this kind goeth not out save by prayer and fasting.* See Mark ix. 29."

The American Standard Version follows the Revised Version.

Where the same incident is recorded in Mark 9:29, the *Authorized Version* text reads:

"This kind can come forth by nothing, but by prayer and fasting."

The Inspired Version follows the text of the Authorized Version.

The Revised Version text of Mark 9:29 is substantially the same (merely substituting "out" for "forth" and "save" for "but") except that "and fasting" is omitted. The marginal note reads:

"Many ancient authorities add *and fasting.*"

The American Standard Version follows the Revised Version.

On these omissions in the Revised Version, Dean Burgon cites the following instances, with the comments given:

"The foregoing enumeration of instances of Mutilation might be enlarged to almost any extent. Take only three more short but striking specimens, before we pass on:—

"(a) Thus, the precious verse (S. Matthew xvii. 21) which declares that '*this kind* [of evil spirit] *goeth not out but by prayer and fasting,*' is expunged by our Revisionists; although it is vouched for by every known uncial *but two* (Bℵ), every known cursive *but one* (Evan. 33) ; is witnessed to by the Old Latin and the Vulgate, — the Syriac, Coptic, Armenian, Georgian, Æthiopic, and Slavonic versions; by Origen, — Athanasius, — Basil,—Chrysostom,—the *Opus imperf.,*—the Syriac Clement, —and John Damascene;—by Tertullian,—Ambrose,—Hilary,— Juvencus, — Augustine, — Maximus Taur., — and by the Syriac version of the *Canons of Eusebius*: above all by the Universal East,—having been read in all the churches of Oriental Christendom on the 10th Sunday after Pentecost, from the earliest period. Why, in the world, then (our readers will ask) have the Revisionists left those words out? . . . For no other reason, we answer, but because Drs. Westcott and Hort place them among the interpolations which they consider unworthy of being even 'exceptionally retained in association with the true Text.' 'Western and Syrian' is their oracular sentence." (Burgon, pp. 91-92, and see *Note Thirty-one*, pp. 310-311.)

Sub-item m. "The Son of man is come to save," Matt. 18:11.

The King James (Authorized) Version text reads:

"For the Son of man is come to save that which was lost."

The Inspired Version of the Prophet Joseph uses the same text as the Authorized Version.

The Revised Version text omits the verse entirely, but adds a marginal note reading:

"Many authorities, some ancient, insert ver. 11 *For the Son of man came to save that which was lost.* See Luke xix. 10."

The American Standard Version follows the Revised Version.

The King James (Authorized) Version for Luke 19:10 reads:

"For the Son of man is come to seek and to save that which was lost."

The Inspired Version text for Luke 19:10 reads:

"For the Son of Man is come to seek and to save that which was lost."

The Revised Version text for Luke 19:10 reads:

"For the Son of man came to seek and to save that which was lost," but there is no annotation in Luke.

The American Standard Version follows the Revised Version as to Luke 19:10.

Upon this state of facts, Dean Burgon says (his citations omitted):

"The blessed declaration, *'The Son of Man is come to save that which was lost,'* — has in like manner been expunged by our Revisionists from S. Matth. xviii. 11; although it is attested by every known uncial except B ℵ L, and every known cursive *except three*: by the old Latin and the Vulgate: by the Peschito, Cureton's and the Philoxenian Syriac: by the Coptic, Armenian, Æthiopic, Georgian and Slavonic versions:—by Origen,—Theodorus Heracl.,—Chrysostom—and Jovius the monk;—by Tertullian, —Ambrose, — Hilary, — Jerome, — pope Damasus — and Augustine:—above all, by the Universal Eastern Church,—for it has been read in all assemblies of the faithful on the morrow of Pentecost, from the beginning. Why then (the reader will again ask) have the Revisionists expunged this verse? We can only answer as before,—because Drs. Westcott and Hort consign it to the *limbus* of their *Appendix;* class it among their 'Rejected Readings' of the most hopeless type. As before, *all* their sentence is 'Western and Syrian.' They add, 'Interpolated either from Lu. xix. 10, or from an independent source, written or oral.' . . . Will the English Church suffer herself to be in this way defrauded of her priceless inheritance, — through the irreverent bungling of well-intentioned, but utterly misguided men?" (Burgon, p. 92.)

Sub-item n.   The Last Twelve Verses of the Gospel of Mark, Mark 16:9-20.

The text of the *King James* (*Authorized*) *Version* reads thus:

"Now when Jesus was risen early the first day of the week, he appeared first to Mary Magdalene, out of whom he had cast seven devils.

"And she went and told them that had been with him, as they mourned and wept.

"And they, when they had heard that he was alive, and had been seen of her, believed not.

"After that he appeared in another form unto two of them, as they walked, and went into the country.

"And they went and told it unto the residue: neither believed they them.

"Afterward he appeared unto the eleven as they sat at meat, and upbraided them with their unbelief and hardness of heart, because they believed not them which had seen him after he was risen.

"And he said unto them, Go ye into all the world, and preach the gospel to every creature.

"He that believeth and is baptized shall be saved; but he that believeth not shall be damned.

"And these signs shall follow them that believe; In my name shall they cast out devils; they shall speak with new tongues;

"They shall take up serpents; and if they drink any deadly thing, it shall not hurt them; they shall lay hands on the sick, and they shall recover.

"So then after the Lord had spoken unto them, he was received up into heaven, and sat on the right hand of God.

"And they went forth, and preached every where, the Lord working with them, and confirming the word with signs following. Amen."

The Inspired Version follows the Authorized Version text, with two or three minor verbal changes.

The Revised Version text has a considerable space between these verses and the last preceding verse (Mark 16:8).

In the British print, the Revised Version has the following marginal note to the beginning of verse 9:

"The two oldest Greek manuscripts, and some other authorities, omit from ver. 9 to the end. Some other authorities have a different ending to the Gospel." Further marginal notes are made in the British print: to the word "new" in the phrase "new tongues" found at the end of verse 17: "Some ancient authorities omit *new*"; and to "devils,"—"Gr. *demons.*"

The American Standard Version is arranged in the same way as the British Version and has identical marginal notes except that the word "demons" is inserted in the text in place of "devils."

This treatment of this text by the Revisers has called forth from the High Textualists, perhaps the most vigorous and voluminous condemnation that has been voiced against any of the changes made by the Revisers. (See *supra, Note Eleven.*)

We may begin with certain observations of Prebendary Scrivener, who, in his section headed "Preliminary Considerations," comments as follows:

"To begin with variations of the gravest kind. In two, though happily in only two instances, the genuineness of whole passages of considerable extent, which are read in our printed copies of the New Testament, has been brought into question. These are the weighty and characteristic paragraphs Mark xvi. 9-20 and John vii. 53—viii. 11. We shall hereafter defend these passages, the first without the slightest misgiving, the second with certain reservations, as entitled to be regarded authentic portions of the Gospels in which they stand." (Scrivener, p. 7.)

Later in his work, Scrivener returns to the subject of Mark 16:9-20, and briefly analyzes the situation as to their genuineness. We shall quote a part of his discussion:

"In Chapter I. we engaged to defend the authenticity of this long and important passage, and that without the slightest misgiving (p. 7). Dean Burgon's brilliant monograph, 'The Last Twelve verses of the Gospel according to S. Mark vindicated against recent objectors and established' (Oxford and London, 1871), has thrown a stream of light upon the controversy, nor does the joyous tone of his book misbecome one who is conscious of having triumphantly maintained a cause which is very precious to him. We may fairly say that his conclusions have in no essential point been shaken by the elaborate and very able counter-plea of Dr. Hort (*Notes*, pp. 28-51). This whole paragraph is set apart by itself in the critical editions of Tischendorf and Tregelles. Besides this, it is placed within double brackets by Westcott and Hort, and followed by the wretched supplement derived from Cod. L (*vide infra*), annexed as an alternative reading (*allos*). Out of all the great manuscripts, the two oldest (א B) stand alone in omitting ver. 9-20 altogether. Cod. B, however, betrays consciousness on the scribe's part that something is left out, inasmuch as after *ephoboynto gar* ver. 8, a whole column is left perfectly blank (*the only blank one in the whole volume*), as well as the rest of the column containing ver. 8, which is usual in Cod. B at the end of every book of Scripture (*see* p. 104). No such peculiarity attaches to Cod. א. . . . Besides these, the twelve verses are omitted in none but some old Armenian codices and two of the Æthiopic, *k* of the Old Latin, and an Arabic Lectionary (IX) No. 13, examined by Scholz in the Vatican." (Scrivener, pp. 583-584.)

After detailed consideration and evaluation of various codices, Scrivener states that the first objector to the paragraphs was Eusebius, and after noting his objections, adds:

"The language of Eusebius has been minutely examined by Dean Burgon, who proves to demonstration that all the subsequent evidence which has been alleged against the passage, whether of Severus, or Hesychius, or any other writer down to Euthymius Zigabenus in the twelfth century, is a mere echo of the doubts and difficulties of Eusebius, if indeed he is not retailing to us at second-hand one of the fanciful Biblical speculations of Origen (*see* pp. 509, 512-3)." (Scrivener, p. 588.)

The fourth edition of Scrivener adds the following:

" . . . Jerome's recklessness in statement has been already noticed (Vol. II. p. 269) ; besides that, he is a witness on the other side, both in his own quotations of the passage and in the Vulgate, for how could he have inserted the verses there, if he had judged them to be spurious?" (Scrivener-Miller, Vol. II, p. 342.)

The third edition continues (we quote this rather lengthy discussion in full, because of the importance of the problem and because the acknowledged scholarship, experience, and wisdom of Scrivener gives unusual weight to his reasonings and conclusions):

"With regard to the argument against these twelve verses arising from their alleged difference in style from the rest of the Gospel, I must say that the same process might be applied —and has been applied—to prove that S. Paul was not the writer of the Pastoral Epistles (to say nothing of that to the Hebrews), S. John of the Apocalypse, Isaiah and Zechariah of portions of those prophecies that bear their names. Every one used to literary composition may detect, if he will, such minute variations as have been made so much of in this case, either in his own writings, or in those of the authors he is most familiar with.

"Persons who, like Eusebius, devoted themselves to the pious task of constructing harmonies of the Gospels, would soon perceive the difficulty of adjusting the events recorded in ver. 9-20 to the narratives of the other Evangelists. Alford regards this inconsistency (more apparent than real, we believe) as 'a valuable testimony to the antiquity of the fragment' (N. T. *ad loc.*) : we would go further, and claim for the harder reading the benefit of any critical doubt as to its genuineness (Canon I. p. 493). The difficulty was both felt and avowed by Eusebius, and was recited after him by Severus of Antioch or whoever wrote the scholion attributed to him. Whatever Jerome and the rest may have done, these assigned the *antilogia*, the *enantiosis* they thought they perceived, as a reason (not the first, nor perhaps the chief, but still as a reason) for supposing that the Gospel ended with *ephoboynto gar*. Yet in the balance of probabilities, can anything be more unlikely than that S. Mark broke off so abruptly as this hypothesis would imply, while no ancient writer has noticed or seemed conscious of any such abruptness? This fact has driven those who reject the concluding verses to the strangest fancies; — namely, that, like Thucydides, the Evangelist was cut off before his work was completed, or even that the last leaf of the original Gospel was torn away.

"We emphatically deny that such wild surmises are called for by the state of the evidence in this case. All opposition to the authenticity of the paragraph resolves itself into the allegations of Eusebius and the testimony of א B. Let us accord to these the weight which is their due: but against their verdict we can appeal to the reading of Irenæus and of both the elder Syriac translations in the second century; of nearly all other versions; and of all extant manuscripts excepting two. So powerfully is it vouched for, that many of those who are reluctant to recognise S. Mark as its author, are content to regard it notwithstanding as an integral portion of the inspired record originally delivered to the Church." (Scrivener, pp. 588-590.)

In the fourth edition of Scrivener the following statement is added at the end of the penultimate sentence of the foregoing:

" . . . but against their verdict we can appeal to a vast body of ecclesiastical evidence reaching back to the earlier part of the second century; to nearly all the versions; and to all extant manuscripts excepting two, of which one is doubtful." (Scrivener-Miller, Vol. II, p. 344.)

As set out in the foregoing comments of Scrivener, Dean Burgon, from whom we have heretofore quoted so extensively, has prepared a volume of 334 pages—*The Last Twelve Verses of the Gospel According to S. Mark, Vindicated Against Recent Critical Objectors and Established*, published by Parker, Oxford, 1871, in which he contends for the genuineness of these twelve verses. (Burgon, p. 37.) This has been characterized by Scrivener as quoted above.

The author might conveniently repeat here the testimony of Mr. Burgon's scholarship given by Prebendary Scrivener, who says, in tendering his acknowledgments for assistance in preparing the second and third editions of his *Plain Introduction*:

" . . . and especially by Dean Burgon, to whom the present edition is more deeply indebted than it would be possible to acknowledge in detail. His series of Letters addressed to me in the *Guardian* newspaper (1873) contains but a part of the help he has afforded towards the preparation of this and the second edition." (Scrivener, n. 1, p. 178.)

Among the many comments which Dean Burgon makes in his *The Revision Revised*, touching the Revisers' treatment of the last twelve verses of Mark (he makes numerous allusions to his work—cited above—in which he deals with the entire subject), the following may be quoted, for though the extracts quoted are somewhat lengthy, they pertain to a most important problem.

"When, however, such an one as Tischendorf or Tregelles,— Hort or Ellicott,—would put me down by reminding me that half-a-dozen of the oldest Versions are against me, — 'That argument' (I reply) 'is not allowable on *your* lips. For if the united testimony of *five* of the Versions really be, in your account, decisive,—Why do you deny the genuineness of the 'last Twelve Verses of S. Mark's Gospel, *which are recognized by every one of the Versions?* Those Verses are besides attested *by every known Copy*, except two of bad character: *by a mighty chorus of Fathers*: *by the unfaltering Tradition of the Church universal.* First remove from S. Mark xvi. 20, your brand of suspicion, and then come back to me in order that we may discuss together how 1 Tim. iii. 16 is to be read. . . .

"We may now proceed with our examination of their work, beginning — as Dr. Roberts (one of the Revisionists) does, when explaining the method and results of their labours—with what we hold to be the gravest blot of all, viz. the marks of serious suspicion which we find set against the last Twelve verses of S. Mark's Gospel. Well may the learned Presbyterian anticipate that—

" 'The reader will be struck by the appearance which this long paragraph presents in the Revised Version. Although inserted, it is marked off by a considerable space from the rest of the Gospel. A note is also placed in the margin containing a brief explanation of this.'

"A *very* brief 'explanation' certainly: for the note *explains* nothing. Allusion is made to the following words—

" 'The two oldest Greek manuscripts, and some other authorities, omit from ver. 9 to the end. Some other authorities have a different ending to the Gospel.'

"But now,—For the use of *whom* has this piece of information been volunteered? Not for learned readers certainly: it being familiarly known to all, that codices B and א *alone of manuscripts* (to their own effectual condemnation) omit these 12 verses. But then scholars know something more about the matter. They also know that these 12 verses have been made the subject of a separate treatise extending to upwards of 300 pages,—which treatise has now been before the world for a full decade of years, and for the best of reasons has never yet been answered. Its object, stated on its title-page, was to vindicate against recent critical objectors, and to establish 'the last Twelve Verses' of S. Mark's Gospel. Moreover, competent judges at once admitted that the author had succeeded in doing what he undertook to do. *Can* it then be right (we respectfully enquire) still to insinuate into unlearned minds distrust of twelve consecutive verses of the everlasting Gospel, which yet have been demonstrated to be as trustworthy as any other verses which can be named?" (Burgon, pp. xxiii, 36-37.)

BURGON'S ANALYSIS OF DESIGNATED OBJECTIONS

After narrating some of the matters of procedure

followed by the Revisers (see pp. 269 ff., *supra*) Dean Burgon continues:

"We naturally cast about for some evidence that the members of the New Testament company possess that mastery of the subject which alone could justify one of their number (Dr. Milligan) in asserting roundly that these 12 verses are '*not from the pen of S. Mark himself*'; and another (Dr. Roberts) in maintaining that 'the passage is *not the immediate production of S. Mark.*' Dr. Roberts assures us that—

" 'Eusebius, Gregory of Nyssa, Victor of Antioch, Severus of Antioch, Jerome, as well as other writers, especially Greeks, testify that these verses were not written by S. Mark, or not found in the best copies.'

"Will the learned writer permit us to assure him in return that he is entirely mistaken? He is requested to believe that Gregory of Nyssa says nothing of the sort—*says nothing at all* concerning these verses: that Victor of Antioch vouches emphatically for their *genuineness*: that Severus does but copy, while Jerome does but translate, a few random expressions of Eusebius: and that Eusebius himself *nowhere* 'testifies that these verses were not written by S. Mark.' So far from it, Eusebius actually *quotes the verses,* quotes them as *genuine.* Dr. Roberts is further assured that there are *no* 'other writers,' whether Greek or Latin, who insinuate doubt concerning these verses. On the contrary, besides *both* the Latin and *all the* Syriac— besides the Gothic and the *two* Egyptian versions—there exist four authorities of the IInd century;—as many of the IIIrd;— five of the Vth;— four of the VIth;—as many of the VIIth;— together with *at least ten* of the IVth (*contemporaries therefore of codices* B and ℵ) ;—which actually recognize the verses in question. Now, when to *every known Manuscript but two* of bad character, besides *every ancient Version, some one-and-thirty Fathers* have been added, 18 of whom must have used copies at least as old as either B or ℵ, — Dr. Roberts is assured that an amount of external authority has been accumulated which is simply overwhelming in discussions of this nature.

"But the significance of a single feature of the Lectionary, of which up to this point nothing has been said, is alone sufficient to determine the controversy. We refer to the fact that *in every part of Eastern Christendom* these same 12 verses— neither more nor less—have been from the earliest recorded period, and still are, *a proper lesson both for the Easter season and for Ascension Day."* (Burgon, pp. 39-40.)

In the course of his discussion of the treatment accorded by the Revisers of Luke 2:14, Dean Burgon has to say further about the last twelve verses of Mark:

"Our Revisionists, so far from holding what follows to be 'canonical Scripture,' are careful to state that a rival ending to be found elsewhere merits serious attention. S. Mark xvi. 9-20, therefore *(according to them)*, is *not certainly* a genuine part of the Gospel; *may*, after all, be nothing else but a spurious accretion to the text. And as long as such doubts are put forth by our Revisionists, they publish to the world that, *in their account* at all events, these verses are *not* 'possessed of full canonical authority.' If 'the two oldest Greek manuscripts' *justly* 'omit from verse 9 to the end' (as stated in the margin), will any one deny that our printed Text ought to omit them also? On the other hand, if the circumstance is a mere literary curiosity, will any one maintain that it is entitled to abiding record in the margin of the *English Version* of the everlasting page? — *affords any warrant whatever for separating 'the last Twelve Verses' from their context?"* (Burgon, pp. 48-49.)

It was a comforting thing to read that these great verses that close Mark's Gospel, are to stand, on the record, and that there was seemingly no reason really to accept the "conjectural emendation," "the individual mind," (Burgon, p. 25) with its pseudo-revelation complex, that these verses should be omitted.

It might be interesting here to note that the verses in question have been wholly eliminated from the text of the American Revised Standard Version and relegated to a note, which is introduced thus: "Other texts and versions add as 16.9-20 the following passage:" and then quotes the verses in question.

This discussion may appropriately close with a repetition (the third or fourth) of the observations of Prebendary Scrivener on the unsupported conclusions embodied in text and marginal notes of the Revised Version, all founded upon the arguments and conclusions reached by Westcott and Hort, for which the latter seems primarily responsible:

"But there is little hope for the stability of their imposing structure, if its foundations have been laid on the sandy ground of ingenious conjecture: and since barely the smallest vestige of historical evidence has ever been alleged in support of the views of these accomplished editors, their teaching must either be received as intuitively true, or dismissed from our consideration as precarious, and even visionary. . . .

"Dr. Hort's system, therefore, is entirely destitute of historical foundation. . . .

". . . we are compelled to repeat as emphatically as ever our strong conviction that the hypothesis to whose proof he has devoted so many laborious years, is destitute not only of historical foundation, but of all probability resulting from the internal goodness of the text which its adoption would force upon us. . . .

" 'We cannot doubt that it [Luke 23:34] comes from an extraneous source' (Hort, *Notes*, p. 68). Nor can we on our part doubt that the system which entails such consequences is hopelessly self-condemned." (Scrivener, pp. 531, 537, 542, 604; see herein, pp. 79, 117, 125, 255, 297, 316.)

NOTE THIRTY-THREE ·
Revised Standard Version (American), Published February, 1946

Item 1. *Character of the New Revised Standard Version.*

Summary. This Version is, in matters of prime importance, substantially the same as the American Standard Version, which is substantially the Revised Version of Great Britain with its eliminations, additions, changes, and doubt-raising comments touching the Messiahship of Jesus. The language of the Version has apparently been modernized. These *Notes* are concerned only with the New Testament text. The Extreme Textualist attitude and philosophy were of predominant influence in the preparation of the printed text. It has been affirmed that "orthodox scholars were not permitted to review the book before it was released to the public." An account is given of and comments made on the pamphlet issued by the Revisers under the title, *An Introduction to the Revised Standard Version of the New Testament.* The character of the approach to the public by the Revisers through their *Introduction* is noted. As in the earlier Revisions (British and American), inconsequential matters are emphasized in the explanations of the Revisers; important matters are either not mentioned or glossed over. Noted are the seeming motives and mechanics of the Revisers.

Looking at this new translation of the Bible, the Revised Standard Version (RSV), after just having finished an examination of the Revised Version (RV), with its various eliminations and doubt-raising comments on vital passages bearing on the Messiahship of Jesus, the author must say that the Revised Standard Version is just more of the same thing, and even worse. For aside from the deliberate destruction of the classic elegance of the King James Version (the most glorious in English literature) and the substitution therefor of a modern English of indifferent literary value, this new Version has taken the doubts raised by the Revised Versions about certain vital passages in the King James Version (Authorized Version) and has boldly adopted these doubts, has discarded the Authorized Version readings in these cases, and has made the doubts the actual texts. The Extreme Textualist translators of the new Revised Standard Version (for on their work they must so be designated) seem still to be driving along lines that will destroy Jesus as the Christ; lines that seem even anti-Christ.

It has been affirmed (on what authority we cannot vouch, but the memorandum hand-out seen is credited to "The New Bible," an article in *The National Revivalist*, Charles Orville Benham, editor, January, 1953) that "orthodox scholars were not permitted to review the book before it was released to the public." This would seem to be the same principle of procedure that was followed by the British Revisers of the 1880's, where apparently little or no opportunity was given for an adequate presentation of the minority views of the translating committee, nor was there any opportunity (it would seem) for examination by others than committee members. (*Note Twenty-seven*, pp. 265 ff.)

Possibly this suggests the depth of the Revisers' apprehensions that the new translation will no more meet with popular approval than did the earlier Revised Version (British and American) which it is reported did not receive general adoption. (See *infra*, p. 355.)

THE REVISERS' "INTRODUCTION" PAMPHLET

The translators of the Revised Standard Version issued a pamphlet entitled, *An Introduction to the*

Revised Standard Version of the New Testament, in which they discuss various phases of their work in connection with their new translation.

As the author begins a very brief summary examination of a few passages of this new translation, he cannot too strongly urge upon the reader an appreciation of the following facts and considerations:

It must never be out of mind that the comments hereinafter quoted from the *Introduction* are explanations and arguments by the translators themselves (Extreme Textualists) who, by more or less plausible discussions that frequently involve primarily inconsequential matters, tend to build up, deliberately or otherwise, a confidence in their work that, having been established as to small, immaterial matters, will carry over into alterations that are fundamental. None of the writers of the chapters of the *Introduction* have elaborated discussions upon such vital matters as their tampering with the Lord's Prayer, the prayer on the cross, the account of the institution of the Sacrament, the omission of the last twelve verses of the Gospel of Mark, with the practical elimination of miracles through the substitution of the word *sign* for the word *miracle,* with the doubt they raise on the virgin birth of Jesus, nor with many other matters of the utmost importance. As will be pointed out later, a reader will look in vain through their whole *Introduction* for any ringing statement that Jesus is the Christ, or that will reiterate Peter's great testimony to the Temple hierarchy in Jerusalem.

The Revised Standard Version has followed the Revised Versions in what some will regard as an anti-Christ attitude.

Readers must not be misled by the elaborate arguments touching the changing of pronouns, of prepositions (though some of these are important), of particles, and what not. These are not of the essence, and it is the essentials that must be looked to. In many essential matters the readings of the Revised Standard Version cannot be accepted by true Christians, as against the Authorized Version, irrespective of the readings of certain manuscripts favored by the Revisers.

THE LANGUAGE OF THE NEW REVISION

A careful reading of this *Introduction* seems to justify the statement that the translators of the Revised Standard Version have sought, by two devices, for popular recognition for their own work:

First, they have cast reflections upon the Revised Version by reiterating, time and again, that it is stiff and stilted in its expressions, is too literal, is a word-for-word translation of the Greek (construing instead of translating), and has failed to use the English idioms in its text. This criticism is belabored again and again by various of the authors of the essays in the *Introduction*.

Next, they have condemned the King James Version (Authorized Version) by declaring it is archaic, ancient in its text, is filled with obsolete words, often uses bad grammar, and, *mirable dictu*, it was translated in an English of too much beauty and elegance, in an English too majestic and divine-like for the writings of New Testament times. So they announce the purpose of getting rid of this magnificent over-plusage and of putting the sacred writings into translations of the language of the street of the first century. They seem to have fairly succeeded. Certainly all too frequently they have polluted or destroyed the glorious literature that belongs to the King James Version (Authorized Version) of the New Testament.

As Professor Goodspeed puts it:

"The New Testament then calls for a direct, familiar style in translation; an elaborate, elegant style is unsuited to it, and in proportion as it is rendered in a conscious literary style, it is misrepresented to the modern reader." (Edgar J. Goodspeed, "The Making of the New Testament: Greek and Roman Factors," *An Introduction*, p. 33; see herein, pp. 378, 381.)

Could any language be too great, too elegant, too beautiful, too majestic, too divine-like to record the doings and sayings of Jesus of Nazareth, the Christ?

Speaking of the Antiochian center and the (asserted but unproved) revisions there made in the texts, Kenyon says:

". . . the principle may have been established by general consent that the best way to deal with divergences of readings was to combine them, wherever possible, to smooth away difficulties and harshnesses, and to produce an even and harmonious text." (Kenyon, *Our Bible*, p. 115; see p. 78, herein.)

May readers not be the victims of another Antiochian Revision era (if there ever was the first one) invoking and using the old devices.

Rev. Bowie of Grace Church, New York, gives away the case of the Revisers (Extreme Textualists), when he says, after quoting the hope that Dr. Philip Schaff expressed that the earlier Revised Versions would be generally adopted:

"But as a matter of fact that Revision was not generally adopted. The 'venerable English version,' the King James Bible, which is now more than three hundred years old, has still continued to hold its place upon the lecterns of the majority of the churches." (Walter Russell Bowie, "The Use of the New Testament in Worship," *An Introduction*, p. 61; see Testimony of Bishop G. Bromley Oxnam, *Hearing Before the Committee on*

Un-American Activities, House of Representatives, Eighty-third Congress, First Session, July 21, 1953; see also p. 379, herein.)

So, since the Revised Version did not supplant the King James Version, the Extreme Textualists seem to be making another try. If this does not succeed, and we think it will not, they will probably some day try again. But the true Christian will detect the heresies in this new translation, the Revised Standard Version, as he did in the Revised Version. He will detect them in the next like translation when that comes.

Item 2.   Organization for the Revised Standard Version Project.

Summary. Rules ("vote") under which the Revisers worked. Manner of working.

In 1928 the International Council of Religious Education (in which were associated the educational boards of forty of the major Protestant Churches of the United States and Canada) appointed an American Standard Bible Committee, "to have charge of the text" (the copyright to the American Standard Version having been acquired in 1928) with an authorization "to undertake further revision if deemed necessary." The "charter" of the Committee stipulated that "all changes in the text shall be agreed upon by a two-thirds vote of the total membership of the Committee." (Luther A. Weigle, "The Revision of the English Bible," *An Introduction*, p. 10.)

The Committee began its work in 1930; it interrupted its work in 1932 for lack of funds; it resumed its work in 1937; the translation was finished and revised in the mid-1940's; the title page of the edition in hand of the complete Bible, bears the date, 1952. The title page of the edition of the New Testament in hand bears date of 1946.

The Committee prosecuted its work under the following "vote" of the International Council of Religious Education:

"There is need for a version which embodies the best results of modern scholarship as to the meaning of the Scriptures, and expresses this meaning in English diction which is designed for use in public and private worship and preserves those qualities which have given to the King James Version a supreme place in English literature. We, therefore, define the task of the American Standard Bible Committee to be that of revision of the present American Standard Bible in the light of the results of modern scholarship, this revision to be designed for use in public and private worship, and to be in the direction of the simple, classic English style of the King James Version." (Weigle, *An Introduction*, p. 11.)

Perhaps further narration of the Committee's work might appropriately be preceded by carefully noting the opening statement of the opening sentence above quoted. The contemplated new Version is *to embody "the best results of modern scholarship as to the meaning of the Scriptures."* "Modern scholarship," not inspiration, not revelation, not the guidance of the Holy Ghost (which the Christ declared the Father would send in Christ's name to teach the disciples all things, and bring all things to their remembrance which he had taught them), not these spiritual endowments, but *scholarship* was to teach "the meaning of the Scriptures." From such a beginning we may wander anywhere, and we do, here and there, wander far afield.

As already indicated, this aim and purpose as to the character of the text, to be in "classic English style of the King James Version" has yet to be realized.

For its work, the Committee was divided into two

sections: the one for the work on the New Testament (which was finished first), and the other for work on the Old Testament (the work on which apparently took some four years longer).

An Advisory Board, made up of representatives of the various denominations affiliated with the International Council of Religious Education, gave advice on occasion when consulted. (*An Introduction*, p. 13.)

Dean Luther A. Weigle (former head of the Yale University Divinity School), outlines the procedure followed in the work of the Committee, but a statement thereon is unnecessary here. (Weigle, *An Introduction*, p. 14; see Testimony of Bishop G. Bromley Oxnam, *Hearing Before the Committee on Un-American Activities, House of Representatives, Eighty-third Congress, First Session, July 21, 1953;* see also the "hand-out," "The New Bible," by the *National Revivalist*, January, 1953, hereinbefore cited.)

Item 3.   Reasons Assigned for Revision—Imperfections of the Revised Version.

Summary. Reasons assigned for the Revision—imperfections of the Revised Version, as explained by these Revisers. Character of the Greek in which the manuscripts were written,—a low grade Greek, and must be translated into casual, popular English.

Since the observations of the Revisers of the Revised Standard Version, as printed in the *Introduction*, constitute the latest statements and arguments of the Extreme Textualists (so far as the author has observed) he has quoted extensively, and sometimes repetitiously, from them, so that their attitude and concepts might be fully understood. It will be seen that they do not contain anything that should give just concern to the true Christian who has an abiding testimony of the truthfulness of the Restored Gospel.

The reasons for undertaking the revision of the English text of the Revisions of the 1880's, and the American Standard Version of 1901, are given by Dr. Weigle as follows:

"1. The English Revised Version of 1881 and its variant, the American Standard Version of 1901, lost some of the beauty and force which made the King James Version a classic example of English literature. They are mechanically exact, literal, word-for-word translations, which follow the order of the Greek words, so far as this is possible, rather than the order which is natural to English. Charles H. Spurgeon, the English preacher of the closing nineteenth century, put it tersely when he remarked that the Revised New Testament was 'strong in Greek, weak in English.' 'The Revisers in their scrupulous and conscientious desire to be perfectly true to the Greek have . . . been too unmindful of the claims of their own language,' was the comment of Dean Perowne. 'They have sometimes been too literal, construing instead of translating; they have inverted the natural order of words in English in order to follow the Greek; and they have carried the translation of the article, and of the tenses, beyond their legitimate limits.' A well-balanced and generally favorable article in the *Edinburgh Review* for July, 1881, concluded by saying: 'The revisers were not appointed to prepare an interlinear translation for incompetent school-boys.' These criticisms, which were made when the English Revised Version was published, apply as well to the American Standard Version. These versions convey the meaning of the Scriptures more accurately than the King James Version, but they have lost much of its beauty and power.

"2. Scholars are better equipped today than they were sixty years ago, both to determine the original text of the Greek New Testament, and to understand its language. This is partly because of the evidence afforded by newly discovered manuscripts of the New Testament itself, but chiefly because of the amazing body of Greek papyri that has been unearthed in Egypt since the last decade of the nineteenth century—private letters, official reports, wills, business accounts, petitions and other such trivial, everyday recordings of the on-going activities of human beings. In 1895 appeared the first of Adolf Deissmann's studies of these

commonplace materials. He proved that many words which
had hitherto been assumed to belong to what used to be called
'Biblical Greek' were current in the spoken vernacular of the
first century A.D. His discoveries revolutionized the study of
New Testament Greek. The New Testament, we now know,
was written in the *Koine,* the Common Greek which was spoken
and understood practically everywhere throughout the Roman
Empire in the early centuries of the Christian era. It was a
language without serious differences of dialect; and it covered
a larger proportion of the civilized world than English does
today. This development in the study of New Testament Greek
has come since the work on the English Revised Version and
the American Standard Version was done. The revisers were
unaware of what was so soon to be learned. The fact that we
today bring to the interpretation of New Testament Greek a
whole new body of resources developed within the past sixty
years, makes a revision of the English version of the New Testament imperative.

"3. In the Bible we have not merely an historical document
and a classic of English literature, but the Word of God. And
the Bible carries its full message, not to those who regard it
simply as a heritage of the past or praise its literary style, but
to those who read it that they may discern and understand God's
Word to men. That Word must not be hidden in ancient phrases
which have changed or lost their meaning; it must stand forth
in language that is direct and clear and meaningful to the people
of today." (Weigle, *An Introduction,* pp. 11-13.)

All of this goes primarily to the matter of literary
style, which varies as to time and somewhat as to place;
it varies as to individuals and peoples. The Bible is a
record of God's dealings with his children and of his
instructions, his commandments to them. The Bible is
read for the purpose of obtaining knowledge of these.
The divine words of the Father and his Son should be
couched in language that will awaken in the reader the
loftiest feelings and aspirations. It is for study and
reflection. It is not for reading as an after-dinner seda-
tive. Principles and doctrines are superior to style and
cannot be sacrificed for it. It will be noted that this

whole apology relates to the language, there is no word about changes of substance in the text, great and important changes, such as were noted in *Note Thirty-two*. There is no word here in explanation of these; no word of the great messages,—just the presumed making-easy the reading.

Yet above and beyond all else we must never forget that Jesus is the Christ, the Redeemer of the World, the First Fruits of the Resurrection, the Savior of Mankind, the only "name under heaven given among men, whereby we must be saved." Remember the ancient anthem of the Revelator: "In the beginning was the Word, and the Word was with God, and the Word was God. The same was in the beginning with God. . . . In him was life; and the life was the light of men."

However, the iniquity of the Extreme Textualists in their translations does not consist in altering the English translation of occasional Greek words. The iniquity consists in omitting whole vital passages, not because of the different meanings of a few words, but because the Greek manuscript which they chose to adopt as controlling as against other manuscripts equally good, had textual changes, or omissions, which appealed to these Revisers as desirable. It seems clear that the papyri records had little or nothing whatever to do with this, because the most important alterations were made in the British and American Revised Versions which were prepared before the papyri were discovered, and these alterations are retained here in the Revised Standard Version.

Item 4. Source Materials Used for New Testament Text Revision.

Summary. Source materials used for New Testament text revision are noted. The reliance of Revisers on Kenyon's work is noted, as likewise the reliance placed upon Kenyon's family classification of manuscripts.

Something more must be said about the source materials—the manuscripts and other documents—upon which these Revisers rely for the Revised Standard Version New Testament Text,—The New Covenant.

Relying upon Sir Frederic Kenyon's works (who seems to be their tutor in these matters), the Revisers affirm through a chapter by Dr. Frederick C. Grant (President, Seabury-Western Theological Seminary), that:

". . . all existing manuscripts of the New Testament go back to ancestors that belonged to one or another of these groups. . . .

"(1) Western, represented by Codex Bezae and the Old Latin version.

"(2) Caesarean, represented by the Koridethi Gospels, etc.

"(3) Alexandrian, represented by Codex Sinaiticus, Codex Vaticanus, and the Coptic version.

"(4) Syriac, represented by the Old Syriac version.

"(5) Other, i. e., a classification for readings that do not fall into any of the preceding groups. . . ." (Grant, *An Introduction*, p. 39.)

The author must in fairness point out that the foregoing classification does not seem to carry the true picture as given by Kenyon in all his works.

This classification seems to be based upon Kenyon's work *The Story of the Bible* (p. 131), the latest reprint available to the author bearing date of September, 1949.

The list as appearing in *The Story* has the following order: (1) the Alexandrian; (2) the Western; (3) the Syriac; (4) the Caesarean; and (5) the residue.

Since *The Story of the Bible* is "A Popular Account of How it Came to Us" (title page), the order of listing is of no real importance.

However, Kenyon before making his list, affirms: "We now seem to find our pre-Byzantine authorities falling into at least five categories." Then follows the listing in the order just quoted. Dr. Grant makes no mention of this restriction on the period covered by the listings.

In this connection the author is reminded that Dr. Kenyon has also said, after calling attention to the Chester Beatty manuscripts:

"What is significant is that they prove that in Egypt in the early part of the third century [i. e. 200 A.D., or say 150 years before the writing of Sinaiticus and Vaticanus] readings were in circulation which were derived from, or which eventually became attached to, all the principal families, together with a not inconsiderable number of which no other witness has survived." (Kenyon, *The Text*, new ed. 1949, p. 250.)

As will be seen in *Note Nineteen, supra,* the Byzantine text (Textus Receptus) appears along with the earliest texts, so the statement of Kenyon that his classification is of the pre-Byzantine manuscripts might be misleading. (*The Story*, p. 131.)

Kenyon in his seemingly better considered, not "popular" writings, makes the following classification under the heading, "The classification now suggested is as follows," (α) the *Byzantine*, the "Received Text"; (β) the *Alexandrian*, substantially identical with Hort's "Neutral"; (γ) the *Caesarean;* (δ) the *Western;* (ε) the *Syriac;* and then a mass of seemingly unassigned manuscripts. (*Our Bible*, 1948 reprint, pp. 177 ff.)

Kenyon introduces in *The Text of the Greek Bible, A Students Handbook,* his somewhat detailed discussion of the same classification with these words:

"It is proposed therefore to deal with them [the several families] under the first letters of the Greek alphabet: (α) the Received Text, of which one of the earliest representatives (in the Gospels) is Codex A; (β) the text which Hort calls Neutral,

headed by Codex B; (γ) the Cæsarean text; (δ) the Western
text headed by Codex D; (ε) the Syrian text; (ζ) such residue
as may be found to be left over." (*The Text*, p. 197.)

It would be observed that in the classifications given
by Kenyon other than in *The Story*, the Byzantine text
heads the list. Therefore, the going forward by Dr.
Grant in his discussion as if the Byzantine text were
either non-existent or disqualified from consideration
does not seem to be justified on the record.

Dr. Grant continues:

"If Kenyon's conclusion is correct—and it is shared by many
other experts—the situation is completely changed from that
in 1881. Instead of tracing back the text to its original in the
autographs by a steady process of convergence following back
to a common source the divergent lines of descent, we shall have
to stop when we get to the second century; and in place of some
rule of preference for one type of text over another, or for their
common agreements over their divergences, we shall have to
trust a great deal more than heretofore to what is called internal
criticism. In fact, this is about the point at which we had arrived
anyway: the style of a New Testament author, for example,
counts for a great deal more in textual criticism at the present
time than it did in the nineteenth century; and Matthew, Luke,
and perhaps even John, are pretty good early witnesses to the
text of Mark, for example; and so on. But now, with Kenyon's
conclusions before us, it is more obvious than ever where our
chief problems lie. 'In the first two centuries this original text
disappeared under a mass of variants, created by errors, by
conscious alterations, and by attempts to remedy the uncertainties thus created. Then, as further attempts to recover the lost
truth were made, the families of text that we now know took
shape. They were, however, nuclei rather than completed forms
of text, and did not at once absorb all the atoms that the period
of disorder had brought into existence.' (*The Text of the
Greek Bible*, p. 242.)" (Grant, *An Introduction*, p. 40; see
p. 210, herein; and for Burgon's comment on the classification
of texts, see *supra*, p. 192.)

This seems a complete abandonment of the Westcott-
Hort theory that there was one original text from which

all others are descended, and the search then was for that original text. The condition described in the last sentence of the foregoing quotation, seems to admit the existence of the situation out of which the Extreme Textualists affirmed the Byzantine text grew and which they unsparingly condemned. This seems to be a square about-face.

Item 5. *Canons of Criticism—Adoption of Westcott-Hort's Greek Text.*

Summary. Rules to be followed in making choice of texts are given, but seemingly the final result was the adoption of texts supporting א and B. Summary observations made on present position of Extreme Textualists, as set out by Kenyon.

After briefly stating the evolutionary development of "canons of criticism" from Gerhard of Maastricht with his forty-three canons, through Griesbach with his reduction to fifteen, with Bengel to one ("let the harder reading prevail"), through Wordsworth and White, who reduced them to two ("the shorter reading is the more probable one," and "the true reading wins out in the end"), and after noting that the "shorter reading" led to Westcott and Hort's preference for the Codex Vaticanus, Dr. Grant states:

"We may venture to state the general situation at present, and the new rules now in force, somewhat as follows:

"1. No one type of text is infallible, or to be preferred by virtue of its generally superior authority.

"2. Each reading must be examined on its merits, and preference must be given to those readings which are demonstrably in the style of the author under consideration.

"3. Readings which explain other variants, but are not contrariwise themselves to be explained by the others, merit our preference; but this is a very subtle process, involving intangible elements, and liable to subjective judgment on the part of the critic.

"With the best will in the world, the New Testament translator or reviser of today is forced to adopt the eclectic principle: each variant reading must be studied on its merits, and cannot be adopted or rejected by some rule of thumb, or by adherence to such a theory as that of the 'Neutral Text.' It is this eclectic principle that has guided us in the present Revision. The Greek text of this Revision is not that of Westcott-Hort, or Nestle, or Souter; though the readings we have adopted will, as a rule, be found either in the text or the margin of the new (17th) edition of Nestle (Stuttgart, 1941)." (*An Introduction*, pp. 41-42; manuscripts principally followed by Westcott and Hort, א and B.)

Dr. Grant continues:

"It was a part of our commission to take into account the progress of modern Biblical research. This most certainly includes textual research or criticism. We have endeavored to discharge this part of our commission as faithfully as we could. And it is really extraordinary how often, with the fuller apparatus of variant readings at our disposal, and with the eclectic principle now more widely accepted, we have concurred in following Westcott and Hort. Not that we agreed in advance in favor of Hort—quite the contrary, there was no such unanimity; our agreement is really a tribute to Westcott-Hort, which is still the great classical edition of modern times. I find that we have adopted only one conjectural emendation (in Jude 5, 'he who . . .'), and this is one that Hort discussed in his notes, and favored. We have made considerable use of the Chester Beatty fragments; in fact we have consulted them constantly, and have occasionally adopted readings from that source, when supported by others. Usually, the Beatty fragments range themselves with Aleph and B, i.e., Sinaiticus and Vaticanus.

"If anyone will take the trouble to go through the footnotes to the new Revision, and list the chief authorities for the reading in the text and for the alternatives cited in the margin, noting especially the passages where we differ from the American Standard Version, he will find that we have followed B-Aleph-Chester Beatty (or some one or two of them) in the following important passages:

"Matthew 3.16; 9.14; 12.47; 17.22. Mark 1.1; 7.4; 8.15; 10.24; 15.44; 16.9-20. Luke 2.14; 4.44; 5.17; 12.39; 15.16; 22.16; 23.38. John 3.13; 5.2; 7.53-8.11; 8.16; 8.57; 9.35. Acts

11.20; 18.7; 19.39. Romans 4.1; 5.1; 5.2; 8.28. 1 Corinthians 1.4; 1.14. 2 Corinthians 3.2. Ephesians 1.1. 2 Thessalonians 2.3. Hebrews 3.2; 3.6; 6.2; 6.3; 9.11. 1 Peter 4.1; 5.2. 2 Peter 1.21. 1 John 2.10. 2 John 8. Revelation 21.3; 22.14." (Grant, *An Introduction,* pp. 41-42.)

The following observations by Professor Cadbury (Harvard University) dealing with the problem and difficulties of translating, are worth noting at this point:

"Although the language of the Greek New Testament has been studied as long and as intensively as that of any body of writings, the resulting knowledge in any generation cannot be regarded as final. The translators of 1611 and 1881 included excellent scholars in this field and their judgments are usually only confirmed by later discovery and by re-examination, yet some additions to their knowledge have been made. These have been taken into account in the present translation.

"It would be a mistake to exaggerate the extent to which such revised judgments of the language can be actually recorded in translation. Improved knowledge of the original is often mainly a matter of slight nuances, of the suggestions that the original phrases hold for one familiar with them, rather than such as to necessitate one English rendering instead of another.

"For example, it is possible now to recognize that the Greek of the New Testament is not uniform. Some authors write a more vernacular style than others, some a more Semitic style, some a more formal style. Even within a single author's work— especially in the two most extensive contributions to the New Testament, Luke-Acts and the letters of Paul—there are differences of style, of tone and of vocabulary. The translator into English can scarcely reproduce these differences by exact equivalents. The variation of style between Thessalonians and Ephesians, between the first chapters of Luke and the last half of Acts, and even between Luke and the parallels in Mark, so far as it involves not merely different vocabulary but differences of cultural quality, could only by a thankless and strained effort be paralleled in English." (Henry J. Cadbury, "The Vocabulary and Grammar of New Testament Greek," *An Introduction,* p. 44; see Scrivener's comments on style, herein pp. 344-345, Scrivener, pp. 588-590.)

Thus it appears that the Extreme Textualists are

aware that they have not the perfect text, that other changes may be necessary. So they proceed to build a new text in exactly the same way that they affirm the Byzantine text was built, which they unmercifully condemn. We need not, therefore, be too much disturbed as to the importance, as against the King James Version, of the changes they have thus far made, perhaps even where those changes cast doubts upon or detract from the divinity of Christ. But certainly we seem not to be under compulsion to regard too seriously matters of English style, particularly where the records are in the Greek vernacular. More learning may cause still further changes.

So in summary we may say: In the first place, it is clear that the great uncials which were basic to the translations of the 1880's and 1901 have lost something, indeed, it seems much, of their favored position in the critical world, though apparently the Extreme Textualists are still following the conclusions of Westcott and Hort as to the value of the two oldest discovered uncials —א and B (see *supra* p. 196). For these, א B, seem still to dominate the field. Notwithstanding this, they point out that the original autographs had disappeared before the end of the second century and that there was widespread corruption in the texts that came after. They admit they do not know whether texts from which א and B were copied, were the purest and best texts that survived the period of corruption, and that they do not know that some of the later uncials and cursives may not be copies of purer texts than the present texts of א and B. As a matter of mere logic and ordinary reason, mere yearly age, in that period, under the circumstances then existing, is a weak premise upon which to base primacy.

In the next place, the Greek New Testament text prepared by Westcott and Hort has lost the place of primacy it held in the 1880's and 1901 translations, though still highly regarded by the Extreme Textualists. Yet the estimates of Scrivener, Burgon, and the rest, regarding the insufficiency of that text (as hereinabove set out) have not been destroyed for anybody except Extreme Textualists, and they seem to be yielding ground.

Attention must again be called to the fact that all the foregoing quoted discussions and observations in the present *Note* are a presentation of the case of the Extreme Textualists.

Perhaps we may quote here—though in part repetitious—a further statement from Dr. Grant, who after calling attention to the length of time the Westcott and Hort text has held the field, adds:

"Their theory of the 'neutral' text has gradually been abandoned even though the manuscripts which they included in that classification are still recognized as of great importance, chiefly Sinaiticus and Vaticanus. There has been a growing recognition among scholars of the importance of the so-called 'Western' text. It contains some good readings, and moreover (as Westcott and Hort themselves recognized) it does not include some of the interpolations that got into all other types of text—most of which are found at the end of the Gospel of Luke." (Grant, *An Introduction,* pp. 39-40.)

Just a word about "interpolations":—hints and comments have been used by Westcott and Hort and their supporters that it might be assumed that these readings of which they complain as *late,* and brought in from one place and another, were in fact pure inventions of some scribe or his principals (whoever they were). But no word has been seen by the author that would certainly exclude or even negative the possibility that they came in from some now unknown manuscript which could have well been as old, indeed older, than manuscripts in which they are now found, and in which they are regarded as depravations.

Item 6. New Source Material Available to Revised Standard Version Translators.

Summary. List of materials made available since the American Standard Version. However, the vital changes made in the Authorized Version and retained here, were seemingly based on א and B.

Since the sources of the 1880's and 1901 translations have thus been subordinated and indeed placed in doubt as to their prime sufficiency, we may here again set out briefly the new source materials that have been brought into use. (See *Note Fourteen* above, for fuller description.) We should keep in mind that the new source materials (the papyri) seem to play little, if any, part in supporting the vital changes in the Revised Version and Revised Standard Version made by the Extreme Textualists. These vital changes seem based upon the great uncials א and B and a very few other favored and concurring manuscripts.

Dr. Grant, in his chapter in the *Introduction*, "The Greek Text of the New Testament," (already quoted from) makes the following observations on this matter. It will be noted that basic to all comments and arguments of the Extreme Textualists is the premise that the original Sacred Autographs were in Greek. (See *Note Six* above.)

Dr. Grant says:

"A mere list of the more important manuscripts and fragments made available to scholars since the last revision is imposing.

"One of the most important discoveries has been a manuscript of the Old Syriac version of the Gospels, found in the monastery of St. Catherine on Mt. Sinai by Mrs. Lewis and Mrs. Gibson in 1892. The text of this version is older than the Curetonian Syriac, and probably dates from the second century. Thus it testifies to the state of the Greek text from which it was translated, perhaps around 150 A.D.

"Related to this is the remarkable discovery of a fragment of Tatian's *Diatessaron* in Greek, found at Dura on the Euphrates by the Yale Expedition in 1933, and edited by Professor Carl Kraeling.

"Another important discovery was the 'Washington' manuscript, purchased at Cairo in 1906 by Mr. Charles Freer of Detroit. It contains a mixed text; i.e., some parts were copied from one type of manuscript, others from other types.

"Even more important was the discovery in 1931 of fragments of twelve manuscripts (eight Old Testament, three New Testament, and one containing part of Enoch), and their purchase by Mr. A. Chester Beatty, an American living in England. These fragments are of extraordinary importance, as the leading experts agree that they were copied for the most part in the third century—a hundred years, presumably, before Vaticanus and Sinaiticus! The Gospels and Acts probably come from the first half of the third century; the fragments of the Pauline letters are certainly not later than 250 A. D.—which is almost unbelievably early, compared with the 'great uncials' upon which Westcott and Hort, and the earlier revisers, had to rely.

"These were not the only discoveries, of course; scores of papyrus fragments, and even some vellum codices have continued to turn up. The famous ninth-century Koridethi Gospels were edited by Beermann and Gregory in 1913. Recent American editions include *The Rockefeller McCormick New Testament* (13th century), *The Four Gospels of Karahissar* (13th century), and *The Elizabeth Day McCormick Apocalypse* (17th century). Even these late Byzantine manuscripts are not to be overlooked; once in a while they are of real importance in establishing the earlier text.

"In addition to the discovery and publication of Greek and Syriac manuscripts, considerable attention has been given to other versions, such as the Sahidic, Armenian, and above all the Latin, especially the Old Latin, perhaps contemporaneous with the Old Syriac, i.e., around 150 A.D. The result has been a quantity of fresh discoveries and new publications including better editions of manuscripts and versions already known.

"All this new material for textual criticism has to be evaluated and assimilated by New Testament scholars. Its influence upon both the editing and the translating of the New Testament is apparent in all the standard editions of its text since 1881, and in many of the newer translations. And it simply demanded a fresh revision of the Revised Version." (Grant, *An Introduction*, pp. 37-38.)

Dr. Grant had previously observed that the Revisers had made use of the Greek texts, in addition to Westcott and Hort, of Nestle and Souter. (*Supra*, p. 366.)

Again it must be pointed out that the critical changes made by the Extreme Textualists in the Revised Standard Version were made in the Revised Version before this newest material was available, indeed before it was discovered, and that the changes were founded primarily on the א and B manuscripts. None of this recently discovered material (since the publication of those earlier Revisions) was available to the Revised Version translators.

However, it will be noted that the critics still go forward, assuming as a fact the fundamental question that the Byzantine text (the Textus Receptus) is an inferior text. But that is the whole problem. Dr. Grant's condescending observation that late Byzantine texts "are not to be overlooked; once in a while they are of real importance in establishing the earlier text," is just a bit patronizing and gratuitous. The Extreme Textualists have already eaten some humble pie. They will probably eat more.

Item 7.   Use of Source Materials.

Summary. Use of source materials, as explained by Revisers.

Dr. Grant continues:

"Now the problem arises, how to make use of these new manuscripts and new editions. Therein lies the whole point of the science of textual criticism. It may be thought that a simple rule would be to count those manuscripts which favor a particular reading; then count up the manuscripts on the other side; or if there are three readings which are competing for recognition, then count up the supporters of all three and choose the reading that has the strongest support in numbers. But such a method would never do, for the reason that the largest number of manuscripts are of a late date; the early manuscripts are more rare.

"So then another method must be devised. Perhaps this would be to 'weight' the manuscripts and give a fifth-century manuscript twice the value of a sixth-century, etc. But the trouble with this scheme is that sometimes a later manuscript turns out to have been copied from a manuscript considerably earlier in date than its immediate rival; in the case just mentioned, the sixth-century manuscript may happen to be copied from a third-century one while the fifth-century manuscript may have been copied from another which was almost contemporary.

"Hence some better system must be devised for evaluating manuscripts; and when the manuscripts have been evaluated some principles must be set up by which the original text of the autographs may be approximated as closely as possible. This is an indispensable procedure, since we do not possess a single autograph of a New Testament document. As in the case of all other ancient books we have only copies of copies. Our oldest fragment of a New Testament book, the tiny little scrap of papyrus giving a few words from the Gospel of John, is not earlier than a little before 150 A.D. That fragment is now in the John Rylands Library at the University of Manchester in England.

"As a result of approximately two hundred and fifty years of modern textual criticism, scholars have come to the conclusion that there existed at the end of the second century five main types of text, that is, all existing manuscripts of the New Testament go back to ancestors that belonged to one or another of these groups." (Grant, *An Introduction*, pp. 38-39, see, *supra*, p. 362.)

It is amusing to note how quickly and unceremoniously Dr. Grant gets rid of the hundreds of Byzantine manuscripts as against the half dozen upon which he and the other Extreme Textualists rely. You must not look to the number of witnesses, he says.

The argument of Dr. Grant that as a matter of fact one of the later manuscripts might be a copy of an earlier manuscript than was the source of an existing earlier manuscript in calendar years seems completely to destroy the age or antiquity argument, upon which the earlier Revisers so fully relied. One should know the master copy of any existing manuscript before giving it a primacy or before casting it aside.

It might be noted here that as to the teachings of Christ as contained in the New Testament, Dr. Goodspeed apparently finds in the Apocrypha, the inspiration for such teachings. He says: "The familiar New Testament groups, scribes and Pharisees, saints and sinners, demons and angels, are not introduced to us in the Old Testament but in the Apocrypha." This surely debases the New Testament record and the status of Jesus. He also comments: "There is even reason to believe that Wisdom 9.1,2 strongly influenced the theology of John." (Goodspeed, *An Introduction*, p. 31.)

The passages referred to by Dr. Goodspeed read, in the Douay translation, as follows:

"God of my fathers, and Lord of mercy, who hast made all things with thy word,

"And by thy wisdom hast appointed man, that he should have dominion over the creature that was made by thee."

These concepts certainly do not enhance the concept of Jesus as the Christ. It may not have been intended that they should.

Item 8. Possible Aramaic Original Text.

Summary. A possible Aramaic original text as against a Greek original text is referred to, with the explanations thereon of one of the translators. Comments thereon.

As bearing upon this whole question of source material, we may note that Professor Millar Burrows, of Yale University, writes a chapter under the heading, "The Semitic Background of the New Testament." Professor Burrows embraces in the word *Semitic*, as used by him, both the Hebrew and the Aramaic languages. Speaking of the Jewish nation in Palestine, he says:

"Their whole cultural and spiritual heritage, for all the Persian and Greek elements it had assimilated, was basically Semitic. Both the form and the content of the New Testament can be understood only in the light of these facts." (Burrows, *An Introduction,* p. 22; see pp. 62-63, *supra.*)

Comments have already been made (*Note Six*) on the possibility that the Syriac is possibly the oldest text of the New Testament that we have, and that (in its original) it could be either a copy or an actual "Sacred Autograph." As bearing upon this possibility, the following comment by Burrows is interesting.

"Since the gospel was first proclaimed in Aramaic, it is not surprising that the recorded words of Jesus and the apostles retain even in translation much that is characteristic of the original Semitic sentence structure and idiom. Whether there was any direct translation of written Aramaic sources, in addition to the preservation of Semitic ways of speaking through tradition and oral translation, is a question on which the members of our Committee do not agree. It is also, however, a question which was never debated in the Committee, because the basic assumption that our responsibility was to translate the Greek text made such considerations irrelevant." (Burrows, *An Introduction,* pp. 27-28; see also *id.,* pp. 46 ff. for Professor Cadbury's comments.)

This stated reason for eliminating the consideration of the possibility of an Aramaic-written source as a foundation for our Greek text, is not too persuasive. In this connection the fact may be noted that no limits, as to the use by the Revisers of outside sources, appear to have been observed where the Revisers are seeking to justify a change they desire to make in the Authorized Version text, particularly where the change is calculated to cast doubt or destroy Jesus as the Christ. It is old wisdom that it is a poor rule that will not work both ways. If confirmatory material (wherever found) is used to break down Jesus, why not use confirmatory evidence (wherever found) to build him up?

Some scholars affirm that the Old Syriac text, which is nearly two centuries older than any Greek manuscript so far discovered, "resembles" and "support(s)" the Received Text (that is, the Greek original of the Authorized Version). It is not to be wondered at under these circumstances that the Extreme Textualists manifest no desire to seek to establish an early Aramaic text, and, on the other hand, invent reasons why possible Aramaic sources should not be searched for.

A complaint regarding this latest Revision, has been read affirming:

"Deception and deceit marked the various steps of the high-pressure promotional program that preceded the appearance of the New Bible. *Orthodox scholars were not permitted to review the book before it was released to the public.* It was to be accepted *before* examination. Yet in no sense is this book the 'authorized' version of modern Christendom. It is 'official' only to the degree that one may attach importance to the claims made by the National Council of Churches." (Italics ours, except *before*.)

Professor Burrows discusses under his chapter heading, "The Semitic Background of the New Testament," such matters as the "transliteration of proper names," the quotations in the New Testament from passages in the Old Testament, "echoes of Semitic ways of speaking," omissions of words and phrases of "Semitic coloring," (among which is the phrase "and it came to pass," of such frequent use in modern scripture), the "de-semitization" of the text by changing such words as *heart* to *mind, seed* to *children, offspring* to *descendants.* Concluding his chapter, Professor Burrows says:

> "The New Testament does not merely have a Semitic background: its foundation is Semitic, for 'no other foundation can any one lay than that which is laid, which is Jesus Christ' and Christ was born of the lineage of David, born under the law. 'Salvation is from the Jews,' says Jesus to the Samaritan woman in John 4:22." (Burrows, *An Introduction,* pp. 23, 26, 28-30; see also *id.,* p. 52, and *Note Six, supra.*)

Item 9.   The Seeming Real Reasons for the Revised Standard Version.

Summary. The seeming real reasons for the Revised Standard Version, is stated by Goodspeed and others of the Revisers,—briefly and clumsily put, the English of the New Testament is too good, it should seemingly be on the level of the ordinary press reporter's style of today. Comments on this suggestion.

Dr. Goodspeed has fairly epitomized the motif of the entire Revision in the sentences now to be quoted. He himself has put forth a modern translation of the New Testament. After speaking of the discovery in the last few decades of Greek papyri that are said to record in the ordinary Greek of the early Christian centuries, accounts of the ordinary and commercial and social life of the peoples of the east Mediterranean coasts, the Doctor says, playing the same chord of too good literature in the Authorized Version Old Testament, which is unfitted for the New Testament:

"This discovery has put New Testament translation in a new perspective. For if it is written in plain informal style, it should be translated in such a style. Here it differs widely from the Old Testament. The prophets and Job used a high style, often imaginative and rhetorical in the extreme. Their books were for the most part poetry. The Psalter is of course poetry. The Old Testament preserves the masterpieces of Hebrew literature from over a thousand years.

"The New Testament is altogether different in literary quality. It owes almost nothing to literary artistry, and everything to the ideas it had to convey. To convey them with the utmost directness, simplicity and vigor was the chief concern of its writers. And if that was indeed the aim of its writers, it should also be that of its translators. The New Testament then calls for a direct, familiar style in translation; an elaborate, elegant style is unsuited to it, and in proportion as it is rendered in a conscious literary style, it is misrepresented to the modern reader.

"This has been the occasion of the modern speech translations of the past half-century. Their makers have sought to take from the New Testament the stiffness of the sixteenth- and seventeenth-century Bibles which really put a mask upon the diction of the New Testament, and to present it in a form much closer to that of the original New Testament. For instance, the recent American revision of the Roman Catholic New Testament (1941) has changed 'ye' to 'you' throughout the Sermon on the Mount. The result of this simple change is to add immensely to the vigor of the Sermon. It seems to speak to us so much more directly and forcibly. To that extent it speaks our language. The same version has abandoned the quaint forms of the third person, goeth, seeketh, findeth, and the like, and substituted the familiar modern forms, goes, seeks, finds. This too results in increased vigor.

"The antique second person singular pronouns 'thee' and 'thou' have come to be associated so closely with Bible diction as to be almost inseparable from it; in fact it is only in the Bible that most people ever encounter them. Yet they certainly impart to the Scriptures a stiff and archaic quality altogether foreign to the actual style of the Greek New Testament, and immediately put the modern reader at a distance. In recognition of this, modern translators for more than a hundred years past have in most places given them up, in favor of the familiar form 'you,' which everybody but the Friends now uses, except in prayer." (Goodspeed, *An Introduction*, pp. 32-33.)

Perhaps this is as good a case as can be made for the abandonment by the Revisers of the classic elegance, the "incomparable beauty" of the English of the King James Version (one of the greatest, if not the greatest, monument in all English literature), and the substitution therefor of a decrepit, commonplace English of the press and street, even though it is the best the Revisers could do.

In passing, it may be remarked that in spite of all this, the Reverend Bowie (Grace Church, New York) declares:

"The 'venerable English version,' the King James Bible, which is now more than three hundred years old, has still continued to hold its place upon the lecterns of the majority of the churches. . . . They [worshipping congregations] have loved it because it has seemed to them incomparably beautiful." (Bowie, *An Introduction*, p. 61.)

Perhaps they love it also because they feel it more nearly expresses the great spiritual truths of Christ's Gospel than do the modern, non-literary translations.

Dr. Weigle (former Dean, Yale University Divinity School), writing under the title, "The English of the Revised Standard Version of the New Testament," notes "the errors and archaic language of the King James Version." (Luther A. Weigle, "The English of the Revised Standard Version of the New Testament," *An Introduction*, p. 53.)

He also affirms, striking a slightly different chord from Goodspeed:

"A requirement that has constantly been kept in mind by the present Committee is that the Bible should be translated into language that is euphonious, readable, and suited for use in public and private worship. It must sound well, and be easy to read aloud and in public. The choice of words and ordering of phrases must be such as to avoid harsh collocations of sound, and consonantal juxtapositions over which tongues will trip and lisp. . . ." (Weigle, *An Introduction,* p. 57.)

He cites as an example of the application of this principle, I Cor. 7:19. *The Authorized Version* reads:

"Circumcision is nothing, and uncircumcision is nothing, but the keeping of the commandments of God."

This has been changed to read in the *Revised Standard Version*:

"For neither circumcision counts for anything nor uncircumcision, but keeping the commandments of God."

It takes a Professor Weigle to perceive that the Revised Standard Version is in this instance either more euphonious, readable, or better suited for reading in private or public, than the King James sentence. Indeed, some would say that the King James sentence is superior in all these relations, and one need not be too much of a purist to say that the two renditions have different meanings. "Is nothing" is not the equivalent of does not "count for anything" and therefore this is an interpretation, not a translation.

The purport of the foregoing comments and of many others of the same tenor in the Revisers' *Introduction,* seems clearly to come to this: We should reduce the New Testament to the dead level of an ordinary reporter's daily newspaper account of the travels, teachings, and happenings of the news of the day, and apply it to Christ's mission in Palestine. The sublime, divine truths of the Master's teachings—unequalled in the other records of the world, save the records of other divine works; the glorious visions of angelic messengers, the visits of the

Father himself; the incidents of the mighty miracles,—the walking on the water, the stilling of the storm, the feeding of the five and of the four thousands, the healings of the sick, the maimed, the deaf, the dumb, and the blind; the transfiguration on the mount, the raising of Lazarus, the Last Supper, the arrest, the trial, the crucifixion, the resurrection,—all are not worthy, the Extreme Textualists tell us, to be told in the magnificent language and poetry of the Old Testament. They say an "elaborate, elegant style" is unsuited for the account of these mighty works and teachings, "and in proportion as it is rendered in a conscious literary style, it is misrepresented to the modern reader." All this they tell us. (Goodspeed, *An Introduction*, p. 33.) The whole effect of the work of these Revisers seems to be to break down Christ, take away his divinity, make him just *man*, though an exceptional one.

How well the Christ knew all this. To the disciples on the Mount of Olives, answering their enquiry as to his second coming, he declared:

"And many false prophets shall rise, and shall deceive many.
"And because iniquity shall abound, the love of many shall wax cold." (Matt. 24:11-12; see 23, 24.)

How fully John described them when he declared:

"And every spirit that confesseth not that Jesus Christ is come in the flesh is not of God: and this is that spirit of antichrist, whereof ye have heard that it should come; and even now already is it in the world. . . .
"For many deceivers are entered into the world, who confess not that Jesus Christ is come in the flesh. This is a deceiver and an antichrist." (I John 4:3; II John 7.)

Item 10. Illustrative Text Changes.

Summary. Professor Craig lists changes allegedly necessary because of the faulty English translation in the Authorized Version, instancing I Thess. 4:15; Matt. 6:25; Mark 6:25; Luke 18:12; John 10:16.

To show some of the changes made by the Revisers in order to make the New Testament a sort of newspaper account of the teachings and works of the Christ, Professor Clarence T. Craig (Oberlin Graduate School of Theology) writes a chapter in the Revisers' *Introduction* under the title, "The King James and the American Standard Versions of the New Testament." In this chapter he notes a number of infelicities in the English of the King James Version. He affirms that the Revisers, following the principles used by Westcott and Hort, "found correction to be necessary at more than five thousand points." He quotes an early charge made against the Authorized Version, that it is "bad theology, bad scholarship, and bad English." (Clarence T. Craig, "The King James and the American Standard Versions of the New Testament," *An Introduction*, pp. 15-16.)

He first calls attention to a series of changes hardly noticed by the average reader. To note one only of these: he takes II Cor. 5:14:

"There the Received Text called for the translation, 'If one died for all, then were all dead.' But Paul did not think that there was anything hypothetical about the representative death of Christ. The apostle wrote, as the American Standard Version translates, 'One died for all.'" (Craig, *An Introduction*, p. 16.)

We think that no reader with average intelligence and the slightest knowledge of the New Testament would ever have a thought that Paul was speaking doubtfully of Christ's vicarious death. The *if* of the passage is quite obviously equivalent to *since*.

We might note that we are not quite clear as to the significance to be attached to Professor Craig's phrase "representative death." We would understand *vicarious death*. Any variation by an Extreme Textualist of the accepted terminology is open to suspicion.

Among other scriptural passages cited by Professor Craig as illustrating the word-obsolescence of the Authorized Version, we may note these:

He cites Matthew 13:21, where *dureth* is used where we would use *endureth;* I Peter 3:11, where *ensue* is used where we would use *pursue;* Mark 7:24, 31, where *coasts* is used "as a synonym for 'borders.' " The Professor calls attention to I Thess. 4:15, with these observations:

> "Unless a reader remembers his Latin he is likely to be misled by the words, 'We which . . . remain unto the coming of the Lord shall not prevent them which are asleep (1 Thess. 4.15). Since we use 'prevent' for 'hinder,' the revisers wisely substituted 'precede.' " (Craig, *An Introduction*, p. 17.)

The Revisers' understanding of the resurrection led them here to interpret rather than to translate.

Matthew 6:25 is cited, where for "Take no thought for your life," the Revisers have substituted, "Be not anxious." Obviously, these two expressions are not equivalent. Here is some more interpreting, not translating.

He refers to the use of *charger*, in place of *platter*, in connection with the presentation of the head of John the Baptist to the daughter of Herodias. (Mark 6:25.)

The Professor cites a number of other cases, but few of them go to the essentials. Of these few, we may note these:

He cites Luke 18:12, where the Lord, in declaring the parable of the Pharisee and the publican, has the Pharisee say: "I give tithes of all that I possess." Professor Craig affirms this is wrong, because Jesus knew that tithes were to be from income. So the Revisers have translated, "All that I get." (Craig, *An Introduction,* p. 18.)

This change seems not to be of translation but of interpretation. Carr points out that the Pharisees paid tithes on certain things that were not tithable under the strict law. (A. Carr, ed., *The Gospel According to St. Matthew, The Cambridge Bible for Schools and Colleges* (Cambridge and London, The University Press, 1893), *Note* to Matt. 23:23.)

Farrar points out that the Savior has the Pharisee boasting about his tithes as about his fasting. (F. W. Farrar, ed., *The Gospel According to St. Luke, Cambridge Bible, Note* to Luke 18:12.)

Jesus was well aware that a Pharisee would not minimize his practices and so he put into the Pharisee's mouth the boastful, though inaccurate, declaration. It is not clear that in ancient Israel a man's capital was ever tithed. The experience of Abraham and his tithing to Melchizedek seems not too clear on the point. The practice as to tithing seems to have varied at different times.

(See W. O. E. Oesterley, "Tithes," *HDB* (*Single Vol.*) ; J. A. MacCulloch, "Tithes," Hastings, *Encyc.*, Vol. XII; Arthur S. Peake, "Tithe," *A Dictionary of the Bible,* James Hastings, ed. (New York, Charles Scribner's Sons, 1902), Vol. IV; Andrew C. Zenos, "Tithe," *A New Standard Bible Dictionary* (New York and London, Funk and Wagnalls Company, 1925) ; J. R. Willis, "Tithes," *Dictionary of the Apostolic Church,* James Hastings, ed. (New York, Charles Scribner's Sons, 1919), Vol. II; C. Goodspeed, "Tithe," *A Dictionary of Christ and the Gospels,* James Hastings, ed., (New York, Charles Scribner's Sons, 1908), Vol. II.)

However, modern scripture is perfectly clear that under certain conditions, a member's capital is to be tithed. (D. C. Sec. 119.)

Professor Craig also discusses John 10:16 as follows:

"The mistake in John 10:16 has a pertinent bearing on the question of Christian unity. The King James Version reads, 'Other sheep I have, which are not of this fold . . . and there shall be one fold, and one shepherd.' But in the Greek there are two different words, both of which are translated here 'fold,' as in the Vulgate. What the gospel says is that there are sheep who do not belong to this fold, but that all belong to one flock." (Craig, *An Introduction*, pp. 18-19.)

The full *Authorized Version* text of John 10:16, reads:

"And other sheep I have, which are not of this fold: them also I must bring, and they shall hear my voice; and there shall be one fold, and one shepherd."

The Inspired Version is except for punctuation, just the same as the Authorized Version.

The Revisers have rendered this passage as follows:

"And I have other sheep, that are not of this fold; I must bring them also, and they will heed my voice. So there shall be one flock, one shepherd." (John 10:16, R.S.V.)

It is not clear just what the new translation does for "Christian unity." Either translation would seem to be acceptable to us. But the Revisers would not have had serious trouble with the passage if they had known of the followers of Christ on the American continent and that following his resurrection, Christ visited them, taught them, and organized his Church among them.

But any of these and all of them together, could have been cured, if they needed curing, by a few well-worded notes. It would not seem they were worth a committee of some thirty odd members of distinguished scholars, working one hundred and forty-five days of some nine hours each, or, some 1305 hours, equalling some forty thousand odd man hours, and a new Revision of the

Bible. It is recorded that in making the British Revised
Version, Hort himself talked, all told, three years. But
these and a few other inconsequential matters (see *Item
11* of this *Note*) are the things they talk about; they say
very little about the important and elemental changes
they made in their Revision, as noted in *Note Thirty-
four* herein.

Item 11.   Some Grammatical and Other Errors in the Authorized Version.

> *Summary.* Professors Craig and Cadbury discuss
> grammatical errors, *cherubims* for *cherubim* (Heb. 9:5);
> giving gender *his* to salt (Matt. 5:13); "though he were
> a Son," false use of subjunctive (Heb. 5:8); *"whom* do
> men say that I am" (Mark 8:27); calling Old Testament
> characters by different names; defects in some geo-
> graphical names; use of word *charity;* faults in vocabu-
> lary; comments on baptism. Improvements are again
> alleged in the Revised Standard Version over the lan-
> guage of both the Authorized and Revised Versions. A
> test of readability of the Bible is given. Two of the Re-
> visers only seem to glimpse the value of spiritual ele-
> ments of the New Testament.

In discussing the grammatical errors of the King
James Version, Professor Craig (covering ground more
or less covered by each of the writers of the *Introduction*), picks up the common instances: *cherubims* as a
false plural (Heb. 9:5); "salt has lost *his* savour" (Matt.
5:13); "though he were a Son," a false use of the sub-
junctive (Heb. 5:8); *"Whom* do men say that I am?"
(Mark 8:27).

He also calls attention to a few matters of the person-
alities involved in "calling the same Old Testament character by three different names, Jeremiah, Jeremias, and
Jeremy," and also notes the same King James Version
defect in some geographical names. He also calls atten-

tion to the use of the word *charity* by Paul. (I Cor. 13; Craig, *An Introduction*, pp. 19-20; see also Cadbury, *An Introduction*, p. 45; *supra*, p. 308.)

He cites some other equally important or unimportant matters of the same sort. But none of them, nor all of them put together, are of the last importance, nor sufficent to justify the making of a new translation.

In a chapter entitled, "The Vocabulary and Grammar of New Testament Greek," Professor Cadbury (Harvard University) deals with changes made on account of grammar and vocabulary. We have already quoted his opening paragraphs, and have made references to other portions which deal with the use and translation of Greek particles, distinctions between words, the matter of tenses in Greek and English. (*Supra*, pp. 367, 375 ff., Semitic element; see Burgon, pp. 161 ff., 402.)

However, none of these require mention here beyond noting his brief comment on *baptism*. He says:

"So when the preposition *eis* is used where we expect *en* we may as well render it the same way without comment since we know that the Greek of the period was not particular in such matters, even with the verb baptize. Compare Mark 1.5 with 1.9 (Jordan), and Acts 8.16 with 10.48 (name). Nor does it seem now necessary to distinguish 'baptize in' (*en* and dative) and 'baptize with' (dative alone). Compare Mark 1.8 with Matt. 3.11." (Cadbury, *An Introduction*, pp. 49-50.)

We of the Church can accept the use of *in* and of *with* in the passages cited, but we cannot accept that there is no difference between *baptize in* and *baptize with*. The difference could be between *immersion* and *pouring* or *sprinkling*.

In a chapter headed, "The English of the Revised Standard Version of the New Testament," Dean Luther A. Weigle, Yale University Divinity School, deals further with this matter of revised renderings. Observing

that the Revisers were not instructed "to return to the
errors and archaic language of the King James Version,
but rather that they were charged to recover its simplicity and directness," qualities that had been lost in the
translations of the British (1880's) and American
(1900-1901). He states the major defeat of these latter
translations "is that these are literal, word-for-word
translations, which follow the order of the Greek words
wherever possible, rather than the order which is natural
to English." (Weigle, *An Introduction*, p. 53.)

Dean Weigle gives three instances to show the way
in which the present Revisers have improved both the
King James Version and the translations of the 1880's
and 1901. They are worth quoting, as showing what has
been thrown away by the Revisers:

"Luke 9.17. KJ: 'And they did eat, and were all filled: and
there was taken up of fragments that remained to them twelve
baskets.' ASV: 'And they ate and were all filled; and there
was taken up that which remained over to them of broken pieces,
twelve baskets.' RSV: 'And all ate and were satisfied. And
they took up what was left over, twelve baskets of broken
pieces.'

"Luke 20.1-2. KJ: 'And it came to pass, *that* on one of
those days, as he taught the people in the temple, and preached
the gospel, the chief priests and the scribes came upon *him* with
the elders, And spake unto him, saying, Tell us, by what authority doest thou these things? or who is he that gave thee this
authority?' ASV: 'And it came to pass, on one of the days, as
he was teaching the people in the temple, and preaching the
gospel, there came upon him the chief priests and the scribes
with the elders; and they spake, saying unto him, Tell us: By
what authority doest thou these things? or who is he that gave
thee this authority?' RSV: 'One day, as he was teaching the
people in the temple and preaching the gospel, the chief priests
and the scribes with the elders came up and said to him, "Tell
us by what authority you do these things, or who it is that
gave you this authority?" '

"Luke 23.8. KJ: 'And when Herod saw Jesus, he was exceeding glad: for he was desirous to see him of a long season,

because he had heard many things of him; and he hoped to have seen some miracle done by him.' (Here is an example, incidentally, of the inaccuracy of KJ. The Greek reads, and good English demands, 'to see' instead of 'to have seen.') ASV: 'Now when Herod saw Jesus, he was exceeding glad; for he was of a long time desirous to see him, because he had heard concerning him; and he hoped to see some miracle done by him.' RSV: 'When Herod saw Jesus, he was very glad, for he had long desired to see him, because he had heard about him, and he was hoping to see some sign done by him.'" (Weigle, *An Introduction*, pp. 53-54.)

As these changes are given as examples of needed changes which led to a new translation and what was done about it, one is somewhat at a loss to perceive where the new texts meet, better than the Authorized Version text, Dr. Weigle's requirement that the new text must be "euphonious, readable, and suited for use in public and private worship." (Weigle, *An Introduction*, p. 57.)

Attention is called to the elimination by the Revisers of the word *miracle* in Luke 23:8, and the substitution of the word *sign*. This matter will be discussed later.

Dean Weigle then calls attention to changes in translating Greek articles; the archaisms in the King James Version in the use of the personal pronouns (see *supra*, *Item 9*, pp. 377 ff.), in the use of words, the meaning of which has been changed, as, for example, *let* for *hinder*, of changes in prepositions, of tenses, in the use of old verb forms, in the use of *shall* and *will*, and in the use of italics to indicate words not found in the Greek text. He boasts of the use of fewer words by the Revisers, and affirms that a requirement constantly kept in mind was:

" . . . that the Bible should be translated into language that is euphonious, readable, and suited for use in public and private worship. It must sound well, and be easy to read aloud and in public. The choice of words and ordering of phrases must be such as to avoid harsh collocations of sound, and consonantal juxtapositions over which tongues will trip and lisp. . . .

"Much even of the prose of the King James Bible has the beauty, and something of the rhythm, of poetry. But it is a mistake to assume that all of the Bible is poetry, or that, to be readable and suited for use in public worship, the translation must be rhythmic." (Weigle, *An Introduction,* p. 57.)

This is more of the same persistent chord sounded by the other Revisers. It must be said in behalf of the Revisers that they have succeeded admirably in achieving their purposes so far as destroying much of the beauty and majesty of the King James Version. Sometimes their work is not too good daily newspaper reporting. May the great English masters, Shakespeare, Milton, Johnson, the airy artistry of Shelley and Keats, and all the rest, be preserved from the hands of such "literary" revisers.

The Reverend Walter Russell Bowie, Grace Church, New York, furnished a short chapter on, "The Use of the New Testament in Worship." He, too, dwells upon the infelicity of the language of the King James Version, but seemingly reluctantly and with a faltering voice. In his heart he seems to hear only the magnificence of the King James text.

President Abdel Ross Wentz (Lutheran Theological Seminary, Gettysburg) provided a chapter on, "The New Testament and the Word of God." He early buttresses his observations about the necessity for translating the New Testament books, by affirming that the existing translations are not readily intelligible to us moderns, and so by a sort of "Pentecostal" concept or manifestation, changes must be made so that each generation, each people, must hear the Word of God in its own tongue. Almost he approaches the principle of continuous revelation.

Each of these last two, in contradistinction to the

other writers, sought to deal with the larger and spiritual aspects, rather than with the critical matters involved in the translation. Their contribution will be noted in the few observations now to be made.

Item 12. Some General Impressions.

Summary. Some general impressions in summary by the author. No one of the Revisers strikes out boldly for Jesus as the Christ, the Son of God, the Redeemer of the World, the First Fruits of the Resurrection.

Out of a careful reading and re-reading of the whole *An Introduction to the Revised Standard Version of the New Testament*, we come away with a few general impressions:

1. Several of the writers take great pains to say that their sole function is to supply a translation of the Greek text. They point out that in their work no one manuscript or group of manuscripts was taken as possessing this text.

2. They largely proceed as if the Sacred Autographs were in Greek, though they distinctly reserve the point (for some of them) that the Aramaic, that is, the Syrian text, represented by the Syriac Versions, may have been original.

3. They condemn all previous translations, though they level their criticism mostly at the King James Version, and are rather severe on the English and American Revised Versions.

4. With what seems to be a rather childish concept, they seem rather studiously to avoid referring to the King James Version as the Authorized Version, or the "Textus Receptus," though this seems to have been the designation used by the critics generally up to this time.

As if the failure to use the term "Authorized Version" would do away with it!

5. The great underlying stated need for and the purpose of a new translation are the infelicities of the English of the King James Version. This consideration is belabored by every one of the authors in the *Introduction*. Their finished work leaves much to be desired on this particular point. The end they sought in this matter, as avowed by some of them, is the elimination of all approaches to the beauty, dignity, and solemnity of the language of the Old Testament, and to reduce the language of the New Testament record to the equivalent of the level of the ordinary daily newspaper of our day. The words of the Lord and of the Apostles are to be preserved in the ordinary language of the street. These latest Revisers have had considerable success in working out this purpose.

6. While finding fault with the mere language of the Revised Versions, English and American, they have (as we shall see) clung rather closely to all changes made in the earlier Revisions on matters of substance. 'The voice is the voice of Jacob, but the hands are the hands of Esau.' The Extreme Textualists are still at work, undermining and, it seems when they dare, eliminating much that proclaims Jesus as the Christ.

7. We have looked in vain for one definite statement in all this *Introduction* that would ring out clearly the message of the great declaration of Peter to the priesthood in Jerusalem, when, responding to their inquiry, "By what power, or by what name, have ye done this?"— healing the lame man at the Gate Beautiful—Peter, filled with the Holy Ghost, declared:

"Be it known unto you all, and to all the people of Israel, that by the name of Jesus Christ of Nazareth, whom ye crucified, whom God raised from the dead, even by him doth this man stand here before you whole.

"This is the stone which was set at nought of you builders, which is become the head of the corner.

"Neither is there salvation in any other: for there is none other name under heaven given among men, whereby we must be saved." (Acts 4:7-12.)

No statement has been found that straitly declares this great truth, the central truth of the New Testament, indeed of all God's words to his children.

President Wentz speaks of Christ in highly rhetorical periods, as "the great unique Personality"; he speaks of the "plumb line of Christian faith," of the "Christian way of life," of the perpetuation by the scriptures of "the body of Christ in the twentieth century," of the fact that the "original writers of the New Testament books were witnesses to Jesus Christ as their Lord and Savior," —he speaks of all these and of related matters, in language of rare eloquence, but in no place does he come to grips with the one basic question of truth,—Was Jesus of Nazareth the Son of God, the Messiah, the Christ that was to come, the Redeemer of the World, the First Fruits of the Resurrection, the Sole Source of our Salvation. He approaches it when he affirms that this "great unique Personality who meets us in the New Testament and speaks to us from its pages is the very center of God's entire revelation." But this is equivocal and does not declare Christ's Messiahship and Godhood. (Abdel Ross Wentz, "The New Testament and the Word of God," *An Introduction*, pp. 64, 65, 68.)

This crucial defect is present in all that the Revisers write in the entire *Introduction*. No other of the Revisers comes as close, in his writings here, to the great truth, as does President Wentz.

As we have said hereinabove, and in the earlier parts
of these *Notes*, one cannot escape the conclusion that the
Extreme Textualists have in too large a measure forsaken
Jesus the Christ and his Godhood, if there can be degrees
in such an apostasy.

NOTE THIRTY-FOUR •
Some Critical Omissions from and Changes Made in the King James Version by the Earlier Revisions and Retained and Added to by the Revised Standard Version

We now come to grips with some of the many matters of first importance. All that has been treated in the preceding *Note* are largely decorative "window dressing," almost (some would think) the airy persiflages of the arguments of gentlemanly scholars.

For convenience, the same matters discussed in considering the Revised Version will be discussed here and generally in the same order (see *Notes Twenty-nine*, *Thirty*, *Thirty-one*, and *Thirty-two*, for discussions of all these *Items*, in the Revised Versions, British and American).

We shall now briefly consider what the Revisers of the Revised Standard Version did to the important changes made in the Revised Versions of the 1880's and 1901, in matters of vital importance to us of the Church. For convenience of reference we shall treat the changes in the order in which they appear in our discussion of the Revised Versions.

Item 1. "Conjectural Emendations."

Summary. See *Note Twenty-nine, Item 2*. The Revisers affirm they virtually abandoned "conjectural emendation" in this Revision; admit only one: Jude 5-6, —angels who kept their *first estate*.

We will first consider the "conjectural emendations," sufficiently explained above (*supra*, pp. 286 ff.). By way of reminder, we may say that "conjectural emendation" is, it appears, a procedure by which the framers of a text arrive at their decisions as to the true text, by a sort of divination, which is used to reach decisions as among two or more texts, or to arrive at a text that is different from all other texts, or, and this is extraordinary, to fill in omissions or make alterations in existing texts without any justifying authority from any text.

Speaking of Westcott and Hort and their new Greek text, and their use of this principle, Burgon derisively challenges: "If these distinguished Professors have enjoyed a Revelation as to what the Evangelists actually wrote, they would do well to acquaint the world with the fact at the earliest possible moment." (Burgon, p. 95, n. 1.)

The new Revisers affirm they have kept but one "conjectural emendation" offered by Westcott and Hort, which is Jude 5. (Grant, *An Introduction*, p. 41.) But this statement may not be too accurate. For example, the "conjectural emendation" criticized by Burgon of II Tim. 1:13 (Burgon, pp. 351-353), seems to have been retained in the Revised Standard Version. But we have not attempted to check others.

As to Jude 5, the *King James Version* (the Authorized Version) reads:

"5. I will therefore put you in remembrance, though ye once knew this, how that the Lord, having saved the people out of the land of Egypt, afterward destroyed them that believed not.

"6. And the angels which kept not their first estate, but left their own habitation, he hath reserved in everlasting chains under darkness unto the judgment of the great day."

The Inspired Version of the Prophet Joseph Smith follows the King James Version.

The particular phrase of interest to the Latter-day Saint is found in verse 6,—"the angels which kept not their first estate."

The English Revision (1881) proposed:

"5. Now I desire to put you in remembrance, though ye know all things once for all, how that the Lord, having saved a people out of the land of Egypt, afterward destroyed them that believed not. [6.] And angels which kept not their own principality, but left their proper habitation, he hath kept in everlasting bonds under darkness unto the judgement of the great day."

The American Standard Version (1901) was identical save for two words: *how* is omitted before "that the Lord" and *which* is changed to *that* after "angels."

The Revised Standard Version—which retains Westcott and Hort's "conjectural emendation"—reads:

"5. Now I desire to remind you, though you were once for all fully informed, that he who saved a people out of the land of Egypt, afterward destroyed those who did not believe. 6. And the angels that did not keep their own position but left their proper dwelling have been kept by him in eternal chains in the nether gloom until the judgment of the great day."

No one with an understanding of the great truths announced in Abraham 3, would have eliminated "first estate." The expression "nether gloom" may be good mythology (we do not know), but it does not describe any Christian concept.

Burgon was not too far away, we may again say, when he challenged Westcott and Hort to declare if they pretended to offer their *conjectural emendations* as revelations. (*Supra, Note Twenty-nine,* p. 287.) Whether revelations or not, need not be determined, but this one "conjectural emendation" was not a revelation from God.

Item 2. "Love" for "Charity."

The word *love* is substituted for *charity* in I Corinthians 13. (For a discussion of this change, see *Note Thirty-one,* p. 308.) Here the Revised Standard Version follows the errors of the Revised Versions of the 1880's and 1901.

The Inspired Version of the Prophet Joseph follows the Authorized Version.

Item 3. Elimination of "Miracles" from the New Text.

The elimination of the word *miracle* from the text and the substitution of the word *sign*: A careful checking of the Revised Standard Version, shows that of 31 times the word *miracle* occurs in the New Testament of the King James Version, it has been twice omitted in the new Version, with rephrasing to avoid its use; it has been changed to *sign* 22 times; it has been retained •nly 7 times, and curiously, all these seven have to do with Paul and his writings: Acts 8:13, 19:11; I Cor. 12:10, 12:28, 12:29; Gal. 3:5; and Heb. 2:4.

This matter has been already discussed hereinbefore. (*Note Thirty-one,* pp. 308-309.) We then observed that there is of course an obvious difference in meaning in English between the word *sign* and the word *miracle* which no one can overlook. The *signs* of the coming of our Lord are wars, etc. etc., but these are not *miracles.* As Burgon points out, a *miracle* may be a sign; but a *sign* is not necessarily a miracle.

Almost all of our Church members have seen instances of miraculous healings. These have not been *signs,* save in the sense that they are evidences of God's power. To eliminate *miracles* from the records of God's dealings with men, is to eliminate the virgin birth of the

Christ, and the resurrection. *Miracles* have been in the past and are today of frequent occurrence among the Saints. We must not lose that truth.

Here the *Revised Standard Version* follows the errors of the Revised Versions of the 1880's and 1901.

The Inspired Version of the Prophet Joseph follows the Authorized Version, except in Mark 6:52.

Item 4. Casting Out of Evil Spirits, Matt. 17:14 ff.

The Revisers have followed the Revised Versions and tampered with the record of the incident of the casting out of the evil spirit from the lunatic. Following the Revised Versions they have substituted *epileptic* for *lunatick*, thus seemingly attempting to cast doubt or destroy the idea of demoniacal possession. (See Matt. 17: 14 ff.) To assist in this, the Revisers have followed also the Revised Versions, and omitted the twenty-first verse: "Howbeit this kind goeth not out but by prayer and fasting." (Matt. 17:14 ff.; for discussion, see *Note Thirty-one*, pp. 310-311; *Note Thirty-two*, pp. 338-339.)

In this also, the *Revised Standard Version* Revisers followed the error of the Revised Versions.

The Inspired Version of the Prophet Joseph follows the Authorized Version, except there is a comma inserted after "howbeit."

Item 5. The Word "Inspiration," II Tim. 3:16.

The word *inspiration* has also been tampered with, following the Revised Versions. The reading of II Timothy 3:16 in the *King James Version* (Authorized Version) reads:

"All scripture is given by inspiration of God, and is profitable for doctrine, for reproof, for correction, for instruction in righteousness."

The Inspired Version of the Prophet Joseph reads substantially as in the Authorized Version:

"And all scripture given by inspiration of God, is profitable for doctrine, for reproof, for correction, for instruction in righteousness."

Following the pattern of the earlier Revised Versions, the Revisers of the *Revised Standard Version* have rephrased this passage. It now reads:

"All scripture is inspired by God and profitable for teaching, for reproof, for correction, and for training in righteousness."

The Revised Versions of the 1880's and 1901 read:

"Every scripture inspired of God is also profitable for teaching, for reproof, for correction, for instruction which is in righteousness."

The omission of *doctrine* is significant; there is a fundamental difference between *doctrine* and *teaching*. The latter does not include the former,—all *doctrines* may be taught, but not all *teaching* is doctrine.

Item 6. The Godhood of Christ.

In Romans 9:4-5 of the *King James Version* (Authorized Version), it is said:

"Who are Israelites; to whom pertaineth the adoption, and the glory, and the covenants, and the giving of the law, and the service of God, and the promises; whose are the fathers, and of whom as concerning the flesh Christ came, who is over all, God blessed for ever. Amen."

The Inspired Version of the Prophet Joseph reads:

"Who are Israelites; of whom are the adoption, and the glory, and the covenants, and the giving of the law, and the service of God, and the promises which are made unto the fathers; and of whom, as concerning the flesh, Christ was, who is God over all, blessed for ever. Amen."

The Revised Standard Version translators render it thus:

"They are Israelites, and to them belong the sonship, the glory, the covenants, the giving of the law, the worship, and the promises; to them belong the patriarchs, and of their race, according to the flesh, is the Christ. God who is over all be blessed for ever. Amen."

It is pointed out that as given in the Authorized Version, this is an unequivocal testimony "to our LORD'S eternal GODhead." (Burgon, p. 211.) The Inspired Version makes this definitely clear.

However, once more the Revised Standard Version follows the lead of the Revised Versions, this time in supporting a Socinian gloss. (See *Note Thirty-one*, pp. 312 ff., for a full discussion of the overwhelming patristic support for the Authorized Version rendering.)

Item 7. Special Vital Omissions.

There now follow herein a number of vital omissions and vital differences between the King James Version and the Revised Standard Version.

These that are named below have already been discussed in connection with the Revised Version. (*Supra*, pp. 316 ff.) In all cases the Revised Standard Version has followed the Revised Version. In substance as to these matters, the Revised Standard Version is merely a copy of the earlier Revised Versions.

Sub-item a. Account of the Birth of Jesus, Matt. 1:25.

The King James Version reads:

"And knew her not till she had brought forth her firstborn son: and he called his name Jesus."

The Inspired Version of the Prophet Joseph agrees

with the Authorized Version, except the changing of *till* to *until*, and *he* to *they*.

The Revised Standard Version text (agreeing with the Revised Versions text) reads:

" . . . but knew her not until she had borne a son; and he called his name Jesus."

The Revised Standard Version omits the significant words, "her firstborn son," which opens the way for a contention regarding Mary's virginity. The overwhelming authority is for the Authorized Version rendering. (See, for further consideration, with a collection of authorities, *supra*, pp. 316 ff.)

Sub-item b.   Jesus, the Son of God, Mark 1:1.

The King James Version reads:

"The beginning of the gospel of Jesus Christ, the Son of God."

The Inspired Version of the Prophet Joseph follows the King James Version.

To the King James Version has been added, both in the *Revised Standard Version* and the earlier *Revised Versions*, a marginal note reading:

"Other (some) ancient authorities omit *the Son of God.*"

This casts a doubt, raises a question, on a text that is all but universally recognized in the manuscripts and in the writings of the Fathers. (*Supra*, p. 318; for a discussion of *marginal notes* and their ill effects, see *supra*, pp. 300 ff.)

The Revised Standard Version again follows the error of the Revised Version.

Sub-item c.   Christ, the Creator, John 1:3-4.

The King James Version reads:

"All things were made by him; and without him was not any thing made that was made. In him was life; and the life was the light of men."

The Inspired Version of the Prophet Joseph follows the King James Version:

"All things were made by him; and without him was not anything made which was made. In him was the gospel, and the gospel was the life, and the life was the light of men."

The Revised Standard Version substitutes *through* for *by* in the phrase *made by him.*

But here again is a doubt-casting marginal note, both in the Revised Standard Version and in the earlier Revised Versions, which would make the text read:

" . . . all things were made through him, and without him was not anything made. That which has been made was life in him . . . "

Critics affirm that this change is a known perversion brought in by the Gnostics of the second century. (*Supra,* p. 319.)

Again the Revised Standard Version has followed the earlier Revised Versions.

Sub-item d.   The Son of Man, "in heaven," John 3:13.

The King James Version reads:

"And no man hath ascended up to heaven, but he that came down from heaven, even the Son of man which is in heaven."

The Inspired Version of the Prophet Joseph retains the phrase omitted in the Revised Standard Version, and reads:

"I tell you, No man hath ascended up to heaven, but he who came down from heaven, even the Son of Man who is in heaven."

The Revised Standard Version reads:

"No one has ascended into heaven but he who descended from heaven, the Son of man." A marginal note states: "Other ancient authorities add *who is in heaven.*"

The Revised Standard Version Revisers adopt the Revised Version text as suggested in the note, and then relegate the whole Authorized Version text to the note, so eliminating it from the text.

Thus the Revised Standard Version translators go beyond the Revised Version Revisers and actually adopt the error of the earlier Revisions.

Here again the overwhelming authority is in favor of the Authorized Version text. (*Supra,* pp. 319 ff.)

Sub-item e.   The Lord's Prayer, Matt. 6:9-13; Luke 11:2-4.

The King James text of Matt. 6:9-13 reads:

"Our Father which art in heaven, Hallowed be thy name. Thy kingdom come. Thy will be done in earth, as it is in heaven. Give us this day our daily bread. And forgive us our debts, as we forgive our debtors. And lead us not into temptation, but deliver us from evil: For thine is the kingdom, and the power, and the glory, for ever.   Amen."

The Revised Standard Version reads:

"Our Father who art in heaven,
Hallowed be thy name.
Thy kingdom come,
Thy will be done,
    On earth as it is in heaven.
Give us this day our daily bread;
And forgive us our debts,
    As we also have forgiven our debtors;
And lead us not into temptation,
    But deliver us from evil."

The omission of the Doxology, "For thine is the kingdom, and the power, and the glory, for ever. Amen," will be observed.

Marginal notes are given as follows:

" . . . our daily bread"—the note reads, "Or *our bread for the morrow.*" " . . . from evil"—the note reads, "Or *the evil one.* Other authorities, some ancient, add, in some form, *For thine is the kingdom and the power and the glory, forever. Amen.*"

LUKE'S ACCOUNT

In the *King James Version*, the Luke 11:2-4 text reads:

"Our Father which art in heaven, Hallowed be thy name. Thy kingdom come. Thy will be done, as in heaven, so in earth. Give us day by day our daily bread. And forgive us our sins; for we also forgive every one that is indebted to us. And lead us not into temptation; but deliver us from evil."

The Inspired Version of the Prophet Joseph made a few changes in the body of the prayers—each of them—but retained the Doxology in Matthew and added a part of it to Luke's text.

The Revised Standard Version text reads:

"Father, hallowed be thy name. Thy kingdom come. Give us each day our daily bread; and forgive us our sins, for we ourselves forgive every one who is indebted to us; and lead us not into temptation." The marginal note to "our daily bread," reads, "Or *our bread for the morrow.*"

These tragic mutilations of the Lord's Prayer are discussed in considerable detail at pp. 321 ff., where it is pointed out that they all may be traced back to "the scalpel of Marcion the heretic," who wrote almost 1800 years ago. (Burgon, p. 35.)

The blighting shadow of the Revised Version again casts itself over the Revised Standard Version.

Sub-item f. The Message of the Heavenly Host, Luke 2:14.

The King James Version reads:

"Glory to God in the highest, and on earth peace, good will toward men."

The Inspired Version of the Prophet Joseph follows the King James Version, with slight changes. It reads:

"Glory to God in the highest; and on earth, peace; good will to men."

The Revised Standard Version reads:

"Glory to God in the highest, and on earth peace among men with whom he is pleased!" A marginal note reads: "Other ancient authorities read, *peace, goodwill among men.*"

Here is another tragic mutilation that must take its place along side the mutilation of the Lord's own words. This time it is a mutilation of the words of the heavenly host who were announcing the mortal birth of the Son of God, the Redeemer of the World. This mutilation has been exhaustively considered at pp. 325 ff., *supra.* Dean Burgon, who is quoted *in extenso* on the subject, concludes his consideration of the matter as follows:

"The history of the reading advocated by the Revisionists is briefly this:—*It emerges into notice in the IInd century; and in the Vth, disappears from sight entirely.*" (Burgon, p. 46.)

The evil shadow of the Revised Version again darkens the Revised Standard Version text.

Sub-item g.   The Institution of the Sacrament, Luke 22:19-20.

The King James Version text reads:

"19. And he took bread, and gave thanks, and brake it, and gave unto them, saying, This is my body which is given for you: this do in remembrance of me.

"20. Likewise also the cup after supper, saying, This cup is the new testament in my blood, which is shed for you."

The Inspired Version of the Prophet Joseph (disregarding punctuation changes) reads as the Authorized

Version text except that *"it"* is omitted after "brake."
(See, for collection and comparison of accounts of King
James Version, author's *On the Way to Immortality
and Eternal Life,* pp. 375-378.)

The Revised Standard Version reads:

"19. And he took bread, and when he had given thanks he
broke it and gave it to them, saying, 'This is my body.' " The
marginal note to the declaration, "this is my body," reads:
"Other ancient authorities add *which is given for you. Do this
in remembrance of me.' "*

The Revised Standard Version omits entirely verse
20, but gives it in the marginal note as follows:

"20. *And likewise the cup after supper, saying, 'This cup
which is poured out for you is the new covenant in my blood.' "*

But it will be observed that this marginal version
omits the vital words found in the Authorized Version,
"which is shed for you."

Other accounts of the Sacrament will be found in
Matt. 26:26-29, and Mark 14:22-24.

For a discussion of the Luke account and the lack
of authority for the changes made therein by the Revised Versions, see *supra,* pp. 329 ff.

Obviously, if the abbreviated text of the Revised
Standard Version is accepted in Luke, the Sacrament
will consist only of the blessing and eating of the bread.
The element of the shedding of blood will be lost. But
this is retained in the other texts.

And here again, the influence of the Revised Version
has even multiplied itself, for while the blood element
was retained in that text (in the Revised Version), with
a marginal note saying that some ancient authorities
omitted it, the Revised Standard Version Revisers *have*

omitted the whole passage from the text and have relegated it to a marginal note.

MATTHEW'S ACCOUNT

Matthew's account (26:26-28) of the *King James Version* reads:

"And as they were eating, Jesus took bread, and blessed it, and brake it, and gave it to the disciples, and said, Take, eat; this is my body. And he took the cup, and gave thanks, and gave it to them, saying, Drink ye all of it; for this is my blood of the new testament, which is shed for many for the remission of sins."

In the *Inspired Version* of the Prophet, the account of Matthew 26:22-24 is given thus:

"And as they were eating, Jesus took bread and brake it, and blessed it, and gave to his disciples, and said, Take, eat; this is in remembrance of my body which I give a ransom for you. And he took the cup, and gave thanks, and gave it to them, saying, Drink ye all of it. For this is in remembrance of my blood of the new testament, which is shed for as many as shall believe on my name, for the remission of their sins."

In the *Revised Version* (British) the text in Matthew reads:

"And as they were eating, Jesus took bread, and blessed, and brake it; and he gave to the disciples, and said, Take, eat; this is my body. And he took a cup, and gave thanks, and gave to them, saying, Drink ye all of it; for this is my blood of the covenant, which is shed for many unto remission of sins." To "bread," a marginal note says, "Or *a loaf*"; to "a cup," a marginal note says, "Some ancient authorities read *the cup*"; to "the covenant," a marginal note says, "Or *the testament*"; to "covenant," a marginal note says, "Many ancient authorities insert *new*" [between *the* and *covenant*].

In the *American Standard Version* (Matt. 26:26-28), these same passages are given the same translation as in the British edition, with the same marginal notes, except:

The phrase "which is shed for many" in the British edition, is made "which is poured out for many," and the marginal note to "the covenant,"—"Or *the testament*" is omitted.

The Revised Standard Version (Matt. 26:26-28) has only slight changes from the American Standard Version. It reads:

"Now as they were eating, Jesus took bread, and blessed, and broke it, and gave it to the disciples and said, 'Take, eat; this is my body.' And he took a cup, and when he had given thanks he gave it to them, saying, 'Drink of it, all of you; for this is my blood of the covenant, which is poured out for many for the forgiveness of sins . . .'"

The changes made in this last text over its predecessor are obvious and need no comment. There is the same marginal note about "new"; the other marginal notes are omitted.

MARK'S ACCOUNT

Mark's account as given in the Inspired Version makes the greatest changes made of any of the Gospels.

The King James Version reads (Mark 14:22-24):

"And as they did eat, Jesus took bread, and blessed, and brake it, and gave to them, and said, Take, eat: this is my body. And he took the cup, and when he had given thanks, he gave it to them: and they all drank of it. And he said unto them, This is my blood of the new testament, which is shed for many."

The Inspired Version reads (Mark 14:20-23):

"And as they did eat, Jesus took bread and blessed it, and brake, and gave to them, and said, Take it, and eat. Behold, this is for you to do in remembrance of my body; for as oft as ye do this ye will remember this hour that I was with you. And he took the cup, and when he had given thanks, he gave it to them; and they all drank of it. And he said unto them,

This is in remembrance of my blood which is shed for many, and the new testament which I give unto you; for of me, ye shall bear record unto all the world."

The account in Mark (14:22-24) in the *Revised Version* (British) reads as follows:

"And as they were eating, he took bread, and when he had blessed, he brake it, and gave to them, and said, Take ye: this is my body. And he took a cup, and when he had given thanks, he gave to them: and they all drank of it. And he said unto them, This is my blood of the covenant, which is shed for many." There are the following marginal notes: To "bread," — "Or, *a loaf*"; to "the covenant," — "Or, *the testament*"; to "covenant,"—"Some ancient authorities insert *new.*"

In the *American Standard Version*, Mark's record (Mark 14:22-24) repeats the text of the Revised Version (British), except:

The phrase "shed for many," reads: "poured out for many." All marginal notes are repeated except the marginal note to "the covenant."

The Revised Standard Version (Mark 14:22-24) reads:

"And as they were eating, he took bread, and blessed, and broke it, and gave it to them, and said, 'Take; this is my body.' And he took a cup, and when he had given thanks he gave it to them, and they all drank of it. And he said to them, 'This is my blood of the covenant, which is poured out for many . . .' " The Revised Standard Version has the same marginal note as to "new," but the other marginal notes are omitted.

Sub-item h. The Agony in the Garden and the Ministering Angel, Luke 22:43-44.

The King James Version reads:

"43. And there appeared an angel unto him from heaven, strengthening him.

"44. And being in an agony he prayed more earnestly: and

his sweat was as it were great drops of blood falling down to the ground."

The Inspired Version of the Prophet Joseph follows the King James Version with inconsequential changes.

The Revised Standard Version reads substantially the same for verse 43, but verse 44 is made to read:

"44. And being in an agony he prayed more earnestly; and his sweat became like great drops of blood falling down upon the ground."

The Revised Version had a marginal note reading:

"Many ancient authorities omit ver. 43, 44."

The Revised Standard Version note reads:

"Other ancient authorities omit verses 43 and 44."

For a critical discussion of this suggested omission of these verses which, as one critic says, "the universal Church has almost erected into an article of the Faith," see *supra*, pp. 331 ff. The basis for casting doubt on these great verses is said to be that they are *"an early Western interpolation . . . a fragment from the Traditions . . . locally current . . . an 'evangelic Tradition' . . . 'rescued from oblivion by the Scribes of the second century.'"* (Burgon, pp. 79, 81, n. 15.) But an analysis of the records made by those who support the authenticity thereof, seems clearly to overcome these contentions.

Here once more, the Revised Standard Version even slavishly follows the Revised Version.

Sub-item i.   The Prayer on the Cross, Luke 23:34.

The King James Version reads:

"Father, forgive them; for they know not what they do."

The Inspired Version of the Prophet Joseph follows

here, also, the Authorized Version, but inserts in brackets, following "they know not what they do," the limiting phrase of responsibility, "meaning the soldiers who crucified him."

The Revised Version has a marginal note which reads:

"Some ancient authorities omit *And Jesus said, Father, forgive them; for they know not what they do.*"

The Revised Standard Version repeats this note:

"Other ancient authorities omit the sentence *And Jesus . . . what they do.*"

Again slavishly the Revised Standard Version follows the Revised Version. Here, as in many other places, the Revised Standard Version translators range themselves with the earlier Extreme Textualists with all their anti-Christ expressions, if not feelings. (*Supra,* pp. 334 ff.)

These words are quoted throughout Christendom as personifying the perfect love and forgiveness, the top-rung of charity. We cannot lose them.

The critical analysis of the record made at pp. 335-336, *supra,* establishes that Christ so spoke on the cross.

Sub-item j. Christ's Salutation to the Apostles in the Upper Chamber, Luke 24:36.

The King James Version reads:

"And as they thus spake, Jesus himself stood in the midst of them, and saith unto them, Peace be unto you."

The Inspired Version of the Prophet Joseph agrees with the King James Version, but substituting *said* for *saith.*

The Revised Version had this marginal note:

"Some ancient authorities omit *and saith unto them, Peace be unto you,*" but retained the words in the text itself.

The Revised Standard Version eliminates from the text the words:

" . . . *and saith unto them, Peace be unto you,*" and adds a marginal note reading, "Other ancient authorities add *and said to them, 'Peace to you!'* "

Once more the influence of the Revised Version multiplied itself so that a doubt-raising marginal note in the Revised Version brings about an elimination from the text of the Revised Standard Version.

Concerning the condition of the record on this point, Dean Burgon says:

"And yet the precious words . . . (Lu. xxiv. 36) are vouched for by 18 uncials (with ℵ A B at their head), and *every known cursive copy* of the Gospels: by all the Versions: and (as before) by Eusebius, — and Ambrose, — by Chrysostom, — and Cyril,—and Augustine." (Burgon, p. 90; see *supra*, p. 337.)

Sub-item k.   Christ Displays His Hands and Feet, Luke 24:40.

The King James Version reads:

"And when he had thus spoken, he shewed them his hands and his feet."

The Inspired Version of the Prophet Joseph follows the King James Version, omitting the initial *and.*

The Revised Version marginal note reads:

"Some ancient authorities omit ver. 40," — the verse just quoted.

Once again the Revised Version has multiplied its influence and the *Revised Standard Version now omits* the questioned words *from the text,* but puts them in a marginal note reading:

"Other ancient authorities add verse 40, *And when he had said this, he showed them his hands and his feet.*"

Again we may quote Burgon:

"The words are found in 18 uncials (beginning with ℵ A B), and in every known cursive: in the Latin, — the Syriac, — the Egyptian,—in short, *in all the ancient Versions.* Besides these, ps.-Justin, — Eusebius, —Athanasius, —Ambrose (in Greek), — Epiphanius,— Chrysostom,— Cyril,—Theodoret,— Ammonius,— and John Damascene—quote them. What but the veriest trifling is it, in the face of such a body of evidence, to bring forward the fact that D and 5 copies of the old Latin, with Cureton's Syriac (of which we have had the character already), *omit* the words in question?" (Burgon, pp. 90-91; see *supra,* p. 338.)

Sub-item l.   Casting Out Evil Spirits, Matt. 17:21.

The King James Version reads:

"Howbeit this kind goeth not out but by prayer and fasting." (See *supra,* pp. 310, 338.)

Again the *Inspired Version* of the Prophet Joseph follows the King James Version.

The Revised Version omits this verse entirely, with a marginal note:

"Many authorities, some ancient, insert ver. 21 *But this kind goeth not out save by prayer and fasting.* See Mark ix. 29."

The Revised Standard Version again follows the Revised Version and omits the entire verse, with the following marginal note:

"Other ancient authorities insert verse 21, *'But this kind never comes out except by prayer and fasting.'* "

MARK'S ACCOUNT

Where the same incident is recorded in Mark 9:29, the *King James Version* text reads:

"This kind can come forth by nothing, but by prayer and fasting."

This is also the text of the *Inspired Version* by the Prophet Joseph.

The Revised Version text of Mark 9:29 is substantially the same (merely substituting *out* for *forth* and *save* for *but*, except that *and fasting* is omitted.

The marginal note reads: "Many ancient authorities add *and fasting.*"

The Revised Standard Version text of Mark 9:29 reads:

"This kind cannot be driven out by anything but prayer," with the marginal note reading: "Other ancient authorities add *and fasting.*"

Burgon, discussing the Revised Version text, shows the same preponderance of evidence for verse 21 that he massed in favor of Luke 24:36, and Luke 24:40, as quoted above.

Sub-item m.   The Son of Man is Come to Save, Matt. 18:11.

The King James Version reads:

"For the Son of man is come to save that which was lost."

The Inspired Version of the Prophet Joseph agrees with the King James Version.

The Revised Version omits this verse entirely, but adds a marginal note reading:

"Many authorities, some ancient, insert ver. 11 *For the Son of man came to save that which was lost.* See Luke xix. 10."

The Revised Standard Version also omits the verse with this marginal note:

"Other ancient authorities add verse 11, *For the Son of man came to save the lost.*"

Thus is eliminated the great declaration of the divine mission of Jesus, the Christ. Burgon again masses his evidence:

" . . . it is attested by every known uncial except B ℵ L, and every known cursive *except three*: by the old Latin and the Vulgate: by the Peschito, Cureton's and the Philoxenian Syriac: by the Coptic, Armenian, Æthiopic, Georgian and Slavonic versions:— by Origen, —Theodorus Heracl.,— Chrysostom—and Jovius the monk;—by Tertullian,—Ambrose,—Hilary, — Jerome, — pope Damasus — and Augustine: — above all, by the Universal Eastern Church,—for it has been read in all assemblies of the faithful on the morrow of Pentecost, from the beginning." (Burgon, p. 92, see *supra*, p. 340.)

Burgon affirms this elimination was made merely on the fiat of Westcott and Hort. (Burgon, p. 92.)

Sub-item n.   The Last Twelve Verses in Mark, Mark 16:9-20.

The Revised Version left a considerable space between these verses and the last preceding verse, Mark 16:8, with a marginal note, *but it printed the verses in the text.* The British and American treatment of these verses was identical both as to arrangement of the text and the marginal notes.

The Revised Standard Version, again yielding to the increased influence of the Revised Version, does not print these verses in the text, but consigns them to a marginal note, which begins:

"Other texts and versions add as 16. 9-20 the following passage." Then follow the omitted verses.

The Revised Standard Version adds, after the insertion of the note containing the last twelve verses which are omitted from the text, the following additional note:

"Other ancient authorities add after verse 8 the following: *But they reported briefly to Peter and those with him all that they had been told. And after this, Jesus himself sent out by means of them, from east to west, the sacred and imperishable proclamation of eternal salvation.*" (Characterized by Scrivener as a "wretched supplement derived from Cod. L. . . . annexed as an alternative reading." See p. 343, herein.)

The Inspired Version of the Prophet Joseph follows the Authorized Version with two or three minor verbal changes.

This treatment of this text of Mark by the Extreme Textualist Revisers, has called forth perhaps the most vigorous and voluminous condemnation that has been brought to bear upon any other one act of the "higher critics" work. Dean Burgon wrote an entire volume in support of the authenticity of these verses. Earlier in our discussion consideration has been given to this whole question, and we refer thereto (*supra*, pp. 341 ff.). There seems little reasonable question but that the evidence established their authenticity.

SOME CLOSING OBSERVATIONS ·

THESE NOTES

It is hoped that the reading of these *Notes* will do for those who patiently read them what their preparation has done for the author,—fortify a conviction in the essential verities of the Authorized Version in all matters of substance to the point where that conviction cannot be shaken by the "higher critics" (including the Extreme Textualists). Furthermore, it is hoped that these *Notes* will help others as they have helped the author to put aside the pettifogging, doubt-raising attacks of these "higher critics" on the matters of basic concern to us Christians and to dismiss all their contentions as unworthy of the serious consideration of any and all believers in Jesus Christ.

THE SPIRIT OF THE APPROACH

It will be recalled that among the stated purposes and necessities given by the Revisers offering the Revised Standard Version was: "There is need for a version which embodies the best results of modern scholarship as to the meaning of the Scriptures." This principle goes to the matter of interpretation not of translation. Indeed, no clear cut statement of the Revisers is noted that, in their work, they either sought or enjoyed the help of the Spirit of the Lord or of the Holy Ghost. So far as their expressions go it would seem the whole Revision was approached in the same spirit they would employ in the translation of any classical work.

How different was the spirit of the approach to their task of the translators of the King James Version of 1611. In their message, "The Translators to the Reader," speaking of their translation, they say:

"Truly, good Christian Reader, we never thought from the beginning that we should need to make a new translation, nor yet to make of a bad one a good one; (for then the imputation of *Sixtus* had been true in some sort, that our people had been fed with gall of dragons instead of wine, with wheal instead of milk;) but to make a good one better, or out of many good ones one principal good one, not justly to be excepted against; that hath been our endeavour, that our mark."

Speaking of the spirit in which the translators worked, they say:

"And in what sort did these assemble? In the trust of their own knowledge, or of their sharpness of wit, or deepness of judgment, as it were in an arm of flesh? At no hand. They trusted in him that hath the key of *David,* opening, and no man shutting; they prayed to the Lord, the Father of our Lord, to the effect that St. *Augustine* did; *O let thy Scriptures be my pure delight; let me not be deceived in them, neither let me deceive by them.* In this confidence, and with this devotion, did they assemble together."

Then their final paragraph:

"Many other things we might give thee warning of, gentle Reader, if we had not exceeded the measure of a preface already. It remaineth that we commend thee to God, and to the Spirit of his grace, which is able to build further than we can ask or think. He removeth the scales from our eyes, the vail from our hearts, opening our wits that we may understand his word, enlarging our hearts, yea, correcting our affections, that we may love it above gold and silver, yea, that we may love it to the end. Ye are brought unto fountains of living water which ye digged not; do not cast earth into them, with the Philistines, neither prefer broken pits before them, with the wicked Jews. Others have laboured, and you may enter into their labours. O receive not so great things in vain: O despise not so great salvation. Be not like swine to tread

under foot so precious things, neither yet like dogs to tear and
abuse holy things. Say not to our Saviour with the *Gergesites*,
Depart out of our coasts; neither yet with *Esau* sell your birthright for a mess of pottage. If light be come into the world,
love not darkness more than light: if food, if clothing, be
offered, go not naked, starve not yourselves. Remember the
advice of *Nazianzene*, *It is a grievous thing* (or dangerous)
*to neglect a great fair, and to seek to make markets after-
wards*: also the encouragement of St. *Chrysostome*, *It is
altogether impossible, that he that is sober* (and watchful)
should at any time be neglected: lastly, the admonition and
menacing of St. *Augustine*, *They that despise God's will inviting them shall feel God's will taking vengeance of them*. It
is a fearful thing to fall into the hands of the living God; but
a blessed thing it is, and will bring us to everlasting blessedness
in the end, when God speaketh unto us, to hearken; when he
setteth his word before us, to read it; when he stretcheth out
his hand and calleth, to answer, Here am I, here we are to do
thy will, O God. The Lord work a care and conscience in us
to know him and serve him, that we may be acknowledged of
him at the appearing of our Lord JESUS CHRIST, to whom with
the Holy Ghost be all praise and thanksgiving. Amen."

MY WITNESS

I am constrained to close this book with my personal
testimony, born of the spirit;

That Jesus of Nazareth was an historic personality,
—the greatest personality in all the history of the world;

That, as John declared: "In the beginning was the
Word, and the Word was with God, and the Word was
God";

That "the same was in the beginning with God";

That "all things were made by him; and without
him was not any thing made that was made";

That "in him was life; and the life was the light of
men";

That he was divinely conceived, and born in mortality to Mary, the very Son of God, the Son of Man;

That, cradled in a manger and reared in the home of a lowly carpenter, yet was he the Sovereign of this earth;

That, growing to manhood, he moved and labored among our Heavenly Father's earthly sons and daughters, he was their Elder Brother;

That "he came unto his own, and his own received him not," yet taught he them the plan of life and salvation which, obeyed, will bring them back into an eternal presence with their Heavenly Father;

That his teaching and service completed, he prepared himself to make the great atoning sacrifice for the Fall of Adam;

That he was arrested, tried, condemned, crucified, and buried;

That, as he had time and again declared, he was, on the morning of the third day, resurrected;

That his resurrection was literal, for he rose with the bones, muscles, and body form that he laid down;

That by his atoning sacrifice, he vicariously suffered and paid the penalty for the Fall,—so that every man and woman born to earth, each and every of them, will, in due time, be resurrected, even as was he;

That he was in truth the Beloved Son, the Only Begotten in the Flesh, the Creator of the Earth, the Redeemer of the World, the Christ that was to come, the First Fruits of the Resurrection, our Intercessor and Advocate with the Father;

That by obedience to his Gospel all mankind may be saved, not only, but exalted in the Kingdom of God;

That in these Latter-days the Holy Priesthood after the Order of the Son of God, taken from among men after the mortal days of the Christ, has been again restored to the earth in this the Last Dispensation, the Dispensation of the Fulness of Times, and along with this Priesthood the Gospel of Jesus Christ has been restored;

That through these, all mankind may be saved and exalted, God's destiny for man as declared to Moses: "For behold, this is my work and my glory—to bring to pass the immortality and eternal life of man."

To all this I bear solemn witness.

APPENDIX

Appendix A

TABLE OF CHIEF UNCIAL MANUSCRIPTS

CENT.	NAME	PLACE		GOSPELS		ACTS AND CATHOLIC EPISTLES		PAULINE EPISTLES	APOCALYPSE
IV.	Vaticanus	Vatican	B	All.	—	All.	—	As far as Heb. 9:14.	All.
	Sinaiticus	St. Petersburg	ℵ	All.	—	All.	—	All.	All.
V.	Alexandrinus	Brit. Museum	A	From Matt. 25:6. Omit John 6:50-8:52.	—	All.	—	Omit 2 Cor. 4:13-12:6.	About ⅔.
	Ephraemi	Paris	C	Fragments=about ⅔ of whole.	—	About ⅔ of whole.	—	About ⅔.	
	Guelpherbytanus B	Wolfenbüttel	Q	235 Verses of St. Luke and St. John.					
VI.	Rossanensis	Rossano	Σ	As far as Mark 16:14.					
	Beza	Cambridge	D_1	All with hiatus . . .	—	All with hiatus.			
	Claromontanus	Paris					D_2	All except Rom. 1:1-7, 27-30.	
	Coislin, 202	Paris and St. Petersburg		486 Verses of all Evangelists.			H_2	12 leaves.	
	Guelpherbytanus A	Wolfenbüttel	P						
	Dublinensis	Dublin	Z	290 verses of St. Matt.					
	Nitriensis	Brit. Museum	R	516 verses of St. Luke.					
	Purpureus	Brit. Museum Rome and Vienna	N	12 leaves and 33 at Patmos.					
	Laudianus	Bodleian			E_2	Acts 1:1-26:29; 28:26-end.			
	Coislin I. (Septuag. Octateuch)	Paris, &c.	Fa	9 verses.	—	7 verses.	—	10 verses.	
VII.	Basiliensis	Basle	E_1	All, except Luke 3:4-15; 24:47-53.					

Cent.	Manuscript	City	Gospels	Acts & Cath.	St. Paul	Apoc.
	Mosquensis	Moscow	V — All, except Matt. 5:44-6:12; 9:18-10:1; 22:14-23:35; 28:17-20. Mark 10:16-30; 15:2-20. John 21:15-25. John 21:12-25. After John 7:39, in Cursives.			
	Barberini	Rome	Y — John 16:3-19:41.			
	Zacynthius	Bible Society	Ξ — Luke 1:1-11:33.			
	Vaticanus, 2066	Vatican				B_2 — All.
IX.	Wolfi B	Hamburg	H — Fragments.			
	Cyprius	Paris	K — All.			
	Augiensis	Cambridge			F_2 — Defective in 4 places.	
	Boreeli	Utrecht	F_1 — Full of hiatus.			
	Mutinensis	Modena		H_2 — Acts, except 4 places.	All, except 2 places.	
	Tischendorfianus IV.	Bodleian	Γ — All Luke, Mark except 105 verses, 531 of the rest.			
	Mosquensis, 98	Moscow		K_2 — Cath. Ep. only.	Defective in 6 places.	
	Sangallensis	St. Gall	Δ — All, except John 19:17-35.			
	Boernerianus	Dresden			G_3 — Down to Heb. 13:10.	
	Angelicus	Rome		L_2 — From Acts 8:10.	All, except 8 places.	
	Petropolitanus	St. Petersburg	Π — All, except Matt. 3:12-4:18; 19:12-20:3. John 8:6-39.			
	Porphyrianus	St. Petersburg		P_2 — All, except 3 places.	All, except 3 places.	
	Campianus	Paris	M — All.			
	Monacensis	Munich	X — With serious defects.			
X.	Nanianus I.	Venice	U — All.			
	Vaticanus, 354	Vatican	S — All.			
	Harleianus	Brit. Museum	G — Fragments.			

ℵ is quoted thus: —ℵ*, the original reading; ℵ^a, second c. (VI.); ℵ^c (VII.), and eight others.

B:—B*, original reading; B^2 or B^3, first corrector (X. or XI.).

C:—C*, or ^2, first corrector (VI.); C**, or ^3, second (IX.); C***, or ^4, third.

D:—corrected, first, by the original penman as Diorthota; afterwards by eight or nine others, some nearly coeval with the Codex, some not very long ago.

D suppl. (IX.) filled up some omissions.—Scrivener, Plain Int., Tischendorf, Prolegomena (C. R. Gregory).

(Edward Miller, A Guide to the Textual Criticism of the New Testament, pp. 108-109.)

Appendix B

The chief Versions have been already noticed. The general dates of them all may be seen together in the following Table:—

CENT.	SYRIAC	LATIN	EGYPTIAN	SINGLE VERSIONS
II.	Peshito (1)	Old Latin (1) sc. a. African b. European	. . . . . ? Memphitic, or Bahiric (2) ? Thebaic, or Sahidic (2)	. . . . . .
III.	. . . . . .	. . . . . .	? Memphitic and Thebaic . . . . . . Bashmuric, or Elearchian (3)	. . . . . .
IV.	? Curetonian (3)	. . . . . . Vulgate (2)	. . . . . .	. . . . . Gothic (2)
V.	Jerusalem (3) Karkaphensian (3)			Armenian (2) Georgian (3) Ethiopian (2)?
VI.	Philoxenian (3) A.D. 508.			
VII.	Harclean (3) A.D. 616.			
		Clementine Revision A.D. 1592.		Slavonic (3) IXth. Anglo-Saxon (4) VIIIth-XIth. Frankish (4) IXth. Persic (4) IXth. Arabic (several) VIIIth, &c.

The figures here attached to the names of the several Versions denote their relative scale of excellence in a critical light according as Dr. Scrivener has classed them. (Miller, pp. 113-114.)

Appendix C

It may be convenient to subjoin an alphabetical list of the ecclesiastical writers, both in Greek and Latin and in other languages (with the usual abridgements for their names), which are the most often cited in critical editions of the New Testament. The Latin authors are printed in italics, and unless they happen to appeal unequivocally to the evidence of Greek codices, are available only for the correction of their vernacular translation. The dates annexed generally indicate the death of the persons they refer to, except when 'fl.' (=*floruit*) is prefixed.

Alcimus (Avitus), fl. 360.

Ambrose, Bp. of Milan, A.D. 397 (Ambr.).

Ambrosiaster, the false Ambrose, perhaps *Hilary* the Deacon, of the fourth century (Ambrst.).

Ammonius of Alexandria, circa 438 (Ammon.) *in Catenis*.

Amphilochius, fl. 380.

Anastasius, Abbot, fl. 650.

Anastasius Sinaita, fl. 570.

Andreas, Bishop of Caesarea, sixth century? (And.)

Andreas of Crete, seventh century.

Antiochus, monk, fl. 614.

Antipater, Bp. of Bostra, fl. 450.

Aphraates, the Syrian, fourth century.

Archelaus and Manes, fl. 278.

Arethas, Bp. of Caesarea Capp., tenth century? (Areth.)

Aristides, fl. 139.

Arius, fl. 325.

Arnobius of Africa, 306 (Arnob.).

Asterius, fourth century.

Athanasius, Bp. of Alexandria, 373 (Ath.).

Athenagoras of Athens, 177 (Athen.).

Augustine, Bp. of Hippo, 430 (Aug.).

Barnabas, first or second century? (Barn.)

Basil, Bp. of Caesarea, 379 (Bas.).

Basil of Cilicia, fl. 497.

Basil of Seleucia, fl. 440 (Bas. Sel.).

Bede, the Venerable, 735 (Bede).

Caesarius of Arles, fl. 520.

Caesarius (Pseudo-) of Constantinople, 340 (Caes.).

Candidus Isaurus, fl. 500.

Capreolus, fl. 430.

Carpathius, John, fl. 490.

Cassianus, fl. 415.

Cassiodorus, 468-560 (?) (Cassiod.).

Chromatius, Bp. of Aquileia, fl. 390 (Chrom.).

Chrysostom, Bp. of Constantinople, 407 (Chrys.).

Chrysostom (Pseudo-), fl. eighth century.

Clement of Alexandria, fl. 194 (Clem.).

Clement, Bp. of Rome, fl. 90 (Clem. Rom.).

Clementines, the, second century.

Corderius.

Cosmas, Bp. of Maiuma, fl. 743.

Cosmas Indicopleustes, 535 (Cosm.).

Cyprian, Bp. of Carthage, 258 (Cypr.).

Cyril, Bp. of Alexandria, 444 (Cyr.).

Cyril, Bp. of Jerusalem, 386 (Cyr. Jer.).

Dalmatius, fl. 450.

Damascenus, John, 730 (Dam.)[1].

Damasus, Pope, fl. 366.

Didache, 80-120.

Didymus of Alexandria, 370 (Did.).

Diodorus of Tarsus, fl. 380.

Dionysius, Bp. of Alexandria, 265 (Dion.).

Dionysius of Alexandria (Pseudo-), third century.

Dionysius (Pseudo-) Areopagita, fifth century (Dion. Areop.).

Dionysius Maximus, fl. 259 (?).

Ephraem the Syrian, 378 (Ephr.).

Ephraem the Syrian (Pseudo-), fourth century.

Ephraim, Bp. of Cherson.

Epiphanius, Bp. of Cyprus, 403 (Epiph.).

Epiphanius, Deacon of Catana, fl. 737.

Erechthius, fl. 440.

Eudocia, wife of Theodosius II, fl. 430.

Eulogius, sixth century.

Eusebius of Alexandria.

Eusebius, Bp. of Caesarea, 340 (Eus.).

Eustathius, Bp. of Antioch, fl. 350.

Eustathius, monk.

Euthalius, Bp. of Sulci, 458 (Euthal.).

Eutherius, fl. 431.

Euthymius Zigabenus, 1116 (Euthym.).

Eutychius, fl. 553.

Evagrius of Pontus, 380 (Evagr.).

Evagrius Scholasticus, the historian, fl. 492.

Facundus, fl. 547.

Faustus, fl. 400.

Ferrandus, fl. 356.

Fulgentius of Ruspe, fl. 508 (Fulg.).

Gaudentius, fl. 405 (Gaud.).

Gelasius of Cyzicus, fl. 476.

Gennadius, fl. 459.

Germanus of Constantinople, fl. 715.

Gregentius, fl. 540.

Gregory of Nazianzus, the Divine, Bp. of Constantinople, 389 (Naz.).

Gregory Naz. (Pseudo-).

Gregory, Bp. of Nyssa, 396 (Nyss.).

Gregory Thaumaturgus, Bp. of Neocaesarea, 243 (Thauma.).

Gregory the Great, Bp. of Rome, 605 (Greg.).

---

[1] Dam[par cod]. i.e. 'Joh. Damasceni parallela sacra ex cod. Rupefuc. saeculi ferè 8.' Tischendorf, N. T., Preface to vol. i of the eighth edition, 1869. He promised full information in his 'Prolegomena,' which never appeared. Here we have a manuscript ascribed to the same century as the Father whose work it contains. One MS. is at Paris (collated by Mr. Rendel Harris, A.D. 1884); another in Phillipps collection at Cheltenham.

Haymo, Bp. of Halberstadt, ninth century (Haym.).
Hegesippus, fl. 180.
Hermas, second century.
Hieronymus (Jerome), 420 (Hier.) or (Jer.).
Hilary, Bp. of Arles, 429.
Hilary, Bp. of Poictiers, fl. 354 (Hil.).
Hilary, the deacon, fourth century.
Hippolytus, Bp. of Portus (?), fl. 220 (Hip.).
Ignatius, Bp. of Antioch, 107 (Ign.).
Ignatius (Pseudo-), fourth century.
Irenaeus, Bp. of Lyons, fl. 178; chiefly extant in an old Latin version (Iren.).
Isidore of Pelusium, 412 (Isid.).

Jacobus Nisibenus, fl. 335.
Jobius, sixth century.
Julian, heretic, fl. 425.
Julius Africanus, fl. 220.
Justin Martyr, 164 (Just.).
Justin Martyr (Pseudo-), fourth century.
Justinian, Emperor, fl. 527-565.
Juvencus, fl. 320 (Juv.).

Lactantius, 306 (Lact.).
Leo the Great, fl. 440.
Leontius of Byzantium, fl. 348.
Liberatus of Carthage, fl. 533.
Lucifer, Bp. of Cagliari, 367 (Luc.).

Macarius Magnes, third or fourth century.
Macarius Magnus, fourth century.
Manes, fl. 278. *See* Archelaus.
Marcion the heretic, 139 (Mcion.), cited by Epiphanius (Mcion-e) and by *Tertullian* (Mcion-t).
Maxentius, sixth century.
Maximus the Confessor, 662 (Max. Conf.).

Maximus Taurinensis, 466 (Max. Taur.).
Mercator, Marius, fl. 218.
Methodius, 311 (Meth.).
Modestus, patriarch of Jerus. seventh century.
Nestorius of C. P., fifth century.
Nicephorus, fl. 787.
Nicetas of Aquileia, fifth century.
Nicetas of Byzantium, 1120.
Nilus, monk, fl. 430.
Nonnus, fl. 400 (Nonn.).
Novatianus, fl. 251 (Novat.).
Oecumenius, Bp. of Tricca, tenth century? (Oecu.)
Optatus, fl. 371.
Origen, b. 186, d. 253 (Or.).
Pacianus, Bp. of Barcelona, fl. 370.
Pamphilus the Martyr, 308 (Pamph.).
Papias, fl. 160.
Paschasius, the deacon?
Paulus, Bp. of Emesa, fl. 431.
Paulus, patriarch of Constantinople, fl. 648.
Peter, Bp. of Alexandria, 311 (Petr.).
Petrus Chrysologus, Archbp. of Ravenna, fl. 440.
Petrus, Deacon, fl. sixth century.
Petrus Siculus, fl. 790.
Philo of Carpasus, fourth century.
Phoebadius, Bp. of Agen, fl. 358.
Photius, Bp. of Constantinople, 891 (Phot.).
Polycarp, Bp. of Smyrna, 166 (Polyc.).
Porphyrius, fl. 290.
Primasius, Bp. of Adrumetum, fl. 550 (Prim.).
Prosper of Aquitania, fl. 431.
Prudentius, 406 (Prud.).
Rufinus of Aquileia, 397 (Ruf.).
Severianus, a Syrian Bp., 409 (Sevrn.).

Severus of Antioch, fl. 510.
Socrates ⎰ Church ⎰ fl. 440 (Soc.).
Sozomen ⎱ Historians ⎱ 450 (Soz.).
Suidas the lexicographer, 980? (Suid.).
Symeon, fl. 1000.
Symmachus, fourth century.
Tatian of Antioch, 172 (Tat.).
Tatian (Pseudo-), third century.
Tertullian of Africa, fl. 200 (Tert.)[1].
Theodore, Bp. of Mopsuestia, 428 (Thdor. Mops.).
Theodoret, Bp. of Cyrus or of Cyrrhus in Commagene, 458 (Thdrt.).
Theodorus of Heracleia, fl. 336.
Theodorus, Lector, fl. 525.
Theodorus Studita, fl. 794.
Theodotus of Ancyra, fl. 431.
Theophilus of Alexandria, fl. 388.
Theophilus, Bp. of Antioch, 182 (Thph. Ant.).

Theophylact, Archbp. of Bulgaria, fl. 1077 (Theophyl.).
Tichonius the Donatist, fl. 390 (Tich.).
Timotheus of Antioch, fifth century.
Timotheus of Jerusalem, sixth century.
Titus, Bp. of Bostra, fl. 370 (Tit. Bost.).
Victor of Antioch, 430 (Vict. Ant.)[2].
Victor, Bp. of Tunis, 565 (Vict. Tun.).
Victorinus, Bp. of Pettau, 360 (Victorin.).
Victorinus of Rome, fl. 361.
Vigilius of Thapsus, 484 (Vigil.).
Vincentius Lirinensis, fl. 434.

Zacharias, patriarch of Jerusalem, fl. 614.
Zacharias, Scholasticus, fl. 536.
Zeno, Bp. of Verona, fl. 463.

Besides the writers, the following anonymous works contain quotations from the New Testament:—

Auctor libri de xlii. mansionibus (auct. mans.), fourth century.
Auctor libri de Promissionibus dimid. temporis (Prom.), third century.
Auctor libri de Rebaptismate (Rebapt.), fourth century.
Auctor libri de singularitate clericorum (auct. sing. cler.), fourth century.

Auctor libri de Vocatione gentium (Vocat.), fourth century.
Acta Apostolica (Syriac), fourth century.
Acta Philippi, fourth century.
Acta Pilati, third or fourth century.
Anaphora Pilati, fifth century.
Apocalypse of Peter, 170 (?).

---

[1] This important witness for the Old Latin version must now be used with H. Roensch's 'Das Neue Testament Tertullian's', Leipzig, 1871, wherein all his citations from the N. T. are arranged and critically examined.

[2] *See* Dean Burgon's Appendix (D) to his 'Last Twelve Verses of St. Mark,' pp. 269-287, which well deserves the praise accorded to it by a not very friendly critic. The Dean discusses at length the genius and character of Victor of Antioch's Commentary on St. Mark, and enumerates the manuscripts which contain it.

Apocryphal Gospels, second century, &c.

Apostolic Canons, third to fifth century.

Apostolic Constitutions, third and fourth centuries.

Chronicon Paschale, 628.

Concilia, Labbè or Mansi.

Cramer's Catena.

Dialogus, fourth or fifth century.

Eastern bishops at Ephesus, 431.

Gospel of Peter, about 165.

Opus Imperfectum, fifth century.

Quaestiones ex utroque Testamento, fourth century[3].

---

[3] It should be stated that some of the dates in the two tables just given are doubtful, authorities differing.

(F. H. A. Scrivener, *A Plain Introduction to the Criticism of the New Testament*, 4th ed., Edward Miller, ed., Vol. II, pp. 171-174.)

BIBLIOGRAPHY •

Allen, Willoughby C., "Criticism (New Testament)," James Hastings, ed., *Encyclopaedia of Religion and Ethics*, New York, Charles Scribner's Sons, 1928, Vol. IV.

... "Matthew, Gospel According to," James Hastings, ed., *A Dictionary of Christ and the Gospels*, New York, Charles Scribner's Sons, 1908, Vol. II.

American Standard Version, National Council of the Churches of Christ in the U.S.A., New York, Thomas Nelson & Sons, 1900-1901.

Andrews, Samuel J., *The Life of Our Lord Upon the Earth; Considered in its Historical, Chronological, and Geographical Relations*, rev. ed., New York, Charles Scribner's Sons, 1891.

Briggs, Charles Augustus, *New Light on the Life of Jesus*, New York, Charles Scribner's Sons, 1909.

Broadus, John A., *A Harmony of the Gospels in the Revised Version, With New Helps for Historical Study*, Archibald Thomas Robertson, rev. ed., New York, George H. Doran Company, 1920.

Bruce, F. F., *The Books and the Parchments, Some Chapters on the Transmission of the Bible*, London, Pickering & Inglis Ltd., 1950.

Burgon, John William, *The Causes of the Corruption of the Traditional Text of the Holy Gospels, Being the Sequel to The Traditional Text of the Holy Gospels*, Edward Miller, ed., London, George Bell and Sons, 1896.

... *The Revision Revised*, London, John Murray, 1883.

Carr, A., *The Gospel According to St. Matthew, The Cambridge Bible for Schools and Colleges*, Cambridge and London, The University Press, 1893.

Clark, George W., *A New Harmony of the Four Gospels in English; According to the Common Version*, rev. ed., Philadelphia, American Baptist Publication Society, 1900.

Davison, W. T., "John, Gospel of," James Hastings, ed., *Dictionary of the Bible*, One Volume Edition, New York, Charles Scribner's Sons, 1920.

Edersheim, Alfred, *The Life and Times of Jesus The Messiah*, 3rd ed., New York, Longmans, Green and Co., 1927.

Ellis, William T., "Roman Census That Caused Famed Bethlehem Journey Proved by Ancient Record," *The Washington Post*, December 19, 1926.

Farrar, F. W., *The Gospel According to St. Luke, The Cambridge Bible for Schools and Colleges*, Cambridge and London, The University Press, 1894.

Fox, John, *Book of Martyrs*, Charles A. Goodrich, ed., Edwin Hunt, Middletown, 1833.

Goodspeed, C., "Tithe," James Hastings, ed., *A Dictionary of Christ and the Gospels*, New York, Charles Scribner's Sons, 1908, Vol. II.

Gwilliam, G. H., "Language of Christ," James Hastings, ed., *Dictionary of the Bible*, One Volume Edition, New York, Charles Scribner's Sons, 1920.

History of the Church of Jesus Christ of Latter-day Saints, Salt Lake City, The Deseret News, 1902-1912.

Inge, William Ralph, "John, Gospel of (II.: Contents)," James Hastings, ed., *A Dictionary of Christ and the Gospels*, New York, Charles Scribner's Sons, 1908, Vol. I.

Introduction to the Revised Standard Version of the New Testament, An, The International Council of Religious Education, 1946.

Johnson, Jotham, "The Language of Homer's Heroes," *Scientific American*, Vol. 190, No. 5 (May, 1954).

Kenyon, Sir Frederic G., "English Versions," "Text of the New Testament," James Hastings, ed., *Dictionary of the Bible*, One Volume Edition, New York, Charles Scribner's Sons, 1920.

... *Our Bible and the Ancient Manuscripts*, 4th ed. rev., London, Eyre & Spottiswoode, 1948.

... *The Story of the Bible, A Popular Account of How It Came to Us*, London, John Murray, 1949.

... *The Text of the Greek Bible, A Students Handbook*, new ed., London, Duckworth, 1949.

MacCulloch, J. A., "Tithes," James Hastings, ed., *Encyclopaedia of Religion and Ethics*, New York, Charles Scribner's Sons, 1928, Vol. XII.

Maclean, Arthur J., "Mark, Gospel According to," James Hastings, ed., *A Dictionary of Christ and the Gospels*, New York, Charles Scribner's Sons, 1908, Vol. II.

Miller, Edward, *A Guide to the Textual Criticism of the New Testament*, London, George Bell and Sons, 1886.

Moulton, James Hope, "Language of the NT," James Hastings, ed., *Dictionary of the Bible*, One Volume Edition, New York, Charles Scribner's Sons, 1920.

New Schaff-Herzog Encyclopedia of Religious Knowledge, The, New York, Funk & Wagnalls Company, 1908-1914.

Oesterley, W. O. E., "Tithes," James Hastings, ed., *Dictionary of the Bible*, One Volume Edition, New York, Charles Scribner's Sons, 1920.

Parallel Bible, The, London, C. J. Clay and Son, 1885.

Peake, Arthur S., "Tithe," James Hastings, ed., *A Dictionary of the Bible*, New York, Charles Scribner's Sons, 1902, Vol. IV.

Price, Ira Maurice "Apocrypha," James Hastings, ed., *Dictionary of the Bible*, One Volume Edition, New York, Charles Scribner's Sons, 1920.

Putnam's Handbook of Universal History, George Haven Putnam, ed., New York and London, G. P. Putnam's Sons, 1914.

Revised Standard Version, Division of Christian Education of the National Council of the Churches of Christ in the U.S.A., New York, Thomas Nelson & Sons, 1946-1952.

Revised Version, University Press, Oxford, 1881-1885.

Roberts, B. H., *A Comprehensive History of The Church of Jesus Christ of Latter-day Saints*, published by the Church, Salt Lake City, Deseret News Press, 1930.

Robertson, A. T., *A Harmony of the Gospels for Students of the Life of Christ (Based on the Broadus Harmony in the Revised Version)*, New York, Richard R. Smith, Inc., 1930.

Robinson, Edward, *A Harmony of the Four Gospels in English; According to the Common Version*, M. B. Riddle, rev. ed., Boston, New York, and Chicago, Houghton, Mifflin and Company, 1886.

Scrivener, Frederick Henry Ambrose, *A Plain Introduction to the Criticism of the New Testament, For the Use of Biblical Students*, 2nd ed. rev., 1874; 3rd ed. rev., 1883; Cambridge, Deighton, Bell & Co. Ltd.; 4th ed. rev., Edward Miller, ed., London, G. Bell & Sons, 1894.

Smith, Joseph Fielding, *Essentials in Church History*, 5th ed., Salt Lake City, Deseret News Press, 1935.

... *Teachings of the Prophet Joseph Smith*, Salt Lake City, Deseret News Press, 1938.

Stevens, Wm. Arnold, and Burton, Ernest DeWitt, *A Harmony of the Gospels for Historical Study*, 12th ed. rev., New York, Charles Scribner's Sons, 1904.

Strachan, James, "Criticism (Old Testament)," James Hastings, ed., *Encyclopaedia of Religion and Ethics*, New York, Charles Scribner's Sons, 1928, Vol. IV.

Strachan, R. H., "John, Gospel of (I.: Critical Article)," James Hastings, ed., *A Dictionary of Christ and the Gospels*, New York, Charles Scribner's Sons, 1908, Vol. I.

Variorum Bible, The (The Sunday School Centenary Bible, Authorized Version), 1880, (Teacher's Edition), 1894, London, Eyre & Spottiswoode, Ltd.

Willis, J. R., "Tithes," James Hastings, ed., *A Dictionary of the Apostolic Church*, New York, Charles Scribner's Sons, 1919, Vol. II.

Wilson, Edmund, "A Reporter at Large, The Scrolls From the Dead Sea," *The New Yorker*, May 14, 1955.

Wright, Arthur, "Luke, Gospel According to," James Hastings, ed., *A Dictionary of Christ and the Gospels*, New York, Charles Scribner's Sons, 1908, Vol. II.

Wright, G. Ernest, "A Phenomenal Discovery," *The Biblical Archaeologist*, Vol. XI, No. 2 (May, 1948).

Zenos, Andrew C., "Tithe," *A New Standard Bible Dictionary*, New York, Funk and Wagnalls Co., 1925.

BIOGRAPHICAL NOTES •

Allen, Willoughby C., M.A., Rector of Saham Toney, Norfolk; Chaplain, Fellow, and Lecturer in Theology and Hebrew at Exeter College, Oxford; works include, "Criticism (New Testament)," Hastings', *Encyclopaedia of Religion and Ethics* (New York, 1928); "Gospel According to Matthew," Hastings', *Dictionary of Christ and the Gospels* (New York, 1908).

Andrews, Samuel J., lawyer, theologian; Pastor, Congregational Church, East Windsor; Catholic Apostolic Church, Hartford; Instructor, Trinity College, Hartford; works include, *Life of Our Lord Upon the Earth* (New York 1862); *God's Revelations of Himself to Man* (1885), *Christianity and Anti-Christianity in Their Final Conflict* (1898).

Bowie, Rev. Walter Russell, B.D., D.D., Grace Church. New York; New Testament American Standard Bible Committee; works include, "The Use of the New Testament in Worship," in *An Introduction to the Revised Standard Version of the New Testament* (1946).

Briggs, Charles Augustus, D.D., D.Litt., Edward Robinson Professor of Biblical Theology, Union Theological Seminary, New York; works include, *New Light on the Life of Jesus* (New York, 1909).

Broadus, John A., D.D. Ll.D., President and Professor of Interpretation of New Testament and Homiletics, Southern Baptist Theological Seminary; Pastor, Baptist Church, Greenville, S.C.; works include, *A Harmony of the Gospels in the Revised Version* (New York, 1920).

Bruce, F. F., M.A., Department of Biblical History and Literature, University of Sheffield; works include, *The Books and the Parchments* (London, 1950).

Burgon, John William, B.D., Dean of Chichester; Church of England scholar, Fellow of Oriel College, Oxford, Gresham Professor of Divinity; works include, *A Plain Commentary on the Four Holy Gospels* (8 vols., 1855); *The Last Twelve Verses of the Gospel According to St. Mark Vindicated and Established* (1871); *The Revision Revised* (London, 1883); and *The Causes of the Corruption of the Traditional Text of the Holy Gospels* (London, 1896).

Burrows, Professor Millar, B.A., B.D., Ph.D., Yale University, Old Testament and New Testament American Standard Bible Committee; works include, "The Semitic Background of the New Testament," in *An Introduction to the Revised Standard Version of the New Testament*.

Burton, Ernest De Witt, D.D., Professor of New Testament Literature and Interpretation, Head of Department of Biblical and Patristic Greek, University of Chicago; editor, *Biblical World, American Journal of Theology;* works include, *Harmony of the Gospels for Historical Study* (New York, 1894; in collaboration with W. A. Stevens).

Cadbury, Professor Henry J., A.M., Ph.D., Litt.D., D.D., Harvard University, New Testament American Standard Bible Committee; works include, "The Vocabulary and Grammar of New Testament Greek," in *An Introduction to the Revised Standard Version of the New Testament* (1946).

Carr, Rev. A., M.A., Fellow of Oriel College, Oxford, Assistant Master at Wellington College; editor of St. Matthew in *The Cambridge Bible* (Cambridge, 1893).

Clark, Rev. George W., American Baptist Publication Society; works include, *A New Harmony of the Four Gospels in English* (1900), *Commentary on the New Testament* (9 vols., Philadelphia, 1870-1907).

Craig, Professor Clarence T., A.B., S.T.B., Ph.D., D.Litt., M.A., D.D., Oberlin Graduate School of Theology, New Testament American Standard Bible Committee; works include, "The King James and the American Standard Versions of the New Testament," in *An Introduction to the Revised Standard Version of the New Testament* (1946).

Davison, Rev. William Theophilus, M.A., D.D., Principal and Professor of Systematic Theology, Richmond College, Surrey; Member of faculty of theology in London University; President, Wesleyan Methodist Conference, 1901; works include, "Gospel of John," Hastings' *Dictionary of the Bible* (1920).

Edersheim, Alfred, M.A. Oxon., D.D., Ph. D., Biblical scholar, Vicar of Loders, Dorsetshire; Warburtonian Lecturer, Preacher to the University of Oxford and Grinfield Lecturer on the Septuagint; works include, *The Temple, Its Ministry and Services as They Were at the Time of Jesus Christ* (London, 1874); *The Life and Times of Jesus the Messiah,* (New York, 3rd ed., 1886, 1927 reprint).

Farrar, the Ven. Frederic William, D.D., F.R.S., Archdeacon of Westminster, Dean of Canterbury; among his numerous publications are, *Life of Christ* (2 vols. 1874); *The Early Days of Christianity* (2 vols., London, 1882); editor of St. Luke in *The Cambridge Bible* (1894).

Goodspeed, Rev. Calvin, D.D., Ll.D., Professor of Systematic Theology in Baylor University, Waco, Texas; works include, "Tithe," Hastings' *A Dictionary of Christ and the Gospels* (New York, 1908).

Goodspeed, Professor Edgar J., A.B., D.D., D.B., Ph. D., University of Chicago, New Testament American Standard Bible Committee; works include, *The Bible: An American Translation* (1935); "The Making of the New Testament: Greek and Roman Factors," in *An Introduction to the Revised Standard Version of the New Testament* (1946).

Grant, Frederick C., B.D., S.T.M., Th.D., D.D., D.C.L., President, Seabury-Western Theological Seminary, New Testament Standard Bible Committee; "The Greek Text of the New Testament," in *An Introduction to the Revised Standard Version of the New Testament* (1946).

Gwilliam, Rev. G. H., B.D., Rector of Remenham, Henley; works include "Language of Christ," Hastings' *Dictionary of the Bible* (New York, 1920).

Hastings, James, M.A., D.D., Fellow of the Royal Anthropological Institute, Member of the Council of the Palestine Exploration Fund; editor of *A Dictionary of the Bible* (5 vols., Edinburgh and New York, 1898-1904); *Dictionary of Christ and the Gospels* (2 vols., 1906-07); *Dictionary of the Bible* (1 vol., 1920); *Dictionary of the Apostolic Church* (1916); *Encylopaedia of Religion and Ethics* (1928); and *The Expository Times*.

Hort, Fenton John Anthony, D.D., Vicar of St. Ippolyts cum Great Wymondley, near Cambridge, Hulsean Professor of Divinity, Cambridge; member New Testament Revision Committee; works include, with Brooke Foss Westcott, *The New Testament in the Original Greek* (2 vols., 1881).

Inge, Rev. William Ralph, D.D., C.V.O., F.B.A., Dean of St. Paul's; Vicar of All Saints', Ennismore Gardens, London, Late Fellow and Tutor of Hertford College, Oxford; works include, "Gospel of John (II. Contents)," Hastings' *A Dictionary of Christ and the Gospels* (New York, 1908).

Kenyon, Sir Frederic G., K.C.B., F.B.A., M.A., D.Litt., Ph.D., Department of Manuscripts in the British Museum, Late Fellow of Magdalen College, Oxford, Formerly Director and Principal Librarian of the British Museum; works include, "English Versions," and "Text of the New Testament," Hastings' *Dictionary of the Bible* (New York, 1920); *Our Bible and the Ancient Manuscripts* (London, 1948); *The Text of the Greek Bible*, (London, 1949); *The Story of the Bible* (London, 1949); *Handbook to the Textual Criticism of the New Testament* (2nd ed., 1951); *The Bible and Archaeology* (1940).

MacCulloch, John Arnott, D.D., Examiner in Comparative Religion and Philosophy of Religion, Victoria University, Manchester; Chaplain to the Bishop of St. Andrews; works include, "Tithes," Hastings' *Encyclopaedia of Religion and Ethics* (New York, 1928); *The Religion of the Ancient Celts*.

Maclean, Arthur John, M.A., D.D., Bishop of Moray, Ross, and Caithness; works include, "Gospel According to Mark," Hastings' *A Dictionary of Christ and the Gospels* (New York, 1908); *Dictionary and Grammar of Vernacular Syriac* (Cambridge and Oxford, 1895-1901); *Ancient Church Orders; Recent Discoveries Illustrating Early Christian Life and Worship* (London, 1904); and editor of *East Syrian Liturgies* (1890-92).

Miller, Edward A., M.A., Fellow and Tutor of New College, Oxford; Wykehamical Prebendary of Chichester, Rector of Bucknell, Oxon; works include, *A Guide to the Textual Criticism of the New Testament* (London, 1886); arranged, compiled, and edited *The Causes of the Corruption of the Traditional Text of the Holy Gospels*, by John William Burgon (1896); editor of 4th ed., F.H.A. Scrivener, *Plain Introduction to the Textual Criticism of the New Testament* (London, 2 vols., 1894).

Moulton, Rev. James Hope, M.A., D. Litt., D.D., D.C.L., Greenwood Professor of Hellenistic Greek in the Victoria University of Manchester; works include, "Language of the NT," Hastings' *Dictionary of the Bible* (New York, 1920).

Oesterley, Rev. W. O. E., M.A., D.D., Rector of St. Mary, Aldermary; Warburton Lecturer in Lincoln's Inn Chapel; Examiner in Hebrew and Greek in the University of London; works include, "Tithes," Hastings' *Dictionary of the Bible* (New York, 1920).

Peake, Arthur S., M.A., D.D., Professor in the Primitive Methodist College, Manchester, and Lecturer in Lancashire Independent College; sometime Fellow of Merton and Lecturer in Mansfield College, Oxford; works include, "Tithe," Hastings' *A Dictionary of the Bible* (New York, 1902).

Price, Ira Maurice, M.A., B.D., Ph.D., Ll.D., Professor of Semitic Languages and Literature in the University of Chicago; works include, "Apocrypha," Hastings' *Dictionary of the Bible* (New York, 1920).

Riddle, Matthew Brown, D.D., Professor of New Testament Exegesis in Hartford Theological Seminary and at Western Theological Seminary; works include, *Story of the Revised New Testament, American Standard Edition* (Philadelphia, 1908); edited, *American Standard Edition of the Revised Version of the Bible;* revised portions of the American edition of *The Ante-Nicene Fathers* (New York, 1886-1888); edited Robinson's *A Harmony of the Four Gospels in English* (Boston, 1889).

Roberts, Brigham Henry, one of Seven Presidents of Seventies, Church of Jesus Christ of Latter-day Saints, editor and writer; works include, *The Gospel* (1888); *Outlines of Ecclesiastical History* (1893); *Defense of the Faith and the Saints; A Comprehensive History of the Church of Jesus Christ of Latter-day Saints; A New Witness for God* (1895).

Robertson, Archibald Thomas, M.A., Litt. D., D.D. Ll. D., Professor of Biblical Introduction and Interpretation of the New Testament, Southern Baptist Theological Seminary; works include, *A Harmony of the Gospels for Students of the Life of Christ* (New York, 1930); edited, John A. Broadus, *A Harmony of the Gospels in the Revised Version* (New York, 1920).

Robinson, Edward, D.D., LL.D., Professor of Biblical Literature in the Union Theological Seminary, New York; works include, *Biblical Researches in Palestine, Mount Sinai, and Arabia Petraea* (1841); *Greek Harmony of the Gospels* (1845); *A Harmony of the Four Gospels in English* (1846); and *A Greek and English Lexicon of the New Testament* (1850).

Scrivener, Frederick Henry Ambrose, M.A., D.C.L., Ll.D., of Trinity College, Cambridge; Rector of St. Gerrans, Cornwall, Prebendary of Exeter, Vicar of Hendon; member of New Testament Revision Committee; works include, *A Plain Introduction to the Criticism of the New Testament* (1861; 2nd ed., 1874; 3rd ed., 1883; 4th ed., enlarged, 2 vols., 1894); *A Supplement to the Authorized English Version of the New Testament* (1845); *Bezae Codex Cantabrigiensis, Gr. and Lat.* (1864); *The New Testament in the Original Greek, According to the Text Followed in the Authorized Version together with the Variations Adopted in the Revised Version* (1881).

Smith, Joseph Fielding, D.Litt., President, Quorum of the Twelve Apostles, and Historian, Church of Jesus Christ of Latter-day Saints; works include, *The Way to Perfection; Signs of the Times; The Progress of Man; Teachings of the Prophet Joseph Smith* (1940); *Essentials in Church History* (1950); *Man: His Origin and Destiny* (1954).

Stevens, William Arnold, Professor of Greek, Denison University; Professor of New Testament Exegesis, Rochester Theological Seminary; works include, *A Harmony of the Gospels for Historical Study* (12th ed. rev., 1904).

Strachan, James, M.A., D.D., Late Professor of Hebrew and Biblical Criticism in Magee College, Londonderry; Cunningham Lecturer; works include, "Criticism (Old Testament)," Hastings' *Encyclopaedia of Religion and Ethics* (New York, 1928).

Strachan, Rev. R. H., B.A. M.A. Minister at Elie; works include, "Gospel of John (I.: Critical Article)," Hastings' *A Dictionary of Christ and the Gospels* (New York, 1908).

Weigle, Dean Luther A., B.A., M.A. Ll.D., Ph.D., D.D., Litt.D., S.T.D., J.U.D., Yale University Divinity School, Old Testament and New Testament American Standard Bible Committee; Chairman, Revision Committee, Revised Standard Version; works include, "The Revision of the English Bible," "The English of the Revised Standard Version of the New Testament," in *An Introduction to the Revised Standard Version of the New Testament* (1946).

Wentz, Abdel Ross, A.B., B.D., Ph.D., D.D., Ll.D., Th.D., President, Lutheran Theological Seminary, Gettysburg, New Testament American Standard Bible Committee; works include, "The New Testament and the Word of God," in *An Introduction to the Revised Standard Version of the New Testament* (1946).

Westcott, Brooke Foss, D.D., Bishop of Durham, Regius Professor of Divinity, Cambridge; member New Testament Revision Committee; works include, with Fenton John Anthony Hort, *The New Testament in the Original Greek* (2 vols., 1881).

Willis, John Rothwell, B.D., Canon of St. Aidans, Ferns, and Rector of Preban and Moyne, Co. Wicklow; works include, "Tithes," Hastings' *Dictionary of the Apostolic Church* (New York, 1919).

Wright, Rev. Arthur, D.D., Fellow, Tutor, and Vice-President of Queens' College, Cambridge; works include, "Gospel According to Luke," Hastings' *A Dictionary of Christ and the Gospels* (New York, 1908).

Wright, G. Ernest, A.B., B.D., A.M., Ph. D., D.D., McCormick Theological Seminary; editor, *The Biblical Archaeologist*.

Zenos, Andrew C., M.A.,D.D., Ll.D., Dean and Professor of Biblical Theology in McCormick Theological Seminary, Chicago, Ill.; works include, "Tithe," *A New Standard Bible Dictionary* (New York, 1925).

INDEX A ·

SUBJECTS

Abbreviations used in the Index:
ASV—American Standard Version (Revised Version)
AV—Authorized (King James) Version
IV—Inspired Version of the Prophet Joseph Smith
MSS—Manuscripts
NT—New Testament
OS—Old Syriac Version
OT—Old Testament
RSV—Revised Standard Version
RV—Revised Version (British)
TR—Textus Receptus (Received Text)
WH—Westcott-Hort

—A—

A Codex—see Alexandrinus
ℵ Codex—see Sinaiticus
ℵ B Text, see Sinaiticus and Vaticanus
 antiquity argument, 122-129, 219
 AV, known to scholars of, 191
 Byzantine contemporary, 156, 209, 219, 225
 Church, rejected by, 222, 224-225
 Erasmus, known to, 191
 errors in, 138
 MSS, agreement of, 134-135, 138, 141, 145-147
 revision of, 222
 value, measured by agreement with, 198
 primacy position decreasing, 196, 211
 versions, agreement with, 158-159, 162-163
α family, see Byzantine, Syrian
Abbott, collation of Codex Dublinensis, 147
Abraham, Book of, papyri, 228
Abyssinia, Ethiopic Version, 160
accents, markings in MSS, 205-206, 240
Achaeans, language of, 19
Acta Philippi, cited by Burgon, 336
Acta Pilati, cited by Burgon, 328, 336
Acts: date, 10
 historical accuracy, 58
 origin, 109
Acts of the App., cited by Burgon, 336
Advisory Board, International Council of Religious Education, 358
Adysh MS, 157

Ælfric English translation, 174
Africa, Roman, Version, 156
African form of Old Latin Version, 161
 family classification, 97
agony in the Garden, treatment of passage, 331-334, 410-411
Akhenaten, mentioned in papyri, 17
Akhmimic Version, 158
Alcala, Complutensian, Latin name for, 195
Alcimus Avitus, cited by Burgon, 313
Alexander II, patron of Tischendorf, 236
Alexandretta, discoveries near, 18
Alexandria: Origen at, 243
 MSS originating in, 138, 139
Alexandrian family β, 96, 99, 362-363
 competition of families, 220-221
 corruption, 115
 development, 214-216
 Egyptian, Syriac variants, 97
 MSS, agreement of, 135, 141, 144-147, 214, 218
 pre-Byzantine classification, 99
 Revised Version, 215
 versions, 75, 158-159, 215
Alexandrian family γ, 91
Alexandrinus, Codex A, illustration, 136; 138-139
 British Museum, 132, 138
 Burgon, cited by, 323, 326-329, 332, 337-338, 413-414
 capital letters, 239
 collation with Cur. and Sin. of OS, 71
 compared with ℵ B C D, 197, 246-248
 corruption, 138, 252-257

Alexandrinus—*Cont'd.*
date, 72, 132, 138, 246
family classification, 91, 96, 224-225,
  363
competition of families, 218-222
form, 88, 250
Lachmann favored, 3
line arrangement, 240
MSS, agreement of, 135, 145-147
origin, 113, 242
Revisions, source of, 5, 269
scribe, 138, 202
textual criticism, place in, 201, 203
Thecla, scribe, 138, 202
Westcott-Hort estimate, 93
Alfred the Great, English MS Bible,
  173
Alford, on last of Mark, 344-345
Allen, Willoughby C.: criticism of
  NT, 108-109
personality of Jesus, 54-59
alterations, see changes, corruption
Ambrose, cited by Burgon, 260, 311,
  313, 317-318, 320, 332, 336-339,
  341, 413, 414, 416
Amenhotep IV, mentioned in papyri,
  17
American Standard Bible Committee, 32, 356-357
American Standard Version, 29-32,
  230-235, 265-273, 282-285
accuracy challenged, 60
British collaboration, 22, 267-268,
  282-283
comparison of texts with other Versions, 316-350, 395-417
date, 31, 230, 283
Greek text (WH), 5, 269
imperfections, 358-361
Prefaces, 282-285
preparation, 29-32, 230-235, 265-273
Revised Version, essentially same,
  22
revision by RSV, 35, 37, 351-394
reasons for, 37, 357-361
sources, 4-5
title page, 39
Amiatinus, Codex of Vulgate, 163-
  164
Ammonian sections, 205
Ammonius of Alexandria, 205
Ammonian sections, 205
cited by Burgon, 260, 338, 414
Amorites, mentioned in discoveries,
  18

Amphilochius, cited by Burgon, 313,
  320
ps.-Amphilochius, cited by Burgon,
  336
Anastasius Ant., cited by Burgon,
  313
Anastasius Sinaita, cited by Burgon, 328, 333, 336
Andreas of Crete, cited by Burgon,
  260, 328, 336
Andrews, Samuel J., harmony of, 45
angel, treatment of word, 310
angels, message of, treatment of
  passage, 294, 405-406
Anglican Church:
Apocrypha, 189
formularies, 324
part in AV, 183
part in RV, 287
protest by Churchmen, 5
Angora, inscriptions at, 50
Anti-Christ: concepts of Revisions,
  6, 232, 353
prophecies, 381
Antioch: Council of, cited by Burgon, 313
version for, 156
Antiochian revision, 75-78, 223, 355
Alexandrinus, Codex, relationship,
  138
development, 220
identical with late Greek MSS, 192,
  199
key to Extreme Textualist theory,
  149
myth, 76-78, 220
phantom scheme, 114, 116
pre-Syrian Text, 79, 114, 125
Scrivener on, 114
Westcott-Hort theory, 113, 125
Antiochus monk, cited by Burgon,
  336
antiquity argument, 122-129, 217,
  374,
age of MSS, 123
Byzantine א B texts, 201, 219
א B, losing potency, 129
columnar arrangement, 250-251
Extreme Textualists theory, 72, 128
of gospels, 9-12
present, as of, 126
Aphraates the Persian, cited by Burgon, 320, 327
Aphroditopolis, Chester Beatty papyri discovered at, 131
Apocalypse: literary style, 344
number of MSS, 89-90

Apocrypha, 188-190
  Authorized Version, 188-189
  books in, 189
  Coverdale Bible, 177
  Geneva Bible, 188-189
  Luther Bible, 177
  Prophet Joseph Smith on, 189, 190
  Revised Standard Version, 374
Apostolic Constitutions, cited by
  Burgon, 327, 336
Apostolos, number of MSS, 154
Aquileia, Council of, cited by Bur-
  gon, 313
Arabic Version, 91, 160
  Burgon, cited by, 327
  Mark, treatment of last verses, 343
Aramaic language, 62-64, 67-83
  antiquity argument, 124
  dialect of ancient Hebrew, 63
  idiom, 165
  Jesus, 11, 62-64, 375
  MSS, see Syriac
  Sacred Autographs, 11, 83, 155,
    375-377, 391
  Syriac dialect, 74
  writing on papyri, Moabite Stone,
    18
Archelaus and Manes, cited by
  Burgon, 336
Arianism, in textual criticism, 27
Ariminum, Council of, 77
Arius, cited by Burgon, 333
Armenian Version, 156-157, 165
  cited by Burgon, 311, 317, 320, 327,
    339-340, 416
  date, 156, 223
  family classification, 96, 99, 223
  MS 989, 157
  Mark, on last verses of, 343
  new attention to, 371
Articles of Faith, Pearl of Great
  Price, 228
Ascension Day lesson, cited by Bur-
  gon, 349
Ashburnham, Lord, on columnar ar-
  rangement, 251
Asia Minor, discoveries in, 17
Asiatic family of Bengel, 216
Astruc, Jean, textual critic, 30, 104
  discovered critical secret, 104
Athanasius, cited by Burgon, 311,
  313, 317, 320, 328, 333, 336, 338-
  339, 414
Augiensis, Codex F₂, 144
  family classification, 91, 97, 225
  form, 250
  MSS agreement, 135, 144

Augustine, Latin Father, 162
  cited by Burgon, 260, 302, 311, 313,
    317-318, 321, 333, 336-337, 339,
    341, 413, 416
  harmony of, 44
Authorized Version, 60-61, 183-193
  Apocrypha omitted, 188
  Bishops' Bible, predecessor, 181
  Byzantine text, 76, 216
  comparison of texts with Revisions,
    314-350, 395-417
  criticism, development of, 3, 103-118
  editions, 185, 188
  errors, 216, 379
  family classification of texts, 91, 216
  Geneva Bible, supplanted, 27
  Greek sources, 2, 172, 185-187, 191-
    193
  Greek Text, 1, 2
    published by Palmer, Scrivener,
    193
  Inspired Version, 43, 61, 127, 227
  Kenyon's appraisal, 27
  language, 386-392
    classic style, 216, 351, 357
    criticized, 382
    grammar, 37, 216
    names, 217
    vocabulary, 37
  literature, compared with RV, 359,
    379
  greatest classic in English, 60
  origin, 2
  position held, 110, 355, 379
  preface to, Translators to the Read-
    er, xxvii-lv, 419, 420
    Smith, Dr. Miles, author, 185
    spirit of approach, 418-420
  preparation, 183-185, 418-420
    rules, 184-185
    time occupied, 184
  reasons for use, 60-61
  Received Text (Textus Receptus),
    2, 22, 76, 391
  revision, need for, 36, 37, 192, 354,
    391
  sources, 2, 172, 185-187, 191-193
  term AV, avoided by Revisers, 391
  theology criticized, 382
  title page, 38-39
  translators:
    preface of, xxvii-lv, 419-420
    scholarship, 382
    spirit of approach, 418-420
  Word of God, 60

—B—

B Codex, see Vaticanus
β family, see Alexandrian, Neutral
Babylonian cuneiforms, 18
Bahiric, see Bohairic
Baptist, treatment of word, 310
baptize, treatment of word, 387
Barker, R., printed Authorized Version, 185
Barnabas' Epistle, 236-237
Baruch, Book of Apocrypha, 189
Bashmuric or Elearchian Version, 160
Basil, cited by Burgon, 311, 313, 317, 318, 320, 328, 331, 336, 339
Basil of Cilicia, cited by Burgon, 320
Basil of Seleucia, cited by Burgon, 328
Basiliensis, Codex E, 143
  family classification, 91, 198-199, 221, 224-225
  value, 198-199, 221
Basle:
  Erasmus Bible printed at, 195
  MSS at, 143, 149, 150
Baur, on date of NT, 9
Beatty, A Chester, see Chester Beatty Papyri
Bede, English MS Bible, 173
Beermann, edited Koridethi Gospels, 371
Bel and the Dragon, 189
Belgium, MSS deposited in, 90
Bengel, textual critic, 292
  Asiatic family, 216
  canons of criticism, 365
  divided NT into paragraphs, 101
  Scrivener's appraisal, 292
Benham, Charles Orville, on RSV, 352, 358
Bentley, textual critic, 292
  Scrivener's appraisal, 292
  Wetstein, disciple, 132
Berat, MSS at, 148
Beratinus, Codex Φ, 148
  family classification, 96, 221, 225
Bessarion, Cardinal, supplied missing portions of Vaticanus, 206, 239
Beza, Theodore, Reformation scholar, 141
  Bible (Greek), 2, 171-172
  Authorized Version, source of, 172 193
  Codex Bezae, discovered, 142, 172
  Geneva Bible, source of, 180
  Revisers' comment, 169

Scrivener edition, 193
  scholarship of, 180
  Traditional Greek Text, 192
Bezae, Codex D, illustration, 217; 141-142
  Beza, discovered by, 142, 172
  Burgon, cited by, 302, 323, 326-331, 336, 338, 414
  Byzantine text, source of, 214, 218
  collation with Cur. and Sin., 71
  columnar arrangement, compared with א A B C, 249-251
  compared with א A B C, 197, 246-248, 253-255
  corruptions, 208, 218, 252-257, 302-303
  date, 141, 247
  family classification, 92, 97, 99, 214, 362, 364
  competition of texts, 113, 218-219, 221-224
  form, 250
  MSS agreement, 134-135, 147-148, 151-152, 217-218
  omissions, number of, 302-303
  pre-Byzantine classification, 99
  Revisions, source of, 5, 269
  Scrivener, edited by, 24-25, 142
  Stephen, used by, 171, 196, 214
  studied by Scrivener, Rendel Harris, Chase, Weiss, Ropes, Clark, 142
  textual criticism, place in, 142, 201, 203
  Textus Receptus, source of, 218, 221, 224
  Trent, taken to Council of, 142
  versions, agreement, 158, 161, 224
Bible commentaries, keyed to AV, 60
Bibliotheque Nationale, Paris, MSS at, 140, 143, 145-146
Bilson, Bishop, put AV through press, 185
birth of Jesus, treatment of passage, 316-318, 401-402
bishop, treatment of word, 310
Bishops' Bible, 2, 180-181
  Authorized Version, source of, 181, 184, 186-187
  Great Bible, supplanted, 181, 186-187
  preparation, 180-181, 186
Blake, on Georgian Version, 157
bloody sweat, treatment of passage, 331-334, 410-411
Bodleian: Genesis MS, 128
  Library (University of Oxford), MSS in, 143, 147, 151

Boernerianus, Codex G₃, 144
family classification, 97
Bohairic Version, 158-159
canon of, 159
family classification, 91, 96, 99
pre-Byzantine classification, 99
value, 116
book-arrangement, 146, 177
Book of Common Prayer, 308
Book of Mormon, accepted Scriptures, 228
Book of Origins, Hexateuch, 106
Book of the Dead, papyri, 17
Borgianus, Codex T, 146
cited by Burgon, 332
family classification, 91, 96, 224
Revised Versions, source of, 5
Bowie, Rev. Walter Russell:
language of AV, 390
use of NT in worship, 355, 390
breathings, markings in MSS, 205-
206, 240
Breviarium, cited by Burgon, 313
Briggs, Charles Augustus, minis-
try of Jesus, 49
British and Foreign Bible Society:
MSS in, 147
omitted Apocrypha, 189
British Empire, MSS deposited in, 90
British Museum: MSS deposited in,
3, 5, 70, 90, 110, 132, 134, 136, 138,
145, 146, 150, 158, 251
Papyri, 134
Sinaiticus, purchase of, 136, 237-238
Broadus, John A.,
list of harmonies, 44, 46
Bruce, F. F., authority cited, 9
Byzantine text, antiquity of, 201
Syriac Version, 80
Bruce, James, Ethiopic Version of,
160
Bull and Pearson, modern divines,
cited by Burgon, 313
Burgon, John William, authority
cited, 23-29
א B, estimate of, 26
causes of corruption, 15
conjectural emendation (ring of genuineness), 287-288, 293-296
list of changes, 297-299
revelation, pseudo, 396
elimination of words charity and
miracles, 308-309
inventory of MSS, 84
Kenyon's appraisal, 25
marginal notes, 301-305

Burgon—Cont'd.
Mark, on last of, 28, 346
Revised Version, critic, 112
scholarship, 346
Scriptures, God mindful of safety,
256
Scrivener's estimate, 27, 346
Sound or High Textualist, 121
Tischendorf, textual criticism, 259
WH Greek text, theories appraised,
263-264, 295
Burkitt, on date of Old Syriac MSS,
71
Burrows, Professor Millar, on Semit-
ic background of NT, 68-69, 375-
377
Burton, Ernest DeWitt, harmony of,
46
Byblos inscriptions, 18
Byzantine Church, Received Text of,
78
Byzantine Text, 95-96, 194-226, 363-
364
א B, contemporary, 150, 209, 225
antiquity, 199, 201, 222, 235, 363
Bezae in, 214
Church, adopted by, 150, 225
date, 167, 199, 222, 225-226, 235, 363
development, 97, 214-216, 364-365
Antiochian Revision, 75-78
Peshitta, 75
Revisions, compared, 77, 368
established in East, 167
Extreme Textualists ignore early
texts, 196
Legg classification, 225
MSS agreement, 72, 75, 145-146,
148-150, 152, 219, 221-222, 225,
363, 371
MSS competition, 217-226
meaning of term, 194, 216
other designations, 216
pre-Byzantine classification, 99
Revisers' estimate, 372, 374
Textus Receptus, 76
version agreement, 75, 156, 164, 223-
224

—C—

C Codex, see Ephraemi
Cadbury, Henry J., on grammar,
vocabulary, 367
Caedmon, English MS Bible, 173
Caesar Augustus, decree inscription,
50
Caesar, Julius, quoted, 111

Caesarea: Eusebius of, 243
  library at, 96
  Origen, home, 243
  origin of MSS, 139
Caesarean family γ, 94, 96, 362-364
  competition of texts, 221
  consideration due, 127, 211
  MSS of, 146-147, 151
  pre-Byzantine classification, 99
  versions of, 157
Caesarius: cited by Burgon, 313
  ps.-Caesarius, cited by Burgon, 333
Cairo: Tischendorf copied ℵ, 236
  Washington MSS discovery, 371
Caliph Omar, textual criticism, 197-
  198
Calvin, Geneva Bible, 179-180
Cambridge University: company of
  AV, 184
  editions of AV, 188
  MSS at, 5, 141, 172
  RV publishers, 22, 268
canonical scripture, 349
canons of criticism, 365-370
Canons of Eusebius:
  cited by Burgon, 311, 339
  meaning of term, 205
Capreolus, cited by Burgon, 321
Carmina Nisibena, Ephraem, cited by
  Burgon, 334
Carr, A., on tithes, 384
Carthage, Cyprian, Bishop of, use of
  Old Latin text, 161
Cassian, cited by Burgon, 313, 320,
  333
catalogue of MSS: Gregory, 92
  von Soden, 92
  Wetstein, 101
Catholic English Bible, 181-182
Catholic Epistles, meaning of term,
  89
census inscriptions, 50
centurion's faith, treatment of passage, 120
changes, see also corruption
  conjectural emendation (ring of
    genuineness) 297-299
  grammar, 306-314
  illustrative textual, 381-386
  MSS, in, 364
  new renderings of words, 306-314
  number, 120, 217
  retained by RSV, 392
  vital not explained, 37, 361, 386

chapter-division: Cardinal Hugo, 102,
  171
  Diatessaron, 74
  Stephen Langton, 102
charger changed to platter, 383
Charles I, received Codex Alexandrinus, 138
charity, substituted by love, 308, 387,
  398
Chase, studied Codex Bezae, 142
cherubims, treatment of word, 386
Chester Beatty Papyri, illustration,
  8; 135
  antiquity argument, 72
  Book of Enoch, 160
  date, 72, 123, 131-132, 218, 363, 371
  discovery, 131, 202, 371
  family classification, 96, 99, 214, 218
    competitive texts in, 214, 218-219
  Kenyon, edited by, 135
    estimate of, 246
  pre-Byzantine classification, 99
  Revisers, use of, 5, 366
  textual criticism, place in, 72
Chichester, Dean of, see John William Burgon, 121
children, seed changed to, 377
Christ displays hands and feet, treatment of passage, 337-338, 413-414
Christ Jesus, 48-59, 62-64
  abandonment, 6, 30, 48-59, 111, 280,
    315, 351-352, 368, 374, 381
  adaption of life to mythology, 55
  Old Testament prophecies, 55
  critics' appraisal, 53-59
  language, Aramaic, 11, 62-64, 83,
    375
  ministry, 48-52
  personality, 6, 38, 53-59
    critics' appraisal, 54-59
  reaction on history, 58
  Wentz on, 393
  Revisers' mention, 281, 284, 391-394
Christ the Creator, treatment of
  passage, 319, 403
Christian Remembrancer, on Codex
  Zacynthius, 148
Christmas Day sermons, cited by
  Burgon, 320, 328
chronology of Scripture, Archbishop
  Ussher, 188
Chrysostom:
  cited by Burgon, 260, 294, 311, 313,
    317, 320, 327-328, 333, 336-339,
    341, 413-414, 416
  era of, 244

Chrysostom—*Cont'd.*
family classification, 91, 95
ps.-Chrysostom, cited by Burgon, 336
church, treatment of word, 310
churchmen, protest against RV, 5
Church of England, see Anglican Church
Clark, A. C., criticism of Codex Bezae, 141-142
Clark, George W., harmony of, 46
Claromontanus, Codex D₂, 143
Beza, used by, 172
family classification, 92, 97
form, 250
MSS agreement, 144
classification of MSS, 86-101, 130-154, 364
classics, textual science applied to, 215, 276, 390
clay tablets: discoveries, 17
library at Ras-Shamra (Ugarit), 18-19
Clement: cited by Burgon, 302
family classification, 92
study of, 116
Clement VIII, edition of Vulgate, 163
Clement, Syriac, cited by Burgon, 311
Clementine Homilies, cited by Burgon, 336
clergy, loss of faith, 30, 111
coasts, word changed to borders, 383
codices: as books, 131
description, 134-151, 250
meaning of term, 87-88
oldest, אA B C D, 136-143
collation, 253-255
columnar arrangement, 249-251
comparison of texts, 246-248
relative corruption, 252-257
Coislinianus 202, Codex H₃, 144
collations: of א A B C D, 71, 240, 244, 246-248, 253-254
Cur. & Sin., 71
Pamphilus, 244
colometrical edition, 144
colophon, meaning of term, 151
columnar arrangement: basis of antiquity argument, 250-251
MSS, 240, 245, 249-251
Colwell, E. C., study of lectionaries, 152
Comestor, harmony of, 44
comparer, meaning of term, 204
competitive texts, 217

Complutensian Polyglott (Greek) of Ximenes, 2, 195
AV, use in, 172
Erasmus, used by, 196
printed, 168-170
Revisers' comment, 169
sources, 169, 240
Stephen, used by, 171, 196
Traditional Greek Text, 192
conflation, meaning of term, 115
Congressional Committee on Un-American Activities, cited, 355-356, 358
Congressional Library, purchase of Gutenberg Bible, 195
conjectural emendation in determining texts, 286-299, 395-397
Burgon on, 118, 293-296
critics' acceptance, 288, 299
list of changes based on, 297-299
Mark, on last of, 349
meaning of term, 286, 287
revelations, as, 349, 396-397
Revisions, in, 292-296, 366, 395-397
Scrivener on, 118, 296-297
Westcott-Hort, theory of, 98, 118, 293-294
Constantine, ordered copies from Eusebius, 204, 244
Constantinople, origin of MSS, 145
Constantinopolitan Church-books of Eusebius, 247
Constantinopolitan family, of Griesback, 216
Convocation of Province of Canterbury (Southern Province), origin of movement of revision, 5, 22, 29, 234, 266
Cook, canon: cited by Burgon, 324
Sound or High Textualist, 121
copyists, see scribes, errors of, 11, 115, 125, 166, 201-202, 208, 241
Coptic (Egyptian) Version, 10-11, 156-160
cited by Burgon, 289, 304, 311, 320, 327, 336, 338-340, 348, 414, 416
date, 155
family classification, 96, 224, 362
competition of texts, 224
variants, 97
origin, 10-11
Scrivener on, 165
correctors of MSS, 141
corruptions (see copyists), 79-80, 241, 249, 339
א A B C D compared, 207-208, 252-257
causes, 11, 15, 125, 200, 210, 253

corruptions—*Cont'd.*
  early, 124, 364, 368
  MSS, in, 288-289, 364
  Marcion, 13
  Prophet Joseph Smith on, 12, 126
  Scrivener on, 13, 256
  Westcott-Hort, 115, 264
Cosmas, cited by Burgon, 320, 328
Council of Jerusalem, Alfred MS
    Bible, 173
countries, MSS deposit, by, 90
Coverdale, English Bible, 2, 176-177
  AV, source of, 184, 186
  editions, 179
  Great Bible revision, 178
  Matthew's Bible revision, 178
  scholarship, 178, 186
Craig, Clarence T., on language of
    NT, 382
Cranmer, Thomas (Archbishop of
    Canterbury):
  Great Bible, 179
  Matthew's Bible, 178
Crete, discoveries at, 17
criticism, textual: aim of, 167
  Authorized Version, 190-191
  Astruc, q. v., 104
  canons of, 365-370
  choice of text, 214
  critical secret, 104
  development, 3, 103-118, 232-234
  higher and lower, meaning of terms,
    230-231
  historical, 108-118
  Hort, Fenton John Anthony, q. v., 4
  Jesus, personality of, 53-59
  Lachmann, q. v., 3
  literary, 108-118
  MSS favored, 240-241, 247
  RSV, criticism not available, 38
  Tischendorf, q. v., 4
  Tregelles, q. v., 4
  Westcott, Brooke Foss, q. v., 4
Cromwell, patron of Coverdale, 176
Cromwell, Thomas (Earl of Essex),
    Matthew's Bible, 178
Crusaders, divided Codex N, 145
Cureton, Dr., discovery of Cur. MS,
    70
Curetonian, MS of Old Syriac, 70, 81,
    151, 371
  cited by Burgon, 311, 331, 338, 340,
    414, 416
  recension, 76, 78
cursives, (see minuscules), 149-151
  classification of MSS, 130
  meaning of term, 86, 131

Cyprian, bishop of Carthage:
  cited by Burgon, 313
  family classification, 92, 97
  Old Latin Version, use of, 161, 162
  pre-Byzantine classification, 99
Cyprius, Codex K, 145
  family classification, 91, 222, 224-
    225
Cyril, Bp. of Alexandria, cited by
    Burgon, 260, 289, 313, 318, 320,
    327-328, 331, 333, 336-338, 413-
    414
Cyril, Bp. of Jerusalem, cited by
    Burgon, 317, 318, 327

—D—

D Codex, see Bezae
Δ Codex, see Sangallensis
δ family, see Western
Damascene, John, cited by Burgon,
    289, 311, 313, 317, 320, 328, 333,
    336-339, 414
Damasus, Bishop of Rome, 162
  cited by Burgon, 341, 416
  Vulgate Version, 162
Davidson, on Codex Bezae, 142
Davison, Dr. W. T., on Diatessaron,
    73
Dead Sea scrolls, discovery of, 50
decree of Caesar Augustus, inscrip-
    tions of, 50
Deissmann, Adolf, studies of new
    papyri, 359
demons, substituted for devils, 342
demotic writing, 157
Denmark, MSS deposited in, 90
depraved texts (see corruptions),
  Codices א A B C D compared, 249,
    253
descendants, offspring changed to,
    377
de-Semitization of NT, 377
designation of MSS, by Wetstein, 101
deWette, textual critic, 105
Diatessaron of Tatian (early Syrian
    Text), 44, 69, 71, 73-74
  antiquity, 124
  date, 72, 81, 223
  family classification, 97
  harmony, 44, 74
  language, 73, 81
  new discovery at Dura, 371
  Kraeling edited, 371
  Scrivener on, 74
  translation, 80
Didymus, cited by Burgon, 313, 317,
    320, 327, 333

Diocletian persecutions, destruction of MSS, 204, 243
Dionysius, Bp. of Alexandria, cited by Burgon, 333
ps.-Dionysius, cited by Burgon, 260, 313, 320
Dionysius, Bishop of Corinth, corruption of letters, 13, 124
disciple, treatment of word, 310
discoveries, recent, 202, 371
effect on textual criticism, 234-235
Divine names, Elohim and Jehovah in textual criticism, 104
Division of Christian Education of National Council of the Churches of Christ in the U.S.A., publication of RSV, 32
Dobbin, Dr., number of omissions in Vaticanus, 140, 241
doctrine, substituted by teaching, 307, 311, 399-400
Doctrine and Covenants, accepted as Scriptures, 228
Domitian persecution, date of Revelation, 10
Douai-Rheims Version, 91, 181-182, scholarship, 186
double brackets, WH use of, 263, 335
Dresden National Library, MSS at, 144
Dublin (see Archbishop Trench and Archdeacon Lee),
MSS at, 146-147, 150
Dublinensis, Codex Z, 146-147
cited by Burgon, 317
family classification, 91, 96, 221, 224
Duhm, textual critic, 107
Dura, new discovery of Diatessaron, 371
dureth, changed to endureth, 383
Durham, Bishop of, see Brooke Foss Westcott

—E—

E Codex, see Basiliensis
E₂ Codex, see Laudianus
E₃ Codex, see Sangermanensis
ε family, see Syriac
Easter season lesson, cited by Burgon, 349
Eastern bishops, cited by Burgon, 328, 333
Eastern Church, cited by Burgon, 327, 339, 341, 348, 416
Ebionite Gospel, cited by Burgon, 302

Ecclesiasticus, Book of Apocrypha, 189
Ecclesiasticus palimpsest, columnar arrangement in, 250
eclectic principle, 366
Edersheim, Alfred, on language of Jesus, 63
Edessa, Syriac revision at, 76, 97
Edinburgh Review, on language of RV, 359
Edward VI, owner of copy of Wyclif Bible, 175
Eerdmans, Prof. B. D., textual critic, 107
Egypt: all families, 213-214
circulation of Byzantine text, 218
discoveries of MSS, 17, 87, 131
MSS deposited, 90
origin of texts, 96, 139, 213
papyri, origin of, 87
Egyptian vernacular, dialects, 158
Egyptian Version, see Coptic
Eichhorn, textual critic, 104-105
appraisal of Cursive 33, 150
Elearchian (Bashmuric) Version, 160
eliminations, see omissions
Elizabeth I: Bibles produced during reign, 187
owned a Wyclif Bible, 175
Elizabeth Day McCormick, new edition of Apocalypse, 371
Ellicott, Charles John, Bishop of Gloucester and Bristol, Chairman of Revisers, 260
Bezae, on, 302
British scholarship, estimate of, 318
Burgon's reply, 314
cited by Burgon, 346
John, Syrian text basis of, 81
marginal readings, 303-304
method of work of Revisers, 269-270
Tischendorf's textual criticism, 259-260
WH Greek text, adopted system of, 296
Ellis, William T., on Roman census inscriptions, 50
Elohim and Jehovah in textual criticism, 104
Elzevir (Bonaventure and Abraham) Greek Bible, 2, 172
Received Text, 2
Traditional Greek Text, 192
England, MSS deposited in, 90
English of AV, see language, literature

English Version, 173-182
  authorized for public use, 178
  demand for, during Reformation, 1
  early narrative, Life of Christ, 174
  Greek text, 2
  MSS Bibles, 173-175
  printed Bible, 175-182
ensue, changed to pursue, 383
Ephraem, Carmina Nisibena, cited by Burgon, 334
Ephraemi, Codex C, illustration, 137; 140
  Burgon, cited by, 323
  compared with ℵ A B D, 197, 246-248
  corruption, 138, 252-257
  date, 140, 246-247
  Ephraim Syrus writing, 140
  family classification, 91, 96, 198, 225
    competition of texts, 218, 220
  MSS agreement, 135, 146-147
  origin, 113
  palimpsest, 140
  rescript codex, 246
  Revisions, source of, 5, 269
  textual criticism, place in, 201, 203
Ephraim Syrus, 74
  cited by Burgon, 317, 327, 333, 336
  writing on Codex Ephraemi, 140
epileptic substituted for lunatic, 310-311, 399
Epiphanius: cited by Burgon, 313, 317, 318, 320, 327, 328, 331, 333, 338, 414
  writings on corruptions, 13
Erasmus, Reformation scholar, 195
  Bible, illustration, 216; 2, 170, 195
  AV, source of, 172
  Byzantine Text, 216
  Coverdale, used by, 179
  editions, 196
  Great Bible, source of, 179
  printed before Complutensian, 170
  scholarship, 195
  Sepulveda, correspondence with on Vaticanus, 240
  sources, 149-150, 191
  Stephen, used by, 171
  Tindale, used by, 176
  Traditional Greek Text, 192
  Vaticanus, knew of, 170, 191, 209
errors, see corruptions
eschatological teaching, in Gospels, 55
Esdras, Book of Apocrypha, 189

Esther, Book of Apocrypha, 189
Estienne, Robert, see Stephen
eternal, substituted for everlasting, 311
Ethiopic Version, 91, 160
  Book of Enoch, 160
  cited by Burgon, 289, 304, 317, 320, 327, 339, 340, 416
  Mark, on last of, 343
  Scrivener's comment, 165
Eulogius, Archbishop of Alexandria, cited by Burgon, 313, 328
Eumenes, King of Pergamum, first use of vellum, 87
eunuch's confession of faith, treatment of passage, 143
Euphrates Valley: discoveries, 17, 371
  Tatian birthplace, 73
  version for, 156
Eusebian canons: cited by Burgon, 311, 339
  meaning of term, 205
  Sinaiticus, use in, 205
Eusebius of Caesarea, 243
  canons of, 205
  changes in MSS, 247
  cited by Burgon, 260, 327, 333, 336-338, 348, 413, 414
  columnar arrangement, 245
  Constantine, order of copies, 204, 244
  Constantinopolitan Church-books, 247
  family classification, 96
  harmony, 44
    difficulties in, 344
  Mark, on last of, 343-345
  pre-Byzantine classification, 99
  successor to Origen, 243
Eustathius, cited by Burgon, 313, 320
Euthalius of Sulca, colometrical edition of Epistles, 144
Eutherius, cited by Burgon, 336
Euthymius Zigabenus, on last of Mark, 344
Evan. 33, cited by Burgon, 339
Evangelistaria (Evangeliaria):
  meaning of term, 89
  number of MSS, 89-90, 153-154
everlasting substituted by eternal, 311
evil spirits, treatment of passage, 338-339, 399, 414-415
Ewald, Heinrich, OT scholar, 105

Extreme Textualists, 21, 48-59, 103-
  118
  anti-Christ attitude, 38, 126, 280,
    394
  Antiochian Revision theory, 75-82,
    149
  antiquity argument, 72, 122-129, 219
  appraisal of Jesus, 38, 48-59
  Arianism, 27
  Byzantine texts, appraisal of, 196
  conjectural emendation, 286-299,
    395-397
  higher critics, 21
  Kenyon, appraisal of, 28-29
  key to theory, 81-82, 149
  Lachmann, K., 109
  Mark, on last of, 417
  meaning of term, 103, 122
  members of, see Lachmann, Tisch-
    endorf, Tregelles, Westcott-Hort
  MSS, favorite, 100, 110, 131-132,
    198
  omissions, 119-121, 231-232
  one original text theory, 66, 81-82,
    209-210
  pre-Erasmus texts, 196
  reasoning processes, 68
  Revisions, responsible for, 5, 29, 35,
    280, 352
  Schools of Extreme and Sound or
    High Textualism, 21, 103, 122-123
  spirit of approach, 53
  Syriac Versions, appraisal of, 81-82
  Textus Receptus, appraisal of, 187,
    190-191, 196

—F—

F₂ Codex, see Augiensis
Facundus, cited by Burgon, 313, 333
faith of Revisers, 283, 285
families, classification of MSS, 86-
  100, 362-365
  see also ℵ B, α, β, δ, ε, γ, ζ,
    Alexandrian, Byzantine, Caesar-
    ean, Neutral, Residual, Syriac,
    Syrian, Western families.
  ℵ B type, coexistent with Byzan-
    tine, 209
  choice of critic, 214
  competition among, in same MS,
    209, 213, 217-219
  development, 214-216
  early appearance, 208-209
  Egypt, all principal in, 213-214
  Fathers, use of, 166
  Grant, Dr., on, 362-364, 373
  Kenyon grouping, 94-100

one original text theory, 209-210
pre-Byzantine grouping, 99-100, 363
reclassification, 92-100, 200
Westcott-Hort grouping, 91-92
Family 1, 150
  family classification, 96, 99
Family 13, 150-151
  family classification, 96, 99
Farrar, F. W., on tithes, 384
Fathers, the, 155, 166-167
  ante-date existing MSS, 166
  family classification, 91, 92, 166
  Origen, scholarship, 166
  table of, Appendix C
  textual criticism, value in, 166, 197
Faustus, cited by Burgon, 302
Fayoum Version, 160
Fayyumic Version, 158
Ferrandus, cited by Burgon, 313
Ferrar, group of MSS, 150
Flemish Latin Bible, columnar ar-
  rangement, 251
formularies, of Church of England,
  324-325
forsook substituted by left, 307
Fragment Hypothesis of Alexander
  Geddes, 105
fragments of MSS, 202
France, MSS deposited in, 90
Francis I, patron of Stephen, 171
Frederick Augustus, King of Saxony,
  patron of Tischendorf, 236
Freer, Charles, discovery of Wash-
  ington MS, 371
Freer Museum, MSS at, 144, 146
French Version of Apocalypse, Eng-
  lish translation, 174
Friderico-Augustanus Codex, 236
Froben, printed Erasmus Bible, 195
Fulgentius, cited by Burgon, 313
Fust and Schoeffer, printed first
  Bible, 168

—G—

G Codex: family classification, 225
  MSS agreement, 135
G₃ Codex, see Boernerianus
γ family, see Alexandrian, Caesarean
Galerius persecutions, destruction of
  Scriptures, 204, 243
Galilee, Aramaic, language of, 63
Gaudentius, cited by Burgon, 260
Gaul, version for Roman, 156
Geddes, Alexander, textual critic, 105
Gelasius Cyz., cited by Burgon, 313
Genesis, Inspired Version of, 227-228

Geneva Bible, 179-180
  Apocrypha, 188
  AV replaced, 27
  source of, 184, 186-187
  Puritan Bible, 181
  scholarship, 186
  verse-division, 180
Gennadius, cited by Burgon, 313, 333
Genoa, MSS at, 145
geographical distribution of witness-
  es, cited by Burgon, 329
Georgian Version, 91, 157
  family classification, 96, 99
  Scrivener on, 165
  cited by Burgon, 317, 320, 327, 339,
  340, 416
Gerhard of Maastricht, canons of
  criticism, 365
German Bible of Zwingli, used by
  Coverdale, 176
German school of textual criticism,
  9, 110, 282
Germanus, cited by Burgon, 328
Germany, MSS deposited in, 90
Gerson, harmony of, 44
Gezer, mentioned in discoveries, 18
Gibson, Mrs., discovery of Sinaitic
  MS of Old Syriac, 71, 371
Gilby, A., Christ's College, Geneva
  Bible, 180
glosses, 310, 312-314, 401
Gnostics: Hegesippus wrote against,
  81
  perversion of texts, 13, 319, 403
Godhood of Christ, treatment of
  passage, 312-314, 400-401
Goodspeed, C., on tithes, 384
Goodspeed, Dr. Edgar J.: on Apoc-
  rypha, 374
  on style of AV, 355
gospel, treatment of word, 310
Gospel of the Separated, Old Syriac
  Version, 71
Gospels, The: date of, 55
  historical accuracy, 57
Gothic Version, 91, 164-165
  cited by Burgon, 304, 327, 348
grace, treatment of word, 310
Graeco-Latin MSS, 147, 172
  family classification, 97, 99
  form, 250
Graeco-Syriac Text: of fourth cen-
  tury, 199
  MS of, 142
  Textus Receptus, 192
Graf, K. H., textual critic, 106-107

Grafian Hypothesis, 106-107
grammar of AV, 37, 306-307, 354,
  367, 386-389
Grant, Dr. Frederick C.: Byzantine
  text, value of, 372
  canons of criticism, 365-367
  conjectural emendation, 298
  family classification of texts, 362-
  364
  science of textual criticism, 373
Great Bible, the 2, 178-179
  AV, source of, 184, 186-187
  editions of, 179
Greece, MSS deposited in, 90
Greek Evangelistarium, columnar
  arrangement, 250
Greek language, Biblical and common, 307, 360
Greek MSS: classification, 130-154
  discovery and publication, 371
Greek Text: Authorized Version, 1,
  193
  Geneva Bible, 179-180
  main text, 24
  Revisions, 1, 269, 366
  Sacred Autographs, 62-64, 65-66, 74,
  83, 155
  scholars unknown, 77
Gregory, Dr. C. R.: catalogue of
  MSS, 24, 92, 132-133
  edited Koridethi Gospels, 371
Gregory of Nazianzus, cited by Bur-
  gon, 260, 327, 333
Gregory of Nyssa, cited by Burgon,
  260, 313, 317, 327, 328, 336, 348
Gregory Thaumaturgus, cited by
  Burgon, 328
Grenfell, Dr. B. P., acquired Rylands
  Fragment, 66
Griesbach, J. J., textual critic:
  canons of criticism, 365
  Constantinopolitan family classifi-
  cation, 216
  Greek main text, 24
  Hort, theories of, 115
  school of criticism, 192
  Scrivener on, 292
Guelpherbytanus, MSS of Gothic
  Version, 164
Guppy, Dr. H., date of Rylands
  Fragment, 136
Gutenberg (Mazarin) Bible, 168, 195
  first printed book, 163
  purchase by United States, 238
Gwilliam, Dr. G. H., on language of
  Jesus, 62-63

—H—

H MS, family classification, 225
H₃ Codex, see Coislinianus 202
Habiru, identified with Hebrew, 18
Hammond, on textual criticism, 197
Hampole, Richard Rolle, hermit of,
    English Version of Psalter, 174
Hampton Court Conference, and the
    AV, 183
Harkleian Syriac Version, 80
    cited by Burgon, 289
harmonies of the Gospels, 44-47
    Ammonian Sections, 205
    chronological, 44
    elements, 44
    list of, 44-47
    Our Lord of the Gospels, 33, 44
Harnack, on date of NT, 9
Harris, Rendel, studied Codex Bezae,
    142
Hazor, mentioned in discoveries, 18
heart changed to mind, 377
heavenly host, message of, treat-
    ment of passage, 325-329, 405-406
Hebrew: language of Jewish scrip-
    tures, 69
    elements in NT, 375
Hebrews, Paul as writer of, 344
Hegesippus: cited by Burgon, 336
    wrote against Gnostics, 81
Hellenistic colony in Egypt, 156
Hellenistic Greek, 307
Henry VI, owned a Wyclif Bible, 175
Henry VII, owned a Wyclif Bible,
    175
Henry VIII: Bibles produced during
    reign, 187
    Coverdale Bible condemned, 176,
        179
    Tindale Bible condemned, 176, 179
Herculanean rolls, Vaticanus resem-
    blance, 239
Hereford, Nicholas, English transla-
    tion, 174
heresies: Irenaeus books, 14
    retained in RSV, 356
heretics, texts of, 124
Hermas' Shepherd, in Sinaiticus, 237
Hesychius: cited by Burgon, 336
    martyrdom of, 243
    on last of Mark, 344
Hexapla, polyglot of Origen, 128
    collations, 244
    corrections, 244
Hexateuch, Book of Origins, origin
    of, 106

hieratic writing, 157
hieroglyphic writing, 157
High or Sound Textualists, 103-118,
    122-123
    support AV, 5-6
higher criticism, see Extreme Tex-
    tualists
    meaning of term, 34, 230-231
Hilary, cited by Burgon, 302, 311,
    313, 320, 332, 333, 336, 339, 341,
    416
hinder, changed to precede, 383
Hippolytus: cited by Burgon, 313,
    320, 333, 336
    study of writings, 116
historical criticism:
    of Jesus, 53-59
    of NT, 108-118
History of Susanna, of the Apocry-
    pha, 189
Hittite writing, 17
Holland, MSS deposited in, 90
Holy Ghost or Spirit, glosses on, 310
homilies, translation by Ælfric, 174
Horner, edition of Bohairic Version,
    158-159
horoscope, MSS papyrus discovery,
    158
Hort, Fenton John Anthony, textual
    critic, 4, 261
    see also Westcott-Hort
    Antiochian Revision theory, q. v.,
        75-78
    conflations, 115
    conjectural emendation, 293
    cursives, appraisal of, 150
    Extreme Textualist, 109-110
    family classifications, 91-92, 363
    Greek, main text, 24
    Greek Text, collaboration with
        Westcott, 261, 264, 293
    Griesbach, theories compared with,
        115
    individual mind, 293
    Kenyon's appraisal, 25
    Mark, on last of, 343
    Revised Versions, influence upon,
        25, 269-270, 286
    time spent, 385-386
    Scrivener's appraisal, 117, 255-256,
        315-316
    Sinaiticus, origin of, 242
    Stanley, Dean, appraisal by, 321
    Vaticanus, omissions, 241
        origin, 242
        scribes, 239-240
Hoskier, on date of Bohairic Version,
    159

host, message of heavenly, treatment
    of passage, 325-329, 405-406
Hug, origin of Vaticanus, 242
Hugo, Cardinal of Santo Caro, chap-
    ter-division of Bible, 102, 171
Hunt, date of Michigan Papyri, 134
Hupfeld, textual critic, 105-106
Hyginus, death of Bishop, 13
hypocrite, treatment of word, 310

—I—

I Codex, see Washingtonianus II
Ibn Ezra, early textual critic, 104
ps.-Ignatius, cited by Burgon, 336
Ilgen, textual critic, 105
imperfections, see corruptions
individual mind, see conjectural
    emendation
inscription on the cross, treatment
    of passage, 120, 336
inscriptions found at: Angora, 50
    Serabit, Byblos, Tell Duweir, 18
inspiration, treatment of word, 311,
    399-400
Inspired Version, 34, 227-229
    comparison of texts with Revisions,
        314-350, 395-417
    preparation, 228
    recension, 227
    supports AV, 3, 7, 43, 61, 127
    title page, 228
internal evidence: see also conjec-
    tural emendations
    cited by Burgon, 335
    meaning of term, 116, 364
    seven rules governing, 292
    textual criticism, use in, 290, 364
International Council of Religious
    Education, publication of RSV,
    32, 356-358
interpolations, cited by Burgon, 341
    meaning of term, 369
    Scrivener on, 113-114
    sources, 369
    Western, 334, 411
    Westcott-Hort on, 330, 339
interpretation, not translation, 380
Introduction to RSV, 42, 351-394
Ireland, MSS deposited in, 90
Irenaeus, cited by Burgon, 304, 313,
    318, 327, 333, 336
    discordant readings, on, 124
    family classification, 92
    heresies, books on, 14
    John, closeness to, 14
    Mark, on last of, 345
    Old Latin, on, 162

Polycarp, relationship to, 14
    study of writings, 116
Isaiah: Dead Sea Scrolls, 50
    differences of literary style, 344
Isidorus, cited by Burgon, 260, 317
Italy: MSS deposited in, 90
    origin of Vaticanus, 139
    version for, 156

—J—

Jacobean divines, AV work of, 186
James I: Alexandrinus offered to,
    138
    Authorized Version, part in, 183
Jasher, Book of Apocrypha, 190
Jehovah and Elohim, Divine names
    in textual criticism, 104
Jerome: cited by Burgon, 260, 313,
    317, 320, 331-333, 336, 341, 348,
    416
    Mark, on last of, 345
    Vulgate of, 160-161, 162-164
    source, 163
Jerusalem: MSS copied at, 147, 151
    mentioned in discoveries, 18
Jerusalem Chamber, place of meet-
    ing of Revisers, 271, 331
Jesus Christ, see Christ
Jesus the Son of Sirach, Book of
    Apocrypha, 189
Jews, Persian and Greek elements
    assimilated by, 375
John: conversed with Polycarp, 124
    Gospel of: accuracy, 48, 59
        composite scholarship, 109
        date, 9, 10, 66
        source, 81
    Irenaeus, relationship, 124
    literary style, 344
    theology, 374
Jonah, Tindale translation, 176
Jovius the monk, cited by Burgon,
    341, 416
Juda, Leo, source of Geneva Bible,
    180
Judea, Aramaic, language of, 63
Judith, Book of Apocrypha, 189
Julian the heretic, cited by Burgon,
    333
Justin Martyr: cited by Burgon,
    302, 331, 333
    family classification, 92
    ps.-Justin Martyr, cited by Burgon,
        336, 338, 414
    Tatian, disciple of, 73
Juvencus, cited by Burgon, 302, 311,
    339

—K—

K Codex, see Cyprius
K, von Soden Byzantine classification, 216, 225
Kagemna on Ethics, early papyri MS, 17
Karahissar, Four Gospels of, new edition, 371
Karkaphensian Syriac text, 80
Kenyon, Sir Frederic G., authority cited, 9
  Antiochian-Syrian Revision, 77
  antiquity argument, 126
  Burgon, on, 25-26
  Byzantine text, 225
  Chester Beatty Papyri, edited, 135
  favorite text, 246
  date of NT books, 9
  family classification of texts, 92-100, 362
  language of Jesus, 63
  one original text thesis, 209-213
  pre-Byzantine classification, 99-100
  reader, any intelligent, 20, 200
  Revisers' estimate, 11-12, 23, 28, 203
  Scrivener, on, 24-25
Kieff, MSS at, 144
King James Version, see Authorized Version
Kish, discovery of tablets by Langdon, 17
Koine, common Greek, 360
Koridethianus, Codex ⊙, 147
  date, 147, 222
  family classification, 96, 99, 222, 362
  new edition, 371
Kraeling, Carl, edited new Diatessaron discovery, 371
Kuenen, textual critic, 107

—L—

L Codex, see Regius
Λ Codex, see Tischendorfianus III
Lachish: inscriptions at, 18
  mentioned in discoveries, 18
Lachmann, K., textual critic, 3, 30, 93, 233
  breaking monopoly of TR, 110
  cited by Burgon, 321
  conjectural emendation, 290
  Extreme Textualist, 109
Lactantius, cited by Burgon, 302
Lake, edited Codex Sinaiticus, 136
Lamsa, George, on Peshitta, 80

Langdon, discovery of tablets at Kish, 17
Langton, Stephen, chapter-division, 102
language:
  Achaeans, Homer's Heroes, 19
  AV, 351, 359-360, 367, 377-390, 391-392
  Jesus, Aramaic, 11, 62-64, 83, 375
  MSS of NT, early, 63-83
  origin of Greek and Hebrew, 18
  Revisions, 354-355, 359-360, 367, 377-390
  Sacred Autographs, 11, 83, 155, 370-371
Latin Versions, 160-163
  cited by Burgon, 289, 311, 320, 327, 329, 338, 348, 414
  date, 155
  new attention to, 371
  origin, 10-11
  Scrivener on, 165
Laudianus, Codex E₂, 143
  family classification, 92
  form, 250
Laura, Monastery on Mt. Athos, MSS at, 144, 148
Laurensis, Codex Ψ, 148
  family classification, 224
  Mark, ending of, 148
Laurentian Library, Florence, MSS at, 164
lectionaries, 151-153
  Apocrypha, 189
  Arabic, on last of Mark, 343
  cited by Burgon, 327, 348
  importance, 153
  meaning of term, 89, 134
  number of MSS, 89-90, 151, 153-154
Lee, Archdeacon of Dublin, position with Revisers, 272
left, sustituted for forsook, 307
Legg, classification of Byzantine family, 225
Leningrad, MSS at, 143, 144, 145, 146, 151
Leo, Bp. of Rome, cited by Burgon, 313
Leo X, patron of Cardinal Ximenes, (Complutensian Polyglott), 169
Leontius Byz., cited by Burgon, 313, 333
Levitical rites, Gospel substituted for, 52
Lewis, Mrs., discovery of Sinaitic MS of Old Syriac, 71, 371

libraries: at Caesarea, 96
  Pamphilus, 244
  Ras-Shamra, discovery at, 18-19
  Ugarit, discovery at, 19
Lietzmann, Dr. H., catalogue of new
  MSS, 134
Life of Christ, early English narra-
  tive, 174
Lightfoot, Bishop, 324
  changes by Revisers, 298
  Egyptian Version, 165
  on Lord's Prayer, 324
  Vaticanus, on omissions in, 241
Lindisfarne Gospels, English MS
  Bible, 174
literary criticism of NT, 108-118
literature of AV: compared with Re-
  visions, 359
  compared with revision of classics,
    390
  criticism, 354-355
  reason for revision, 377
  style, 359-360, 378-381
Lloyd, Bp., collation of Luke, 253-254
Long, Ciceronis Verrin, cursives
    children of respectable ancestors,
    258
Long Parliament, on Apocrypha, 188
Lord's Prayer, treatment of, 321-
    325, 353, 404-405
love, substituted for charity, 308, 398
lower criticism, meaning of term,
    230-231
Lower Sahidic Version, 160
Lucar, Cyril, Patriarch of Alexan-
    dria, offered Alexandrinus to
    Britain, 138
Lucian, martyrdom, 243
  text of Septuagint, 164
Lucifer, cited by Burgon, 320
Luke: date, 10
  historical accuracy, 48
  Marcion edition, 13
  one original text theory, 212
  origin, 108-109
  Q text, 211
  testimony as to many texts, 82, 211
lunatic, substituted by epileptic, 310,
    399
Luther, early textual critic, 104
  arrangement of books, 177
  Coverdale, used by, 176-177
  Tindale, used by, 176
Lyons, Latin Version, 161
  columnar arrangement, 250

—M—

M MSS, family classification, 91, 225
MacCulloch, J. A., on tithes, 384
Maccabees, Books of Apocrypha, 189
Mai, Cardinal: edition of Vaticanus,
    239, 241
Mainz, Fust and Schoeffer printers,
    first printed book, 168
Malan, Rev. S. C., on Egyptian Ver-
    sion, 165
Malchion, cited by Burgon, 313
Manasses, Prayer of, Book of Apoc-
    rypha, 189
Manchester University, MSS in, 373
Manes and Archelaus, cited by Bur-
    gon, 336
manuscripts, 84-100
  א, full canon, 84
  Byzantine Text, majority, 149, 216
  catalogues and inventories, 84, 92,
    101, 132-134
  classification, families, 91-100
    material and writings, 86-91, 130-
    134
  codices, age and form, 250-251
  competitive families, 217-219
  copies of copies, 201, 332, 373
  countries, arranged as to, 90
  cursives, see minuscules
  designations, 92, 101, 132, 133
  destruction under persecutions, 243
  earliest recovered, 66
  early, 11
  form, 250
  language of early, 65-83
  markings, 205-206, 240
  materials, see papyri, vellum
  minuscules, 149-150
    date, 153
  new discoveries, 42, 359-361, 373
  number of, 84-85, 89-90, 149, 153-
    154
  preparation, 201-203
  rolls, 250-251
  uncials, 136-149
  valuation, 128-129, 198, 373
  various readings, 85, 197
  writing, see cursives, minuscules,
    uncials
Marchalianus, Codex, 128, 239
Marcion, 13
  cited by Burgon, 323-324
  edition of NT, 13, 323

Marcion—*Cont'd.*
Lord's Prayer, treatment of, 323-324, 405
recension, 323
marginal notes, 231, 300-305, 366, 402
alternative readings, 282
authorities cited not given, 305
Authorized Version, in, 184
Burgon on, 301-305
Geneva Bible, in, 180
Ellicott, Bp., on, 303-304
MSS referred to, 300, 305
Nestle edition, 366
Scrivener on, 301, 315-316
wording of, 300

Marius Mercator, cited by Burgon, 313, 321

Mark, Gospel of: Caesarean family established in, 96
date, 10
historical accuracy, 48
origin, 108-109
Q text, basis, 211

Mark, Last Twelve Verses of, 6, 119, 341-350, 416-417
age of authorities, 345, 348
Alford, testimony of antiquity, 344-345
American Standard Version, 342
separated, note in margin, 342
Arabic Lectionary No. 13, omits, 343
Armenian, some old codices omit, 343
Ascension Day, attested by lesson for, 349
attested by:
Curetonian MS, 70
ecclesiastical evidence, 345
Eusebius, 348
Fathers, 345, 347, 348
18 as old as אֲ B, 348
Irenaeus, 345
Jerome, 344-345
Lectionaries, 348-349
lessons for Easter and Ascension Day, 349
MSS, all but אֲ B, 206, 248, 343, 345-348
Laurensis, adds short ending, 148
Regius, adds short ending, 145

Mark—*Cont'd.*
Vaticanus (B) doubtful, 206, 343, 345
tradition of the Church, 347
Versions, every ancient, 343, 345, 346, 348
except: Armenian, some old codices, 343
Ethiopic, two MSS, 343
Old Latin MS k, 343
Vulgate, 344
Burgon defends, 294, 297, 343-344, 346-349
canonical scripture, 349
Curetonian MS, attests, 70
Easter lesson, attests, 349
ecclesiastical evidence, 345
Ethiopic MSS, two omit, 343
Eusebius, 343-345, 348
אֲ B, possibly prepared under his direction, 248
difficulty in adjusting to harmony, 344-345
first objector to passages, 343-344, but see, 348
quotes as genuine, 348
speculation of Origen, 344
Fathers attest, 347, 348
18 as old as אֲ B, 348
Grant citations, 366
Gregory of Nyssa, 348
Irenaeus attests, 345
Jerome attests, 344-345
translates Eusebius, 348
Vulgate attests, 344
Laurensis (Ψ), both short and long ending, 148
Lectionaries, attest, 348-349
except Arabic No. 13, 343
Mark, writer of, vindicated, 344, 345, 348
Eusebius, does not state Mark not writer, 348
Milligan, quoted, 348
Roberts, quoted, 348
style discussed, 344
Miller, list of vital omissions, 119
Milligan, quoted, states Mark not writer, 348
Old Latin MS k, omits, 343
Omitted only by:
אֲ B, 206, 343, 345-348
Arabic Lectionary No. 13, 343
Armenian, some old codices, 343
Ethiopic, two MSS, 343
Old Latin MS k, 343

Mark—*Cont'd.*
  Revised Standard Version, which
    relegates to margin, 416-417
  Origen, speculation of, 344
  Regius (L), both short and long
    ending, 145
  Revised Standard Version,
    ending in margin, 349, 353
    Grant cites authority, 366
    short ending added in margin, 416-
    417
  Revised Version, separated, note in
    margin, 342, 347
  Roberts, quoted: explains marginal
    notes, 347
    states Mark not writer, 348
  Scholz, examined Arabic Lection-
    ary, 343
  Scrivener, defends verses, 248, 342-
    345
  Severus of Antioch, copies Eusebi-
    us, 345, 348
  short ending added: by Laurensis
    (Ψ), 148
    Regius (L), 145
    Revised Standard Version (in mar-
    gin), 416-417
    Westcott-Hort, 343
  Sinaiticus (ℵ), with Vaticanus (B),
    omitted, 206, 248, 343, 345-348
    cited by Grant, 366
    copied under Eusebius inspection,
    248
  Syriac Version, of 2nd century,
    attests, 345
  Thucydides, fanciful explanation,
    345
  Tischendorf, sets off passage, 343
  tradition of the Church, attests, 347
  Tregelles, sets off passage, 343
  Vaticanus (B), with Sinaiticus (ℵ),
    omit, 206, 248, 343, 345-348
    cited by Grant, 366
    exclusion doubtful, 345
    leaves blank column, 206, 343
    copied under Eusebius inspection,
    248
  Versions, every ancient attests, 343,
    345, 346, 348
    except: Armenian, some old codi-
    ces, 343
      Ethiopic, two MSS, 343
      Old Latin MS k, 343
    Syriac of 2nd cent. attests, 345
  Victor of Antioch, vouches for gen-
    uineness, 348
  Vulgate attests, 344

Mark—*Cont'd.*
  Westcott-Hort, 263
    admit ring of genuineness, 297
    counter-plea against Burgon, 343
    placed in double brackets, 263, 343
    printed separately, 263
    short ending annexed, 294, 343
  markings: in MSS, 205-206, 240
  Martin, Gregory, Douai-Rheims
    Bible, 181
  Mary, virginity of, 317, 402
  Mary, Queen of England, circulation
    of English Versions, 179
  Massoretic Text, adoption of, 265
  Matthew, Gospel of: date, 10
    historical accuracy, 48
    Inspired Version, 227-228
    origin, 108-109
    Q text, basis, 109, 211
  Matthew's Bible, Thomas, 2, 177-178
    AV, source of, 184, 186
    editions, 179
    scholarship, 186
  Maundy-Thursday lesson, cited by
    Burgon, 332
  Maximus Taurinensis, cited by Bur-
    gon, 260, 313, 321, 331, 333, 336,
    339
  Mazarin Bible, see Gutenberg
  McCormick, Elizabeth Day, new edi-
    tion of Apocalypse, 371
  Medici, ownership of Codex Ephra-
    emi, 140
  Megiddo, mentioned in discoveries, 18
  Memphis, discoveries at, 17
  Memphitic Version, see Bohairic
  Mercian Dialect Bible, 174
  Merivale, Dr., position with Revisers,
    272
  Mesopotamia: Aramaic language of,
    63
    excavations, 17
  message of heavenly host, treatment
    of passage, 325-329, 405-406
  Messiahship, see Christ
  Methodius, cited by Burgon, 302, 313,
    328
  Metropolitan Church, Byzantine text
    in, 96
  Michigan Papyri, P38, 134-135
    competitive texts, 217-218
    date, 217
    family classification, 217-218
  Michigan University, MSS at, 134-
    135
  Middle Egyptian Version, 160
  Middleton, Bishop, on grammar, 311

Milan:
  MSS at, 151
  Genesis Fragment, columnar arrangement, 250
Mill: number of MSS, 85
  Stephen text, 172
  textual critic, 292
Miller, Edward W., authority cited, 14-15, 26, 67
  א B, origin of, 204, 243-245
  Antiochian Revision, 76-78
  Kenyon's appraisal, 26
  list of eliminations, 119-121
Milligan, Dr., on last of Mark, 348
mind, substituted for heart, 377
ministering angel, treatment of passage, 331-334, 410-411
minuscule (cursive) MSS, 130-131, 149-151
  ancestors, representatives of respectable, 258
  Burgon, cited by, 304, 313, 317, 318, 333, 335, 337-340, 413, 414, 416
  Byzantine Text, 91, 96, 149, 225
  date, 153
  family classification, 91, 96, 149, 225
  full canon, 85
  meaning of term, 86, 130-131
  number, 89, 131, 149, 153-154
  textual criticism, place in, 197-198
    Caliph Omar's argument, 197-198
  Tischendorf on, 258
  value, 368
Minuscules, partial list:
  Family 1, 96, 99, 150
  Family 13, 96, 99, 150-151
  1, 149, 198
  2, 150
  13, 150, 332
  33, 91, 96, 150, 151, 198
  38, 336
  61, 150, 198
  69, 198, 332
  81, 96, 150
  124, 332
  157, 96, 150-151, 198
  259, 198
  346, 151, 332
  383, 151
  435, 336
  473, family classification, 92
  565, 151
  579, 151
  614, 151
  629, 150

miracles: converts through, 51
  historical accuracy, 55, 57-58
  pool of Bethesda, 120
  treatment of word, 308-310, 353, 389, 398-399
mixed texts, development, 213
Moabite Stone, 18
Moberly, Bishop of Salisbury, attendance at meetings, 271, 273
Moesia, translation by Bishop Ulfilas for Goths, 164
Monumenta Sacra Inedita of Tischendorf, 236
Mosaic law, Gospel substituted for, 51
Moscow, MSS at, 144
Moses, Book of, Inspired Version, 228
Moulton, Dr. James Hope, on language of NT, 63
Mount Athos, MSS at, 144
Mount Sinai, discovery of Sinaiticus by Tischendorf, 4, 209, 236
Munster, Sebastian: Latin translation, 179
  Great Bible, source of, 179
musical notes, markings in MSS, 205
mutilation of scriptures, see corruption

—N—

N Codex, see Purpureus Petropolitanus
Nablous Samaritan Pentateuch, columnar arrangement, 250
names in OT, transliteration of, 377, 386-387
Napoleon, Vaticanus in Paris, 139
National Council of the Churches of Christ in the U.S.A., publication of RSV, 32
National Revivalist, on RSV, 352, 358
nativity, hymn of angels, treatment of passage, 325-329, 405-406
Nelson, Thomas & Sons, printers of American Revisions, 230
Nestle, of Stuttgart, Greek Text, 366, 372
Nestorius, cited by Burgon, 313, 333
Neutral family (β), 91, 97, 363, 366
  development, 214-216
  MSS in, 75, 91
  position of, 93, 369
  pre-Byzantine classification, 100
  Revisions' foundation, 94, 215
  Westcott-Hort appraisal, 115

New Greek Text, RV, 232-233
  Westcott-Hort, 261-264
newspaper language, 379-380, 382
New Testament: book-arrangement,
  146, 177
  chapter-division, 102
  date, 8-11, 55
  historical criticism, 108-118
  historically accurate, 55-57
  language, 62-64, 74
  literary criticism, 108-118
  Semitic background, 68-69
  style of writers, 364
  supported by modern discoveries, 98
  textual criticism, 108-118
  verse-division, 102
Newth, Dr.: attendance of Revisers,
  270
  method of work of Revisers, 270
Nicaea, Council of, 77
Nicetas, cited by Burgon, 317
Nicolas V, Pope, on Vaticanus, 238
Nippur, clay tablets found at, 17
Nisibis, Syriac revision at, 76
Nitrian Desert, Curetonian MS of
  Old Syriac found in, 70
Nitrian Syriac, British Museum, co-
  lumnar arrangement, 251
Nitriensis, Codex R, 146
  cited by Burgon, 332
  family classification, 91, 96, 224
  Revised Version, source of, 5
  value, 198
Nolan, Dr., on Eusebius, 247
Nonconformists, on Apocrypha, 188
Nonnus, cited by Burgon, 260, 320
Northern Syria, discoveries in, 17
Northumbrian Dialect Bible, 174
notes, markings in MSS, 205
Notitia Ed. Cod. Sinaitici of Tisch-
  endorf, 236
Novatian, cited by Burgon, 313, 320

—O—

O Codex, see Sinopensis
O fragments, 146
Ω Codex, family classification of,
  225
Oesterley, W.O.E., on tithes, 384
offspring, changed to descendants,
  377
Old Latin Version, 161-162
  cited by Burgon, 302, 304, 318, 326,
    330, 331, 336, 338-340, 414, 416
  columnar arrangement, 251

Old Latin Version—Cont'd.
  family classification, 92, 97, 362
    competition with other texts, 224
    pre-Byzantine classification, 99
  Jerome, revision, 70, 163, 164
  MSS agreement, 143, 146
  Mark, on last of, 343
  new attention to, 371
  variations surviving in, 113
  versions, agreement, 158
  Vulgate, revision, 70, 163-164
Old Syriac Version, 70-72, 156
  antiquity, 124
  columnar arrangement, 251
  Curetonian MS, 81, 371
  date, 71, 371
  family classification, 92, 97, 362
    competition of texts, 223
    pre-Byzantine classification, 99
  Greek, translation from, Bruce
    quoted, 80
  MSS agreement, 151
  new attention to, 371
  Peshitta revision, 69-70, 75-80
  Sinaitic MS, 81, 371
  Textus Receptus, agreement, 376
Old Testament: criticism, 103-107
  prophecies, life of Jesus adapted to,
    55
  quotation in NT, 377
  transliteration of names, 386-387
  writing, 16
O mirificam, title of Stephen Bible,
  171
omissions (see also corruptions),
  119-121
  number of, 207-208, 241, 302-303
  Revisions, by, 6, 287, 361
  seven most important, 231
  vital not explained, 37, 361, 386
  Westcott - Hort explanation, 287,
    297-299, 334
one original text thesis, 206, 209-213,
  249, 364
  Luke quoted, 211
  Paul quoted, 212
Opiza MS, 157
Opus imperf., cited by Burgon, 311,
  317, 336, 339
Oriental, Semler family classification, 216
Oriental bishops, cited by Burgon,
  333
Oriental Church, cited by Burgon,
  339
Oriental Monasteries, MSS deposited in, 90

Origen:
Alexandria, home, 243
Ammonius of Alexandria, relationship, 205
Burgon, cited by, 260, 311, 313, 320, 327, 336, 339, 340, 416
Caesarea, home after troubles in Alexandria, 243
Eusebius, relationship, 243
family classification of texts, 91, 96, 99
Hexapla (polyglott), 128, 244
Mark, on last of, 344
scholarship, 166
study of writings, 116
original text, see Sacred Autographs
orthodox scholars, review of Revisions, 376
other sheep, treatment of passage, 385
Oxford University:
AV company of translators, 184
AV editions, 188
Bodleian Library, MSS at, 143, 147, 151
RV, publishers of, 22, 268
Oxnam, Bishop G. Bromley, cited, 355-356, 358
Oxyrhynchus Papyri, 134

—P—

P₂ Codex, see Porphyrianus
Φ Codex, see Beratinus
Ψ Codex, see Laurensis
Pagninus Latin Version, source of English versions, 176, 180
Palestine: Aramaic language of, 62-63
dialect, OS text, 71, 80
MSS deposited in, 90
palimpsest MSS, 71, 140, 146-147, 246, 250
meaning of term, 71, 140, 246
Palladius the Arian, cited by Burgon, 313
Palmer, Archdeacon: edition of Greek Text of AV, 193
columnar arrangement, 245
Pamphilus, MSS of, 137, 144, 243-244, 247
Papias, on language of Sacred Autographs, 63-64, 81
papyrus:
classification of MSS, 130
codices, 87-88
date, 17, 88
description of important, 134-136

earliest recovered, Rylands Fragment of John, 8, 66, 136
new discoveries, 42, 359, 377
origin, Egypt, 17, 87
rolls, 87, 131, 250
textual criticism, part in, 361, 370
writing material, 1, 87, 130
paradise, treatment of term, 310
paragraph-division, by Bengel, 101
parchment, writing material, 87
origin of term, 87
Paris, MSS at, 5, 144, 150-151, 172, 191
Pasinus, Catalogue, 251
Pastoral Epistles, see Paul
Patmos: columnar arrangement of Patristic MS, 250-251
MSS at, 145
Paul, date of writings, 10
literary style, 344
one original text theory, 212
Paulinus, cited by Burgon, 333
Paulus, bishop of Emesa, cited by Burgon, 313, 320, 328, 333
Peake, Arthur S., on tithes, 384
Pearl of Great Price: accepted Scripture, 228
Inspired Version, 227
Pearson and Bull, modern divines, 313
Pentateuch: criticism by Astruc, 30
date of writing, 16
English translation, 176
writers J E P, 106
Pentecost lessons, cited by Burgon, 339, 341, 416
Pergamum, King Eumenes of, origin of term parchment, 87
pericope adulterae, 157
Perowne, Dean, on language in RV, 359
Perpinian, harmony of, 44
persecutions of Diocletian and Galerius, 243
Persian elements assimilated by Jews, 375
Persian Version, 91, 160
Peschito, see Peshitta
Peshito, see Peshitta
Peshitta Version, 69, 75-81
Antiochian Revision, 78-83
antiquity, 124
authorized Bible of Syrian Church, 97-98
cited by Burgon, 304, 317, 340, 416
family classification, 75, 91
Greek, translation of, Bruce quoted, 80

Peshitta version—*Cont'd.*
  Rabbula, revision, 75
  pre-Peshitta text, 125
  received text of Syrian Church, 75
  Scrivener on, 165
  vernacular revision of Old Syriac,
    70, 75
  writers of, 201
Peter: conversion, 51-52
  testimony, 353
  visit to sepulchre, treatment of
    passage, 336
Philastrius, cited by Burgon, 260
Philo of Carpasus, cited by Burgon,
    327
Philoxenian Syriac Version, 80
  cited by Burgon, 304, 317, 340, 416
Phoenicia: mentioned in discoveries,
    18
  writing of, 18
Photius, cited by Burgon, 317, 333
piercing of Lord's side, treatment of
    passage, 120
Polycarp, relationship to John and
    Irenaeus, 14, 124
Porphyrianus, Codex P₂, 146
Porphyry, Archimandrite (Bishop),
    part of ℵ Sinaiticus MS, 237
  cited by Burgon, 318
Praxapostolos, Lectionaries of, num-
    ber of MSS, 89-90, 153-154
Prayer of Manasses, Book of Apoc-
    rypha, 189
prayer on the cross, treatment of
    passage, 334-336, 353, 411-412
pre-Byzantine classification, 99-100,
    363-364
Prefaces of Revisions, 274-285, 351-
    391, 418
Presbyterian, on Revising Commit-
    tee, 347
prevent, substituted for hinder, 383
Primasius: Old Latin Version, 162
  family classification of text, 97
printed Bible, 163, 168-172, 175-182
Priscillian: Old Latin Version, 162
  family classification of text, 97
Privy Council, review of AV, 184
Proclus, abp Constantinople, cited by
    Burgon, 313, 317, 328
Propaganda Library, Rome, MSS at,
    146
propaganda of RSV, 36
Ptah-Hetep, papyrus MS on gnomic
    philosophy, 17

Ptolemy of Egypt, use of papyrus, 88
punctuation in MSS, 205
Puritans: Bible of, Geneva, 179-181
  part in AV, 183
purple MSS, designation, 96, 225
Purpureus Petropolitanus, Codex N,
    145
  family classification, 96, 221, 225
  MSS agreement, 146, 148
Purvey, John, Version of Wyclif
    Bible, 175

—Q—

Q, collection of sayings of Jesus, 109,
    211

—R—

R Codex, see Nitriensis
Rabbula, Bishop of Edessa: produced
    Peshitta, 75-76, 97
Ras-Shamra, clay tablet library, 18-
    19
reader, Kenyon's any intelligent, 20,
    231
readings: alternative, rejected, vari-
    ous, placed in margins, 282, 301
  discordant, settlement, 124
Received Text, see Textus Receptus
recensions, 35, 141, 230
  meaning of term, 91
Reformation, demand for English
    Bible during, 1
Regius, Codex L, 145
  cited by Burgon, 340, 416
  family classification, 91, 96
  MSS agreement, 145, 148, 151, 163
  Mark, last of, 145, 294, 343, 417
  Revisions, source of, 5
  Scrivener's estimate, 417
  textual criticism, place in, 198
Reiche, Dr. J. G., Sound or High
    Textualist, 121
rescript codex, see palimpsest
residue family (ζ), 98-99, 199, 362-
    364
resurrection, miracle of, 399
revelation, see conjectural emenda-
    tion
Revised Standard Version, 351-394,
    395-417
  accuracy, 60
  anti-Christ effect, 351-352, 381, 392
  changes, 395-417
    number of, 217
  character, 351-356

Revised Standard Version—*Cont'd.*
comparison of texts with AV, IV,
    RV, ASV, 395-417
conjectural emendation, 298-299
criticism of, 38, 121
date, 31
depraved text, 217
development, compared with Byzan-
    tine Text, 216, 368
instructions, 356-357, 391
Introduction, publicity pamphlet,
    36-38, 42-43, 352-356
language, 354-356
  grammar and vocabulary, 386-390
  Sacred Autographs, 375, 391
making of, 31-32, 216-217
Mark, treatment of last verses, 348-
    349, 416-417
one original text thesis, 210
organization for revision, 356-358,
    385
orthodox scholars, review by, 352,
    376
reasons for, 357, 361, 377-381
Revisions, recension of earlier, 22,
    35, 37, 392
  comparison of texts, 395-417
scholarship, 357, 418-419
source material: 4-5, 36, 366, 372
  family classification, 361-365
  Greek Text, 5, 391
  new discoveries, 370-372
spirit of approach, 357, 418-420
time spent, 385
title page, 39
vital changes and omissions, not ex-
    plained, 37, 361, 386

Revised Version (British), 29-30,
    230-242, 265-273
acceptance, 110, 352, 355
accuracy, 60, 286
American collaboration, 267-268
AV sources, 169, 187
Burgon, critic, 112
Cambridge University, publisher,
    268
changes: grammar and vocabulary,
    306-314
  number of, 120, 273, 382
comparisons of text with AV, IV,
    ASV, 314-350; RSV, 395-417
conjectural emendation, 292-296
date, 30-31, 230, 275-276
Greek Text, 1, 5, 264, 269, 289
Hort, see Westcott-Hort
marginal notes, 282, 300-301
Newth, Dr., method of work, 270

Revised Version—*Cont'd.*
organization for revision, 230-235
attendance, 270-273
attitude and motives, 233-235
method of work, 264, 269-273, 307
origin, 29-30, 266
qualifications, 274
rules, 230, 232, 266-267, 301
time consumed, 264, 267, 276
omissions, summary of, 119-121
Oxford University, publishers, 268
Preface to NT, 276-282
spirit of approach, 233-235, 270-
    273, 275-282, 285
Preface to OT, 275-276
revision by RSV, 351-417
  reason for, 354, 358-361, 372, 391
  changes retained, 22, 37, 392
  comparison of texts, 395-417
Scrivener, position of, 264, 269-270,
    289
sources, 4-5, 34, 112, 137, 203, 217
  family classification, 215
textual criticism, product of, 3, 29,
    230, 280
Unitarian, 280
Westcott-Hort, position of, 5, 34-35,
    112, 261, 263-264, 269-270, 286
  time consumed, 385-386
Reuss, Eduard, critic of OT, 106
Revelation, date, 10
revelation, pseudo: conjectural
    emendation, 349, 396-397
Reynolds, Dr., Pres. Corpus Christi
    College, Oxford, new English
    Version, 183
Rheims-Douai Bible, 181-182
Riddle, D. W., study of lectionaries,
    152
Riddle, M. B., ed. Robinson harmony,
    46
ring of genuineness: see conjectural
    emendation
Rival School of Sound or High Tex-
    tualism, 103
Roberts, Dr., position with Revisers,
    272
Mark, last of, 347-348
Robertson, Archibald Thomas,
    harmony of, 46, 47
Robinson, Edward, harmony of, 46
Rockefeller McCormick NT, edition,
    371
Roe, Sir Thomas, British Ambassa-
    dor, offered Alexandrinus for
    King James I, 138
Rogers, John, Matthew's Bible, 177-
    178

Rolle, Richard, hermit of Hampole, English Version, 174
rolls, see papyrus
Roman Church: American revision, 378
Vulgate Version of Jerome, 160-164
Rome, MSS at, 5, see also Vatican
Ropes: comparison of ℵ B, 137
studied Codex Bezae, 142
Rossano in Calabria, MSS at, 148
Rossanensis, Codex Σ, 148, 239
family classification, 96, 221, 225
MSS agreement, 146, 148, 221
royal road to recovery of original text, 126
Russia, Emperor of, patron of Tischendorf, 236
Russia, MSS deposited in, 90, 145, 235
Russian Archimandrite Porphyry, brought Sinaiticus from Mt. Sinai, 237
Rylands Fragment of John, P52, Papyri illustration, 9; 136, 168, 373
date, 8, 66
Rylands Library, MSS at, 136

—S—

S Codex, family classification, 91, 225
Σ Codex, see Rossanensis
sacrament, treatment of passage, 120, 329-331, 353, 406-410
Sacred Autographs: ℵ B, relationship, 113, 117, 249
corruption of, 117, 368
date, 123
disappearance, 43, 65, 123, 364, 368
Fathers, use of, 166-167
language, 11, 62-66, 83, 155, 370-371, 375, 391
meaning of term, 11, 155
one original text thesis, 206, 209-213, 364
royal road to recovery, 126
Syriac, relationship, 375
Sahidic Version, 158
cited by Burgon, 311
family classification, 91, 92, 96, 99
Graeco-Sahidic MS, 146
new attention to, 371
St. Andrews, Bishop of, see Wordsworth
St. Catherine Monastery, Mt. Sinai: ℵ Sinaiticus, discovered at, 136, 236
Sinaitic MS (Syriac) discovered at, 371

St. Ephraem of Syria (see Ephraim Syrus), writer of 4th century, 74
St. Gall, MSS at, 144, 147
St. Petersburg, MSS at, 235
Salisbury, Bishop of, see Moberly
salt has lost his savour, treatment of passage, 386
salutation in Upper Chamber, treatment of passage, 120, 337, 412-413
Samaritan Pentateuch at Nablous, columnar arrangement, 250
Sampson, Thomas, Geneva Bible, 180
Sanders, date of Michigan Papyri, 134
Sangallensis, Codex Δ, 147
MSS agreement, 144
value, 198
Sangermanensis, Codex E₃, 143-144
copy of known copy, 170, 201
family classification, 97
Satan, thrust into Lord's Prayer, 324-325
Schaff, Dr. Philip, cited by Revisers, 355
scholars, 4, 23-28
anti-Christ, 30
antiquity of Byzantine Text, 201
arguments of, 395
authorities cited, 23-28
Extreme Textualists, 4, 28-29
orthodox, review of RSV, 376
Sound or High Textualists, 121
textual critics, not churchmen, 4-5
scholarship:
Authorized Version, 186, 367, 418-420
Beza, 180
English Versions, 178, 186
Erasmus, 195
Revisers, 285, 367, 418-419
Prefaces of Revisers devoted to, 276
spirit of approach, 277-282, 357, 418-419
scholion of Severus of Antioch, on last of Mark, 345
Scholz, J. M. A.:
cataloguing system, 132
last of Mark, 343
textual critic, 291
schoolmen, textual critics, 4-5
Schools of Textual Criticism, 48-59, 103-118, 122-123
Schubart, date of Michigan Papyri, 134
Scillitan martyrs, Latin Version at time of, 161

Scotland, MSS deposited in, 90
scribes, see also copyists
  training of, 202
scripture, treatment of word, 310
Scriptures, regard of the Lord for
  preservation of, 256
Scrivener, Frederick Henry Ambrose,
  authority cited, 23-25
  ℵ B, appraised, 137
  history, 235-242
  relationship to A C D, 247-248
  scribes, 244
  various readings of ℵ A B C D, 255
  Alexandrinus, Codex, 138
  Antiochian theory, 78-79
  AV, published Greek Text of, 193
  Bezae, Codex, edited, 24-25, 142
  Burgon, estimate of, 27, 343, 346
  catalogue of MSS, 24, 84, 132
  conjectural emendation, 289-292,
    296-297
  corruption of texts, 13-14
  Diatessaron, importance of, 74
  Griesbach, theories of, 115
  Kenyon's appraisal, 24-25
  MSS appraisal, 197
  marginal notes, 301, 315-316
  Mark, last of, 342-346
  Plain Introduction, editions of, 14-
    15, 24
  Revised Version:
    attitude toward, 272-273
    position among Revisers, 25, 264,
      269-270, 289
    published Greek Text, 289
    textual critic, 121, 272
  Tischendorf, appraisal of, 258, 260
  Versions, 164-165
  Westcott-Hort, appraisal of Greek
    Text and theories of, 24, 112, 117,
    255-256, 262-263, 296-297, 315-
    316, 349-350
scrolls, see also papyrus
  discovery near Dead Sea, 50
section-division, 144, 205
Sedulius, cited by Burgon, 260
seed changed to children, 377
Sectarians, alliance with RV, 287
Seminarian stage of Constantine, 244
Semitic background of NT, 68-69,
  367, 375-377
Semitic language, 62
Semitic writing, 18
Semler, Oriental family classification
  of texts, 216

Septuagint:
  English Versions, 177
  Jerome revision, 163
  Lucianic Text, 164
  Vaticanus, treatment by, 295
  writers of, 77, 201
sepulchre, substituted by tomb, 307
Sepulveda, correspondence with
  Erasmus on Vaticanus, 240
Serabit inscriptions, 18
Serapion, cited by Burgon, 318
Severianus, Bishop of Gabala, cited
  by Burgon, 313, 318
Severus of Antioch: cited by Burgon,
  260, 313, 320, 348
  Mark, on last of, 344, 345
sheep, other, treatment of passage,
  385
sign substituted for miracle, 309-310,
  353, 398-399
Simon, Richard, early critic, 104
Sinaitic (Sin.) MS of Old Syriac,
  70-71, 81
  family classification, 92

Sinaiticus, Codex ℵ (see also ℵ B
  Text), illustration, 248; 136-137,
  235-238
  acceptance by church, 224-225
  Alexander II, given to, 110
  Ammonian sections in, 205
  antiquity argument, 122-129
  British Government, purchased by,
    110, 132, 237-238
  Burgon, cited by, 311, 317, 323-324,
    326-329, 337-340, 347-348, 413-414,
    416
  canon of, full, 84
  collation with Cur. and Sin. of OS,
    71
  columnar arrangement, 245, 249-251
  compared with four oldest uncials,
    A B C D, 197, 246-248
  competition of texts, 363
  corruption, 26, 79-80, 93, 117, 125,
    127, 138, 203-206, 208-209, 218,
    252-257
  critical character, 233, 237, 246-251
  date, 72, 123, 132, 217, 371
  description, 88, 136-137, 236-239,
    250
  Egypt, preservation of text, 213-
    214, 363
  Eusebian canons in, 205
  evaluation, 198
  facsimile of, 237
  family classification (see ℵ B Text),
    91, 96, 219, 224, 363

Sinaiticus—*Cont'd.*
  competition of texts, 218-226, 237
  history, 94, 113, 204, 211, 235-238,
    242, 244, 247, 249
  MSS agreement of, 135, 139, 144-
    145, 147-148, 152, 221, 224-225
  Mark, on last of, 206, 343, 345
  markings, 205
  one original text thesis, 210-211
  preparation, 243-245
  preservation, 209
  reliability, 246-251
  Revisions, source of, 203, 269, 366,
    370, 372
  Sacred Autographs, relationship,
    113, 249
  Septuagint published as Friderico-
    Augustanus Codex, 236
  scribes, 204-205, 207, 244
  Scrivener appraisal, 137
  textual criticism, position in, 93, 99,
    110, 115, 201, 203, 211, 234-235,
    247, 368-369
  Tischendorf: discovered by, 4, 110,
    132, 136, 236
    appraisal by, 246, 295
  United States, bid for, 237-238
  Vaticanus (B), agreement, 137, 206-
    208, 237, 245
  Westcott-Hort: appraisal by, 93,
    115, 234
    Greek Text, basis of, 4-5, 34, 246
single original text, see one original
  text thesis
Sinopensis, Codex O, 146
  family classification, 148, 221
  MSS agreeing with, 148
Sixtus V, edition of Vulgate, 163
Slavonic Version, cited by Burgon,
  317, 327, 339, 340, 416
Smith, Prophet Joseph: Apocrypha,
  189-190
  corruption of the Scriptures, 12, 126
  Inspired Version, 3, 227-229
  Pearl of Great Price, 228
Smith, Dr. Miles: Authorized Ver-
  sion, published, 185
  Translators to the Reader, wrote,
    185, xxvii-lv
Societa Italiana, Florence, MSS at,
  135
Societa Italiana Fragment, P48, 135-
  136
Socinian glosses, 312-314, 401
Solomon, Wisdom of, Book of
  Apocrypha, 189
Son of man in heaven, treatment of
  passage, 319-321, 403-404

Son of man is come to save, treatment of passage, 340-341, 415-416
Song of the Three Holy Children,
  of the Apocrypha, 189
Sorbonne, criticism of Stephen Bible,
  171
Soter, Bishop of Rome, correspond-
  ence with Dionysius tampered
  with, 13, 124
Sound or High Textualists, 103
א B, appraisal of, 235
  Authorized Version, support, 5-6
  Jesus, appraisal of, 56-57
  meaning of term, 122-123
  members of, 121
  omissions, on, 231-232
  source materials, 212-213, 361-364,
    372-374
  new, 370-372
  Q, of Gospel texts, 211
Souter Greek Text, 366, 372
Spain, MSS deposited in, 90
Spinoza, early critic of OT, 104
Spitta, NT critic, 109
Spurgeon, Charles H., on English-
  Greek of RV, 359
Stanley, Dean, appraisal of Dr. Hort,
  321
  inspected Sinaiticus, 237
Stephen, Henry, son of Robert
  Stephen, 171
Stephen, Robert, Bible of, 171, 196
  Authorized Version, source of, 172
  Byzantine Text, 216
  Geneva Bible, source of, 179
  Greek Text, 2, 171, 196
  published by Palmer, 193
  MSS agreement, 147
  Received Text, 191
  Revisers' comment, 169
  sources, 142, 169, 196, 214
  Traditional Greek Text, 192
  verse-division, 102, 179
Stephanus Bible, see Robert Stephen
Stevens, William Arnold, harmony
  of, 46
stops, markings in MS, 205-206, 240
Story of Bel and the Dragon, Book
  of the Apocrypha, 189
Strachan, Dr. James, on OT criti-
  cism, 103-107
style of Biblical writers, 344, 364-
  365, 367-368, 378-381
subjective criticism, 290-291
Supplement Hypothesis, OT criti-
  cism, 106
Susanna, History of, Book of the
  Apocrypha, 189

Sweden, MSS deposited in, 90

Switzerland, MSS deposited in, 90

Synoptic Gospels: date, 10
  historical accuracy, 48
  origin, 108-109

Syria: discoveries in, 17-19
  language, dialect of Aramaic, 63, 74
  writing ability of Syrians, 82

Syriac Clement, cited by Burgon, 311, 339

Syriac (ε) family classification of texts, 94, 97, 362-364
  Byzantine text, 216
  date, 223
  competition of texts, 222-223
  consideration due, 127, 211
  pre-Byzantine classification, 99
  Textus Receptus, 192, 199
  Traditional Greek Text, 192, 199
  variants from, 97

Syriac revision, myth of, see Antiochian revision

Syriac (Syrian) Version, 67-83, 91, 156
  Antiochian revision, q. v., 76-83, 113-118
  Aramaic, language, 67
  cited by Burgon, 311, 320, 327, 338-339, 341, 348, 414
  date, 81, 155, 223, 375
  family classification, see Syriac family above
  Graeco-Syriac Text, late Greek MSS of, 192, 199
  Greek, translation of, Bruce quoted, 80
  Kenyon on Antiochian revision, 77-78
  Mark, on last of, 345
  Miller on Antiochian revision, 76-78
  new discoveries, 371
  origin, 10-11, 70, 73, 75
  Sacred Autographs, relationship, 81-82, 375, 391
  scholars producing, 77
  Scrivener on Antiochian revision, 78-79
  summary on, 81
  Textus Receptus, 72, 192, 199

Syrian (α) family, 91, 95-96

Syrian text, used by John, 81

—T—

T Codex, see Borgianus

Θ Codex, see Koridethianus

Tatian, 73-75
  ps.-Tatian, cited by Burgon, 317, 333, 336
  date of, 73
  Diatessaron of, 44, 73-75, 97
  fragment found at Dura, 371
  disciple of Justin Martyr, 73
  sources, 81

Taverner English Bible, 2, 178

Tbet' MS, 157

teachings substituted for doctrine, 307, 311, 399-400

Tell Duweir, inscriptions, 18

Tell el-Amarna, papyri discoveries, 17

Tertullian: cited by Burgon, 311, 313, 339, 341, 416
  corruptions, on, 13
  Latin Text, 161-162

texts, classification of, see family classification

texts, development of, 214-217

textual criticism, 103-118
  applied to classics, 215
  conjectural emendation, 286-299
  development of, 3, 103-118, 232-234
  Extreme and Sound or High, Schools of, 122-123
  higher and lower, meaning of term, 230-231
  German school, 9, 110, 282
  internal evidence, rules of, 290, 292
  new material, position of, 371-372
  one original text thesis, 209-210
  principles of, 14, 20, 197, 292, 364, 373
  reader, Kenyon's any intelligent, 20
  Revised Version, offspring of, 230
  scholars, not churchmen, 4
  subjective criticism, 290-291

Textus Receptus (Received Text), 194-226
  Authorized Version, 2, 22
  Alexandrinus in, 138
  Byzantine Text, 76, 78, 95, 194, 216
  Bezae, source of, 224
  development of, 195, 215-216, 220, 222
  earliest texts, co-existent with, 363
  first use of term, 172
  MSS agreement, 72, 135, 138, 141, 147-149, 224
  MSS revised to conform, 213, 222
  meaning of term, 194, 199
  OT adopted by Revisers, 265
  Revisers avoid use of term, 391
  Syrian Version, agreement, 91, 376

Textus Receptus—*Cont'd.*
textual criticism of, 41, 108-118, 121, 123, 196, 263
Traditional Greek Text, 123, 172, 192, 199
Westcott-Hort Greek Text, departure from, 41, 263
Thebaic (Sahidic) Version, 158
necessity for study of, 116
Thebes, discoveries at, 17
Thecla, scribe of Alexandrinus, 138, 202
Theodore of Mopsuestia, early critic of OT, 104
cited by Burgon, 260, 313, 320, 333
Theodoret, cited by Burgon, 313, 320, 327, 331, 333, 336, 338, 414
Theodorus haeret, cited by Burgon, 333
Theodorus Heracl., cited by Burgon, 320, 336, 340-341, 416
Theodosius Alex., cited by Burgon, 333
Theodotus of Ancyra, cited by Burgon 313, 327
Theophilus Alex., cited by Burgon, 313
Thompson, (Mr.) E. Maude, columnar arrangement of MSS, 251
Three Holy Children, Song of, Apocrypha, 189
Thucydides, theory on last of Mark, 345
Tiflis, MSS at, 147
Tindale English Bible, 2, 175-176
arrangement of books, 177
Authorized Version, source of, 184, 186-187
editions, 179
first English translation from Greek, 175-176
Henry VIII, condemned by, 176
Jonah, translation of, 176
martyrdom of, 175
Pentateuch, translation from Hebrew, 176
scholarship, 178, 186

Tischendorf, Constantine, textual critic, 4, 109, 234
cited by Burgon, 321, 331, 336, 346
editions of NT, 258-260
instability of textual criticism, 258-260
Mark, on last of, 343
MSS unknown to, 334
Received Text, returned to, 258, 260

Tischendorf—*Cont'd.*
Samaritan Pentateuch at Nablous columnar arrangement, 250
Sinaiticus (ℵ), 258-260
discovery of, 4, 109, 136, 203, 236
edition, 248
favorite text, 246, 295
scribes, 207, 244, 247
Vaticanus: edition of, 139
inspection of, 139, 209
scribes, 207, 240, 244, 247
Tischendorfianus III, Codex Λ, 147
tithes, treatment of passage, 383-384
Titus of Bostra, cited by Burgon, 318, 327
Tobit, Book of Apocrypha, 189
tomb, substituted for sepulchre, 307
Tomson, Laurence, revision of NT, 180
traditions, evangelic, 334, 347, 411
Traditional Greek Text, 123, 172, 192, 199
transcriptional probability, 335
Tregelles, Samuel Prideaux, textual critic, 4, 109, 233
cited by Burgon, 321, 346
ignored TR, 110, 233
Mark, treatment of last of, 343
Sinaiticus, inspected, 237
subjective criticism, 290
Vaticanus: favorite text, 234, 246
Sepulveda correspondence with Erasmus recalled, 240
tracing of, 239
Trench, Archbishop of Dublin, attitude toward Revision, 271, 273
Trent, Council of, on Apocrypha, 189
Bezae taken to, 142
Trinity College, Cambridge, MSS at, 144
Trinity College, Dublin, MSS at, 146
Turin: MSS at, 144
Minor Prophets MS, columnar arrangement, 251
Turkey, MSS deposited in, 90
Tutankhamen, connected with papyri discovery, 17
Tyconius, family classification of text, 97

—U—

U Codex, family classification, 225
Ugarit, discovery of clay tablet library, 19
Ulfilas, Bishop, translation for Goths, 164

uncials, 136-148
antiquity argument, 72, 122-129
family classification, 91-92, 95-100, 225, 362-365
five oldest, א A B C D, position in textual criticism, 197
later, value of, 91, 96, 128-129, 197, 225, 368
list of important, 136-148
MSS classification, 130
number of, cited by Burgon, 304, 318, 333, 335, 337-340, 413, 414, 416
meaning of term, 86, 130
number of MSS, 90, 131, 153-154
Sinaiticus, only, contains full NT text, 84
Table of, see Appendix A
Unitarian, among Revisers, 280
United States: bid for Sinaiticus, 237-238
MSS deposited in, 90
purchase of Mazarin-Gutenberg Bible, 238
Ur, discovery of clay tablets, 17
Ussher, Archbishop, chronology of Scripture, 188
Utrecht Psalter, columnar arrangement, 251

—V—

V Codex, family classification, 225
Valentinus, additions to text, 13
Variorum Bible: Robinson harmony in, 46
AV, Translators to the Reader, 185
various readings: development, 113, 213
Diatessaron, in, 74
five oldest codices, א A B C D, 113, 247-248, 253-255
judging character of, 198
marginal notes, placed in, 301
number of, 85
one original text theory, 210-213
source of, 200
Vatican Dio Cassius, columnar arrangement, 250
Vatican Library, MSS in, 3, 139, 140, 145, 148, 209, 238, 343
Vaticanus, Codex B, illustration, 249; 139-140, 238-242, 243-245
acceptance by Church, 150, 224-225
antiquity argument, 122-129
Bessarion, Cardinal, supplied portions, 206, 239

Vaticanus—Cont'd.
Burgon, cited by, 311, 317, 323-324, 326-329, 332, 336-340, 347-348, 413-414, 416
Byzantine Text, antiquity compared, 150, 219, 225
collation, attempts at, 240
with Cur. and Sin. of OS, 71
columnar arrangement, 245, 249-251
compared with four oldest uncials, א A C D, 197, 246-248
competition of texts, 363
conjectural emendation, 294
corruption, 26, 79-80, 93, 117, 125, 127, 138, 206-209, 218, 252-257
critical character, 233, 246-251
date, 72, 123, 132, 217, 371
description, 88, 139-140, 239, 250
editions, 239
Egypt, preservation of text, 213-214, 363
Erasmus, known to, 170, 191, 196, 209, 240
family classification (see א B Text), 91, 96, 219, 224, 363
competition of texts, 218-226, 237
Herculanean Rolls, resemblance to, 239
history of, 94, 113, 203-204, 211, 238-242, 244, 247, 249
Lachmann favored, 3
MSS, agreement, 135, 144-145, 147-148, 150, 152, 221, 224-225
Mark, treatment of last of, 206, 343, 345
markings, 206
omissions, 140, 207-208, 241
one original text thesis, 210-211
preparation of, 243-245
preservation, 209
reliability, 246-251
Revisions, position in, 203, 269, 286, 366, 370, 372
Sacred Autographs, relationship to, 113, 249
scribes, 204, 207, 244
Scrivener appraisal, 137
section numeration, 144
Septuagint Version in, 295
Sinaiticus, agreement, 137, 206, 208, 237, 245
textual criticism, place in, 93, 99, 110, 115, 201, 203, 211, 234-235, 247, 368-369
Tischendorf, inspection, 209
Tregelles, appraisal, 234, 246
Vatican, in Library at, 132, 139

Vaticanus—*Cont'd.*
Westcott-Hort, appraisal, 115, 234,
    246, 295, 365
  Greek Text, basis of, 4-5, 34, 210,
    246, 261
Vaticanus 2066, Codex 046, 140, 148
  MSS agreeing with, 135
Vatke, textual critic, 106
vellum, writing material, 1, 130
  codices, 88
  meaning of term, 87
verse-division, 102
  Geneva Bible, 179-180
  Stephen Bible, 102, 171
  Whittingham Version, 180
versions, 156-165
  Byzantine type, 223-224
  Greek text, translation of, 66
  majority of, cited by Burgon, 318,
    333, 335, 337, 338, 345, 348, 413,
    414
  MSS classification, 66-67
  meaning of term, 66, 91, 155
  Scrivener on versions, 165
  Table of, see Appendix B
  textual criticism, place in, 197
Victor of Antioch, cited by Burgon,
    260, 304, 318, 348
Victorinus, cited by Burgon, 313,
    318, 320
Vienna, Latin Version at, 161
  MSS at, 145
Vigilius, cited by Burgon, 321
virgin birth, miracle of, 353, 398
virginity of Mary, treatment of
    passage, 402
vocabulary in AV, RSV, 37, 367, 386-
    389
von Dobschutz, continued Gregory's
    catalogue, 134
von Soden, H.: catalogue of MSS,
    84, 92, 133, 134
  K classification of texts, 216, 225
Vulgate Version of Jerome, 70, 91,
    160-164
  Authorized Version, source of, 172
  cited by Burgon, 317, 339, 340, 416
  Coverdale, used by, 177
  Douai-Rheims, source of, 181-182
  Erasmus, used by, 170
  established in West, 167
  sources, 163
  official Bible of Roman Church, 163
  printed book, first, 163, 168, 195
  Tindale, used by, 176
  Wyclif translation of, 175

—W—

W Codex, see Washingtonianus I
Washingtonianus I, Codex W, 146
  family classification, 96, 225
  competition of texts, 221
  new discovery, 371
Washingtonianus II, Codex I, 144-
    145
  family classification, 99
  new discovery, 371
Weigle, Luther A., Chairman, RSV,
    32, 356, 358
  English of RSV, 379-381
  language of Revisions, 359
  reasons for revising previous
    Revisions, 359-360
Weiss, studied Codex Bezae, 142
Wellhausen, textual critic, 106-107,
    109
Wentz, Abdel Ross, RSV, 393
  personality of Jesus, 393
  NT as Word of God, 390
Westcott, Brooke Foss, Bishop of
    Durham, textual critic, 4, 109,
    261, see Westcott-Hort
Westcott-Hort, textual critics, 233-
    234
  ℵ B Text, 99
  Antiochian revision theory, 76-78,
    113-118, 199
  antiquity theory, 124-129
  canons of criticism, 365
  cited by Burgon, 321, 331, 333, 339,
    341, 416
  conjectural emendation, 286-299,
    366, 396
  divinity of Jesus, 287
  eclectic principle, 366
  family classification, 91-92, 93, 99
  favorite texts, 93, 99, 210, 234, 246,
    295
  Greek Text, 233-234, 246, 261-264,
    293, 396
  Burgon appraisal, 264, 295
  position of, 368-369
  rejected readings in margin, 300
  Revisions, source, 5, 34-35, 269,
    286, 293, 366-369, 372
  Scrivener appraisal, 262-263
  sources of, 4, 234, 246
  TR, substituted for, 41, 110
  title page, 261
  reliability, 286
  interpolations, 369
  Lord's Prayer, treatment of, 324
  Mark, treatment of last of, 263,
    294, 297, 343

Westcott-Hort—*Cont'd.*
omissions, explanation of, 334
one original text thesis, 210-213, 364-365
Scrivener opposed, 24, 112, 349-350
Vaticanus, appraisal of, 93, 99, 210, 234, 246, 295

Western family, (δ), classification of texts, 75, 91-92, 94, 97, 362-364
cited by Burgon, 339, 341
consideration due, 127, 211, 369
corruption, 115
development, 214-216
MSS agreement, 135, 141, 214, 218
pre-Byzantine classification, 99
re-grouping, 93-94
Scrivener on, 113
variants in, 97

Westminster College, company of AV translators, 184
Wetstein, J. J., textual critic, 132
designation of MSS, 101
Scrivener on, 291
Whitchurch's Bible, source of AV, 184
White, canons of criticism, 365
White, Rev. H. J., on Vulgate, 164
Whittingham, W., published Geneva Bible, 179
Wiclif, see Wyclif
Wilberforce, Bishop, attendance at meetings of Revisers, 271
Chronicle of Convocation, cited, 281
Wilcken, date of Michigan Papyri, 134
Willis, J. R., on tithes, 384
Wilson, Edmund, on Dead Sea Scrolls, 50
Wisdom of Jesus, the Son of Sirach, Book of Apocrypha, 189
Wisdom of Solomon, 189, 250, 374
woman taken in adultery, treatment of passage, 294

Woolley, Sir Leonard, discovery of clay tablets at Ur, 17
words: meaning of changed, 389
miscellaneous changes, 309-310
obsolescence of, 383-385
Wordsworth, canons of criticism, 365
Wordsworth, John, Bishop of Salisbury, on Vulgate, 164
Wordsworth, Bishops Charles and Christopher, 121
address on Revised Version, quoted, 281
attendance at meetings, 271
criticized changes, 273
writing, early, 16-18
Wyclif Bible, 174-175
arrangement of books, 177

—X—

Ξ Codex, see Zacynthius
Ximenes, Cardinal, Complutensian Polyglott, 2, 168-170, 195
sources, 169

—Y—

Y MS, family classification of text, 225
Yale Expedition, new discovery of Diatessaron at Dura, 371

—Z—

Z Codex, see Dublinensis
ζ family, 364
Zacagni, tracing of Vaticanus, 239
Zacynthius, Codex Ξ, 147-148
MSS agreement, 221-222, 224
Zechariah, literary style, 344
Zeno, cited by Burgon, 321
Zenos, Andrew C., on tithes, 384
Zurich, German Bible of Zwingli, 176
Zwingli German Bible, used by Coverdale, 176

INDEX B ·

SCRIPTURAL REFERENCES

Chapter Verse	Page	Chapter Verse	Page	Chapter Verse	Page
Matthew		**Mark (Cont'd)**		**Luke (Cont'd)**	
1...16	151	6...11	303	43-44......70, 119, 298,	
25......297, 316, 401		20	292		305, 331,
3...11	387	25	383		335, 410
16	366	52	399	23...8......310, 388, 389	
5...13	386	7...4	366	17	298
22	255	24	383	34......70, 119, 297	
37	324	25-30	52		298, 305, 316,
39	324	31	383		334, 350, 411
6...9-13......70, 119, 297,		8...15	366	38	298, 366
	321, 404	27	386	24...12	298
25	383	27-30	52	36......337, 412, 415	
8...1-17	52	9...29	338, 414	40......337, 413, 415	
9...14	366	10...24	366	51	120
12...47	297, 366	14...22-24......407, 409		53	115
13...19	324	15...44	366		
21	383	16...9-20......6, 70, 119,		**John**	
38	324		145, 146, 148,		
15...21-28	52		155, 206, 248,	1...1-2	420
16...2-3	297		263, 294, 297,	3-4......319, 321,	
4	51		341-350, 353,		403, 420
13-20	52		366, 416	11	420
17...14-21	399			3...13......116, 298, 319,	
21......297, 310,		**Luke**			321, 366, 403
	338, 414	1...1-4......82, 211		4...4-42	52
22	366	2...1	50	22	377
18...11......297, 340, 415		14......325, 349,		5...2	**366**
19...17	255		366, 405	3-4	298
23...23	384	3...22	302	6...66	51
24...11-12	381	23	49	7...53......157, 263, 298,	
23-24	381	4...33-41	52		343, 366
26...26-28......406, 408		44	366	8...1-11...157, 263, 298,	
39-40	332	5...17	366		343, 366
27...49	294	6...1	298	16	366
		8...35-44	253	57	366
Mark		9...17	388	9...35	366
1...1......318, 321,		54-56	298	10...16	385
	366, 402	10...41-42......298, 302		14...13	279, 280
5	387	11...2-4......119, 321, 404		26	53, 279
8	387	12...39	366	15...16	280
9	387	15...16	366	16...23	279, 280
18	307	18...12	383	18...31-33......8, 66, 136	
20	307	19...10	340, 415	37-38......8, 66, 136	
21-26	52	20...1-2	388	19...34	294
27	248	22...16	366	21...22	142
27-45	52	19-20....120, 329, 406		25	53, 259

Chap-ter	Verse	Page	Chap-ter	Verse	Page	Chap-ter	Verse	Page

Acts

3	1-11	52
4	7-12	43, 111, 392
7	46	292
8	13	398
	16	387
	37	143
9	31-42	52
10	11-22	52
	23-33	52
	34-43	53
	48	387
11	20	367
13	32	292
15	23-29	173
17	12-16	158
18	7	367
19	11	398
	39	367
	40	292
20	28	247
26	28	292

Romans

4	1	367
5	1	367
	2	367
8	2	292
	28	367
9	4-5	400
	5	312
12	9	324

I Corinthians

1	4	367
	14	367
	18	111
7	19	380
12	2	292
	10	398

1 Corinthians (Cont'd)

	28	398
	29	398
13	1-13	308, 387, 398
	3	256

II Corinthians

3	2	367
	6	27
5	14	382

Galatians

3	5	398

Ephesians

1	1	367
2	11	292
6	16	324

Philippians

2	1	256

I Thessalonians

4	15	383

II Thessalonians

2	3	367

I Timothy

3	16	247, 314, 347
6	7	292

II Timothy

1	13	396
3	16	311, 399
4	13	212

Hebrews

2	4	398
	14	325
3	2	367
	6	367
5	8	386
6	2	307, 367
	3	367
9	5	386
	11	367
	14	139

I Peter

1	23	256
3	11	383
4	1	367
5	2	367

II Peter

1	21	367
3	10	288, 292
	12	292

I John

2	10	367
3	8	325
4	3	381
5	7-8	150, 247

II John

	7	381
	8	367

Jude

	5	292, 298, 366, 396
	5-6	396
	22-23	292

Revelations

21	3	367
22	14	367